AMERICAN CIVICS

◀ **Freedom Edition** ▶

AMERICAN CIVICS

William H. Hartley
William S. Vincent

 Holt, Rinehart and Winston, Inc.
Harcourt Brace Jovanovich, Inc.

Austin • Orlando • San Diego • Chicago • Dallas • Toronto

Authors

WILLIAM H. HARTLEY, a former classroom teacher, is Professor of Education, Emeritus, at the Towson State University, Baltimore, Maryland. He is well known to teachers of the social studies as a past president of the National Council for the Social Studies. His monthly article "Sight and Sound" was for many years a highlight of *Social Education*. Dr. Hartley has written several textbooks, a number of motion picture and filmstrip scripts, and many articles in the field of education.

WILLIAM S. VINCENT, a former teacher of junior high school social studies, was Professor of Education, Emeritus, at Teacher's College, Columbia University, where he organized and directed the Citizen Education Project. Dr. Vincent has written several books on citizenship and has produced a number of educational films. He authored *Indicators of Quality*, a method of training teachers to measure the educational quality of schools and school systems.

Consultants and Reviewers

Larry L. Bybee
Secondary Social Studies Supervisor
Northside Independent School
  District
San Antonio, Texas

Bernice Craig
Social Studies Teacher
Woodrow Wilson Junior High School
Tampa, Florida

George G. Dawson
Emeritus Professor of Economics
Empire State College
State University of New York
Old Westbury, New York

Roy Erickson
Coordinator of Social Studies and
  Multicultural Education
San Juan Unified School District
Carmichael, California

Kay Cooper Gabbert
Education Chairperson
Nashville League of Women Voters
Nashville, Tennessee

Michael Lamanna
Associate Professor of Education
State University of New York
Albany, New York

Marcus Shannon
Lecturer in Education, Retired
George Peabody College for
  Teachers at Vanderbilt University
Nashville, Tennessee

George B. Sherman
Educational Consultant
Department of History
University of Connecticut
Old Lyme, Connecticut

Irving J. Sloan
Social Studies Teacher
Scarsdale Middle High School
Scarsdale, New York

Elizabeth Zuniga
Social Studies Teacher
Roosevelt High School
East Chicago, Indiana

For permission to reprint copyrighted material, grateful acknowledgment is made to the following sources:

Joan Davies: From *I Have a Dream* by Martin Luther King, Jr. Copyright © 1963 by Martin Luther King, Jr.

Office of the Texas Secretary of State, Voter Registration Application.

Printed in the United States of America

ISBN 0-03-054019-4

2 3 4 5 6 7 062 9 8 7 6 5 4

Contents

UNIT SIX
THE AMERICAN ECONOMY   307

Reference Section

Civics Skills

CITIZENSHIP SKILLS

LIFE SKILLS

SOCIAL STUDIES SKILLS

Charts, Graphs, and Maps

Citizenship in Action

Focus on Freedom

Our Living Constitution: A Legacy of Two Hundred Years

The Beginnings of the Constitution

The Articles of Confederation was the Republic's first plan of government. The plan created a central government that did not have enough power to solve the young nation's problems. One of these problems was trade. Alexander Hamilton called for a meeting of delegates to discuss issues of commerce. This meeting is known today as the Annapolis Convention. It met in September 1786 with delegates from only five states attending. Plans were then made for another meeting in Philadelphia, which took place in May 1787. Delegates from 12 of the 13 states gathered for the meeting, which is now called the Constitutional Convention. At first the delegates planned to strengthen the Articles. They soon realized, however, that the young Republic needed a new and stronger form of central government. As a result, they drew up the United States Constitution.

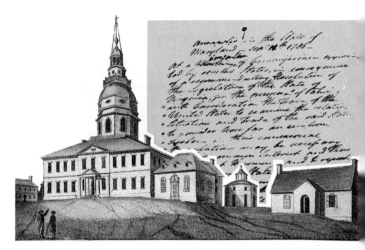

The delegates to the Annapolis Convention met in Maryland's capitol (above).

The delegates in Philadelphia elected George Washington (standing, right) to preside over the Constitutional Convention.

Compromises

The United States Constitution has been called "a bundle of compromises." The delegates from the agricultural South and the industrial North had different interests. They wisely resolved their differences through compromise.

At the opening of the Convention, Edmund Randolph of Virginia introduced a plan of government. Called the Virginia Plan, it favored the interests of the large states and was opposed by delegates from the small states. William Paterson of New Jersey then presented a plan that favored the small states. It was called the New Jersey Plan. A third plan proposed by Roger Sherman of Connecticut resolved the differences between the Virginia and New Jersey plans. Sherman's plan was called the Great Compromise. It formed the basic structure of the government's legislative branch.

Other compromises were also made at the Convention. One settled the method of electing the President. Another resolved the government's commerce and taxing powers. Still another settled the counting of slaves to determine representation in Congress.

Virginia's governor, Edmund Randolph, proposed that representation in Congress be based on population.

Roger Sherman's compromise gave the government a two-house legislature. In the House of Representatives each state's representation was based on population. In the Senate each state had two seats.

William Paterson's plan called for each state, regardless of its population, to have one vote in Congress.

The North's economy was based on trade and manufacturing (left). Northern delegates wanted a tax on imports to protect their growing industries.

The South's economy was agricultural (below). The South exported its goods to foreign countries. Southern delegates agreed to the tax on imports in exchange for no taxes on exports.

In a final economic compromise, the delegates agreed that laws regulating commerce within the United States would be decided by a simple majority of Congress.

The question of counting slaves as a part of a state's population was settled by the Three-Fifths Compromise. In this compromise the North agreed to count a slave as three-fifths of a free person.

Guarantees of Freedom and Civil Liberty

The Bill of Rights was added to the Constitution in 1791. Its ten amendments protected mainly the civil rights of the white, male voting population and prevented the federal government from infringing on these rights.

The amendments added after 1791 have extended these basic civil rights to all American citizens. For example, the Fifteenth, Nineteenth, Twenty-third, and Twenty-sixth amendments extended voting rights to other groups in American society. Through the amendment process, the Constitution has been able to meet the needs of a growing and changing society. In 1991, Americans commemorate the Bicentennial of the Bill of Rights.

Freedom of assembly is closely related to freedom of speech. Freedom of assembly is essential in a democracy.

The First Amendment guarantees freedom of speech. People in the United States are free to express their opinions and ideas.

Voting is a right and a responsibility of citizenship. Voting enables American citizens to have a say in how they are governed and who governs them.

Freedom of the press protects the right of Americans to be informed about their government and about events around the world (left). Freedom of the press is also closely related to freedom of speech.

In the United States, a person accused of a crime is considered innocent until proven guilty by a jury of peers. The Sixth Amendment guarantees a prompt, fair trial.

Under freedom of religion, Americans are free to practice a religion of their own choosing, or to choose none at all. American citizens are thus free to worship in such places as a church (left), a synagogue (center), or a mosque (right).

Congress: The First Branch

The framers of the Constitution believed that good government begins with good laws. The legislature was so important to them that they discussed Congress first. Article 1 of the Constitution set up a two-house Congress—the House of Representatives and the Senate. Today Congress has 435 representatives and 100 senators.

Members of Congress pass laws on such topics as taxes, the federal budget, and the nation's armed forces. The decisions of Congress affect all Americans.

Congress meets in the Capitol.
The Capitol is a symbol of the American system of government.

Three outstanding senators of the 1800's were Henry Clay (left), Daniel Webster (center), and John C. Calhoun (right). These three senators made lasting contributions to the nation's government.

"'The Old House of Representatives" shows the House at work in the early 1820's. At that time the House had 183 members representing 24 states.

An important part of a senator's job (left) is discussing issues with other senators.

Senators (right) also keep voters informed about new laws.

The Presidency: Upholding the Constitution

Article 2 of the Constitution describes the office of the Presidency. The President is our nation's highest elected official. The President's most important duty is to uphold the Constitution of the United States. The President signs bills into law and, through various departments and agencies, sees that the laws are carried out.

The President of the United States is a symbol of the American nation, its laws, and its people. American citizens often regard Presidents as leaders who are responsible for the nation's achievements and its greatness.

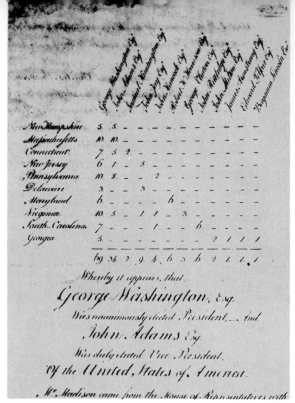

The election of George Washington as the first President in 1789 was recorded in the *Journal* of the United States Senate (above).

George Washington kept the young Republic on a steady course.

Thomas Jefferson doubled the size of the United States with the purchase of the Louisiana Territory.

Andrew Jackson was called a President of the "common people." He helped make the nation more democratic.

Abraham Lincoln governed the nation during the Civil War. He upheld the Constitution by saving the Union.

The White House is the official residence of the President.

The Oval Office is the scene of many important Presidential decisions.

Theodore Roosevelt brought many reforms to the United States and started the National Park System.

Woodrow Wilson sought to bring lasting peace to the world after World War I.

Franklin D. Roosevelt was elected to four terms. He governed the nation during the Great Depression and World War II.

George Bush, elected in 1988, pledged to make education a top priority of his administration.

The Supreme Court: Interpreting the Constitution

The Supreme Court is the only Court named in the Constitution. Its chief duty is to interpret the laws of the nation in light of the Constitution. The decisions of the Court affect the lives of all Americans. Cases reach the Supreme Court by petition or on appeal. By turning to the Court for final decisions, the American people have kept the Constitution as the supreme law of the land for two centuries.

The Chief Justice of the United States presides over the Court and greatly influences the Court's decisions. Portraits of some noteworthy Chief Justices are shown to the right.

John Jay presided over the first session of the Supreme Court.

The phrase over the Supreme Court Building, "Equal Justice Under Law," sums up the goal of the Court—to interpret the Constitution fairly and to provide equal justice for all Americans.

John Marshall established the principle of judicial review.

William Howard Taft was the only Chief Justice to have been President of the United States.

The Supreme Court under Earl Warren reflected his commitment to civil rights and civil liberties.

The Justices of the Supreme Court today are (standing, left to right) David Souter, Antonin Scalia, Sandra Day O'Connor, and Anthony Kennedy; (seated, left to right) John Paul Stevens, Thurgood Marshall, Chief Justice William Rehnquist, Byron White, and Harry Blackmun.

The Constitution Preserved

The Constitution is preserved in the National Archives in Washington, D.C. The four parchment pages of the original document are very fragile. They must be preserved from the effects of light, heat, and moisture in a special viewing exhibit.

Glass cases house the pages of the Constitution. Deep yellow filters block out the harmful effects of light. The temperature and humidity are also strictly controlled.

Only the first page and the signature page of the Constitution are displayed every day of the year. Each night, these two pages are lowered into a vault 20 feet (6 meters) below the floor. Once a year—on September 17, Constitution Day—the complete document is displayed to commemorate its signing.

The stately National Archives Building houses the Constitution, the Bill of Rights, and the Declaration of Independence.

Two beautiful paintings showing the framers of the Constitution decorate the walls of the rotunda of the National Archives Building.

Each year, thousands of visitors view the original Constitution.

The special glass and bronze cases are filled with helium gas to preserve the Constitution.

Celebrating the Constitution: Then and Now

The American people are proud of the Constitution and the government that it established. Throughout the nation's history, Americans have celebrated the Constitution and all that it symbolizes.

The Constitution was formally ratified on September 17, 1787. In 1887, Americans celebrated the Centennial of its signing with much pomp and splendor. In 1987, Americans commemorated the Bicentennial of its signing.

The United States Constitution, a legacy of two hundred years, is a triumph of government by the people. It is the foundation of the greatest democratic nation in the world.

An engraving from the late 1800's reflects the people's confidence in the Constitution.

New Yorkers celebrated their state's ratification of the Constitution in July 1788 with a great parade.

25 Cts.   25 Cts.

GA. SC. NC. VA. MD. DEL. PA. N.Y. N.J. CONN. R.I. MASS. N.H.

OFFICIAL PROGRAMME
OF THE
CONSTITUTIONAL
CENTENNIAL CELEBRATION.

PHILADELPHIA, SEPTEMBER 15·16·17.

·1887·

J. F. DICKSON & CO.
PRINTERS, BINDERS AND PUBLISHERS,
SEVENTH AND ARCH STREETS, PHILADELPHIA.

The Centennial of the Constitution in
1887 (above) was commemorated
with a grand celebration in
Philadelphia and in other cities
across the nation.

UNITED STATES ★ CONSTITUTION
★ 1787-1791 ★ BICENTENNIAL ★ 1987-1991 ★

We the People

The logo of the Bicentennial of the
Constitution includes the first words of
the Preamble, *We the People.*

Planning for the Constitution's Bicentennial Celebration began in 1985.

The Philadelphia Orchestra performed for the Bicentennial Celebration.

The United States Army Band practiced for the Celebration.

Citizenship in Our Democracy

CHAPTER 1

We the People

Chapter Sections

Chapter Focus

The United States is built on a dream—the hope of a better life for everyone. This dream has been shared by millions of people who have believed that in this nation all men and women could be truly free. The dream began in colonial times, and its power is still so great that it draws thousands of people to our shores each year.

What does freedom mean to Americans? For many people, it has meant religious freedom. For those who fled from poverty, it has meant the chance for a new start and a better life. For still others, it has meant safety from political persecution and wars.

Throughout our history, America has held the promise of excitement, adventure, and a better life. It seemed a good place to invest energy, time, and money. Who could tell how far an ambitious, hard-working person could go in a growing land? This idea is still part of the American Dream.

But the American Dream can have meaning only in a free nation. Each one of us must help protect our precious heritage of freedom so that the American Dream can come true. We accept this responsibility as **citizens**—as members of our nation.

Study Guide

As you begin to explore citizenship in the United States, look for answers to the following questions:
★ What is civics, and what does it mean to be an American citizen?
★ Who were the early immigrants to America, and how do people become American citizens today?
★ What does the census tell us about Americans, and how is the American population changing?

1 Civics in Our Lives

What is civics? Why do we study this subject in school? What does civics have to do with my life? These are some of the questions you may be asking as you begin your civics course.

Many of the subjects you take in school teach you about the American way of life and the priceless rights you enjoy as an American. The civics course you are about to begin will explain how you, as a citizen of the United States, can help to keep this heritage alive.

The Meaning of Civics

Civics is the study of what it means to be an American citizen. The word "civics" comes from the Latin *civis*, meaning "citizen." The meaning of this word has changed greatly since the ancient Romans first used it many hundreds of years ago. At that time, only a small group of wealthy people who owned property could be Roman citizens. Today almost everyone is a citizen of a nation.

The rights and responsibilities of being a citizen also have changed over time. Moreover, they differ from nation to nation. They depend upon the kind of government a nation has. **Government** is the authority, or power, that rules on behalf of a group of people. Under the American system of government, citizens have many rights and many kinds of responsibilities. Your civics course will help you discover the most important ones.

You will discover that American citizenship means more than being a responsible member of the nation. It includes being a useful and sharing member of society. Almost all Americans belong to a family, go to school for a number of years, and work with other people. Americans also are members of their local communities—villages, towns, or cities—and of states. Being an effective citizen of the United States means fulfilling your duties and responsibilities as a member of each of these groups.

American Ideals

The importance of being a responsible citizen cannot be stressed too much. As a citizen of the United States, there are many different reasons you can take pride in your nation. It is a land of great natural beauty and a land of many wonders built by its people. Even more important are the **ideals,** or beliefs, of our great nation.

The government of the United States and the American way of life are based on the ideals of freedom and equality. As a citizen of this nation, each one of us is guaranteed the same rights and freedoms. These rights and freedoms are protected by our laws and cannot be taken from any citizen. As a citizen of the United States, you must be willing to do your share to protect this great heritage of freedom, or liberty. It has been handed down to us from one generation to another for over 200 years.

The success of the United States depends on well-educated citizens. These students know that studying is the key to a good education.

Our Heritage of Freedom

One important American freedom concerns you directly as you read this. It is the freedom to learn. Americans believe that every young citizen should have the opportunity to learn about our nation and our world by receiving a well-rounded education. Therefore, our states and communities spend billions of dollars each year to provide free public schools for all young citizens. Each state also has public and private universities for those who wish to continue their education.

Another important freedom is the freedom to choose a job or career. Americans believe that all persons qualified for a job should have an equal opportunity to try for it.

As Americans, we also are proud of many other freedoms. Consider how important they are in our lives. We may live as we wish as long as we respect the rights of others. We are free to own a house, marry the person of our choice, and raise a family. We may start our own business and travel or live anywhere in the nation. We are free to speak and write what we wish as long as our words do not harm another person. We may not be arrested or imprisoned without just cause.

Government by the People

The leaders who planned our government created a system that would guarantee our freedom. The form of government that they established continues strong today. Under our American form of government, the people rule through the officials they elect.

These elected officials are responsible to the people. Citizens are free to vote for new officials at election time if those in office do not do their jobs properly. Officials also can be removed from office before the end of their terms if necessary. By making our officials answerable to the people they represent, the founders of our country made sure that our system of government would continue to serve the American people.

The Role of the Citizen

As an American citizen, you have many freedoms. Being a citizen also involves many responsibilities. Voting in elections is one of the most important of these responsibilities. However, you can help choose the men and women who will govern us in other ways as well. You can work for a political party, for example. Anyone who answers telephones, stuffs envelopes, or helps prepare for meetings of a political party is playing a part in the American system of government.

It is also your responsibility as a thoughtful citizen to inform officials of your needs or disagreements with government actions. You can do this by taking direct action. For example, you can write or call public officials or write to newspapers.

Knowing how your government works will help you carry out your duties and responsibilities as a citizen. The study of civics will teach you how the powers of government are divided between the nation, the states, and the local communities. As you study the functions of these governments, you will learn what an important part each of them plays in your life.

Qualities of a Good Citizen

As an American citizen and a future voter, you will play a vital role in determining the future of our nation. Your participation in American government is necessary for our form of government to continue to work. Therefore, each of you must study and train to become an effective citizen.

How can you become an effective citizen? What qualities will you need? Here is a list of ten characteristics of a good citizen. You probably can think of several you would like to add.

1. Good citizens are responsible family members.

2. Good citizens respect and obey the laws of the land.

3. Good citizens respect the rights and property of others.

4. Good citizens are loyal to their nation and proud of its accomplishments.

5. Good citizens take part in and improve life in their communities.

6. Good citizens take an active part in their government.

7. Good citizens use our natural resources wisely.

8. Good citizens try to be well informed on important issues.

9. Good citizens believe in equality of opportunity for all people.

10. Good citizens respect individual differences and ways of life that are different from their own.

Like these baseball players, citizens in a free nation must act as members of a team. For our government to work, everyone must obey the rules and cooperate.

The Importance of Civics

It is important for every American citizen to understand how our system of government operates. It is equally important for every American to understand why he or she must take part in it. Participation in government has always been a basic principle of our American form of government.

In your study of civics, you will learn a great deal about American government. Your study also will include many other topics that concern all American citizens. You will study how American communities serve their people and some of the problems our communities face today. Your study of civics will deal with citizenship in the family.

You will also read about our nation's free economic system and how it provides opportunities for all people. You will learn why citizens must pay taxes. You will study jobs and careers and learn what training and abilities they require. You will discover how America's schools are run and how you can get the most from your school years. You will read about America's relations with other nations and learn how over the years our nation has taken a position as a world leader.

Being an American citizen is something we often take for granted. To become a responsible and effective citizen requires effort and training, just as becoming a good athlete or musician does. Our nation needs citizens who are well informed and who are willing to take part in determining how our nation acts. Meeting the obligations of American citizenship is an important challenge. This textbook was written to help you meet that challenge.

Our training as members of a family is our first lesson in civics. With other members of our family, we learn to work together toward shared goals.

 SECTION 1 REVIEW

Define citizens, civics, government, ideals

1. **Seeing Relationships** (a) How does the American form of government guarantee that citizens have freedom? (b) What are some of the freedoms held by Americans?
2. **Understanding Ideas** (a) List the ten characteristics of good citizenship. (b) Why is civics an important area of study?

Thinking Critically You head a committee to encourage good citizenship in your community. Explain how your committee will pursue this goal.

2 Who Are American Citizens?

America's heritage of freedom and equality was formed bit by bit as groups from different parts of the world settled here. These people brought with them their hopes and dreams. Today all Americans can be proud of the interesting and wonderful background they share. For we are all **immigrants**—people who came here from other lands—or descendants of immigrants. From their countries of origin, the immigrants brought different languages, ideas, and customs. These different ways of life mixed with the ideas already developed in America. This blend has given a special energy to our nation that would not be possible without our multicultural heritage.

Early Americans

As you know from your study of American history, the first people to settle in America were the Indians, or Native Americans. Many scientists believe that the ancestors of the Indians came here from Asia at least 25,000 years ago. Gradually, over thousands of years, they moved into many parts of North and South America.

The Vikings came next, but did not stay very long. The Spaniards were the first Europeans to build lasting settlements in the Americas. They settled in Mexico, South America, and what are now Florida, California, and the Southwest in the United States.

The original 13 colonies were settled mostly by people from England. Colonists from other countries included German settlers in Pennsylvania, the Dutch along the Hudson River, and the Swedes in New Jersey and Delaware. Many black people also came to America from Africa. Unlike other immigrants, most of them were brought to America as slaves. They and their children were forced to live in bondage for many years.

America's Immigration Policy

Over the years, the United States has been settled and populated by people from all over the world. During our early history, the new American nation had to struggle hard to survive. Therefore, most immigrants were welcomed to the United States. Farm and factory workers were needed as our nation expanded

Did you know that...

all the people of the Western Hemisphere really could be called Americans? After all, the two continents that make up this hemisphere are North *America* and South *America*. Why aren't the people of Canada, or Mexico, or Brazil called Americans too?

The answer is that the United States was the first *independent* nation in the hemisphere. By the time Mexico and the other nations won their independence in the 1800's, the "American" label already had a specific meaning. It meant a citizen of the United States.

from the Atlantic Ocean to the Pacific Ocean. During the first half of the 1800's, our government adopted an "open shore" policy, allowing unlimited immigration. The only persons who were not admitted were criminals and those with certain diseases.

However, as America began to fill up and land became less available, some Americans wanted to change our immigration policies. Slowly the United States began to limit the number of people who were allowed to immigrate to this country. During the 1880's the government began to place restrictions on immigration. It was not until the 1920's, however, that a **quota,** or definite limit, was established on the number of immigrants who could be admitted each year.

The faces of America show the many lands from which our citizens have come. Though our backgrounds may be very different, we are all Americans.

Today the number of immigrants allowed to enter the United States is still limited, as it is in most nations. In 1965 the quota was set at 290,000 immigrants a year. The quota is not used for **refugees,** or homeless people fleeing their nations. It also is not used for the immediate relatives of American citizens, who are admitted under special laws.

In recent years more than 600,000 immigrants, including refugees and others not subject to limitations, have been admitted to the United States each year. More than 40 percent of the new arrivals come from Asia. A slightly higher percent come from Latin America, with large numbers from Mexico.

Citizenship by Birth

Millions of immigrants have become American citizens. Some American citizens belong to families that have lived here for many generations. Other Americans were born in foreign countries. American citizens are of many different races and religions. All citizens, regardless of their background, have the same legal rights and responsibilities.

Americans gain their citizenship either by birth or by a special legal process called naturalization. Since citizenship by birth is the way most of us became citizens of the United States, let us review it first.

If you were born in any one of the 50 states or in any American territory, you automatically became a **native-born citizen.** If your parents were United States citizens, you were a citizen by birth even if they were living in a foreign land when you were born. Citizenship, then, can be acquired by the place of birth or through one's parents.

What about children born in this country whose parents are citizens of a foreign country? Are they citizens of the United States? In most cases they are, if their parents were under the authority of the United States at the time the children were born.

What about children born here whose parents are officials representing a foreign country? They are not United States citizens, because their parents are under the authority of another country. All cases involving claims to American citizenship are handled by the United States Department of Justice.

Aliens in America

Several million people living in the United States are citizens of other countries. These people are called **aliens.** Some are here on a visit. Others live and work here or attend school here but expect someday to return to their homelands. Many aliens in the United States expect to live here permanently.

While in thc United States, all aliens must obey the laws of this country. They are also entitled to be protected by its laws. Aliens enjoy most of the benefits of American citizenship. They cannot, however, vote or hold public office. Moreover, various state laws prohibit aliens from working at certain jobs, such as teaching in public schools.

All aliens living in the United States must register with the **United States Immigration and Naturalization Service,** an agency of the Department of Justice. They also must keep the agency informed of their current address.

Illegal Aliens

Several million aliens live in the United States illegally. No one knows exactly how many illegal aliens there are, but estimates range from 4 million to 12 million. In 1986 a law was passed to legalize the status of illegal aliens who met certain requirements, but the flow of illegal immigration still remains high.

More than half the illegal aliens come from Mexico. Most come to the United States to find work and a better life. However, life is often difficult for illegal aliens. Many become migrant workers, moving from farm to farm picking crops. Illegal aliens often have to work for very low wages and under poor working conditions. Some citizens resent these aliens, who they feel are taking jobs away from them. Moreover, illegal aliens always face the danger of being caught and forced to leave the United States.

How an Alien Becomes a Citizen

Under certain circumstances, citizens of other countries may become citizens of the United States. The legal process by which an alien may become a citizen is called **naturalization.** The first part of this process is entering the United States legally.

By learning English, these aliens are taking an important step toward becoming American citizens.

To be eligible to enter the country, foreigners must prove that they can support themselves and that they can read and write. They must prove they do not have certain diseases and are not mentally ill, drug addicts, or criminals. There are a number of other restrictions that bar people from entering the United States. One of them bars persons who favor violent revolution, that is, the overthrow of the government by force.

Only immigrants, or aliens admitted as permanent residents, may become citizens. This excludes visitors, students, and others who do not plan to stay in the United States.

Although not required, immigrants may file a declaration of intention, stating that they plan to become citizens. Some employers ask for this document as evidence that the employee plans to stay in the country.

Aliens may apply for citizenship after they have lived in this country for five years. This period is reduced to three years for an alien married to a citizen. Aliens must be at least 18 years old to apply for citizenship.

The first step is to fill out an application called a petition for naturalization. When immigration authorities receive this application, they set a date for the person to appear before a naturalization official for an examination.

During the examination the applicant must show that he or she is a person of good moral character who believes in the principles of the United States Constitution. The applicant also must prove that he or she can read, write, and speak English acceptably and knows something about American history and government. After the examination the applicant files the petition for naturalization in a naturalization court.

Before they become citizens, applicants may be investigated to check their qualifications. If they prove to have the background needed to become citizens, they are called to court for a final hearing. There they take an oath of allegiance to the United States and are granted a certificate of naturalization. Children automatically become citizens when their parents' naturalization is completed.

Naturalized citizens have the same rights and duties as native-born Americans. There is only one exception. Naturalized citizens are not eligible to become President or Vice President of the United States.

How an Alien Becomes a Citizen

DECLARATION OF INTENTION (Optional)
An alien may file this declaration in any naturalization court. This written statement declares that the alien plans to seek American citizenship.

PETITION FOR NATURALIZATION
After an alien has lived in the United States at least 5 years (or 3 years if married to an American citizen), he or she files an application called a petition for naturalization.

EXAMINATION
A naturalization examiner conducts an examination in which the applicant must show that he or she is a person of good moral character who believes in the principles of the Constitution. The applicant also must prove that he or she can read, write, and speak English and knows about the history and government of the United States.

FINAL HEARING
If the applicant meets all of the qualifications, he or she is granted citizenship at a final hearing. There, the alien swears an oath of allegiance and is given a certificate of naturalization.

 SECTION 2 REVIEW

Define immigrants, quota, refugees, native-born citizen, aliens, naturalization

Identify United States Immigration and Naturalization Service.

1. **Summarizing Ideas (a)** Who were the early settlers to America? **(b)** Summarize the history of America's immigration policy.
2. **Composing a Paragraph** Write a paragraph explaining the two ways in which a person can be an American citizen by birth.
3. **Organizing Ideas (a)** Describe the lives of legal and illegal immigrants. **(b)** What are the steps in the naturalization process?

Thinking Critically If you could, how would you change the requirements for becoming a naturalized citizen? Explain your answer.

3 The American People Today

The leaders who planned the American government knew that they would need to know how many people—citizens as well as noncitizens—lived in the nation. They decided that every ten years the national government would make an official count of the number of people living in the United States. This count is called a **census.** The most recent census was taken in 1990.

What the Census Tells Us

The main purpose of the census is to find out the size of each state's population. This information is used for many purposes, including to determine how many people from each state will be elected to Congress.

The census also tells us a great deal about the United States and the people who live here. For example, it tells us how many children there are in each family, how many people have moved and where, and something about the standard of living of Americans. In addition, the census indicates the rate of population growth in the United States. This and other information gathered by census takers helps the government, business, and individuals to plan for the future. It also helps us learn something about ourselves.

Population Growth

When the first census takers counted our nation's population in 1790, they reported fewer than 4 million people living in the original 13 states. Since that time, our nation has grown greatly in both size and population. Instead of 13 states, there are now 50. And, according to current projections, the population will exceed 268 million by the year 2000. How did the United States grow to its present size and population?

All nations grow in three ways. One way is by natural increase in population. A natural population increase occurs when the birth rate is greater than the death rate. The **birth rate** is the number of births per 1,000 members of the population over a period of one year. The **death rate** is the number of deaths per 1,000 persons over a period of one year.

The second way a nation grows is by adding new territory. The United States has gained new territory from time to time through war, purchase, and annexation. The people living in these new lands have added to the size of our population.

The third source of population growth has been immigration, or the arrival of people from other lands. Since 1820 over 53 million immigrants from all over the world have come to the United States to live.

How America's Population Grew

As the United States expanded from the Atlantic coast to the Pacific coast, it needed a rapidly growing population. However, in the early years of our nation, the population grew slowly.

Life was very difficult in those pioneer days. Many infants died and the death rate of

(continued on page 14)

CITIZENSHIP IN ACTION

Learning About "The Good Old Days"

What was life like for teenagers in Springfield, Massachusetts, during the city's "golden years" in the early 1900's? That's what a group of students in Springfield wanted to know, and they set out to discover the facts in an interesting way.

Interviewing Takes Patience

Teenagers from two high school clubs formed an interviewing team. Over a six-week period they taped the comments of senior citizens who had lived through the city's golden years. At first the students were nervous about the oral history project. Many of them had never spent much time talking to older people. The students also had to learn how to use recording equipment and how to conduct an interview. They discovered that interviewing takes a lot of patience.

Learning from Each Other

The major purpose of the oral history project was to help teenagers learn about the past by talking to those who had lived through it. Yet the program had another important result. Young and old realized that each group had something to offer the other. The students and older people became friends during the taping sessions. They called each other by their first names and looked forward to Wednesday afternoons together.

What did the teenagers learn? One elderly man told them that Springfield in the 1920's was alive with baseball teams— just as it is today. There was a difference, however. In those days the teams built their own baseball diamonds. "We'd go to a big field with shovels and rakes," the man recalled. "We'd make our own ballfield."

The idea of having to work to have fun was new to many of the students. Now they say they are more understanding when their older relatives tell them, "We didn't have it easy, as people have it today." Questioning the senior citizens about

their schools, work, and recreation taught the teenagers that, indeed, people worked very hard in the 1920's—even at play.

Then, as now, people enjoyed canoeing on nearby lakes and rivers.

The teenagers also learned that some events were the same, yet different. One example is the celebration of Independence Day on July Fourth. This was as important a holiday in the 1920's as it is today. People in Springfield lit up the sky then too. Instead of using fireworks, however, they used lanterns, which were strung on the streets and in the park.

When the older people were asked what they thought about the oral history project, they were very enthusiastic. It meant a lot to them to share their memories of the past with people who were really interested.

Thinking it Over

1. How do you think students can benefit from an oral history project? How can the people they interview benefit?
2. Besides conducting interviews, what else might the students have done to learn about Springfield's past?

Americans was high. Disease was common, and there were few doctors. Moreover, little was known about diseases and how to cure them. Of course, some Americans lived to a very old age. Nevertheless, disease, poor diet, and the hazards of pioneer living made the average life span short.

Between 1790 and 1830, the population of the nation more than tripled, reaching nearly 13 million. Almost all of this growth was the result of births in the United States. It was common for families to have as many as 10 to 12 children. Large families were a necessity at this time. Most people lived on farms, and large families could help get all the work done. Thus, even though many children died young and the death rate was high, the population grew.

Beginning in the 1830's, great numbers of immigrants started to arrive in the United States. Between 1830 and 1840, more than 500,000 immigrants came, mainly from Ireland. Over the next ten years, a million and a half new immigrants arrived. The population had reached 23 million by 1850.

By 1920 our nation's population had risen to 106 million. Immigrants from many lands, particularly the nations of southern and eastern Europe, accounted for a large part of this huge increase in our total population. However, after 1920, as you have read, the United States began to limit the number of immigrants admitted into our country each year. Most of the population growth after this time was due to natural increase.

Today's Smaller Population Growth

Today the population of the United States continues to grow, though not as rapidly as in the past. In 1970, for example, 203 million people lived in the nation—nearly 24 million more than in 1960. By 1980, however, a new trend had appeared. Although the population increased by 23 million, this represented a change of only 11 percent since 1970. This was the second smallest increase in any ten-year period since 1790. Population projections indicate that the rate of increase will continue to drop, falling to 7 percent by the year 2000. One reason the American population is growing at a slower rate is that many people are having smaller families.

A People on the Move

Where do the people of the United States live? The first census found most Americans living on farms, with a smaller number living in villages and in a few medium-sized cities. Over the years this changed. The farm population has gotten smaller every year. In 1988 only about 5 million people lived on farms in the United States.

Beginning in the 1800's, Americans began to move away from **rural areas,** or regions of farms and small towns. Most of them went to live in **urban areas,** or cities, in order to work in factories and offices. As early as 1820, the census showed that urban areas were growing faster than rural areas. With each new census, the proportion of Americans living in or near cities continued to grow. By 1920 the census showed that more Americans lived in urban areas than in rural areas.

As the population continued to grow rapidly and people moved to the cities, urban areas became overcrowded. Many Americans could afford to buy automobiles, which made it possible to travel longer distances to work. Therefore, beginning in the mid-1900's, the people of the cities started to move out into the surrounding areas—the **suburbs.**

They moved to the suburbs in search of better homes, schools, and communities. Thirteen of the nation's 25 largest cities lost population between 1960 and 1970. Only one, Los Angeles, showed a gain. Today the people who live in the suburbs outnumber those who live in the cities.

Taken together, however, cities and their suburbs account for a vast majority of the nation's population. Today more than three fourths of the American population live in **metropolitan areas,** or areas made up of cities and their suburbs. Nearly half live in areas with populations of 1 million or more.

Another Population Shift

Throughout our nation's history, Americans have been on the move. This movement continues today, with many Americans moving to different parts of the nation. Such movement of people from region to region is called **migration.** The migration pattern in the United States in recent years has been from the middle of the country and the Northeast to the South and West.

The older industrial areas of the North and East have been losing population. Americans from these areas are moving to states in the South and West. These states are known as the **Sunbelt.** People are moving to the Sunbelt because of the region's warmer climate. Also, they are looking for better jobs and a better life.

California is now the state with the largest population. Nevada, Arizona, Florida, and Alaska are among the fastest growing, with increases of about 30 percent in the past ten years. States such as Michigan, Iowa, West Virginia, and Pennsylvania, however, are losing population or have very low growth rates.

Because of the population shift to the Sunbelt, cities in the South and West are growing. San Diego, California, and Phoenix, Arizona, are now among the nation's ten largest cities. San Antonio, Texas, is one of the fastest growing. At the same time, cities in the North and East such as Buffalo, New York; Detroit, Michigan; and Pittsburgh, Pennsylvania, are losing population. Despite this trend, New York City remains the most populous city.

A Diverse Population

The United States has been shaped by people from all over the world. Today's Americans

People are attracted to Phoenix, Arizona, because of its warm climate and many job opportunities.

come from many different cultural backgrounds and represent a wide variety of racial and ethnic groups. Despite this diversity, however, the people are united by a common bond—they are all Americans (see page 549).

The 29 million African Americans in the United States today make up about 12 percent of the population, forming the largest minority group. The fastest growing minority group, however, is the second largest—Hispanics. The Hispanic population has increased to about 19 million, up 30 percent since 1980. During the same time period the non-Hispanic population has increased by only 6 percent. Asians form the country's third largest minority group—a group that also is growing rapidly. Today Asians account for about 6 million Americans.

Smaller Families

Recent statistics also show that other changes are taking place in the United States. The size of American households has decreased since 1970. Many couples are having fewer children.

Many people, too, now live alone. Therefore, today there are more households with fewer people living in them. Since 1970 the total number of households increased from 63.4 million to over 91 million. However, the average number of persons living in a household declined from more than 3 people to fewer than 3 people.

Another change currently taking place in American families is the increase in the number of one-parent families. Since 1970 the number of one-parent families in the United States has doubled. As more couples divorce, more women are becoming heads of households. Generally, women remain responsible for taking care of the children. Today less than one third of the nation's households include the traditional family of mother, father, and one or more children.

Our older citizens stay active for many years past retirement. Here, some older Americans experience the excitement of white water rafting.

Changing Life Styles

Along with changes in the family have come changes in the life styles of American men and women. Today there are about 6 million more women than men in the United States. Perhaps one of the most significant changes in life style has come about as more women have expanded their role from the traditional one of homemaker. For the first time in the nation's history, more women than men are entering college. And, after receiving their educations, more women than ever before are entering the work force.

In 1970 about 31 million women worked outside the home. Today more than 54 million women work outside the home, and projections indicate that this number will reach 60 million by 1995. Most women work for the same reason that most men do—economic necessity. Women who live alone or who head households depend on a job as a source of income. So do many married women. Today more than half the married women in the United States work outside the home. One result of the increased participation of women in the labor force has been that more women are entering professions that once were open only to men.

An Older Population

Recent statistics also show that our nation is "growing older" every year. In the early years of our nation, when both birth and death rates were high, ours was a young population. In 1820, for example, half the population was under the age of 16. By 1900 half the population was under 23. Until the 1970's, the largest age group in our population was under 25.

Today Americans between the ages of 25 and 65 make up the largest group in the population. In this group of over 120 million people are most of our nation's wage earners and heads of families. They hold most of the responsible positions in our nation. They control business, government, and courts. They greatly influence America's standards of living and conduct.

An increasing part of our population consists of Americans who are 65 or older. This trend has resulted from a drop in both the birth and death rates. The birth rate dropped steadily beginning in the 1960's before finally leveling off in the 1980's. Also, most Americans are living longer. In 1900 the average American lived 49 years. Currently the average life expectancy is 75 years.

Today about 30 million Americans are 65 or older. This means that a large number of Americans are retired. However, many older Americans are eager to remain in the work force. Some work part-time, and others have started new careers or returned to school.

Most older citizens continue to be active and productive. Yet, many are troubled by the problems of low income and poor health. Using the experience and talents of senior citizens offers both a challenge and an opportunity for our nation.

 SECTION 3 REVIEW

Define census, birth rate, death rate, rural areas, urban areas, suburbs, metropolitan areas, migration, Sunbelt

1. **Seeing Relationships (a)** Why is it important for us to know how many people live in the United States? **(b)** Identify and discuss the three ways in which a nation's population may grow.
2. **Composing an Essay** Write a short essay describing the growth and movement of the American population.
3. **Summarizing Ideas** Summarize what we know from recent statistics about each of the following groups: African Americans, Hispanics, Asians, families, women, older Americans.

Thinking Critically Imagine that you are living in the year 2010. Thinking back to today, how did the changing trends in American life influence your decisions about your life?

Civics is the study of what it means to be an American citizen. It teaches us our responsibilities and rights as members of our nation. As citizens, we must help keep alive the ideals of freedom on which our nation was built. We also have important citizenship responsibilities as members of our local community and state. In fact, citizenship is important in every group to which we belong, including our family and school.

Citizenship in our nation is gained by birth or by naturalization. Naturalized citizens enjoy the same rights as native-born citizens. The one exception is that naturalized citizens are not eligible to become President or Vice President.

The national government has taken a census every ten years since 1790 to determine how many people live in the United States. The information gathered by census takers has told us how our nation has grown and changed over the years. A nation of farms has become a nation of cities and suburbs.

Recent statistics reveal that Americans are living longer, having smaller families, and moving to the Sunbelt. The number of African Americans, Hispanics, and Asian Americans is increasing, as is the number of women entering the work force.

CHAPTER 1 SUMMARY

SOCIAL STUDIES SKILL
Using Your Textbook

Have you ever heard the phrase "tools of the trade"? These are the tools that help people do their jobs. Right now, your job is studying civics. Your basic learning tool is your textbook.

Even though you've already had a great deal of practice using textbooks, remember that each textbook is a specialized tool. You have to treat this book as you would any new tool. You need to explore all its features to discover how it works and how it can best serve you.

How to Use the Textbook

To get the most from your textbook, follow these guidelines.

1. **Use the Table of Contents.** Look first at the Table of Contents, which begins on page v. The Table of Contents will give you an overview of the topics in the textbook and show you how the book is organized.
2. **Study each unit's opening page.** Begin each unit by looking at the unit's opening page. For example, review the opening page of Unit One (page 1). Read the title of the unit and the titles of the chapters found in the unit. Note what the unit title says about the chapters in the unit.
3. **Begin at the beginning.** Turn to pages 2–3 for the opening of Chapter 1. Look at the chapter title, the section titles, and the illustration. Note what these items say about the theme of the chapter. Next read the Chapter Focus and Study Guide features. These features will guide you in studying the chapter.
4. **Preview the chapter.** Skim the chapter, noting all section titles (pages 3, 6, and 11). Read the subheadings in each section. These give you clues about the details that support the section's main ideas. Note the photographs and other visuals in each sec-

tion. Glance at the first Section Review (page 6). Previewing will give you a firm foundation on which to base your study.

5. **Read the chapter carefully.** Careful reading will help you get the most out of your textbook. First, use the headings and subheadings as clues to main ideas and supporting details. Second, note the words printed in bold black type. These **boldfaced terms** are highlighted to indicate their importance to the study of civics. The meaning of a boldfaced term can be learned from the sentences surrounding it. Use the Section Review at the end of each section to check your progress. Then read the Chapter Summary (page 17).
6. **Study the special features.** Each unit of the textbook contains a number of special features that will add to your knowledge of and enjoyment of civics. Be sure to read each feature carefully.
7. **Review your learning.** The textbook contains Chapter Reviews (page 19) and Unit Reviews (page 92). Each of these reviews will help you to check your understanding.
8. **Use the end-of-book material.** The textbook contains a large Reference Section, including a Glossary and an Index, that will add to your study of civics. Familiarize yourself with this material now so that you may use it as needed (beginning on page 529).

Applying the Skill

Complete the following activities.

1. Turn to the Table of Contents. **(a)** How many units and chapters are contained in the textbook? **(b)** What is the title of Unit Six?
2. Turn to the Glossary beginning on page 567. **(a)** What does the term "currency" mean? **(b)** What is the second entry under "G"?

Reviewing Terms

On a separate sheet of paper, supply the term from the list below that correctly completes each sentence.

immigrants   citizens
government   naturalization
refugees   quota
census

1. _____ is the authority, or power, that rules on behalf of a group of people.
2. The legal process by which aliens may become American citizens is called _____.
3. Members of a nation are called the nation's _____.
4. The term _____ refers to homeless people who flee their nation in order to find safety in a foreign nation.
5. _____ are people who come to the United States from other nations in order to settle here permanently.
6. The official count of the United States population that is taken every ten years is called the _____.
7. A _____ is the limit placed on the number of immigrants admitted to a nation in any one year.

Using Thinking Skills

1. **Comparing Ideas** (a) Compare America's immigration policy before 1880 with its policy after 1880. (b) Where do today's immigrants come from?
2. **Organizing Ideas** What are the main steps by which an alien becomes an American citizen?
3. **Expressing Ideas** What do recent statistics tell us about migration patterns in the United States?
4. **Drawing Conclusions** (a) How did the founders of our government make sure that government would serve the people? (b) Why is it important to study civics?

5. **Seeing Relationships** (a) Why is the size of the American household decreasing? (b) How are the lives of women changing? (c) Why is our nation growing older?
6. **Identifying Ideas** Who were the early settlers to America?
7. **Summarizing Ideas** List the ten characteristics of good citizenship.
8. **Understanding Ideas** (a) What are the three ways by which a population may grow? (b) Describe the growth of the American population. (c) What are the three largest minority groups in the United States?

Practicing Civics Skills

1. **Locating Information** (a) How many chapters are contained in Unit Four? (b) What is the title of Chapter 19? (c) Where in the textbook did you look to find the answers to these questions?
2. **Identifying Sources** Identify the sources in the Reference Section you would use to find the following information: (a) a definition of the term "citizen"; (b) the name of the 14th President of the United States; (c) the population of your state; (d) the page on which the Constitutional Convention is first mentioned.

Being a Good Citizen

1. Interview an older relative or neighbor who immigrated to the United States in the early decades of the 1900s. Record his or her experiences to present to the class.
2. Work with a committee of students to prepare and display posters on such topics as "The American Dream," "Immigration to America," and "Good Citizenship."
3. Write a short paper describing the history of contributions made to American society by one of the following groups: African Americans, Hispanics, Asian Americans.
4. Invite a naturalized citizen to class to describe how he or she became a citizen.

CHAPTER 2
Foundations of Our Government

Chapter Sections

Chapter Focus

What do we mean by the word "government"? You probably have a fairly good idea of what government is. The chances are, however, that you have never before tried to describe it in a few words.

When you think of government, perhaps you think of the Capitol Building in Washington, D.C., or your state capital, or the city hall in your own community. Perhaps you think of the President of the United States, the governor of your state, or the mayor of the town in which you live. Perhaps you think of laws you must obey or the rules of the student council in your school. If you do think of government in this way, you are on the right track.

Yet government is not only buildings and leaders and laws. It includes all of these—and much more. **Government** is the entire system of authority, or power, that acts on behalf of a group of people.

Our American government is a government "of the people, by the people, and for the people." Its main purpose is to serve the people. It protects our rights as individuals and safeguards our freedom. The American government is you—it is all of us.

Study Guide

As you begin to read about how and why our government was created, look for answers to the following questions:

★ What types of government exist around the world, and why is government necessary?
★ What was the nation's first plan of government, and why was it a weak plan?
★ How did the Constitutional Convention create a strong new nation?

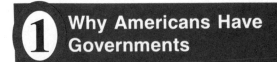

① Why Americans Have Governments

To govern means to rule. A government is any organization set up to make and enforce rules. You actually live under three different governments. The city or town where you live has a government. It makes and enforces rules for the people in your community. Your state government makes and enforces rules for the people in your state. Our national government makes and enforces rules for all the people in the United States.

Governments Differ

Every nation in the world has a government. These governments, however, are not all alike. There are many important differences in the way they govern. They differ in the way their rulers are chosen and in the amount of power held by their people. Each nation's government has been shaped by the beliefs of the people and by their history.

In times past, the governments of many nations were controlled by kings or queens. They often held all the power in their nation's governments, and they were able to rule by force. For this reason, they were called **absolute monarchs.** Today there are few absolute monarchs left. Most nations that have monarchs greatly limit their power.

In some nations, one person or a small group of people holds all the power. The government has total control over the lives of the people. It rules the nation by force. We call this type of government a **dictatorship** or a **totalitarian government**.

Other nations have a democratic form of government. In a **democracy,** the people of a nation rule directly or they elect officials who will act for them. The word "democracy" comes from an ancient Greek term meaning "rule of the people."

There are different forms of democracy. In a **direct democracy,** all the voters in a community meet together at one place to make laws and decide what actions to take. This works only in small communities.

In a **representative democracy,** the people elect representatives to carry on the work of government for them. This system of government is also called a **republic.** It is the form of government we have in the United States.

Americans are fortunate to live in a republic. We believe that the people should rule themselves. We have a form of government in which the leaders are responsible to the people. The term **American government** refers to the authority that Americans have set up to help them rule their own affairs.

Why Do We Need Government?

Wouldn't it be possible for all of us to live as we choose? Couldn't we manage our own affairs without a government? Do we really need rules for getting along with one another? In order to answer these questions, it is important to understand the basic purposes of government.

Government Makes It Possible for People to Live Together

Whenever large groups of people have lived together, they have found it necessary to have a government. Under early forms of government, the strongest person was often made the leader of the people. This person could best help the people defend themselves against their enemies. When food was scarce, the best hunter might be the leader, because a hunter could help get a good food supply. In other matters, such as whether the people should move to better land, a group of the oldest and wisest leaders might decide.

One of the earliest lessons people learned was that cooperation was useful. It was easier to hunt and kill a large animal for food if the group worked together. The people could better protect themselves against enemies when they were united. Even the simplest form of government helped to make life safer, easier, and more pleasant.

Government Performs Many Services

Over the years, government has grown more and more complex. Yet its basic purposes have remained the same. It provides ways for people to live and work together. It also enables a large group of people to get things done. It might be possible for each person in the group to do some of these things alone. However, it usually would be more difficult and expensive for each person to do so.

For example, what would happen if each family in your community had to educate its own children? Even if parents had time enough to teach, would they be able to teach well? How would they teach subjects they had forgotten or perhaps had never studied when they went to school? By establishing schools, our government makes it possible for all children to receive a good education.

Government also performs other services that would be difficult or impossible for in-dividual citizens to provide for themselves. Government protects the people from enemy nations. It also provides police to protect our lives and property. Our homes are protected by fire departments.

Because of government, American citizens can travel over highways that stretch from sea to sea and from border to border. A system of money makes it easy for Americans to buy and sell things and to know the value of these things. Trash is collected, and health laws are enforced. Libraries are built and operated. These and many more services are provided by government.

Government Provides Rules, or Laws

Large groups of people need rules to help them live together in peace. When there are rules, all people know what they may and may not do. Without rules, any disagreement would probably end with the strongest members of the group settling things their way.

Providing rules of conduct for the group is therefore one of the most important reasons for establishing governments. These rules are known as **laws.** They are written down so that people can know them and obey them. Laws are written by our government to guide, as well as to protect, all of us.

For example, if you own a house on a city or village street, a law may require you to keep your sidewalk in good repair. If you allow cracks to form, someone may fall and be injured. This law also protects you and your family, since you must depend on your neighbors to keep their sidewalks in good condition.

Many of the laws under which we live are contained in **constitutions,** or written plans of government. Americans have used constitutions to establish their national and state governments. A constitution states the purposes of the government. It describes how the government is to be organized, or set up. It also contains the most important laws the government is to uphold.

Our government provides its citizens with hundreds of services, such as free public libraries and the maintenance of community-owned trees.

Government Enables a Nation to Put Its Ideals into Practice

A nation's government helps put into practice the ideals of the people, the things in which they believe. Americans believe that the people should rule themselves. We also believe that each person is important and that no one should be denied his or her rights.

What are these rights? In the Declaration of Independence (which you will read about later in this chapter), they are described as "life, liberty, and the pursuit of happiness." This means that all Americans have the right to live their own lives in liberty, or freedom, and to seek happiness for themselves.

To safeguard a citizen's liberty, our government guarantees certain freedoms, such as freedom of speech, freedom of the press, and freedom of religion. These freedoms can never be taken away from any American citizen by the government. Nor can they ever be restricted, except to keep people from using these freedoms to violate the rights of others.

For example, free speech and a free press do not mean freedom to tell lies or write false statements about another person. Each citizen has the right to have his or her reputation protected from efforts to hurt or destroy it with untruths.

Americans believe that if any citizen is denied his or her rights, the liberty of all is endangered. Our government has helped its people put their ideals into practice by passing and enforcing laws that guarantee equal rights for all citizens. For example, we have laws requiring that all Americans be given equal opportunities to get an education, to vote, and to find jobs.

 SECTION 1 REVIEW

Define government, absolute monarchs, dictatorship, totalitarian government, democracy, direct democracy, representative democracy, republic, American government, laws, constitutions

1. **Identifying Ideas (a)** What two factors shape a nation's government? **(b)** Identify who holds the power in each of the various types of government around the world.
2. **Contrasting Ideas** Explain how a direct democracy differs from a representative democracy.
3. **Summarizing Ideas (a)** What are the four basic purposes of government? **(b)** Give an example of the way in which the American government fulfills each of its purposes.

Thinking Critically Imagine that all governments and government services suddenly disappear. Describe how your life will be affected.

As you may remember from your study of American history, our nation was once ruled by Great Britain. However, Great Britain was far away on the other side of the Atlantic Ocean. This great distance made it easy for the American colonists to make their own rules and regulations without interference from British leaders.

When the British government under King George III began to enforce its rules and regulations in the colonies, the Americans were angry. They had become used to doing things their own way. They resented being told what they could and could not do. They especially resented being forced to obey laws they considered unjust. Americans wanted to be free to govern themselves. They fought the Revolutionary War to gain their independence as a nation and to be free.

The Declaration of Independence

When fighting broke out between the American colonies and Great Britain in 1775, the Americans were not yet officially seeking independence. The next year, however, leaders from all 13 colonies met in Philadelphia. At this meeting, called the Second Continental Congress, they named a committee to draw up a **Declaration of Independence.** Most of the Declaration was written by Thomas Jefferson. It was approved by members of the Continental Congress on July 4, 1776.

The Declaration explains the reasons the 13 colonies decided to separate from Great Britain and form a free nation. By doing so it upholds the philosophical position that the power of government comes from the consent of the governed—the people. If a government ignores the will of the people, the people have a legitimate right to change their government.

Yet the Declaration of Independence is much more than a document to justify in-

The artist John Trumbull painted this version of the signing of the Declaration of Independence. The tallest figure in the center is its author, Thomas Jefferson.

dependence. It also is a statement of American ideals. It explains to the world, in clear and inspiring language, that the purpose of government is to protect **human rights,** the basic rights to which all people are entitled as human beings.

Ideals of American Government

These basic human rights are clearly defined in the Declaration of Independence:

> We hold these truths to be self-evident: That all men are created equal; that they are endowed by their Creator with certain unalienable rights; that among these are life, liberty, and the pursuit of happiness.

This passage is one of the most famous in American writing. Over the years it has come to mean that all Americans—members of all races and both men and women—are equal under the law.

For example, the right of each individual to life, liberty, and happiness must be equal to that of every other individual. In other words, no person has the right to consider his or her own life and liberties more important than those of others.

The leaders who signed the Declaration of Independence realized that these ideals would be difficult to achieve. Yet they believed these ideals were worth "our lives, our fortunes, and our sacred honor."

The Declaration of Independence is one of the greatest documents in the history of our nation. Although written more than 200 years ago, it has remained a lasting symbol of American freedom. (You will find the complete text on pages 35–37.)

A Government for the New Nation

The Declaration of Independence did not provide a government for the new American nation. In 1777, while the Revolutionary War

Did you know that...

there was no official ceremony for the signing of the Declaration of Independence? Although paintings show delegates to the Second Continental Congress signing the document as a group, such a ceremony did not actually take place.

The Congress did adopt the Declaration on July 4, 1776—the occasion we celebrate as Independence Day. But only John Hancock, president of the Congress, signed the Declaration on that day. Other signers added their names between then and November 4. The last signature on the Declaration was not added until 1781!

Maybe you have seen a copy of Hancock's signature on the Declaration. He wrote it with such a flourish that we still use the expression "John Hancock" to mean a person's signature.

was still being fought, the Continental Congress drew up a new plan of government. It was approved by the 13 states and began to operate in 1781. This plan of government was called the **Articles of Confederation.**

The Articles of Confederation

A **confederation** is a loose association rather than a firm union of states. The Articles of Confederation, the young nation's first plan of government, set up a "firm league of friendship" among the 13 states. Each state in the

Can you imagine what would happen if each state issued its own money today? That is what the states did under the Articles of Confederation.

nation was to have equal powers and in most ways was independent of the other states. The central, or national, government was given very limited powers. The people of the 13 states did not want a strong central government. They feared that such a government might use its power to limit the freedom of the separate states.

Under the Articles of Confederation, the national government consisted of a lawmaking body of one house, called Congress. The states sent representatives to Congress. Each state had one vote in Congress, regardless of the number of people living in the state.

There was no provision in the Articles for a President or executive branch to carry out the nation's laws. Instead, the Articles gave the states the power to enforce the laws passed by Congress. In part, this was because the people were suspicious of strong leaders after their experience with King George III of Great Britain. The Articles also did not establish a national court system to interpret the nation's laws and punish lawbreakers.

During the Revolutionary War, the 13 states were willing to work together and make sacrifices to achieve victory. Things were dif-ferent in the years following the Revolution, however. Many Americans suffered difficult times after the war. Property had been destroyed. Trade with other nations had been cut off. American business was badly hurt. Moreover, the war left the young nation deeply in debt. The new government tried its best to handle these difficult problems. But it was too weak to solve them.

The Weaknesses of the Confederation

There were many reasons for the weakness of our nation's government under the Articles of Confederation. Congress had trouble passing laws, because a vote of 9 of the 13 states was needed to pass important measures. Without a President or executive branch, there were no officials to see that the laws passed by Congress were carried out. Moreover, there were no national courts to interpret the laws or to judge those who broke them.

In addition, it was very difficult to change the Articles of Confederation in order to make the national government stronger. Changes in the Articles required the unanimous vote of all 13 states.

One of the main weaknesses of the new national government was that Congress lacked the power to collect taxes. Congress could ask the states to contribute money to help the national government meet its expenses. But Congress had no power to force states to make these contributions.

Without money, Congress could not pay its debts or carry on any government programs that might be needed. Congress also could not pay the soldiers who had fought in the Revolutionary War or repay the money it owed to foreign nations.

Under the Articles of Confederation, the national government also lacked other important powers. It could not regulate, or control, trade between the states or with foreign nations. Each state regulated its own trade. This caused many disputes among the states and with other nations. In addition, most of the states issued their own money.

The states were acting more like small separate nations than states that were members of a confederation. The states often refused to obey the laws of Congress. As a result, relations between the states and Congress grew steadily worse.

Why the Confederation Failed

The Articles of Confederation succeeded in establishing a new nation. This was a major achievement. Yet the national government set up by the Articles failed in a number of important ways.

The real trouble with the government set up by the Articles of Confederation was that the states refused to give the national government enough power to operate effectively. The states feared a strong central government and kept most of the real power in their own hands.

The people of each state continued to think of themselves as belonging to their particular state rather than to the nation as a whole. This was natural because the states were separated by great distances and transportation was poor. Also, there was little contact between many of the states. It took years before the states began to think of themselves as parts of a single nation.

The weaknesses of the national government became clear as new problems faced the American nation. The states began to quarrel over the location of boundary lines. They got into disputes over trade. The national government was powerless to end these disagreements. It seemed as if the new American nation was about to break up into several small nations.

A growing number of leaders began to favor strengthening the national government. As a result, in 1787 Congress called upon the states to send representatives to a meeting to consider what could be done to improve the American government.

SECTION 2 REVIEW

Define human rights, confederation

Identify Declaration of Independence, Articles of Confederation

1. **Seeing Relationships (a)** What was the outcome of the Second Continental Congress? **(b)** Why was the outcome of this meeting so important?
2. **Expressing Ideas (a)** Describe the weaknesses of the nation's first plan of government. **(b)** How did the lack of a strong national government create problems?

Thinking Critically You are a delegate to the Second Continental Congress. Write a letter to one of your relatives in Great Britain that explains why Americans believe they must be free to govern themselves.

3 Writing and Approving the Constitution

On May 25, 1787, a group of the nation's most outstanding leaders met in Independence Hall in Philadelphia. They had been sent as **delegates,** or representatives, of their states to find ways to improve the national government. The delegates soon became convinced that simply changing the Articles of Confederation was not enough. They decided instead to draw up a completely new plan of government, a new constitution.

The meeting became known as the **Constitutional Convention.** The leaders who attended wrote a constitution that established a government for the United States that has lasted for more than 200 years. The new plan of government the delegates drafted is the **Constitution of the United States.** It is the world's oldest written constitution still in effect.

The Delegates

The 55 delegates who attended the Constitutional Convention included some of the most famous leaders in the nation. George Washington had led the American army to victory over the British in the Revolutionary War. Respected by all, he was chosen to preside over the Convention. He called on speakers and kept the meetings moving smoothly. Benjamin Franklin—diplomat, inventor, writer—was world famous. Then 81 years old, Franklin was the oldest delegate to the Constitutional Convention.

Among the other delegates to the Constitutional Convention were James Madison, Alexander Hamilton, James Wilson, Roger Sherman, William Paterson, and Edmund Randolph. They had all been involved in the nation's struggle for independence.

The English Background

These leaders knew history well, and they had learned many important lessons from the past. The delegates wanted the American people to enjoy the rights the English had fought for and won during past centuries.

This heritage from England included the rights mentioned in the **Magna Carta** (the Great Charter), which the English people had won from King John in 1215. This important document guaranteed that free people could not be arrested, put in prison, or forced to leave their nation unless they were given a trial by other free people who were their equals. It also guaranteed that citizens of England were to be judged only according to English law.

The members of the Constitutional Convention also wished the new American nation to have the rights contained in the English Bill of Rights of 1689. One of these rights was the right to petition, or request, the government to improve or to change laws. Another was the right to a fair punishment if a citizen were found guilty of a crime.

The Convention delegates in Philadelphia also studied carefully the example of the British Parliament. **Parliament** is the law-making body of the British government. It is **bicameral.** That is, it consists of two parts, or houses. It is made up of the House of Lords, appointed by the monarch, and the House of Commons, elected by the people. This enables each house to check on and improve the work of the other house. The leaders in Philadelphia wanted no part of royalty or nobility. However, they could see the advantages of a two-house lawmaking body.

Secret Meetings

The delegates to the Constitutional Convention held their meetings in secret. They were forbidden to discuss any of the business of the Convention with outsiders. This rule was put into effect so that the delegates could speak freely. Many delegates feared that if they spoke publicly on a particular issue, they might be subjected to pressure from outsiders. Taking a public stand would also make it more difficult for delegates to change their minds after debate and discussion. Some delegates criticized the secrecy rule. Without it, however, agreement on difficult issues might have been impossible.

If the meetings were held in secret, how do we know today what took place at the Convention? We know because of James Madison of Virginia. Madison kept a journal, or record, of the happenings at each meeting. His journal, which was kept secret until after his death, is our chief source of information about the Convention.

Writing the Constitution

The delegates agreed that the national government had to be given greater power. At the same time, most of the members agreed that the states should keep the powers needed to govern their own affairs. In order to achieve

The Constitutional Convention owed much of its success to the wisdom and work of these two delegates—Benjamin Franklin (left) and James Madison (right).

this, the delegates established a system of government known as a federal union, or a **federal system.** In a federal system, the powers of government are divided between the national government, which governs the whole nation, and state governments, which govern the people of each state.

The delegates worked out the new plan of a federal system at their meetings during the hot summer months of 1787. They discussed many ideas and proposals. They had to resolve many disputes as they worked on the Constitution. The delegates settled these differences of opinion by a series of compromises. A **compromise** is an agreement in which each side gives up part of its demands.

The most serious disagreement arose over the question of representation in the new national **legislature,** or lawmaking body. The larger states favored a legislature in which representation would be based on the size of a state's population. The smaller states wanted

each state to have an equal number of representatives in the legislature.

For weeks the delegates argued over this issue. Finally both sides agreed to a compromise. Their agreement provided for a lawmaking body of two houses, called Congress. In one house, the Senate, the states were to have equal representation. In the other house, the House of Representatives, each state was to be represented according to the size of its population. This agreement is known as the **Great Compromise.**

A Strong New Nation Is Created

Many other compromises were reached as the Convention delegates worked on the Constitution. The delegates agreed to take away some of the powers of the states and to increase the powers of the new national gov-

Weaknesses of Government Established by the Articles of Confederation (1781)

ONE-HOUSE CONGRESS

NO PRESIDENT

NO COURT SYSTEM

States given most powers; few powers given to the national government.

★ Congress elected by the state legislatures.

★ Laws were difficult to pass (approval of 9 out of 13 states required).

★ Congress had no power to collect taxes.

★ Congress had no power to regulate trade.

★ Congress had no power to coin money.

★ Congress had no power to establish armed forces—each state kept its own troops.

★ No President or executive branch.

★ No system of national courts.

Strengths of Government Established by the Constitution (1789)

TWO-HOUSE CONGRESS

A PRESIDENT

A COURT SYSTEM

States keep many powers; important powers given to the national government.

★ Congress elected by the people (after the 17th Amendment).

★ Laws easier to pass (majority vote required).

★ Congress given power to collect taxes.

★ Congress given power to regulate interstate and foreign trade.

★ Congress given power to coin money.

★ Congress given power to establish an army and a navy to defend the nation.

★ President given powers to enforce the laws.

★ National court system, including a Supreme Court, given power to interpret the laws.

---

ernment. The national government was given the power to tax, to regulate trade among the states and with foreign nations, to raise armed forces, and to coin and print money. Provision was made for a President to carry out the nation's laws. A Supreme Court and other national courts would interpret these laws. The chart on this page shows the major differences between the Articles and the Constitution.

By September 1787 the delegates had completed their work. Probably no delegate was satisfied with every part of the document. Benjamin Franklin, for example, did not approve of parts of the Constitution. Yet he believed that the delegates had written the best Constitution possible. For this reason, he urged the delegates to sign the Constitution.

Most of the members shared Franklin's feeling. Of the 42 delegates present that day, 39 signed the Constitution. After a farewell dinner, the delegates left for home.

Approving the Constitution

The work of the members of the Constitutional Convention was not over even after they left Philadelphia. The Constitution now had to be sent to the states and the people for their approval, or **ratification.** Before the Constitution could go into effect, it had to be approved, or ratified, by 9 of the 13 states. Each state set up a special convention of delegates to vote on the Constitution.

People quickly divided into two groups over the Constitution. Some supported it. Others were opposed to it. The public was swamped with pamphlets, letters to newspapers, and speeches by both groups.

Federalists and Anti-Federalists

Supporters of the Constitution were called **Federalists.** They favored a strong central, or national, government. The Federalists argued that the government under the Articles of Confederation was too weak to keep the country united. Unless the Constitution was adopted, they feared the United States would break up into 13 separate nations.

People who opposed the new Constitution were called **Anti-Federalists.** They feared that a Constitution that established a strong central government defeated the purpose of the recent war against Great Britain. The Anti-Federalists did not believe the new Constitution would protect the power of the states and the freedom of the people.

The Constitution Is Ratified

Gradually those who favored the Constitution gained support. However, many citizens were upset that the Constitution did not contain a list of the rights of the people. Finally it was agreed that such a list, or bill, of rights for the

George Washington was inaugurated as the first President of the United States in New York City on April 30, 1789.

people would be added if the new Constitution were ratified.

Most of the states ratified the Constitution in 1787 and 1788. The new government of the United States began to operate in March 1789. Two states, North Carolina and Rhode Island, did not approve the Constitution until after it went into effect.

New York City was chosen as the nation's temporary capital. There, on April 30, 1789, George Washington was sworn in as the first President of the United States. Members of the new Senate and House of Representatives arrived to begin their work. The nation's new government was under way.

The Constitution of the United States is such a remarkable and important document that every American citizen should read and study it carefully. (The complete text of the Constitution can be found on pages 55–75.) You will learn more about the government established by the Constitution in the next chapter.

 SECTION 3 REVIEW

Define delegates, bicameral, federal system, compromise, legislature, ratification

Identify Constitutional Convention, Constitution of the United States, Magna Carta, Parliament, Great Compromise, Federalists, Anti-Federalists

1. **Drawing Conclusions** What ideas of government did the delegates borrow from Great Britain?
2. **Seeing Relationships** In what ways did the Constitution strengthen government?
3. **Understanding Ideas (a)** What was the basis of the argument between the Federalists and the Anti-Federalists, and how was it settled? **(b)** What happened after the Constitution was ratified?

Thinking Critically You are a delegate to the Constitutional Convention. Write an entry in your journal describing the debate over the decision to hold secret meetings.

CHAPTER 2 SUMMARY

Government serves many important purposes. Above all, government makes it possible for people to live and work together. Government provides many services that citizens acting alone could not perform.

Americans believe that our people should rule themselves. We also believe that no person should be denied his or her rights. These ideals of the American people are clearly set forth in the Declaration of Independence, one of the greatest documents in the history of our nation.

The Articles of Confederation established the first government of the 13 states. Under this plan, the weak national government could not operate effectively.

In 1787 delegates to the Constitutional Convention wrote a new plan of government for the nation. This plan, the Constitution of the United States, has lasted for more than 200 years. It created a stronger national government. It established a lawmaking body of two houses, called Congress. It also provided for a President to carry out the laws and for national courts to interpret the laws. The Constitution was approved by the states in 1789.

★ CIVICS
SKILLS

SOCIAL STUDIES SKILL
Learning from Pictures

According to an old saying, "One picture is worth a thousand words." A picture, however, does not speak for itself. You have to know how to read and interpret a picture before you can fully grasp its meaning. Fortunately, there are easy guidelines you can follow that will help you learn to get the most information from the pictures in your textbook.

How to Gather Information from Pictures

To effectively gather information from pictures, follow these guidelines.

1. **Determine the subject of the picture.** Look at the people who are portrayed in the picture and take note of any objects that surround these people. Try to determine what the people portrayed in the picture are doing. Check the title of the picture or read the caption that accompanies it for clues to its subject matter.
2. **Examine the details.** Study the details of the picture, including the picture's background. Remember that *all* of the visual evidence in a picture is important to your understanding of a historical event or time period.
3. **Determine the artist's point of view.** Most people think that a picture presents only facts. But this is not the case. Any photograph or picture also expresses the artist's own ideas and feelings about a subject. Certain details are emphasized over the rest. Other details are left out of the picture. With this in mind, try to determine whether the artist is portraying the events in the picture favorably or unfavorably. Ask yourself what impact the picture might have on other viewers.
4. **Use the information carefully.** Try to determine whether the information presented in the picture is an accurate description of the actual events. Remember that a picture is an artist's interpretation of an event. Therefore, consider what you already know about the event or time period. Knowing whether or not the picture is accurate will give you clues about how to use the information.

Applying the Skill

Carefully examine the painting below, which shows George Washington addressing the delegates to the Constitutional Convention. Then answer the following questions.

1. Which details in the painting is the artist trying to emphasize?
2. **(a)** How does the artist want you to feel about George Washington? **(b)** Which details in the painting support your answer?
3. Using what you have learned about the Constitutional Convention from the textbook, why do you think the artist made George Washington the center of attention?

Chapter 2 Foundations of Our Government 33

Reviewing Terms

On a separate sheet of paper, write each of the following terms. Then read the definitions below. Choose the definition that best fits each term. Write the definition next to the proper term.

confederation	ratification
republic	compromise
laws	delegates
constitution	federal system

1. The approval of the Constitution by the states.
2. Representatives sent by the states to attend the Constitutional Convention.
3. A written plan of government.
4. An organization in which powers are divided between the national government and the state governments.
5. A form of government in which the people elect representatives to carry on the work of government for them.
6. A league of states loosely bound together.
7. An agreement in which each side gives up part of its demands.
8. Rules of conduct for a group of people to follow.

Using Thinking Skills

1. **Expressing Ideas** (a) What were the main purposes of the Declaration of Independence? (b) What rights were guaranteed by the Magna Carta and the English Bill of Rights?
2. **Comparing Ideas** (a) Explain how various governments around the world differ. (b) What factors shape a nation's government?
3. **Seeing Relationships** (a) Why did the delegates to the Constitutional Convention decide to hold secret meetings? (b) How do we know today what occurred at the Convention?
4. **Composing a Paragraph** Write a paragraph that explains the purposes of government.

5. **Summarizing Ideas** What evidence shows that the nation's new government got under way soon after the Constitution went into effect?
6. **Organizing Ideas** (a) What are the three types of government under which you live? (b) Explain the difference between a direct democracy and a representative democracy.
7. **Drawing Conclusions** (a) Describe the weaknesses of the American government under the Articles of Confederation. (b) How did the Constitution correct these weaknesses?
8. **Understanding Ideas** (a) Explain how the delegates settled the question of representation in the national legislature. (b) What was the basis of the argument between supporters and opponents of the Constitution? (c) What agreement led to ratification of the Constitution?

Practicing Civics Skills

Analyzing a Painting Look at the painting on page 31 of your textbook and answer the following questions. (a) What event does the painting show? (b) What details does the artist emphasize? (c) How would you describe the expression on the faces of most of the people in the painting? (d) What do you think the artist wanted the painting to "say"?

Being a Good Citizen

1. Work with a committee to prepare a bulletin-board display on "The Great Ideals of American Government."
2. Read a biography of Thomas Jefferson. Then write a report describing his role in the writing of the Declaration of Independence.
3. Organize groups to report on special topics. Topics might include "Why We Need Governments," "How Governments Began," and "The Role Played by George Washington in the Constitutional Convention."

The Declaration of Independence

In Congress, July 4, 1776
The Unanimous Declaration of the Thirteen United States of America

Why the Declaration Was Written

When, in the course of human events, it becomes necessary for one people to dissolve the political bands which have connected them with another, and to assume, among the powers of the earth, the separate and equal station to which the laws of nature and of nature's God entitle them, a decent respect to the opinions of mankind requires that they should declare the causes which impel them to the separation.

Statement of Basic Human Rights

We hold these truths to be self-evident: That all men are created equal; that they are endowed by their Creator with certain unalienable rights; that among these are life, liberty, and the pursuit of happiness.

Government Must Safeguard Human Rights

That to secure these rights, governments are instituted among men, deriving their just powers from the consent of the governed;

That whenever any form of government becomes destructive of these ends, it is the right of the people to alter or to abolish it, and to institute a new government, laying its foundation on such principles, and organizing its powers in such form, as to them shall seem most likely to effect their safety and happiness. Prudence, indeed, will dictate that governments long established should not be changed for light and transient causes; and accordingly all experience hath shown that mankind are more disposed to suffer while evils are suffer-able, than to right themselves by abolishing the forms to which they are accustomed. But when a long train of abuses and usurpations, pursuing invariably the same object, evinces a design to reduce them under absolute despotism, it is their right, it is their duty, to throw off such government, and to provide new guards for their future security.

Abuses of Human Rights by the King

Such has been the patient sufferance of these colonies; and such is now the necessity which constrains them to alter their former systems of government. The history of the present King of Great Britain is a history of repeated injuries and usurpations, all having in direct object the establishment of an absolute tyranny over these states. To prove this, let facts be submitted to a candid world.

He has refused his assent to laws the most wholesome and necessary for the public good.

He has forbidden his governors to pass laws of immediate and pressing importance, unless suspended in their operation till his assent should be obtained; and, when so suspended, he has utterly neglected to attend to them.

He has refused to pass other laws for the accommodation of large districts of people, unless those people would relinquish the right of representation in the legislature, a right inestimable to them, and formidable to tyrants only.

He has called together legislative bodies at places unusual, uncomfortable, and distant from the depository of their public records, for the sole purpose of fatiguing them into compliance with his measures.

He has dissolved representative houses repeatedly, for opposing, with manly firmness, his invasions on the rights of the people.

He has refused, for a long time after such dissolutions, to cause others to be elected, whereby the legislative powers, incapable of annihilation, have returned to the people at large for their exercise; the state remaining, in the mean time, exposed to all the dangers of invasion from without and convulsions within.

He has endeavored to prevent the population of these states; for that purpose obstructing the laws of naturalization of foreigners, refusing to pass others to encourage their migrations hither, and raising the conditions of new appropriations of lands.

He has obstructed the administration of justice, by refusing his assent to laws for establishing judiciary powers.

He has made judges dependent on his will alone for the tenure of their offices, and the amount and payment of their salaries.

He has erected a multitude of new offices, and sent hither swarms of officers to harass our people and eat out their substance.

He has kept among us, in times of peace, standing armies, without the consent of our legislatures.

He has affected to render the military independent of, and superior to, the civil power.

He has combined with others to subject us to a jurisdiction foreign to our constitution, and unacknowledged by our laws; giving his assent to their acts of pretended legislation:

For quartering large bodies of armed troops among us;

For protecting them, by a mock trial, from punishment for any murders which they should commit on the inhabitants of these states;

For cutting off our trade with all parts of the world;

For imposing taxes on us without our consent;

For depriving us, in many cases, of the benefits of trial by jury;

For transporting us beyond seas, to be tried for pretended offenses;

For abolishing the free system of English laws in a neighboring province, establishing therein an arbitrary government, and enlarging its boundaries, so as to render it at once an example and fit instrument for introducing the same absolute rule into these colonies;

For taking away our charters, abolishing our most valuable laws, and altering, fundamentally, the forms of our governments;

For suspending our own legislatures, and declaring themselves invested with power to legislate for us in all cases whatsoever.

He has abdicated government here, by declaring us out of his protection and waging war against us.

He has plundered our seas, ravaged our coasts, burnt our towns, and destroyed the lives of our people.

He is at this time transporting large armies of foreign mercenaries to complete the works of death, desolation, and tyranny already begun with circumstances of cruelty and perfidy scarcely paralleled in the most barbarous ages, and totally unworthy the head of a civilized nation.

He has constrained our fellow citizens, taken captive on the high seas, to bear arms against their country, to become the executioners of their friends and brethren, or to fall themselves by their hands.

He has excited domestic insurrections amongst us, and has endeavored to bring on the inhabitants of our frontiers the merciless Indian savages, whose known rule of warfare is an undistinguished destruction of all ages, sexes, and conditions.

Colonial Efforts to Avoid Separation

In every stage of these oppressions we have petitioned for redress in the most humble terms; our repeated petitions have been answered only by repeated injury.

A prince whose character is thus marked

by every act which may define a tyrant is unfit to be the ruler of a free people.

Nor have we been wanting in our attentions to our British brethren. We have warned them, from time to time, of attempts by their legislature to extend an unwarrantable jurisdiction over us. We have reminded them of the circumstances of our emigration and settlement here. We have appealed to their native justice and magnanimity; and we have conjured them, by the ties of our common kindred, to disavow these usurpations, which would inevitably interrupt our connections and correspondence. They, too, have been deaf to the voice of justice and consanguinity. We must, therefore, acquiesce in the necessity which denounces our separation, and hold them, as we hold the rest of mankind, enemies in war, in peace friends.

assembled, appealing to the Supreme Judge of the world for the rectitude of our intentions, do, in the name and by the authority of the good people of these colonies, solemnly publish and declare, That these united colonies are, and of right ought to be, free and independent states; that they are absolved from all allegiance to the British crown, and that all political connection between them and the state of Great Britain is, and ought to be, totally dissolved; and that, as free and independent states, they have full power to levy war, conclude peace, contract alliances, establish commerce, and to do all other acts and things which independent states may of right do. And, for the support of this declaration, with a firm reliance on the protection of Divine Providence, we mutually pledge to each other our lives, our fortunes, and our sacred honor.

The Colonies Declare Independence

We, therefore, the representatives of the United States of America, in General Congress

John Hancock

President

NEW HAMPSHIRE
Josiah Bartlett
William Whipple
Matthew Thornton

MASSACHUSETTS
Samuel Adams
John Adams
Robert Treat Paine
Elbridge Gerry

RHODE ISLAND
Stephen Hopkins
William Ellery

CONNECTICUT
Roger Sherman
Samuel Huntington
William Williams
Oliver Wolcott

NEW YORK
William Floyd
Philip Livingston
Francis Lewis
Lewis Morris

NEW JERSEY
Richard Stockton
John Witherspoon
Francis Hopkinson
John Hart
Abraham Clark

PENNSYLVANIA
Robert Morris
Benjamin Rush
Benjamin Franklin
John Morton
George Clymer
James Smith
George Taylor
James Wilson
George Ross

DELAWARE
Caesar Rodney
George Read
Thomas McKean

MARYLAND
Samuel Chase
William Paca
Thomas Stone
Charles Carroll
of Carrollton

VIRGINIA
George Wythe
Richard Henry Lee
Thomas Jefferson
Benjamin Harrison
Thomas Nelson, Jr.
Francis Lightfoot Lee
Carter Braxton

NORTH CAROLINA
William Hooper
Joseph Hewes
John Penn

SOUTH CAROLINA
Edward Rutledge
Thomas Heyward, Jr.
Thomas Lynch, Jr.
Arthur Middleton

GEORGIA
Button Gwinnett
Lyman Hall
George Walton

The American Constitution

Chapter Sections

Chapter Focus

The United States has a **constitutional** form of government. This means that we are governed according to the provisions of our Constitution. Our rights are written into the Constitution and must be respected by the government. The Constitution is the highest law of the land. Everyone, even the President of the United States, is required to obey the Constitution.

A famous English leader, William Pitt, said many years ago that the Constitution of the United States "will be a pattern for all future constitutions and will receive the admiration of all future ages." Time has proved the truth of these words. The Constitution is now the world's oldest written plan of government still working successfully.

Our Constitution has been successful because it is based upon many great ideals concerning government. At the same time, it provides us with a system of government that enables us to put these ideals into action.

Study Guide

As you begin to learn about the Constitution and about the workings of our nation's government, look for answers to the following questions:

★ What ideals are expressed in the Constitution of the United States?

★ What are the branches of government, and how does the Constitution control their power?

★ How does the Constitution provide for changing needs and changing conditions?

1 Great Ideals in the Constitution

The Declaration of Independence states that governments should receive their powers from "the consent [approval] of the governed [people]." This is one of the basic ideals upon which our nation was founded.

This ideal, treasured by the writers of the Constitution, can be traced in part to the **Mayflower Compact** (see page 535). The Compact was drawn up on November 11, 1620, when the Pilgrims on the *Mayflower* reached the New World. They were far off course and had no charter from the king to settle in New England or to form a government. The Pilgrim leaders wrote the Compact to create a new government, one based on cooperation and the consent of the people.

Consent of the Governed

Government by consent of the governed, or **popular sovereignty,** is one of our most cherished ideals. It is stated in the opening sentence of the Constitution, which is known as the **Preamble.** The Preamble is an introduction that explains why the Constitution was written.

The Preamble begins with the words "We the people." They are very meaningful words. The writers of the Constitution wanted to emphasize the importance of the people. These words stress that our government was established by the people. As the Preamble clearly states, "We the people of the United States, . . . do ordain [order] and establish this Constitution. . . ."

Six Goals of the Constitution

The Preamble itself is not law. Rather, it is a statement of goals. (See page 55.)

The Preamble lists these six goals for the government of the United States:

1. "To Form a More Perfect Union." The new government should be a better union of states than the one the people had under the Articles of Confederation.

2. "To Establish Justice." The government should make laws and establish a system of courts that are fair to all.

3. "To Insure Domestic Tranquillity." The government should preserve peace within the country.

4. "To Provide for the Common Defense." The government should be able to protect the nation from its enemies.

5. "To Promote the General Welfare." The government should help ensure the well-being of all the people.

6. "To Secure the Blessings of Liberty." The freedom of the people should be carefully safeguarded now and in the future.

These goals reflect the belief that the government should serve its citizens. They remain the goals of our nation today.

Our Representative Democracy

The representative democracy, or republic, that was set up by our Constitution is based upon the consent of the people who are governed. What happens, though, if the people become dissatisfied with the way their representatives are governing them? In that case, the people can let their representatives know what they think should be done. If people do not approve of their representatives' actions, at the next election they can elect new representatives who they hope will do a better job.

Our republic works successfully because Americans believe in **majority rule.** The majority is more than half of the people. When disagreements occur, the decision of the majority is accepted by all. However, under our system of government, the majority must always respect the rights of the minority—the smaller group of people. Moreover, the minority must be free to express its views on issues and to try to convince the majority to accept its ideas.

Government Based on a Federal System

As you learned in the last chapter, the delegates at the Constitutional Convention agreed to establish a federal system of government for the United States. Under **federalism** the powers of government are divided between the national government, which governs the whole nation, and state governments, which govern the people of each state.

The national government is usually called the **federal government.** It is important

How the Powers of Government Are Divided

FEDERAL GOVERNMENT POWERS (Delegated Powers)	POWERS SHARED by Federal and State Governments (Concurrent Powers)	STATE GOVERNMENT POWERS (Reserved Powers)
To regulate interstate and foreign trade	To collect taxes	To regulate trade within the state
To coin and print money	To borrow money	To establish local governments
To conduct foreign relations	To establish courts	To conduct elections
To establish post offices and roads	To enforce laws and punish lawbreakers	To determine qualifications of voters
To raise and support armed forces	To provide for the health and welfare of the people	To establish and support public schools
To declare war and make peace		To incorporate business firms
To govern American territories and admit new states		To license professional workers
To pass naturalization laws and regulate immigration		To keep all powers not granted to the federal government nor prohibited to the states
To make all laws "necessary and proper" to carry out its powers		

to remember that the term "federal government" refers to the national government, which is centered in Washington, D.C. The term "federal system" is used to refer to our entire system of government and includes both the federal government and the 50 state governments.

Under our federal system, the federal government is given certain important powers. All powers that are not given to the federal government remain with the states.

Powers of the Federal Government. The powers of the federal government, called **delegated powers,** are meant to apply to matters concerning all the people. For example, only the federal government can coin money. Only the federal government has the power to control trade with foreign nations. The federal government alone has the power to provide for the common defense, because an attack on the United States would threaten all Americans.

You recall that under the Articles of Confederation, the federal government did not have these important powers. It was hoped that our new government would now be strengthened.

Powers of the State Governments. The Constitution leaves to the states many important powers to manage their own affairs. Under our federal system, the states or the people have all the powers not specifically given to the federal government by the Constitution. These are known as **reserved powers** because they are reserved, or set aside, for the states or the people. The state governments, for example, conduct elections, regulate trade within the state, and help provide schools.

Shared Powers. The federal and state governments also share many powers. These are known as **concurrent powers.** Both the federal and state governments, for example, can raise funds through taxation. Both also have the power to borrow money. Moreover, they share the power to establish courts, to enforce laws and punish lawbreakers, and to provide for the health and welfare of the American people.

Responsibility for running the nation's Postal Service is one of the powers given to the federal government. Why do you suppose that this is so?

Whenever a state law disagrees with the Constitution or with a federal law, the state must give way to the federal government. The writers of the Constitution made this clear by saying that the Constitution and the laws of the federal government shall be "the supreme law of the land."

Government in Which Powers Are Limited

By establishing the American federal system, the writers of the Constitution set up the stronger national government that our new nation needed. They were determined,

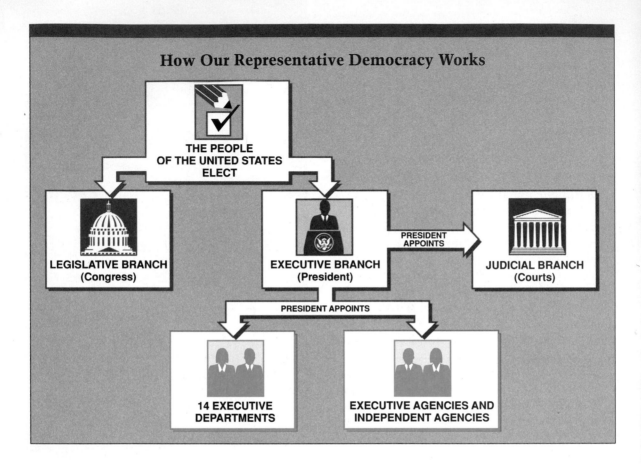

How Our Representative Democracy Works

THE PEOPLE
OF THE UNITED STATES
ELECT

LEGISLATIVE BRANCH
(Congress)

EXECUTIVE BRANCH
(President)

PRESIDENT
APPOINTS

JUDICIAL BRANCH
(Courts)

PRESIDENT APPOINTS

14 EXECUTIVE
DEPARTMENTS

EXECUTIVE AGENCIES AND
INDEPENDENT AGENCIES

however, to keep the new federal government from becoming too powerful. This ideal of **limited government** led our founders to spell out very carefully the powers of the federal government. Because of this, American citizens know exactly what the powers of the federal government are.

The Constitution also provides that all powers not mentioned are reserved for the states or the people. Furthermore, the Bill of Rights (which will be discussed in the next chapter) specifies certain powers that are forbidden to both the federal government and the states. It describes the many freedoms that belong to every American citizen.

As you have read, the writers of the Constitution believed that all governments should have the consent of the people. They made sure the new government could have only as much power as the people wanted to give it.

The American people clearly wanted to limit, or to check, the powers that their federal government would have. But why?

Nearly all Americans at the time of the Constitutional Convention were against strong governments. They feared that a strong national government might limit their freedom, as the British king had attempted to do. They wanted to be sure that their new government would be responsible to the American people.

SECTION 1 REVIEW

Define constitutional, popular sovereignty, majority rule, federalism, federal government, delegated powers, reserved powers, concurrent powers, limited government

Identify Mayflower Compact, Preamble

1. **Seeing Relationships** How did the Pilgrims influence our nation's founders?
2. **Summarizing Ideas** (a) List the goals of American government. (b) Explain the principle of majority rule.
3. **Understanding Ideas** Why does the Constitution limit the powers granted to the federal government?

Thinking Critically Which of the goals of government is most important? Explain.

② The Three Branches of Government

There are several provisions in the Constitution designed to prevent any person or group of people, or any part of the government, from taking too much power. In the last section, you read how our federal system divides powers between the national and state governments. Another provision of the Constitution sets up three separate branches, or divisions, in the federal government.

This three-way division of power is known as the **separation of powers.** It ensures that no branch of the federal government can become too powerful. The three branches of government are the legislative branch, the executive branch, and the judicial branch. They were created by the first three articles of the United States Constitution.

Legislative Branch

Article 1 of the Constitution established Congress as the **legislative branch,** or lawmaking branch, of the government. Congress is made up of two houses—the Senate and the House of Representatives.

The writers of the Constitution placed great emphasis on Congress. It is the first branch of government mentioned in the Constitution. The workings of Congress are described in greater detail than either of the other two branches of the federal government. In addition, the other branches must depend on Congress for the money they need to carry out their responsibilities. You will read more about Congress in Chapter 5.

Executive Branch

The **executive branch,** described by Article 2 of the Constitution, is responsible for seeing that the nation's laws are carried out. It is headed by the President, who is the nation's Chief Executive. The executive branch also

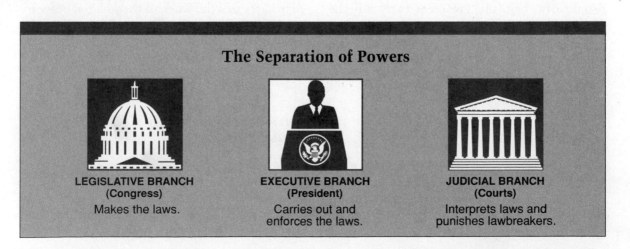

The Separation of Powers

LEGISLATIVE BRANCH
(Congress)
Makes the laws.

EXECUTIVE BRANCH
(President)
Carries out and enforces the laws.

JUDICIAL BRANCH
(Courts)
Interprets laws and punishes lawbreakers.

Checks and Balances in the Federal Government

POWERS		CHECKS ON POWERS
Passes bills into laws. Can pass laws over the President's veto if two thirds of the Congress approve the law. Approves appointments of federal court judges.	 THE CONGRESS	President can veto bills. The Supreme Court can rule that a law is unconstitutional.
Can approve or veto laws. Carries out the laws. Appoints federal court judges.	 THE PRESIDENT	Congress can pass laws over the President's veto by a two-thirds vote. Congress may impeach and remove the President for high crimes or for misdemeanors. Senate approves the President's appointments to the federal courts.
Interprets the meaning of laws. May rule that laws passed by Congress and actions taken by the executive branch are unconstitutional.	 THE SUPREME COURT	Congress (or the states) may propose an amendment to the Constitution if the Supreme Court rules that a law is unconstitutional. Senate may refuse to approve the appointments to the federal courts. Congress may impeach and remove a federal judge from office.

includes the Vice President and many other people who help the President carry out the executive duties.

As our nation's Chief Executive, the President represents all the American people. You will read more about the executive branch in Chapter 6.

Judicial Branch

Article 3 established the **judicial branch,** or federal court system, to interpret the laws and punish lawbreakers. The Constitution makes the Supreme Court the head of the judicial branch. The Constitution also gives Congress the power to establish lower federal courts to help carry out the work of the judicial branch.

The Supreme Court can declare a law invalid if it is in conflict with the Constitution. You will read more about the judicial branch in Chapter 7.

Government with Checks and Balances

To make sure that no branch of the federal government becomes too powerful, a system of **checks and balances** was included in the Constitution. Each branch of the government has powers that check, or limit, the powers of the two other branches. In addition, each branch has its own powers, which no other branch can assume. In this way, the powers of government are balanced by being divided three ways.

How does this system of checks and balances work? Let's consider lawmaking as an example. Congress is the legislative branch of the federal government. However, the President has the power to **veto,** or turn down, a proposed law. With this power to approve or disapprove laws passed by Congress, the President can check the lawmaking power of Congress.

Does this mean that the President can prevent any law passed by Congress from taking effect? That would give the President too much power. Therefore, the Constitution balances the President's power. It does so by giving Congress the power to pass laws over the President's veto. A two-thirds vote of both houses of Congress is required before Congress can pass any law that the President has vetoed. In this way, Congress can check the lawmaking power of the President.

The Supreme Court can also become involved in lawmaking. It has the power to interpret, or decide the meaning of, laws. In addition, the Court can declare that a law is in conflict with the Constitution and must not be enforced.

There are many other checks and balances in the working of our federal government. You will learn more about how the three branches check and balance each other as you study our American government in the chapters that follow.

★ SECTION 2 REVIEW

Define separation of powers, legislative branch, executive branch, judicial branch, checks and balances, veto

1. **Understanding Ideas** Why does the Constitution provide for the separation of powers in the federal government?

2. **Composing a Paragraph** Write a short paragraph that accurately describes the purpose of each of the three branches of the federal government.

3. **Organizing Ideas** How does the system of checks and balances in the federal government work?

Thinking Critically If the system of checks and balances were suddenly eliminated, which branch of government do you think would become the most powerful? Why would this be dangerous?

③ A Flexible Constitution

Changing times may call for changes in our government. In 1787, when our Constitution was written, the United States was a nation of 13 states with fewer than 4 million people. Today our 50 states are home to more than 250 million people. Our nation has changed in other ways as well. How can the Constitution, which was written in the age of sailing ships, meet the needs of our nation in the space age? The answer is that our nation's founders were wise enough to plan a government that could be changed to meet changing conditions. Our Constitution truly is a "living document."

The Constitution Provides for Change

One of the most important features of the American Constitution is that it is flexible. The writers of the Constitution knew that the plan of government they were creating would have to meet the changing needs of a growing nation. They could not possibly foresee all the changes the United States would undergo. Yet (continued on page 50)

CITIZENSHIP IN ACTION

Watergate—A Test of the Constitution

A few pieces of tape were the first clue. They had been placed over the door latches so that the doors would not lock shut. While on his rounds, a guard named Frank Wills found the pieces of tape and removed them. He thought they had been left there by building workers. However, when Wills returned, he found the doors taped again. He called the police—and set off a chain of events that eventually led to the resignation of the President of the United States.

The Watergate Break-in

In June 1972 the Watergate Building in Washington, D.C., where the taped doors were found, housed the headquarters of the national committee of the Democratic Party. Before dawn on June 16, five burglars broke into these offices. One of them taped the doors so that the others could get in.

When the burglars were arrested, the police found that they were carrying large sums of money, listening equipment, two-way radios, and cameras. It soon became clear that this was not just a routine burglary case. Reporters immediately began asking questions. Why would anyone want to break into the offices of the Democratic Party? What did they hope to find? Slowly the evidence grew. It seemed to point to some assistants to the President in the White House.

The Senate Watergate Committee was created in 1973 in order to investigate charges stemming from the Watergate break-in.

The White House Is Involved

The year 1972 was a Presidential election year. Some people wondered if the burglars had been looking for something that might help defeat Democratic candidates and reelect President Richard M. Nixon, a Republican. However, most people did not believe that anyone in the White House would take part in such actions. President Nixon was reelected by a huge margin.

After the election, though, reporters and others continued to ask if there was a link between the Watergate break-in, the

Committee for the Reelection of the President, and the White House. Early in 1973 the Watergate burglars were tried and found guilty. It was expected that they would go to jail and that would be the end of the case. But Judge John Sirica, who had tried the case, did not believe the whole truth had come out during the trial. He told the burglars that they would be sent to prison for as long as 40 years unless they told what they knew. One of the burglars broke his silence. He described conversations with top aides in the White House.

Executive Privilege

The Senate formed a special committee—the Senate Watergate Committee—to investigate the charges against President Nixon's aides. At first the President refused to allow his aides to appear before the committee. He claimed executive privilege—the right and need of the President and his aides to keep silent about official conversations. This was the first step in a conflict between the President and the Congress.

Senate Watergate Committee leaders Sam Ervin (center) and Howard Baker (far left) examine evidence with their aides.

Some Americans worried that the President was trying to cover up illegal activities in the White House. Members of Congress grew increasingly angry and, as a result, President Nixon changed his mind. He announced that he would permit his aides to testify. Before the hearings began, reports in the news media made it clear that some people in the White House had been involved in the Watergate break-in. Moreover, they had tried to cover up their actions. In April 1973 the President's top aides resigned.

The Senate Watergate Committee began public hearings in May. One Presidential aide, John Dean, testified that President Nixon knew about the cover-up. The President denied the charge.

But the question remained. Was President Nixon involved in the cover-up? Then it appeared there was a way to find out who was telling the truth. The public learned that every conversation between the President and his aides had been recorded on tape. Hidden recording machines had been placed in the White House by order of the President himself. He had hoped that the tapes would serve as a record for future historians of his time in office.

Conflict over the Tapes

The Senate committee and Archibald Cox, the special prosecutor who had been appointed to investigate Watergate, immediately requested a number of the tapes dealing with that subject. The President refused to turn them over, again claiming executive privilege. In October 1973 a federal court of appeals denied this claim of executive privilege. The court ruled that the President must turn over the tapes so that a criminal investigation could go forward. "The President," the court said, ". . . is not above the law's command."

In response President Nixon offered to release a written summary of the tapes and ordered Cox not to request any additional tapes. When Cox refused to obey the President's orders, he was fired. These actions led to great protests from the public and Congress. The President then agreed to release the tapes and appointed a new special prosecutor, Leon Jaworski.

Then came another shock. The White House announced that some of the requested tapes were missing. Criticism of President Nixon grew, and many Americans began to demand that he be impeached. Under the Constitution, impeachment is the responsibility of the House of Representatives. An official impeached by the House is then tried by the Senate.

The House Judiciary Committee began its investigation into the possible impeachment of the President—the first such investigation in more than 100 years. The committee asked for additional tapes. Finally, in April 1974, President Nixon released written transcripts, or copies, of the tapes. Many people were angered by the contents and the President's seeming lack of respect for the law. On one tape the President discussed paying "hush" money to the Watergate burglars to keep them from talking about what they knew.

President Nixon announced on television that he was releasing written transcripts of the Watergate tapes.

The House committee and the special prosecutor continued to demand the tapes. Finally the question of the tapes was put before the Supreme Court. On July 24, 1974, the Court ruled that President Nixon had to release the tapes.

President Nixon Leaves Office

On the day of the Supreme Court decision, the House Judiciary Committee began a televised debate. The committee voted to recommend impeachment on three counts: obstruction of justice, abuse of power, and contempt of Congress and the courts. It was now up to the full House to vote.

Before the House of Representatives could act, the newly released tapes proved that President Nixon had been involved in the cover-up of the Watergate break-in. It quickly became certain that the President would be impeached by the House and tried by the Senate. He was under great pressure from both Republicans and Democrats to resign.

In an emotion-filled speech on television, President Nixon announced that he would resign the next day. On August 9, 1974, he left the nation's capital—the only American President ever to resign from the Presidency.

Vice President Gerald R. Ford became President and declared that "our long national nightmare is over." He went on to say that "our Constitution works; our great Republic is a government of laws and not of men. . . ."

The Watergate case proved that the system of checks and balances set up by the Constitution works. Together the courts and Congress had restrained a President engaged in wrongdoing. Moreover, they reminded the world that even a President is not above the law in the United States.

Richard Nixon waved goodbye to onlookers as he prepared to leave Washington, D.C., and the Presidency on August 9, 1974.

Thinking It Over

1. No one ever proved that President Nixon had anything to do with the Watergate burglary. Why then was he thought to be guilty of crimes in the Watergate case?
2. What are the steps by which a President is impeached?
3. How did the Watergate case prove that the system of checks and balances set up by the Constitution works?

the Declaration of Independence, the Constitution, and the Bill of Rights all are on display at the National Archives Building in Washington, D.C.? These valued safeguards of American liberties are displayed in a special glass case that prevents air and moisture from seeping in.

Every evening, at the touch of a button, special machinery lowers the documents through the floor. They remain in a vault made of steel and reinforced concrete until morning, when the documents go back on display.

the government established by our Constitution has been able to change and adapt to new circumstances and challenges.

There are three ways in which the Constitution and the government can adapt to the changing needs and conditions of the nation. These three ways are amendment, interpretation, and custom.

The Amendment Process

An **amendment** is a written change made in the Constitution. The process for amending, or changing, the Constitution is set forth in Article 5 of the Constitution (see page 65). It is not easy to amend our Constitution.

All proposed amendments require the approval of three fourths of the states. Also, amendments may take a long time to pass. This makes it more likely that long, careful thought will be given to any proposed amendment before it is passed. Since the Constitution went into effect in 1789, only 26 amendments have been added to it. (These amendments to the Constitution will be discussed in Chapter 4 and can be read in their entirety on pages 67–75.)

Proposing an Amendment. Both Congress and the states must be involved in the process. An amendment may be proposed in two ways. The first way is to have Congress propose an amendment by a two-thirds vote in both houses. Since a two-thirds vote in Congress is difficult to obtain, members must be sure the change is really needed.

The second way of proposing an amendment to the Constitution begins with the states. With this method, the legislatures of two thirds of the states—34 out of 50—can ask Congress to call a national convention to propose an amendment. This method has never been used successfully. However, it could be used if Congress should refuse to propose an amendment that the American people believed was necessary.

Ratifying an Amendment. After an amendment has been proposed, it then must be approved by three fourths, or 38, of the states. There are two ways an amendment may be approved, or ratified. The method of ratification must be described in each proposed amendment.

The proposed amendment may be sent to the state legislatures for approval. All but one of the 26 amendments have been approved in this way. Or the proposed amendment may be sent to state conventions elected by the people of each state to consider the amendment. This method has been used only once, to ratify the Twenty-first Amendment.

After an amendment has been approved by the required number of states, it becomes part of the written Constitution. What happens if the people decide they do not like the way an amendment is working? In that case, the amendment in question can be canceled, or **repealed,** by another amendment. Only one of the amendments to the Constitution, the Eighteenth Amendment, has been repealed.

Interpreting the Constitution

Our government also changes when some part of the Constitution is interpreted in a new way. Congress may interpret a certain clause in the Constitution as giving it the right to pass a particular law.

For example, Congress has passed laws setting the minimum wage that workers must be paid. A minimum wage is not mentioned anywhere in the Constitution. However, the Constitution does give Congress the right to control trade among the states. The goods made by workers usually travel from one state to another. Therefore, Congress interpreted the Constitution to mean that it could pass laws affecting working conditions, including wages.

The Supreme Court has the power to decide if Congress has interpreted the Constitution correctly. The Court's ruling is final.

Custom and the Constitution

A number of changes in our nation's federal government also have come about through custom and tradition. For example, the Constitution did not provide for regular meetings of the leaders in the executive branch of our federal government. However, President

Congress used its power over interstate trade to outlaw child labor, which once was common in American factories and mines.

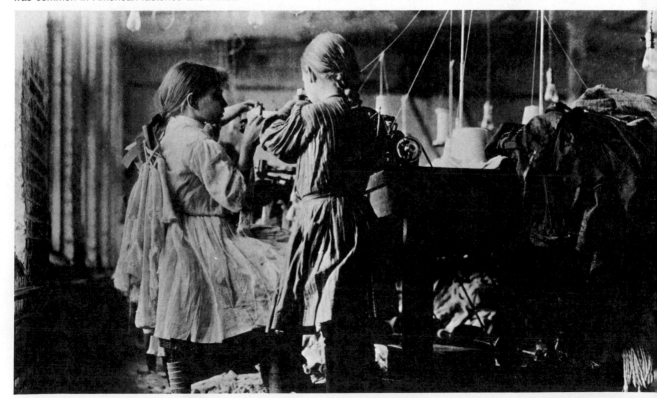

Can You Guess?

How many people come to see the Declaration of Independence and the Constitution in Washington, D.C., each year?

Answers are on page 594.

George Washington brought these leaders together regularly to serve as his advisers, or **Cabinet.** Since that time, regular meetings between a President and the Cabinet have become an accepted part of the tradition of our government.

Many other important traditions have developed in our nation's government. These traditions are followed regularly. Yet they have seldom been written down or made into laws. For this reason, they are sometimes called our **unwritten Constitution.**

SECTION 3 REVIEW

Define amendment, repealed, Cabinet, unwritten constitution

1. **Evaluating Ideas** Why can it be said that our Constitution is a "living document"?
2. **Understanding Ideas** (a) Describe the amendment process. (b) How can an amendment to the Constitution be canceled, or repealed?
3. **Summarizing Ideas** (a) How does interpretation of the Constitution help the government change to meet changing times? (b) What role does the Supreme Court play in this process? (c) Explain how custom works to change American government.

Thinking Critically You are a delegate to the Constitutional Convention. Write a short speech that will convince the other delegates how important it is to make the Constitution a flexible document.

CHAPTER 3 SUMMARY

Our nation's government is based on the Constitution of the United States. This Constitution, together with its amendments, provides us with a workable plan of government.

The United States government is based upon the ideal of popular sovereignty, or the consent of the people who are governed. It is a federal system in which certain powers are given to the federal government and other powers are left to the states and the people. Certain other powers are shared by both the federal and state governments.

The Constitution set up three separate branches of government—the legislative branch, the executive branch, and the judicial branch. This separation of powers is designed to prevent any person or group of people from taking too much power. Each branch of government has powers that check, or limit, the powers of the other two branches.

Our Constitution and government have been able to meet the needs of a growing and changing nation. The Constitution can be amended, and it can be interpreted in a new way. Changes can also come about through custom and tradition. The Constitution truly is a "living" document.

SOCIAL STUDIES SKILL
Reading a Flow Chart

A flow chart is a diagram that presents information in a simple, easily understandable way. Its main purpose is to show the various steps through which a process, such as the amendment process, can go. Once you learn how to read a flow chart, you will be able to trace the movement of the process through time.

How to Read a Flow Chart

To read a flow chart effectively, follow these guidelines.

1. **Determine the subject of the flow chart.** Read the title of the chart to determine its subject matter. Look at any major headings to get an overview of the process shown in the flow chart.
2. **Identify the beginning and the end points.** Study the arrows in the chart, noting their direction. This will tell you how the process

begins and how it ends. Remember that any process may have more than one beginning and more than one end.

3. **Study the middle stages.** The middle stages show you movement through time by connecting all the stages in the order they occur. They also show you where the process may become stalled.

Applying the Skill

Examine the flow chart below, which shows the amendment process. Then answer the following questions.

1. What happens if two thirds of the state legislatures request a constitutional convention?
2. What evidence in the flow chart supports the following statement: "A majority of the people have to favor an amendment before it can be added to the Constitution."

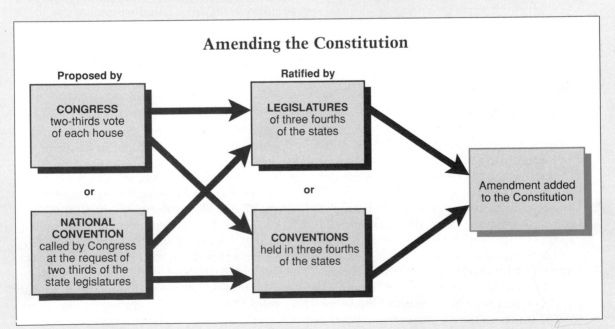

Amending the Constitution

Proposed by

CONGRESS
two-thirds vote
of each house

or

NATIONAL CONVENTION
called by Congress
at the request of
two thirds of the
state legislatures

Ratified by

LEGISLATURES
of three fourths
of the states

or

CONVENTIONS
held in three fourths
of the states

Amendment added
to the Constitution

Reviewing Terms

On a separate sheet of paper, supply the term from the list below that correctly completes each sentence.

reserved	Cabinet
delegated	Preamble
constitutional	veto
amendment	federalism

1. A(n) _____ is a written change in the Constitution.
2. The powers that are given to the federal government by the Constitution are called _____ powers.
3. The _____ is the power of the President to turn down a law that is passed by Congress.
4. The _____ is the introduction to the Constitution that explains why the Constitution was written.
5. Another term for our federal system of government is _____
6. Leaders who act as advisers to the President of the United States make up the President's _____.
7. The powers that are set aside for the states are called _____ powers.
8. To say that we have a _____ form of government means that we are governed by the provisions of the Constitution.

Using Thinking Skills

1. **Drawing Conclusions (a)** How does the introduction to the Constitution emphasize the importance of the people? **(b)** What are the six goals of the Constitution?
2. **Understanding Ideas** How do interpretation and custom help the government change to meet the changing needs and conditions of our nation?
3. **Organizing Ideas (a)** How does the principle of majority rule work in our republic? **(b)** Describe how the minority should be treated under majority rule.

4. **Composing a Paragraph** Write a short paragraph explaining how the Constitution ensures that no branch of the federal government can become too powerful.
5. **Summarizing Ideas (a)** Summarize the steps in the amendment process. **(b)** What can be done if an amendment is not serving the people?
6. **Expressing Ideas (a)** Explain the relationship between the Mayflower Compact and the ideal of popular sovereignty. **(b)** How are powers divided between the federal government and the states?
7. **Seeing Relationships** Why did the founders of our nation make the Constitution a flexible document?

Practicing Civics Skills

Interpreting a Flow Chart Examine the flow chart on page 42 of your textbook and answer the following questions. **(a)** Who sets the "flow" of representative democracy in motion? **(b)** Which government officials are elected? **(c)** Which government officials are appointed? **(d)** What conclusions can you draw from the flow chart about our American system of government?

Being a Good Citizen

1. Organize the class into groups to collect newspaper articles that show examples of powers shared by your state and the federal government. Make a bulletin board of the articles to display in class.
2. Draw a chart that has six columns. Label each column with one of the six goals from the Preamble to the Constitution. Under each goal list current activities of the federal government that support that goal.
3. Write a report on one of the following topics: the history of child-labor laws in the United States; the establishment of the minimum wage; the duties of the President's Cabinet.

The Constitution of the United States

The parts of the text crossed out in blue have been changed by the passing of time or by later amendments. Explanations and comments are also in blue.

Preamble

We the people of the United States, in order to form a more perfect union, establish justice, insure domestic tranquillity, provide for the common defense, promote the general welfare, and secure the blessings of liberty to ourselves and our posterity, do ordain and establish this CONSTITUTION for the United States of America.

The **Preamble,** or introduction, to the Constitution states the purposes of the Constitution. It also makes clear that the government is established by consent of the governed. "We the people, . . . ordain and establish" the government.

By separating the functions of government among branches concerned with making laws (Article 1), executing laws (Article 2), and interpreting laws (Article 3), the writers of the Constitution were applying the principle of **separation of powers.** They were also developing a system of **checks and balances.** They hoped it would prevent any part of the federal government from becoming too powerful.

ARTICLE 1. Legislative Branch

SECTION 1. Congress

All legislative powers herein granted shall be vested in a Congress of the United States, which shall consist of a Senate and a House of Representatives.

The power to make laws is given to Congress. Congress is made up of two houses—the Senate and the House of Representatives.

SECTION 2. House of Representatives

1. Election of Members and Term of Office. The House of Representatives shall be composed of members chosen every second year by the people of the several States, and the electors in each State shall have the qualifications requisite for electors of the most numerous branch of the State Legislature.

Members of the House of Representatives are chosen every two years. They are elected directly by the voters who are qualified to vote for members of their state legislatures.

2. Qualifications. No person shall be a Representative who shall not have attained to the age of twenty-five years, and been seven years a citizen of the United States, and who shall not, when elected, be an inhabitant of that State in which he shall be chosen.

Members of the House of Representatives must be at least 25 years old, United States citizens for at least 7 years, and residents of the states that they represent.

3. Division of Representatives and Direct Taxes Among the States. Representatives and direct taxes shall be apportioned among the several States which may be included within this Union, according to their respective numbers, which shall be determined by adding to the whole number of free persons, including those bound to service for a

The number of representatives for each state is based on its population.

A **census,** or count of the population, must be taken by the federal government every ten years.

Vacancies in the House of Representatives are filled by special elections called by the governor of the state.

The House of Representatives has the power to choose its **Speaker,** or presiding officer, and other officers. It also has the power to **impeach,** or accuse, an official in the executive branch or a federal judge. The trial of the impeached official takes place in the Senate. (See Section 3, Clause 6.)

In the Senate, each state is represented equally by two senators. [Amendment 17 provides for the direct election of senators.]

One third of the senators are elected every two years for a six-year term. As a result, the terms of senators overlap, making the Senate a "continuing" body.
Under Amendment 17, Senate vacancies are filled by new senators appointed by the governor of the state.

Senators must be at least 30 years old, United States citizens for at least 9 years, and residents of the states that they represent.

The Vice President is the presiding officer of the Senate but may vote only in the case of a tie.

The Senate elects a temporary presiding officer from among its members. The **president** *pro tempore* serves when the Vice President is absent or becomes President.

term of years, and excluding Indians not taxed, three fifths of all other persons. The actual enumeration shall be made within three years after the first meeting of the Congress of the United States, and within every subsequent term of ten years, in such manner as they shall by law direct. The number of Representatives shall not exceed 1 for every 30,000, but each State shall have at least one Representative; and until such enumeration shall be made, the state of New Hampshire shall be entitled to choose three; Massachusetts, eight; Rhode Island and Providence Plantations, one; Connecticut, five; New York, six; New Jersey, four; Pennsylvania, eight; Delaware, one; Maryland, six; Virginia, ten; North Carolina, five; South Carolina, five; and Georgia, three.

4. Filling Vacancies. When vacancies happen in the representation from any State, the Executive authority thereof shall issue writs of election to fill such vacancies.

5. Officers; Impeachment. The House of Representatives shall choose their Speaker and other officers; and shall have the sole power of impeachment.

SECTION 3. Senate

1. Number of Members and Term of Office. The Senate of the United States shall be composed of two Senators from each State, chosen by the Legislature thereof, for six years; and each Senator shall have one vote.

2. Classification; Filling Vacancies. Immediately after they shall be assembled in consequence of the first election, they shall be divided as equally as may be into three classes. The seats of the Senators of the first class shall be vacated at the expiration of the second year, of the second class at the expiration of the fourth year, and of the third class at the expiration of the sixth year, so that one third may be chosen every second year; and if vacancies happen by resignation, or otherwise, during the recess of the Legislature of any State, the executive thereof may make temporary appointments until the next meeting of the Legislature, which shall then fill such vacancies.

3. Qualifications of Members. No person shall be a Senator who shall not have attained to the age of thirty years, and been nine years a citizen of the United States, and who shall not, when elected, be an inhabitant of that State for which he shall be chosen.

4. President of the Senate. The Vice President of the United States shall be President of the Senate, but shall have no vote, unless they be equally divided.

5. Other Senate Officers. The Senate shall choose their other officers, and also a President *pro tempore*, in the absence of the Vice President, or when he shall exercise the office of President of the United States.

6. Trial of Impeachments. The Senate shall have the sole power to try all impeachments. When sitting for that purpose, they shall be on oath or affirmation. When the President of the United States is tried, the Chief Justice shall preside; and no person shall be convicted without the concurrence of two thirds of the members present.

The Senate has power to try impeachment cases. A two-thirds vote is needed to convict an impeached official.

7. Penalty for Conviction in Impeachment Cases. Judgment in cases of impeachment shall not extend further than to removal from office, and disqualification to hold and enjoy any office of honor, trust, or profit under the United States; but the party convicted shall nevertheless be liable and subject to indictment, trial, judgment, and punishment, according to law.

If the Senate convicts an impeached official, it can only punish the official so far as to remove him or her from office and disqualify him or her from holding office again. An official who has been impeached and convicted may also be tried in a court of law if he or she has broken the law.

SECTION 4. Both Houses

1. Holding Elections. The times, places, and manner of holding elections for Senators and Representatives shall be prescribed in each State by the Legislature thereof; but the Congress may at any time by law make or alter such regulations, except as to the place of choosing Senators.

Election regulations are set by the states. But Congress may pass laws overruling the state regulations.

2. Meetings. The Congress shall assemble at least once in every year, and such meeting shall be on the first Monday in December, unless they shall by law appoint a different day.

Congress must meet at least once a year. The meeting time of Congress was set by Amendment 20 at January 3.

SECTION 5. The Houses Separately

1. Organization. Each house shall be the judge of the elections, returns, and qualifications of its own members, and a majority of each shall constitute a quorum to do business; but a smaller number may adjourn from day to day, and may be authorized to compel the attendance of absent members, in such manner, and under such penalities, as each house may provide.

Each house of Congress decides whether its members are qualified and have been elected fairly. A **quorum**, or a majority of the members, must be present to carry on the work of each house. Members of either house of Congress may be compelled to attend in order that business may be carried on.

2. Proceedings. Each house may determine the rules of its proceedings, punish its members for disorderly behavior, and, with the concurrence of two thirds, expel a member.

Each house may establish rules for carrying on its business and may punish members who break these rules. In either house, a two-thirds vote is required to expel a member of that house.

3. Journal. Each house shall keep a journal of its proceedings, and from time to time publish the same, excepting such parts as may in their judgment require secrecy; and the yeas and nays of the members of either house on any question shall, at the desire of one fifth of those present, be entered on the journal.

Each house of Congress must keep and publish an official record of its activities. *The Congressional Record* is published every day that Congress is in session. It furnishes a daily account of what the members of Congress do and say.

4. Adjournment. Neither house, during the session of Congress, shall, without the consent of the other, adjourn for more than three days, nor to any other place than that in which the two houses shall be sitting.

The two houses of Congress must remain in session for the same period of time and in the same place.

SECTION 6. Privileges and Restrictions

1. Pay and Privileges. The Senators and Representatives shall receive a compensation for their services, to be ascertained by law, and paid out of the treasury of the United States. They shall in all cases, except

Members of Congress are paid salaries and receive additional sums of money for certain expenses.

Members of Congress cannot be sued or arrested for anything they say in Congress. But they can be arrested for major crimes while Congress is in session.

Members of Congress cannot hold any other federal office while serving in Congress. Nor can members resign and then accept federal jobs that were created during their term in Congress.

treason, felony, and breach of the peace, be privileged from arrest during their attendance at the session of their respective houses, and in going to and returning from the same; and for any speech or debate in either house they shall not be questioned in any other place.

2. Members Cannot Hold Other Offices. No Senator or Representative shall, during the time for which he was elected, be appointed to any civil office under the authority of the United States, which shall have been created, or the cmoluments whereof shall have been increased, during such time; and no person holding any office under the United States shall be a member of either house during his continuance in office.

SECTION 7. Method of Passing Laws

1. Revenue Bills. All bills for raising revenue shall originate in the House of Representatives; but the Senate may propose or concur with amendments as on other bills.

Revenue, or money-raising, bills must begin in the House of Representatives. But the Senate can suggest changes in these bills.

A bill passed by Congress must be sent to the President. If the President approves and signs the bill, it becomes a law. If the President **vetoes,** or refuses to sign, the bill, it is returned to the house in which it started.

The President's veto may be overruled by a two-thirds vote of each house of Congress. The President can let a bill become a law without signing it by holding it for ten days (excluding Sundays) while Congress is in session. But a bill sent to the President during the last ten days of a session of Congress is rejected by a ''pocket veto'' if the President does not sign it.

2. How a Bill Becomes a Law. Every bill which shall have passed the House of Representatives and the Senate shall, before it becomes a law, be presented to the President of the United States; if he approve he shall sign it, but if not he shall return it with his objections to that house in which it shall have originated, who shall enter the objections at large on their journal, and proceed to reconsider it. If after such reconsideration two thirds of that house shall agree to pass the bill, it shall be sent together with the objections, to the other house, by which it shall likewise be reconsidered, and, if approved by two thirds of that house, it shall become a law. But in all such cases the votes of both houses shall be determined by yeas and nays, and the names of the persons voting for and against the bill shall be entered on the journal of each house respectively. If any bill shall not be returned by the President within ten days (Sundays excepted) after it shall have been presented to him, the same shall be a law, in like manner as if he had signed it, unless the Congress by their adjournment prevent its return, in which case it shall not be a law.

The President must sign or veto every resolution, except those on adjournment, passed by both houses.

3. Presidential Approval or Veto. Every order, resolution, or vote to which the concurrence of the Senate and House of Representatives may be necessary (except on a question of adjournment) shall be presented to the President of the United States; and, before the same shall take effect, shall be approved by him, or, being disapproved by him, shall be repassed by two thirds of the Senate and House of Representatives, according to the rules and limitations prescribed in the case of a bill.

SECTION 8. Powers Granted to Congress

The Congress shall have power

The specific powers delegated, or granted, to Congress are:
to levy and collect uniform taxes in order to pay government debts and provide for the defense and general welfare of the nation.

1. To lay and collect taxes, duties, imposts, and excises, to pay the debts and provide for the common defense and general welfare of the United States; but all duties, imposts, and excises shall be uniform throughout the United States;

to borrow money

2. To borrow money on the credit of the United States;

3. To regulate commerce with foreign nations, and among the several states, and with the Indian tribes;

to regulate interstate and foreign commerce, or trade

4. To establish a uniform rule of naturalization, and uniform laws on the subject of bankruptcies throughout the United States;

to set up uniform laws concerning **naturalization,** or becoming a citizen, and concerning bankruptcy

5. To coin money, regulate the value thereof, and of foreign coin, and fix the standard of weights and measures;

to coin money and set standards of weights and measures

6. To provide for the punishment of counterfeiting the securities and current coin of the United States;

to provide for the punishment of counterfeiting

7. To establish post offices and post roads;

to establish post offices and post roads

8. To promote the progress of science and useful arts, by securing for limited times to authors and inventors the exclusive right to their respective writings and discoveries;

to issue patents and copyrights

9. To constitute tribunals inferior to the Supreme Court;

to set up a system of federal courts

10. To define and punish piracies and felonies committed on the high seas, and offences against the law of nations;

to define and punish piracy

11. To declare war, grant letters of marque and reprisal, and make rules concerning captures on land and water;

to declare war

12. To raise and support armies, but no appropriation of money to that use shall be for a longer term than two years;

to raise and support armies

13. To provide and maintain a navy;

to provide and maintain a navy

14. To make rules for the government and regulation of the land and naval forces;

to make rules and regulations for the armed forces

15. To provide for calling forth the militia to execute the laws of the Union, suppress insurrections, and repel invasions;

to provide for calling out the **militia** (National Guard)

16. To provide for organizing, arming, and disciplining the militia, and for governing such part of them as may be employed in the service of the United States, reserving to the States respectively, the appointment of the officers, and the authority of training the militia according to the discipline prescribed by Congress.

to help states maintain their militias

17. To exercise exclusive legislation, in all cases whatsoever, over such district (not exceeding ten miles square) as may, by cession of particular States, and the acceptance of Congress, become the seat of the government of the United States; and to exercise like authority over all places purchased by the consent of the Legislature of the State in which the same shall be, for the erection of forts, magazines, arsenals, dock-yards, and other needful buildings; and

to establish and govern the nation's capital, the District of Columbia, and govern other federal property

18. To make all laws which shall be necessary and proper for carrying into execution the foregoing powers, and all other powers vested by this Constitution in the government of the United States, or in any department or officer thereof.

to make all "necessary and proper" laws for carrying out the powers of the federal government. This clause is the **elastic clause,** which allows Congress to take many actions not named in the Constitution.

SECTION 9. Powers Forbidden to the Federal Government

[Amendments 1 to 10 also directly or indirectly limit the powers of the federal government.]

The powers forbidden to Congress are:

[to interfere with the foreign slave trade before 1808]

1. The migration or importation of such persons as any of the States now existing shall think proper to admit, shall not be prohibited by the Congress prior to the year one thousand eight hundred and eight, but a tax or duty may be imposed on such importation, not exceeding ten dollars for each person.

to suspend the **writ of _habeas corpus_** except during emergencies. The guarantee of the writ of _habeas corpus_ means that people may not be held in jail on little or no evidence.

2. The privilege of the writ of _habeas corpus_ shall not be suspended, unless when in cases of rebellion or invasion the public safety may require it.

to pass **bills of attainder** or _ex post facto_ laws. A bill of attainder is a law, passed by the legislature, that condemns and punishes a person without a jury trial. An _ex post facto_ law is a law that punishes a person for doing something that was not illegal at the time it was done.

3. No bill of attainder or _ex post facto_ law shall be passed.

to levy direct taxes except in proportion to population [See Amendment 16.]

4. No capitation or other direct tax shall be laid, unless in proportion to the census or enumeration herein before directed to be taken.

to tax exports

5. No tax or duty shall be laid on articles exported from any State.

to pass any laws that would favor the trade of a particular state

6. No preference shall be given by any regulation of commerce or revenue to the ports of one State over those of another; nor shall vessels bound to, or from, one State, be obliged to enter, clear, or pay duties in another.

to spend money without appropriating it by law.

7. No money shall be drawn from the treasury, but in consequence of appropriations made by law; and a regular statement and account of the receipts and expenditures of all public money shall be published from time to time.

to grant or accept any title of nobility

8. No title of nobility shall be granted by the United States; and no person holding any office of profit or trust under them shall, without the consent of the Congress, accept of any present, emolument, office, or title, of any kind whatever, from any king, prince, or foreign state.

The powers forbidden to the states are:

SECTION 10. Powers Forbidden to the States
[Supplemented by Amendments 14 and 15]

to make treaties or alliances
to coin money
to pass a bill of attainder
to pass an _ex post facto_ law
to pass a law excusing people from carrying out lawful obligations
to grant titles of nobility

1. No State shall enter into any treaty, alliance, or confederation; grant letters of marque and reprisal; coin money; emit bills of credit; make anything but gold and silver coin a tender in payment of debts; pass any bill of attainder, _ex post facto_ law, or law impairing the obligation of contracts; or grant any title of nobility.

to levy taxes or tariffs on goods sent into or out of the state without permission of Congress

2. No State shall, without the consent of the Congress, lay any imposts or duties on imports or exports, except what may be absolutely necessary for executing its inspection laws; and the net produce of all duties and imposts, laid by any State on imports and exports, shall be for the use of the Treasury of the United States; and all such laws shall be subject to the revision and control of the Congress.

3. No State shall, without the consent of Congress, lay any duty of tonnage, keep troops or ships of war in time of peace, enter into any agreement or compact with another State, or with a foreign power, or engage in war, unless actually invaded, or in such imminent danger as will not admit of delay.

to keep troops or warships in peacetime or deal with another state or a foreign nation without consent of Congress or engage in war unless invaded

ARTICLE 2. Executive Branch

SECTION 1. President; Vice President

1. Term of Office. The executive power shall be vested in a President of the United States of America. He shall hold his office during the term of four years, and, together with the Vice President, chosen for the same term, be elected as follows:

Executive power is given to the President, who holds office for a four-year term.

2. The Electoral System. Each State shall appoint, in such manner as the Legislature thereof may direct, a number of Electors equal to the whole number of Senators and Representatives to which the State may be entitled in the Congress; but no Senator or Representative, or person holding an office of trust or profit under the United States shall be appointed an Elector.

The President and Vice President are elected by **electors,** or members of the **Electoral College,** chosen by the voters. Each state is entitled to the number of electors equal to the number of its senators and representatives.

3. A Discarded Way of Using the Electoral System. The Electors shall meet in their respective States, and vote by ballot for two persons, of whom one at least shall not be an inhabitant of the same State with themselves. And they shall make a list of all the persons voted for, and of the number of votes for each; which list they shall sign and certify, and transmit sealed to the seat of the government of the United States, directed to the President of the Senate. The President of the Senate shall, in the presence of the Senate and House of Representatives, open all the certificates, and the votes shall then be counted. The person having the greatest number of votes shall be the President, if such number be a majority of the whole number of Electors appointed; and if there be more than one who have such majority, and have an equal number of votes, then the House of Representatives shall immediately choose by ballot one of them for President; and if no person have a majority, then from the five highest on the list the said house shall in like manner choose the President. But in choosing the President, the votes shall be taken by States, the representation from each State having one vote; a quorum for this purpose shall consist of a member or members from two thirds of the States, and a majority of all the States shall be necessary to a choice. In every case, after the choice of the President, the person having the greatest number of votes of the Electors shall be the Vice President. But if there should remain two or more who have equal votes, the Senate shall choose from them by ballot the Vice President.

This procedure for electing the President and Vice President was changed by Amendment 12.

4. Time of Elections. Congress may determine the time of choosing the Electors, and the day on which they shall give their votes; which day shall be the same throughout the United States.

Today, Presidential elections are held on the first Tuesday after the first Monday in November. Electoral votes are cast on the first Monday after the second Wednesday in December.

The President must be a natural-born citizen of the United States, at least 35 years old, and a resident of the United States for at least 14 years.

If the President dies, or for any reason cannot carry out the duties of office, the Vice President will act as President. In the event that both officials are unable to serve, Congress has declared that the order of succession is as follows: (1) Speaker of the House, (2) President *pro tempore* of the Senate, and (3) the Cabinet members in the order in which their offices were created. [See Amendment 25 also.]

The President receives a salary, the amount of which may not be changed during the term of office.

The President takes an oath of office, or is sworn in, before beginning the duties as **Chief Executive.**

The President is **Commander in Chief** of the armed forces.
The head of each executive department is, in practice, a member of the President's **Cabinet.**
The President may grant pardons for offenses against the United States, except in cases of impeachment.

The President has the power to make treaties and to appoint such officers as ambassadors, federal judges, and Presidential advisers provided that the Senate approves them.

The President may appoint officials to fill vacancies temporarily without the consent of the Senate if Congress is not in session.

5. Qualifications for the President. No person except a natural-born citizen, or a citizen of the United States at the time of the adoption of this Constitution, shall be eligible to the office of President; neither shall any person be eligible to that office who shall not have attained to the age of thirty-five years, and been fourteen years a resident within the United States.

6. Filling Vacancies. In case of the removal of the President from office, or of his death, resignation, or inability to discharge the power and duties of the said office, the same shall devolve on the Vice President, and the Congress may by law provide for the case of removal, death, resignation, or inability, both of the President and Vice President, declaring what officer shall then act as President, and such officer shall act accordingly, until the disability be removed, or a President shall be elected.

7. Salary. The President shall, at stated times, receive for his services a compensation, which shall neither be increased nor diminished during the period for which he shall have been elected, and he shall not receive within that period any other emolument from the United States, or any of them.

8. Oath of Office. Before he enter on the execution of his office, he shall take the following oath or affirmation:–"I do solemnly swear (or affirm) that I will faithfully execute the office of President of the United States, and will, to the best of my ability, preserve, protect, and defend the Constitution of the United States."

SECTION 2. Powers of the President

1. Military Powers. The President shall be Commander in Chief of the army and navy of the United States, and of the militia of the several States, when called into the actual service of the United States; he may require the opinion, in writing, of the principal officer in each of the executive departments, upon any subject relating to the duties of their respective offices, and he shall have power to grant reprieves and pardons for offences against the United States, except in cases of impeachment.

2. Treaty-making Power; Power of Appointment. He shall have power, by and with the advice and consent of the Senate, to make treaties, provided two thirds of the Senators present concur; and he shall nominate, and, by and with the advice and consent of the Senate, shall appoint ambassadors, other public ministers, and consuls, judges of the Supreme Court, and all other officers of the United States, whose appointments are not herein otherwise provided for, and which shall be established by law; but the Congress may by law vest the appointment of such inferior officers, as they think proper, in the President alone, in the courts of law, or in the heads of departments.

3. Filling Vacancies. The President shall have power to fill up all vacancies that may happen during the recess of the Senate, by granting commissions which shall expire at the end of their next session.

SECTION 3. Duties of the President

He shall from time to time give to the Congress information of the state of the Union, and recommend to their consideration such measures as he shall judge necessary and expedient; he may, on extraordinary occasions, convene both houses, or either of them, and in case of disagreement between them, with respect to the time of adjournment, he may adjourn them to such time as he shall think proper; he shall receive ambassadors and other public ministers; he shall take care that the laws be faithfully executed, and shall commission all the officers of the United States.

The President is required to send or to read a report on the state of the Union—the condition of the nation—at the opening of each session of Congress. The President also sends special messages to Congress.

The President may call special sessions of Congress.

The President is required to receive ambassadors, to make sure that the laws of the nation are carried out, and to sign papers that give officers in the armed forces the right to hold their positions.

SECTION 4. Impeachment

The President, Vice President, and all civil officers of the United States, shall be removed from office on impeachment for, and conviction of, treason, bribery, or other high crimes and misdemeanors.

The President and all civil officers may be removed from office if impeached and convicted of treason, bribery, or other high crimes. [See Article 1, Section 3, clauses 6 and 7 also.]

ARTICLE 3. Judicial Branch

SECTION 1. Federal Courts

The Supreme Court and Lower Federal Courts. The judicial power of the United States shall be vested in one Supreme Court, and in such inferior courts as the Congress may from time to time ordain and establish. The judges, both of the Supreme and inferior courts, shall hold their offices during good behavior, and shall, at stated times, receive for their services a compensation, which shall not be diminished during their continuance in office.

Judicial power is given to a Supreme Court and lower federal courts established by Congress.

Federal judges hold office for life. But they may be removed by impeachment.

SECTION 2. Jurisdiction of the Federal Courts

1. General Jurisdiction. The judicial power shall extend to all cases, in law and equity, arising under this Constitution, the laws of the United States, and treaties made, or which shall be made, under their authority; to all cases affecting ambassadors, other public ministers and consuls; to all cases of admiralty and maritime jurisdiction; to controversies to which the United States shall be a party; to controversies between two or more States, between a State and citizens of another State [see Amendment 11], between citizens of different States, between citizens of the same State claiming lands under grants of different States, and between a State, or the citizens thereof, and foreign states, citizens, or subjects.

Federal courts may try cases involving the Constitution, federal laws, treaties, and laws relating to ships on the high seas and navigable waters. They may also try cases involving the United States government itself, foreign diplomatic officials, two or more state governments, citizens of different states, and a state or its citizens versus foreign countries or citizens of foreign countries.

2. The Supreme Court. In all cases affecting ambassadors, other public ministers, and consuls, and those in which a State shall be party, the Supreme Court shall have original jurisdiction. In all the other cases before mentioned, the Supreme Court shall have appellate jurisdiction, both as to law and fact, with such exceptions, and under such regulations, as the Congress shall make.

Cases involving ambassadors or officials of foreign nations and cases involving states are tried in the Supreme Court. Other cases begin in lower courts but may be appealed to the Supreme Court.

3. Conduct of Trials. The trial of all crimes, except in cases of impeachment, shall be by jury; and such trial shall be held in the

Every person accused of a federal crime, except someone undergoing impeachment, is guaranteed a jury trial in the state where the crime took place.

State where the said crimes shall have been committed, but when not committed within any State, the trial shall be at such place or places as the Congress may by law have directed. [Expanded by Amendments 5, 6, and 7.]

SECTION 3. Treason

Treason is carefully defined as waging war against our nation or helping its enemies. A person cannot be convicted of treason without the testimony of two witnesses to the same act, unless the person confesses in court.

1. Definition. Treason against the United States shall consist only in levying war against them, or in adhering to their enemies, giving them aid and comfort. No person shall be convicted of treason unless on the testimony of two witnesses to the same overt act, or on confession in open court.

Punishment for treason is determined by Congress and may not extend to the family of the convicted person.

2. Punishment. The Congress shall have power to declare the punishment of treason, but no attainder of treason shall work corruption of blood, or forfeiture, except during the life of the person attainted.

ARTICLE 4. Relation of the States to Each Other

SECTION 1. Official Acts

All states are required to honor each other's laws, records, and legal decisions.

Full faith and credit shall be given in each State to the public acts, records, and judicial proceedings of every other State. And the Congress may by general laws prescribe the manner in which such acts, records, and proceedings shall be proved, and the effect thereof.

SECTION 2. Privileges of Citizens

Each state must treat citizens of other states as it treats its own citizens.

1. Privileges. The citizens of each State shall be entitled to all privileges and immunities of citizens in the several States.

An accused person who flees to another state must be **extradited**, or returned, to the state in which the crime was committed. However, the governor of a state cannot be forced to extradite a prisoner if the governor feels that such action will result in injustice to the accused person.

2. Fugitive Criminals. A person charged in any State with treason, felony, or other crime, who shall flee from justice, and be found in another State, shall, on demand of the executive authority of the State from which he fled, be delivered up, to be removed to the State having jurisdiction of the crime.

This provision for fugitive slaves was in effect until 1865, when Amendment 13 abolished the institution of slavery.

3. Fugitive Slaves. No person held to service or labor in one State, under the laws thereof, escaping into another, shall in consequence of any law or regulation therein, be discharged from such service or labor, but shall be delivered up on claim of the party to whom such service or labor may be due.

SECTION 3. New States and Territories

New states may not be formed by dividing or joining existing states without the consent of the state legislatures and Congress. New states may be admitted into the Union by Congress.

1. Admission of New States. New States may be admitted by the Congress into this Union; but no new State shall be formed or erected within the jurisdiction of any other State; nor any State be formed by the junction of two or more States, or parts of States, without the consent of the Legislatures of the States concerned, as well as of the Congress.

Congress has power to make laws for the territories and for federal property.

2. Powers of Congress Over Territories and Other Property. The Congress shall have power to dispose of and make all needful rules and regulations respecting the territory or other property belonging to the United States; and nothing in this Constitution shall be so construed as to prejudice any claims of the United States, or of any particular State.

SECTION 4. Guarantees and Protection for the States

The United States shall guarantee to every State in this Union a republican form of government, and shall protect each of them against invasion; and on application of the Legislature, or of the Executive (when the Legislature can not be convened), against domestic violence.

Each state is guaranteed a republican form of government; that is, government by representatives of the people. The federal government must protect the states against foreign attack or violence within their borders.

ARTICLE 5. How Amendments Are Made

The Congress, whenever two thirds of both houses shall deem it necessary, shall propose amendments to this Constitution, or, on the application of the Legislature of two thirds of the several States, shall call a convention for proposing amendments, which, in either case, shall be valid to all intents and purposes, as part of this Constitution, when ratified by the Legislatures of three fourths of the several States, or by conventions in three fourths thereof, as the one or the other mode of ratification may be proposed by the Congress; provided that no amendment which may be made prior to the year one thousand eight hundred and eight shall in any manner affect the first and fourth clauses in the ninth section of the first article; and that no State, without its consent, shall be deprived of its equal suffrage in the Senate.

Amendments may be proposed by a two-thirds vote of each house of Congress or by a national convention at the request of two thirds of the states. Amendments may be **ratified,** or approved, by the legislatures of three fourths of the states, or by conventions in three fourths of the states.

No amendment may deprive a state of its equal vote in the Senate.

ARTICLE 6. General Provisions

1. Public Debt. All debts contracted and engagements entered into, before the adoption of this Constitution, shall be as valid against the United States under this Constitution as under the Confederation.

The federal government will honor all debts and contracts of the United States made before the adoption of this Constitution.

2. The Supreme Law. This Constitution, and the laws of the United States which shall be made in pursuance thereof, and all treaties made, or which shall be made, under the authority of the United States, shall be the supreme law of the land; and the judges in every State shall be bound thereby, anything in the constitution or laws of any State to the contrary notwithstanding.

The Constitution, federal laws, and treaties of the United States are the supreme law of the nation. No state or local laws may conflict with them.

3. Oaths of Office. The Senators and Representatives before mentioned, and the members of the several State Legislatures, and all executive and judicial officers, both of the United States and of the several States, shall be bound by oath or affirmation to support this Constitution; but no religious test shall ever be required as a qualification to any office or public trust under the United States.

All federal and state officials must promise to support the Constitution.

Religion may not be a qualification for federal office.

ARTICLE 7. Ratification

The Constitution was to become the law of the nation when it was ratified, or approved, by nine states.

The ratification of the conventions of nine States shall be sufficient for the establishment of this Constitution between the States so ratifying the same.

DONE in Convention, by the unanimous consent of the States present, the seventeenth day of September, in the year of our Lord one thousand seven hundred and eighty-seven, and of thc Independence of thc United States of America the twelfth. *In Witness* whereof we have hereunto subscribed our names.

(Signed by) *G. Washington,*
PRESIDENT AND DEPUTY FROM VIRGINIA

NEW HAMPSHIRE

John Langdon
Nicholas Gilman

NEW YORK

Alexander Hamilton

NEW JERSEY

William Livingston
David Brearley
William Paterson
Jonathan Dayton

MARYLAND

James McHenry
Daniel of St. Thomas Jenifer
Daniel Carroll

VIRGINIA

John Blair
James Madison

MASSACHUSETTS

Nathaniel Gorham
Rufus King

DELAWARE

George Read
Gunning Bedford
John Dickinson
Richard Bassett
Jacob Broom

SOUTH CAROLINA

John Rutledge
Charles Cotesworth Pinckney
Charles Pinckney
Pierce Butler

CONNECTICUT

William Samuel Johnson
Roger Sherman

PENNSYLVANIA

Benjamin Franklin
Thomas Mifflin
Robert Morris
George Clymer
Thomas FitzSimons
Jared Ingersoll
James Wilson
Gouverneur Morris

NORTH CAROLINA

William Blount
Richard Dobbs Spaight
Hugh Williamson

GEORGIA

William Few
Abraham Baldwin

Attest: William Jackson,
SECRETARY

Amendments to the Constitution

The first ten amendments to the Constitution are called the **Bill of Rights.** The Bill of Rights limits the powers of the federal government and protects the rights of the people.

The date in parentheses is the year in which ratification of each amendment was completed and in which the amendment was therefore adopted.

AMENDMENT 1. Freedom of Religion, Speech, Press, Assembly, and Petition (1791)

Congress shall make no law respecting an establishment of religion, or prohibiting the free exercise thereof; or abridging the freedom of speech, or of the press, or the right of the people peaceably to assemble, and to petition the government for a redress of grievances.

Congress may not set up an official church nor pass laws that limit freedom of religion, speech, the press, assembly, and the right to petition.

AMENDMENT 2. Right to Keep Arms (1791)

A well regulated militia being necessary to the security of a free state, the right of the people to keep and bear arms shall not be infringed.

The right of states to have a militia (National Guard) is guaranteed. The right of citizens to keep weapons to resist a tyrannical government is also protected.

AMENDMENT 3. Quartering of Soldiers (1791)

No soldier shall, in time of peace, be quartered in any house, without the consent of the owner, nor in time of war, but in a manner to be prescribed by law.

In peacetime, troops may not take over private houses.

AMENDMENT 4. Search and Seizure; Warrants (1791)

The right of the people to be secure in their persons, houses, papers, and effects, against unreasonable searches and seizures, shall not be violated, and no warrant shall issue but upon probable cause, supported by oath or affirmation, and particularly describing the place to be searched, and the persons or things to be seized.

*The government is limited in its right to search and take custody of persons and property. A **search warrant** can be issued by a judge only if there is a good reason for its use and if it describes the place to be searched and the persons or property to be seized.*

AMENDMENT 5. Rights of Persons Accused of Crime (1791)

No person shall be held to answer for a capital, or otherwise infamous crime, unless on a presentment or indictment of a grand jury, except in cases arising in the land or naval forces, or in the militia, when in actual service in time of war or public danger; nor shall any person be subject for the same offense to be twice put in jeopardy of life or limb; nor shall be compelled in any criminal case to be a witness against himself, nor be deprived of life, liberty, or property, without due process of law; nor shall private property be taken for public use without just compensation.

*A person cannot be tried for an important crime unless first **indicted**, or accused, by a grand jury. An accused person cannot be tried twice for the same crime nor forced to testify against himself or herself. No person can be deprived of life, liberty, or property except by lawful means. The government cannot take private property for public use without paying a fair price for it.*

AMENDMENT 6. Right to Speedy Trial (1791)

An accused person is entitled to a speedy, public trial by a jury in the state where the crime was committed. The accused person must be told of the charge against him·or her and is entitled to have a defense lawyer. The accused person has the right to question anyone who gives testimony against him or her and to call defense witnesses.

In all criminal prosecutions, the accused shall enjoy the right to a speedy and public trial, by an impartial jury of the State and district wherein the crime shall have been committed, which district shall have been previously ascertained by law, and to be informed of the nature and cause of the accusation; to be confronted with the witnesses against him; to have compulsory process for obtaining witnesses in his favor, and to have the assistance of counsel for his defense.

AMENDMENT 7. Jury Trial in Civil Cases (1791)

A jury trial in civil cases is guaranteed when the matter amounts to more than $20.

In suits at common law, where the value in controversy shall exceed twenty dollars, the right of trial by jury shall be preserved, and no fact tried by a jury shall be otherwise reexamined in any court of the United States, than according to the rules of the common law.

AMENDMENT 8. Excessive Bail or Punishment (1791)

Bails, fines, and punishments must not be unreasonable.

Excessive bail shall not be required, nor excessive fines imposed, nor cruel and unusual punishments inflicted.

AMENDMENT 9. Powers Reserved to the People (1791)

The listing of these rights guaranteed in the Constitution does not mean that these are the only basic rights. Nor does it mean that other basic rights may be restricted.

The enumeration in the Constitution of certain rights shall not be construed to deny or disparage others retained by the people.

AMENDMENT 10. Powers Reserved to the States (1791)

All powers not given to the federal government nor denied to the states are left to the states and to the people.

The powers not delegated to the United States by the Constitution, nor prohibited by it to the States, are reserved to the States respectively, or to the people.

AMENDMENT 11. Suits Against States (1798)

Any suit brought against a state by a citizen of another state or of a foreign country must be tried in the courts of the state that is being sued and not in a federal court.

The judicial power of the United States shall not be construed to extend to any suit in law or equity, commenced or prosecuted against one of the United States by citizens of another State, or by citizens or subjects of any foreign state.

AMENDMENT 12. Election of President and Vice President (1804)

This amendment changes Article 2, Section 1, Clause 3. Before this amendment, the electors (members of the Electoral College) voted for two persons without specifying which person was to be President and which Vice President.

The Electors shall meet in their respective States, and vote by ballot for President and Vice President, one of whom, at least, shall not be an inhabitant of the same State with themselves; they shall name in their ballots the person voted for as President, and in distinct ballots the person voted for as Vice President; and they shall make distinct lists of all persons voted for as President, and of all persons voted for as Vice President, and of the number of votes for each, which lists they shall sign and certify, and transmit sealed to the seat of the government of the United States, directed to the President of the Senate;—the President of the Senate shall, in the presence of the Senate and House of Representatives, open all the certificates, and the votes shall then be counted;—the person having the greatest number of votes for President shall be the President, if such number be a majority of the whole number of Electors appointed; and if no person have such majority, then from the persons having the highest numbers not exceeding three on the list of those voted for as President, the House of Representatives shall choose immediately, by ballot, the President. But in choosing the President, the votes shall be taken by States, the representation from each State having one vote; a quorum for this purpose shall consist of a member or members from two thirds of the States, and a majority of all the States shall be necessary to a choice. And if the House of Representatives shall not choose a President, whenever the right of choice shall devolve upon them, before the fourth day of March next following, then the Vice President shall act as President, as in the case of the death or other constitutional disability of the President. [See Amendment 20.] The person having the greatest number of votes as Vice President shall be the Vice President, if such number be a majority of the whole number of Electors appointed, and if no person have a majority, then from the two highest numbers on the list the Senate shall choose the Vice President; a quorum for the purpose shall consist of two thirds of the whole number of Senators, and a majority of the whole number shall be necessary to a choice. But no person constitutionally ineligible to the office of President shall be eligible to that of Vice President of the United States.

The candidate receiving the majority of electoral votes became President; the person with the next largest number became Vice President. In the election of 1800, there was a tie. Amendment 12 was established to prevent such situations. It instructs electors to cast separate ballots for President and for Vice President.

AMENDMENT 13. Slavery Abolished (1865)

SECTION 1.

Neither slavery nor involuntary servitude, except as a punishment for crime whereof the party shall have been duly convicted, shall exist within the United States, or any place subject to their jurisdiction.

Slavery is abolished.

SECTION 2.

Congress shall have power to enforce this article by appropriate legislation.

AMENDMENT 14. Rights of Citizens (1868)

SECTION 1. Citizenship Defined

All persons born or naturalized in the United States, and subject to the jurisdiction thereof, are citizens of the United States and of the State wherein they reside. No State shall make or enforce any law which shall abridge the privileges or immunities of citizens of the United States; nor shall any State deprive any person of life, liberty, or property, without due process of law; nor deny to any person within its jurisdiction the equal protection of the laws.

Citizenship is given to black Americans. The states are forbidden to deny equal privileges and protection by law to any citizen. In effect, the basic protections of the Bill of Rights apply to state governments as well as to the federal government.

SECTION 2. Apportionment of Representatives

A state's representation in Congress may be reduced if the state denies the right to vote to any eligible [adult male] citizen.

Representatives shall be apportioned among the several States according to their respective numbers, counting the whole number of persons in each State, ~~excluding Indians not taxed.~~ But when the right to vote at any election for the choice of electors for President and Vice President of the United States, Representatives in Congress, the executive and judicial officers of a State, or the members of the Legislature thereof, is denied to any of the **male** inhabitants of such State, being ~~twenty-one years of age and~~ citizens of the United States, or in any way abridged, except for participation in rebellion or other crime, the basis of representation therein shall be reduced in the proportion which the number of such **male** citizens shall bear to the whole number of **male** citizens ~~twenty-one years~~ of age in such State.

SECTION 3. Disability for Engaging in Insurrection

Certain former officials of the Confederate states were barred from holding public office.

No person shall be a Senator or Representative in Congress, or Elector of President and Vice President, or hold any office, civil or military, under the United States, or under any State, who, having previously taken an oath, as a member of Congress, or as an officer of the United States, or as a member of any State Legislature, or as an executive or judicial officer of any State, to support the Constitution of the United States, shall have engaged in insurrection or rebellion against the same, or given aid or comfort to the enemies thereof. But Congress may, by a vote of two thirds of each house, remove such disability.

SECTION 4. Public Debt

All debts of the federal government connected with the Civil War are to be paid. All debts of the Confederate states are declared illegal and will not be paid by the federal government. No payment will be made for the loss of former slaves.

The validity of the public debt of the United States, authorized by law, including debts incurred for payment of pensions and bounties for services in suppressing insurrection or rebellion, shall not be questioned. But neither the United States, nor any State shall assume or pay any debt or obligation incurred in aid of insurrection or rebellion against the United States, ~~or any claim for the loss or emancipation of any slave;~~ but all such debts, obligations, and claims shall be held illegal and void.

SECTION 5. Enforcement

The Congress shall have power to enforce, by appropriate legislation, the provisions of this article.

AMENDMENT 15. Right of Suffrage (1870)

SECTION 1.

Citizens cannot be denied the right to vote because of their race or color, or because they were formerly slaves.

The right of citizens of the United States to vote shall not be denied or abridged by the United States, or by any State, on account of race, color, or previous condition of servitude.

SECTION 2.

The Congress shall have power to enforce this article by appropriate legislation.

AMENDMENT 16. Taxes on Income (1913)

The Congress shall have power to lay and collect taxes on incomes, from whatever source derived, without apportionment among the several States, and without regard to any census or enumeration.

Congress is given the power to pass a law taxing personal incomes. [This amendment changes Article 1, Section 9, Clause 4.]

AMENDMENT 17. Election of Senators (1913)

SECTION 1.

The Senate of the United States shall be composed of two Senators from each State, elected by the people thereof, for six years; and each Senator shall have one vote. The electors in each State shall have the qualifications requisite for electors of the most numerous branch of the State legislatures.

Senators are to be elected by the voters of each state. [This amendment changes Article 1, Section 3, Clause 1, under which senators were elected by state legislatures.]

SECTION 2.

When vacancies happen in the representation of any State in the Senate, the executive authority of such State shall issue writs of election to fill such vacancies. Provided, that the Legislature of any State may empower the executive thereof to make temporary appointment until the people fill the vacancies by election as the Legislature may direct.

A vacancy in the Senate may be filled by a special election. Or the governor of the state may be given the power by the state legislature to appoint someone temporarily to fill the vacancy.

SECTION 3.

This amendment shall not be so construed as to affect the election or term of any Senator chosen before it becomes valid as part of the Constitution.

AMENDMENT 18. National Prohibition (1919)

SECTION 1.

After one year from the ratification of this article the manufacture, sale, or transportation of intoxicating liquors within, the importation thereof into, or the exportation thereof from the United States and all territory subject to the jurisdiction thereof, for beverage purposes is hereby prohibited.

The making, sale, and transportation of alcoholic beverages in the United States are prohibited. [This amendment was repealed by Amendment 21.]

SECTION 2.

The Congress and the several States shall have concurrent power to enforce this article by appropriate legislation.

SECTION 3.

This article shall be inoperative unless it shall have been ratified as an amendment to the Constitution by the Legislatures of the several States as provided in the Constitution within seven years from the date of the submission hereof to the States by the Congress.

AMENDMENT 19. Women's Suffrage (1920)

SECTION 1.

The right of women to vote is guaranteed.

The right of citizens of the United States to vote shall not be denied or abridged by the United States or by any State on account of sex.

SECTION 2.

Congress shall have power to enforce this article by appropriate legislation.

AMENDMENT 20. "Lame Duck" Amendment (1933)

SECTION 1. Beginning of Terms of Office

A defeated candidate who holds office after his or her replacement has been elected has little influence and therefore is called a "lame duck." This amendment shortens the time in office of "lame ducks." The President and Vice President are to take office on January 20 (instead of March 4). Members of Congress are to take office January 3. (Previously, new members of Congress had to wait 13 months before taking their seats.)

Congress is to meet at least once a year.

The terms of the President and Vice President shall end at noon on the 20th day of January, and the terms of Senators and Representatives at noon on the 3d day of January, of the years in which such terms would have ended if this article had not been ratified; and the terms of their successors shall then begin.

SECTION 2. Beginning of Congressional Sessions

The Congress shall assemble at least once in every year, and such meeting shall begin at noon on the 3d day of January, unless they shall by law appoint a different day.

SECTION 3. Presidential Succession

If the President-elect should die before January 20 or fail to qualify, the office of President is to be filled temporarily by the Vice President.

If, at the time fixed for the beginning of the term of the President, the President-elect shall have died, the Vice President-elect shall become President. If a President shall not have been chosen before the time fixed for the beginning of his term, or if the President-elect shall have failed to qualify, then the Vice President-elect shall act as President until a President shall have qualified; and the Congress may by law provide for the case wherein neither a President-elect nor a Vice President-elect shall have qualified, declaring who shall then act as President, or the manner in which one who is to act shall be selected, and such person shall act accordingly until a President or Vice President shall have qualified.

SECTION 4. Filling Presidential Vacancy

This amendment gives Congress the power to decide what to do in the event a Presidential candidate dies when the election must be decided by the House. Congress may also make a determination in similar cases when a candidate dies and the Senate must elect a Vice President.

The Congress may by law provide for the case of the death of any of the persons from whom the House of Representatives may choose a President whenever the right of choice shall have devolved upon them, and for the case of the death of any of the persons from whom the Senate may choose a Vice President whenever the right of choice shall have devolved upon them.

SECTION 5. Effective Date

Sections 1 and 2 shall take effect on the 15th day of October following the ratification of this article.

SECTION 6. Limit on Time for Ratification

This article shall be inoperative unless it shall have been ratified as an amendment to the Constitution by the Legislatures of three fourths of the several States within seven years from the date of its submission.

AMENDMENT 21. National Prohibition Repealed (1933)

SECTION 1.

The eighteenth article of amendment to the Constitution of the United States is hereby repealed.

Amendment 18 is repealed.

SECTION 2.

The transportation or importation into any State, Territory, or possession of the United States for delivery or use therein of intoxicating liquors, in violation of the laws thereof, is hereby prohibited.

States may prohibit the sale of alcoholic beverages.

SECTION 3.

This article shall be inoperative unless it shall have been ratified as an amendment to the Constitution by conventions in the several States, as provided in the Constitution, within seven years from the date of the submission hereof to the States by Congress.

AMENDMENT 22. Two-Term Limit for Presidents (1951)

SECTION 1.

No person shall be elected to the office of the President more than twice, and no person who has held the office of President, or acted as President, for more than two years of a term to which some other person was elected President, shall be elected to the office of the President more than once. But this article shall not apply to any person holding the office of President when this article was proposed by the Congress, and shall not prevent any person who may be holding the office of President, or acting as President, during the term within which this article becomes operative from holding the office of President, or acting as President, during the remainder of such term.

A President is limited to two full terms in office. If a Vice President has already served more than two years as President, this person may be elected President only once.

This amendment did not apply to Harry Truman, who was President when the amendment was proposed.

SECTION 2.

This article shall be inoperative unless it shall have been ratified as an amendment to the Constitution by the Legislatures of three fourths of the several States within seven years from the date of its submission to the States by the Congress.

AMENDMENT 23. Presidential Electors for District of Columbia (1961)

SECTION 1.

The District constituting the seat of Government of the United States shall appoint in such manner as Congress may direct: A num-

Residents of Washington, D.C., are given the right to vote for President and

Vice President. In effect, this amendment gives the District of Columbia three electoral votes.

ber of Electors of President and Vice President equal to the whole number of Senators and Representatives in Congress to which the District would be entitled if it were a State; but in no event more than the least populous State; they shall be in addition to those appointed by the States, but they shall be considered, for the purposes of the election of President and Vice President, to be Electors appointed by a State; and they shall meet in the District and perform such duties as provided by the twelfth article of amendment.

SECTION 2.

The Congress shall have power to enforce this article by appropriate legislation.

AMENDMENT 24. Prohibition of Poll Taxes for National Elections (1964)

SECTION 1.

A poll tax may not be a requirement for voting for federal officials. In 1966 the Supreme Court ruled that poll taxes were also illegal as a requirement for voting in state and local elections.

The right of citizens of the United States to vote in any primary or other election for President or Vice President, for Electors for President or Vice President, or for Senator or Representative in Congress, shall not be denied or abridged by the United States or any State by reason of failure to pay any poll tax or other tax.

SECTION 2.

The Congress shall have power to enforce this article by appropriate legislation.

AMENDMENT 25. Presidential Disability and Succession (1967)

SECTION 1. Filling the Empty Office of President

If a President dies or resigns from office, the Vice President becomes President.

In case of the removal of the President from office by his death or resignation, the Vice President shall become President.

SECTION 2. Filling the Empty Office of Vice President

If the office of Vice President becomes empty, the President may appoint someone to fill this office. The appointment must be approved by a majority vote in both houses of Congress.

Whenever there is a vacancy in the office of the Vice President, the President shall nominate a Vice President who shall take the office upon confirmation by a majority vote of both houses of Congress.

SECTION 3. When the Vice President Acts as President

If the President feels unable to carry out the duties of office, the President is to notify Congress in a written message. The Vice President takes over as Acting President until the President is again able to carry out the duties of office.

Whenever the President transmits to the President *pro tempore* of the Senate and the Speaker of the House of Representatives his written declaration that he is unable to discharge the powers and duties of his office, and until he transmits them a written declaration to the contrary, such powers and duties shall be discharged by the Vice President as Acting President.

SECTION 4. When Congress Decides Who Shall Be President

If the Vice President and a majority of the Cabinet members feel the President

Whenever the Vice President and a majority of either the principal officers of the executive departments, or of such other body as Congress may by law provide, transmit to the President *pro tempore* of the Senate and the Speaker of the House of Representatives their written declaration that the President is unable to discharge the powers and duties of his office, the Vice President shall immediately assume the powers and duties of the office as Acting President.

Thereafter, when the President transmits to the President *pro tempore* of the Senate and the Speaker of the House of Representatives his written declaration that no inability exists, he shall resume the powers and duties of his office unless the Vice President and a majority of either the principal officers of the executive departments, or of such other body as Congress may by law provide, transmit within four days to the President *pro tempore* of the Senate and the Speaker of the House of Representatives their written declaration that the President is unable to discharge the powers and duties of his office. Thereupon Congress shall decide the issue, assembling within 48 hours for that purpose if not in session. If the Congress, within 21 days after receipt of the latter written declaration, or, if Congress is not in session, within 21 days after Congress is required to assemble, determines by two-thirds vote of both houses that the President is unable to discharge the powers and duties of his office, the Vice President shall continue to discharge the same as Acting President; otherwise, the President shall assume the powers and duties of his office.

is unable to carry out the duties of office, they are to notify Congress in a written message. The Vice President then takes over as Acting President.

When the President feels ready to carry out the duties again, the President may notify Congress. But if the Vice President and a majority of the Cabinet members do not agree, then Congress must decide who is President by a two-thirds vote within 21 days.

AMENDMENT 26. Voting Age Lowered to 18 (1971)

SECTION 1.

The right of citizens of the United States, who are 18 years of age or older, to vote shall not be denied or abridged by the United States or any state on account of age.

The minimum voting age is lowered to 18 in all federal, state, and local elections.

SECTION 2.

The Congress shall have the power to enforce this article by appropriate legislation.

CHAPTER 4

Duties and Rights of Citizenship

Chapter Sections

1 **The Bill of Rights**
2 **Guaranteeing Other Rights**
3 **Citizens' Duties and Responsibilities**

Chapter Focus

Birthdays are special days in your life. You may celebrate with candles on a cake. You may receive cards and gifts from friends and family. Your 18th birthday will be particularly special. On that day you will receive the right to vote. Why is this so important? From that day on, you can fully take part in our government. You can vote on important issues and help elect our nation's leaders.

Many of us take voting for granted. Yet the right to vote has not always been given to all Americans. For example, if you had been a woman living in the 1800's, you would not have been able to vote for President. Why? Women in the United States were not guaranteed the right to vote until 1920. Before then, only men could cast ballots in national elections.

Voting is only one of the many rights we have as American citizens. We have the right to express our ideas both in speech and in writing. We have the right to live in any town, city, or state in our country. We have the right to own property. Each of these rights has been guaranteed to all Americans by the Constitution.

We can add many other rights to this list. However, we must also realize that rights are accompanied by responsibilities. In exchange for our rights, we must fulfill certain duties. For example, in exchange for the right to a free education, we have the responsibility to do our best to learn as much as we can. Both duties and rights enable us to be good citizens.

Study Guide

As you begin to read about the rights, duties, and responsibilities of American citizens, look for answers to the following questions:
★ What is the Bill of Rights, and why is it important?
★ How has the Constitution changed over time to better guarantee our rights?
★ What are your duties and responsibilities as an American citizen?

① The Bill of Rights

Most of the writers of the Constitution believed that the safeguards written into that document would protect the rights of Americans. However, when the Constitution was sent to the states in 1787 for ratification, or approval, many Americans were not happy with it. As you have read, they demanded that a bill, or list, of rights be added to the Constitution. A number of states ratified the Constitution only on condition that a bill of rights would be added.

The new American government went into effect in 1789. Two years later the **Bill of Rights** was added as the first ten amendments to the Constitution. Congress discussed nearly 200 proposals for amendments before it presented these ten to the states for approval. The states ratified these amend-

ments, and they became part of the Constitution of the United States in 1791. (The complete text of the Bill of Rights can be seen on pages 67–68.)

The First Amendment

The rights described in the First Amendment of the Constitution are probably the most familiar to us because they are so close to our daily lives. First Amendment rights are basic rights that are essential to a free people.

Freedom of Religion. The first right, or freedom, guaranteed in the Bill of Rights is **freedom of religion.** This freedom guarantees to all Americans the right to practice any religion they choose, or to practice no religion at all.

The First Amendment forbids Congress from establishing an official national religion, or from favoring one religion in any way. This division between religion and government is known as the **separation of church and state.**

Like all rights in the Bill of Rights, freedom of religion had its origins in colonial times. As you know, several colonies were established mainly by settlers who were seeking the freedom to practice their religion in their own way. However, some of these colonies denied this freedom to people with different beliefs.

Gradually, the ideal of religious freedom developed in America. This right eventually was guaranteed to all Americans by the First Amendment.

Freedom of Speech. The right to express your ideas and opinions when you speak is called **freedom of speech.** Freedom of speech also means the right to listen to the ideas and opinions of others. This freedom guarantees that Americans are free to express their thoughts and ideas about anything. We may talk freely to our friends and neighbors or deliver a speech in public to a group of people.

The First Amendment guarantees Americans the right to express opinions about our government and to criticize the actions of

A ride down any country road gives evidence of the freedom of the press guaranteed by the First Amendment. How does this picture show that freedom?

Freedom of the Press. The freedom to express your ideas in writing is known as **freedom of the press.** This freedom is closely related to freedom of speech and is also guaranteed by the First Amendment.

Americans struggled in colonial times for this important right. At that time newspapers were not allowed to criticize the government or public officials. An important court case, however, led to more freedom of the press.

A printer named John Peter Zenger was arrested and jailed in 1734 for publishing newspaper articles that criticized the royal governor of New York. According to the law, Zenger was guilty even if what he had written were true. However, the jury found Zenger not guilty. The jury agreed with his lawyer that writing the truth was not a crime.

Freedom of the press gives all Americans the right to express their thoughts freely in writing, provided they do not state falsehoods that damage a person's reputation. If they do, they may be sued for **libel.**

The courts have decided that freedom of the press applies to electronic media as well as to written works such as books. Thus, television and radio broadcasts also are protected under the First Amendment.

Freedom of Assembly. Another of the priceless freedoms guaranteed by the First Amendment is **freedom of assembly,** or freedom to hold meetings. Americans are free to meet to discuss their problems and plan their actions. They can gather together to express their views about government decisions. Of course, such meetings must be peaceful.

Freedom of Petition. The right to ask your government to do something or stop doing something is **freedom of petition.** The First Amendment also contains this guarantee. Freedom of petition gives you the right to write to your representatives in Congress and ask them to work for the passage of laws you favor. You are free to ask your representatives to change laws you do not like. The right of petition also helps government officials know what Americans think and what actions they want the government to take.

government officials. In contrast, people living under a totalitarian government have no right to speak freely. They do not dare to criticize the actions of the government. If they do, they may be punished.

Of course, people cannot use their freedom of speech to injure others. People do not have the right to tell lies about others. If they do, they may be sued in court for **slander,** or knowingly making false statements that hurt another person's reputation.

Furthermore, the right of free speech cannot be exercised in a way that might cause physical harm to others. A person does not have the right to call out "Fire!" in a crowded room just to see what might happen. Such an action could cause panic, and many people could be injured in the rush to get out.

In other words, like all our freedoms, the right of free speech is not an absolute freedom. There are limits based on the rights of others and on what is good for all.

The Second Amendment

The Second Amendment to the Constitution guarantees Americans the **right to bear arms.** The government cannot forbid Americans to own firearms, such as handguns and rifles.

During the colonial period, Americans organized militias, or volunteer armies, to defend their communities. The militias played an important part in the American Revolution. Later, in the early years of our nation, Americans needed weapons in order to serve in the militias that were established to defend the states. The militias provided protection during emergencies, too. Many Americans believed that, without weapons, they would be powerless if the government tried to overstep its powers and rule by force. For these reasons, the right to bear arms was included in the Bill of Rights.

Today, because of the increase of crime in the United States, gun control is widely debated. Some people have demanded that guns be regulated. They say that gun control laws would lower the crime rate. Other people argue that the Second Amendment prevents the government from passing laws that limit the right to bear arms.

The Third Amendment

The Third Amendment states that the government cannot force Americans to quarter, or give housing to, soldiers in peacetime. Under British rule, the colonists were sometimes forced to house and feed British soldiers. As a result, Americans wanted a "no quartering" right in the Bill of Rights.

The Fourth Amendment

The Fourth Amendment protects people from unreasonable searches and seizures. This means that in most cases our persons or property cannot be searched and our property cannot be taken from us by the government.

However, a search is considered reasonable if a judge has issued a **search warrant.** This is a legal document that describes the place to be searched and the persons or things to be seized. A search warrant can be issued only if there is good reason to believe that evidence about a crime will be found.

The Fifth Amendment

The Fifth Amendment contains several provisions protecting the rights of a person accused of a crime. Before a person can be brought to trial, he or she must be **indicted,** or formally accused of a crime, by a group of citizens known as a grand jury. This protects an accused person from hasty action on the part of the government.

The Fifth Amendment also protects an accused person against **self-incrimination,** or having to testify against oneself. Furthermore, it protects people from **double jeopardy.** This means that people cannot be tried a second time for the same crime.

These citizens are attending a town meeting in Vermont to give their views and to listen to the views of other American citizens.

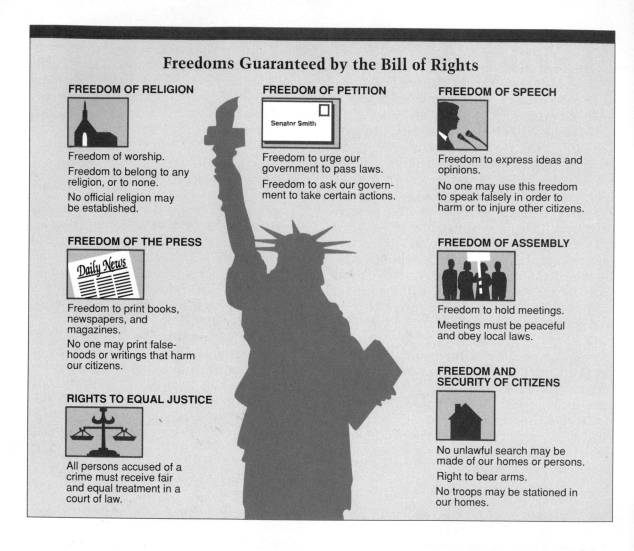

Freedoms Guaranteed by the Bill of Rights

FREEDOM OF RELIGION

Freedom of worship.

Freedom to belong to any religion, or to none.

No official religion may be established.

FREEDOM OF THE PRESS

Daily News

Freedom to print books, newspapers, and magazines.

No one may print falsehoods or writings that harm our citizens.

RIGHTS TO EQUAL JUSTICE

All persons accused of a crime must receive fair and equal treatment in a court of law.

FREEDOM OF PETITION

Senator Smith

Freedom to urge our government to pass laws.

Freedom to ask our government to take certain actions.

FREEDOM OF SPEECH

Freedom to express ideas and opinions.

No one may use this freedom to speak falsely in order to harm or to injure other citizens.

FREEDOM OF ASSEMBLY

Freedom to hold meetings.

Meetings must be peaceful and obey local laws.

FREEDOM AND SECURITY OF CITIZENS

No unlawful search may be made of our homes or persons.

Right to bear arms.

No troops may be stationed in our homes.

Another Fifth Amendment protection says that no person can be denied life, liberty, or property without **due process of law.** This means that a person can be punished for a crime only after receiving a fair trial.

The last clause of the Fifth Amendment guarantees all Americans the **right to own private property.** It states that the government cannot take private property for public use without paying a fair price for it. For example, if the government needs to build a road or a school, property owners may have to give up their property to make way for a public need. However, the government must pay a fair price for the property.

The government's power to take private property for public use is known as **eminent domain.** Property may be taken only for the public good and with just compensation.

The right to own private property is one of our nation's basic freedoms. Our free economic system is based upon this right.

The Sixth and Seventh Amendments

The Sixth Amendment guarantees a person accused of a crime the right to a prompt, public trial by a jury. Accused people must be informed of the crimes they are charged with committing. They also have the right to hear and question all witnesses against them and to call witnesses to appear in court.

The Sixth Amendment also guarantees a person accused of a crime the right to have the help of a lawyer. In recent years, the Supreme Court has ruled that if the accused person cannot afford a lawyer, the judge will assign one. The government will pay the lawyer's fee.

The Seventh Amendment provides for a trial by jury in certain kinds of cases that involve conflicts over money or property.

The Eighth Amendment

The Eighth Amendment says that the court cannot set bail that is excessive, or too high. **Bail** is the money or property an accused person gives the court to hold as a guarantee that he or she will appear for trial. After the bail is paid, the accused person is allowed to leave jail. The bail is returned after the trial.

Furthermore, the Eighth Amendment forbids "cruel and unusual punishments." The exact meaning of these words has been debated for a long time.

The Ninth Amendment

The writers of the Bill of Rights did not want to give the idea that the people had only those rights that are specifically mentioned in the Constitution and in the first eight amendments. To make sure that Americans would enjoy every right and freedom possible, they added the Ninth Amendment. This amendment states that the people of our country enjoy many other basic rights that are not listed in the Constitution. These rights are just as important and valuable as those that are mentioned in the Constitution. Among these rights are:

1. Freedom to live or travel anywhere in our nation.

2. Freedom to work at any job for which we can qualify.

3. Freedom to marry and raise a family.

4. Freedom to receive a free education in public schools.

5. Freedom to join a political party, a union, and other legal groups.

The Tenth Amendment

As a final guarantee of our rights, the Tenth Amendment set aside, or reserved, many powers of government for the states or for the people. This amendment says that all powers not expressly given to the federal government or forbidden to the states by the Constitution are reserved for the states or for the people. This provision leaves with the states the power to act in many ways to guarantee the rights of their citizens.

 SECTION 1 REVIEW

Define separation of church and state, slander, libel, right to bear arms, search warrant, indicted, self-incrimination, double jeopardy, due process of law, right to own private property, eminent domain, bail

Identify Bill of Rights, freedom of religion, freedom of speech, freedom of the press, freedom of assembly, freedom of petition

1. **Identifying Ideas (a)** What is the Bill of Rights? **(b)** Why was the Bill of Rights added to the Constitution?
2. **Expressing Ideas (a)** What rights are guaranteed by the First Amendment? **(b)** Why are they "so close to our daily lives"?
3. **Categorizing Ideas (a)** What rights are guaranteed to a person accused of a crime? **(b)** What are some rights Americans have that are not found in the Bill of Rights?

Thinking Critically Which freedom in the Bill of Rights do you think is most important?

Focus on Freedom

Students Speak Out for Change

The freedom to express our ideas and opinions is a priceless right guaranteed to us by the First Amendment. This right allows us not only to express our thoughts freely, but also to question actions we believe to be wrong or unfair. It also lets us propose new actions we consider to be right and fair. Recently, students at a university in our nation's capital proved— to themselves and the nation—how valuable the right to free speech truly is.

A Surprising Decision

Gallaudet (gal·uh·DEHT) University, founded in 1864, is the only liberal arts university for deaf people in the world. Known for its excellent teaching, Gallaudet has trained approximately 95 percent of the nation's hearing-impaired professionals. Until 1988, however, Gallaudet, whose 2,100 students are all hearing-impaired, had never had a deaf president.

The long-standing practice of appointing only hearing presidents came under fire when the university's board of trustees had to choose a new president in 1988. Since two of the candidates for the position were hearing-impaired, the students eagerly anticipated the historic moment when a deaf person would begin to lead the university.

This moment was not to be, however. Students and faculty were shocked to learn that the trustees had chosen a hearing person for the university's highest position. Their shock turned to outrage when it became clear that the new president had no experience in educating the deaf. Moreover, the new president did not know sign language—the only language used by most of the Gallaudet students.

The Protests Begin

Protests over the decision erupted within minutes of the announcement. The students argued that, by choosing a hearing person to lead a university for the deaf, the trustees had sent

The slogan "Deaf President Now" expressed the goal of the Gallaudet students to have a president who would serve as their role model.

the message that disabled people need able-bodied people to take care of them. The students wanted a president who could serve as a role model. They wanted a president who could show the nation that disabled people are entitled to the same freedom of opportunity granted to all Americans. They wanted a president who, like themselves, was hearing impaired.

"Deaf President Now"

For four long days, the students waged their peaceful but active protests. They blocked the gates of the university and marched on the White House, located only a mile from the school. Many chanted slogans that they themselves could not hear. Most used sign language to communicate their outrage. Colorful banners and posters expressed the students' demand, summed up by the simple phrase "Deaf President Now."

Faced with this outcry, the new president resigned on the fourth day of the protests. Soon after, the board of trustees appointed a hearing-impaired person as president. The students had won their fight, and they had struck a blow for the rights of disabled people everywhere. Most important, they had proved the value—and power—of free speech.

Our First Amendment right to free speech helped the Gallaudet students change a long-standing practice.

Protecting Our Freedom

Freedom of speech is essential to a democracy. Only when citizens are free to express themselves can a government truly reflect the wants and needs of the people. Benjamin Franklin knew this. He said that, "Whoever would overthrow the liberty of a nation must begin by subduing the freeness of speech. . . ." The students of Gallaudet also knew the importance of this priceless right. To protect our democracy, we must all guard our First Amendment right to free speech.

Questions to Consider

1. Where is Gallaudet University, and what makes it unique?
2. Why did the Gallaudet students protest the decision made by the board of trustees? What did the students hope to accomplish with their protest?
3. What was the result of the students' actions?

② Guaranteeing Other Rights

Since the passage of the Bill of Rights, other amendments have been added to the Constitution. These amendments were passed as changing conditions in our nation and changing beliefs brought about new needs. Today our Constitution has 26 amendments in all. Some amendments changed the way the government works. (You will read about these in later chapters.) In this section we will look at the amendments that expanded the rights of the American people.

Extending Civil Rights

Rights guaranteed to all American citizens are called **civil rights.** Our Constitution, especially the Bill of Rights, is the foundation for civil rights in this nation. However, until after the Civil War, the protection of civil rights was left largely to the individual states. The Thirteenth and Fourteenth Amendments were added after the Civil War to protect the rights of newly freed black Americans.

The Thirteenth Amendment. The Thirteenth Amendment, ratified in 1865, outlawed slavery in the United States. President Abraham Lincoln had ordered an end to slavery in the Confederate States during the Civil War. But his order, the Emancipation Proclamation (see page 542), had led to the freedom of very few slaves. The Thirteenth Amendment officially ended slavery in all the states and in all lands ruled by the United States.

The Fourteenth Amendment. The Fourteenth Amendment, ratified in 1868, was intended mainly to protect the rights of black Americans. However, it contains important rights for all the American people.

The first part of the amendment grants full citizenship to blacks. Next the amend-

Women held marches and demonstrations for years before finally gaining the right to vote with the ratification of the Nineteenth Amendment in 1920.

ment says that no state can take away a citizen's "life, liberty, or property, without due process of law." Also, no state can deny citizens the equal protection of the laws. Thus the Fourteenth Amendment protects citizens against unfair actions by state governments, just as the Fifth Amendment protects American citizens against unfair actions by the federal government.

Voting Rights

One of our most important civil rights is the right to vote, or **suffrage.** The struggle to gain the right to vote for all Americans was not won easily. Voting rights are the subject of six amendments to the Constitution.

The Constitution at first made no mention of voting rights. It was left to the states to decide who could vote. Most states limited the vote to white males over the age of 21 who owned a certain amount of property. Furthermore, some states only allowed those who held certain religious beliefs to vote.

Gradually the states did away with property and religious qualifications for voting. Between the late 1800's and the 1970's, amendments to the Constitution extended the right to vote to all American citizens.

The Fifteenth Amendment. Black Americans were guaranteed the right to vote by the Fifteenth Amendment, ratified in 1870. It says that no person can be denied the right to vote because of race or color. However, in the late 1800's and early 1900's many states, especially in the South, passed laws that kept blacks from voting. Finally, in the 1960's, Congress passed a number of civil rights laws that truly brought about equal voting rights for black Americans.

The Seventeenth Amendment. The right of eligible voters in a state to elect the state's United States senators was granted by the Seventeenth Amendment. Before this amendment was ratified in 1913, United States senators were chosen by members of the state legislatures.

The Nineteenth Amendment. American women were granted the right to vote by the Nineteenth Amendment. Women won this right only after a long, hard struggle. It was led by such courageous women as Lucretia Mott, Elizabeth Cady Stanton, Susan B. Anthony, and Carrie Catt. They argued that the women of our nation should not be treated as second-class citizens.

In 1869 Wyoming became the first state in the nation to give women the right to vote. Gradually other states began to grant the vote to women. The suffragists, those who fought for the right of women to vote, finally won in 1920, when the Nineteenth Amendment was ratified. Because women make up about half of our population, the amendment doubled the eligible voting population of the United States.

The young people here show their eagerness to take advantage of the Twenty-sixth Amendment. They are registering to cast their first votes in an election.

The Twenty-third Amendment. The Twenty-third Amendment, ratified in 1961, further extended voting rights. It gave people living in the District of Columbia (Washington, D.C.), the nation's capital, the right to vote for President and Vice President. Before this amendment, they could not vote in national elections.

The Twenty-fourth Amendment. Beginning in the 1890's, some states established a requirement that all persons must pay a special tax, called a **poll tax,** in order to vote. Many Americans believed this tax was aimed at the poor, and especially at black Americans, to discourage them from voting. In 1964 the Twenty-fourth Amendment forbade the use of a poll tax as a qualification for voting in national elections. In 1966 the Supreme Court ruled that the poll tax is also unlawful in state elections.

The Twenty-sixth Amendment. The right to vote was extended to another large group of Americans in 1971. In that year the

Twenty-sixth Amendment lowered the voting age in national, state, and local elections to 18. Previously, most states had set 21 as the age at which people could vote for the first time. With the adoption of this amendment, young Americans were given a greater voice in our government.

✔️ SECTION 2 REVIEW

Define civil rights, suffrage, poll tax

1. **Understanding Ideas (a)** Why can we call the Thirteenth and Fourteenth Amendments "Civil War Amendments"? **(b)** How did these amendments extend civil rights?
2. **Summarizing Ideas** Write a paragraph that explains how constitutional amendments have extended voting rights to various groups of American citizens.

Thinking Critically The Fourteenth Amendment is often referred to as the most important amendment to the Constitution. Why do you think this is so?

③ Citizens' Duties and Responsibilities

So far in this chapter, you have been learning about the rights that are guaranteed to all American citizens. Along with their rights, the citizens of our nation also have important duties and responsibilities.

Duties of Citizenship

Certain actions are the duty of all American citizens. These duties are the "musts" of citizenship. That is, all American citizens are required by law to perform these actions. The duties required of all citizens are described in the Constitution of the United States and in the laws of our nation and states.

Most Americans are familiar with these duties of citizenship, but sometimes we forget how important they really are. The success of our system of government depends upon all citizens fulfilling these duties.

Obeying the Law. One of the most important duties of citizenship is to obey the law. Our American government can work in an orderly way only if citizens respect and obey its laws. Of course, it is important to know what the laws are. For example, when you learn to drive a car, you must also learn the traffic laws. "Ignorance of the law excuses no one" is an old saying that continues to hold true today.

Attending School. One of the first duties of all Americans is to attend school. Our nation places a very high value on educating its citizens. Free public schools guarantee all young Americans the opportunity to study and learn in order to develop their talents and abilities. Education also gives us the skills and knowledge needed to fulfill the duties and responsibilities of good citizenship. In order to ensure our freedoms and the future of our nation, our citizens must be educated.

Paying Taxes. Another of the important duties of citizenship is to pay taxes. Our taxes pay for the many different services that government provides. In paying taxes, we are paying for police and fire protection, good streets, schools, electricity, and countless other services. Tax money also pays for the costs of maintaining our nation's military defenses. The United States must be able to defend itself in order to protect the rights and freedoms of American citizens.

Serving in the Armed Forces. As an American citizen, you have a duty to help your nation if it is threatened. You may be called upon to help defend the nation by serving in the armed forces.

During several periods in our history, the United States has used the **draft.** That is, men were required to serve in the military. Since 1975 the United States has used only volunteers in the armed forces. Since 1980, however, 18-year-old men have had to **register,** or sign up, for military service. This lets the government know the names and addresses of all men of draft age. Registration ensures that if a war or other crisis requires that the nation quickly expand its armed forces, the draft could be used again.

Appearing in Court. American citizens must, if called, serve as members of a jury. Citizens must also testify in court if called as witnesses. Appearing in court sometimes is seen as an inconvenience. Often we must take time out from our regular work to attend court. However, our right to a trial by jury depends on citizens fulfilling their duty to serve on juries and appear as witnesses.

These young Americans are aware that our recreational areas are more enjoyable for all people when everyone respects and obeys the rules.

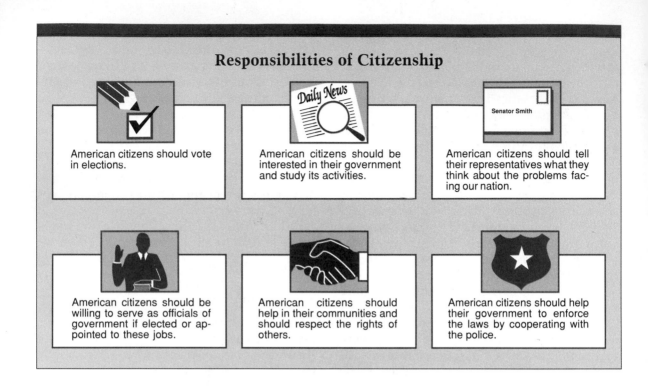

Responsibilities of Citizenship

American citizens should vote in elections.

American citizens should be interested in their government and study its activities.

American citizens should tell their representatives what they think about the problems facing our nation.

American citizens should be willing to serve as officials of government if elected or appointed to these jobs.

American citizens should help in their communities and should respect the rights of others.

American citizens should help their government to enforce the laws by cooperating with the police.

Responsibilities of Citizenship

In addition to the duties of citizenship, Americans have many responsibilities of citizenship. These responsibilities are the "shoulds" of citizenship. That is, American citizens are not required by law to carry out these actions. Most Americans, though, accept these responsibilities because they are so important to the success of our nation and the welfare of its citizens.

Voting. As you read earlier in this chapter, voting is one of the most important rights of American citizens. Voting is also one of our most important responsibilities. By voting, each citizen plays a part in deciding who will be the leaders of our government. Each voter also helps to determine what actions our government will take, since the people we elect to office plan our government's activities. Voting is one of the great privileges the citizens of our nation are given.

The vote of every citizen counts. Only by exercising the right to vote can citizens carry out our great constitutional ideal of government by consent of the governed.

Being Informed. In order to cast their votes wisely, American citizens have a responsibility to be well informed. Of course, education helps prepare citizens for this important responsibility.

Americans should take an active interest in the programs and activities of the government. They also should learn what policies are favored by each candidate running for office. Furthermore, Americans have a responsibility to tell their representatives what they think about public issues.

Taking Part in Government. Citizens should be concerned with their government either as members of a political party or as independent voters. In addition, American citizens should be willing to serve as officials of government if they are asked to serve by election or appointment to public office. The quality of any government depends upon the quality of the people who serve in that government.

Helping Your Community. One of the most important ways to be a responsible citizen is to take pride in your community and make sure that your community can take pride in you. For example, it is essential that all members of the community respect the property of others. Being careful not to litter, and even picking up after those who do, is an important part of citizenship.

It is also important to take an active part in the affairs of your community. Citizens should be willing to give their time to help improve their neighborhood, town, or city. Local groups can assist in the library, for example. Cooperating with the police is another important way to help the community.

Respecting and Protecting the Rights of Others. The success of our nation depends on the rights of its citizens. You can play an important role in protecting these priceless rights. By knowing what rights all people share, you can be sure to respect those rights. You will also know when people's rights are being violated, and seek to protect those rights. All Americans must take part in defending human rights for our nation to truly have a "government of the people, by the people, for the people."

 SECTION 3 REVIEW

Define draft, register

1. **Understanding Ideas (a)** Name the duties of citizenship. **(b)** Name some responsibilities of citizenship.
2. **Comparing Ideas** What is the difference between a citizen's duties and a citizen's responsibilities?

Thinking Critically Create a plan of action to help your community. Identify a local problem that needs to be solved, decide how best to meet that need, and list the specific steps that will help achieve your goal.

Our Constitution has 26 amendments. The first ten amendments, known as the Bill of Rights, clearly define the rights of all Americans. These amendments guarantee such priceless rights as freedom of speech and press, freedom of assembly, freedom of religion, and the right to a speedy and fair trial by a jury. Moreover, the Ninth Amendment says that the rights mentioned in the Constitution are not the only rights held by the American people. The Tenth Amendment sets aside, or reserves, to the states and to the people all powers not specifically given to the federal government by the Constitution.

Later amendments to the Constitution further expanded the rights of all Americans. The Thirteenth and Fourteenth Amendments protected the rights of the newly freed black Americans after the Civil War. Six other amendments to the Constitution expanded the voting rights of the American people.

Along with the rights and freedoms of American citizenship go important duties and responsibilities. Our nation can remain free and strong only if its citizens respect and obey its laws and carry out the other duties and responsibilities of citizenship.

SOCIAL STUDIES SKILL
Reading a Bar Graph

On November 8, 1988, over 91 million Americans turned out to cast their votes for President. Although this sounds like an impressive figure, it represents about 50 percent of the voting-age population.

How often have you heard statements such as the one above? If you are like most Americans, you probably encounter figures like these nearly every day. One effective way to make sense of this information is to use graphs.

Graphs are important tools for helping us understand data. A single graph can condense large amounts of written information into one easy-to-read diagram. Graphs enable you to understand a great deal of information easily, often with only a quick glance.

How to Read a Bar Graph

To read a bar graph effectively, follow these guidelines.
1. **Identify the type of graph.** The graph on this page is called a bar graph, because it uses bars to show amounts. Other graphs use different symbols, such as lines, pictures, or parts of circles to display data.
2. **Determine the subject matter of the graph.** Read the title of the graph to determine the subject and purpose of the graph.
3. **Study the labels.** Bar graphs usually have two labels. One label runs sideways across the bottom of the graph. This label identifies the data on the line called the horizontal axis. Now look at the label that sits on top of the line running up and down. This line is called the vertical axis. What information is indicated by the label for the vertical axis? Studying the labels will help you understand the information presented in the graph.
4. **Analyze the data.** Compare the height of the bars in the graph. Use these bars to determine how the groups of voters identified on the horizontal axis differ.
5. **Put the data to use.** Use the data to draw conclusions about the subject of the graph.

Voter Participation in 1988 Presidential Election

Percentage of eligible voters

Voter age groups: 18–24, 25–44, 45–64, 65 and over

Applying the Skill

Complete the following activities.
1. **(a)** Based on the bar graph on this page, what conclusions can you draw about the relationship between age and voter participation? **(b)** How might a Presidential candidate use the graph on this page?
2. **(a)** Write a paragraph that summarizes the data presented in the bar graph. **(b)** Which is more effective in describing the data—the graph or your paragraph? Explain.

Reviewing Terms

On a separate sheet of paper, supply the term that correctly answers each question below.

1. What term refers to the government's power to obtain private property for public use?
2. What is the right to vote called?
3. What word is used to refer to falsehoods spoken about another person that damage that person's reputation?
4. What term refers to the rights guaranteed to all American citizens?
5. What legal document describes the place to be searched and the person or things to be seized?
6. What are the first ten amendments to the Constitution called?

Using Thinking Skills

1. **Expressing Ideas (a)** Why was the Bill of Rights added to the Constitution? **(b)** Why was the Ninth Amendment added to the Bill of Rights?
2. **Organizing Ideas (a)** What amendments focus on the rights of people accused of crimes? **(b)** What rights do these amendments guarantee?
3. **Contrasting Ideas (a)** Explain the difference between freedom of speech and freedom of the press. **(b)** What other rights are guaranteed by the First Amendment? **(c)** What is the difference between slander and libel?
4. **Drawing Conclusions (a)** Why is it important that Americans fulfill their duties as citizens? **(b)** What might happen to the country if people did not fulfill their responsibility to vote?
5. **Summarizing Ideas** How have the amendments that deal with voting rights made the United States more democratic?
6. **Understanding Ideas** Explain why the Second Amendment to the Constitution is so controversial.

7. **Seeing Relationships** Why did Americans want a "no quartering" right in the Bill of Rights?
8. **Identifying Roles** What responsibilities do all American citizens have?

Practicing Civics Skills

1. **Graphing Data** The data below show the percentage of American voters that participated in Presidential elections from 1968 to 1988.

Year	Percentage
1968	67.8
1972	63.0
1976	59.2
1980	59.2
1984	59.9
1988	57.4

On a separate sheet of paper, show this same information in a bar graph. Give your graph a title and label the horizontal and vertical axes.
2. **Analyzing Data** Study your bar graph. What general statements can you make on the basis of your graph?

Being a Good Citizen

1. Interview some relatives or neighbors. Ask them to list the duties and responsibilities of citizenship. Compare their ideas to the duties and responsibilities that are listed in your textbook.
2. Create a Bill of Rights scrapbook. Collect newspaper and magazine articles that focus on the first ten amendments to the Constitution of the United States.
3. Organize the class into two teams for a debate on voter participation. One team will argue that voting should be required by law (a duty). The other team will argue that voting should remain voluntary (a responsibility).

Reviewing the Facts

1. (a) What is a constitution? (b) How did our nation's founders make sure that government would serve the people?
2. (a) What is a census? (b) Describe the three ways in which a nation's population may grow.
3. (a) What is the Bill of Rights? (b) Why did Americans want a Bill of Rights added to the Constitution?
4. (a) What is the Preamble? (b) What six goals of government are listed in the Preamble to the Constitution?
5. (a) What is libel? (b) What is slander? (c) What freedoms are guaranteed by the First Amendment to the Constitution?

Using Critical Thinking

1. **Expressing Ideas** Explain how our nation's founders were influenced by the Mayflower Compact, the Magna Carta, and the English Bill of Rights.
2. **Organizing Ideas** (a) Which amendments to the Constitution focus on voting rights? (b) Explain how these amendments to the Constitution have made the United States a more democratic nation.
3. **Understanding Roles** (a) Why is it important for Americans to study civics? (b) How do the duties of citizenship differ from the responsibilities of citizenship?
4. **Understanding Ideas** (a) How did the delegates to the Constitutional Convention settle the argument over representation in the legislature? (b) Why did the founders of our nation make the Constitution a flexible document?
5. **Composing a Paragraph** (a) Why can it be said that the United States is a nation of immigrants? (b) Write a short paragraph describing the history of America's immigration policy.
6. **Summarizing Ideas** Describe the steps involved in the amendment process.

7. **Evaluating Ideas** (a) How are the Thirteenth and Fourteenth Amendments related to the Civil War? (b) How did the ratification of the Nineteenth Amendment affect women's lives?
8. **Drawing Conclusions** (a) Over what issue did the Federalists and the Anti-Federalists argue? (b) How does the Preamble to the Constitution emphasize the importance of the people?

Applying What You Know

1. Make a flow chart that shows the steps a person must take to become a naturalized citizen.
2. Draw a bar graph showing voter participation by age groups in a recent election in your community. A good source for this information is the League of Women Voters. Use the graph to draw conclusions about voter participation in your community.
3. Write a short essay describing how the changes in household and family size might affect the need for new schools and new hospitals in your community.
4. Contact your local Chamber of Commerce to find out how you can volunteer your services to help your community.

Expanding Your Knowledge

Day, Carol Olson, *The New Immigrants*, Franklin Watts. An examination of America's immigration policies.

Lieberman, Jethro K., *The Enduring Constitution: An Exploration of the First Two Hundred Years*, Harper & Row. A study of government structure, constitutionalism, and current constitutional issues.

Padover, Saul K., *The Living Constitution*, New American Library. A guide to the Constitution of the United States, including important Supreme Court cases and their meaning.

The Federal Government

UNIT 2

CHAPTER 5

Congress Makes Our Nation's Laws

Chapter Sections

Chapter Focus

The third day of January is always a busy and exciting day in Washington, D.C. In the Capitol Building, where the Congress of the United States holds its meetings, doorkeepers take their places. Clerks prepare to keep careful records of the proceedings. Members of the Senate and the House of Representatives take their seats. A new session of Congress is about to begin.

What is the job of the members of Congress? According to the Constitution, their job is to make our nation's laws. As lawmakers they make decisions that affect the lives and welfare of the American people.

Members of Congress may have to decide such important questions as how large our armed forces should be or how high federal taxes should be. Only Congress holds "the power of the purse." This means that only Congress has the right to tax, to regulate interstate and foreign commerce, and to coin and borrow money for the federal government. Members of Congress may declare war. They may propose amendments to the Constitution. Also, of course, they must keep in touch with the people of their home states and take care of their problems.

Study Guide

As you begin to learn about Congress and how Congress makes our nation's laws, look for answers to the following questions:

★ What is the purpose of Congress, and how is its membership determined?

★ How is Congress organized, and what are its powers and limitations?

★ How does a bill become a law?

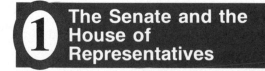

1 The Senate and the House of Representatives

As you know, the work of our national government is divided among three separate branches—the legislative branch, the executive branch, and the judicial branch. The writers of the Constitution believed the legislative branch was so important that they discussed it first, in Article 1 of the Constitution (see pages 55–61).

The Two Houses of Congress

The work of the legislative branch is carried out by the **Congress** of the United States. Congress is the lawmaking body of our national government. The Constitution of the United States provides that the Congress shall be composed of two houses—the Senate and the House of Representatives.

The leaders who drew up our plan of government in 1787 had two main reasons for creating a lawmaking body of two houses, or a **bicameral legislature.** First, a lawmaking body of two houses would help to "check and balance" the work of this branch of the government. Having two houses to share the responsibility of making the nation's laws allows each house to check the actions of the other. As a result, there is less danger that Congress will pass laws in haste or pass laws that are not needed or wanted by the people.

Second, the writers of the Constitution established a bicameral Congress in order to settle a dispute between the large and the small states. As you read in Chapter 2, the smaller states feared they would be dominated by the larger ones. The dispute was settled by the Great Compromise. It provided that the states should be represented equally in the Senate and according to the size of their population in the House of Representatives.

The House of Representatives

The **House of Representatives,** or the House, as it is sometimes called, has 435 members. It is the larger of the two houses of Congress. Members of the House are referred to as **representatives.** According to the Constitution, the number of representatives each state may elect to the House is based on the size of the state's population. Each state, regardless of its population, is entitled to at least one representative.

Originally, each state elected one representative for every 30,000 people living in the state. In the first Congress, which met in 1789, there were 59 representatives in the House. Then, as new states joined the union and the nation's population increased, the House steadily grew in size. To prevent the membership from growing too large, Congress finally limited the size of the House of Representatives. In 1929 Congress set the limit at 435 members. Today each member of the House represents over 500,000 people.

How Membership Is Divided. Every ten years, after the census is taken, Congress determines how the 435 seats in the House are to be **apportioned,** or distributed. Congress itself divides these seats among the states according to population.

If a state's population decreases from one census to the next, the number of its representatives may be reduced. On the other hand, states whose populations grow may be entitled to more representatives. But the total size of the House of Representatives can never be more than 435 members. The map on this page shows the number of representatives each state sends to the House as a result of the 1990 census.

Congressional Districts. Each of our representatives is elected from a **congressional district.** Each state legislature is responsible for dividing the state into as many congressional districts as it has members in the House. The boundaries must be drawn so that each district is nearly equal in population. After every census, the state legislature must redivide the state's congressional districts if the population has changed.

Electing Representatives. Elections for members of the House of Representatives are held in November of each even-numbered year. All representatives are elected for two-year terms. They may be reelected, and there is no limit on the number of terms they may serve. Because representatives often are reelected, there are always experienced lawmakers in the House. If a representative dies or resigns before the end of a term, the governor of the home state must call a special election to fill the vacancy.

The Senate

The **Senate** is the smaller of the two houses of Congress. The Constitution provides that each state, regardless of size, be represented in the Senate by two members. These members are known as **senators.**

The first Senate consisted of 22 senators, representing 11 states. (Two of the 13 states, North Carolina and Rhode Island, had not yet approved the Constitution.) Today the Senate has 100 members—two senators elected from each of the 50 states. Each senator represents his or her whole state.

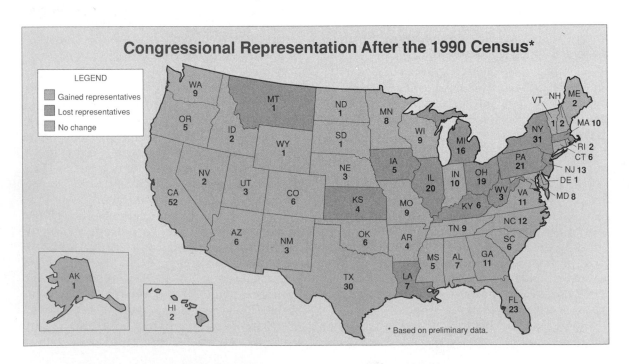

Congressional Representation After the 1990 Census*

LEGEND
Gained representatives
Lost representatives
No change

WA 9, OR 5, ID 2, MT 1, WY 1, ND 1, SD 1, MN 8, WI 9, MI 16, VT, NH, ME 2, NY 31, MA 10, RI 2, CT 6, PA 21, NJ 13, DE 1, MD 8, NV 2, UT 3, CO 6, NE 3, IA 5, IL 20, IN 10, OH 19, WV 3, VA 11, CA 52, AZ 6, NM 3, KS 4, MO 9, KY 6, NC 12, OK 6, AR 4, TN 9, SC 6, MS 5, AL 7, GA 11, TX 30, LA 7, FL 23, AK 1, HI 2

* Based on preliminary data.

Senators are elected to Congress for six-year terms and may be reelected any number of times. Elections for senators, like those for representatives, are held in November of each even-numbered year. Only one third of the Senate's membership comes up for election every two years. Therefore, a new Senate begins its work with at least two thirds of the members having had experience in the Senate.

The senator from each state who has served the longer period of time is called the state's **senior senator.** If a senator dies or resigns before the end of his or her term of office, the governor of the state may appoint someone to fill the vacancy until the next regular election or until a special state election is held.

Qualifications of Members of Congress

The Constitution lists the qualifications that members of Congress must meet. These are the qualifications for members of the House of Representatives:

1. A representative must be at least 25 years old.

2. A representative must have been a citizen of the United States for at least seven years.

3. A representative must be a legal resident of the state he or she represents. Usually a representative lives in the district from which he or she is elected. However, the Constitution does not make this a requirement for office.

The qualifications for members of the Senate differ slightly from those for representatives. The Constitution lists these qualifications for senators:

1. A senator must be at least 30 years old.

2. A senator must have been a citizen of the United States for at least nine years.

3. A senator must be a legal resident of the state he or she represents.

In addition to these qualifications, members of Congress traditionally have shared a number of other characteristics. Most have attended college. A majority are lawyers. Many others are business people or bankers. Their average age is about 52.

Traditionally, most members of Congress have been white men. In recent years, however, the number of women, African Americans, Hispanic Americans, and Asian Americans in Congress has been increasing. Their numbers, though, still are far below their actual percentages in the population.

Members of Congress usually have had previous political experience, often in their state legislature. Most members of Congress also have been active members of community and volunteer organizations.

Salary and Benefits of Members of Congress

Representatives receive a yearly salary of $125,100. Senators receive $101,900. (The Senate allows members to receive up to $27,500 a year for outside speaking engagements.) In addition, both receive many benefits free or at low cost. All members of Congress have offices on Capitol Hill. To help run their offices, they receive an allowance to pay staff members.

All members get free trips to their home states, an allowance for local district offices, and a stationery allowance. They also have the **franking privilege**—the right to mail official letters free of charge. In addition, senators and representatives frequently have the opportunity to make free trips abroad on congressional business.

Members of Congress cannot be arrested when they are attending Congress or are on

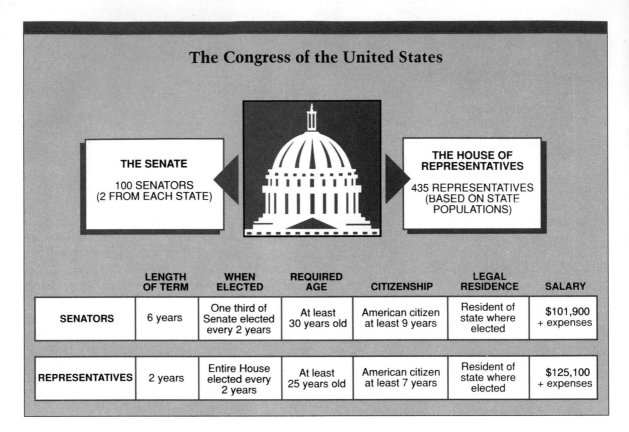

The Congress of the United States

THE SENATE

100 SENATORS
(2 FROM EACH STATE)

THE HOUSE OF REPRESENTATIVES

435 REPRESENTATIVES
(BASED ON STATE POPULATIONS)

	LENGTH OF TERM	WHEN ELECTED	REQUIRED AGE	CITIZENSHIP	LEGAL RESIDENCE	SALARY
SENATORS	6 years	One third of Senate elected every 2 years	At least 30 years old	American citizen at least 9 years	Resident of state where elected	$101,900 + expenses
REPRESENTATIVES	2 years	Entire House elected every 2 years	At least 25 years old	American citizen at least 7 years	Resident of state where elected	$125,100 + expenses

their way to or from a meeting of Congress, unless they have committed a serious crime. This **congressional immunity** ensures that no one can interfere needlessly with federal lawmakers as they perform their duties.

Members of Congress cannot be sued for anything they may say while they are speaking in Congress. This provision in the Constitution is intended to protect their freedom to debate. On the other hand, members of Congress are not free to behave just as they wish. Both the Senate and the House have rules of conduct that members must follow.

Rules of Conduct

Both houses of Congress have the right to decide who shall be seated as members. This means that if the Senate or House questions the methods by which any member was elected, the member may not be seated until an investigation is made. If either house finds that dishonest or questionable methods were used, it can refuse to seat this member. The Senate or the House can also require the state to hold a new election. Fortunately, Congress seldom has to refuse to seat a member.

The House and Senate have passed strict codes of conduct for their members. For example, members may not use campaign funds for personal expenses. There is a limit on the amount of outside income they may earn. In addition, members of Congress are required to make a full disclosure of their financial holdings.

Serious misconduct by a member of the Senate or House may result in **expulsion** from office by a vote of two thirds of the senators or representatives. Expulsion of a member means that the member must give up his or her seat in Congress. Grounds for expulsion are limited to the most serious offenses, such as treason or the acceptance of bribes.

Less serious offenses may bring a vote of **censure,** or formal disapproval of a member's actions. A censured member must stand alone at the front of the House or Senate and listen as the charges are read.

SECTION 1 REVIEW

Define bicameral legislature, apportioned, congressional district, franking privilege, congressional immunity, expulsion, censure

Identify Congress, House of Representatives, representatives, Senate, senators, senior senator

1. **Seeing Relationships** For what two reasons did the writers of the Constitution create a bicameral legislature?
2. **Summarizing Ideas (a)** Write a short paragraph discussing House membership and how representatives are elected. **(b)** Write a short paragraph discussing Senate membership and how senators are elected.
3. **Comparing Ideas** Compare the qualifications for members of the House and Senate.
4. **Organizing Ideas (a)** What benefits do members of Congress receive? **(b)** How does Congress deal with misconduct by members?

Thinking Critically You are a new member of Congress. How will you stay informed about the needs of the people in the state or district you represent?

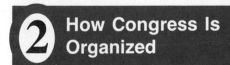

2 How Congress Is Organized

Beginning with the first Congress in 1789, each Congress has been identified by number. Thus the Congress that began its term in 1789 was known as the First Congress. The Congress that began its term in 1991 is called the 102nd Congress.

Terms and Sessions of Congress

In each term of Congress, there are two regular **sessions,** or meetings. The first session begins on January 3 in the odd-numbered year following the congressional election in November. The second session begins on January 3 of the next year.

Each session may last as long as Congress wishes. In the past, sessions usually lasted from January 3 until August or September. In recent years, the growing workload has led to longer sessions. Both houses of Congress must agree upon the date to adjourn, or end, the session.

Sometimes serious problems come up after Congress has adjourned its regular session. In such cases, the President of the United States may recall Congress for a **special session.** Usually the President calls both houses into special session. However, the President may decide to call only one of the two houses.

Under certain circumstances, the House of Representatives and the Senate will meet together. This is known as a **joint session** of Congress. For example, a joint session will be called if the President wants to address the Congress. Such sessions are often televised.

The Organization of Congress

The Constitution provides for only three congressional officers. First, it directs the House of Representatives to select a presiding officer. Second, it names the Vice President of the United States as president of the Senate. Third, it calls for the selection of a senator to preside in the Vice President's absence. These are the only directions given by the Constitution about the organization of Congress.

Over the years, Congress has developed procedures to organize itself. Shortly after the opening day of each term, the Republican and Democratic members in each house gather separately in private meetings. These private meetings are called **party caucuses.** At these caucuses, the Republican members of each house choose their own leaders, and the Democratic members choose theirs.

The political party that has more members in each house is known as the **majority party.** The political party that has fewer members is called the **minority party.**

Leaders of the House

According to the Constitution, the presiding officer of the House of Representatives is the **Speaker** of the House. The Speaker is the most powerful officer in the House. No representative may speak until called upon, or recognized, by the Speaker. The Speaker also has great influence in deciding the order of business in the House.

The Speaker, because of these important responsibilities, is paid $160,600 a year. The Speaker is always a member of the majority party. Like other leaders in the House and Senate, the Speaker is usually a longtime member of Congress.

House members also choose a number of other leaders. At their private caucuses, House Democrats and Republicans each choose a floor leader and a party whip. The **floor leader** of each party guides the party's proposed laws through Congress. The floor leader of the majority party is called the majority leader. The floor leader of the minority party is the minority leader. Each floor leader is assisted by a **party whip,** who tries to persuade members to vote for party-sponsored legislation.

Leaders of the Senate

The Constitution provides for the Vice President of the United States to serve as the presiding officer of the Senate. However, the Vice President is not a senator and therefore cannot take part in Senate debates. The Vice President may vote only in the case of a tie.

In recent years, the Vice President has had many other responsibilities and has spent little time in the Senate. During the Vice President's absence, the Senate is presided over by the **president *pro tempore*** (pro TEM·pa·ree), a president "for the time being." This leader is elected by the members of the Senate. The president *pro tempore* is by custom the longest serving member of the majority party.

The Senate and the House of Representatives meet together in a joint session when the President wants to address Congress.

The most powerful officers of the Senate are the majority leader and the minority leader. Like the floor leaders of the House, the majority leader and the minority leader are elected in party caucuses. They too are assisted by party whips.

Congress Works Through Committees

Every year Congress has to consider thousands of **bills,** or proposed laws. Members of the First Congress could have read every one of the 268 bills they considered. Today Congress handles as many as 20,000 bills in a two-year term. It would be impossible for all the members of each house to consider every bill that is proposed. Therefore, the members divide their work among many smaller groups, or **committees.**

Most of the work of Congress is done in committees. The congressional committees study all bills before they are considered by Congress. To get information needed to do their work, committees hold meetings and conduct investigations.

Standing Committees. Each house of Congress has a number of permanent committees, or **standing committees.** As you can see in the chart on page 102, the Senate has 16 standing committees. The House has 22. Each committee is responsible for a special area. In the House, for example, the Ways and Means Committee handles all matters concerning taxes. In the Senate, bills related to taxes go to the Finance Committee.

Before any bill is considered by Congress, it is carefully studied by a standing committee. The committee holds special meetings called hearings to gain information on the good and bad points of a bill. Committee members may revise a bill. It is then sent to the entire membership for consideration, with the committee's recommendation for or against it. This recommendation usually determines whether the members will or will not approve the bill.

The teenagers shown here on the steps of the Capitol are congressional pages, who carry messages for members of Congress.

Subcommittees. Each standing committee is divided into **subcommittees.** These subcommittees deal with specific issues in the area handled by the committee as a whole. For example, the subcommittees of the Senate Foreign Relations Committee include those on Africa, Asia, Europe, and the Western Hemisphere.

Select Committees. From time to time, each house of Congress will appoint **select committees** to deal with issues that are not handled by the standing committees. Select committees have investigated government scandals, for example. After holding hearings on a problem area, a select committee recommends solutions that may lead to new laws. Select committees are disbanded when they have finished their work.

Joint Committees. Congress also has committees made up of an equal number of representatives and senators. These **joint committees** are set up when the two houses of Congress decide they can take care of certain matters better by working together. One example of a joint congressional committee is the Taxation Committee.

Conference Committees. Another kind of House-Senate committee is known as a **conference committee.** This is formed to work out a compromise when the House and Senate pass different versions of the same bill. Each conference committee is temporary and considers only one bill.

Standing Committees of Congress

HOUSE COMMITTEES

Agriculture
Appropriations
Armed Services
Banking, Finance,
    and Urban Affairs
Budget
District of Columbia
Education and Labor
Energy and Commerce
Foreign Affairs
Government
    Operations
House Administration
Interior and
    Insular Affairs
Judiciary
Merchant Marine
    and Fisheries
Post Office and
    Civil Service
Public Works
    and Transportation
Rules
Science, Space, and
    Technology
Small Business
Standards of
    Official Conduct
Veterans' Affairs
Ways and Means

SENATE COMMITTEES

Agriculture, Nutrition,
    and Forestry
Appropriations
Armed Services
Banking, Housing,
    and Urban Affairs
Budget
Commerce, Science,
    and Transportation
Energy and
    Natural Resources
Environment and
    Public Works
Finance
Foreign Relations
Governmental Affairs
Judiciary
Labor and
    Human Resources
Rules and
    Administration
Small Business
Veterans' Affairs

Membership on Committees

Each member of the House usually serves on only one of the major standing committees. This enables each representative to specialize in one subject area. In the Senate, each senator serves on at least two of the major standing committees. Members of Congress eagerly seek assignment to the most important standing committees.

The membership of the standing committees is divided in proportion to the number of members each party has in each house. If the Senate contains 60 Republicans and 40 Democrats, a ten-member committee would include six Republicans and four Democrats. Thus the majority party has a great advantage over the minority party. It is able to control much of a committee's work.

Each party in each house of Congress has its own **committee on committees.** This group nominates, or names, members of the party to serve on the various standing committees. Then a party caucus reviews the nominations. Loyal party members and longtime members of Congress usually are rewarded with important committee assignments.

Committee Chairpersons

Since congressional committees are so important, their chairpersons are very powerful. They decide when a committee will meet and when it will hold hearings. Chairpersons create subcommittees and hire and fire committee staff. Their importance gives them great influence in Congress.

How does someone get this position? For many years, the post of committee chairperson automatically went to the member of the majority party who had the most years of service on the committee. This **seniority system** was a long-established custom.

Some people believe the seniority system works well. They say it assures experienced leadership. In recent years, some people have questioned the use of seniority in choosing committee chairpersons. Critics believe that younger members with fewer years of service might provide more vigorous leadership.

As a result of such criticism, Congress has changed its method of selecting chairpersons. The majority party in each house now chooses the heads of committees by secret vote in a party caucus. However, the person with the longest service is almost always chosen.

Congressional Staffs

Congressional staffs include special assistants, clerks, and secretaries. Members of Congress need large staffs to run their offices in Washington and in their home districts or states. Their staffs also provide information on bills being considered by Congress. In addition, staff members help keep senators and representatives informed on important issues. Furthermore, they keep members of Congress informed on how the people they represent feel about issues being considered.

 SECTION 2 REVIEW

Define sessions, special session, joint session, party caucuses, majority party, minority party, bills, committees, standing committees, subcommittees, select committees, joint committees, conference committee, committee on committees, seniority system

Identify Speaker, floor leader, party whip, president *pro tempore*

1. **Understanding Ideas (a)** When does each session of Congress begin? **(b)** How long does each regular session of Congress last, and how is an end date chosen?
2. **Summarizing Ideas (a)** Name the three congressional positions for which the Constitution makes provision, and explain why they are important. **(b)** How are the leaders in each house of Congress chosen?

3. **Drawing Conclusions (a)** Why does Congress work through committees? **(b)** What usually determines whether or not Congress will approve a bill?

4. **Seeing Relationships (a)** How are committee assignments made? **(b)** Who usually gets the important congressional committee assignments?

Thinking Critically Congress has chosen you as the person who will decide how committee assignments are made. What system will you use to choose the committee chairpersons? Explain your answer.

 The Powers of Congress

The Congress of the United States is very powerful. Under the Constitution, Congress's most important job is to make laws. These laws do not simply tell us what we can and cannot do. They affect us in many other ways as well. For example, laws passed by Congress determine how high our taxes are. They provide for the building of highways and dams. They decide what military equipment we will sell to other nations. Thus Congress's actions affect the lives of millions of people in the United States and throughout the world.

The Powers Given to Congress

Article 1, Section 8, of the Constitution lists the powers granted to Congress. As you know, these powers are called delegated powers because they are granted, or delegated, to Congress by the Constitution. They give Congress the right to make laws in the following five important areas:

1. **Financing Our Government.** Congress can raise and collect taxes, borrow money, and print and coin money. It can use

a member of Congress once declared his horse to be a "public document"? As you recall, every member of Congress has the franking privilege—the right to send official mail without paying postage. Instead of a stamp, a copy of the congressperson's signature appears on the envelope. In the past, the franking privilege was sometimes abused. The most extreme example of this abuse involved a senator in the 1800's. He put his signature on his horse's bridle and had him shipped home—for free!

the funds it collects to pay the debts of the United States and to provide for the country's defense and for the general welfare.

2. Regulating and Encouraging Trade and Industry. Congress can regulate trade with foreign countries and among the states. It can also help American businesses by setting a uniform standard of weights and measures and by passing laws that protect the rights of inventors. Congress also establishes post offices and builds roads that help business and industry in our nation. In addition, Congress can set punishments for piracy and other crimes committed against American ships on the seas.

3. Defending the Nation. Congress has the power to declare war and to maintain an army and a navy. It also can provide for a citizen army that can be called to duty during wartime or national emergencies.

4. Enforcing the Nation's Laws. Congress can pass laws concerning such crimes as counterfeiting and treason. To see that these and other federal laws are upheld, Congress can establish a system of national courts.

5. Providing for the Nation's Continuing Growth. Congress has the power to govern the nation's territories and to provide for the admission of new states. Congress also has the power to regulate immigration and to pass naturalization laws. Naturalization laws make it possible for aliens to become American citizens.

The Elastic Clause

The last power listed in Section 8 of Article 1 is among the most important. It says that Congress has the power "to make all laws which shall be necessary and proper for carrying into execution [carrying out] the foregoing powers."

This is the famous **elastic clause.** It is called the elastic clause because it has allowed Congress to stretch the delegated powers listed in the Constitution in order to cover many other subjects. The clause has permitted Congress to pass laws covering situations that developed long after the Constitution was written.

For example, Congress has set up national military academies to train army, navy, and air force officers. The Constitution does not specifically give Congress this power. But Congress says that the academies are "necessary and proper" in order for it to carry out its constitutional right to establish an army and a navy. Congress claims that this part of the Constitution implies, or suggests, that Congress has the right to establish military academies to train military officers. For this reason, the powers that Congress claims under the elastic clause are sometimes called **implied powers.**

The Power to Impeach

The Constitution gives Congress other important powers in addition to lawmaking. One of Congress's most serious responsibilities is its power to accuse high federal officials of serious crimes against the nation and to bring them to trial. The highest officials in our government—including the President, Vice President, and federal judges—may be removed from office if they are found guilty of treason or some other serious crime.

The charges against the accused official must be drawn up in the House of Representatives. The list of charges is read before the entire House. Then the representatives vote. If a majority of them vote in favor of the list of charges, the official is formally accused, or impeached, and will be put on trial. The procedure of drawing up and passing the list of charges in the House is called **impeachment.**

The trial on the impeachment charges is held in the Senate. During this trial, the Senate becomes a court. The Vice President usually acts as the judge. If the President is impeached, however, the Chief Justice of the Supreme Court presides instead. That is because the Vice President would become President if the President were found guilty.

The members of the Senate act as the jury. They hear the evidence and examine all witnesses. Then they vote on whether the official is innocent or guilty. Two thirds of the Senate must find the official guilty before he or she can be dismissed from office.

The impeachment process has been used rarely. Altogether, 14 federal officials have been impeached. Only five of them, all judges, were found guilty and dismissed from office. Only one President, Andrew Johnson, has ever been impeached. In his impeachment trial in the Senate in 1868, President Johnson was found not guilty by only one vote. In 1974 the threat of impeachment caused President Richard M. Nixon to resign.

Special Powers of Each House

The Constitution gives each house of Congress a number of special powers. The House of Representatives has three special powers:

1. The House alone can start impeachment proceedings.

2. All bills for raising money must start in the House.

3. If no candidate for President receives the number of votes needed to be elected, the members of the House of Representatives choose the President.

The Senate has four special powers:

1. All impeachment trials must be held in the Senate.

Powers of Congress

THE SENATE   **THE HOUSE OF REPRESENTATIVES**

DELEGATED POWERS

Collect taxes to pay for the cost of the federal government

Regulate foreign and interstate trade

Set a uniform standard of weights and measures and grant patents and copyrights

Declare war and make peace

Raise armed forces to defend our nation

Establish post offices and roads

Print and coin money

Make rules about naturalization and immigration

Govern the District of Columbia and the nation's territories

Admit new states to the Union

Borrow money

Establish a system of national courts

IMPLIED POWERS

To make all laws "necessary and proper" to carry out the delegated powers

To provide for the "general welfare" of the United States

Members of Congress, such as Senator Barbara Mikulski, meet often with their constituents.

2. If no candidate for Vice President receives the number of votes needed to be elected, the members of the Senate choose the Vice President.

3. All treaties, or written agreements, with foreign nations must be approved by the Senate by a two-thirds vote.

4. Certain high officials appointed by the President must be approved by the Senate by a majority vote.

Limits on the Powers of Congress

The powers of Congress are limited in several important ways. The Supreme Court has the power to decide when Congress has gone beyond the powers granted to it by the Constitution. (You will read more about this in Chapter 7.) When the Court rules that Congress passed a law that exceeds Congress's constitutional powers, this law has no force.

Another limit of Congress's powers is the Tenth Amendment to the Constitution. It declares that the states shall keep all the powers not actually granted to the national govern-ment. These powers, as you recall, are the reserved powers. They include the states' authority with regard to elections, education, and marriage.

In addition, Article 1, Section 9, of the Constitution denies certain powers to Congress. The Constitution specifically forbids the following powers to Congress:

1. Congress Cannot Pass *Ex Post Facto* Laws. A law that applies to an action that took place before the law was passed is called an ***ex post facto* law.** For example, it is not against the law today to buy and sell foreign automobiles. If tomorrow Congress forbids the buying and selling of foreign cars, a person cannot be arrested for having bought or sold one of these cars in the past.

2. Congress Cannot Pass Bills of Attainder. A law that sentences a person to jail without granting the person a trial is called a **bill of attainder.** The Constitution provides that anyone accused of a crime must be given a trial in a court of law.

3. Congress Cannot Set Aside, or Suspend, the Writ of *Habeas Corpus.* A person accused of a crime has the right to a **writ of *habeas corpus.*** This is a court order requiring that the accused person be brought to court to determine if there is enough evidence to hold the person for a trial. If Congress had the right to set aside the writ of *habeas corpus*, a person might be kept in jail indefinitely with no formal charges being brought. The only exception to this rule is in times of rebellion or invasion.

4. Congress Cannot Tax Exports. Goods that are sent to other countries are called exports. A tax on exports would harm our foreign and domestic trade. Congress can, however, tax imports—goods that are brought into the country from abroad.

5. Congress Cannot Pass Any Law That Violates the Bill of Rights. The first ten amendments to the Constitution, as you recall, spell out the rights and freedoms of all American citizens. (See pages 67–68.) Congress is forbidden to pass any law that violates these rights.

6. Congress Cannot Favor the Trade of One State over That of Other States. Congress cannot pass a law giving any state or group of states an unfair advantage in trade. Of course, Congress can pass laws regulating trade. But these laws must apply equally to all states.

7. Congress Cannot Grant Titles of Nobility to Any American Citizen. Americans believe that all people are created equal. Therefore, they are opposed to establishing a noble class, or small group of persons with rights superior to those of other citizens.

8. Congress Cannot Withdraw Money from the Treasury Without a Law. Congress must pass a law telling how money shall be spent and the exact amount to be spent before the public funds are made available. This means that Congress must pass money laws to provide the money for carrying out the other laws it passes.

Other Roles of Congress

Over the years, the job of members of Congress has expanded greatly. Their responsibilities have grown to include roles that were not anticipated in the Constitution.

Helping Constituents. One of the most important jobs of members of Congress is to serve the interests of the people who live in their home districts or states. These people are called their **constituents.**

Members of Congress receive thousands of letters from their constituents every week. Some of this mail gives opinions on issues. Other letters ask a representative or senator to vote for or against a certain bill.

Most of the mail is from people asking for help. For example, a disabled veteran may complain that the Department of Veterans Affairs has lost his claim. The owner of a small company may ask how to apply for a government contract.

Conducting Investigations. Another important responsibility of Congress is its power to conduct investigations. Either house of Congress may investigate national issues. The purpose of these investigations usually is to determine whether a new law is needed or if an existing law is being carried out as Congress intended.

SECTION 3 REVIEW

Define elastic clause, implied powers, impeachment, *ex post facto* law, bill of attainder, writ of *habeas corpus*, constituents

1. **Organizing Ideas (a)** Name the five powers that are delegated to Congress by the Constitution. **(b)** Give an example of how Congress uses each of these five powers.
2. **Seeing Relationships (a)** How does the elastic clause help us to have a flexible government? **(b)** Describe the procedure for impeachment.
3. **Understanding Ideas (a)** What special powers does the House of Representatives have? **(b)** What special powers does the Senate have?
4. **Identifying Ideas** Identify four ways in which the Constitution limits the power of Congress.

Thinking Critically You are a new member of Congress. How will you vote on issues—according to your own beliefs or according to the wishes of your constituents? Why?

4 How a Bill Becomes a Law

Each day that Congress is in session, an interesting scene takes place. As the members of the House enter their legislative hall, some of them approach the front of the chamber. Then they drop papers into a box on the clerk's desk. The box is called the hopper. The papers dropped into it are bills, or written proposals for laws.

Of course, not all these proposals become laws. The process of getting a law passed is long and difficult. This sometimes makes us think that government is not responsive enough. In the long run, however, the process helps to ensure that our nation's laws will be good laws.

How the Idea for a Bill Begins

Each year the Senate and the House of Representatives consider thousands of bills. These bills may be introduced in either house. The only exception to this rule is an **appropriation bill,** or bill approving the spending of money. An appropriation bill must originate in the House of Representatives. Every bill must be passed by both houses of Congress before it may be signed by the President and becomes a law. A law is also known as an **act.**

Where do the ideas for all of these bills begin?

1. Ideas for Bills May Come from Any American Citizen.   The people are a powerful force in influencing laws. When a large number of constituents request a law, a representative or senator usually introduces a bill containing their ideas.

2. Ideas for Bills May Come from Organized Groups.   Members of Congress sometimes introduce bills because they are requested to do so by certain groups. For example, business people may want to limit competition from industries in other countries. Labor groups may call for laws establishing improved working conditions or higher hourly wages.

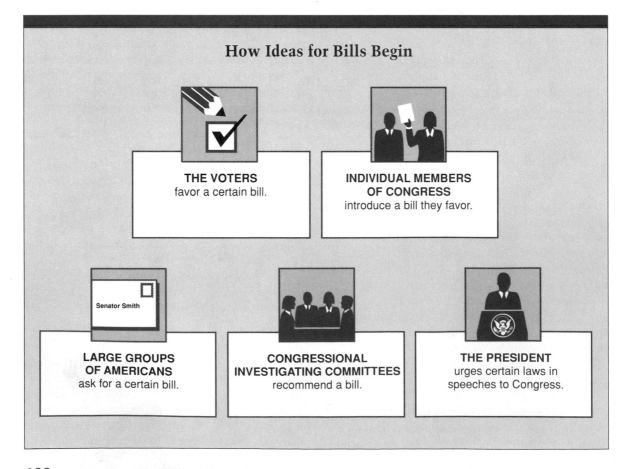

How Ideas for Bills Begin

THE VOTERS
favor a certain bill.

INDIVIDUAL MEMBERS OF CONGRESS
introduce a bill they favor.

Senator Smith

LARGE GROUPS OF AMERICANS
ask for a certain bill.

CONGRESSIONAL INVESTIGATING COMMITTEES
recommend a bill.

THE PRESIDENT
urges certain laws in speeches to Congress.

3. Ideas for Bills May Come from Committees of Congress. Many bills begin in Congress itself. Suppose that a congressional investigating committee conducts a study of certain kinds of crime. Suppose that its findings convince the committee that the federal government needs a new law for crime control. The committee can then draw up a bill and introduce it in Congress.

4. Ideas for Bills May Come from Members of Congress. Members of Congress often become experts in certain fields. A senator or representative who has had long experience with farm problems, for example, may introduce a bill to help agriculture.

5. Ideas for Bills May Come from the President of the United States. The President has great influence on bills introduced into Congress. Early in each session of Congress, the President appears before a joint session of the two houses to deliver a State of the Union Address. In this speech, the President recommends laws that the President believes are needed to improve our nation's well-being. Many of these ideas are soon introduced as bills by members of Congress.

How an Idea Becomes a Bill

Although anyone can suggest an idea for a bill, only members of Congress can introduce the bill itself. Suppose, for example, that a group of citizens favors creating a new national park. They write to their senators or representatives and explain their idea. The leader of the group arranges for a personal meeting with a senator or representative.

At this meeting, the leader of the group provides facts and figures on the subject and urges that a bill be introduced. If the senator or representative is convinced that the group's idea is a good one, he or she may agree to introduce the bill.

To see how a bill becomes a law, let us study the progress of this bill as it is considered first by the House of Representatives and then by the Senate.

The Bill Is Introduced in the House

How does the representative introduce this bill in the House? First the proposed bill is carefully written out. Bills are not always written by representatives. In fact, many bills are written by a committee, by the group who suggested the bill, or by an assistant to the representative.

After the bill is dropped into the hopper, it is given letters and a number. Let us suppose that the bill to create a new national park is marked HR 1215. The letters *HR* show that the bill is being considered by the House of Representatives. The number *1215* shows its place among all the bills presented in this particular session of Congress.

What happens to the bill after it is introduced? First it is sent to one of the standing committees for study. Usually the subject of the bill determines which committee will study it. In some cases, two committees may be interested in studying the bill. The Speaker of the House then decides to which committee it will be sent.

The Bill Is Sent to a Committee

In the case of HR 1215, the Speaker sends the bill to the House Interior and Insular Affairs Committee. This committee deals with all bills concerning the national park system.

Each bill is given careful attention by the committee to which it is sent. Many of the bills are found to be unnecessary. These are set aside and are never sent back to the House for further action. In this way the committees cut down on the amount of legislation Congress must consider.

The Committee Holds Hearings

HR 1215 is not set aside. Instead, the House Interior and Insular Affairs Committee holds special meetings, called **hearings,** to consider the bill. Most committee hearings are open

Congressional committees hold hearings to get information on bills they are considering. Here witnesses testify before a Senate committee.

to the public. Some important hearings are shown on television. At the hearings, the committee calls witnesses to testify for and against the bill. These witnesses help give the committee members the information they need in order to recommend that the bill be accepted, rejected, or changed.

Some of the witnesses who testify may be lobbyists. A **lobbyist** is a person who is paid to represent a certain group's point of view, or interests, at committee hearings. Lobbyists and expert witnesses, letters and telegrams from citizens, and evidence that committee members gather from many sources—all these help the committee reach a decision on the bill.

The Committee Studies the Bill

In the case of HR 1215, the Interior and Insular Affairs Committee decides to change the bill in certain ways. Members reword lines and add new sections to parts of the bill. When they are finished, the bill is very different from the one they originally received. The majority of committee members decide to recommend

that the House pass the bill as amended, or changed, by the committee.

The House Considers the Bill

When HR 1215 is reported out of committee and sent back to the House of Representatives, it is placed on the House calendar. The **calendar** is the schedule that lists the order in which bills are to be considered. In an emergency, a bill can be moved up on the calendar so that action may be taken quickly.

HR 1215 must be given three readings in the House of Representatives. By the time its turn comes on the calendar, the first reading really has already occurred. It took place when the Speaker first read the title of the bill to the House before sending it to the appropriate committee. The second reading will occur while the bill is debated.

The Rules Committee decides how much time will be given to debate on this bill. The time to be spent in debate, or discussion, is divided evenly between those members who are in favor of the bill and those members who are against the bill.

How a Bill Becomes a Law

This chart shows a bill that begins in the House of Representatives.

The same procedure is followed when a bill begins in the Senate.

HOUSE OF REPRESENTATIVES

Representative
A representative introduces the bill.

Clerk of the House
The clerk reads the bill's title to the House, gives the bill a number, and has it printed.

Speaker of the House
The Speaker of the House sends the bill to the proper committee.

House Committee
The committee or one of its sub-committees holds hearings on the bill, and may amend, kill, or approve the bill. If the full committee approves the bill, it is placed on the House calendar.

Floor of the House
The bill is read and debated. The House amends it, returns it to the House committee for revision, or approves it and sends it to the Senate.

Passed by the House

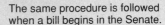
Sent to the Senate

SENATE

Clerk of the Senate
The bill is given a number, its title is read, and it is printed.

Presiding Officer of the Senate
The presiding officer of the Senate sends the bill to the proper committee.

Senate Committee
The committee or one of its sub-committees holds hearings on the bill, and may amend, kill, or approve the bill. If the full committee approves the bill, it is placed on the Senate calendar.

Floor of the Senate
The bill is read and debated. The Senate amends it, returns it to the House committee for revision, or approves it. If the Senate approves a version different from the House version, the bill is sent to a conference committee of the House and Senate.

President
The President signs or vetoes the bill or allows it to become law without signing it. Congress can override a veto by a two-thirds vote of both houses.

Conference Committee
The conference committee irons out differences between the House and Senate versions of the bill. It returns the revised bill to both houses for approval.

For the debate, the House usually acts as a **Committee of the Whole.** As one committee, the House can act less formally and really turn the meeting into a work session. The bill now is given its second reading. A clerk reads a paragraph, and then amendments may be offered. Debate on each amendment is usually limited to five minutes for each member who speaks. A vote is then taken on the amendment. It is usually a voice vote with all in favor saying "yea" and those opposed, "nay."

Each paragraph of the bill is read and amended in similar fashion until the entire bill has been considered. When the House meets again in formal session, a member may demand a "quorum call." A **quorum,** or majority of the members, must be present in order to do business.

The House Votes on the Bill

When a quorum is present, the House is ready for the third reading. This reading is usually by title only. However, any member may demand that the bill be read in its entirety. The vote is then taken. A majority of the members present is required to pass a bill.

On important bills, a **roll-call vote** is usually taken. Each member's name is called and a record is made of his or her vote. Our bill to create a new national park, as amended, passes the House. But it is not yet a law. Like all bills, it must now be considered by the other house of Congress, the Senate.

The Senate Acts on the Bill

In the Senate, the bill is called S 2019. The way in which a bill is handled in the Senate is similar to the process followed in the House. Bill S 2019 is read by title, for its first reading. It is then sent to the Senate Energy and Natural Resources Committee.

After holding hearings, the committee revises S 2019. The committee then recommends that the bill be passed by the Senate.

The senators usually are not limited in their debate, as are members of the House of Representatives. In the Senate, speeches may go on and on. Some senators have talked for many hours in order to prevent the Senate from taking a vote on a bill. This method of delay by making lengthy speeches is called a **filibuster.** Senators have sometimes tried to "talk a bill to death." Debate in the Senate can be limited only if three fifths of the full Senate vote to limit it. Limit on debate in the Senate is called **cloture.**

After the members of the Senate finish their debate on S 2019, a roll call is taken. Bill S 2019 passes. What happens next?

The House and the Senate Must Agree on the Final Bill

When a bill passes the House and Senate in identical form, it is ready to be sent to the President. Usually, however, the two houses pass different versions of the same bill. If a bill is changed in any way, it must be sent back to the house in which it originated. In our example, the House of Representatives does not agree to the Senate changes. When this happens, a conference committee must be called.

A conference committee meets to try to reach an agreement on the bill. The committee is made up of an equal number of senators and representatives. The committee members from each house may have to give up something in order to reach a compromise.

Finally a compromise bill is sent back to both houses. Usually both houses approve the work of their conference committee.

The President Approves the Bill

The bill as passed by both houses is sent to the President of the United States. The President may take one of three possible actions on a bill:

1. The President may sign the bill and declare it to be a law.

2. The President may refuse to sign the bill and send it back to Congress with a message giving the reasons for rejecting it. This action, as you have read, is called a **veto.**

3. The President may keep the bill for ten days without signing it. If Congress is in session during this ten-day period, the bill becomes a law without the President's signature. However, if Congress is not in session and the President does not sign the bill within ten days, the bill does not become a law. When this happens, we say the bill has been killed by a **pocket veto.**

The President does not use the veto often. Even then, Congress can pass a bill over the President's veto by a two-thirds vote of both houses. In the case of our national park bill, it becomes a law and goes into effect after the President signs it.

The long and involved process of making laws may be slow. However, it prevents hasty legislation while providing a way for the national government to pass needed laws.

SECTION 4 REVIEW

Define appropriation bill, act, hearings, calendar, quorum, roll-call vote, filibuster, cloture, veto, pocket veto

Identify lobbyist, Committee of the Whole

1. **Understanding Ideas** From which sources may the ideas for bills introduced into Congress originate?
2. **Summarizing Ideas** Summarize the steps by which a bill becomes a law.
3. **Identifying Ideas** (a) What three possible actions can the President take on a bill that has been passed by both houses of Congress? (b) What can Congress do if the President does not approve a bill?
4. **Seeing Relationships** How does the fact that lawmaking is a lengthy process benefit the nation?

Thinking Critically Imagine that you are the leader of the group that favors creating a new national park. Write a short letter to your senator or representative explaining your idea.

The legislative, or lawmaking, branch of our federal government is called Congress. It consists of two houses, the House of Representatives and the Senate. Each state is represented in the Senate by two senators. The number of representatives each state elects to the House of Representatives is based on the size of the state's population.

Congress meets for a two-year term. The two houses organize their work and operate in similar ways. Much of the actual work of Congress is done by committees.

Congress has been given many important powers by the Constitution. The delegated powers set forth specific functions of Congress. The elastic clause has permitted Congress to exercise powers not specifically granted to it. The Constitution also limits the powers of Congress. It reserves certain powers for the states and specifically forbids some powers to Congress.

Congress considers thousands of bills, or proposed laws, each year. To become a law, each bill must be passed by both houses of Congress before being signed by the President.

CHAPTER
5
SUMMARY

DEVELOPING CIVICS SKILLS

CITIZENSHIP SKILL
Interpreting Political Cartoons

Most Americans recognize him at a glance. He has been wearing the same outfit for more than 100 years: striped pants, a cutaway coat, and a stovepipe hat decorated with stars. His name is Uncle Sam—the figure that has come to represent the United States.

You see Uncle Sam and many other famous characters all the time. They appear regularly in political cartoons. Political cartoons typically are found in the editorial sections of newspapers. These cartoons use pictures to express a point of view. Because the pictures often are funny, your first reaction might be to laugh. It is important, however, to look beyond the humor. Every political cartoon has a serious message.

How to Interpret a Political Cartoon

To get the most from political cartoons, follow these guidelines.

1. **Identify the symbols used.** As you look at the cartoon, keep in mind that the artist often uses symbols, or drawings with special meanings. Some symbols, such as Uncle Sam represent groups of people or places. Other symbols represent ideas. Justice, for example, often is shown as a blindfolded woman holding a set of scales.
2. **Identify the caricatures.** Caricatures are sketches that exaggerate, or distort, a person's features. Caricatures can be positive or negative, depending on the cartoonist's point of view. Try to identify whether the cartoonist is portraying the subject in a favorable or unfavorable manner.
3. **Read all labels.** Editorial cartoons often use labels to identify people, objects, events, or ideas. Determine how the labels help express the cartoonist's point of view.
4. **Read the caption.** Many cartoons carry a caption in addition to the labels. If the cartoon has a caption, note how it relates to the cartoon. Identify whose point of view is being expressed in the caption—the cartoonist, the cartoon figure, or some other person.

Applying the Skill

Examine the political cartoon below. Then answer the following questions.
1. What is the subject of the cartoon?
2. Why do you think the cartoonist chose to portray the seniority system as an old king?
3. **(a)** What is the cartoonist's opinion of the seniority system? **(b)** Do you agree with this opinion? Why or why not?

American Revolution Bicentennial

Reviewing Terms

On a separate sheet of paper, copy the paragraph below. Then fill in each blank, using the correct term from the following list.

bills
committees
House of
   Representatives
President
lobbyists
filibuster
Speaker of the House
bicameral
President *pro*
   tempore
Senate

     A civics class visiting Washington, D.C., learned that Congress is a two-house, or (1) _____, legislature. Its two houses are the (2) _____ and the (3) _____. In a representative's office, they saw people called (4) _____ try to persuade the representative to vote a certain way. Then, in the Senate, they watched several senators conducting a (5) _____, or making long speeches to delay a vote. They saw the (6) _____, the presiding officer of the Senate. In the House of Representatives, the presiding officer is the (7) _____. The members of Congress were discussing (8) _____ that might become laws if they passed both houses and were signed by the (9) _____. To manage all their work, both houses divide their work among small groups called (10) _____.

Using Thinking Skills

1. **Drawing Conclusions (a)** Why do we have a two-house national legislature? **(b)** Why is lawmaking such a lengthy process?
2. **Understanding Ideas (a)** Explain how membership in the House is divided. **(b)** When are elections for representatives and senators held, and how long are their terms? **(c)** What qualifications are required of members of Congress?
3. **Organizing Ideas (a)** List the benefits received by members of Congress. **(b)** What are Congress's rules of conduct, and how does Congress deal with misconduct?

4. **Comparing Ideas (a)** Compare the special powers held by the two houses of Congress. **(b)** What are the things that Congress cannot do? **(c)** Who are the presiding officers in the houses?
5. **Summarizing Ideas** Summarize the process by which a bill becomes a law.
6. **Contrasting Ideas (a)** What is the difference between a conference committee and a joint committee? **(b)** Why is most of the work of Congress accomplished through committees?
7. **Seeing Relationships (a)** What are the five powers delegated to Congress by the Constitution? **(b)** How does the elastic clause help our government meet the nation's changing needs?

Practicing Civics Skills

Interpreting a Political Cartoon Look through a newspaper or newsmagazine to find a political cartoon that focuses on the subject of Congress. Mount this cartoon on a piece of paper. Study the cartoon and answer the following questions. **(a)** What symbols are used in the cartoon? **(b)** What caricatures are used? **(c)** What is the main point of the cartoon? **(d)** Is the cartoonist presenting a negative or a positive view of Congress?

Being a Good Citizen

1. Imagine that you have just been elected to Congress. Write a diary entry describing what a typical day at work is like for you.
2. Conduct research to provide answers for the following questions: **(a)** Who represents your congressional district? **(b)** Who are the senators from your state? **(c)** How many representatives does your state have?
3. Imagine that there is an issue that you consider important enough to deserve attention in Congress as a bill. Describe how you would go about gaining a large group of citizen supporters for your cause.

The President Carries Out Our Nation's Laws

Chapter Sections

Chapter Focus

"The terms of the President and Vice President shall end at noon on the 20th day of January . . . and the terms of their successors shall then begin."

—Amendment 20,
Constitution of the United States

The day on which the new President takes office is called Inauguration Day. It is an exciting day in Washington, D.C., and indeed throughout the nation. Visitors pour into the nation's capital from our 50 states and from foreign lands.

The inaugural ceremony is held on a large, flag-draped platform set up at the Capitol. The highlight of the ceremony is the swearing in of the President. The President-elect places one hand on the Bible and repeats the oath of office. The Chief Justice of the

United States administers the oath, reading these words from the Constitution:

"I do solemnly swear (or affirm) that I will faithfully execute the office of President of the United States, and will, to the best of my ability, preserve, protect, and defend the Constitution of the United States."

The President then delivers an Inaugural Address. People throughout the world listen carefully to this speech. They know they are listening to one of the most powerful people in the world: the person who will lead the United States for the next four years.

Study Guide

As you begin to read about how the President carries out the nation's laws, look for answers to the following questions:
★ What are the President's powers and roles?
★ How is the executive branch organized?
★ What are the executive departments and the independent agencies?

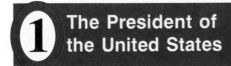

1 The President of the United States

The executive branch of the federal government, described in Article 2 of the Constitution, is headed by the **President** of the United States. In 1789 George Washington became the nation's first President. Since then only 40 other men have served as President. Hundreds of people, however, have sought the office. The President is the nation's most powerful elected official.

Qualifications

The Constitution sets forth certain qualifications that the President of the United States must meet:

1. The President must be a native-born American citizen.

2. The President must be at least 35 years of age.

3. The President must have been a resident of the United States for at least 14 years.

These are the only qualifications for President mentioned in the Constitution. However, there also have been a number of unwritten rules about who could be elected President. For example, all American Presidents have been men. All have been white. All have been Christian. Most Presidents have attended college. Many have been lawyers. Most have held other political offices before becoming President.

These unwritten rules, however, can change. For most of our nation's history, only Protestants were elected President. John F. Kennedy, who was a Roman Catholic, broke that unwritten rule when he was elected President in 1960.

Recently, more women and minority group members have become involved in Presidential politics. In 1984 Geraldine Ferraro was the Democratic nominee for Vice President. Jesse Jackson, an African American, made a strong bid for the Presidency in 1984 and again in 1988.

Term of Office

The President is elected to a four-year term and may be reelected for a second term of office. The original Constitution did not state how many terms the President could serve.

Can You Guess?

- **How young was the youngest person ever elected President? Who was he?**
- **How old was the oldest person ever elected President? Who was he?**

Answers are on page 594.

The President of the United States conducts much of the nation's business in the Oval Office of the White House.

George Washington set the tradition of a limit of two terms. He refused to run for the Presidency a third time when he was urged to do so. This two-term tradition was not broken until Franklin D. Roosevelt was elected to a third term as President in 1940. In 1944 he won a fourth term.

In 1951 the length of time a President could serve was limited by passage of the Twenty-second Amendment (see page 73). This amendment set a two-term limit to the Presidency.

Salary and Benefits

The salary the President receives is fixed by Congress. However, Congress cannot change the salary during a President's term of office. This restriction was included in the Constitution to prevent Congress from punishing or rewarding a President.

Today the President is paid a salary of $200,000 a year plus $50,000 for official expenses. Since the President must travel fre-

quently, there is also an annual allowance for travel costs.

The President is provided with many additional benefits. The President's family lives in the White House. This beautiful building has been the home of all American Presidents since John Adams. The White House is also the site of the President's office and the offices of the President's closest assistants. Parts of the White House are open to visitors.

For special meetings and for relaxation on weekends or holidays, the President can use Camp David, in the mountains of Maryland. A large fleet of cars, helicopters, and planes—including the special jet *Air Force One*—is also available to the President.

The Vice President

The Constitution provides that if the President dies, resigns, or is removed from office, the **Vice President** becomes President. The Constitution gives the Vice President only one other job—to preside over the Senate. Because the power of the Vice President is so limited, John Adams, the country's first Vice President, called the office "the most insignificant" ever invented.

However, nine Vice Presidents have succeeded to the office of President. The first was John Tyler. He became President in 1841 when President William Harrison died. In this century, five Vice Presidents have succeeded to the Presidency.

The Vice President thus holds a very important position. Moreover, in recent years Presidents have given their Vice Presidents more responsibilities. Vice Presidents must be fully informed and prepared to take over the important job that could become theirs.

The Vice President must meet the same constitutional qualifications as the President. The Vice President also serves a four-year term, and receives a salary of $160,600 a year plus a sum for official expenses.

Vice Presidential candidates often are chosen for their ability to help the Presidential candidates win election. Increasingly, political parties have also chosen Vice Presidential nominees who are fully qualified by experience to succeed to the Presidency.

Presidential Succession

Eight Presidents of the United States have died while in office. One President resigned. In each case, the Vice President took the oath of office and became President as provided by the Constitution.

What would happen if both the President and the Vice President should die while in office? The Constitution gave Congress the right to decide who should then fill the office of President. This is known as the order of **Presidential succession.**

According to a law passed by Congress in 1947, the Speaker of the House of Representatives becomes President if both the regularly elected President and Vice President die or are removed from office. If the Speaker dies or is removed from office, then the president *pro*

tempore of the Senate succeeds to the Presidency. Following them in succession to the Presidency are the members of the Cabinet, in the order in which their departments were created.

The Twenty-fifth Amendment

If the President dies or resigns and is succeeded by the Vice President, who then becomes Vice President? Until 1967 the answer to this question was, no one. The office of the Vice President remained empty when the Vice President moved up to the Presidency. Under the Twenty-fifth Amendment (see page 74), the new President nominates a new Vice President. The nomination must then be approved by a majority vote of both houses of Congress.

The first test of the Twenty-fifth Amendment came in 1973. Vice President Spiro Agnew resigned after he was charged with income tax evasion. President Richard M.

Chief Justice Warren Burger swore in Gerald Ford as the 38th President of the United States on August 9, 1974, the day that President Richard Nixon resigned.

Nixon nominated Gerald R. Ford as the new Vice President. The nomination was confirmed by Congress.

The amendment was used again in 1974. When President Nixon resigned because of the Watergate scandal, Vice President Ford became President. Ford then nominated Nelson A. Rockefeller as Vice President, and Congress approved the nomination. For the only time in our history, the nation had a President and a Vice President who had not been elected by the people.

The Twenty-fifth Amendment also provides that if the President is too ill to serve, the Vice President will serve as Acting President until the President is well again. Suppose, however, that the President wants to serve again, but the Vice President and the Cabinet do not think the President is fit to do so. Then Congress must decide by a two-thirds vote whether the President will return to office or whether the Vice President will continue as Acting President.

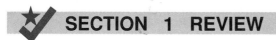

SECTION 1 REVIEW

Define Presidential succession

Identify President, Vice President

1. **Organizing Ideas (a)** What are the constitutional qualifications for the President of the United States? **(b)** What have been some of the "unwritten rules" for becoming President?
2. **Understanding Ideas (a)** Why did John Adams call the office of Vice President "insignificant"? **(b)** How has the role of the Vice President changed in recent years?
3. **Summarizing Ideas (a)** Summarize the provisions of the Twenty-fifth Amendment. **(b)** Why was this amendment added?

Thinking Critically You are a nominee for President of the United States. What qualities will you look for in a Vice Presidential candidate? Why?

② The Powers and Roles of the President

Article 2, Section 1, of the Constitution provides that "the executive power shall be vested in [given to] a President of the United States of America." This means that the President is responsible for executing, or carrying out, the laws passed by Congress. Because the President has the job of executing the nation's laws, the President is often called the nation's **Chief Executive.** As Chief Executive, the President must take an active role in all phases of government.

The President Influences Legislation

The President plays a large role in shaping the laws of the United States by recommending, or suggesting, needed laws to Congress. In fact, the Constitution requires that the President "shall from time to time give to the Congress information of [about] the state of the Union, and recommend to their [Congress's] consideration such measures as he shall judge necessary. . . ."

To carry out this constitutional provision, the President delivers several messages to Congress each year. These messages may be delivered as speeches before Congress or in writing.

Every year, usually in late January, the President delivers to Congress a **State of the Union Address.** As you read in Chapter 5, this speech sets forth the programs and policies that the President wants Congress to put into effect as laws.

The President also sends Congress a budget message, recommending how the federal government should raise and spend its money. In an economic message to Congress, the President reviews the nation's economic condition and recommends various laws to help the economy.

The President's Veto Power

The President also influences legislation by the power to veto, or reject, laws. Sometimes the threat of a Presidential veto discourages Congress from passing a bill. Congress knows how difficult it is to pass a bill after it has been vetoed by the President. For this reason, Congress considers carefully before passing a bill it knows the President does not approve.

Commander in Chief

As head of the armed forces of the United States, or **Commander in Chief,** the President has important powers. All military officers, in time of war or in peacetime, take their orders from the President. The President does not actually lead American forces into battle. However, the President is in constant touch with our nation's military leaders. The President also has the final word in planning how a war is to be fought. This is a serious responsibility in our age of modern weapons.

Under the Constitution, only Congress can declare war. As Commander in Chief of the armed forces, however, the President may send American forces into any part of the world where danger threatens. Presidents have sent troops into action in foreign countries many times in our nation's history.

Sending American troops into certain situations sometimes involves the risk of war. Therefore, Congress passed the **War Powers Act** in 1973 to try to limit the President's military power. This act requires that troops sent abroad by the President be recalled within 60 days unless Congress approves the action.

Foreign Policy Leader

The President, as Chief Executive of one of the most powerful nations of the world, must give constant attention to our **foreign policy,** our nation's plan for dealing with the other

As foreign policy leader, President Jimmy Carter helped Anwar Sadat (left) of Egypt and Menachem Begin (right) of Israel work out a peace agreement.

nations of the world. As the person in charge of conducting America's foreign policy, the President seeks to secure friendly relations with foreign governments while preserving the security of the United States.

To conduct our relations with other governments, the President appoints officials to represent the United States in foreign nations. The President also meets with leaders of other nations and with their representatives in the United States. In addition, the President often travels abroad to meet with foreign leaders.

Treaty-Making Power. The government of the United States makes written agreements, called **treaties,** with other nations. The President is responsible for making these treaties with foreign governments. Other officials do most of the actual work in reaching agreements with other nations. The President, however, assumes the final responsibility for all treaties.

All treaties must be made with the advice and consent of the Senate. The Senate must approve a treaty by a two-thirds vote before it becomes effective. If the treaty is approved, it is the President's job to see that its provisions are carried out.

Chief Diplomat

Great skill and tact are required in dealing with friendly and unfriendly nations. The art of dealing with foreign governments is called **diplomacy,** and the President is our chief diplomat. The President often visits foreign nations to build up international friendship and security.

Powers of the President

THE PRESIDENT OF THE UNITED STATES

Approves or vetoes all bills passed by Congress

Is Commander in Chief of the armed forces

Appoints Cabinet members, ambassadors, and federal judges

Proposes laws and programs to Congress

Keeps Congress informed about the state of the nation and the economy

Prepares the federal government's budget

Receives foreign ambassadors

Conducts America's foreign relations and makes treaties

May pardon those guilty of crimes against our federal government

As the nation's chief diplomat, the President often corresponds with the heads of foreign governments. These written communications are called **diplomatic notes.** In addition, the President has access to a computerized communications system. This system enables the President to make a direct connection with the government of the Soviet Union very quickly in an emergency. Such a method of communication between world leaders is very important. It can prevent governments from taking actions that might have dangerous consequences for our nation and the world.

Judicial Powers

The Constitution of the United States gives the President the power to appoint Supreme Court Justices and other federal judges. These appointments must be approved by the Senate by a majority vote.

The President also has the power to grant reprieves and pardons to those who have committed certain federal crimes. A **reprieve** postpones the carrying out of a sentence. It gives a convicted person the opportunity to gather more evidence to support his or her case or to appeal for a new trial. A **pardon** forgives a person convicted of a crime and frees him or her from serving out the sentence. The President also has the judicial power known as **commutation,** or making a convicted person's sentence less severe.

Other Presidential Roles

Over the years, the President has also taken on other roles that are not mentioned in the Constitution. These roles include Chief of State and leader of a political party.

As **Chief of State,** the President is the symbol of the United States and its people. It is the President who greets visiting foreign leaders and travels to other countries to strengthen ties and improve relations. The

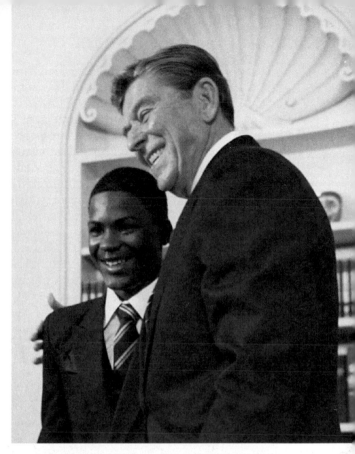

Presidents, such as President Ronald Reagan, enjoy meeting with young Americans.

President performs many ceremonial duties. These include awarding medals to honor worthy citizens, lighting the nation's Christmas tree, and throwing out the first baseball to open the baseball season.

The President is also the leader of a political party. Members of the President's party worked hard to help elect the President. In return the President makes speeches to help other party members who are running for office. The President helps the party raise money for its political campaigns.

The President's Day

In addition to making many important decisions, the President must find time to carry on a wide range of other activities from day to day. At all times, the President's office must be in touch with other high officials of the nation's government. Thus the President can never be far away from the telephone.

The activities that occupy the President's time are varied. Many hours of the day are spent in meetings with Presidential advisers. When Congress is in session, the President may have a breakfast or luncheon meeting with congressional leaders. Meetings are also held with members of the President's political party to talk over the bills before Congress, appointments of officials, or political plans important to the party. In addition, the President meets regularly with members of the Cabinet.

The President delivers speeches by the dozen. President Franklin D. Roosevelt established the custom of reporting directly to the American people. He did so by radio talks, which he called "fireside chats." Today the President appears on television to speak directly to the people, to inform them of proposed new programs and ask for their support. The President also holds press conferences to explain government decisions and answer questions from reporters.

In addition, the President must find time to attend to many other important duties. The President must sign (or veto) bills, write speeches, appoint officials, and examine budget figures. The President must also deal with matters of foreign policy and reach decisions on national defense problems. Furthermore, the President must find time to read newspapers and magazines and to study reports received from government officials at home and abroad. The President must stay informed about events occurring throughout the world.

★ SECTION 2 REVIEW

Define State of the Union Address, War Powers Act, foreign policy, treaties, diplomacy, diplomatic notes, reprieve, pardon, commutation

Identify Chief Executive, Commander in Chief, Chief of State

1. **Identifying Roles** (a) How does the President of the United States influence legislation? (b) How does the President influence the judicial process?
2. **Summarizing Ideas** Write a brief summary of the President's foreign policy powers.
3. **Forming Opinions** (a) Identify what duties the President performs as Chief of State. (b) In your opinion, how important are these duties? Why?

Thinking Critically Imagine that you are President of the United States. What will you try to achieve? Make a list of the goals of your administration. Explain why you believe each goal is important.

3 The Executive Departments and the Cabinet

The duties of the executive branch of the federal government have grown greatly since George Washington served as the nation's first Chief Executive. During the early years of our nation, Presidents could carry out their duties with the help of a few assistants. Today, there are more than 5,000 people assisting our nation's President.

The Executive Office of the President

The President's closest advisers and assistants are part of the **Executive Office of the President.** The Executive Office was established in 1939. It has been reorganized by every President since then. The agencies and offices that make up the Executive Office advise the President on important domestic and international matters.

The Council of Economic Advisers, for example, furnishes the President with facts and figures about the nation's economy. It recommends programs to help economic growth and stability.

Another agency of the Executive Office is the Office of Management and Budget. It assists in the preparation of the federal budget, which the President must present to Congress.

The National Security Council (NSC) is the President's top-ranking group of advisers on all matters concerning the nation's defense and security. The Office of National Drug Control Policy coordinates federal, state, and local activities designed to stop the use of illegal drugs. The Council on Environmental Quality monitors the environment and makes recommendations to the President.

The White House Office includes the President's closest personal and political advisers. Also part of this office are researchers, clerical staff, social secretaries, and the President's doctor. Members of the White House staff perform many important jobs for the President. They schedule appointments and write speeches. They help maintain relations with Congress and with other departments and agencies of the government. The **press secretary** represents the President to the news media and the public.

The Executive Departments

The people who wrote the Constitution drew up a plan of government with plenty of room for growth. They did not try to work out every detail of government. For example, they did not try to plan for each person who would help the President carry out the laws. The Constitution made no mention of the President's assistants except to state that "he may require the opinion, in writing, of the principal officer in each of the executive departments. . . ."

Today there are 14 **executive departments** in the federal government. Each has specific

Did you know that...

HIS HIGHNESS   MR. PRESIDENT

when George Washington became the nation's first President, no one knew what to call him? Vice President John Adams wanted to call him "His Highness, The President of the United States and Protector of the Rights of the Same." The Senate called him "His Highness." This was the title used for the British king.

It was the House of Representatives that began to refer to the nation's Chief Executive as "the President of the United States." This simple title soon won everyone's approval.

areas of responsibility. The chart on page 131 shows you the main duties of each executive department.

Congress has the power to establish executive departments, combine several under one head, or even drop a department. The President must then direct these departments, working within the structure set up by Congress.

The Cabinet

George Washington had the help of only three executive departments: the Departments of State, Treasury, and War. He met frequently with the heads of these departments to discuss policy and get their advice on important matters. The heads of these executive departments, as you recall, became known as the

President's **Cabinet.** Every President since Washington has followed his custom of holding Cabinet meetings.

The Cabinet consists of the heads of the 14 executive departments and any other officials the President chooses. The President often invites other key government officials, such as the Vice President, to attend Cabinet meetings. Cabinet meetings are led by the President.

Members of the Cabinet are appointed by the President. However, these appointments must be approved by a majority vote of the Senate. The title of most Cabinet members is **Secretary.** For example, the head of the Department of State is the Secretary of State. The head of the Treasury Department is the Secretary of the Treasury. The head of the Justice Department, however, is known as the **Attorney General.**

On the next few pages, you will read about how each of the 14 executive departments works to improve the lives of all Americans.

Department of State

The conduct of our nation's relations with other countries is the special responsibility of the Department of State. The Secretary of State heads a large staff of officials in Washington, D.C., who direct the worldwide work of the department. In addition, the officials who are sent to other countries to represent our nation report to the Department of State.

Ambassadors are the highest-ranking American representatives in foreign countries. The official residence of an ambassador in a foreign country is called an **embassy.** In a few smaller countries, the United States is represented by officials called **ministers.**

There is also another kind of representative, called a **consul.** An American consul's office, or **consulate,** can be found in most large foreign cities. The consuls and the members of their staffs work hard to build up our foreign trade and commerce. They also help to protect citizens of the United States who do business and own property in foreign lands. Citizens of the United States traveling in foreign lands may go to the consulate if they need help.

At home the Department of State is the keeper of the Great Seal of the United States. The Great Seal is put on all laws and treaties. In addition, the Department of State issues documents known as passports and visas. **Passports** allow our citizens to travel abroad. **Visas** allow people from other nations to come to the United States.

These pictures show the steady growth of the size of the Cabinet from President Washington's time (left) to President Bush's time.

Department of the Treasury

The Department of the Treasury manages the nation's money. It collects taxes from our citizens and pays out the money owed by our national government. When necessary, the Department of the Treasury borrows money for our government. It also supervises the coining and printing of money, and it keeps the President informed about the financial condition of our country.

There are several important divisions within the Department of the Treasury. The Internal Revenue Service (IRS) collects personal and corporate income taxes. The Customs Service collects taxes on goods brought into the country. The Secret Service protects the President and helps prevent counterfeiting—making or distributing fake money.

Inspectors for the Department of the Treasury study all bills to see that they are properly printed.

Department of Defense

Until 1947 the nation's armed forces were administered, or directed, by two separate departments—the Department of War and the Department of the Navy. Then in 1947 Congress placed all the armed forces—the Army, Navy, Air Force, and Marine Corps—under one department, the Department of Defense. Its head, the Secretary of Defense, is always a civilian. However, the Secretary has many military officers as assistants. These officers help the Secretary plan the military defense of our nation and provide for the training and equipping of the armed forces.

There are three major divisions within the Department of Defense. The Department of the Army commands our land forces. The Department of the Navy has charge of our seagoing forces and includes the Marine Corps. The Department of the Air Force is responsible for our air defenses. Each of these divisions of the Defense Department is headed by a civilian Secretary.

The highest-ranking military officers of the Army, Navy, and Air Force are members of the **Joint Chiefs of Staff.** The head of the Marine Corps attends all meetings of the Joint Chiefs and takes part as an equal member when matters concerning the Marines are discussed. Members of the Joint Chiefs of Staff have the duty of advising the President on military matters.

Training Our Military Leaders. The Department of Defense is also responsible for our four officer-training schools. These are the Military Academy at West Point, New York, the Naval Academy at Annapolis, Maryland, the Air Force Academy at Colorado Springs, Colorado, and the Coast Guard Academy at New London, Connecticut.

Candidates for the various academies are nominated by the representative from their district or by one of the senators from their state. Usually four candidates are named for each vacancy, or opening. All candidates must have good high school records. They must also pass scholastic and physical tests.

The successful candidate receives a free four-year college education and upon graduation becomes an officer in one of the military services. Since 1976 women have been (continued on page 130)

Focus on Freedom

Debating the Meaning of the Second Amendment

Guns have played an important role in American history. Colonists used muskets to hunt food for their families and to win the American Revolution. As our country expanded westward, rifles and pistols were used for hunting game, settling disputes, and defending against cattle rustlers.

Guns are still an important part of American life. Over 70 million Americans own firearms. Americans use their guns primarily for recreation—hunting, target shooting, and collecting. Many people keep guns in their homes for self-protection.

Unfortunately, firearms have a darker side. About 30,000 Americans are killed by firearms each year. Most of these deaths involve crimes. But gun accidents kill about 1,400 Americans annually. And firearms kept for self-protection often end up injuring or killing friends or family members instead of warding off intruders.

Because so many Americans are hurt and killed by firearms, many citizens want the government to restrict gun ownership. Other people argue that gun ownership is a basic right guaranteed to all Americans. At the center of this hotly debated issue is the Second Amendment to the Constitution.

"A Well Regulated Militia"

The Second Amendment states that "A well regulated militia being necessary to the security of a free state, the right of the people to keep and bear arms shall not be infringed."

This amendment allows each state to form and arm its own "well regulated militia," what we know today as the National Guard. National Guard units maintain the internal security of each state during emergencies. The amendment also gives local, state, and federal governments the right to establish and arm security forces, such as police departments.

Few people would argue against giving police and military officials the right to use weapons to maintain the peace and security of our nation. But what about average citizens? Does the Second Amendment give everyone the right to own and use guns?

As the colonists in this engraving illustrate, firearms were a common sight in early America.

Interpreting the Constitution

In 1981, the town of Morton Grove, Illinois, became the first town to completely ban handguns. The United States Court of Appeals ruled that the Morton Grove law did not violate the Second Amendment, and the Supreme Court refused to hear the case, allowing the lower court's ruling to stand.

The Morton Grove decision is in keeping with the judiciary's view of the Second Amendment. In fact, every Supreme Court and federal court decision involving the amendment has held that the amendment does not *guarantee* the right of individuals to own or to carry arms. Thus, gun control laws are constitutional.

The federal government, most states, and many communities have restrictions on gun ownership. Still, many people disagree with the courts' rulings, and are challenging gun control laws.

Both the supporters and the opponents of handgun ownership believe strongly in their positions. Because of this, the topic is hotly debated.

Battling Over Gun Control

America's gun battle is being fought most vigorously in Washington, D.C., where opposing groups are fighting to win the votes of Congress. The National Rifle Association (NRA) is a highly vocal supporter of gun ownership. The NRA's 2.7 million members argue that the Second Amendment guarantees Americans "the right to keep and bear arms."

Opposing the NRA are a number of smaller groups that are working for laws to restrict gun ownership. Among the most prominent of these groups is Handgun Control. Handgun Control argues that stronger gun control laws, by keeping guns out of the hands of criminals, would reduce the number of Americans killed and injured by guns each year.

Questions to Consider

1. What role have guns played in American life?
2. Why do some people support gun control laws? Why do others oppose these laws?
3. Find out what, if any, gun control laws exist in your community or state. Are they too strict? Not strict enough? Explain.

admitted into all the service academies on an equal basis with men.

Department of Justice

The Department of Justice, under the Attorney, General, enforces federal laws. It also defends the United States in court when a lawsuit is brought against the federal government for any reason.

The Federal Bureau of Investigation (FBI) is an important agency of the Justice Department. The FBI investigates crimes that break federal laws and arrests those accused of crimes against the United States. The Immigration and Naturalization Service (INS) and the Bureau of Prisons are also within the Justice Department.

Department of the Interior

The Department of the Interior manages our nation's natural resources. Its duties are to encourage the wise use of America's land, minerals, water, fish, and wildlife. The department also manages our national parks and federal dams.

There are several important divisions within the Department of the Interior. The Bureau of Indian Affairs deals with matters involving Native Americans. The Bureau of Reclamation sponsors irrigation, flood control, and hydroelectric power projects. Other divisions include the National Park Service, the Bureau of Mines, and the United States Fish and Wildlife Service.

Department of Agriculture

The Department of Agriculture helps American farmers in the important task of raising and marketing crops. Special agencies in the department, such as the Agricultural Research Service and the Soil Conservation Service, encourage better methods of farming. The de-

partment also prepares reports on market conditions for crops and livestock to assist farmers in their planning and planting.

Other divisions within this department include the Farmers Home Administration (FHA), which provides loans for buying and operating farms, and the Forest Service, which helps to protect our nation's woodlands. The Food and Nutrition Service manages the Food Stamp and National School Lunch Programs.

Department of Commerce

American trade and business are encouraged by the Department of Commerce. There are many important agencies within this department. For example, the Bureau of Economic Analysis studies business conditions in the United States. The Minority Business Development Agency assists in creating and strengthening minority-owned businesses. The Patent and Trademark Office protects the rights of inventors. The National Telecommunications and Information Administration promotes the effective use of telecommunications.

Also within this department is the Bureau of the Census, which counts the United States population every ten years. The National Weather Service, which monitors and forecasts the nation's weather, is also part of the Department of Commerce.

Department of Labor

The American worker receives important services from the Department of Labor. It gathers information on working conditions in various businesses and industries. The Wage and Hour Division is responsible for carrying out federal laws that regulate the wages and hours of workers in businesses engaged in interstate commerce.

Another division of the Department of Labor is the Bureau of Labor Statistics, which collects information about employment and

Principal Duties of the Executive Departments

DEPARTMENT OF STATE (1789)[1]
Conducts our foreign relations
Protects our citizens abroad
Issues passports and visas

DEPARTMENT OF THE TREASURY (1789)
Prints, coins, and issues money
Collects taxes and pays bills
Manages government funds

DEPARTMENT OF JUSTICE (1789)[2]
Investigates violations of federal laws
Prosecutes cases before courts
Administers naturalization laws
Enforces immigration laws

DEPARTMENT OF THE INTERIOR (1849)
Controls our public lands
Maintains our public parks
Supervises Indian reservations
Controls our water resources

DEPARTMENT OF AGRICULTURE (1862)
Conducts studies to help farmers
Manages Food Stamp and School Lunch
  Programs
Helps farmers raise and market crops
Directs soil conservation programs

DEPARTMENT OF COMMERCE (1903)
Sets standards for weights and measures
Encourages and regulates foreign trade
Publishes reports on business and trade

DEPARTMENT OF LABOR (1913)
Determines standards of labor
Publishes employment information
Directs public employment services

DEPARTMENT OF DEFENSE (1949)
Maintains our armed forces
Conducts military studies
Operates military bases

**DEPARTMENT OF HEALTH AND
HUMAN SERVICES (1953)[3]**
Directs our public health services
Operates the Social Security program
Sees that our foods and medicines are safe

**DEPARTMENT OF HOUSING AND
URBAN DEVELOPMENT (1965)**
Helps urban housing programs
Helps cities plan traffic control
Helps cities plan mass transportation
Cooperates with metropolitan area planners

**DEPARTMENT OF
TRANSPORTATION (1966)**
Helps develop our nation's transportation
  policy
Supervises federal-aid highway program
Promotes transportation safety

DEPARTMENT OF ENERGY (1977)
Helps develop our nation's energy policy
Promotes conservation of energy
Regulates hydroelectric power

DEPARTMENT OF EDUCATION (1979)
Sets guidelines for granting financial aid to
  schools
Conducts research on educational subjects
Administers federally sponsored education
  programs

**DEPARTMENT OF VETERANS
AFFAIRS (1989)**
Administers medical and disability benefits
  to veterans and their families
Provides pensions and death benefits for
  veterans
Guarantees home loans to veterans

1. Year in parentheses indicates the year the department was established.
2. Attorney General position established in 1789; department set up in 1870.
3. Department of Health, Education, and Welfare established in 1953; split into Department of Education
   and Department of Health and Human Services in 1979.

labor-management relations. The Women's Bureau is responsible for promoting the opportunities and well-being of wage-earning women.

Department of Health and Human Services

The Department of Health and Human Services gathers information, conducts research, and runs programs to promote the health and well-being of all citizens. It was created from the Department of Health, Education, and Welfare (HEW) in 1980. The largest division of Health and Human Services is the Social Security Administration.

Department of Housing and Urban Development

The Department of Housing and Urban Development (HUD) seeks to improve the living conditions in America's cities. It runs programs to help people purchase homes. The department also helps city and state governments provide public housing and improve older neighborhoods.

Department of Transportation

The Department of Transportation helps to coordinate and develop our nation's rail, highway, and air transportation. It also promotes safety and deals with problems of mass transportation. The Coast Guard is part of the Department of Transportation in peacetime. In wartime it becomes part of the Navy.

Department of Energy

The Department of Energy helps plan and manage the nation's energy policy. One of the department's main goals is to lessen the amount of energy that is wasted in our nation.

In addition, it is responsible for carrying out our energy laws. The Department of Energy also regulates the development and use of our hydroelectric power, gas and oil pipelines, and energy deposits.

Department of Education

The Department of Education provides advice and information to the nation's school systems. It is also responsible for distributing federal funds to schools throughout the United States.

Department of Veterans Affairs

The Department of Veterans Affairs replaced the Veterans Administration (VA), a government agency, in 1989. The department is responsible for administering government benefits to veterans and their families. These benefits include health care, pensions, and education loans.

Changing the Executive Departments

As you have read, Congress has the authority to make changes in the executive departments. It may vote to create, disband, or reorganize any of the departments. The President, as Chief Executive, has a great deal of influence in these decisions. Changing the executive departments helps our nation adapt to changing times.

 SECTION 3 REVIEW

Define press secretary, executive departments, Cabinet, Secretary, Attorney General, ambassadors, embassy, ministers, consul, consulate, passports, visas

Identify Executive Office of the President, Joint Chiefs of Staff

1. **Understanding Ideas** What is the purpose of the Executive Office of the President?
2. **Seeing Relationships** What is the relationship between the Cabinet and the executive departments?
3. **Summarizing Ideas** Name the 14 executive departments.

Thinking Critically Imagine the President has asked you to take charge of one of the executive departments. Which of the 14 executive departments would you choose to lead? Why?

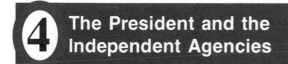

4 The President and the Independent Agencies

In addition to the executive departments, Congress has set up a number of **independent agencies.** These agencies help the President carry out the duties of office. The independent agencies are separate from the executive departments because they perform specialized duties that often do not fit into any regular department. In addition, some of these agencies serve all the departments. Therefore, they function best as separate and independent organizations.

Independent Agencies

There are about 60 independent agencies. Each was created by Congress to perform a specific job. For example, the Commission on Civil Rights collects information about discrimination and makes recommendations to the President and Congress. The Farm Credit Administration helps farmers obtain loans. The Nuclear Regulatory Commission regulates the use and safety of nuclear power plants. The National Aeronautics and Space Administration (NASA) runs our nation's space program.

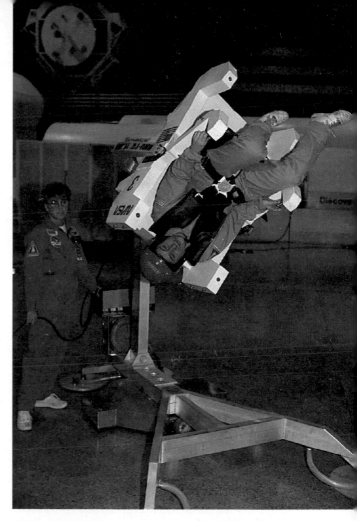

NASA operates Space Camp, where young people can train like the astronauts and learn about space.

Several independent agencies assist the work of the entire government. For example, the Office of Personnel Management gives tests to people who apply for jobs with the federal government. The General Services Administration buys supplies for the federal government. It also builds and maintains federal buildings.

Regulatory Agencies

A number of independent agencies have the power to make rules and bring violators into court. These are called **regulatory agencies.** Their decisions often have the force of law.

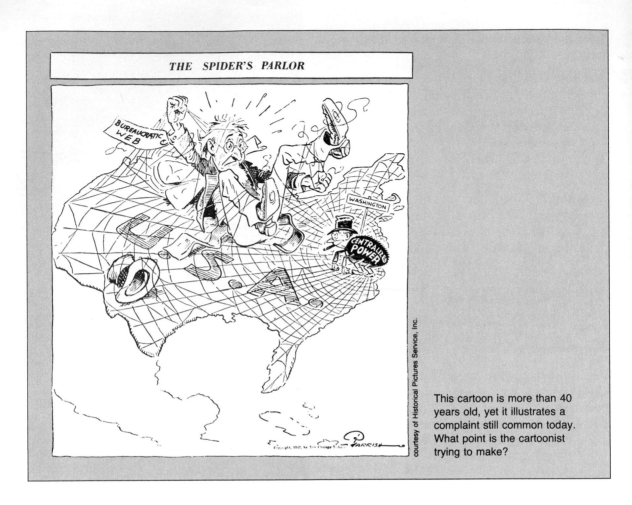

THE SPIDER'S PARLOR

courtesy of Historical Pictures Service, Inc.

This cartoon is more than 40 years old, yet it illustrates a complaint still common today. What point is the cartoonist trying to make?

The Interstate Commerce Commission (ICC), for example, regulates railroad, bus, truck, and water transportation that crosses state lines. The commission has the power to regulate rates and services. Established by Congress in 1887, it is the nation's oldest independent regulatory agency.

The Consumer Product Safety Commission (CPSC) sets and enforces safety standards for consumer products. It also conducts safety research.

The Securities and Exchange Commission (SEC) helps enforce laws regulating the buying and selling of stocks and bonds. This helps protect Americans when they invest their money in stocks and bonds.

The National Labor Relations Board (NLRB) helps enforce federal labor laws. It also works to prevent and remedy unfair labor practices.

Who Runs the Regulatory Agencies?

The regulatory agencies were given independence so that they could have the freedom they need to do their jobs. The heads of these agencies are appointed by the President, with the approval of the Senate. However, they have long terms, often as long as 14 years. This means that no President can appoint more than a few agency leaders.

The independence of the regulatory agencies has often been criticized on the grounds that it makes them too powerful. Some people say that these agencies regulate too much and interfere too much in our lives. Other people defend these agencies. They say that their regulations are needed to protect the public.

The Bureaucracy

The many departments and agencies in the executive branch of the government form the federal **bureaucracy.** More than two million people work in the bureaucracy. They include administrators, lawyers, scientists, doctors, engineers, secretaries, and clerks. People in the bureaucracy do the day-to-day work of the executive branch. They work in Washington, D.C., in other cities throughout the United States, and in other nations.

The bureaucracy has many rules and regulations for carrying out a wide range of activities. Often these rules and regulations lead to bureaucratic delay, or "red tape." People dealing with a government agency often must spend a lot of time filling out forms. They must stand in seemingly endless lines. Sometimes they must go from department to department before getting the help they need. Yet in spite of these problems, the people in the bureaucracy keep the executive branch functioning under every President.

 SECTION 4 REVIEW

Define independent agencies, regulatory agencies, bureaucracy

1. **Understanding Ideas** Why are the independent agencies separate from the rest of the executive branch?
2. **Identifying Ideas** Identify three independent agencies and briefly explain their functions.
3. **Seeing Relationships** (a) In what way are independent agencies and regulatory agencies similar? (b) In what way are they different?

Thinking Critically Why do you think the government creates so much "red tape"? Why do agencies require us to fill out so many forms?

As the head of the executive branch, the President is responsible for seeing that our nation's laws are carried out. The President is elected for a four-year term.

The President has a difficult and demanding job. The President must provide leadership in such vital areas as setting our foreign policy, planning our nation's defense needs, and promoting our nation's prosperity. As Chief Executive of one of the world's most powerful nations, the President plays a large part in shaping the history of our nation and the world.

For help in these tasks, the President turns to the members of the Cabinet—the heads of the executive departments. These departments carry on much of the work of the executive branch of the federal government. A number of independent agencies also assist in the day-to-day work of the executive branch. These agencies deal with such matters as interstate commerce, protection of the environment, national defense, and many other important activities of government.

CHAPTER 6 SUMMARY

SOCIAL STUDIES SKILL
Reading an Organizational Chart

A highly effective way to visualize the executive branch is to use an organizational chart. An organizational chart is a diagram that helps you see how the various parts of an organization are related to each other. The organization represented by the diagram may be a business, a club, or a government.

Organizational charts have two basic parts: boxes and lines. The boxes represent certain offices or people. The lines that connect the boxes represent lines of communication and authority. Generally, the offices or people with the most authority are at the top and those with the least authority are at the bottom of the chart.

How to Read an Organizational Chart

To use an organizational chart effectively, follow these guidelines.
1. **Determine the subject of the chart.** Read the title to learn which organization is being diagrammed.
2. **Identify the symbols and colors.** The key included in the chart identifies what the symbols and colors in the chart represent.
3. **Study the chart.** Carefully examine the chart. Read the labels of the various boxes, and notice how the lines of authority and communication connect the boxes.
4. **Put the information to use.** Draw conclusions about the organization from the chart.

Applying the Skill

1. **(a)** To whom does the Chief of Staff of the Air Force report? **(b)** To whom does the Secretary of the Air Force report? **(c)** Who reports directly to the Commander in Chief?
2. **(a)** What role is played by civilians in the Department of Defense? **(b)** Why do you think this is so?

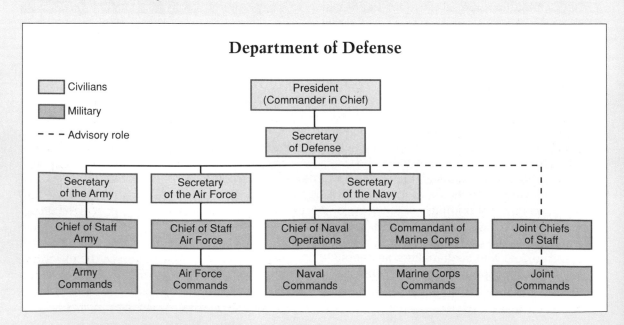

Department of Defense

Reviewing Terms

On a separate sheet of paper, identify or define each term in the list below and tell how it is related to the powers and duties of the President of the United States.

Chief Executive
independent
  agencies
Secretary
Cabinet
executive
  departments
Commander in
  Chicf

foreign policy
State of the Union
  Address
Vice President
Chief of State
diplomatic notes
Executive Office of
  the President

Using Thinking Skills

1. **Comparing Ideas (a)** Compare the duties of the Vice President of the United States with those of the President. **(b)** How have the responsibilities of the Vice President changed in recent years?
2. **Organizing Ideas (a)** What are three ways in which the President can influence lcgislation? **(b)** Explain how the President can influence the judicial branch of the federal government.
3. **Understanding Ideas (a)** What is Presidential succession? **(b)** What is the purpose of the Twenty-fifth Amendment to the Constitution?
4. **Drawing Conclusions** Why are some federal agencies independent of the rest of the executive branch?
5. **Identifying Roles** What is the President's role in American foreign policy?
6. **Identifying Ideas (a)** How does the President of the United States communicate with the American people? **(b)** How does the President stay informed about important issues?
7. **Summarizing Ideas** Name the 14 executive departments, whose heads are members of the President's cabinet.

8. **Expressing Ideas (a)** What Presidential role gives the President the authority to send American troops into battle? **(b)** What limits the military power of the President?

Practicing Civics Skills

1. **Charting Information** There are three main levels of authority in our federal government. At the top is the Constitution. The next level consists of the three branches of government. Below the executive branch are the 14 executive departments you read about in this chapter.

   Draw an organizational chart that shows the relationship among these different levels. If you need help in drawing your chart, study the organizational charts in references such as the *United States Government Manual.*
2. **Using a Diagram (a)** Who or what has authority over the President of the United States? **(b)** Is one branch of the federal government more powerful than the others? How does the chart help you see this?

Being a Good Citizen

1. Work with several other students to prepare and display a detailed organizational chart of the United States federal government.
2. Keep a record of news reports that tell about the President's daily activities. Explain how each of the President's activities are related to Presidential responsibilities. To which responsibility has the President been devoting most of his time? What reasons can you find for the President's use of time? Report your findings to the class.
3. Write a report on a person in the executive branch who is a member of one of the following groups: women, African Americans, Hispanics, Asian Americans.

CHAPTER 7

The Federal Courts Interpret Our Nation's Laws

Chapter Sections

Chapter Focus

Whenever people play a game together, they are governed by a set of rules. If a player breaks the rules, that player is penalized. Sometimes the players in a game disagree about what the rules are or what a certain rule means. In these cases, officials make the final decisions about the rules. In a football game, for example, the referees interpret the rules and set penalties if the rules are broken.

Our government also needs officials to interpret its rules, or laws, and to decide how those people who disobey the laws should be punished. The officials who interpret the laws of our government are the members of our court system.

The goal of our court system is to provide equality under the law. In accordance with the American ideal of justice, our courts seek to protect, defend, and uphold the rights guaranteed to American citizens by the Constitution of the United States.

The ideal of equal justice for all is essential to our free nation. The way our courts interpret and apply the law is one of democracy's great achievements.

Study Guide

As you begin to learn about the roles of the federal courts in our government, look for answers to the following questions:

★ How do our laws guarantee equal justice for all citizens?

★ How is the federal court system organized?

★ What role does the Supreme Court play in the court system, and how do Supreme Court decisions affect our lives?

1 Providing Equal Justice Under Law

Carved in marble over the entrance of the Supreme Court Building in Washington, D.C., is the motto "Equal Justice Under Law." It proclaims that in the United States all citizens are considered equal and are guaranteed equal protection by our laws.

Laws for the Good of All

We enjoy freedom in the United States because we have laws to protect our rights. Of course, some laws limit our freedom. A law against robbery, for example, denies the robber's freedom to steal. However, it gives the rest of us freedom to use and enjoy our own property.

Laws usually represent what the majority of us believe to be right and wrong. When most of the American people believe strongly that something should or should not be done, a law is passed on this issue. If the American people later change their position on the issue,

the law can be changed. In this way, our laws grow and change with the times.

Every American citizen has the duty to know and obey the laws. It is our responsibility to get to know the laws that concern any activity we expect to undertake. If you ride a bicycle, for example, you must learn about road signs and traffic regulations. The law-abiding citizen realizes that laws are passed for the good of all. By learning and obeying the nation's laws, you are practicing good citizenship.

Kinds of Laws

There are four different kinds of laws in the United States. All these laws must follow the principles set forth in the Constitution, which is the supreme law of the land.

Statutory Law. Laws that are passed by lawmaking bodies are known as **statutory laws.** They are passed by Congress and by state and local governments. For example, a state law that requires fire exits in all public buildings is a statutory law.

Common Law. What happens if there is no statutory law covering a specific situation? Then we follow certain rules that have been accepted by Americans as the proper ways in which to act. Some of these rules are based on both common sense and common practice.

For example, before automobiles became a major form of transportation, there were no laws about driving them. Suppose that someone was driving an automobile at its top speed and ran into a horse-drawn wagon, crushing the wagon. The driver might argue that his case should be dismissed because there is no law regulating the speed of automobiles.

The judge might reply that there is an established principle that people cannot use their property to injure others. Thus the judge would apply the rule of common sense and common practice in such a case.

The judge's decision might be remembered by another judge hearing a similar case. Eventually most judges might follow the same

precedent, or earlier decision, in such cases. In time, those guilty of recklessly driving their automobiles would be punished according to this customary rule. This rule would become a part of our customary, or common, law. **Common law,** therefore, is law that comes from judges' decisions.

In time, most common law is passed as statutory law by the nation's lawmaking bodies. In this way, it is written down so that all of the nation's citizens may know it.

Administrative Law. Many of the laws that affect our daily lives are made by government agencies. These laws are known as **administrative laws.** For example, the Consumer Product Safety Commission is making an administrative law when it rules that a toy is unsafe and must immediately be taken off the market.

Constitutional Law. The Constitution of the United States, as you know, is supreme above all other types of laws. Therefore, if any law comes into conflict with the Constitution, the Constitution prevails. **Constitutional law** is law based on the Constitution and on Supreme Court decisions interpreting the Constitution.

The Idea of Courts

These different kinds of laws are used by courts to help settle disputes. Disputes between people, between people and the government, and between governments are brought before a court. The court applies the law and reaches a decision in favor of one side or the other.

To be just, a law must be enforced fairly. For example, it is against the law for workers in a nuclear power plant to give or sell secrets about their work to a foreign government. What would happen if an FBI agent found an engineer who worked in a nuclear power plant talking to a foreign spy? Could the federal government arrest the engineer on suspicion of treason and put the engineer in prison for years? The answer is no. Under our American system of justice, the engineer must be given a fair public trial.

To guarantee justice in the United States, we have accepted the important idea that a person is innocent until proven guilty. The proper way to determine whether or not a person is guilty is to hold a trial in a court of law. Our courts are made up of persons who have been given the authority to administer justice. We believe that only a system of courts can assure equal justice to all people.

The Right to a Fair Trial

The Constitution guarantees every American the right to a fair public trial. It is important that you understand this guarantee as you study our federal court system and learn how equal justice under the law works in the United States. What does the right to a fair trial mean? Consider our example of the engineer who is accused of giving secret information to a foreign government.

1. The Right to Have a Lawyer. All persons accused of crimes are entitled to the services of a lawyer. The lawyer will represent them in court and help protect their rights. If the engineer cannot afford a lawyer, the court will appoint one and pay the lawyer's fees out of public funds.

2. The Right to Be Released on Bail. A person accused of a crime does not ordinarily have to spend months in prison waiting for the case to come to trial. Usually the accused person may be released if he or she can put up bail. Bail, as you have read, is a sum of money deposited with the court as a pledge that the accused will appear in court at the time of trial. The amount of bail is set by a judge. However, a person accused of a serious crime, such as murder or treason, may be denied bail and have to remain in jail until the trial is held.

3. Indictment by a Grand Jury. Just because a person is arrested on suspicion of a crime does not mean that this person must come to trial. There must be enough evidence against someone to justify bringing that person into court for trial. The group that decides whether there is enough evidence to bring the accused person to trial is called the **grand jury.** In federal courts, the grand jury is made up of 12 to 23 citizens who live in the court district in which the trial is to be held.

The grand jury examines the evidence against the accused person. It questions witnesses and investigates the facts in the case. If a majority of the grand jury decides that the evidence against the accused is strong enough, the person is **indicted,** or formally accused of a crime. In the case of the engineer, suppose the grand jury finds the evidence strong enough. As a result, the engineer will be indicted and held for trial.

4. The Right to a Jury Trial. Individuals who go on trial must be judged on the basis of the evidence for and against them. But who shall judge the evidence? The Sixth Amendment to the Constitution guarantees an accused person the right to be tried before a **trial jury.** A trial jury is also called a **petit jury.** It is usually made up of from 6 to 12 persons who live in the community. The men and women of the trial jury who judge the evidence are called **jurors.**

Jurors on trial juries and grand juries are selected from a list of people who live in the community. A court official draws the names and sends notices ordering the people to report for **jury duty.** From this group, or panel of jurors, the required number of jurors is chosen for the trial.

The trial jury must reach a decision, or **verdict,** in the case. Usually the jury's verdict must be a unanimous vote. This means that all the members of the jury must agree on whether the accused person is guilty or innocent.

5. Innocent Until Proven Guilty. The burden of proof in a jury trial rests with those who bring charges against the person on trial. They must prove their case "beyond a reasonable doubt." Accused persons cannot be forced to testify against themselves. Their lawyers have the right to question all witnesses to make sure their testimony is accurate and honest. Accused persons have the right to call

The right to a jury trial is a cornerstone of the American system of justice. This system relies on the willingness of all citizens to serve on juries.

The Right to a Fair Trial

The right to have a lawyer.

The right to be released on reasonable bail before the trial is held.

The accused person is innocent until proven guilty.

The grand jury must find there is enough evidence to indict the person of the crime.

The right to a speedy trial.

The accused person cannot be forced to testify against himself or herself.

The right to hear and question all witnesses.

The right to appeal the verdict if there is reason to believe that the person did not receive a fair trial.

their own witnesses to help them defend themselves.

Suppose the nuclear engineer accused by the federal government of selling secrets is found guilty by a trial jury. This means the jury believes that the lawyers for the government have proved the engineer's guilt "beyond a reasonable doubt."

6. The Right of Appeal. Since courts are made up of human beings, they sometimes make mistakes. To make sure that cases are decided fairly, our court system provides the right to **appeal,** or ask for a review of the case. If there is reason to doubt that justice was not done in the case of the engineer, the engineer can appeal to a higher court.

3. **Expressing Ideas** Why do we have courts?
4. **Organizing Ideas (a)** What rights to a fair trial are guaranteed by the Constitution? **(b)** To which right is the phrase "beyond a reasonable doubt" related? **(c)** What does this phrase mean?
5. **Drawing Conclusions** Why do we have the right to appeal?

Thinking Critically Imagine that all of the courts in the United States have suddenly disappeared. How will people now settle their disputes?

 SECTION 1 REVIEW

Define statutory laws, precedent, common law, administrative laws, constitutional law, grand jury, indicted, trial jury, petit jury, jurors, jury duty, verdict, appeal

1. **Seeing Relationships (a)** How does majority rule affect our laws? **(b)** Why is it our duty to know and obey the laws?
2. **Understanding Ideas (a)** Describe the four kinds of laws found in the United States. **(b)** Which type of law prevails? Why?

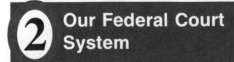

② Our Federal Court System

Under our federal system of government, the United States has two court systems. One is the federal court system. The other is the system of state courts. (You will read about the state court system in Chapter 8.)

Article 3 of the Constitution of the United States provides that "the judicial power of the United States shall be vested in one Supreme Court, and in such inferior [lower] courts as the Congress may from time to time . . . establish." The First Congress used this constitutional power to set up a system of federal courts.

In 1789 Congress passed the Judiciary Act, which established what has grown into one of the great court systems of the world. This system of federal courts makes up the judicial branch—the third branch—of our federal government.

Cases Tried in Federal Courts

The Constitution grants the federal courts jurisdiction in several different kinds of cases. **Jurisdiction** means the authority to interpret and administer the law. Listed below are the kinds of cases that are brought to trial in federal courts:

1. Any person accused of disobeying any part of the Constitution, including the amendments, is tried in a federal court.

2. Anyone accused of violating a treaty of the United States is tried in a federal court.

3. Anyone accused of breaking laws passed by Congress is brought before a federal court.

4. Federal courts have jurisdiction when a foreign nation sues the government of the United States or a citizen of the United States.

5. American ambassadors and consuls are tried in federal courts if they are accused of breaking the laws of the nation in which they are stationed.

6. Crimes committed on American ships at sea are tried in federal courts.

7. Crimes committed on certain federal property are tried in federal courts.

8. Disagreements between states are tried in federal court. However, the Eleventh Amendment provides that any lawsuit against a state brought by a citizen of another state or of a foreign country shall be tried in a state court.

9. Lawsuits between citizens of different states are brought before federal courts. Most federal court cases are of this type.

How Our Federal Courts Are Organized

Federal courts are organized into several levels. They are also classified according to their jurisdiction. The lowest courts are trial courts, which have **original jurisdiction.** This means they are the first courts in which most federal cases are heard.

Above these trial courts are courts that have **appellate jurisdiction.** That is, they review decisions made by lower courts. *Appellate* means "dealing with appeals." Every convicted person has the right to appeal his or her case to an appellate court. An appeal is usually made when lawyers believe the law was not applied correctly in the lower court. A case can also be appealed if new evidence is found.

United States District Courts

There are three main levels of federal courts. The chart on page 144 shows the relationship of courts in the federal system.

At the base of our federal court system are the **district courts.** There is at least one district court in each of the 50 states and the District of Columbia. Some of the larger states are divided into as many as four federal court districts, each with its own district court. Today, there are 91 federal district courts in the United States.

The district court is the only federal court in which jury trials are held. District courts have original jurisdiction in most federal cases. They cannot hear appeals from other courts.

The Constitution is definite about where federal cases shall be tried. Article 3, Section 2, states in part that "such trial shall be held in the state where the said crimes shall have been committed. . . ."

The reason for this provision is to make sure that the accused person receives a fair and convenient trial. The witnesses who will testify are usually close at hand. No one has to travel long distances to be heard. Furthermore, the jury will be familiar with the location of the crime, and it can judge the truth of the evidence more intelligently.

District Court Officials

Most district courts are presided over by a single district court judge. In very busy districts, there may be a number of judges. All district court judges are appointed for life. District court judges decide matters of court procedure and explain the law involved in the case to the jury. They decide the sentence if the accused person is found guilty.

A number of other officials are needed to help the district courts work smoothly. Each district court has a United States **marshal.** Marshals arrest persons accused of breaking federal laws. They also deliver official court orders called **subpoenas,** which require persons to appear in court. The United States marshal also sees that the court's verdict is carried out.

Each district court also has a United States **magistrate.** This official hears the evidence against an accused person and decides

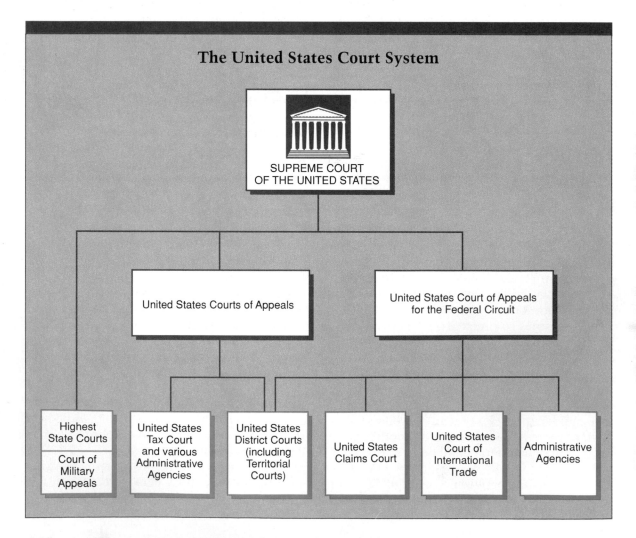

The United States Court System

SUPREME COURT OF THE UNITED STATES

United States Courts of Appeals

United States Court of Appeals for the Federal Circuit

Highest State Courts

Court of Military Appeals

United States Tax Court and various Administrative Agencies

United States District Courts (including Territorial Courts)

United States Claims Court

United States Court of International Trade

Administrative Agencies

whether the case should be brought before a grand jury. Magistrates also try certain minor cases themselves.

Another district court official is the **United States attorney.** This official is a lawyer for the federal government. It is the job of the United States attorney to try to prove to a jury that the accused person is guilty of the crime he or she is charged with committing.

United States Courts of Appeals

The next level of the federal court system consists of **courts of appeals.** These courts review cases that are appealed from the district courts. Courts of appeals also hear appeals from decisions of federal regulatory agencies. For instance, a railroad company might believe that the rates for fares set by the Interstate Commerce Commission are unfair. If so, it can ask a court of appeals to review the commission's decision.

There are 12 United States courts of appeals. Each covers a large judicial district known as a **circuit.** The 50 states are divided into 11 circuits. The twelfth circuit is the District of Columbia. There is also a court of appeals for the federal circuit. This court of appeals has national jurisdiction. Each court of appeals has 6 to 28 judges. The senior judge of each circuit serves as the chief judge. The judges of the courts of appeals are appointed for life.

Jury trials do not take place in the courts of appeals. Instead, a panel of at least three judges reviews the evidence and makes the decision. The judges examine the records of the district court trial and hear arguments by the lawyers for both sides. The judges do not determine whether the accused person is guilty or innocent. They are not holding another trial of the case. That is not their job. Their job is to determine if the person who appealed the case was granted full legal rights during the trial.

In the American court system, judges are sworn to act "without fear or favor" in making their decisions.

The judges reach their decision by majority vote. If the court of appeals finds that justice was not done, it sends the case back to the district court for a new trial. If the court of appeals finds that justice was done, it upholds, or accepts, the decision of the district court. In most cases the decision of the court of appeals is final. Sometimes, however, another appeal is made. This final appeal is made to the United States Supreme Court.

United States Supreme Court

Our highest court is the **Supreme Court** of the United States, which meets in Washington, D.C. It works chiefly as an appeals court. It reviews cases that have been tried in lower federal courts and in state courts.

In addition, the Constitution gives the Supreme Court original jurisdiction in the following three types of cases.

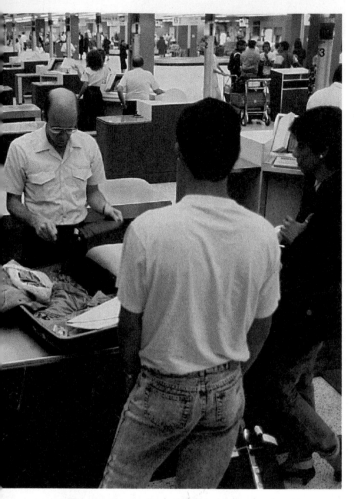

These people are going through customs on entering the United States. They can appeal to the Court of International Trade if they think they are being taxed unfairly.

1. Cases involving diplomatic representatives of other nations.

2. Cases involving disputes between states. For example, the Supreme Court once settled a dispute between Arizona and California over use of waters from the Colorado River basin.

3. Cases involving a state and the federal government. The ownership of public lands has often been a source of conflict between states and the federal government.

Decisions of the Supreme Court are final. Its decisions cannot be appealed.

Other Federal Courts

Congress also set up a number of special courts to handle specific types of cases. You can see each of these courts identified in the diagram of the federal court system on page 144 of your textbook.

The **United States Claims Court** hears cases involving money claims against the federal government. If the court rules against the government, the person bringing the suit is usually granted a sum of money. Congress must then authorize the payment of the claim.

The **United States Court of International Trade** hears cases involving import taxes, or tariffs. An individual or a business importing certain goods into the United States from another country must pay taxes on those goods. People who think that the tax is too high, for example, may take their cases to the United States Court of International Trade. This court is in New York City, but it also hears cases in other port cities.

Territorial courts were established by Congress to bring justice to the people living in the territorial possessions of the United States. There is one each in the Northern Mariana Islands, Guam, the Virgin Islands, and Puerto Rico. These courts handle the same kinds of cases as district courts. In addition, these courts hear the types of cases that would go to a state court.

The **United States Tax Court** hears appeals from those taxpayers who disagree with rulings of the Internal Revenue Services (IRS) concerning their payment of federal taxes. The United States Tax Court is actually an independent agency, but it has powers like those of a court.

The **Court of Military Appeals** is the appeals court for the nation's armed services. People in the armed services who are accused of breaking a military law are tried at a **court-martial.** This is a trial conducted by military officers. The Court of Military Appeals consists of three civilian judges. Its decisions usually cannot be appealed.

Federal Court Judges

All the federal courts are presided over by judges. Federal court judges are appointed by the President. Their appointment must be approved by the Senate by majority vote.

Federal judges are appointed for life. The job is theirs for as long as they want it. They can be removed from office only by impeachment. Congress may not lower a judge's salary during her or his time in office. These guarantees were written into the Constitution to ensure that judges could not be punished or rewarded for their decisions. Judges are assisted in their work by many other people, including clerks and court reporters.

SECTION 2 REVIEW

Define jurisdiction, original jurisdiction, appellate jurisdiction, subpoenas, circuit, court-martial

Identify district courts, marshal, magistrate, United States attorney, courts of appeals, Supreme Court, United States Claims Court, United States Court of International Trade, territorial courts, United States Tax Court, Court of Military Appeals

1. **Understanding Ideas** What kinds of cases are brought to trial in federal courts?
2. **Expressing Ideas** Why are federal cases tried in the same states in which the crimes are committed?
3. **Drawing Conclusions** What is the purpose of the courts of appeals?
4. **Identifying Roles (a)** In what types of cases does the Supreme Court have original jurisdiction? **(b)** Describe the special courts set up by Congress. **(c)** What guarantees for federal court judges are written into the Constitution?

Thinking Critically You head a committee to choose a student judge to decide cases in your school. What qualities will you look for in making your choice?

3 The Supreme Court

The Supreme Court is the head of the judicial branch of the federal government. It is the only court actually established by the Constitution. Decisions of the Supreme Court affect the lives of all Americans.

Justices of the Supreme Court

The size of the Supreme Court is determined by Congress. The number of **Justices,** or judges, of the Supreme Court has been fixed at nine since 1869. The Court has a Chief Justice and eight Associate Justices.

Supreme Court Justices, like other federal judges, are appointed by the President. Their appointments must be approved by a majority of the Senate. Justices are appointed for life and can be removed from office only by the impeachment process. The annual salary of the Chief Justice is $160,600. Associate Justices are paid $153,600 per year.

The Constitution did not set any requirements for Supreme Court Justices. However, all have been lawyers. Many have served as judges on lower courts. Others have taught law or held public office. Until 1981, all Justices were men. In that year, Sandra Day O'Connor became the first woman to serve on the Supreme Court.

Presidents generally try to appoint Justices who share their political beliefs. Once appointed, however, a Justice of the Supreme Court may make decisions with which the President disagrees.

Power of Judicial Review

The Supreme Court has the power to study and review any law passed by Congress. Before it may do so, however, someone must challenge the law and bring a case to court.

(continued on page 150)

The Tinkers Take a Stand

Mary Beth Tinker, her brother John, and Christopher Eckhart did not set out to get their names in American law books. All they wanted to do was take a stand on an important national issue. That's why they wore black armbands to school in December 1965. Little did they realize that their actions would lead to a Supreme Court case.

Protesting the War

In 1965 the United States was deeply involved in a war between North Vietnam and South Vietnam in Southeast Asia. Many Americans were in favor of American support for South Vietnam. However, others thought that the United States should stay out of the war.

Mary Beth Tinker and John Tinker went all the way to the Supreme Court in their fight to wear the black armbands they are holding.

A group of students in Des Moines, Iowa, where the Tinkers and Chris Eckhart lived, decided to wear black armbands to school to protest the war. The armbands were meant to be a symbol of mourning for the American soldiers who were dying in Vietnam.

Members of the Des Moines school board heard about the armbands and became worried. They thought the armbands might cause trouble and banned them from the schools. When several students wore the armbands, the students were suspended from school.

The Supreme Court Hears the Case

The Tinker family took the school board to court on behalf of Mary Beth, John, and Chris Eckhart. Their lawyers argued that the school board had denied them their constitutional right of free speech.

The case went all the way to the Supreme Court of the United States. The Justices agreed to hear the case because they thought it raised two important questions. First, was wearing an armband really a form of free speech? Second, how far did the right of free speech apply to students? Schools must keep discipline in order to allow students to learn.

The Supreme Court announced its decision in the case of *Tinker v. Des Moines Independent Community School District* in 1969. The Court ruled that wearing a symbol, such as an armband, is a form of speech. It is therefore protected by the Constitution. The second question, however, was more difficult to decide. All the Justices stressed that schools must be protected against disturbances. What the Justices could not agree upon was whether or not wearing armbands had caused trouble in school.

Two Justices sided with the school board. They thought that wearing armbands had taken the students' minds off their studies. Therefore, the schools had acted properly in banning the armbands.

The majority of the Justices supported the students. They thought there was no evidence that the armbands had caused any disturbances in class. The Court's opinion ruled that the ban on armbands was unfair. The Justices pointed out that schools had allowed students to wear campaign buttons for political candidates. Wearing buttons is also a form of "speech."

The Supreme Court Justices did not say that schools could never limit the expression of opinions by students. What they said was that in this case the students had acted within their rights.

The Court's ruling is now part of United States law. As a result, students and school officials have a clearer idea of the rights of free speech for students and teachers.

Thinking It Over

1. What were the two main questions that the Supreme Court had to decide in the Tinker case?
2. What reasons can you think of for allowing students to express their political opinions in school? What reasons can you think of for not allowing them to do so?

The most unique feature of the Supreme Court is its power of **judicial review.** This means that the Court has the power to determine whether a law passed by Congress or a Presidential action is in accord with the Constitution. If the Supreme Court decides that a law is in conflict with the Constitution, that law is declared **unconstitutional,** and it is no longer in force.

The Constitution does not say that the Supreme Court has the power of judicial review. This power was established for the Court by John Marshall. As Chief Justice from 1801 to 1835, Marshall laid the foundations for the Supreme Court's great power.

The Influence of John Marshall

During his 34 years as Chief Justice, John Marshall established three basic principles of American law. Marshall stated the idea of judicial review for the first time in 1803, in the case of *Marbury v. Madison.* The case involved William Marbury, who had been promised appointment as a justice of the peace, and Secretary of State James Madison.

Marbury claimed that the Judiciary Act of 1789 gave the Supreme Court the power to order Secretary of State Madison to give him the promised appointment. In his now-famous opinion, Chief Justice Marshall found that the Judiciary Act was in conflict with the Constitution. The act gave the Supreme Court powers not granted by the Constitution. Since the Constitution is the "supreme law of the land," the act passed by Congress was unconstitutional.

Under Chief Justice Marshall, the Supreme Court also established the principle that laws passed by state legislatures could be set aside if they were in conflict with the Constitution. The third important principle established by Marshall was that the Supreme Court had the power to reverse the decisions of state courts. Over the years, the Supreme Court came to have the final power to decide what the Constitution means.

John Marshall was one of our nation's most influential Chief Justices. Under his leadership, the Supreme Court made some of its most important decisions.

The Supreme Court Decides What Cases to Hear

As you have read, the Supreme Court cannot begin a case itself. It must wait until a person files an appeal or a lawsuit. All cases heard by the Court involve real legal disputes. A person cannot simply ask the Supreme Court for an opinion about whether or not a law is constitutional.

The Supreme Court itself decides what cases it will hear. Several thousand cases are appealed to the Court each year. However, the Court turns down about 80 percent of the applications it receives for review. If the Court had to review all cases that were appealed to it, it would still be deciding cases that originated in the 1950's!

How, then, does the Supreme Court decide what cases it will hear? The Justices accept only those cases that involve issues of significant public interest. Cases heard by the

The Supreme Court serves as the final court of appeals. Shown here are (standing, left to right) Justices Souter, Scalia, O'Connor, and Kennedy; (seated; left to right) Stevens, Marshall, Chief Justice Rehnquist, White, and Blackmun.

Supreme Court generally deal with important constitutional or national questions. At least four of the nine Justices must vote to hear a case. If the Supreme Court refuses to review a case, the decision of the lower court remains in effect.

The Supreme Court in Action

The Supreme Court begins its session each year on the first Monday in October. It usually adjourns in late June. The Justices spend much of their time reading written arguments, hearing oral arguments, and holding private meetings.

After the Supreme Court has agreed to hear a case, the lawyers for each side prepare a **brief.** This is a written statement explaining the main points of one side's arguments about the case. Each Justice then studies the briefs.

The next step takes place in a public session. The lawyers for each side appear before the Court to present an oral argument. Each side is limited to a half hour, and the time limit is strictly enforced. The Justices often question the lawyers about the case. The entire procedure is designed to bring out the facts and issues in each case as quickly as possible.

On most Fridays, the Justices meet in private to discuss and vote on the cases they have heard. Each Justice has one vote, but all Justices do not have to vote. Decision is by majority vote. If there is a tie vote, the decision of the lower court remains in effect.

Supreme Court Opinions

One of the Justices who supported the majority decision is assigned to write the **opinion** of the Court. This explains the reasoning that led to the decision. The Court's opinion is binding on all lower courts.

Sometimes a Justice agrees with the decision of the majority, but for different reasons. In that case the Justice may decide to write a **concurring opinion.**

OYEZ! OYEZ!

the words "Oyez, oyez, oyez!" are called out as the Supreme Court Justices file into the courtroom? "Oyez" sounds like "Oh, yes." An odd way to open a court? Actually, the word means "Hear ye," and it comes from the French language. It is one of many French words that are used in conducting government business.

Justices who disagree with the decision of the Court may explain their reasoning in a **dissenting opinion.** Although dissenting opinions have no effect on the law, they can still be important. Many dissenting opinions have eventually become the law of the land when the beliefs of society and the Justices changed.

Checking the Power of the Supreme Court

The Supreme Court has gained great power over the years. What can the other branches of government do to check the powers of the Supreme Court?

Let us take a closer look at what happens if the Supreme Court rules that a law passed by Congress is unconstitutional. As you know, this means that the law has no force. However, Congress may pass a new law that

follows the Constitution and that the Supreme Court may uphold. In this way, laws may be improved while the rights of people under the Constitution remain protected.

Another way to make a desired law constitutional is to change the Constitution. Let us see how this happens. In 1895 the Supreme Court declared that an income tax law passed by Congress was unconstitutional. The Court pointed out that the Constitution (Article 1, Section 9, Clause 4) states that direct taxes must be apportioned according to the population of each state. In other words, such taxes must fall evenly on all people.

The income tax did not meet this constitutional requirement and thus was unconstitutional. However, in 1913 the states ratified the Sixteenth Amendment, which gave Congress the power to tax incomes. The income tax then became legal and constitutional.

The Supreme Court Can Change Its Opinion

The Supreme Court has helped to make the Constitution a long-lived document by interpreting it differently at different times. In this way, the Court has helped the Constitution meet the demands of changing times. Supreme Court Justices are aware of changing social, political, and economic conditions. In reaching decisions, they take into account the beliefs of the people and the advancing ideas of justice for all.

Let us consider one example of the Court's changing attitude to meet new ideas. In the late 1800's, many of the states passed **segregation laws.** These laws segregated, or separated, black Americans. This meant that black people and white people could not share the use of such public services as trains, schools, hotels, and hospitals.

A Decision for Segregation. In 1896 an important case about segregation was brought before the Supreme Court. The case, *Plessy v. Ferguson,* challenged a Louisiana law that required blacks and whites to ride in separate railroad cars. Homer Plessy, who was part black, had taken a seat in a passenger car that had a sign reading "For Whites Only." When he refused to move to a car for blacks, he was arrested.

Plessy was found guilty of breaking the Louisiana law and appealed the decision to the Supreme Court. He argued that the segregation laws of Louisiana denied him the "equal protection of the law" guaranteed by the Fourteenth Amendment of the United States Constitution.

The Supreme Court did not accept Plessy's argument. It ruled that segregation laws did not go against the Fourteenth Amendment if the separate facilities provided for blacks were equal to those for whites. This decision established the "separate but equal" principle. That is, the decision made legal "separate but equal" facilities for blacks in all areas of life.

A Decision Against Segregation. In most places, however, facilities for blacks clearly were not equal to those for whites. For example, schools for blacks often were overcrowded and lacked much of the equipment provided for white students.

After World War II, conditions in the nation began to change. Many Americans began to realize that the nation's black citizens were not being treated fairly under the system of segregation.

In 1954 the Supreme Court decided another important segregation case (see page 544). The case of **Brown v. Board of Education of Topeka** concerned eight-year-old Linda Brown, a black girl living in Topeka, Kansas. The school only five blocks from Linda's home was for whites only. So Linda had to travel 21 blocks to a school for blacks. Her father sued the school district. He claimed segregated schools were unconstitutional.

In a unanimous decision, the Supreme Court agreed. It ruled that segregated schools were not equal and therefore violated the Fourteenth Amendment. Segregated schools, said the Court, denied students equal

One of these pictures was taken in the 1930's and the other was taken fairly recently. What evidence tells you which one came earlier and which later?

protection under the law. Therefore, the Court ruled that public schools in the United States should be desegregated "with all deliberate speed." Thus the Supreme Court had reversed its earlier decision.

Strengthening Our Constitutional Rights

In recent years, decisions of the Supreme Court have made far-reaching changes in three areas of American life—the rights of accused persons, voting, and civil rights.

The Rights of Accused Persons. A number of Supreme Court decisions in the 1960's greatly strengthened the rights of accused persons. For the most part, these decisions applied to the time immediately following a person's arrest.

In the famous 1966 case of *Miranda v. Arizona,* the Supreme Court declared that the police must inform suspects of their rights before they may question them. They must inform suspects that they have the right to remain silent, that anything they say may be used against them, and that they have the right to have a lawyer present when they are questioned. If they cannot afford to hire a lawyer, a lawyer will be appointed for them.

There have been differences of opinion over the Supreme Court decisions involving the rights of accused persons. Some Americans have argued that the Court's decisions protected criminals. Others have said that they guaranteed justice to all Americans. What is the proper balance between the rights of the individual and the rights of society as a whole? This is an important question in a democratic nation such as ours.

"One Person, One Vote." The Supreme Court also made several important decisions in the 1960's in the area of voting and representation in state legislatures and the House of Representatives. The "one person, one vote" decision was the most far-reaching of these rulings. According to this decision, election districts for choosing representatives

to Congress and the state legislatures must be divided by population as equally as possible. This means that every citizen's vote must be equal in value and will result in genuinely representative government at both the state and federal levels.

Civil Rights and Civil Liberties. The third area in which the Supreme Court's rulings have had important results is in civil rights and civil liberties. The 1954 *Brown* decision against segregated schools has not completely ended segregation in American schools or American life. The Court's decision, however, struck a blow against segregation in our nation by suggesting that all segregation laws were unconstitutional.

The civil rights movement and civil rights legislation followed. Laws providing for segregation were removed one by one. Laws were passed guaranteeing black Americans the precious right to vote. By its decisions, the Court has provided leadership in showing that the rights guaranteed in the Constitution apply to all Americans.

The Prestige of the Supreme Court

Throughout its history, the prestige and dignity of the Supreme Court have grown. The Supreme Court Justices, for the most part, have not become involved in politics and have not been influenced by favors or bribes. Most Americans believe the Court is an important part of our democratic system.

The decisions of the Supreme Court have not, however, been free of controversy. Some Courts have seemed too liberal and others too conservative. In the late 1930's, President Franklin D. Roosevelt attempted to change the nature of the Supreme Court by adding more Justices to the Court. But public outcry caused Roosevelt to drop his plan. Americans did not want to change the balance of power among the executive, legislative, and judicial branches. They wanted the Court to remain free of political influence.

The debate over the Supreme Court's power continues today. Nevertheless, it must be remembered that the Court's power is limited. The Court makes important decisions that affect American policy and American life. It cannot, however, enforce these decisions. The Court must depend on the executive branch to carry out its decisions. Finally, the cooperation of the public is necessary if Supreme Court decisions are to be effective.

 SECTION 3 REVIEW

Define judicial review, unconstitutional, brief, opinion, concurring opinion, dissenting opinion, segregation laws

Identify Justices, *Marbury v. Madison*, *Plessy v. Ferguson*, *Brown v. Board of Education of Topeka*, *Miranda v. Arizona*

1. **Identifying Ideas (a)** How are appointments to the Supreme Court made? **(b)** What three principles of American law did John Marshall establish?
2. **Seeing Relationships (a)** How does the Supreme Court decide which cases to hear? **(b)** What happens if the Supreme Court refuses to review a case?
3. **Understanding Ideas** How is the power of the Supreme Court limited by Congress?
4. **Drawing Conclusions** Why is it important that the Supreme Court can change its opinion?
5. **Comparing Ideas** How is *Brown v. Board of Education of Topeka* related to *Plessy v. Ferguson?*

Thinking Critically Imagine you are a Justice on the Supreme Court in 1954. Write the majority opinion for *Brown v. Board of Education of Topeka*. Explain how segregated public schools are unconstitutional.

The federal courts make up the judicial branch of our federal government. The job of these courts is to interpret laws and to bring to trial those accused of breaking laws. In the United States, we believe in the idea of government by law. These laws, however, must be enforced fairly. Thus the federal courts also make sure that every accused person enjoys the Constitution's guarantee of a fair trial.

There are four different kinds of laws in the United States. These are statutory law, common law, administrative law, and constitutional law.

The Constitution gives the federal courts jurisdiction, or authority, to hold trials in a wide variety of cases and to judge these cases. District courts are the only federal courts in which juries are used. Under certain conditions, convicted persons may take their cases next to a court of appeals and then perhaps even to the Supreme Court.

The United States Supreme Court is the highest court in the land. It hears appeals from lower federal courts and from state courts. Its decisions are final. A unique feature of the Supreme Court is the power of judicial review. That is, it hears cases to decide if the laws involved are constitutional. Decisions of the Supreme Court affect the lives of all Americans.

LIFE SKILL
Making Decisions

The judges of our federal courts and the Justices of the Supreme Court are very powerful people. The decisions they make directly affect the lives of all Americans. Thus, it is important that judges and Justices make the right decisions.

You, too, must make important decisions. You must decide, for example, how best to study for your tests. You must decide what extracurricular clubs to join. In fact, you will be making decisions every day for the rest of your life. And many of the decisions you make have important effects on you and the people around you. Thus, it is important that you—just like the judges of our nation—make the right decisions.

How to Make Decisions

To make an effective decision, follow these guidelines.

1. **Define the problem.** It often helps to write down the decision facing you in the form of a question, such as "Should I take an after-school job?" Writing the question down helps you to clarify the problem. It also helps you see if you are asking the right question. For example, instead of deciding if you need an after-school job, you might first need to decide if you need more money.

2. **Determine the importance of the decision.** Many decisions are simple. For example, you decide what you will eat for lunch each day. Other decisions are much more complex. Deciding where you will go to college, for example, is important. Take more time and care when making important decisions.

3. **Identify your options.** For some decisions, your options are limited. For example, if the question before you is "Should I write a research paper on the Supreme Court?" your only options are yes or no. But if the question

is "What should be the topic of my research paper?" then you are faced with a great many more options. Make a list of your options. Then write down the advantages and disadvantages of each option.

4. **Choose an option.** Once you have identified the advantages and disadvantages of each of your options, you can weigh your options and reach a decision. Take your time studying the lists you have made. Rule out less desirable options.

5. **Carry out your decision.** Once you have made your decision, follow through with it.

6. **Evaluate your decision.** After you have carried out your decision, decide if you made the correct one. Judging whether or not you made a mistake will help you make wise decisions in the future.

Applying the Skill

Read the following situation. Then answer the questions.

Should Rosa take a part-time job at the ice cream shop? She needs to save at least $500 a year for college, and she might not find work this summer. The hours could be a problem—three hours every day after school and all day every Saturday. She would have to miss basketball practice. And she would have much less time to study. Her grades could drop, and she might not even be accepted into college. What should she do?

1. What are Rosa's options in this situation?
2. What are the advantages and disadvantages of each of her options?
3. If you were in Rosa's position, which choice would you make? Explain your reasoning.

Reviewing Terms

On a separate sheet of paper, identify or define each term in the list below.

jurisdiction

Supreme Court

judicial review

opinion

administrative law

grand jury

district courts

courts of appeals

unconstitutional

common law

precedent

Using Thinking Skills

1. **Contrasting Ideas** (a) What is the difference between common law and statutory law? (b) What is the difference between original jurisdiction and appellate jurisdiction?
2. **Expressing Ideas** (a) How do our laws change with the times? (b) What are six rights that guarantee a person a fair trial?
3. **Seeing Relationships** (a) What is the relationship between precedent and common law? (b) How did common law begin?
4. **Comparing Ideas** (a) What was the significance of *Plessy v. Ferguson*? (b) Why was the outcome of *Brown v. Board of Education of Topeka* so important? (c) How are the two cases related?
5. **Identifying Roles** (a) How can Congress make constitutional a law declared unconstitutional by the Supreme Court? (b) How does the Supreme Court check the power of Congress?
6. **Drawing Conclusions** Why are federal judges appointed for life?
7. **Evaluating Ideas** (a) Explain the Supreme Court's ruling in *Miranda v. Arizona*. (b) Why do some people disagree with the ruling?
8. **Summarizing Ideas** What is the role of a grand jury?
9. **Understanding Ideas** (a) Explain the Supreme Court's decision in *Marbury v. Madison*. (b) What principles of American law were established by John Marshall?

Practicing Civics Skills

In the famous Tinker case, the Supreme Court faced a difficult decision: Did students have the right to wear black armbands to school to protest the Vietnam War? Place yourself in the position of a Supreme Court Justice. Analyze the Tinker decision by answering the following questions:

1. What options, or choices, did the Supreme Court have?
2. What were some of the possible outcomes of each of these options?
3. Which alternative did the majority of the Justices choose? Why?
4. Would you have made the same choice? Explain.

Being a Good Citizen

1. Select a local, state, or federal court that interests you. Write the presiding judge to arrange a visit to the court. After you have visited the court, report what you learned to the class.
2. Invite a local attorney or judge to visit your class. Prepare a set of questions about court procedures.
3. The men who have been Chief Justices are a diverse and fascinating group. Read a biography of one, and prepare a report on his work as Chief Justice.
4. Read *Gideon's Trumpet*, by Anthony Lewis. This book tells how Clarence Gideon's fight for justice resulted in a landmark decision by the Supreme Court.
5. Conduct research on the life and career of Sandra Day O'Connor, the first female Justice of the Supreme Court. Prepare a short biography of Justice O'Connor and present it to the class.
6. Organize the class into small groups to create bulletin-board displays of pictures that illustrate our American system of justice. Display these in class.

Reviewing the Facts

1. (a) What is Congress? (b) Why is it divided into two houses? (c) What was the Great Compromise?
2. (a) What are the four kinds of laws in the United States? (b) What is a precedent?
3. (a) What is the Supreme Court? (b) What is judicial review, and why is judicial review important?
4. (a) What is the President's Cabinet? (b) How is the Cabinet related to the executive departments?
5. Explain how the President functions as: Chief Executive, Chief of State, and Commander in Chief.
6. (a) What is a bill? (b) Where do ideas for bills come from?

Using Critical Thinking

1. **Summarizing Ideas** Explain how a bill becomes a federal law.
2. **Contrasting Ideas** (a) What is the difference between a conference committee and a joint committee? (b) What are standing committees?
3. **Seeing Relationships** How does the Supreme Court influence the lives of all Americans?
4. **Classifying Ideas** (a) What powers are given to Congress by the Constitution? (b) What is the elastic clause, and how is it used?
5. **Composing a Paragraph** Write a short paragraph describing the President's role in American foreign policy.
6. **Understanding Ideas** (a) What rights guarantee a person a fair trial? (b) How are the leaders of Congress chosen?
7. **Evaluating Ideas** (a) How does the President influence the judicial branch of government? (b) How does the President influence the legislative branch of government?

8. **Organizing Ideas** (a) Why is lawmaking such a complicated process? (b) How does the complexity of the process benefit America?
9. **Expressing Ideas** (a) Why are some federal agencies independent of the rest of the executive branch? (b) How do regulatory agencies differ from other independent agencies?
10. **Drawing Conclusions** (a) What is the purpose of the War Powers Act? (b) What Presidential role gives the President the authority to send American troops into action?

Applying What You Know

1. Select an issue at the local, state, or federal level that interests you and portray it in a political cartoon. Use symbols, caricatures, labels, and a caption to express your point of view.
2. Create an organizational chart of your local government. For information about how your community government is organized, contact city officials or the local chapter of the League of Women Voters.
3. Keep a decision-making log for a period of one week. Note when you make decisions and what your options for each decision are. Also record the reasons you choose the options you do.

Expanding Your Knowledge

Alotta, Robert I., *Number Two: A Look at the Vice Presidency*, Messner. Examines how our nation's Vice Presidents have influenced the government.

Coffer, Wayne R., *How We Choose a Congress*, St. Martin's Press. Discusses the history and organization of Congress.

Kane, Joseph, *Facts About the Presidents*, Wilson. Biographical and historical information about our nation's Presidents.

State and Local Government

UNIT 3

CHAPTER 8

How State Governments Serve Their Citizens

Chapter Sections

Chapter Focus

The United States is made up of 50 states. They differ in many ways. For example, Texas covers a much greater area than Rhode Island. California has a larger population than Delaware. Colorado's climate is colder than Florida's. When people in Colorado are ice skating or skiing, people in Florida are sunbathing.

The governments of the states also differ from one another. Yet they have important similarities. Like the federal government, every state has three branches of government—legislative, executive, and judicial.

The actions of your state government directly affect your daily life. For instance, the state government decides how many days you must attend school each year. It helps pay the costs of all the public schools and colleges in the state. It often decides what should be taught and which textbooks will be used.

States provide other basic services as well. State governments build and maintain highways and bridges. They run hospitals. They help care for the needy.

Study Guide

As you begin to learn about how state governments serve their citizens, look for answers to the following questions:
★ What powers do the states have, and what is included in state constitutions?
★ How are state legislatures organized, and how does a bill become a state law?
★ What is the state executive branch, and how is it organized?
★ How do state courts carry out their work?

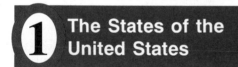

The States of the United States

When the American colonies won their independence, the original 13 states acted like small nations. Under the Articles of Confederation, you may recall, each state issued its own money. Each state regulated trade crossing its borders and often treated neighboring states as though they were foreign nations. Moreover, there was no provision for a President or system of national courts, and the Congress had little power. For a while it looked as though the United States would break up into 13 small, weak nations.

In 1787 the delegates to the Constitutional Convention worked long hours to establish a better form of government. The Constitution that they wrote created a stronger national government. The delegates agreed to take away some of the powers of the states in order to form "a more perfect union." The states, however, were allowed to keep certain powers for themselves. The resulting form of government, as you read earlier, is known as federalism, or a federal system.

The Division of Powers

In our federal system, the powers of government are divided between the 50 states and the federal government. What powers were given to the federal government, and which ones were retained by the states?

The states gave to the federal government those powers that affected all the people of the nation. Only the federal government can regulate trade between the states, coin money, and conduct foreign affairs. The federal government alone can set up a postal service and maintain an army and a navy.

The states still have many powers. Furthermore, the states and the federal government share some important powers. Although the powers of government have been divided between the states and the federal government, the states have remained strong. The states have considerable power to govern the people who live within their borders. State governments are close to the people and provide them with many needed services.

The Reserved Powers of the States

When the states approved the Constitution, they wanted to make certain that the rights of the state governments would always be protected. Therefore, the Tenth Amendment was added to the Constitution. As you have read, it provided that "the powers not delegated [given] to the United States by the Constitution, nor prohibited by it to the states, are reserved to [set aside for] the states respectively, or to the people." These reserved powers make it possible for states to govern their inhabitants effectively.

State governments are responsible for conducting elections. States decide most of the qualifications for voting. Of course, states must respect the federal Constitution's provisions about voting. States also set up procedures for holding all local, state, and national elections. Our federal system of government depends on the states to see that Americans are given the opportunity to elect their own representatives.

Another important function of state governments is education. The power to establish and maintain schools belongs to the state governments. The states have the power to decide what kinds of schools they will have. However, state school regulations cannot conflict with the United States Constitution or with the rulings of the Supreme Court.

The states make laws concerning marriage and divorce. They regulate traffic on the highways. State laws deal with health, safety, welfare, and the regulation of business within their borders. In addition, state governments have control over all local governments within their boundaries—cities, towns, townships, and counties. Local governments get their powers from the states.

Concurrent Powers

The states also share many powers with the federal government. These shared powers, as you recall, are called concurrent powers. Just because the federal government was granted certain powers in the Constitution does not mean that state governments do not also have these powers. Unless a power is forbidden to the states by the United States Constitution, state governments may exercise that power.

A good example of a shared, or concurrent, power is the power of taxation. Both the federal government and the state governments have the power to tax. They both collect various kinds of taxes to carry on their activities. State governments may raise money by taxing such items as gasoline, liquor, cigarettes, real estate, income, and personal property. The money raised through state taxes is used to

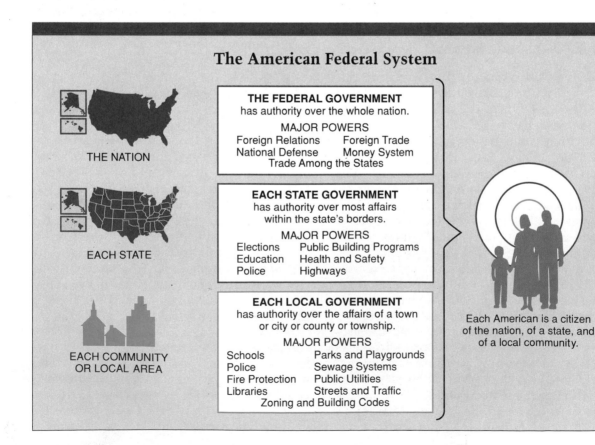

The American Federal System

THE NATION

THE FEDERAL GOVERNMENT
has authority over the whole nation.

MAJOR POWERS
Foreign Relations   Foreign Trade
National Defense   Money System
Trade Among the States

EACH STATE

EACH STATE GOVERNMENT
has authority over most affairs within the state's borders.

MAJOR POWERS
Elections   Public Building Programs
Education   Health and Safety
Police   Highways

EACH COMMUNITY OR LOCAL AREA

EACH LOCAL GOVERNMENT
has authority over the affairs of a town or city or county or township.

MAJOR POWERS
Schools   Parks and Playgrounds
Police   Sewage Systems
Fire Protection   Public Utilities
Libraries   Streets and Traffic
Zoning and Building Codes

Each American is a citizen of the nation, of a state, and of a local community.

pay for education, highways, health and safety programs, public assistance, and other activities of the states.

From 13 States to 50 States

The 13 original states became part of the United States when they approved the Constitution. Most of the other states that were added later, however, were once territories of the United States. A **territory** is an area, governed by the United States, that is eligible to become a state.

In 1787, under the Articles of Confederation, Congress passed an important law called the **Northwest Ordinance.** It provided a way for territories to join our nation as new and equal states.

Under the Northwest Ordinance, a territory was eligible to become a state once it had a population of 60,000 or more inhabitants. Then the territory lawmakers sent a petition to Congress asking to be organized as a state. If Congress agreed to the request, it asked the lawmakers of the territory to write a state constitution. This constitution had to be approved by the people of the territory and by Congress. After these steps were completed, Congress voted to admit the territory as a new state.

The United States has admitted 37 states since it became an independent nation. In 1959 Hawaii became our 50th state. In the future, the United States could grow still larger.

State Constitutions

Each of our 50 states has its own constitution. Your own state constitution probably interests you most of all, and it is worth careful study. This written plan of government for your state contains the rules that direct how your state government is to be organized and how it is to carry on its work. Most state constitutions contain the following parts.

A state police officer is enforcing the law in an area over which each state has control—safety along the state's highways.

1. A preamble, or beginning, which states the basic ideas and ideals on which the state government is founded.

2. A bill of rights, sometimes called a declaration of rights, that lists the rights and freedoms guaranteed to all citizens who live in the state.

3. An outline of the organization of the state's government, with the duties of the legislative, executive, and judicial branches carefully spelled out.

4. Provisions for elections, including qualifications for voting that must be met by the citizens of the state, as well as rules for conducting elections.

5. Provisions for managing state affairs, including education, keeping law and order, building highways, regulating business, and raising money by means of taxes.

6. Methods of amending, or changing, the state constitution, and a list of the amendments passed.

Most state constitutions have gone through the amendment process many times. This has been necessary because the powers and duties of state governments have changed greatly since their constitutions were first written. The Texas constitution, for instance, has been amended more than 300 times. During recent years, a number of states have drawn up new constitutions. Several states have had more than six new constitutions. A new constitution usually is drawn up at a state constitutional convention by delegates who are elected by the people.

The States as Good Neighbors

In joining the Union, the states agreed to work together in harmony. One way they promised to cooperate is stated in Article 4, Section 1, of the Constitution of the United States. It states that "Full faith [belief] and credit [acceptance] shall be given in each state to the public acts, records, and judicial proceedings [court decisions] of every other state."

The **full faith and credit clause** makes certain that each state will accept the decisions of courts in other states. If a court in Texas, for instance, decides that one of its citizens owns a certain piece of land, the other states will accept this legal decision. Another example of the full faith and credit clause is the acceptance of the official records of other states. A marriage certificate, birth certificate, will, contract, or deed issued by any state is accepted by all other states.

States work together in other ways, too. For example, a person accused of a crime cannot escape justice by fleeing to another state. If a person commits a crime in Utah and flees to Arizona, the governor of Utah can ask the governor of Arizona to return the person. This method of returning fugitives from justice is called **extradition.**

States cooperate on many projects. A bridge that crosses a river bordering two states is built and maintained by the governments of both. States also work together to reduce water and air pollution.

The States and the Federal Government

In our federal system, it is important that the 50 states and the federal government cooperate. What are some of the ways in which the federal and state governments join to provide services for Americans?

The Constitution of the United States, in Article 4, Section 4, promises that "The United States shall guarantee to every state in this Union a republican form of government. . . ." As you have read, in a republican form of government the people elect representatives to carry out the work of government. Every state, as it joined the Union, has been required to provide for a republican form of government in its state constitution.

The Constitution of the United States also promises that the federal government will "protect each of them [the states] against invasion." Therefore, it is the responsibility of the federal government to provide strong military forces to defend the states and the nation against attack.

In addition, the Constitution says that the federal government must stand ready to help any state put down "domestic violence" within its borders. An example of domestic violence might be rioting in a town when a mob has gotten out of control. The governor may call on the National Guard of the state if local police cannot control the disorder. In extreme cases, the state legislature or the governor may ask the federal government for assistance.

The federal and state governments share the costs of furnishing a number of services to the American people. Federal and state governments work together to build highways, assist jobless workers, help the needy, and conserve natural resources. Together the federal and state governments provide low-cost lunches for schoolchildren and offer job training for disabled people. These are some of the important ways in which state governments and the federal government cooperate to serve the American people.

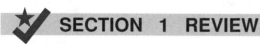

SECTION 1 REVIEW

Define territory, extradition

Identify Northwest Ordinance, full faith and credit clause

1. **Seeing Relationships (a)** What powers are reserved to the states by the Constitution? **(b)** How did the Articles of Confederation provide for the addition of new states?
2. **Understanding Ideas** List the six parts that make up most state constitutions.
3. **Summarizing Ideas** Describe how the states cooperate as good neighbors.

Thinking Critically Which is more important—cooperation among states or cooperation between the states and the federal government? Explain your answer.

2 State Lawmakers

Each state has a lawmaking body elected by the people of the state. In 26 states, this lawmaking body is called the Legislature. The term General Assembly is used in 19 states. In Montana, North Dakota, and Oregon, the lawmaking body is the Legislative Assembly. In Massachusetts and New Hampshire, it is the General Court. In this chapter we shall use the general term **state legislature.**

State Lawmaking Bodies

All but one of the states have a bicameral, or two-house, legislature. The larger of the two houses usually is called the House of Representatives. The smaller house is known as the Senate. Only Nebraska has a one-house legislature, or **unicameral legislature,** called the Senate.

State legislatures vary greatly in size. Alaska has the smallest legislature, with 40 representatives and 20 senators. The largest legislature is in New Hampshire, which has 400 representatives and 24 senators.

The members of each state legislature are elected by the people of the state. Each member represents the people who live in a particular district of that state. The state legislature divides the state into election districts.

Originally, the upper house (Senate) of the state legislature usually had one senator from each county or from each election district into which the state was divided. The counties or districts, however, often were unequal in population. Therefore, sparsely populated areas of the state often had as many senators as heavily populated areas.

In 1964 the United States Supreme Court ruled that all state election districts must be equal in population—or as nearly equal as possible. As you read in Chapter 7, this was the famous "one person, one vote" ruling. Since this decision, the states have set up election districts of nearly equal population.

Qualifications and Terms of State Lawmakers

Members of a state legislature must be citizens of the United States. They must live in the state and district that they represent. In most states, a state senator must be at least 25 years of age. A representative must be at least 21 years old. Some states have lowered the age requirement to 21 for senators and 18 for representatives.

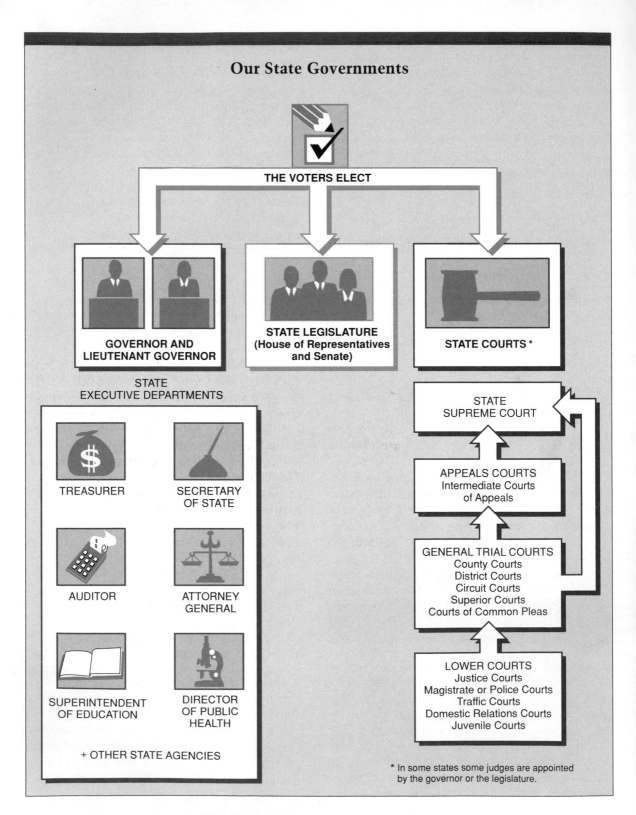

Our State Governments

THE VOTERS ELECT

GOVERNOR AND LIEUTENANT GOVERNOR

STATE LEGISLATURE
(House of Representatives and Senate)

STATE COURTS *

STATE
EXECUTIVE DEPARTMENTS

TREASURER

SECRETARY
OF STATE

AUDITOR

ATTORNEY
GENERAL

SUPERINTENDENT
OF EDUCATION

DIRECTOR
OF PUBLIC
HEALTH

+ OTHER STATE AGENCIES

STATE
SUPREME COURT

APPEALS COURTS
Intermediate Courts
of Appeals

GENERAL TRIAL COURTS
County Courts
District Courts
Circuit Courts
Superior Courts
Courts of Common Pleas

LOWER COURTS
Justice Courts
Magistrate or Police Courts
Traffic Courts
Domestic Relations Courts
Juvenile Courts

* In some states some judges are appointed
by the governor or the legislature.

In most states, senators are elected for four-year terms and representatives for two years. In a few states, however, both senators and representatives are elected for four-year terms. In some states, they both serve two years. The senators who serve in Nebraska's one-house legislature are elected for four-year terms. In all states, members of the legislature may run for reelection and serve any number of terms.

How State Legislatures Are Organized

The legislatures in more than half the states meet in regular sessions every year. Other state legislatures meet once every two years. California has a two-year session that meets for that entire period. In other states, a session can last from 20 days to six months or more. The governor, or sometimes the state legislature, may call special sessions to meet emergencies.

At the beginning of the session, the presiding officer and other leaders are chosen. Committees are appointed. In most states, there is a lieutenant governor who presides over the Senate. In the other states, the Senate chooses its own presiding officer. Members of the lower house in all states choose their own presiding officer, who is usually called the Speaker.

As in the United States Congress, most of the work of the state legislatures is done in committees. In the upper house, committee members are chosen by the presiding officer or by all the members of the house. In the lower house, the Speaker usually appoints the committee members.

How State Legislatures Pass Laws

The lawmaking process in state legislatures is similar to the procedure followed in Congress. Almost every step you studied in the

making of federal laws (Chapter 5) is followed by state legislatures. Here is a brief summary of the way in which a bill becomes law in a state legislature.

1. A Bill Is Introduced. Any member of either house may introduce a bill, or proposed law. It is first handed to the clerk and given a number. The presiding officer reads the title of the bill aloud and sends it to the appropriate committee.

2. The Bill Goes to a Committee. The committee listens to various witnesses for and against the bill and then questions them to obtain necessary information. The members may discuss the bill for many hours. The committee may vote to pass the bill, to change it, or to kill it.

3. The Bill Reaches the Floor. If the committee approves the bill, it is sent back to a full meeting of the house. The bill is read aloud, line by line. The members of the house now begin to debate the bill. Each part of the bill is discussed. Amendments may be offered, and if passed they become part of the bill.

Then the members vote on the bill. Bills that are passed are signed by the presiding officer and sent to the other house.

4. The Bill Goes to the Second House. When the bill is introduced in the second house of Congress, it is sent to a committee. If the bill survives the hearings, debates, and changes in this committee, it is sent

The state legislature is the lawmaking branch of state government. Here members of the Texas House of Representatives debate a bill under consideration.

back to the floor of the second house. Here it is debated, perhaps changed again, and then voted upon.

Bills that pass one house and fail in the second house are dead. If both houses of the legislature pass a bill in the same form, it is then sent to the governor to be signed. Frequently, however, both houses pass the bill, but in different forms. In this case, it is sent to a joint conference committee.

5. The Bill Goes to a Joint Conference Committee. This committee is made up of members selected from both houses. They must try to reach a compromise, or agreement, that will be acceptable to both houses. The compromise bill worked out by the joint conference committee is then voted on by the two houses. Usually each house accepts this final version of the bill.

6. The Bill Is Sent to the Governor. The final step in making a state law is to send the bill to the governor. If the governor signs the bill, it becomes a law. In all states except North Carolina, the governor may veto a bill he or she does not support. In most states, the governor also has the power to veto only one part, or item, of a money bill. This is known as an **item veto.** The legislature can pass a bill over the governor's veto by a two-thirds vote in each house.

Direct Action and Legislation

Some state constitutions allow the people to take a direct part in making laws. Citizens are able to initiate, or start, new legislation through a process called the **initiative.**

First they must draw up a petition describing the proposal. Then they must get a required number of voters to sign the petition. If they succeed, the proposed law appears on the ballot at the next general election. If enough people vote for the bill, it becomes law.

In many states, certain bills passed by the legislature must be approved by the voters before they can become law. This method of referring questions directly to the people is called a **referendum.**

Some states also provide voters with the means to remove elected officials from office. This process, known as a **recall,** begins when a required number of voters sign a petition. A special election is then held. If a majority of voters favors recall, the official is replaced.

 SECTION 2 REVIEW

Define state legislature, unicameral legislature, item veto, initiative, referendum, recall

1. **Seeing Relationships** Why must election districts within states have nearly equal populations?
2. **Understanding Ideas (a)** What are the qualifications for members of state legislatures? **(b)** How long do members of state legislatures serve?
3. **Composing an Essay** Write an essay that explains how a bill becomes a state law.

Thinking Critically Why can it be said that the initiative, referendum, and recall are our three basic instruments of direct democracy?

③ The State Executive Branch

The state's legislative branch makes the laws for the state. These laws are carried out by the state's executive branch. The executive branch is headed by the **governor.** It also includes other officials, as well as numerous agencies, who assist the governor.

Qualifications and Terms of the Governor

The governor is the chief executive in each state. He or she is elected by the people of the state in a statewide election. The qualifications for governor are set forth in each state constitution. In general, a candidate for governor must be a citizen of the United States and must have lived in the state for a certain number of years. Most states require a governor to be at least 30 years old. A few, however, allow persons at least 25 years of age to run for governor.

Most governors serve four-year terms. In other states, they are elected for two years. In three states, Kentucky, New Mexico, and Virginia, governors cannot serve two terms in a row.

The salaries of the governors vary greatly from state to state. For example, the governor of New York receives $130,000 a year and the Texas governor, $93,342. The governor of North Dakota receives $65,000. In addition to a salary, governors usually receive an allowance for expenses. In most states, governors and their families live in an official residence in the state capital.

The Governor's Powers and Duties

The main job of the governor, as chief executive of the state, is to carry out the laws. Like the President of the United States, however, many governors also have legislative and judicial responsibilities.

Chief Legislator. Only the state legislature can pass laws. The governor, though, plays an important part in proposing new laws. The governor usually appears before the state legislature at one of the early meetings. At this meeting, the governor outlines laws he or she thinks should be passed. From time to time, the governor talks to leaders of the legislature, urging them to pass specific bills. State legislators know that if they pass a bill the governor opposes, it may be vetoed.

After the legislature has passed a law, it is the responsibility of the governor to put it into force. If the legislature passes a new tax law, for example, it is the duty of the governor to issue orders that will determine how the taxes are to be collected. The orders that set up methods of enforcing laws are called **executive orders.** Almost every new law requires such executive orders.

Chief Executive. In most states, one of the governor's most important responsibilities is to draw up a budget for the state. The **budget** is a plan of income and spending. A budget director or a budget bureau assists the governor. Long hours are spent in figuring out the amount of money the state will need during the next one- or two-year period, and the taxes that will be required to meet this need. The completed budget is sent to the legislature for approval.

As chief executive of the state, the governor also may appoint a number of officials with the approval of the state Senate. The governor works with these officials to carry out state laws.

Political Party Leader. The governor is the head of his or her political party in the state. State senators and representatives pay close attention to what the governor says. They know the governor can help them during their next election campaigns.

Other Powers. The governor has many other powers. The heads of the state police force and militia report to the governor.

In times of emergency, such as floods or hurricanes, the governor may call out the National Guard to help keep order. The governor also has the judicial power to pardon, or free, certain prisoners. A reprieve issued by a governor will postpone a prisoner's sentence.

Other State Executive Officials

The voters of each state elect a number of officials in addition to the governor to help run the state government. The following officials are the more important members of

The Powers and Duties of the Governor

Carries out state laws and supervises the work of the executive department

Sends messages to the state legislature suggesting new laws

Approves or vetoes bills

May pardon criminals and grant reprieves

Controls the state police force and the state militia

Calls special sessions of the legislature

Appoints and removes certain state officials

Draws up and sends the budget to the legislature

Performs other duties— represents the state at ceremonies and public events

each state's executive branch. In most states, these officials are elected by the voters. In some states, however, they are appointed by the governor. Most of these officials are in charge of the executive departments of the state government.

Lieutenant Governor. All but seven states have a **lieutenant governor.** The lieutenant governor becomes head of the state executive branch if the governor dies, resigns, or is removed from office. In some states, it is possible for the lieutenant governor and the governor to belong to different political parties. The lieutenant governor often serves as presiding officer of the state Senate.

Secretary of State. The **secretary of state** keeps state records, carries out election laws, and fulfills other duties described in the state constitution. Only Alaska, Hawaii, and Utah do not have this official. In states that do not have a lieutenant governor, the secretary of state serves as governor if the office of governor becomes vacant.

Attorney General. The **attorney general** takes care of the state's legal business, or matters concerning the law. If any state official wants advice about the meaning of a law, the attorney general gives it. The attorney general or an assistant represents the state in court when the state is involved in a lawsuit. The attorney general may also assist local officials in the prosecution of criminals.

State Treasurer. The **state treasurer** is in charge of handling all state funds. This official supervises the collection of taxes and pays the state's bills.

State Auditor. The **state auditor** makes sure no public funds are paid out of the state treasury unless payment is authorized by law. Usually the treasurer cannot pay any bills without a written order that is signed by the auditor. This order to pay out money is called a **warrant.** The auditor also examines the state's financial records from time to time to make sure they are correct. The auditor is sometimes called the **comptroller.**

Superintendent of Public Instruction. The most important duty of the **superintendent of public instruction** is to carry out the policies of the state Board of Education (known in some states by other titles). The state board makes regulations, under state law, that govern the various local school districts. The superintendent is in charge of the distribution of state funds to the local school systems according to the law. This official is sometimes called the superintendent of public schools or the state commissioner of education.

The Governor's Cabinet

In some states the officials you have just read about are a part of the governor's Cabinet. In other states they are not considered members of the Cabinet unless they are appointed by the governor. Like the President's Cabinet, the governor's official advisers head the executive departments of the state government.

Most states have a Department of Justice (headed by the attorney general), a Department of Labor, a Department of Agriculture, and a Department of Transportation. In addition, there is a Department of Public Safety, which includes the state police. The Department of Public Works is responsible for all public construction projects in the state except work done on highways.

State Executive Agencies

A number of state agencies exist to help the governor carry out the laws. These agencies are also part of the executive branch of our state governments. They are sometimes called boards, commissions, or departments.

Most state agencies are headed by officials appointed by and responsible to the governor. In some states, the heads of the agencies are appointed by the state legislature. They are responsible directly to the legislature.

Each state agency has a specific area of responsibility. For example, the state Board of Health enforces health laws and recommends measures to improve the health of state citizens. The Department of Human Services supervises programs that help people who are poor, unemployed, or disabled. The state Civil Service Commission is in charge of hiring most of the people who work for the state. Other state agencies administer state laws on agriculture, highways, and conservation. Other agencies regulate banks and public utilities.

State Government Employees

Our state governments employ a great many people. Most state employees get their positions through the state Civil Service Commission. State examinations are given as a means of choosing the most qualified workers. Other state jobs are not controlled under civil service. These jobs are filled through recommendations of political party leaders and office holders. Such jobs often go to those people in the party who have helped in some important way during the election campaign. However, most state government jobs are controlled under civil service. These jobs are open to any qualified citizen.

 SECTION 3 REVIEW

Define executive orders, budget, warrant

Identify governor, lieutenant governor, secretary of state, attorney general, state treasurer, state auditor, comptroller, superintendent of public instruction

1. **Understanding Ideas (a)** What are the qualifications for governor in most states? **(b)** How long do most governors serve?
2. **Composing an Essay** Write a short essay describing the duties of a governor.
3. **Summarizing Ideas** What services do state agencies perform for the state's citizens?

Thinking Critically The organization of the executive branch varies from state to state. Should the federal government require the states to have the same type of organization? Explain your answer.

 State Courts

Each state government has the power to keep peace and order within its boundaries. It exercises this power through all three branches of state government. The legislature passes laws to provide for the welfare and safety of the people of the state. The executive branch sees that these laws are put into effect. The judicial branch—the state court system—has the job of interpreting these state laws and punishing those who break them.

The Work of the State Courts

Federal and state courts handle both criminal and civil cases. **Criminal cases** deal with violations of the law. They involve acts that harm individuals or the community as a whole. A criminal act is considered an offense against society. In such a case, a lawyer for the state presents the evidence against the accused. He or she represents the people of the state, because breaking a state law is a crime committed against the people of the state. Serious crimes such as burglary, kidnapping, or murder are **felonies.** Less serious offenses, such as traffic violations, disorderly conduct, or violation of health laws, are **misdemeanors.**

Civil cases deal with disputes between individuals or businesses. They may also involve disputes between a business and the government or an individual and the government. These disputes are usually over property or money. For example, if one person claims that another person owes him or her money and asks a state court for help in collecting the money, the case would be a civil case. Another example of a civil case might be one company's lawsuit against another company for not carrying out its part of a business contract. In a civil case, the state court must judge who is right and must award damages in the case.

How Our State Courts Are Organized

Each state has its own system of courts to interpret the law and punish lawbreakers. The organization of state courts varies from state to state. Four types of courts are found in most states: lower courts, general trial courts, appeals courts, and a state supreme court. The chart on page 166 shows the organization of most state court systems.

1. Lower Courts. The **lower courts** generally hear minor cases. These include misdemeanors and civil cases involving small amounts of money. In most rural areas and small towns, these cases are heard by a **justice of the peace.** This elected official presides over a justice court and tries misdemeanors and civil cases involving small sums. For misdemeanors the justice of the peace can hand down fines or short jail sentences.

In larger towns and small cities, such cases are handled by a magistrate's court or police court. These courts usually are presided over by an elected judge. All cases are heard by the judge and not by a trial jury.

Many large cities have set up **municipal courts.** These are often divided into smaller courts that handle special matters. Traffic courts, for example, hear cases involving traffic violations. Domestic relations courts hear

cases involving family disputes. Juvenile courts hear cases involving young persons under 18 years of age.

In these special lower courts, judges with special legal training are usually in charge. These judges conduct hearings without a jury. They are usually more interested in getting at the cause of the trouble and preventing further difficulty than in handing out fines or jail sentences. Judges in juvenile and domestic relations courts work closely with social workers to help families who are in trouble. The decisions of the judges in serious cases may be appealed to a trial court.

2. General Trial Courts. Major criminal and civil cases are handled in **general trial courts.** Most cases are heard by a jury, and a judge presides. In about three fourths of the states, the judges are elected by the people of the county or district in which they serve.

Larger cities usually have several general trial courts. Sometimes one of these courts hears only civil cases, and another hears only criminal cases.

About one third of our states have trial courts called county courts. The county court

(continued on page 176)

Many cities have set up various special lower courts. In this domestic relations court, the judge must consider the best interests of the child.

Bill of Rights

Focus on Freedom

Protecting the Rights of the Accused

If you have ever seen an action-packed movie or television show dealing with crime, you are familiar with the following scene: A robbery is committed and the police jump into action. After an exciting chase, the officers corner the fleeing suspect. As one officer handcuffs the suspect, the other officer pulls out a small card and reads a statement similar to the following:

You have the right to remain silent. If you give up the right to remain silent, anything you say can and will be used against you in a court of law. You have the right to be represented by an attorney and to have an attorney present during questioning. If you cannot afford an attorney, one will be provided for you.

This does not just happen in the movies. Real-life police officers are required to read this statement, known as the "Miranda Warning," to all suspects before they are arrested. This requirement comes from a landmark 1966 Supreme Court decision. At the heart of the decision are important freedoms guaranteed to all Americans in the Fifth and Sixth Amendments of the Constitution.

Ernesto Miranda is Arrested

In 1963, a young woman was kidnapped near Phoenix, Arizona. A few days after the kidnapping, the police arrested Ernesto Miranda, a warehouse worker, and took him to the police station. After he was questioned by the police for several hours, Miranda confessed to the crime.

At the trial, the arresting officers testified that they had warned Miranda that anything he said could be used against him in court. They also testified that no threats or force had been used to get Miranda to confess to the crime. The officers admitted, however, that they had not told Miranda about his right to remain silent or to have an attorney. Nevertheless, Miranda was found guilty and given a prison sentence of 20 to 30 years.

Police officers must inform suspects of their legal rights before they can arrest them. They do this by reading the Miranda Warning.

The Supreme Court Decides

Miranda's lawyers appealed the decision to the Arizona Supreme Court, arguing that Miranda had not been informed of his rights and that he had been denied consultation with a lawyer. The Arizona Supreme Court justices were unconvinced, however, and upheld Miranda's conviction. The lawyers then appealed the case to the United States Supreme Court.

In Court, the lawyers argued that the Fifth Amendment gives citizens the right to refuse to give information about themselves. In other words, people have the right to remain silent. Under the Sixth Amendment, the lawyers argued, persons accused of crimes are guaranteed the right to an attorney. The Supreme Court agreed. It ruled that, by taking Miranda's confession without informing him of his rights to silence and an attorney, the police officers had deprived Miranda of these rights. Although Miranda was later reconvicted at a new trial, his case forever changed the way that the police must treat suspects.

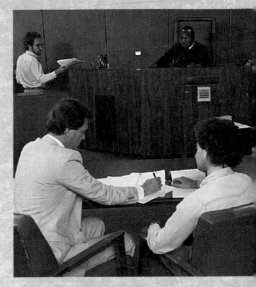

The right to be represented by a lawyer is guaranteed by the Sixth Amendment to the Constitution.

Innocent Until Proven Guilty

If the police or the courts fail to follow the guidelines put down by the Fifth and Sixth Amendments, charges against a suspect—even a guilty one—may be dropped. Because the Miranda ruling makes it possible for real criminals to escape justice because of a technicality, some people argue that the Constitution goes too far in protecting the rights of criminals.

We must remember, however, that our entire judicial system is based on the belief that people are innocent until proven guilty. In order to protect the innocent, we must guard the rights of all who are accused of crimes.

Questions to Consider

1. What is the "Miranda Warning"? What is its purpose?
2. According to the Supreme Court, which of Miranda's constitutional rights were violated?
3. Why is it important to protect the rights of the accused?

The right to sue in a law court and the right to appeal a lower court's decision are protected in our nation. These rights, however, have a price. What is it?

is located in the county seat, which is the center of county government in most states. In other states, trial courts are called district courts. There are also circuit courts, in which the judge travels a circuit (complete route) from one county to another to hold court. Other names for trial courts in some states are superior courts or courts of common pleas.

3. Appeals Courts. Sometimes a person believes his or her case was not handled fairly in a trial court. That person may appeal the decision to an **appeals court.** These courts are often called intermediate courts of appeals. The usual basis for appeal is that the trial judge violated one of the rights to a fair trial guaranteed to all citizens by the Constitution.

There is no jury trial in an appeals court. Instead, a group of judges study the trial record of the lower court and hear the arguments of lawyers. They decide the case by majority vote. The judges must decide whether the trial in the lower court gave the person on trial all the rights guaranteed under the Constitution. If the person is still not satisfied with the decision, he or she can appeal to the state supreme court.

4. State Supreme Court. This is the highest court in most states. The judges who sit on the **state supreme court** hear cases on appeal in much the same way as does the Supreme Court of the United States. In some states, the state supreme court is called the court of appeals.

State supreme court judges are elected in most states. In others they are appointed by the governor with the consent of the state Senate. The decision of the state supreme court is final unless a federal law or a question about the United States Constitution is involved. Then the case may be appealed to the Supreme Court of the United States.

Small Claims Courts

Most states have established special courts that hear civil cases involving small amounts of money. These are called **small claims courts.** They usually handle cases involving $1,000 to $2,000. No lawyers are needed. The people in the dispute explain their side of the argument to the judge. The judge questions each side to try to get all the facts. Then the judge makes a decision in the case.

Our Overcrowded State Courts

There have been many proposals in recent years for the reform of our state court systems. The state courts are overburdened with work. So many cases come before them that the court calendar is often a year or more behind schedule. It is not unusual to find automobile accident cases that have waited two or three years for a court settlement.

In many of our largest cities, the jails are crowded with accused persons who are awaiting trial. Some have waited for more than a year. They may or may not be guilty. They have remained in jail because they do not have the money to post bail. They have not been brought to trial because there are so many cases ahead of them.

This backlog of cases makes it impossible to fulfill the constitutional guarantee of a speedy public trial. Critics point to three reasons for this situation. First, there are more cases than ever before and not enough judges to handle the increasing caseload. Second, trials are long and slow. The very guarantees that protect us often cause trials to take a long time. Third, some courts are not conducted in an efficient manner. Judges call frequent recesses, or breaks, in a trial. Lawyers sometimes use delaying tactics.

Many people say that courts have not kept up-to-date. They suggest the courts use modern business tools, such as computers, to make court work more efficient.

The conditions in our courts are becoming quite serious. Their improvement is an issue well worth the concern and attention of every American citizen.

 SECTION 4 REVIEW

Define criminal cases, felonies, misdemeanors, civil cases

Identify lower courts, justice of the peace, municipal courts, general trial courts, appeals court, state supreme court, small claims court

1. **Summarizing Ideas** Describe the four types of courts found in most states.
2. **Understanding Ideas** What action can citizens take if they are not satisfied with decisions made in appeals court?
3. **Contrasting Ideas** How do small claims courts differ from other courts?

Thinking Critically You have been appointed to help your state court system clear up its backlog of cases. What recommendations will you make?

Each of our 50 states has its own state government. The state government manages the internal affairs of the state. Like the federal government, every state government is based on a written constitution.

In the Constitution of the United States, many powers are left to the states. The states have power over such areas as public education, elections, highways, and the establishment of local governments. The states share with the federal government such powers as taxation, law enforcement, and the protection of the health, safety, and welfare of the people.

Each state government has a legislative branch, executive branch, and judicial branch. Most states have a two-house legislative body similar to Congress. The process of passing state laws is similar to that of putting federal laws through Congress.

The governors of the states are the chief executive officers of the state governments. They see that state laws are carried out. Governors are assisted in their work by other executive officials and state executive agencies.

State courts interpret state laws and bring to trial those people accused of breaking state laws. The court system in the states includes lower courts, general trial courts, appeals courts, and state supreme courts.

CHAPTER
8
SUMMARY

CITIZENSHIP SKILL
Writing to Your Legislator

One of the best ways to let your legislator know what you are thinking is to write a letter. Well-written letters receive more attention than poorly written ones. Fortunately, there are some basic rules to follow to make sure that yours is the kind of letter that gets an answer.

How to Write to Your Legislator

To write an effective letter, follow these guidelines.

1. **Include your return address.** Make sure that your return address is on the letter. This will help your legislator get back to you.
2. **Use the proper term of address.** Always address a legislator as *"The Honorable (name)."* This applies to both the inside address and the address on the envelope.
3. **Use the correct opening and closing.** In the salutation, or greeting, use the person's correct title. For members of the United States House of Representatives, "Dear Representative (name)," "Dear Congresswomen (name)," or "Dear Congressman (name)" are all acceptable. For members of the Senate, "Dear Senator (name)" is the usual style. Titles of state officials vary. Find out the exact title of a state official before you write. End your letter with the proper closing, such as "Respectfully yours," or "Sincerely yours." Then add your signature.
4. **Put your writing skills to work.** Keep the body, or main part, of the letter as brief as possible. Clearly state your position or request in the first paragraph. Point out the facts that will help your legislator understand why you are concerned.
5. **Be considerate of your reader.** Put yourself in the legislator's place. Be polite—even if you are angry. Also, your letter will get more attention if it is neatly typed or handwritten.

Applying the Skill

Use the letter on this page to answer the following questions.
1. **(a)** To whom is the letter addressed?
   (b) What issue is Peter Gill concerned about in his letter?
2. Why might a letter from Peter Gill be more convincing than a telephone call?

---

32 Wadel Avenue
Elkhart, IN 46516
January 15, 1991

The Honorable Ann Downing
The State House
Indianapolis, IN 46204

Dear Representative Downing:

   As you know, there is a bill currently before the legislature that would create 3,000 summer jobs for teenagers in our state. I strongly urge you to support this bill.
   Passage of Bill HR 1026 will give many teenagers the chance to earn money for school. It will also provide them with experience for future jobs. Finally, the state stands to benefit from all the work these teenagers will be doing in our parks, hospitals, and civic centers.
   I would appreciate knowing your position on this important issue.

                    Sincerely yours,

                    Peter Gill
                    Peter Gill

Reviewing Terms

On a separate sheet of paper, supply the term from the list below that correctly completes each sentence.

executive orders territory
referendum   misdemeanors
extradition   felonies
recall   item veto

1. A _____ is an area governed by the United States that is eligible to become a state.
2. Serious crimes, such as burglary, kidnapping, and murder, are called _____.
3. Orders issued by the governor that set up methods of enforcing laws are called _____ _____.
4. _____ is the procedure for returning criminals to the state from which they fled.
5. Citizens may remove an elected official from office by using the _____.
6. _____ is the method of referring new bills to the voters before the bills can become laws.
7. Less serious crimes, such as traffic violations, are called _____.
8. The _____ _____ refers to the power of the governor in most states to turn down only one part of a money bill.

Using Thinking Skills

1. **Comparing Ideas (a)** How are state constitutions similar to the Constitution of the United States? **(b)** In what ways are the state governments similar to the federal government?
2. **Identifying Roles** Explain the role of each of the following in state government: governor, lieutenant governor, secretary of state, state treasurer, state auditor, attorney general.
3. **Summarizing Ideas** Summarize the process by which a bill become a state law.

4. **Expressing Ideas (a)** Why was the Tenth Amendment added to the Constitution? **(b)** What are some of the problems facing state courts today?
5. **Understanding Ideas (a)** How does a territory become a state? **(b)** How does the Constitution ensure that the states will be good neighbors? **(c)** How do the states and the federal government cooperate?
6. **Identifying Ideas** Describe the three methods by which citizens can take a direct part in state lawmaking.
7. **Classifying Ideas (a)** What kinds of cases are heard in general trial courts? **(b)** Why do citizens use appeals courts?

Practicing Civics Skills

Expressing Points of View Write a letter to one of the state legislators representing your election district. Request information about some aspects of your state government or express your thoughts on an issue currently in the news. If you do not know the names or exact titles of your state legislators, check with your school librarian or call the League of Women Voters.

Being a Good Citizen

1. Arrange to visit a state court and listen to cases being tried. Report to the class on your experiences.
2. Organize the class into groups to draw maps showing your state's congressional districts. Outline in red the district in which your community is located. Display the maps in class.
3. Write a report on your state's constitution. Include the following information: when and how the constitution was adopted, the number of amendments that have been made, and any outstanding or unusual features that are included.
4. Organize a group of students to conduct an interview with one of your state legislators.

CHAPTER 9

How Local Governments Serve Their Citizens

Chapter Sections

Chapter Focus

Local governments were our first governments. The primitive tribe that chose the oldest leaders to form a council was seeking a better, safer life for all.

In the same way, the first English settlers who landed in Jamestown, Virginia, in 1607 soon realized they needed rules and leaders. At first the settlers had to look out for themselves. They had to find their own food and build their own shelter. As food supplies began to run low and the colonists faced hunger and disease, they realized that their survival depended on working together.

The colonists formed a council to make laws, and chose Captain John Smith as president. His job was to carry out the laws. This Jamestown government was the first local government in colonial America.

Today local government is still the first and most important government in our lives. We see the work of our local government every day, and how well it does its job affects each of us directly.

Study Guide

As you begin to learn about how local governments serve their citizens, look for answers to the following questions:
★ Why do we need local government?
★ How did towns and villages develop, and how do township governments work today?
★ How do city governments differ in the way they are organized?
★ In what ways do our various levels of government both cooperate and compete?

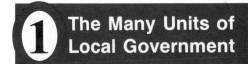

1 The Many Units of Local Government

Local government has grown as our nation has grown. As the American people settled in rural communities, towns, cities, and suburbs, they set up local governments. Americans have found that good local governments make their lives easier, safer, and more pleasant.

How Local Governments Are Established

All local governments are established by and receive their powers from the state governments. State constitutions direct the state legislatures to set up a government for each village, town, county, and city within the state borders. The people of a town or city can change the way their local government is organized, or operates, only with the approval of the state legislature. State governments, however, give local units of government considerable power to manage their own affairs.

Most local governments receive charters from the state. A **charter** is the basic plan of government for a local governmental unit that defines its powers, responsibilities, and organization. Some units of local government are incorporated by the state, which means they have the legal status of corporations. These units, called **municipalities,** include cities, villages, and boroughs. Municipalities, established by petition and election of the residents, have a large degree of self-government. As corporations, municipalities may own property, make contracts, and sue and be sued in court.

Why We Need Local Government

The people who live in each local area or community depend upon local government to serve them in many ways. We take for granted such conveniences as running water in our homes, sidewalks, trash collection, roads, and sewage systems. A great deal of planning by local officials is necessary to make such conveniences possible. Usually only when something goes wrong with local services do we appreciate them.

All these services depend upon a well-run local government. Some services, such as electricity and public transportation, may be provided by privately owned companies. Local government, however, is very much concerned that these services be kept economical and well regulated.

It might be possible for individuals working alone to perform all the services local governments provide. Each person might bury trash in the backyard or hire someone to haul it away. Each person might be able to guard against fire by keeping a fire extinguisher in the home. However, life would be more difficult if every citizen had to do all these things alone. The people in American communities find that by working together they can secure better and more efficient services than by working alone.

Local and State Cooperation

Local governments work closely with state governments to make our communities better places to live. Local lawmaking bodies have the power to pass **ordinances,** regulations that govern the community. An ordinance has the force of law, but it must be in compliance with state and national laws. Local governments also enforce the laws that are passed by the state.

What are some state laws that are enforced by local governments? One is the election law. Elections are carried out according to state rules. However, the polling places, where citizens go to vote, and the officials who supervise them are provided by local governments. Another example concerns weights and measures. In most states, the scales on which a butcher weighs meat must meet certain standards required by state law. Yet these controls are often enforced by local inspectors. The police departments of local governments enforce both state laws and local ordinances.

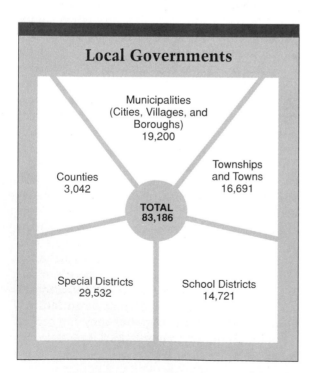

Local Governments

Municipalities (Cities, Villages, and Boroughs) 19,200

Counties 3,042

Townships and Towns 16,691

TOTAL 83,186

Special Districts 29,532

School Districts 14,721

Kinds of Local Governments

There are many kinds of local governments in the United States. These include counties, towns, townships, villages, boroughs, and cities. The chart on this page shows the number of different kinds of local governments in the nation.

Although these governments differ, they also have much in common. The main job of any local government is to provide services for citizens. The first type of local government that we will examine is the county government.

County Governments

Most of our states are divided into parts called **counties.** The number and size of these counties vary from state to state. The state of Texas has 254 counties, while Delaware and Hawaii each have 3. Altogether there are more than 3,000 counties in the United States. In Louisiana, counties are called **parishes.** In Alaska, they are called **boroughs.**

In many states, the county government is the largest unit of local government. Counties help carry out state laws. They also serve as court districts and conduct elections.

Connecticut and Rhode Island have counties, but these are geographical areas only, without county governments. In the New England states, most counties are judicial districts. There, the functions of county governments usually are performed by towns.

The county form of government began in the Southern colonies. In this region, agriculture was the main industry and the population was scattered. Tobacco, rice, indigo, and cotton plantations were often located long distances from each other. The county form of government, borrowed from England, seemed well suited to the settlers' needs.

Each Southern colony was divided into a number of counties. The plantation owners in each county met regularly in a central, easy-to-reach town, which became known as the

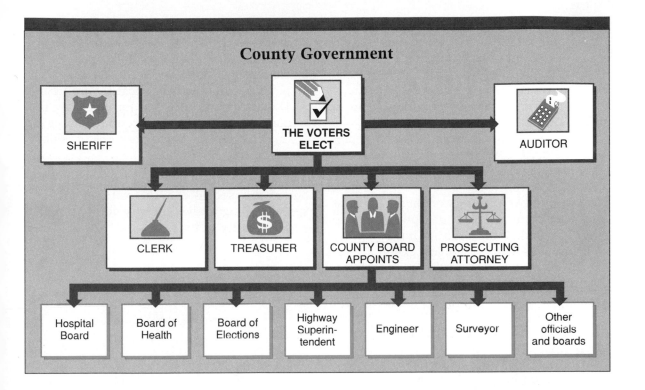

County Government

SHERIFF

THE VOTERS ELECT

AUDITOR

CLERK

TREASURER

COUNTY BOARD APPOINTS

PROSECUTING ATTORNEY

Hospital Board

Board of Health

Board of Elections

Highway Superintendent

Engineer

Surveyor

Other officials and boards

county seat. At these meetings, the plantation owners passed the laws of the county government. The chief official in this early form of government was a sheriff, the title of a similar official in England. The sheriff's job was to see that the laws of the county were enforced.

Today, in states where counties are important, county governments serve two main purposes. First, they help the state government collect various state taxes, supervise elections, and enforce state laws. Second, they serve the people by providing them with roads, schools, libraries, health and welfare services, and law enforcement.

County Officials

At the head of a strong county government is a group of officials elected by the voters. This governing body is often called the **county board.** Other names for this group are county commissioners, county council, fiscal court, county court, or board of county supervisers.

The county board is the legislative body of the county. It may pass local laws regulating health and safety. It may collect taxes on real estate or personal property in the county. The county board also supervises such county buildings as the courthouse and jail.

Many counties have no leader for the executive branch of their government. Instead they have several county officials, each with separate responsibilities. These officials are elected by the people of the county.

The **sheriff** enforces the law. He or she selects deputies to help in law enforcement. The sheriff arrests lawbreakers and carries out the orders of the courts. In many places, the sheriff has charge of the county jail.

The **county clerk** keeps a record of the actions and decisions of the county board. The clerk also keeps records of births, deaths, marriages, and election results. Usually he or she informs the public of all laws and regulations passed by the county board.

The **county treasurer** takes care of the county's money. The treasurer sees that no money is spent unless the county board approves. Sometimes the treasurer collects taxes. Often, however, counties elect a **tax collector** to do this job.

The **county auditor** examines the official records of taxes received and money spent to make sure they are kept properly.

The **county prosecuting attorney** represents the state government in county trials. He or she is also known as the district attorney or state's attorney.

The number of county officials varies not only from state to state but from county to county as well. Some counties have as many as 70 officials. They include a coroner, purchasing agent, public defender, park commissioner, and register of deeds.

The Rise of the County Manager

As the population of areas outside the cities has grown, there has been a demand for better county government. With the approval of the voters and the state legislature, a number of counties have reorganized their governments. Many have established the position of **county manager,** or county executive.

This official is usually appointed by the county board but in some places is elected by the voters. The county manager supervises the county government and organizes it in a businesslike manner. This type of county government places responsibility in the hands of a single executive, with the aim of making the government more efficient.

★ SECTION 1 REVIEW

Define charter, municipalities, ordinances, counties, parishes, boroughs, county seat, county board

Identify sheriff, county clerk, county treasurer, tax collector, county auditor, county prosecuting attorney, county manager

1. **Identifying Ideas (a)** How are local governments established? **(b)** In what ways are municipalities like corporations?
2. **Composing an Essay** Write an essay explaining why we need local governments.
3. **Understanding Ideas (a)** Explain how the county system of government began. **(b)** What are the main purposes of county government?

Thinking Critically You are campaigning for one of the elected county positions. Write a speech telling the voters why you will make a good county official.

2 Town, Township, and Village Governments

Although counties are the largest of all units of local government, they are not always the most important. In a number of states, counties serve only as election districts, with the real work of local government carried on by other units. In all states, counties must share the job of local government with other units of government.

The Development of Towns and Villages

The **town** form of government began in the New England colonies. Each colony received a grant of land from the British king. The colonists established small towns, where they built their homes and churches.

At the edges of the towns, the settlers established their farms. Every day they left their homes and worked on the farms. The colonists considered these outlying farms to be part of their towns. Later some of the settlers moved to the farms. As long as these farms were located within the town limits, the people who lived on them were counted as members of that town. New England towns stretched out into the countryside, as did counties in other settlements.

In New Amsterdam (now called New York), the settlers set up a **village** government. Only the village itself, which included the homes of the settlers as well as other buildings, belonged to the village government. The outlying parts of the settlement were not considered part of the village, and they later came under the rule of the county government.

As other people pushed farther west, they established new settlements. Some of them called their settlements towns. In Pennsylvania, settlements were often called boroughs. Thus many different names were used for these small settlements.

Early Town Government in New England

The people of the early New England towns worked out a simple yet effective form of local government—the **town meeting.** All the people who lived in a town, as well as those from the surrounding farms, met together regularly in the town hall. At these public meetings, citizens discussed their problems and decided how they should be handled.

Every citizen had a chance to speak on any question. After all opinions were heard, the people at the meeting voted on the question. Thus, each citizen had a direct vote in the government. A New England town meeting was direct democracy in action. Some small New England towns still carry on their business in this way. Town meetings are also held in several states in the Midwest.

The Town Meeting Today

In New England towns today, the regular town meeting is usually held in the spring. A **warrant,** or notice of the town meeting, is posted in various parts of town well before the meeting. It is the official notice of the time

This town meeting is taking place in Lancaster, Massachusetts. Here the tradition of town meeting government, begun in colonial times, continues today.

of the meeting, and it lists the town business to be discussed.

On meeting day, the voters gather in the town hall. Before the meeting gets under way, the town elections are held. Some towns, however, wait until after the meeting to hold their elections. The voters elect several (usually three or five) officials, called **selectmen.** These men and women are responsible for managing the town's affairs during the period between regular town meetings. The voters also elect the other town officials. These officials include a town clerk, members of the school board, a tax collector, a tax assessor, and fish and game wardens. Some towns elect these officials on a separate election day rather than at the town meeting.

Before or after the elections, the voters discuss the town's business. They elect a **moderator** to preside over this part of the meeting. The selectmen who have been in office for the past year report on their activities. The treasurer gives the financial report, explains the debts the town has incurred, and asks the citizens to vote to pay these debts.

Then comes a discussion of town business for the coming year. The voters may be asked to give their opinions on such matters as street lighting, the building of a new school, or the purchase of more snow removal equipment. After the discussion ends, a vote is taken on each item. Voting is usually by voice vote. On important issues, the townspeople stand up to cast their vote.

The Representative Town Meeting

The town meeting form of government works well in areas that have small populations. Direct democracy is practical in such towns because it is easy for all the voters to gather in one central location. For many other towns, however, increases in population and the need for more local services have led to changes.

Some towns have abolished the town meetings and hired town managers to take their place. Other towns have turned to **representative town meetings.** In this type of town government, the voters elect representatives to attend the town meetings and make decisions for them.

Early Township Governments

In the Middle Atlantic states (New York, Pennsylvania, New Jersey, and Delaware), counties were divided into smaller units of local government called **townships.** These served many of the same purposes as the towns in New England. Townships were responsible for maintaining local roads and rural schools and for looking after the poor.

As county governments grew in the Middle Atlantic states, township governments became less important. In time these states developed a form of local government called **county-township government.** In this mixed form of local government, county and township officials worked side by side.

A stronger type of township developed in those Midwestern states that were carved out of the old Northwest Territory between the Ohio and the Mississippi rivers. In 1785 Congress worked out a system of surveying, or measuring, this vast area. According to the system, the Northwest Territory was divided into areas 6 miles square (9.6 kilometers square) called **congressional townships.**

Early congressional townships were not units of government. They were only divisions of land. As settlers from New England moved into this territory, they set up governments similar to the town governments in the states from which they came. The new units of government were called **civil townships.** Sometimes a civil township occupied the same area as a congressional township, but usually it included more territory.

Township Government Today

Township government generally has decreased in importance. In many areas, municipal and county governments have taken over the services once provided by townships. Found today in 20 states—mostly Middle Atlantic and Midwestern states—townships mainly serve rural areas.

Township governments vary from state to state. Usually the township is headed by a chairperson, or **township supervisor.** This official is elected by the voters. The voters also elect a **township board of commissioners,** or **board of trustees,** who make the laws or regulations for the township. Laws are enforced by **constables,** and minor cases are tried by a justice of the peace. Most townships also elect an assessor, a treasurer, a tax collector, and school board members.

Special Districts

Often people living in a certain area within their local unit of government have a special need not shared by others living within the area. In such cases, the people may go directly to the state legislature and ask for a charter setting up a **special district.**

For example, in a farming area in a large Western county, the farmers may wish to have irrigation water for their crops. To pay for the pipes, ditches, and other equipment to supply this need, the state legislature may set up an irrigation district. This special district has no purpose other than to supply water and tax land at a rate sufficient to pay the costs. All other local government services remain in the hands of the county.

As you can see from the chart on page 182, special districts are the most numerous of the nation's local governments. They have been formed to meet many different special needs. Some of these, in addition to supplying water, are sewage disposal, fire and police protection, parks and recreation centers, libraries, public transportation, and gas and electric systems. The legislature usually provides for an elected or appointed commission to handle the details of the special district.

The most common special districts are those set up by each state to provide local schools. There are about 15,000 **school districts** in the United States. Each district has its own governing body called a **board of education.** An executive, usually called a **superintendent of schools,** is employed to manage the schools' day-to-day operations.

Village and Borough Governments

Village government, as you have read, is another unit of local government. When rural communities grow to a population of 200 to 300 people, their inhabitants often have problems that require them to work and plan together. They may then decide to organize their community as a village or borough and set up their own local government.

Libraries are an important service that local governments provide, whether they are public libraries or libraries in public schools.

The request to establish a village or borough government must be sent to the state legislature. If the legislature approves, it permits the village or borough to establish self-government as a municipality. As a municipality, the village or borough can collect its own taxes, set up fire and police departments, and provide other needed services.

The village or borough is often governed by a three- to nine-member council, or board of trustees. The voters also elect an executive called the **chief burgess,** or president of the board of trustees, to carry out the laws. This person is also sometimes called the mayor of the village.

In small boroughs or villages, most of the local officials serve on a part-time basis. There is usually not enough village business to occupy them full time. However, there may be a full-time clerk, constable, street commissioner, and engineer.

If the population of a village or borough becomes large enough, the people may ask the legislature to grant the community a city charter. The number of people needed to qualify as a city varies from state to state. Many states require a population of several thousand people before a city charter is granted.

★ SECTION 2 REVIEW

Define town, village, town meeting, warrant, representative town meetings, townships, county-township government, congressional townships, civil townships, special district, school districts

Identify selectmen, moderator, township supervisor, township board of commissioners, board of trustees, constables, board of education, superintendent of schools, chief burgess

1. **Seeing Relationships (a)** Why is the New England town meeting a form of direct democracy? **(b)** Why have some towns turned to representative town meetings?

2. **Summarizing Ideas (a)** How did townships develop? **(b)** Explain the main purposes served by township government.
3. **Understanding Ideas (a)** Why are special districts formed? **(b)** Identify five needs served by special districts. **(c)** How are school districts run?
4. **Drawing Conclusions** What advantages might a rural community gain by becoming a village?

Thinking Critically You are present at your town meeting. Convince the citizens that your town needs a town manager.

---

③ City Government

More Americans live under city government than under any other unit of local government. A **city** is the largest type of municipality. Some cities, such as New York and Los Angeles, contain over 1 million residents. Often a large population is crowded into a small area. As a result, cities sometimes have more difficult problems than other units of local government.

The city government has to handle a variety of problems dealing with health, education, and safety. It must keep traffic flowing smoothly through neighborhood streets. Police patrols and squad cars must be on the alert to prevent crime. Trash collections must operate efficiently. Street lighting, transportation, water supply, traffic signals, sewage systems—all these and hundreds of other services are the daily business of city governments.

Besides providing such services, city government helps provide cultural activities that are an important part of city life. Cities help support libraries, museums, and parks. City government often contributes to universities, hospitals, and musical groups. Many city governments encourage architects to design buildings that make the city more attractive.

The Organization of City Government

City governments, like all other local governments, are established by state legislatures. That is, they receive charters, or plans of government, from the state legislatures. Increasingly, however, states have been granting to cities what is called **home rule.** Under home rule, a city has the power to write its own municipal charter and to manage its own affairs. The charter must, of course, uphold state law.

Depending on its charter, a city government may take one of three forms: the mayor-council government, the commission government, or the council-manager government. The diagrams on page 190 show the organization of these various forms.

Mayor-Council Government

The oldest and most common form of city government is the **mayor-council plan.** In this kind of government, the lawmaking body is called the **city council.** The chief executive of the city government is the **mayor,** who sees that city laws, or ordinances, are enforced. The mayor and members of the city council are elected by the voters of the city. Their term of office varies, but in most cases it is either two years or four years.

Under the mayor-council government, the city is divided into districts called **wards.** Each ward elects one member of the council. In some cities, though, the people elect several **council members-at-large.** That is, they are chosen by all the voters in the city. Almost all city councils are unicameral.

City voters also elect other officials, including a treasurer, judges of the municipal courts, a city attorney, or solicitor, and tax assessors. Other officials, either elected or appointed, are the heads of departments for police, firefighting, traffic, water, health and welfare, parks and playgrounds, civil defense, housing, licenses, and purchasing.

Can You Guess?

- **What is the oldest city in the United States?**
- **What city has the tallest building in the United States?**
- **What city in the United States has the most people?**
- **In what city is the NASA Space Center located?**

Answers are on page 594.

Weak-Mayor Plan. During the early years of our nation's growth, the American people were slow to grant power to their mayors. The experience of colonists with British governors who did not listen to the people's wishes made Americans fear officials who might have too much power. For this reason, some cities developed the **weak-mayor plan.**

Under the weak-mayor plan of city government, the city council holds more power than the mayor. For example, the council appoints the heads of city departments. These heads report directly to the city council. In addition, the mayor must obtain the consent of the council in order to spend money or take other actions. The weak-mayor plan often results in conflicts between the mayor and the council.

Strong-Mayor Plan. In recent years, most mayor-council cities have tried to make their governments more efficient by following the **strong-mayor plan** of city government. Under the strong-mayor plan, the mayor has chief responsibility for running the city's government.

The mayor appoints most of the city officials and can also dismiss them if they do not do a good job. The mayor can also veto bills passed by the council. It is the mayor's responsibility to draw up the city budget. When the council has approved a budget, the mayor must see that the city's money is spent properly. Under this strong-mayor plan, the

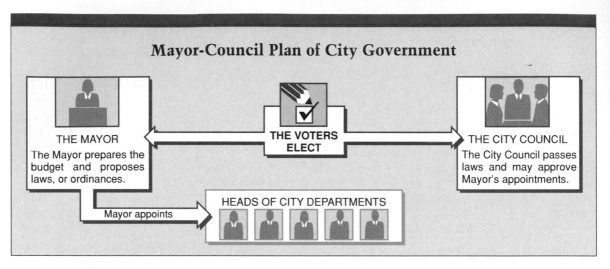

Mayor-Council Plan of City Government

THE VOTERS ELECT

THE MAYOR
The Mayor prepares the budget and proposes laws, or ordinances.

THE CITY COUNCIL
The City Council passes laws and may approve Mayor's appointments.

Mayor appoints

HEADS OF CITY DEPARTMENTS

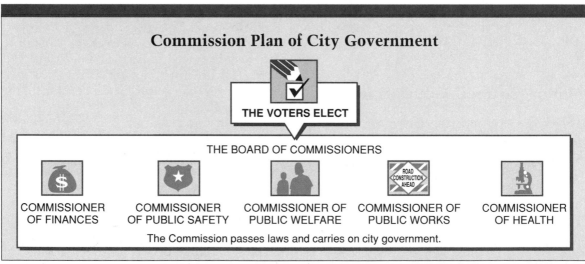

Commission Plan of City Government

THE VOTERS ELECT

THE BOARD OF COMMISSIONERS

| COMMISSIONER OF FINANCES | COMMISSIONER OF PUBLIC SAFETY | COMMISSIONER OF PUBLIC WELFARE | COMMISSIONER OF PUBLIC WORKS | COMMISSIONER OF HEALTH |

The Commission passes laws and carries on city government.

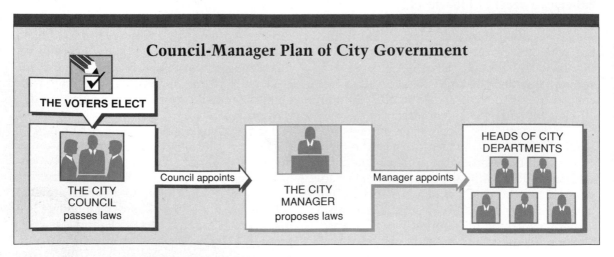

Council-Manager Plan of City Government

THE VOTERS ELECT

THE CITY COUNCIL
passes laws

Council appoints

THE CITY MANAGER
proposes laws

Manager appoints

HEADS OF CITY DEPARTMENTS

mayor takes the lead in carrying on the city's business.

Commission Government

A new form of government grew out of a hurricane that struck Galveston, Texas, in 1900. A huge tidal wave swept across the city, flooding homes and businesses and causing millions of dollars in damages. Nearly 7,000 of the city's 37,000 residents lost their lives. The city's mayor and council were unable to handle the disaster. Yet something had to be done.

Leading citizens in Galveston asked the state legislature for permission to set up a new form of city government. It was called the **commission plan.** Within a few years, this plan of government had been adopted by several hundred other cities.

Under the commission plan, a city is governed by a **commission,** usually consisting of five elected officials. The commission is the city's lawmaking body as well as its executive body. The commission passes the city's ordinances. Each commissioner heads an important department of city government.

One commissioner usually is the head of the department of public safety, which includes the police and firefighters. Another commissioner, in charge of public works, must see that the city has an adequate supply of pure water and that the streets are kept in good repair. A third commissioner oversees the city's finances, including tax collections. Another runs the public welfare department, which helps the poor, the aged, and the unemployed. The health department is managed by a commissioner who supervises hospitals, clinics, and health inspectors.

The commissioners meet as a group to make the city laws. However, they enforce the laws individually. Each commissioner carries out the laws that apply to his or her own department. Either the voters or the commissioners choose one of the commissioners to be mayor. The mayor under this plan has no special powers. Except for presiding over meetings of the commission, the mayor has the same powers as other commissioners.

In some cases, the commission form of city government has had certain disadvantages. The voters sometimes have found it impossible to elect officials who know how to run a department of the city's government. Then, too, there are activities of city government that can come under the jurisdiction of several departments. Sometimes commissioners disagree about who should handle these activities. Therefore, the commission plan is now used by fewer than 10 percent of American cities.

Council-Manager Government

In 1908 Staunton, Virginia, was the first city to set up a **council-manager plan** of government. Today this plan of government is used by a growing number of cities.

Under the council-manager plan, voters elect a city council to act as the city's lawmaking body. The council then appoints

Keeping city streets in good repair is just one of the many services provided by city governments.

a **city manager.** The city manager, as the city's chief executive, appoints the heads of the departments. They report directly to the city manager. Under this plan, the city is run much like any big business firm by specially trained people.

City managers are appointed, not elected, so that they will not take part in party politics or be under any political pressure. They are given a free hand to run city governments efficiently and economically. If a city manager does not do a good job, the council may dismiss him or her and appoint a new manager.

The council-manager plan of government has certain disadvantages. Some smaller cities cannot afford the salary required to hire a good manager. Other cities believe they are better governed when the voters themselves elect the officials who are to run the city's government.

 SECTION 3 REVIEW

Define city, home rule, mayor-council plan, wards, weak-mayor plan, strong-mayor plan, commission plan, council-manager plan

Identify city council, mayor, council members-at-large, commission, city manager

1. **Understanding Ideas (a)** Explain why cities sometimes have more problems than other units of local government. **(b)** How are city governments established?
2. **Comparing Ideas** Describe the advantages and disadvantages of each of the three main kinds of city government.
3. **Identifying Ideas (a)** Why were Americans slow to grant power to mayors during our nation's early years? **(b)** Why have cities recently turned to the strong-mayor plan?

Thinking Critically You head a panel chosen to identify the major social problems currently plaguing our cities. Name the two most pressing problems and explain why you chose them.

4 How Our Governments Work Together

You live under three levels of government—local, state, and national. If each level of government paid no attention to the work of the others, life would become difficult and confusing. City governments might pass city laws that conflicted with state laws. State governments might ignore federal laws and do whatever they wished. No citizen could be sure which set of laws to obey.

How Powers Are Divided Among Our Governments

Fortunately, under our federal system of government, the powers of each level of government are clearly defined and understood. The Constitution of the United States is the "supreme law of the land." All levels of government must obey it.

Our state constitutions, in turn, set up rules that govern the people of each state. These state constitutions must not, of course, take away from the people any of the rights guaranteed in the federal Constitution.

Local units of government, as you have read, have their powers defined for them by the state legislatures. These powers are explained in their charters. In this way, each level of government has its own work to do. Each level is given the powers needed to do its job.

Why Our Governments Work Together

Many of our nation's problems call for cooperation among local, state, and national governments. Consider, for example, the way our modern highway system was built.

Back in colonial days, the building of a road was considered a local project. If the peo-

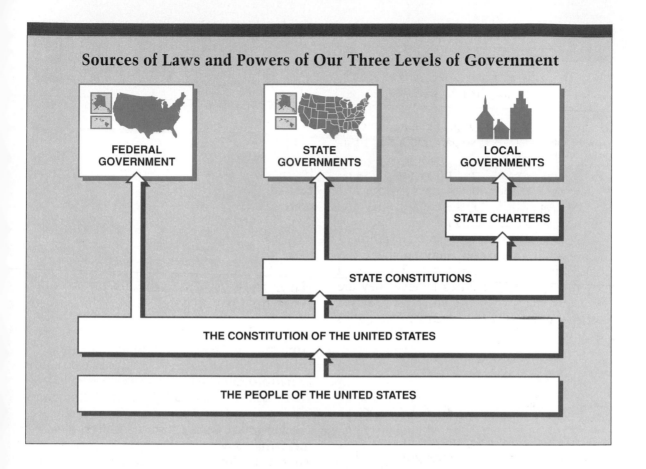

Sources of Laws and Powers of Our Three Levels of Government

FEDERAL GOVERNMENT

STATE GOVERNMENTS

LOCAL GOVERNMENTS

STATE CHARTERS

STATE CONSTITUTIONS

THE CONSTITUTION OF THE UNITED STATES

THE PEOPLE OF THE UNITED STATES

ple of any town wanted a road, they had to build it themselves. As towns spread westward, each county undertook to build connecting roads. The county called upon local farmers and townspeople to supply the labor or provide money to hire workers.

These early roads were often twisting and rutted, dusty in dry weather, and muddy after rain. They were, however, cheap to build and repair. Local governments could easily plan and pay for such roads.

As our nation grew, highways were needed to connect the East with the growing West. Therefore, Congress voted to have the federal government build some main roads to the West. The most important of these early roads was the **National Road** (or Cumberland Road). It started at Cumberland, Maryland, and went as far west as Vandalia, Illinois.

Still, for a long time, most roads were built by local governments or private companies. These roads were paid for by collecting **tolls,** or fees, from the people who used them. When the automobile was invented, it became clear that road building was no longer a local problem alone. Motorists needed highways that would stretch across their home state and connect with roads in other states.

Governments Cooperate in Road Building

Late in the 1800's, even before automobiles were in common use, New Jersey was the first state to use state funds to help its counties improve their local roads. Massachusetts
(continued on page 196)

Saving the Covered Bridges

There once were more than 10,000 covered bridges in the United States. Today only about 1,000 of these wooden structures are still standing. A group of students in Scio (SY-oh), Oregon, decided to try to help save some of them.

Opinion Is Divided

Oregon was in the midst of a debate over which of the state's 56 covered bridges should be placed on the *National Register of Historic Places.* Bridges placed on this register are considered historical landmarks and cannot be torn down. Some people favored listing as many bridges as possible. They thought this might make it easier to get money from the federal government to preserve the bridges. Others argued that listing the bridges would cause the federal government to become too involved in local affairs.

Linn County, where the small town of Scio is located, has ten covered bridges. County officials were divided over a plan that called for placing five of the bridges on the register. In general, officials opposed the plan. They were afraid that paying for the upkeep of the bridges would cause taxes to rise.

The Scio Bridge Brigade

Since eight of the ten bridges in Linn County were near Scio, the townspeople were very interested in the county's decision. It was the students, though, who acted. Many of them passed through a covered bridge every day on their way to and from school. They had fond thoughts about the bridges. One student remembered catching his first fish from a covered bridge. Another thought of the many times she had stopped her bicycle to rest under the roof of a covered bridge. Still others knew what the bridges meant to their parents and grandparents and what they would mean to people in the future. According to one student, "We need touches of the past for our future."

At the urging of a social studies teacher, the students organized themselves into the Scio Bridge Brigade. They wrote down their thoughts about the bridges and sent them to county officials. The students didn't stop there. They went from door to door trying to win support for their cause. They spoke about the bridges at public hearings. They wrote letters to newspapers. They invited the Covered Bridge Society of Oregon to meet in Scio. From money they made from a jog-a-thon, brigade members published a pamphlet of their poems and drawings about the bridges. They carried on their campaign in as many ways as possible.

The members of the Scio Bridge Brigade were successful. As a result of their efforts, five of the county's ten covered bridges have been listed on the *National Register of Historic Places*. For its work the Scio Bridge Brigade won an award from the National Trust for Historic Preservation. The students succeeded in preserving part of our nation's heritage because they cared enough to take action.

Thinking It Over

1. What were the arguments for and against placing the covered bridges on the *National Register of Historic Places*?
2. Why do you think the students were able to convince public officials to preserve some of the bridges?
3. Do you think a special effort should be made to preserve links to America's past, such as covered bridges? Explain. What other links with our nation's past can you think of?

These members of the Scio Bridge Brigade provide a valuable example of citizenship in action.

This well-traveled highway in Texas is part of a vast coast-to-coast highway system. It is just one example of cooperation between federal and state governments.

went a step further in 1894, when it began to build a statewide highway system. Other states soon followed the lead of New Jersey and Massachusetts and set up state highway departments to build main roads.

Today, most well-traveled roads are built and maintained by the state. Each year state governments spend billions of dollars to build and improve roads and keep them safe.

The federal government also has an important role in our states' road-building programs. It pays a large part of the cost of new state highways. It does so because good roads contribute to the welfare of all American citizens.

The **interstate highway system,** planned by the federal government, now connects all parts of the nation. It is a joint project of the federal and state governments. The states plan the routes and supervise construction of the roads. The roads must meet federal requirements.

The federal government pays 90 cents of every dollar of the cost of building and maintaining our nation's highways. This money comes from a highway trust fund to which motorists contribute when they pay taxes on gasoline. The federal government also assists state and local governments in building other highways, bridges, and tunnels.

Other Ways in Which Governments Cooperate

Our local, state, and federal governments work together in many other ways. For example, local and state police cooperate with the Federal Bureau of Investigation to capture suspects. Most states have crime laboratories, whose services also are used by local police officials. State and local police may obtain helpful information, such as fingerprints, from FBI files. Suspects arrested and convicted by local governments are often sent to prisons maintained by state governments.

Stores and businesses must obey many state laws that promote good business practices. Workers in local factories or mines are protected by state inspectors who see that safety regulations are obeyed. State bank inspectors help keep your savings safe.

State governments also serve local communities by setting up state licensing boards. These boards give examinations and issue licenses to doctors, dentists, lawyers, engineers, nurses, teachers, and accountants. This service helps ensure that communities have qualified professional workers.

Local, State, and Federal Cooperation in Education

Public education is one of the most important areas in which our governments cooperate to serve the public. State governments grant funds to local communities to help them operate their schools. State boards of education provide services for local school districts and see that they obey state laws. Actual control of the schools, however, is left to local boards of education. These local boards know the needs of the students in their schools.

The federal government cooperates by helping with special funds for schools. Schools with a large number of students from poor areas receive special federal aid to enrich their educational programs. The federal government also provides school lunch programs for needy students. In addition, the federal government supports research in education.

Other Federal Aid Programs

The federal government provides state and local governments with funds to help them carry out important programs. **Grants-in-aid** are federal funds given to state and local governments for specific projects, such as airport construction or pollution control. The receiv-

ing government must meet certain standards and conditions, and often must provide some money of its own for the project. Grant-in-aid projects are subject to supervision by the federal government.

Block grants are funds given by the federal government for broad purposes. State and local governments develop and carry out the programs, and decide how the funds will be spent. They must, however, develop a spending plan and report how the funds were spent.

City Governments Work Together

Our cities face many common problems. For example, city governments are concerned about how to get more money for police officers, firefighters, and teachers. They look for ways to lessen air pollution and to dispose of trash safely. The **United States Conference of Mayors** meets regularly so that the mayors of our cities may compare problems and discuss possible solutions.

As neighboring cities grow closer together, they often share many problems. For

Through the FBI, the federal government keeps millions of sets of fingerprints on file. Local and state criminal investigators often make use of this file.

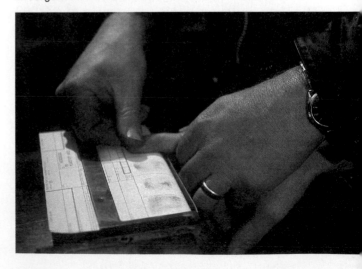

All communities face the risk of fires. Therefore, our local governments must have the funds to keep fire departments always ready for action.

example, many villages and townships make up Nassau County on Long Island, New York. The population of this area grew from 300,000 in 1947 to nearly a million and a half in 1970. Soon one community had merged into the next in an almost continuous line. The officials of the various local units realized that close cooperation by all Nassau County communities was becoming a necessity.

For greater efficiency and better service, the officials of the various localities got together and agreed that their communities should combine and share most of their services. Fire alarms are now answered by the fire departments of several neighboring communities. Local schools are shared, which allows students to attend schools offering special courses they need. The costs of trash collec-

tion, water, and other services are shared. Only the police departments are maintained separately by the various towns, but even here Nassau County communities cooperate closely.

Governments Also Compete

Although cooperation among our various governments is growing, governments also compete with one another. The various levels of government often compete for taxes. For example, a family may have to pay income taxes to both state and federal governments. There may be a city income tax as well. Residents may also have to pay a sizable real estate tax to their local governments.

States compete with each other to attract industry. They offer businesses lower taxes, a good supply of labor, good highways, and favorable laws to encourage industry to move to their state. Cities compete for trade and industry in similar fashion.

The federal government and federal laws sometimes seem to interfere or compete with local laws and customs. For example, the federal government may challenge the election procedures in a state or locality if such procedures conflict with federal law.

Our combined system of federal, state, and local governments is complex. It would be surprising if there were not instances of conflict. Only by working together can we make our democratic form of government work.

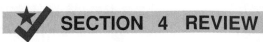

SECTION 4 REVIEW

Define tolls, interstate highway system, grants-in-aid, block grants

Identify National Road, United States Conference of Mayors

1. **Summarizing Ideas (a)** Trace the history of our highway system. **(b)** Why is the federal government interested in better roads?
2. **Composing an Essay** Write an essay that discusses how our governments both cooperate and compete with each other.

Thinking Critically You are a farmer living in the early 1800's. Write a letter to the President that will convince him of the need for the National Road.

Each of us is directly affected by local government. The governments of our cities, towns, townships, and counties take care of many of the practical needs of our lives. They provide fire and police protection, a water supply, a sewer system, trash removal, and other necessary services.

County governments serve the common needs of people over a fairly large area. In some states, more and more power has been given to the towns and cities, and the counties serve mainly as election districts.

Town meetings still serve much of New England and some parts of the Middle West. The rapid growth of population, however, has caused larger New England towns to hire town managers or set up representative town meetings.

Town and township governments in many areas work with the county in governing and in providing services to their communities. Special districts, especially in rural areas, provide such services as sewage systems, water supply, and local schools.

City government has had to meet many special problems in recent years. Some cities have kept the mayor-council plan of government. Others have turned to the commission plan or are using the council-manager plan of government.

Federal, state, and local governments cooperate in many ways. Sometimes, though, the various governments compete for taxes, trade, and industry.

CHAPTER
9
SUMMARY

LIFE SKILL
Reading a Newspaper Article

Important decisions are being made on a daily basis in the United States. Moreover, we live in a rapidly changing world in which the events happening in far-away nations can have an impact on our everyday lives. In fact, the world is fast becoming a global community. This means that there is increasing interdependence and cooperation among the nations of the world.

It is therefore important for citizens to stay informed about what is happening in the nation and around the world. The best source of information on current events is the newspaper. Newspaper articles generally are written according to a standard format. Learning to recognize that format is the key to becoming an informed citizen.

How to Read a Newspaper Article

To get the most out of newspaper articles, follow these guidelines.

1. **Read the headlines.** A headline is a short statement printed in large, bold type above the article. It contains key words designed to capture your attention and present the main point of the article.
2. **Notice the dateline and the byline.** The dateline and the byline are located just below the headline. If a news story happens outside the area in which you live, it will probably contain a dateline. The dateline tells you where the article was written, and may include the date when it was written. The byline tells you who wrote the article—either a reporter or a news service. The two largest news services are United Press International (UPI) and Associated Press (AP).
3. **Skim the lead.** The lead, or first sentence, of a news article is designed to tell you who did what, where, when, how, and often, why.

4. **Read the body for details.** The paragraphs following the lead make up the body of the article. The body usually contains the "why," of the story, including quotations and details. Reading the body of the article will give you a well-rounded picture of the event or situation.
5. **Distinguish between news and editorials.** What you should *not* find in a news article is the writer's opinion or point of view. Writers present their points of view in editorials, found on the editorial pages of the newspaper. Citizens who disagree with editorials or who want to express their own opinions may write letters to the editor.

Applying the Skill

The article below reports a community event. Read it to answer the following questions.
1. **(a)** What does the dateline tell you? **(b)** What does the byline tell you?
2. What questions are answered by the facts given in the lead?

LAKEVILLE, Mich. (AP)—"It was the most successful celebration we've ever seen," said Lakeville officials just one day after the city's annual July Fourth cleanup.

In what has by now become a tradition, people in Lakeville once again did more than watch parades on Independence Day—they also swept sidewalks, planted flowers, and picked up litter.

The idea first caught on in 1976 when Lakeville decided to do something different for the nation's 200th birthday. Response to a city-wide cleanup was so enthusiastic, the city council decided to make it a regular event.

CHAPTER ⑨ REVIEW

Reviewing Terms

On a separate sheet of paper, supply the term that correctly answers each question.

1. What does Louisiana call its counties?
2. What term identifies a local governmental unit formed to meet a special need?
3. What is the largest type of municipality?
4. What term refers to a local governmental unit's plan of government?
5. What word identifies the group of officials who manage a town's business?
6. What are the regulations that govern a community called?
7. What word is used to describe the fees paid by people who use certain roads?
8. What term describes the power of a city to write its own plan of government?

Using Thinking Skills

1. **Contrasting Ideas (a)** How do grants-in-aid differ from block grants? **(b)** How do representative town meetings differ from traditional town meetings?
2. **Identifying Roles** Describe the role of each of the following in local government: county clerk, moderator, constable, chief burgess, mayor.
3. **Identifying Ideas (a)** Explain how local governments are established. **(b)** What would a unit of local government gain by becoming incorporated? **(c)** What services are provided by local governments?
4. **Summarizing Ideas** List and describe the three main types of city government.
5. **Seeing Relationships (a)** How does a county serve both the state and the people in that state? **(b)** How were congressional townships formed, and how did they become civil townships?
6. **Expressing Ideas (a)** How do federal, state, and local governments cooperate in road building? **(b)** In what other ways do these units of government cooperate?

7. **Understanding Ideas (a)** Discuss some of the problems faced by city governments. **(b)** How do city governments provide for the cultural needs of their citizens?

Practicing Civics Skills

Interpreting Sources Using a copy of your local newspaper, select one recent news story about your local government and one recent news story about the government of a foreign nation. For each of these stories, answer the following questions: **(a)** What information is given in the headline? **(b)** What information is given in the byline? **(c)** What facts are given in the lead?

Being a Good Citizen

1. Organize the class into groups to prepare maps of your community. Show the most important streets, buildings, and parks. Display the maps in class.
2. Invite the mayor, a council member, or some other local official to talk to your class and explain how your community is governed.
3. Interview a member of a volunteer service organization in your community to find out what it is the organization does and how students can become involved. Report to the class on your findings.
4. Organize the class into groups. Have each group choose one city in the United States and conduct research to learn how that city's government is organized and how it operates. Construct an organizational chart of the city's government to display in class.
5. Visit your school library or a local library to read about the history of your community. Report to the class the main facts about the founding and growth of your city or town. Also talk about the early leaders of your community.

Reviewing the Facts

1. **(a)** What is extradition? **(b)** How does it uphold the full faith and credit clause of the Constitution?
2. **(a)** What is a county? **(b)** Whcre and how did the county form of government begin in the United States?
3. **(a)** What is an initiative? **(b)** What is a referendum? **(c)** What is a recall?
4. **(a)** What are municipalities? **(b)** How are they established?
5. **(a)** What is a town meeting? **(b)** Why can it be said that the town meeting is a form of direct democracy? **(c)** Why do some towns use representative town meetings?
6. **(a)** What is a territory? **(b)** How did the Northwest Ordinance help our nation grow to its current 50 states?

Using Critical Thinking

1. **Summarizing Ideas** Describe the powers and duties of a state governor.
2. **Understanding Ideas (a)** Why are special districts formed? **(b)** How are school districts governed?
3. **Comparing Ideas (a)** How do felonies differ from misdemeanors? **(b)** How do criminal cases differ from civil cases? **(c)** Why do people use appeals courts?
4. **Identifying Ideas (a)** Why did some cities develop the weak-mayor plan of government? **(b)** What duties does a mayor have under the strong-mayor plan?
5. **Composing a Paragraph** Write a paragraph that traces the process through which a bill becomes a state law.
6. **Expressing Ideas** Explain why it can be said that our interstate highway system is a joint project of the federal and state governments.
7. **Identifying Roles** Describe the role of each of the following in state or local government: lieutenant governor, moderator, Speaker, county prosecuting attorney.

8. **Drawing Conclusions (a)** What six parts are contained in most state constitutions? **(b)** Explain how a charter is like a state constitution.

Applying What You Know

1. Choose an article from your local newspaper that reports a recent action taken by your state legislature. Read the article carefully. Then write a letter to the editor of the newspaper expressing your point of view concerning the action of the legislature.
2. Organize the class into groups. Have each group conduct library research to find newspaper and magazine articles about teenage volunteers who are helping their communities. Summarize each of the articles to share with the class.
3. Suppose that a criminal suspect was thought to be hiding out in your community. How might the local, state, and federal governments work together to find the suspect?
4. Conduct a mock town meeting in your class. Post a warrant giving the date and time of the meeting and listing the town business to be discussed. Elect a moderator to preside over the meeting. Have students act as town citizens to discuss issues that would concern a town.

Expanding Your Knowledge

Batchelor, John E., *States' Rights*, Franklin Watts. Discussion of conflicts between state legislatures and national government.

League of Women Voters Education Fund, *Know Your Community*, League of Women Voters. How you can learn about your local government.

Lefkowitz, William, *Government at Work: From City Hall to State Capitol*, Alemany Press. Discussion of the workings of government at various levels.

The Citizen in American Government

Electing Our Leaders

Chapter Sections

Chapter Focus

Are you ready to vote? The Twenty-sixth Amendment to the Constitution of the United States gives you the right to vote when you are 18 years of age. At that time you will be faced with the challenge of casting your vote intelligently for national, state, and local officials. Your vote will help choose the leaders of our nation and determine the way billions of dollars will be spent. The policies of our nation as well as of your state and local community will be determined in part by you.

Great attention is focused every four years on the Presidential election. Choosing a person to lead our nation is important to all of us. Equally important, however, are congressional, state, and local elections.

To make your vote count most, you should take an active part in our political system. Working to elect candidates you believe in is an excellent way to participate in politics.

Study Guide

As you begin to learn about how Americans choose their leaders, look for answers to the following questions:

★ What are political parties, and what purposes do they serve?

★ Why are there two main political parties in the United States?

★ How are political parties organized?

★ How are our leaders nominated and elected?

1 Our Two-Party System of Politics

Nowhere in the Constitution will you find any provision for political parties. They are not an official part of the organization of our government. Anyone who has lived in our country at election time, however, knows that political parties are a very important part of our democratic way of life.

What Is a Political Party?

A **political party** is an organization made up of citizens who usually have similar ideas on public issues and who work to put their ideas into effect through government action. To achieve their purposes, political parties try to get the voters to elect to public office those whom the party favors. Parties also work hard to get laws that they favor passed.

In the United States, political parties are voluntary. All citizens are free to join the party of their choice. Or they may decide not to join any party. Americans who join a political party usually do so because they agree with most of that party's ideas. Of course, not all members of a political party agree on every issue. If members are in serious disagreement with a party on important issues, they are free to leave the party. They may then join another

political party or decide not to belong to any party at all.

As members of a political party, Americans can join with other citizens in trying to put their party's ideas to work in our local, state, and national governments. Political parties play a large role in helping the American people govern themselves.

Why We Have Political Parties

Why do we have political parties in the United States? The reason is simple. Political parties offer a practical way for large numbers of people with similar ideas to get things done. Political parties are concerned with practical politics. This means that the parties are concerned with what actions our governments should take.

Everyone's life is affected by practical politics. When you complain about the high cost of living, you are taking a practical interest in politics. If you just complain, you are not very effective. If you join with other citizens who agree with you, however, you can make your voice heard in a way that gets better results. Political parties serve this purpose.

Political parties also **nominate**, or select, candidates for public office. **Candidates** are the men and women who run for election to offices at various levels of our government. Most of the people who serve in public office in the United States have been elected to their offices as candidates of political parties. It is not impossible, but it is very difficult, for a person to run for office without the support of a political party.

Political parties also take positions on public issues. They try to get laws passed. During the election campaign, each party tries to convince the voters that it offers the best program.

After an election, the winning candidates become the leaders of our government—the ones who make and carry out our laws. The political party to which these leaders belong tries to make sure they do a good job. In this

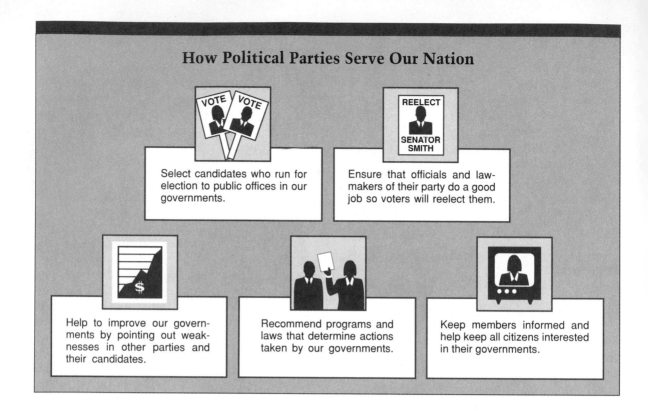

How Political Parties Serve Our Nation

Select candidates who run for election to public offices in our governments.

Ensure that officials and law-makers of their party do a good job so voters will reelect them.

Help to improve our governments by pointing out weaknesses in other parties and their candidates.

Recommend programs and laws that determine actions taken by our governments.

Keep members informed and help keep all citizens interested in their governments.

way, it hopes to ensure that the party's candidates will win again in the next election. The party whose candidates lost the election will be watching for any weaknesses or mistakes the new leaders may make while in office. This party also will be quick to inform the public if the winning party's candidates do not keep their campaign promises after they are elected.

How Our Two-Party System Started

The history of political parties dates back to the late 1700's, when our government first began to operate under the Constitution. The first political parties began during President George Washington's administration. As you read in Chapter 2, those people who favored a strong federal government were called Federalists. Those people who favored limiting the power of the central government were called Anti-Federalists. Later they were known as Democratic-Republicans.

Alexander Hamilton became the leader of the Federalists. He proposed policies that would make the federal government strong. Thomas Jefferson, the leader of the Democratic-Republicans, opposed Hamilton and the Federalist Party. Jefferson and the Democratic-Republicans tried to limit the power of the federal government.

As President Washington watched these two different points of view lead to the establishment of political parties, he became worried. He feared that the growth of parties would weaken the new nation. In his Farewell Address as President, Washington warned Americans that political parties were dangerous because they could divide the nation.

Washington's warnings, however, were soon forgotten. Political parties became a lasting part of government in the United States. Throughout most of our history, the United States has had two strong political parties.

Beginnings of the Democratic and Republican Parties

For more than 135 years, the Democratic Party and the Republican Party have been our nation's two major political parties. The present **Democratic Party** traces its roots to Jefferson's Democratic-Republican Party. In the 1820's, that party split into several groups.

One group, led by Andrew Jackson, became the Democratic Party. Jackson believed that the government was being run for the benefit of the wealthy. He was determined that the federal government should represent frontier settlers, farmers, and city laborers—the common people. Jackson was elected President in 1828, and the Democratic Party he established began its long history.

The present **Republican Party** was formed in 1854. In that year, several small groups that opposed the policies of the Democratic Party joined together. The Republican Party was started by people who were against slavery and who opposed the spread of slavery into the territories. In 1860 Abraham Lincoln became the first candidate nominated by the Republican Party to be elected President of the United States.

Advantages of a Two-Party System

Since then, these two political parties have had almost equal strength. Beginning with Jackson, the Democrats have elected 13 Presidents who, up to 1990, served for a total of 72 years. The Republicans, starting with Lincoln, have had 18 Presidents who, up to 1990, served for a total of 81 years.

Thomas Jefferson (left) and Alexander Hamilton (right) disagreed about how government should operate. They were the leaders of our first political parties.

Theodore Roosevelt was one of our nation's most popular third-party candidates. His spirited speeches always attracted a large and enthusiastic crowd.

Coalition governments, however, have certain disadvantages. Often the political parties disagree, and the coalition breaks apart. This makes the government and the nation weak. Several European nations have this **multi-party system.** Some nations, such as Italy, have had great difficulty in governing themselves because of the many small political parties. However, in the Netherlands and other nations this system has worked well.

Third Parties

Besides the two strong political parties in the United States, there are also a number of minor political parties. In national elections, there are always several candidates who have been nominated by these minor political parties. Minor parties usually are called **third parties.** At certain times in our history, they have had great influence.

In 1912 Theodore Roosevelt was denied the Presidential nomination of the Republican Party and started a third political party, called the Progressive Party. Roosevelt ran for President as the nominee of this party. He was not elected. But he took away enough votes from the Republican candidate, William Taft, to permit the Democratic candidate, Woodrow Wilson, to win.

At other times in American history, third parties have proposed new ideas that were opposed at first by the major political parties but were later adopted. For example, in the late 1800's the Populist Party was formed by a group of Americans that favored several new ideas. One of these ideas was the election of United States senators directly by the voters. The leaders of the two major parties favored the election of senators by state legislatures as provided in the Constitution.

When Populist ideas began to find favor with the American people, some of these ideas were taken over by the major parties. In time some of these ideas, such as the direct election of senators, were put into effect. The method of electing United States senators was

This **two-party system,** as we call it, has worked remarkably well. When one party fails to please a majority of voters, there is another strong party ready to take over. The newly elected party often tries different programs and policies in dealing with the nation's problems.

If we had more than two strong political parties, all of about equal strength, no one party would be able to win a majority of votes. In order to run the government, then, two or more of the political parties would have to work out a compromise and agree to work together. This agreement between two or more political parties to work together to run the government is called a **coalition.**

changed by the Seventeenth Amendment to the Constitution.

Recent Third-Party Trends

Minor political parties have been active throughout most of the nation's history. Third-party candidates continue to run for office. Usually they receive very few votes.

Sometimes, though, third-party candidates attract many voters. In 1968 George Wallace, former governor of Alabama, ran for President as the candidate of the American Independent Party. He received 9.9 million votes, or 13.5 percent of the votes. Representative John Anderson of Illinois, an Independent Presidential candidate, won 7 percent of the votes in 1980.

One-Party Governments

In nations with more than one political party, the voters have a choice. They can decide which party to join and for which party to vote. In many other nations, governments have been based on a **one-party system.** That is, there is just one political party in the nation. All other political parties are forbidden by law. Such nations are sometimes called dictatorships.

In a dictatorship, as you have read, all power is in the hands of one person or a group of people. In a one-party government, a single party controls the government. It dictates, or commands, and the people must obey.

Italy under Benito Mussolini and Germany under Adolf Hitler had such governments. Today Vietnam, the People's Republic of China, and other communist nations are dictatorships with one political party. Our nation has traditionally opposed dictatorships, because such governments do not allow freedom of thought and action for their people. Americans consider such freedoms essential because they believe government should be responsible to the people.

 SECTION 1 REVIEW

Define political party, nominate, candidates, two-party system, coalition, multi-party system, third parties, one-party system

Identify Democratic Party, Republican Party

1. **Understanding Ideas** What purposes do political parties serve?
2. **Summarizing Information** (a) Explain how the two-party system in America began. (b) What are the major advantages of a two-party system?
3. **Drawing Conclusions** Why do coalition governments often last only a short period of time?
4. **Seeing Relationships** How have third parties influenced elections?

Thinking Critically Imagine that you are living in a country that has a one-party system of government. Write a paragraph in which you consider how your life would be different from the way it is now.

2 The Organization of Political Parties

In order to work effectively, a political party must be well organized. It must have leaders, committees, and workers who are able to carry out the party's program. It must be organized at the local, state, and national levels. The party must also be able to raise money to pay for its expenses. The party must nominate its candidates for office and plan its campaign to get these candidates elected. There are hundreds of details that have to be given careful attention.

Today, our two major parties operate the way they do because their members have worked out these procedures over the years. Interestingly, both major parties are organized in much the same way.

Party Committees and Their Jobs

The planning for each political party is done through a series of committees. Each political party has a national committee, state central committees, county committees, and city committees. Each of these party committees is headed by a chairperson. The members are usually elected by the party voters at election time. Sometimes, however, the committee members are chosen at meetings of party leaders. These meetings of party leaders are known as **caucuses.**

The National Committee. The largest party committee is the national committee. Membership on this committee carries great distinction. For many years, it consisted of one committeeman and one committeewoman from each state, each territory, and the District of Columbia. In the 1970's, though, each party enlarged the membership of its national committee.

Members of the national committee may be chosen in three ways. They may be elected by a state convention or by voters in a statewide election, or they may be chosen by the state central committee. The chairperson of the national committee is often chosen by the party's Presidential candidate.

The national committee selects the city in which the **national nominating convention** is to be held. At this convention, or official meeting of the party, the party's Presidential candidate is chosen. The national committee is responsible for setting the date and drawing up rules for the convention.

During an election year, the national committee publishes and distributes party literature and arranges for campaign speakers. It also helps the Presidential candidate to plan and conduct the campaign. Another job of the national committee is to raise money for the party.

State Central Committees. Each political party has a state central committee to supervise the party's operation within each of the 50 states. The chairperson of the state central committee is one of the party's most prominent members in the state. He or she is often a member of the national committee.

The state central committee represents the party organization in each state. Like the national committee, it is busiest at election time. The state chairperson works with the members of the state central committee to keep up a strong state organization and to maintain party harmony. The committee works to raise money for campaigns and to help candidates win elections.

Local Committees. At the local level are county committees and city committees. Township committees are sometimes found in rural areas. Members of local committees are elected by party members. The chairperson of each committee is elected by its members. He or she is the local party leader.

The party's success or failure often depends on what the local committees and their leaders do. The county or city committee is responsible for conducting all campaigns on the local level. It raises money for the party and its candidates. Through the local chairperson, the committee makes recommendations for political appointments and for candidates for office. A strong local chairperson may stay in office for many years and become powerful in the party.

Local Party Organization

To make voting easier for our citizens, counties, cities, and wards are divided into voting districts called **precincts.** The voters in each precinct vote at the same place, which is called a **polling place.** A rural precinct may cover large areas of countryside. A precinct in a crowded city may cover just a few blocks. The party leader in the precinct is called the **precinct captain.** The precinct captain encourages all voters to get out and vote for the party's candidates.

At election time, precinct captains are very busy. They organize volunteers to hand out the party's campaign literature. They see

How Our Political Parties Are Organized

NATIONAL COMMITTEE

STATE CENTRAL COMMITTEES

COUNTY COMMITTEES

CITY COMMITTEES

WARD COMMITTEEMEN AND COMMITTEEWOMEN

PRECINCT CAPTAINS (LOCAL COMMITTEEMEN AND COMMITTEEWOMEN)

THE AMERICAN VOTERS WHO ARE MEMBERS OF THE PARTY

that pictures of the party's candidates are displayed in local shops and on neighborhood billboards. Precinct captains may arrange to have disabled voters driven to the polling place. They also see that party workers telephone voters, urging them to cast their votes for the party candidates. The precinct captains are also busy between elections getting to know the people in the neighborhood.

Political Party Finances

Running for political office is very expensive. Candidates for President, for example, need millions of dollars to run their campaigns. Their costs include office rent, secretaries, printing posters and handbills, radio and television broadcasts, and traveling expenses. From where does all this money come?

Until recently all political campaigns were paid for entirely with private contributions. Most campaigns are still paid for this way. Voters are urged to contribute to the political party of their choice. Business groups, labor unions, farm organizations, and many other kinds of groups contribute to the political party that they believe best represents their interests.

Political parties work hard to raise money. Several times a year, they hold large fund-raising dinners. The money raised at these dinners goes into the party's treasury.

Whenever large campaign contributions are made, however, people worry about corruption. Will a big contributor receive special favors in return for helping the winning candidate? To lessen the possibility of political corruption, the United States Congress passed the Federal Election Campaign Act and the accompanying Revenue Act in 1971.

The Federal Election Campaign Act requires every political candidate to report the name of every person who contributes $200 or more to his or her election campaign. The Revenue Act limits individual contributions to candidates to only $1,000 for primary

(continued on page 214)

Teenagers Help Their Parties

Even though this teenager is too young to cast her vote, she understands the importance of becoming involved in our political system.

Janet Benson and Bill Chan live far apart and have never met. She's from Minot, North Dakota, and is a Republican. He's from Phoenix, Arizona, and is a Democrat. Yet the two teenagers have something in common. They both are active in party politics and have great respect for the work carried out by their political parties.

To Janet and Bill, politics is not something that happens every four years, when a President is elected. It's an ongoing part of life. Long before they reached high school, the two students were rounding up votes for the party of their choice.

An Active Republican

Janet's interest in politics began when she was six years old. Her parents are active Republicans, who for a time advised a club of teenage Republicans. Janet began helping Republican candidates by putting up posters and passing out leaflets. Later, in high school, she became an officer of her local TAR (Teen-Age Republican) Club. With other officers she went to Washington, D.C., for a national TAR conference.

While still in high school, Janet became convinced that politics would remain a key interest in her life. "Some people want a career in science or sports," she says. "For me, it's politics. I love it." She believes that "politics doesn't end when an election is over." Members can help their political party at all times. They can, for example, hold discussions of bills being considered by the state legislature or by Congress. They also can find out what should be done to help those in need.

An Active Democrat

Like Janet, Bill Chan had an early introduction into politics. His mother held elective office and served on the Democratic national committee. To help her, Bill began stuffing campaign leaflets in doorways when he was nine years old.

As a high school junior, Bill went with his mother to a Democratic committee meeting in Washington, D.C. The purpose of the meeting was to help draw up the party platform for the national Democratic convention. Bill read over the proposals with his mother and discussed them with other Democrats. Later he went to the White House and shook hands with the President.

In high school Bill joined the Young Democrats. He enjoys "working the polls" on election day. This means taking up a post outside a polling (voting) place, talking to voters, and passing out leaflets.

Janet and Bill support different political parties. Yet both learned at an early age how important it is to take an active part in our country's political life.

Thinking It Over

1. What might be some of the advantages and disadvantages of joining a political party at a young age?
2. Do you think joining a party organization is a good way to have a say in government? Why or why not?

Teenagers such as these help their political parties by talking to the voters.

Campaigning for candidates in whom you believe is an important way to make your voice heard in government.

Fund-raising dinners are held in communities all over the country. They are used by candidates to help raise the money needed to run for political office.

elections and another $1,000 for general elections. The provisions of these laws are enforced by the Federal Election Commission.

Public Financing

The Revenue Act of 1971, which has been amended several times, also introduced public financing of Presidential elections. How does public financing work? The money comes from the Presidential Election Campaign Fund in the United States Treasury. By checking a box on the federal income tax form, Americans can contribute one dollar of their taxes to the election fund. This neither raises nor lowers the amount of tax a person pays.

The money is distributed to the candidates by the Federal Election Commission. To be eligible to receive federal money, a candidate trying to win a party's nomination for President must first raise at least $100,000 from private contributions. Then the candidate can receive up to $5 million in matching

funds. The more money a candidate raises, the more he or she receives from the federal government. However, to receive matching funds, candidates must limit their spending in nomination campaigns to $10 million.

After winning nomination, Presidential candidates of the major parties, who accept public financing, cannot accept private contributions. Their campaigns must be paid for only with the federal funds they receive. In 1988 the spending limit for each major party's Presidential candidate was $46 million. Candidates of minor parties receive federal funds after the election if they win at least 5 percent of the vote. The amount of money they receive is based on the number of votes they get.

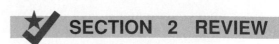

SECTION 2 REVIEW

Define caucuses, national nominating convention, precincts, polling place

Identify precinct captain

1. **Summarizing Ideas** Discuss the general organization of political parties.
2. **Understanding Ideas (a)** From what sources do political parties obtain most of their funds? **(b)** Why did Congress pass laws to regulate the amount of money people and organizations could contribute to political parties? **(c)** What are the basic provisions of the Federal Election Campaign Act of 1971?

Thinking Critically Imagine that you have been appointed the chief fund raiser for your political party in your community. How will you go about seeking contributions?

③ The Right to Vote

At the age of 18, all citizens have the right to vote in national, state, and local elections. Your right to vote is one of your most important rights as an American citizen. It is the way you can most directly affect how our government is run.

State Qualifications for Voting

Each state has the right to decide qualifications for voting in state elections. However, all states must follow the provisions about voting in the Constitution of the United States. The Constitution forbids any state to deny a citizen the right to vote because of race, color, or sex. To ensure the voting rights of all citizens, Congress in 1965 passed the Voting Rights Act (see page 548). Extensions of this law, passed in 1970 and in 1982, prohibit any state from using **literacy tests,** or reading tests, as a requirement for voting.

Many states deny the right to vote to certain citizens who they believe are not eligible to vote. In many states, a person who is convicted of a serious crime loses the right to vote. Most states also deny the right to vote to mentally ill persons confined in hospitals.

Registering to Vote

When a person goes to the polls to vote, how do the officials know that he or she is a qualified voter? Most states make sure of this by requiring all voters to **register** ahead of time. This means that your name is placed on the official roll of eligible voters. When you register to vote, you give your name, address, date of birth, and other information showing that you meet the qualifications for voting.

Almost all states have permanent registration. This means you must register only once as long as you live at the same address. Some of these states, however, require a voter who does not vote in a certain number of elections to register again. A few states have periodic registration in some or all areas. This means that you must register before each election or at regular intervals to remain a qualified voter.

To register, a citizen usually goes to the city hall or some place set up for this purpose. When you have registered, your name will be placed on the voters' list. You may be given a card showing that you are a registered voter.

When you register to vote, you may also be asked to register as a member of the political party of your choice. You may change your party membership at a later date by registering again. You may also choose to register as an **independent voter,** and not become a member of a political party. However, if you do not register as a member of a political party, you may not be able to vote in the primary elections.

Primary Elections

Two separate elections are held in most states. The **primary election** comes first, before the **general election.** The primary election is usually held in the spring. This election gives voters a chance to choose the candidates from each party who will run for public office in the general election.

There are two types of primary elections, the open primary and the closed primary. In the **closed primary,** only voters who are registered in the party can vote to choose the party's candidates. Most states use the closed primary. Thus in most states only registered Democrats can vote for Democratic candidates, and only registered Republicans can vote for Republican candidates. Those who have registered as independent voters cannot vote in the closed primary.

In the **open primary,** voters may vote to choose the candidates of either major party, whether or not they belong to that party. They can vote only for the candidates of one party, however.

In most states, the candidate who receives the highest number of votes is the winner of the primary election. The winning candidate does not have to get a majority, or more than 50 percent of the vote. In some states, espe-

cially in the South, the winner must get a majority of the votes. If no candidate receives a majority, there will be a **runoff election** between the two leading candidates to decide the winner. The winning candidate in the primary election then becomes the party's candidate in the general election.

Nomination by Convention

In some states, political parties choose their candidates in a nominating convention. The people who attend and vote in the convention are elected as delegates by the various committees in the state's political organization. In a state convention, the county and city committees select the delegates. In a national convention, the state committees often select the delegates.

Independent Candidates

What about independent candidates who belong to no political party but wish to run for office? An independent candidate who can get enough supporters to sign a petition can have his or her name printed on the ballot in the general election. Independent candidates do not get elected as often as major party candidates. But they do win some elections, mostly for local offices.

It is even possible for a person to be elected to an office when his or her name is not printed on the ballot. In some states, space is included on the ballot to "write in" the name of a person the voter prefers. It is difficult to get elected by **write-in votes,** but it does happen.

General Elections

Congress has set the date for the general elections of the President and Congress as the first Tuesday following the first Monday in November. A Presidential election takes place

To help get Americans to register to vote, registration tables may be set up on the street to make the process as easy and convenient as possible.

every four years. Congressional elections occur every two years. Most general elections for state officials are also held in November. The President and members of Congress are elected in even-numbered years. Some states elect their state officials in odd-numbered years. But elections are held at different times in different states.

On election day, the American voter faces a great responsibility and privilege of citizenship. The voter must make a choice among the candidates of the various parties. In many local elections, third parties may be strong, or write-in candidates may be well worth considering. Even in national elections, the choice is never simple.

The intelligent voter has studied hard to find the candidate whose views most closely resemble his or her own. The voter has read newspapers and magazines, listened to the candidates on radio and television, and talked about the candidates with other people.

As voters enter the polling place, they may see several neighbors at work. They are acting as inspectors, or **poll watchers.** Each party has its own poll watchers to see that the elections are conducted fairly.

Voting in the Past

During the first part of the 1800's, voting in the United States was by voice vote. Voters announced aloud to the election official the name of the candidate for whom they wanted to vote.

This system of voice voting made it possible to influence the way a person voted. Suppose a person's boss was standing in line. The boss could hear how the employee voted and might fire the employee who did not vote the way the boss wanted.

In 1888 a new system of voting was adopted. A paper ballot was used. This is a paper containing the names of the candidates and a place for the voter to mark a choice. This ballot was marked in secret, so that no one knew for whom a person voted. This

Did you know that...

many terms used to describe elections were first used to describe horse races? Elections often are referred to as *races*. This is natural, since candidates *run* (often with *running mates*) to see who will *win*. A *dark horse* (or *long shot*) is a candidate who seems to have little chance to be elected. The candidate who is ahead is called the *front runner*—but the finish may be *neck and neck*, after all.

method of voting is called the **secret ballot.** It helped make American elections fairer and more honest.

Voting Today

More than half of all American voters use a **voting machine** instead of a paper ballot. The voting machine is a large, curtained booth. The voter enters the booth and pulls a lever to close the curtains. On the front of the voting machine, the voter sees several rows of small metal bars or levers with the name of a candidate under or next to each lever. A party's candidates are sometimes all on one row.

The voter may vote a **straight ticket**—that is, for all the candidates of one party. Or the voter may vote a **split ticket**—that is, for the candidates of more than one political party. When the voter has finished, he or she pulls back the lever that opens the curtains. This

Voters cast their ballots for candidates by pulling levers on a voting machine. The ballots are then quickly and accurately counted by computers.

1. **Understanding Ideas** What are some provisions of the Voting Rights Act?
2. **Seeing Relationships** (a) Why are voters required to register? (b) How do people register to vote?
3. **Contrasting Ideas** (a) How do primary and general elections differ? (b) How do closed and open primaries differ?
4. **Drawing Conclusions** (a) How can an independent candidate get listed on a ballot? (b) How does voting today differ from voting in the past?

Thinking Critically Although voting is a great privilege of American citizenship, nearly half of those people who are eligible to vote in Presidential elections do not vote. Write a paragraph in which you discuss what you can do to encourage people to vote.

action automatically records the vote in the machine. All the levers shift back into position, so they are ready to be pulled down by the next voter.

Voting machines keep a running count of the votes cast for each candidate. When the final vote is cast, election officials open the voting machine and read the total vote for each candidate.

On election day, the polls are usually open from early in the morning until evening. In many states, election day is a public holiday, so that there is no excuse for failing to vote. In other states, the law provides that all employers must give time off during the day to any employee who needs time to vote.

 SECTION 3 REVIEW

Define literacy tests, register, primary election, general election, closed primary, open primary, runoff election, write-in votes, secret ballot, voting machine, straight ticket, split ticket

Identify independent voter, poll watchers

4 Nominating and Electing Our Leaders

Every four years, our nation is stirred with excitement as the time for the Presidential election draws near. Americans like a good, hard-fought battle. And the election of the President is one of the best. Most Americans eagerly follow the election campaign as newspapers, magazines, radio, and television report about it.

"A Hat in the Ring"

Long before election day, leading party members who want to be candidates begin to make speeches. They hope these speeches will make them better known to the public. At an appropriate time, some of these candidates announce that they intend to run for the highest office in the land—the Presidency. In the language of politics, they "throw their hats in the ring."

Choosing Convention Delegates

In each state, members of each political party choose delegates to go to their party's nominating convention. Convention delegates may either be elected in Presidential primaries or selected by party leaders.

In recent years, Presidential primaries have grown in importance. Today more than half our states and the District of Columbia hold **Presidential preference primaries.** In preference primaries, voters indicate which candidate they want the delegates to vote for at the national nominating convention.

In some states, the candidate who gets the most votes wins all the delegate votes from that state. In other states, each candidate gets some of the delegate votes based on the proportion of primary votes received. In still other states, the primaries indicate only the voters' preference. Delegates from these states may vote as they wish at the convention.

In states that do not hold primaries, the delegates are chosen by the state's party leaders in state or local party conventions. Or they are selected by state committees.

Larger states send more delegates to the national nominating convention than smaller states. The Democratic and Republican parties have different formulas for determining how many delegates each state will send to the convention. Because the formulas are different, the number of delegates at each party's convention is different.

Each state may send additional delegates if the party's candidate won in that state at the last Presidential election. Both parties use complicated formulas to choose these extra delegates. States also send alternates who vote if regular delegates become ill.

The National Nominating Convention

Each party's national nominating convention is held during the summer of the Presidential election year. On the opening day of the convention, a series of exciting events begins to occur. The delegates from each state are seated throughout the great convention hall. Sometimes there are rival delegates who claim to represent the regular party organization of their state. The credentials committee of the convention must then decide which delegation to seat.

Bands play, convention delegates walk about talking to one another, the chairperson of the convention calls for order. The chairperson has been selected by the national committee beforehand from among the party's prominent members. A **keynote speaker** then delivers an opening address to both the delegates and the radio and television audience.

Then the convention gets down to business. The **party platform** is presented by a committee. This written statement outlines the party's views on important issues and sets forth a proposed program for our nation. This is the program the party promises to put into action if its candidate is elected. Each part of the platform is called a **plank.** For example, the party platform may include a plank calling for an increase in defense spending or for a reduction in the federal income tax. After strong and often heated debate, the platform is voted on and adopted by the delegates.

Choosing the Presidential Candidate

The convention now tackles its most important item of business—choosing the party's candidate for President.

Nominations. First there is a roll call of the states. As each state is called, one of its delegates may give a speech nominating, or naming, a candidate. Each nominating speech then is followed by one or more seconding speeches.

Then supporters demonstrate in favor of their candidate. The band plays. Delegates who support the candidate parade around the convention floor. They wave signs and carry pictures of the candidate.

Not all state delegations, of course, nominate candidates. There may be half a dozen or more candidates nominated. Many of these nominees will have run in Presidential preference primaries. When the political party has a President in power who is eligible to run again, the convention almost always nominates this person for a second term.

Favorite Sons and Daughters. Some of the candidates named are **favorite sons or daughters.** They are the party leaders who are popular in their home states. These men and women usually are governors or senators. In most cases, favorite sons and daughters have little chance of winning their party's Presidential nomination.

Why, then, do states nominate them? Sometimes the name of a favorite son or daughter is presented to honor the state's party leader. In other cases, a state names a favorite son or daughter in order to delay a decision on which of the well-known candidates it will support. These delegates vote for their favorite son or daughter on the first bal-

lot. In later ballots, they usually switch their votes to one of the leading candidates.

Balloting. After all the candidates have been placed in nomination, the balloting begins. To win the nomination, a candidate must receive a majority of the votes of all the delegates at the convention. A roll call of the states is taken again. A delegate from each state announces how many votes the delegation is casting for each candidate.

In recent decades, one of the candidates has almost always been nominated on the first ballot. When no one candidate is strong enough to win a majority, many ballots may be needed. Supporters of the leading candidates may meet with state delegations to try to win them over. In some cases, a great deal of bargaining takes place.

When a candidate wins a majority of the delegates' votes, the huge convention hall is filled with noise and excitement. The delegates cheer and demonstrate to show their enthusiasm for the candidate who is to represent the party in the November election.

Accepting the nomination for President is an exciting moment for any candidate, as Michael Dukakis (left) and George Bush (right) showed in 1988.

Choosing the Vice Presidential Candidate

The delegates turn next to the nomination of the Vice President. Vice Presidential candidates often are chosen for their vote-getting ability. Sometimes they are from a part of the nation whose support the party needs. The Vice Presidential candidate must be well qualified to be President. This person, after all, is next in line for the Presidency if the party wins the November election.

The nominee for President has the strongest voice in deciding who the Vice Presidential candidate will be. In 1984, Democratic Presidential candidate Walter Mondale made a historic Vice Presidential choice. He chose Geraldine Ferraro, a three-term Congresswoman from New York, as his running mate. This choice marked the first time that a woman was nominated for the Vice Presidency by a major party.

The Reverend Jesse Jackson ran a strong campaign for the 1984 and 1988 Democratic Presidential nominations. Jackson took his campaign to voters across the country.

Acceptance Speeches

Finally the party's nominees for Vice President and President appear before the cheering delegates. Each gives an acceptance speech. In these speeches, the nominees set forth their position on key issues. They urge party members to unite and work for victory in November. Then, its job done, the convention is brought to a close for another four years.

The Election Campaign

The Presidential election campaign gets under way soon after the convention ends. One of the most widely used methods of campaigning is the personal-appearance tour. Jet planes enable the candidates to criss-cross our nation many times in an election campaign.

Television is another effective campaign device. Millions of Americans watch and listen as the candidates discuss their ideas and programs. Sometimes the candidates debate their views on television. As a result, Americans are able to get to know the candidates and to hear their ideas.

Election Day

The actual campaigning ends on the night before the election. Even so, election day itself is a busy one for party workers. They are busy telephoning and urging citizens to vote.

On election night, most Americans watch the election returns on television. They are able to hear complete details of all the political races across the United States. Because of the time difference, the first election returns come from the Eastern states. Gradually the election returns start coming in from the Western states. The last reports usually come in from California, Hawaii, and Alaska. Many Americans stay up late until they know who won. Sometimes the final results are not known until the next morning.

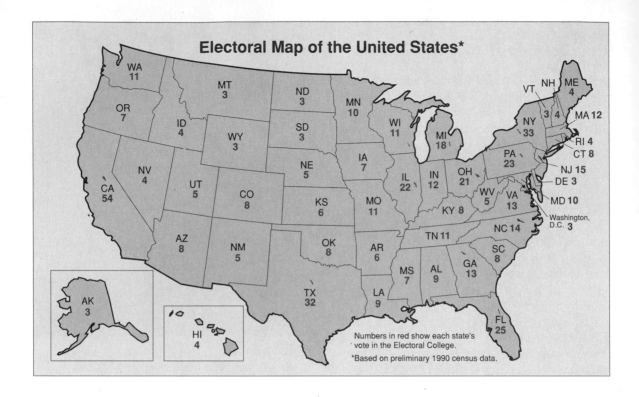

Electoral Map of the United States*

WA 11
OR 7
MT 3
ND 3
MN 10
WI 11
MI 18
VT 3
NH 4
ME 4
MA 12
NY 33
RI 4
CT 8
ID 4
WY 3
SD 3
IA 7
PA 23
NJ 15
DE 3
NV 4
UT 5
CO 8
NE 5
IL 22
IN 12
OH 21
WV 5
VA 13
MD 10
CA 54
KS 6
MO 11
KY 8
NC 14
Washington, D.C. 3
AZ 8
NM 5
OK 8
AR 6
TN 11
SC 8
MS 7
AL 9
GA 13
TX 32
LA 9
FL 25
AK 3
HI 4

Numbers in red show each state's vote in the Electoral College.
*Based on preliminary 1990 census data.

The Electoral College

In a Presidential election, Americans do not vote directly for the President. The votes they cast are known as the **popular vote.** This vote is actually for people called electors. **Electors** cast the official vote for President.

The names of the electors may or may not appear on the ballot. A vote for the Democratic candidate is a vote for the Democratic electors. A vote for the Republican candidate is a vote for the Republican electors. Each state has as many electors as it has senators and representatives in Congress. In addition, Washington, D.C., has three electoral votes. The whole group of 538 electors is known as the **Electoral College.**

In each state, the electors gather in the state capital on the first Monday after the second Wednesday in December. The electors of the party whose candidate won a majority of the popular votes in the state in the November Presidential election cast all the state's electoral votes at this December meeting.

For example, if the Democratic Presidential candidate won a majority of the state's votes in November, it is the Democratic electors who cast the state's **electoral votes.** If the Republican candidate won, it is the Republican electors who gather at the state capital to cast the official vote. The electors are not required to vote for their party's candidate. However, only rarely are votes cast for someone else.

The votes cast by the electors are then sent to the president *pro tempore* of the Senate. On January 6, following the Presidential election, both houses of Congress gather in the House of Representatives. The votes of the electors are opened and officially counted. The candidate who receives a majority of the electoral votes is officially declared the next President of the United States.

What happens if no Presidential candidate receives a majority of the votes in the Electoral College? In that case, the President is chosen by the House of Representatives from among the three leading candidates. If no candidate receives a majority of votes for Vice President, that official is chosen by the Senate. The choice is made from among the two candidates with the highest number of electoral votes. As you may know from your study of American history, this method has seldom been used.

The Electoral College was originally set up in the Constitution because those who planned our government were uncertain just how successful the people of the new republic would be in picking wise leaders. You will recall that they also provided for members of the Senate to be elected by state legislatures rather than directly by the people.

In recent years, many plans have been proposed for a system of direct election by popular vote to replace the Electoral College. Many Americans favor the direct election of the President and Vice President. Others favor keeping the present system.

SECTION 4 REVIEW

Define Presidential preference primaries, party platform, plank, popular vote, electoral votes

Identify keynote speaker, favorite sons or daughters, electors, Electoral College

1. **Summarizing Ideas (a)** How are delegates to each party's national nominating convention chosen? **(b)** What are the key events of the national nominating conventions?
2. **Expressing Ideas** How can voters learn about the views of the Presidential candidates?
3. **Understanding Ideas** What is the origin of the Electoral College?

Thinking Critically When you become eligible to vote, what qualities will you look for in candidates? Why?

Elections are important and exciting events in our national life. On election day the voters choose their government leaders. Although political parties are not mentioned in the Constitution, they have become an important part of our system of government. Political parties choose the candidates who run for office and become our leaders. Political parties offer a practical way for persons to work together to put their ideas and programs into effect in our government.

Today the United States has a strong two-party system. The Republican and Democratic parties are organized at local, state, and national levels. Both parties work through a series of committees to get their candidates elected. Throughout our history, there have also been many minor political parties.

American voters may belong to a political party, or they may decide not to join a party. In any case, voters are free to vote for any person or party they wish. The Constitution provides that the states set most of the qualifications for voting, subject to the restrictions set by the Constitution and by Congress.

The Presidential election, held every four years, is a dramatic event. Americans closely follow the party nominating conventions, the election campaign, and the election results.

CHAPTER 10 SUMMARY

Developing Civics Skills

CITIZENSHIP SKILL
Registering to Vote

Voting for candidates is a right we enjoy as citizens. All states require you to be at least 18 years old to vote. Some states require you to live in the state for a certain period of time before you can register to vote. Many states require you to register in person; other states allow you to register by mail. Whatever the requirements in your state, it is important that you fulfill them so that you too can vote.

How to Register to Vote

To register to vote, follow these guidelines.

1. **Find out your state's registration procedure.** The registration process varies from state to state. To find out how to register, contact your state's election office. You should request a registration form, and find out what deadlines you must meet.

2. **Follow the procedure carefully.** Usually,

registering to vote is as simple as filling out a form. The forms in most states ask for basic information: your name, your age, your residence, and whether you are a citizen. You must also sign the form, swearing that the information you have given is correct.

Applying the Skill

The registration form shown on this page is the one used in Texas. Other states use slightly different forms. The following questions will help you understand the form.

1. Which section should not be filled in? Why?
2. What do you think is the main purpose of the "Place of Birth" section?
3. Why must you sign a voter registration form?
4. Why do you think the form shown on this page is written in Spanish as well as English?

VOTER REGISTRATION APPLICATION *(SOLICITUD PARA REGISTRO DE VOTANTE)*

PLEASE COMPLETE ALL OF THE INFORMATION BELOW. PRINT IN INK OR TYPE.
(POR FAVOR COMPLETE LA SIGUIENTE INFORMACION. ESCRIBA EN LETRA DE MOLDE CON TINTA O ESCRIBA A MAQUINA.)

For Official Use Only
PCT   Cert. Num.   EDR

Last Name (Apellido)	First Name (NOT HUSBAND'S) (Nombre de Pila) (NO DEL ESPOSO)	Middle Name (If any) (Segundo Nombre) (si tiene)	Maiden Name (Apellido de Soltera)

Sex (Sexo)	Date of Birth (Fecha de Nacimiento) month, day, year (el mes, el dia, el año)	Place of Birth (Lugar de Nacimiento) city or county (ciudad o condado) state or foreign country (estado o país extranjero)	County and Address of Former Residence (Condado y direccion de su residencia previa)

Permanent Residence Address: Street Address and Apartment Number, City, State, and ZIP. If none, describe location of residence. (Do not include P.O. Box or Rural Rt.) *(Dirección de Residencia Permanente: Calle y Número de Departamento, Ciudad, Estado, y Zona Postal; si no tiene, describa la localidad de su residencia. No incluya su caja postal o ruta rural.)*

Social Security Number *(Número de Seguro Social)*

Mailing Address, City, State and ZIP: If mail cannot be delivered to your permanent residence address. *(Dirección Postal, Ciudad, Estado y Zona Postal) (si es imposible entregar correspondencia a su dirección permanente)*

Telephone Number (Optional) *(Numero de Telefono) (No obligatorio)*

Precinct Number (If known) *(Numero de precinto) (si lo sabe)*

The applicant is a citizen of the United States and a resident of this county. Applicant has not been finally convicted of a felony or, if a felon, is eligible for registration under Section 13.001(a)(4) of the Texas Election Code. I understand that the giving of false information to procure the registration of a voter is a misdemeanor. *(El suplicante es ciudadano de los Estados Unidos y es residente de este condado. El suplicante no ha sido probado culpable finalmente de un crimen, o, si es criminal, está elegible para registrarse para votar bajo las condiciones de la Sección 13.001(a)(4) del Código de Elecciones de Texas. Yo entiendo que es un delito menor dar información falsa con motivo de conseguir el registro de un votante.)*

X _____

Signature of Applicant or Agent or Printed Name of Applicant If Signed by Witness *(Firma del Suplicante o Agente, o Nombre del Suplicante En Letra de Molde Si Fue Firmado Por Un Testigo)*

Court of Naturalization, If Applicable *(Corte de Naturalización, Si Aplicable)*

FOR AGENT (PARA AGENTE): Application may be made by agent, who must be a qualified voter of this county or have submitted a registration application and must otherwise be eligible to vote and must be the applicant's husband, wife, father, mother, son or daughter. *(La solicitud podrá estar dirigida por un agente que deberá ser un votante capacitado de este condado o que habrá presentado una solicitud para registrarse para votar, y de otro modo deberá ser elegible para votar. El agente deberá ser el esposo, esposa, padre, madre, hijo o hija del suplicante.)*

Relationship (Parentesco) _____

FOR WITNESS (PARA TESTIGO):
Signature (Firma)
___ Check here if applicant is unable to make mark. *(Marque aquí si el suplicante no puede hacer su marca.)*

Printed name (Nombre En Letra de Molde)   Address (Dirección)

* The disclosure of social security number is voluntary. It is solicited by authority of Sec. 13.122 and will be used only to maintain the accuracy of the registration records. *(No es obligatorio dar su numero de seguro social. Se solicita bajo la autoridad de la Sec. 13.122 y se usará solamente para mantener la exactitud de los archivos.)*

Reviewing Terms

On a separate sheet of paper, copy the paragraph below. Then fill in each blank, using the correct term from the following list.

electors	candidates
nominate	popular
convention	register
independent	keynote
machine	electoral
platform	

Every four years we vote for the President and Vice President. Before the names of the (1) _____ appear on the ballot, however, political parties must (2) _____, or choose, who they want to represent them. This process is carried on at the national nominating (3) _____ of each party. After the (4) _____ speaker gives an opening address, a committee presents the party (5) _____, or statement that outlines the party's view on the issues. Then the candidates are chosen. On Election Day, American voters cast the (6) _____ vote. Many Americans belong to political parties, but many others are (7) _____ voters. Regardless, all citizens who wish to vote must (8) _____ before they can vote. Most ballots are cast with a voting (9) _____, instead of with paper ballots. The official votes for President and Vice President, however, are cast by (10) _____, and not by the American people. The vote of these 538 people is called the (11) _____ vote.

Using Thinking Skills

1. **Evaluating Ideas (a)** Why do we have political parties in the United States? **(b)** What are the advantages of a two-party system?
2. **Summarizing Ideas (a)** How do political parties raise money? **(b)** What do they use the money for? **(c)** How has Congress regulated political fund raising?

3. **Expressing Ideas** With what do some people want to replace the Electoral College?
4. **Drawing Conclusions** Why must people register in order to vote?
5. **Seeing Relationships** Why is it important to vote in primary elections as well as in general elections?
6. **Comparing Ideas** How does each of the major political parties in our country select its Presidential candidate?
7. **Identifying Roles** What part does the precinct captain play in a campaign?
8. **Identifying Ideas (a)** What are coalition governments? **(b)** What makes them unstable?
9. **Understanding Ideas (a)** How do voters learn about the qualifications and opinions of political candidates? **(b)** How has television influenced Presidential campaigns?

Practicing Civics Skills

Registering to Vote Contact the election office in your community and request a copy of the voter registration form used in your state. After you have received the form, use it to answer these questions.

1. Does the form include a space for you to enroll in a political party?
2. Is any of the information requested on the form optional? Which information?
3. Are you required to sign the form?

Being a Good Citizen

1. Hold a mock political election, complete with speeches, posters, and campaigning.
2. Attend a political rally or other meeting of voters. What is the purpose of the meeting? What activities were completed? What speeches were made? Report your findings to the class.
3. Prepare a written report on one of America's current third parties. Tell what the party's goals are and how effective it is in getting its message across to the voters.

Taking Part in Our Political System

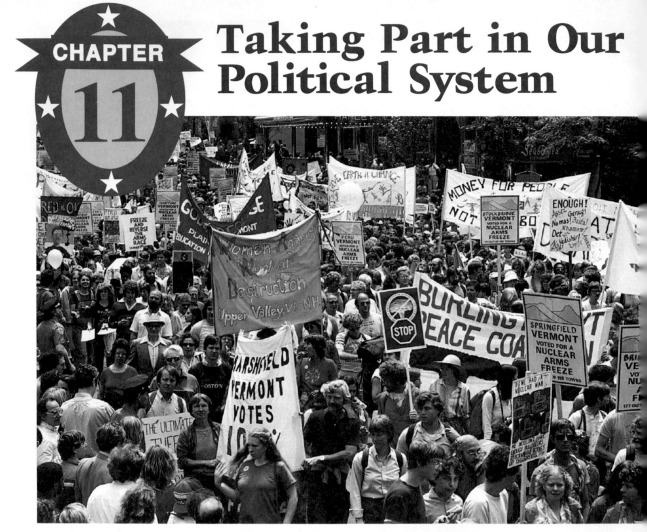

Chapter Sections

1 **Shaping Public Opinion**
2 **Interest Groups Influence Government**
3 **Taking an Active Part in Government**

Chapter Focus

You have been studying how our democratic government operates and how it serves you and all Americans. We turn now to one of the most important features of the American po-

litical system. That is how we, as citizens, can participate directly in our government.

Obviously, every one of us cannot actually serve as an official in the government. Instead, we elect other people to represent us. Each of us is affected by the decisions made by these public officials. Therefore, it is our responsibility to inform them of the actions we want them to take.

Taking part in our political system is an important responsibility of citizenship. It is not something that should be left for others to do. It is essential that citizens form opinions on public issues and express them. One of the most important ways people make their opinions known is by voting.

There are many ways we can make our voices heard in government. Working to help elect candidates of our choice is just one way. No matter how we choose to participate, our action is the key to democracy.

Study Guide

As you begin to learn about how citizens can influence government, look for answers to the following questions:

★ What is public opinion, and how does propaganda attempt to influence it?

★ What are interest groups, and how do they work to influence government?

★ Why is it important for all Americans to take an active part in government?

① Shaping Public Opinion

What is your opinion? You have no doubt been asked that question many times. Our **opinions,** what we believe to be true, are important to us. They can also influence what others believe or how they act.

In our American government, the opinions of the people greatly influence public affairs. For example, an elected public official who ignores the opinions of the people is likely to lose the next election. But what are the opinions of the people? When do the opinions of individuals become public opinion?

What Is Public Opinion?

We have all heard such statements as "Public opinion demands that something be done." People often think that public opinion is one opinion shared by all Americans. There are, however, very few issues on which all Americans agree. On any particular issue, there are a number of opinions held by a number of

groups. These groups are made up of people who share the same opinion. Each group makes up a "public." Because each issue has many publics, **public opinion** is the sum total of the opinions held concerning a particular issue. Thus "public opinion" really means many opinions.

What Shapes Our Opinions?

Our opinions are shaped by influences from many sources. The first influence on our opinions is our family. It is only natural for the ideas and beliefs of our family to become part of our own attitudes or values. Since we share so many of the same experiences with our family, we frequently have similar responses to many issues. As we grow older, other people and experiences also influence what we believe. Friends, teachers, and clubs play a major role in shaping our opinions.

Information is also important in shaping our opinions. Much of the information we need to make wise decisions about public issues comes from newspapers, television, radio, books, and magazines. These sources of information are called the **mass media.**

Having information, however, does not always mean that we are well informed. Sometimes the information we receive is inaccurate or one-sided. A newspaper, for example, might give more favorable coverage to the political candidate it supports.

Effective citizenship requires us to think critically about what we see or hear or read. It is essential to be able to recognize the difference between fact and opinion. We must therefore try to get our information from reliable sources.

Propaganda and Public Opinion

Many of the ideas we get from the mass media have been directed at us for a purpose. Somebody is trying to get us to do something—to buy something, to believe something, or to

courtesy of Field Enterprises, Inc.

"You're wasting your time! .. My mind is totally controlled by what the mass media feeds into it!"

Think for a minute and try to identify what shapes your opinions on public issues. Are you like this man or do other factors affect your thinking?

act in a given way. Ideas used to try to influence us are called **propaganda.**

It has been said that we live in the propaganda age. Propaganda is certainly nothing new. But it has come into its own in recent years. One reason for this development is rather easy to understand. The tremendous growth of the mass media has meant that propaganda can be spread farther and faster than ever before.

There are always many people, groups, and advertisers using propaganda to try to influence public opinion. Propaganda is used by advertisers hoping to get us to buy their products. Political candidates use propaganda to try to convince us to vote for them. When a political party tries to win public support, it is using propaganda.

People often think of propaganda as negative. Under totalitarian governments, this is true. In these societies, propaganda tech-niques often are used to control people and limit their freedoms. In democratic societies, on the other hand, most propaganda is neutral—neither good nor bad. It is simply a technique designed to give one side of an issue. Propaganda is used to influence people's attitudes, opinions, and behavior.

Two Kinds of Propaganda

Citizens must be alert to propaganda. We must be able to recognize it and be aware of the different methods used by propagandists. When propaganda ideas are presented as facts and their sources are kept secret, they are called **concealed propaganda.** Concealed propaganda tries to fool you without letting you know it is trying to influence you.

Sometimes concealed propaganda is relatively harmless. For example, press agents may make up interesting stories about television stars to give these stars publicity. At other times, concealed propaganda may be used to create a harmful impression. A photograph may be taken in a certain way or may be retouched to make a political candidate look bad. False rumors may be spread in order to harm someone.

Revealed propaganda is much more common in the United States. In revealed propaganda, readers or listeners are aware that someone is using ideas to influence them. Almost all advertising is revealed propaganda. You know when you see most advertisements that somebody wants you to buy something or to believe as they do.

Television and radio commercials are direct appeals to the public to buy various products. During an election campaign, political parties often run commercials in an effort to get voters to support their candidates. These commercials must be clearly labeled as paid advertisements.

Your civics book also contains revealed propaganda. It is openly spreading the idea that all Americans should understand and take part in our political system.

Propaganda Techniques

Propaganda experts sometimes use cleverly designed half-truths to mislead people. Some of these propaganda methods are difficult to spot. Others can easily be seen through by those who know how to recognize them. What are some of the propaganda techniques?

1. Testimonials. Political candidates and advertisers often seek endorsements from famous people. Advertising writers know, for instance, that people admire sports heroes. Therefore, they pay famous athletes to say they use and like their product.

They know that if a football hero says he drives a certain automobile, many people will believe the automobile must be good. These people like the football hero, so they will trust his judgment. However, people who think for themselves know that this testimonial by a great athlete proves very little. A football player may be the greatest quarterback of all time, but this does not make him an expert on automobiles.

2. Bandwagon. People who write propaganda know that if you say something often enough and loud enough, many people will believe it. If you can win some people over to your ideas, in time more and more people will come over to your side. This is known as the bandwagon technique of propaganda. "Everybody's doing it! Get on the bandwagon!" This method of propaganda appeals to people's desire to do what their friends and neighbors are doing.

3. Name Calling. Another propaganda technique is name calling. This is the use of an unpleasant label or description to

Propaganda Techniques

TESTIMONIALS

"I always drive a Volta car," says Connie Effort.

NAME CALLING

"The mayor is a puppet controlled by the party leaders."

GLITTERING GENERALITIES

"Lotion X will make your skin glow."

BANDWAGON

"Everyone is switching to Float soap!"

PLAIN-FOLKS APPEAL

"Vote for candidate Smith, who understands the problems of our town."

CARD STACKING

"Party X must win this election because Party Z lacks experience."

Each of the campaign slogans below was used by a successful Presidential candidate. Which President used each slogan?

Tippecanoe and Tyler Too
Return to Normalcy
A New Deal
I Like Ike

Answers are on page 594.

harm a person, group, or product. Name calling is sometimes used to harm political candidates. During an election campaign, name calling is often used by both sides. For example, you may hear that some candidate favors "reckless spending" or that another is "opposed to progress." The question to ask yourself is, What proof is given?

4. Glittering Generalities. Another method of influencing people's thinking is the glittering generality. This method uses words that sound good but have little real meaning. Many advertising slogans are glittering generalities. For example, a statement such as "It contains a miracle ingredient" has very little meaning.

Political candidates often use vague statements with which everyone would agree. These glittering generalities tell voters nothing about what a candidate really believes. This type of propaganda often uses such words as *home, baseball, country, freedom, patriotic,* and *American.* These words are chosen because most people in our nation approve of what they stand for.

5. Plain-Folks Appeal. During election campaigns, many candidates describe themselves as plain, hard-working American citizens. They claim to understand the problems of average Americans. This plain-folks appeal is designed to get votes. Candidates work hard to show the people that, as one of them, they can best represent the interests of the average citizen.

6. Card Stacking. Another propaganda technique is card stacking. This method uses facts in a certain way in order to favor a product, idea, or candidate. Newspapers, for example, may give front-page attention to the activities of the candidates they favor. The other political party and its candidates may be given smaller headlines or be reported only on the inside pages. The news is slanted to favor one party over another.

Measuring Public Opinion

The goal of our government officials is to carry out the wishes of the people. How, then, do government officials find out what the public wants? The most obvious test of public opinion is an election. Another way to measure public opinion is to conduct a **public opinion poll,** or survey.

Polls are used to find out what people think about specific issues and about politicians and their policies. A poll attempts to measure public opinion by asking the opinions of a sample, or portion, of the public.

Choosing a Sample

Great care must be taken to choose a sample that is representative of the public being measured. An unrepresentative sample can cause serious errors in a poll's results. Suppose, for example, your school principal decides to conduct a poll to find out if people want the cafeteria to remain open during the whole school day. If only teachers and cafeteria workers are polled, the result will probably be different than if students are also included in the polling sample.

A well-known example of a sampling error occurred in 1936. A popular magazine called *Literary Digest* conducted a poll to predict the outcome of the Presidential election. President Franklin D. Roosevelt, the Democratic candidate, was opposed by the Republican candidate, Alfred M. Landon.

The *Digest* mailed out more than 10 million ballots. They were sent to people chosen at random from telephone directories and automobile registration lists. More than 2 million people filled out these ballots and mailed them back to the magazine. Based on the poll results, the *Digest* predicted that Landon would be elected. The actual election results were very different. Roosevelt won by a landslide, with 60 percent of the vote.

What went wrong with the poll? It failed because in 1936 only high-income people could afford to own telephones and automobiles. Thus, the sample did not represent the voting population.

Once a representative sample has been chosen, care must also be taken in deciding what questions to ask. The way questions are phrased often affects the answers that will be given. For example, the neutral question "Should more firefighters be hired?" might get one answer. The question "Should taxes be raised to hire more firefighters?" might get a different answer.

Using Polls Carefully

Polls are a valuable tool for measuring public opinion. Some critics fear, however, that polls influence public opinion as well as measure it. For example, some people want to be on the winning side. Imagine that two days before the election, a poll predicts that Candidate Z will win by 15 percent. Might some voters decide in favor of Z in order to support a winner?

Polls can help us evaluate public opinion only if we do more than just look at the percentages given in the results. Other information to look for is the wording of the questions asked, the number of people responding, and the sample population chosen.

Especially important is the number of people responding as "undecided." Frequently, the number of people who are undecided is so great that no prediction is possible. In election campaigns, candidates

address their strongest appeal to the group of undecided voters.

SECTION 1 REVIEW

Define opinions, public opinion, mass media, propaganda, concealed propaganda, revealed propaganda, public opinion poll

1. **Expressing Ideas (a)** What sources influence our opinions? **(b)** Why is it that we can have information and yet not be well informed?
2. **Seeing Relationships (a)** How is propaganda used in totalitarian societies? **(b)** How is it used in democratic societies?
3. **Summarizing Ideas** Describe the six types of propaganda discussed in the section.
4. **Understanding Ideas (a)** Why is it important that polls use representative samples? **(b)** Why do some people criticize polls?

Thinking Critically You are running for Student Council president. Choose four propaganda techniques and write four different campaign slogans for yourself, identifying each technique.

Interest Groups Influence Government

Americans have many ways in which they can express their opinions to government officials and try to influence government policy. One of the most effective ways is through an interest group.

What Is an Interest Group?

Many people are members of one or more **interest groups.** These are organizations of people with a common interest who try to influence government policies and decisions. An interest group is also known as a **pressure group,** or **lobby.**

Interest groups differ from political parties. Both seek to influence government. Interest groups, however, are not primarily concerned with electing candidates to office. They often support a particular candidate. Yet their main interest is in influencing government policies that affect their group.

Interest groups are not new. They have been in existence throughout our nation's history. For example, people favoring the Constitution organized to work for its approval. Before the Civil War, people opposed to slavery organized to demand that it be outlawed.

Kinds of Interest Groups

There are many different kinds of interest groups. They include business associations, labor unions, farm organizations, senior citizens' groups, veterans' organizations, teachers' associations, consumer groups, and

Farmers are just one of the nation's many interest groups. Here they drive their tractors into Washington, D.C., to try to influence government policies.

religious groups. Each group works to promote the interests of its members. The various organizations often have very different views on issues.

Many interest groups represent the economic interests of their members. These include such groups as the National Association of Manufacturers, the United Mine Workers, and the American Farm Bureau Federation. Members of these and many other economic interest groups seek to influence government policies that affect them.

For example, the American Farm Bureau Federation is an organization of farmers and ranchers. It works to get bills passed that will help its members, and to block the passage of bills that do not favor the group's interests.

Some interest groups consist of people whose concerns are issue-oriented. That is, they focus on a specific issue or cause. For example, the National Association for the Advancement of Colored People (NAACP) works to promote racial equality. The National Organization for Women (NOW) seeks to protect the rights of women.

Other groups, called **public interest groups,** seek to promote the interests of the general public rather than just one part of it. These include groups working to protect consumers, wildlife, and the environment.

How Interest Groups Work

Interest groups vary greatly in size, goals, and budgets. Most, though, use similar methods to try to influence government decisions. They often encourage members to write to the President or their senators or representatives about a specific bill. Many interest groups also hire **lobbyists** who will represent their interests. Lobbyists work at all levels of government, although most are located in Washington, D.C.

Lobbyists get their name from the way they operated many years ago. In the past, they waited for lawmakers in the lobbies outside the legislatures' meeting rooms. There they tried to talk to lawmakers and influence their decisions. The term "lobbying" has been used since the 1830's.

Today lobbyists usually are highly skilled people with a staff of research assistants. Some lobbyists were once members of the legislatures or public agencies they now seek to influence. Other lobbyists are lawyers, public relations experts, journalists, or specialists in different fields.

Influencing the Government. Many of the nation's laws are the result of a struggle among interest groups. One example is the minimum wage law. This law says that workers may not be paid less than a certain amount an hour. Labor groups often seek an increase in the minimum wage. Business groups generally oppose such an increase. Lobbyists for both interest groups present their arguments to Congress. After listening to both sides and considering all the facts, Congress makes its decision.

The minimum wage has been increasing over the years. The amount of each increase, though, has been a compromise between those people wanting a higher increase and those wanting a smaller one.

Lobbyists use a number of different methods to promote the action they want. They argue in support of bills they favor and against bills they oppose. Sometimes lobbyists ask members of Congress to sponsor bills favored by members of their interest group. They supply facts for the bill. They may even help write the bill. Frequently, government officials contact lobbyists to learn the position of interest groups on issues that affect them.

Lobbyists often testify at committee hearings. Frequently lobbyists from different interest groups present evidence on opposite sides of the issue. Each lobbyist comes to the hearings prepared with well-developed arguments and statistics.

In fact, supplying information is one of a lobbyist's most important jobs. As you read in Chapter 5, members of Congress are faced with over 20,000 bills a year covering many different subjects. No lawmaker can be fully

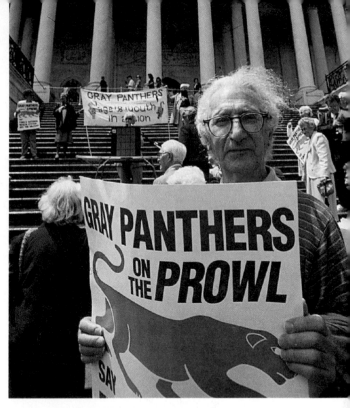

Our older citizens are a steadily growing percentage of the population. As their numbers increase, so does their power as an interest group.

informed in all these areas. Lawmakers often appreciate the help provided by lobbyists.

One way lobbyists influence government officials is by getting to know them. They meet with government officials in their offices or call them on the telephone to discuss their group's opinions. The lobbyists may also invite officials to lunch or dinner for more informal discussions.

Influencing Public Opinion. Interest groups attempt to influence not only the government but public opinion as well. For example, interest groups place advertisements in the mass media in support of their position. They often promise to help government officials in their next election campaign by supplying workers and contributions. Sometimes lobbyists urge local groups and individuals to send letters and telegrams to public officials. They hope that public support will influence the lawmakers' decisions.

(continued on page 236)

Focus on Freedom

From Tragedy to Triumph

You may sometimes think that there is nothing you can do to change something you believe to be wrong. It may seem that the odds are so against you that any action you take will go unnoticed. But under the First Amendment right of petition, you—like all Americans—are free to work toward any cause you believe to be right. Recently, one woman used her First Amendment right of petition to turn a personal tragedy into a triumph for people all across our nation.

A Child Is Killed

In May 1980, 13-year-old Cari Lightner was struck and killed by an automobile as she walked near her home in California. The driver of the automobile was drunk. Candy Lightner, the young victim's mother, was horrified to learn that the driver had been arrested in the past for drunk driving. Moreover, Lightner was told by the police that the driver probably would not go to jail, even though Cari had died in the accident. Why would the driver not go to jail? Because according to California law, driving under the influence of alcohol was a misdemeanor, or minor crime.

Lightner knew that there was nothing she could do to bring back her daughter. But the grieving mother also knew that something had to be done to protect other people from her daughter's tragic fate.

A Mother Takes Action

Lightner decided that her first plan of action would be to work for stronger laws against drunk driving. To this end, she formed an organization called Mothers Against Drunk Driving, or MADD. She and the other concerned citizens of MADD then contacted dozens of elected officials in the state of California, including the governor. Lightner used her First Amendment right of petition to urge these officials to work for stiffer penalties for drunk drivers. California lawmakers soon saw the wisdom of MADD's arguments and strengthened the laws.

Mothers Against Drunk Driving (MADD) is an organization with branches throughout the nation. This organization began when one woman exercised her First Amendment right of petition.

A Nation Responds

Acting as the voice of concerned citizens across the country, Lightner then took her fight to all the states in the nation. As a result, all 50 states have strengthened their drunk driving laws in recent years. Many states, for example, have raised the drinking age from 18 or 19 to 21. Some states take away the driver's license of drivers convicted of driving while intoxicated. And the state of Massachusetts now has a mandatory prison sentence for drunk drivers who are repeat offenders.

The work of MADD continues to this day. The organization now has about one million members nationwide and a budget of $13 million. Located in every state in the nation, MADD's members petition for stricter laws against drunk driving, provide assistance to victims of drunk drivers, serve on advisory boards, sponsor workshops, and give speeches about the dangers of driving and drinking.

Students Against Drunk Driving (SADD), an offshoot of MADD, reflects the commitment of our nation's young people to keep drunk drivers off the road.

Everyone Can Make a Difference

Candy Lightner did not let her personal tragedy keep her from doing what she believed needed to be done. Lightner focused the attention of the entire nation on a serious social problem. One woman made a difference in all of our lives. Our First Amendment right of petition gives all Americans the power to make such a difference.

Questions to Consider

1. Why did the driver of the car that killed Cari Lightner not go to jail?
2. Why did Candy Lightner form MADD?
3. What have been the results of Lightner's actions?

Regulating Interest Groups

Interest groups use any legal means to influence public officials and the public itself. To keep the activities of lobbyists in the open, federal and state governments require lobbyists to register. They must indicate for whom they are working and how much money they spend in lobbying. In recent years, laws regulating lobbying have been made very strict. New laws have closed many of the loopholes, or ways of evading the laws.

The Role of Interest Groups

Lobbyists once were viewed with suspicion because many of them worked in secret. Today, however, most lobbyists work in the open. They are welcomed as sources of information and help by overworked lawmakers and government officials.

Some people are critical of interest groups and their lobbyists. They believe these groups play too great a role in the lawmaking process. Critics charge that too much attention is paid to the interest group that is best organized and has the most money. As a result, important interests—such as those of the poor, the disabled, and many minorities—do not always get an equal hearing.

Despite this, interest groups play an important role in our free society. You are probably a member of a number of interest groups even though you may not be aware of it. Interest groups are the people—in our roles as students, business people, consumers, farmers, workers, or veterans. In our free society, we have the right to make our opinions known to our government leaders. Interest groups are evidence of political freedom.

✔️ SECTION 2 REVIEW

Define interest groups, pressure group, lobby, public interest groups

Identify lobbyists

1. **Contrasting Roles** How do interest groups differ from political parties?
2. **Summarizing Ideas** (a) Describe the various kinds of interest groups that exist. (b) Why have interest groups been criticized?
3. **Composing an Essay** Write a short essay explaining how lobbyists attempt to influence government and public opinion.

Thinking Critically What kinds of problems might arise if the law did not regulate interest groups?

③ Taking an Active Part in Government

In this chapter we have been discussing the ways in which Americans can influence government decisions. We have already considered the importance of public opinion and interest groups. Now we turn to the most direct way in which we, as citizens, can make government responsive to our will. This is by taking an active part in government.

There are many different ways for Americans to take part in government. We can vote in elections—local, state, and national. We can become active in a political party. Helping our local community and speaking out on public issues are also important. As you recall, all these activities are responsibilities of citizenship. They are necessary to the workings of our democratic government.

Voting: Democracy in Action

Voting is the most important opportunity for citizens to participate in our government. Only a small percentage of citizens can actually serve in the government. Instead, we elect people to represent us. All citizens, however, can take part in selecting the people who will lead and represent us.

Elections offer every citizen the chance to be involved in governing our nation. Each voter helps to determine what actions our government will take. We are making our opinions known on public issues when we vote. When we choose candidates, we are expressing our opinion not only of their abilities but of their programs as well.

Voting is not only a right, it is an important responsibility. Yet millions of American citizens do not vote. In recent Presidential elections, little more than half the voting-age population has voted. In 1988 only about 50 percent of the voting-age public voted for our nation's President. In non-Presidential elections, the percentage of voters is even smaller. This is especially the case in state and local elections.

The United States has the lowest turnout of eligible voters of any free government in the world. This low election turnout leaves the selection of our government officials to a small percentage of the people.

Why do so few people vote? Some people have not registered and thus are not eligible to vote. Some people do not like any of the candidates. Some are ill and cannot get to the polling places on election day. Some are unexpectedly away from home and cannot reach the polling places at which they are registered to vote. Others have moved so recently that they do not meet residency requirements for voting.

Every Vote Counts

The most common reason for not voting, however, is a person's belief that his or her vote will not make a difference in the outcome of an election. Of course, this is not true. The vote of every individual helps determine who wins or loses an election. Only by exercising our right to vote can Americans influence the laws and policies that greatly affect our lives. The importance of every vote can be seen by looking at the results of two close Presidential elections.

What is the cartoonist saying about voter participation in our nation? What do you think could be done to encourage more Americans to vote? What can you do to prepare yourself to vote?

In 1916 Charles Evans Hughes, the Republican candidate, went to bed believing he had been elected President. Hughes would have been right if 1,983 people in California had voted for him instead of for the Democratic candidate, Woodrow Wilson. However, since Wilson received a majority of California's popular vote, he was awarded all of that state's electoral votes. California's electoral votes gave Wilson the votes he needed to win the election.

In 1976 Jimmy Carter, the Democratic candidate, defeated Gerald Ford, the Republican candidate, by nearly 1,700,000 popular votes. However, a shift of 5,599 votes in Ohio and 3,687 votes in Hawaii would have changed the electoral vote enough to give the election to Ford. Clearly, every American's vote is important.

Taking Part in a Political Campaign

Another way to influence political decisions is to take part in an election campaign. Although you must be 18 years old to vote, people of any age can work as volunteers in a political campaign. **Volunteers** are people who work without pay to help others. Playing an active role as a volunteer in a political party is a good way to have a say about who represents you in government.

Political parties need the help of great numbers of people. Widespread citizen participation in campaigns is essential to a healthy democratic system. There are many jobs for volunteers during an election campaign. You can ring doorbells or make phone calls to tell voters about your candidate. You can encourage your friends and family members to vote. People are always needed to pass out campaign literature to passersby on the street. Envelopes must be addressed and stuffed with information about the candidate.

On election day, campaign workers urge people who support their candidate to vote. They may stay with young children to enable voters to get to the polling places. All this work can make the difference in the outcome of an election.

Interest Groups and Political Campaigns

Interest groups also take part in political campaigns. One way they do this is by providing volunteers to help candidates who are sympathetic to their causes. Another way they take part is by making financial contributions.

Although interest groups are prohibited by law from contributing money directly to candidates, they may contribute through **political action committees (PACs).** PACs collect voluntary contributions from members and use this money to fund candidates and issues they favor. The number of PACs has risen dramatically in recent years—from 608 in 1975 to about 5,000 today. Together, these PACs contribute hundreds of millions of dollars.

Contacting Public Officials

Suppose you believe the street corner near your home needs a traffic light. Or you oppose a proposed 15-cent increase in your city's bus fare. Or the House of Representatives is voting soon on an issue important to you. How can you make your opinion known quickly?

Writing a letter to local officials or members of Congress is an excellent way to let them know what is on your mind. As you read in Chapter 5, members of Congress receive a lot of mail. They welcome these letters as a way of learning what the people they represent think about the issues.

You can also contact public officials by telephone or telegram. A personal visit to an official's office is another way to express your opinions. Many officials have regular office hours for meeting with their constituents. Of course, it is always best to call first and make an appointment.

Signing petitions for causes in which you believe is one way you can influence our officials.

Community Action

The activities of our local government touch our lives most often and most directly. The quality of life in our town or city depends to a large extent upon how our local government serves us. It is therefore important for all Americans to take part in our local communities. Citizens can greatly influence our local governments.

Citizens often enjoy working together in community groups. For example, **block associations** have been formed in many cities by people working to improve their neighborhoods. Residents of an apartment house might form a **tenants' group** to try to improve the condition of their building. Citizens in a town might organize to raise money to buy new books for the town library or repair the school's baseball field.

Community groups are active in large and small cities, in towns, and in villages. Working together makes it easier for citizens to bring about the needed improvements and changes in our communities. Citizen involvement helps make democracy work.

 SECTION 3 REVIEW

Identify volunteers, political action committees (PACs), block associations, tenants' group

1. **Summarizing Ideas** In what ways can citizens participate in government?
2. **Understanding Ideas (a)** Why is it important for all eligible citizens to vote? **(b)** Why do so few Americans vote?
3. **Composing a Paragraph** Write a paragraph describing the ways in which interest groups take part in political campaigns.

Thinking Critically The President of the United States has invited you to the White House to deliver a speech. The topic of your speech is "How to Encourage Citizen Participation in Politics." Write a draft of the speech you will deliver at the White House.

In our democratic republic, it is important that the government be aware of the concerns and needs of all the people. One way to measure public opinion is by using public opinion polls. If used carefully, these polls can provide helpful information to candidates and government officials.

Opinion is shaped by many different sources, beginning with our families. Information provided by the mass media also plays a major role in shaping opinions. Propaganda is often used to try to influence people. We must be able to recognize propaganda and be aware of the various propaganda techniques.

Interest groups play an important role in influencing government decisions. They also help shape public opinion. Interest groups often hire lobbyists to promote the policies they favor.

Responsible citizens take an active part in public affairs. Exercising our right to vote is an essential part of American government. By voting in elections, citizens can help select the officials who will represent us and make decisions that affect our lives. Other ways to make our opinions known include taking part in political campaigns and working with community groups.

CHAPTER 11 SUMMARY

CITIZENSHIP SKILL
Understanding a Poll

Each year millions of Americans participate in polls. Chances are that someday you will be asked by pollsters to give your opinions on particular topics. Moreover, the results of these polls very often are reported in the media. By learning how to understand polls, you can gain insight into what Americans think about important issues.

How to Understand a Poll

To get the most out of opinion polls, follow these guidelines.

1. **Examine the wording of the questions.** Questions must be worded in such a way that they mean the same thing to every person in the poll. Confusing questions often bring inaccurate answers. Questions also must be neutral. If they lean toward any one answer, they will not truly measure public opinion.

2. **Make note of the answer categories.** Pollsters rarely ask people to supply answers of their own. Rather, they provide a limited set of answers and let people choose the ones that apply to them. Pollsters use limited answers because they make it easy to put large numbers of people into a very few answer categories. Otherwise, if pollsters questioned 1,000 people, they might get 1,000 different responses.

3. **Examine the results carefully.** When a poll is complete, the pollsters compute the percentage of people who selected each answer. These figures are the poll's facts. Pollsters use these facts to make generalizations, or broad statements that describe the patterns and relationships among the facts. Every generalization *must* be supported by the facts. If any of the facts do not fit, the generalization is not valid, or correct.

For example, consider this statement: "I like tacos, chili, and nachos." This statement lists the facts. A generalization that supports these facts is "I like Mexican food."

Applying the Skill

Use the results from the poll on this page to answer the following questions.

1. **(a)** Does the question posed meet the standards for a good question? Explain. **(b)** What are the facts of the poll?
2. "Only some people have a great deal of confidence in television news." Is this a valid generalization? Why or why not?

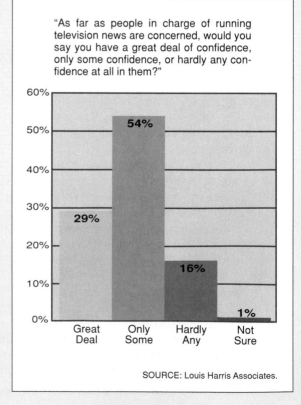

"As far as people in charge of running television news are concerned, would you say you have a great deal of confidence, only some confidence, or hardly any confidence at all in them?"

SOURCE: Louis Harris Associates.

CHAPTER (11) REVIEW

Reviewing Terms

On a separate sheet of paper, supply the term from the list below that correctly completes each sentence.

propaganda   interest groups
lobbyists   public opinion
revealed   mass media
volunteers   concealed

1. The _____ _____ is made up of newspapers, magazines, books, radio, and television.
2. _____ propaganda is propaganda presented as fact and whose source is kept secret.
3. _____ are people hired by interest groups to represent the groups' interests.
4. _____ _____ is the sum total of the opinions held concerning a particular issue.
5. Organizations of people with common interests who try to influence government decisions and policies are known as _____ _____.
6. Ideas used to try to influence us are called _____.
7. Propaganda that openly attempts to influence people is called _____ propaganda.
8. People who work without pay to help others are called _____.

Using Thinking Skills

1. **Contrasting Ideas** (a) How does the use of propaganda differ in totalitarian and democratic societies? (b) How do interest groups differ from political parties?
2. **Identifying Ideas** Explain why it can be said that our legal minimum wage is actually a compromise.
3. **Expressing Ideas** (a) How do lobbyists help interest groups? (b) How do they help government officials? (c) Why do interest groups attempt to influence public opinion?

4. **Summarizing Ideas** Describe six kinds of propaganda techniques.
5. **Drawing Conclusions** (a) What is the purpose of polls? (b) Explain why polls must use representative samples.
6. **Seeing Relationships** (a) What do critics mean when they say that polls can influence public opinion? (b) What things must we pay attention to when evaluating polls?
7. **Understanding Ideas** (a) Write a paragraph on the importance of voting. (b) Write an essay explaining how volunteers and interest groups participate in politics.

Practicing Civics Skills

Interpreting a Poll "Which level of government is closest to the people?" That was just one of the questions recently asked by a pollster to find out what Americans think about their state governments. The following list shows the responses to this question:

State legislatures	77%
Congress	13%
No Difference	4%
Not Sure	6%

Now complete the following activities: (a) Make a generalization about the facts above. (b) Write a good question that will measure public opinion of your state government.

Being a Good Citizen

1. Organize the class into groups to collect examples of propaganda techniques from newspapers and magazines.
2. Obtain several different editorials from your local newspaper on an issue of current importance. Compare the editorials and note their differences and similarities.
3. Consult with your school librarian to obtain a list of interest groups in the United States. Choose one of these groups and write for information concerning the issues about which the group is concerned.

Paying the Costs of Government

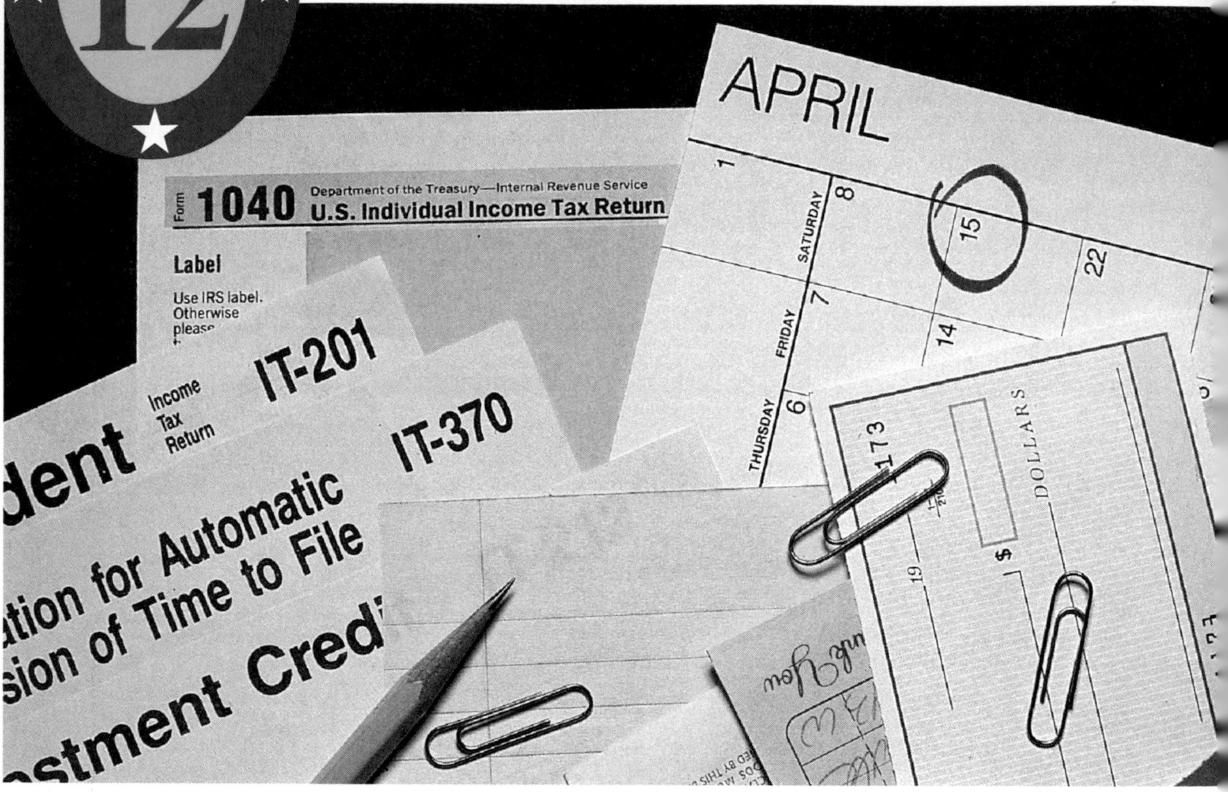

Form **1040** Department of the Treasury—Internal Revenue Service
U.S. Individual Income Tax Return

Label

Use IRS label.
Otherwise
please

APRIL

IT-201

Income Tax Return

IT-370

dent

tion for Automatic
sion of Time to File

stment Cred

ment Cred

DOLLARS

Chapter Sections

Chapter Focus

The many activities of government cost money—huge sums of money. Our federal government alone spends more than $1 trillion a year. State and local governments spend many more billions of dollars. The largest share of this money goes to help individual citizens. Large sums are needed, too, for national defense. Governments also spend money to protect our lives and property and to pay for various programs and services.

In recent years, the costs of government have risen sharply. From where does all the needed money come? It comes from the American people. We must pay for the services our governments provide.

However, the money raised from taxpayers does not cover the enormous costs of government. As a result, the government borrows money from the people, from banks, and from other sources. This borrowing adds to the national debt, which rises each year. The interest alone on this debt is many billions of dollars each year. And it must be paid. As responsible citizens, we should all be aware of how our government spends our money.

Study Guide

As you begin to learn about how our government raises and spends money, look for answers to the following questions:

★ How does the government raise money?

★ What are the different kinds of taxes?

★ How does the government manage our money?

1 How the Government Raises Money

Each year our federal, state, and local governments spend huge amounts of money. Our local governments provide the American people with police and firefighters. Public health programs and schools are paid for largely by local governments. They also provide paved streets, sewers, trash removal, parks, playgrounds, and many other services.

State governments provide highways and state police. They give help to public schools and to people who have lost their jobs. State governments also provide funds to people who cannot afford food and housing.

The federal government provides for our nation's defense. It helps business, labor, and agriculture. It provides agencies to protect the public's health, helps in highway construction, and serves its citizens in hundreds of other ways. All of these government services must be paid for.

Rising Costs of Government Services

One important reason why our governments cost so much money today is that the United States has a larger population than ever before. Our federal government, for example, serves a population of about 250 million people. Another reason is that during the past 50 years the activities of our governments have increased enormously.

The cost of government also has gone up in recent years because of the rising cost of living. Today's dollar will not buy as much as a dollar did in past years. Furthermore, the services and programs of our federal government have grown much larger and more costly.

For example, in 1913 a single two-lane highway cost a few thousand dollars a mile. Today this distance on a six-lane superhighway, with overpasses and cloverleafs, costs more than $5 million. The cost of defense, too, has risen sharply. In 1913 our nation's defense dollars were spent largely for supporting soldiers and their field supplies. Today, however, we spend billions of dollars on missiles, nuclear-powered submarines and aircraft carriers, jet fighter planes, and electronic communication systems.

Establishing Priorities

Many Americans complain about the high costs of government. It is understandable that they do so. All citizens have the right to expect that their government will spend their—the taxpayers'—money wisely.

In recent years, taxpayers have questioned the need for many government programs and criticized wasteful spending practices. Taxpayer revolts across the nation have forced governments to cut back on spending. In a number of states and local communities, taxpayers have voted to place limits on the amount they can be taxed.

Government officials, therefore, are faced with difficult decisions. What government programs need money most? What programs will bring the greatest benefits to the most people?

The first thing government officials do is list those activities that need money. These are listed in order of their urgency and need. This is called establishing **priorities.** Programs at the top of the list have high priority. Programs lower on the list have lower priority. Our government officials try to spend funds for those high on the list. Programs of very low priority may have to be left out. In recent years, there has been much debate over our priorities.

The Purpose of Taxes

All of our American governments—federal, state, and local—raise most of the money to pay for services and programs by collecting taxes. A **tax** is a payment of money that citizens and businesses are required to make in order to help pay for the costs of government. A tax is compulsory. That is, citizens have to pay it whether they want to or not.

The chief purpose of taxes is to raise money, or **revenue.** This revenue pays for the costs of government. Another purpose of taxes

is to regulate, or control, some activity. How are taxes used to regulate activities?

Taxes on imports, for example, are sometimes fixed at a high level. Their aim is not to raise large sums of money but to discourage imports in order to encourage business activity in our own country. High taxes on cigarettes and alcoholic beverages are partly intended to discourage their use.

Some Rules of Taxation

Our governments try to follow certain rules, or principles, when they set up taxes. They follow these rules to try to make taxes as fair as possible for all our citizens. What are these principles of taxation?

1. Taxes Should Be Based on Ability to Pay. Taxes should not be so high that they are difficult for many people to pay. In order to make it possible for all citizens to pay, taxes on the money people earn should be lower for those citizens with low incomes and higher for those with high incomes. Other taxes, such as those on things people buy, are at a fixed rate for all citizens within a given area. These taxes should be set at a reasonable level that all can pay.

2. Taxes Should Be Applied Equally to All. A local tax on property, for example, should be the same for all property worth the same amount of money. Taxes collected on the goods we buy should be the same for anyone purchasing these goods.

3. Taxes Should Be Easy to Pay. The American people want to pay their taxes quickly and easily. Therefore, a large part of some taxes is taken out of workers' paychecks before they receive their checks. These taxes are withheld by employers, who send the tax money directly to the government.

4. Taxes Should Be Collected at Convenient Times. Suppose that all taxes had to be paid at the time of the Christmas holidays when many people have bills to pay. Most Americans would find paying taxes then particularly difficult. Our governments try to

"Only two things are certain," goes an old saying, "death and taxes." In recent years, though, Americans have been protesting that taxes are too high.

Why the Costs of Our Federal Government Have Increased

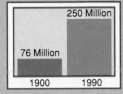

America's population has grown.

Prices have increased, and the cost of living has risen.

The national debt has grown rapidly and requires huge interest payments.

Our federal government now provides more services.

Larger sums are spent for America's defense.

collect taxes at a time when it is easier for citizens to pay them. The United States government also tries to make it easier for citizens to pay certain taxes by collecting part of the total tax each month instead of requiring that the entire tax be paid in full all at once.

Other Methods of Raising Revenue

Other means of raising money for governmental needs include fees, fines, and payments for special services.

Governments raise money by charging **fees,** or small payments, for various licenses — hunting licenses, dog licenses, marriage licenses, and so forth. State governments raise large sums of money from the fees they charge for drivers' licenses and automobile license plates.

Money paid by a citizen as a penalty for breaking certain laws is a **fine.** Fines add to the funds of local governments especially.

Such fines are those paid for illegal parking, speeding, and jaywalking.

Governments provide special services that are paid for directly by those who use these services. For example, the federal government sells timber from national forest reserves and electricity from certain federal dam projects. Those who receive this timber or electric power must pay for it directly. State governments collect payments from drivers who use certain toll roads and bridges. Local governments sometimes install parking meters to collect payments from those who wish to park their cars on the street.

Government Borrowing

Although our governments raise most of their funds through taxes and other forms of revenue, their needs are sometimes so great that they must borrow money. In recent years, our federal government has been trying in various ways to reduce the amount that it spends.

Not many local governments would have on hand the millions of dollars that it costs to build a school like this. So they borrow, often by issuing school bonds.

However, it still spends more money each year than it takes in. As a result, our federal government is in debt for more than $3 trillion.

On state and local levels, a large project, such as a school or a bridge, costs so much to build that it usually cannot be paid for fully out of the government's income in any single year. Therefore, state and local governments must borrow the additional money they need from their citizens.

Our governments borrow the money they need by issuing bonds. A government **bond** is a certificate stating that the government has borrowed a certain sum of money from the owner of the bond. The government promises to pay interest on this money. **Interest** is the payment made for the use of the money. It is generally a certain percentage of the amount borrowed. Furthermore, the government promises to repay the full amount of the loan on a given date.

 SECTION 1 REVIEW

Define priorities, tax, revenue, fees, fine, bond, interest

1. **Understanding Ideas** Why are the costs of government increasing?
2. **Seeing Relationships** What is the relationship between government priorities and government spending?
3. **Summarizing Ideas** (a) What are the purposes of taxes? (b) List and describe the four principles of taxation.
4. **Expressing Ideas** (a) Describe the methods used by our governments to raise money. (b) Why must the government borrow money?

Thinking Critically Imagine you are a local government official whose job it is to help set priorities for government spending. Which government services do you think should have the highest priority? The lowest priority?

② Many Kinds of Taxes

When we walk on a sidewalk or drive on a street, we are enjoying a government service that has cost a great deal of money. When we watch telecasts of American spaceships circling the planets, we are seeing the results of an important government research program that costs billions of dollars each year.

How are these and the other government services and programs paid for? Taxes are the main source of money for our federal, state, and local governments. All levels of government depend on many kinds of taxes to raise the large sums of money needed.

Personal Income Tax

The largest source of revenue for our federal government is the **personal income tax.** This is a tax on the income a person earns. It is not based on a person's total income. The personal income tax is based on the amount left over after certain amounts have been subtracted from the total income.

How Much Do We Pay? All taxpayers are allowed to deduct, or subtract, a certain amount of money for each dependent—each person they support in a family. These amounts are called **exemptions.** The amount of the exemption depends on the rate of inflation. If prices increase, the amount of the exemption also increases. In 1990, the exemption was $2,050.

Taxpayers are also allowed to deduct certain expenses. These amounts are called **deductions.** For example, taxpayers can deduct their charitable contributions and part of their medical bills. Other deductions include interest on house mortgages and business expenses.

The amount left over after all subtractions have been made is called **taxable income.** This is the amount on which personal income tax is paid.

The personal income tax is a progressive tax. A **progressive tax** is a type of tax that takes a larger percentage of income from high-income groups than from low-income groups. For example, a person who has a taxable income of $10,000 might pay an income tax that equals 15 percent of his or her income, or $1,500. A person who has a taxable income of $40,000 might pay an income tax of 28 percent, or $11,200.

The amount of income taxes that people have to pay changes. Congress changes tax

How the Federal Government Spends Its Money

THE FEDERAL GOVERNMENT

SOURCES OF INCOME	EXPENDITURES
Personal income taxes	Health, labor, and welfare
Employment taxes	Defense
Corporate income taxes	Interest on debt
Excise taxes	Veterans' benefits
Import taxes (tariffs)	Education
Borrowing (public debt)	Transportation and commerce
Estate taxes	Grants to states and local areas
Inheritance taxes	Foreign relations
Gift taxes	Space exploration
	Assistance to farmers

rates when it wants to help the economy. It also does so to encourage saving, to encourage or discourage some kinds of spending, or to improve our system of taxation.

How Do We Pay? American taxpayers must fill out and mail their tax forms on or before April 15 each year. Most taxpayers do not pay all their income tax at the time they file tax returns. Income tax payments have already been taken out of each paycheck by their employers, who forward the tax money to the government.

Filling out the tax forms shows taxpayers how much they must pay. Sometimes people learn they will get back some of the tax money withheld by their employers during the year. Sometimes they find they owe the government more money. The system of making small tax payments each payday makes it easier for most Americans to pay their personal income taxes.

State and Local Taxes. The personal income tax is a very successful means of raising money to support the activities of federal government. All but a few of our state governments also collect a personal income tax. In addition, it is collected by some city governments. Each of these states and cities has its own income tax law and fixes its own income tax rate.

Some states use the amount of federal income tax a person pays to determine the amount of state income tax he or she will pay. For example, a person might pay 5 percent of what he or she owes in federal income tax to the state government. Most states, however, create their own tax rates that are not based on federal income tax. Like city income tax rates, state income tax rates are much lower than those for the federal income tax.

Social Security Tax

Another kind of income tax that Americans pay is the **Social Security tax.** This is used mainly to pay income to retired people. All working people pay the Social Security tax at the same rate up to a certain amount, above which they are not taxed. The tax paid by each worker is matched by the employer. You will read more about how Social Security works in Chapter 18.

Corporate Income Tax

The second largest source of income for the federal government is the **corporate income tax.** It also is an important source of income

This paycheck stub shows the kinds of deductions that employers take from workers' paychecks for taxes. Employers then send this tax money to the government.

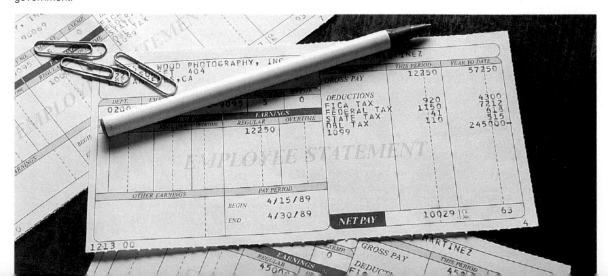

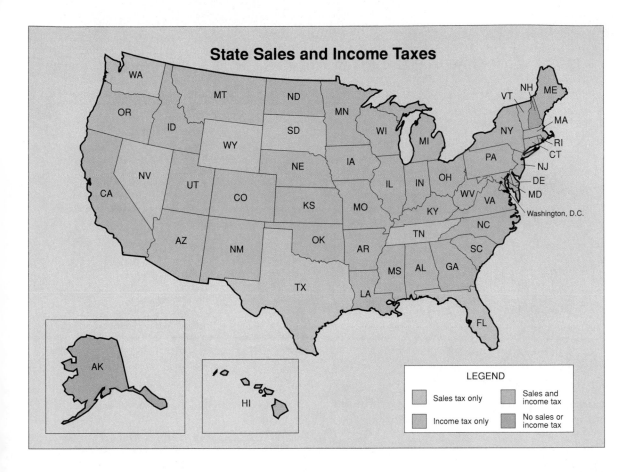

State Sales and Income Taxes

LEGEND

- Sales tax only
- Income tax only
- Sales and income tax
- No sales or income tax

for our state governments. This tax is not based on the total income received by the corporation. It is based only on a corporation's profits. **Profit** is the income a business has left after expenses.

Like individuals, corporations may deduct certain amounts to lower their taxable income. For example, they may subtract money paid to buy new machinery or for employee salaries. Also like individuals, corporations with high taxable incomes are usually taxed at a higher rate.

Sales Tax

Most states and many cities have a **sales tax.** It is collected on most products we buy. For example, if the sales tax is 5 percent, you must pay $1.05 for something that costs $1.00.

Stores send the extra 5 percent they collect to the government.

Sales tax is a regressive tax. A **regressive tax** is a type of tax that takes a larger percentage of income from low-income groups than from high-income groups. Because everyone pays the same tax, regardless of their income, regressive taxes hit lower-income groups harder.

Excise Tax

Excise taxes are similar to sales taxes. The **excise tax,** though, is collected only on certain services and goods produced and sold in the United States, usually on "luxury" items. Some of the items on which excise taxes are collected are tobacco, alcoholic beverages, gasoline, automobiles, and air travel. Excise

How State and Local Governments Spend Their Money

STATE GOVERNMENTS

SOURCES OF INCOME	EXPENDITURES
Federal government	Education
General sales taxes	Public welfare
Personal income taxes	Highways
Cigarette, gasoline, and liquor taxes	Health and hospitals
Corporate income taxes	Police
Inheritance taxes	Public building programs
Licenses and fees	

LOCAL GOVERNMENTS

SOURCES OF INCOME	EXPENDITURES
Federal and state governments	Schools
Property taxes	Public welfare
School taxes	Fire and police protection
Licenses and permits	Health and hospitals
Fines	Utilities
Amusement taxes	Streets and roads
Personal property taxes	Sewage systems
	Parks and playgrounds
	Libraries

taxes are collected by the federal government and by several of our state governments.

Property Tax

The chief source of income for most local governments is the **property tax.** This is a tax on the value of the property owned by a person or a business. Property taxes are collected on two different kinds of property, real and personal.

Real Property and Personal Property. **Real property** consists of land and buildings. **Personal property** includes such things as stocks, bonds, jewelry, cars, and boats. Since it is more difficult to determine the value of an individual's personal property, most governments use the property tax to cover only real property. If personal property is taxed, the rate is usually very low.

How Real Property Is Taxed. To determine the value of property for tax purposes, local governments depend upon local officials called tax assessors. These assessors visit the

property and assess it, or make a judgment of its value.

When the tax assessors complete their work, the local government adds up the assessed value of all the property in the locality. The local government then figures the total amount of money it must raise by the property tax. To decide on the tax rate, it divides this amount by the total assessed value of property in the town.

To see how this works, take the example of a small town that needs revenue amounting to $100,000 from its property tax. Suppose that the total assessed value of property within the boundaries of the town is $3 million. To figure the amount that property owners will have to pay, we divide $100,000 by $3 million. This gives us a tax rate of 3 cents on each dollar, or $3 on each $100 of assessed property value. This 3 percent tax rate means that a house and land assessed at $40,000 will be taxed $1,200 a year.

School Taxes. In many of our states, public schools are supported by a local tax on property, sometimes called a **school tax.**

The school tax is collected by the town, village, county, or school district in which the school is located. The tax money is turned over to the local school board. In most cases, public school districts also receive funds from the state government to help pay the cost of schools.

Tariff, or Import Tax

The United States government collects import taxes on many products imported from foreign countries. This import tax is called a **tariff**, or sometimes a customs duty. In the early days of our nation, the tariff was one of the largest sources of income for the federal government.

Today, however, the United States generally uses tariffs to regulate trade rather than raise money. Our government places protective tariffs on certain products. A **protective tariff** protects American industries against foreign competition.

Many foreign countries can manufacture goods at a far lower cost than they could be manufactured for in the United States. Lower manufacturing costs would allow those goods to be imported and sold here for far less than an American manufacturer would have to charge. American industry would lose business, and some American workers might lose their jobs.

A tariff on the imported product raises its price, making it as expensive as, or more expensive than, the American product. Tariffs thus protect industry. In some cases, though, tariffs hurt American consumers by raising the prices they must pay for certain products.

Estate, Inheritance, and Gift Taxes

When a person dies, the heirs may have to pay several taxes on the real estate, money, and personal property that are left behind. First there is the **estate tax.** This is a federal tax on all the wealth a person leaves. Some states also collect an estate tax. The rate at which the tax is paid by the heirs depends upon the value of the estate they receive.

Then there is a state tax on the share of the estate an individual inherits, or receives. Be sure that you understand the difference between the two taxes. The estate tax is based on the value of the entire estate before it is divided. The **inheritance tax** is based on the amount an individual receives as a share of the estate.

Even a gift of money may be subject to a tax by the federal government. A **gift tax** must be paid by any person giving a gift worth more than a certain amount.

SECTION 2 REVIEW

Define personal income tax, exemptions, deductions, taxable income, progressive tax, Social Security tax, corporate income tax, profit, sales tax, regressive tax, excise tax, property tax, real property, personal property, school tax, tariff, protective tariff, estate tax, inheritance tax, gift tax

1. **Summarizing Ideas (a)** On what is personal income tax based? **(b)** What determines how much personal income tax we pay? **(c)** How do citizens pay income taxes?
2. **Contrasting Ideas (a)** How do sales taxes differ from excise taxes? **(b)** On what kinds of goods are excise taxes usually collected?
3. **Seeing Relationships (a)** On what is corporate income tax based? **(b)** How are corporate income taxes similar to personal income taxes?
4. **Understanding Ideas (a)** How is real property taxed? **(b)** How does a protective tariff work?

Thinking Critically Many American citizens think that regressive taxes are unfair. They maintain that most or all taxes should be progressive. Do you agree? Explain your answer.

3 Managing Our Nation's Money

One of the most important jobs of the various governments in the United States is to manage the public money wisely. As you know, our federal, state, and local governments collect and spend many billions of dollars each year. Therefore, our governments have set up separate divisions to handle public funds. In addition, each of our governments checks on the way public funds are spent.

Collecting Public Money

Each of our governments has a department that collects taxes. In the federal government, income taxes are collected by the **Internal Revenue Service (IRS).** The Internal Revenue Service is an agency of the Department of the Treasury, and it has branches throughout the nation. Tariffs on imports are collected by the Customs Service, another division of the Department of the Treasury. State and local governments have their own tax collection bureaus.

After tax money is collected, it is sent to the treasuries of the various governments. The tax funds of the federal government are handled by the **treasurer** of the United States. It is the treasurer's job to see that all federal tax money is kept safe and that it is paid out only as authorized by the Secretary of the Treasury.

Can You Guess?

In colonial times, the taxes in several Southern colonies were often paid in the form of a major crop. Which crop was it? (Hint: It goes up in smoke.)

Answer is on page 594.

The Secretary may spend money only when authorized to do so by Congress.

In our state and local governments, the official who acts as the "watchdog of the treasury" is the **comptroller.** Comptrollers have a job similar to that of the treasurer of the United States. These state and local officials have the job of seeing that public funds are spent only as authorized by the state legislature or the city council.

Planning Government Spending

All governments have budgets. A **budget** is a plan for raising and spending funds. The budget lists the amount of revenue, or money income, as well as the sources from which this revenue will be collected. It also lists the expenditures, or money to be spent, for various public purposes. A budget usually covers the government's operations for one year.

The responsibility for managing public funds is divided among the three branches of government. The chief executive of each of our governments is responsible for drawing up the budget. In municipalities the mayor, city manager, or other executive officer plans and draws up the budget. In most state governments, the governor prepares the yearly budget of the state's spending and income. The President is responsible for budget planning in the federal government.

The legislative branch must approve the budget before any public money can be spent. The head of the executive branch must see that the money is spent according to the budget's plan. The courts in the judicial branch settle disputes over the collecting and spending of the public money.

Preparing the Federal Budget

In the federal government, the President recommends how public funds may be raised and how they may be spent. The job of planning the federal budget is so complicated that the

President needs the help of several government agencies.

One of the chief agencies involved in helping the President prepare the federal budget is the **Office of Management and Budget (OMB).** This important agency makes studies of our nation's economy. It then forecasts the amount of tax income the government will receive in the coming year.

Each of the executive departments makes a careful estimate of how much money it plans to spend the following year. All these estimates are submitted to the President. Then the President and the director of the OMB study the many requests. Priorities are established for the various items. Some requests may be cut in order to bring the total expenditures closer to estimated revenues.

After the budget is prepared each year, it is published in book form. This huge budget book contains hundreds of pages, listing thousands of separate items.

This scene is a common one each year as April 15 approaches. It is time to take out bills, receipts, and check stubs and fill out an income tax form.

Congress and the Budget

When the budget is in its finished form, the President sends it to Congress. Along with the budget, the President sends a message explaining the budget and urging that it be passed. Sometimes the President addresses a joint session of Congress to seek support for the budget.

Congress then makes its own study of the proposed budget. As you recall, only Congress has the power to raise funds and spend them. The House of Representatives and the Senate debate the various items in the budget and make changes. Both houses of Congress must approve the final version of the budget. The revised budget is then sent back to the President to be approved or vetoed.

This process of preparing the budget takes many months. There is a great deal of give and take before the final budget is approved. When finally completed, the budget becomes the law under which money will be spent during the coming year.

Balancing the Budget

When a government has a **balanced budget,** the amount of revenue equals the amount of expenditures. That is, the amount of money received equals the amount of money spent.

Sometimes a government budget is not balanced, however. When its budget is not balanced, the government's expenses usually are greater than its income from taxes and other sources. This shortage of income is called a **deficit.** A government may, however, receive more income than it planned, so that its revenues exceed its expenditures. This excess, or extra, income is called a **surplus.**

Deficits in a government budget must be made up by borrowing. Governments obtain short-term loans by borrowing enough money from banks to tide them over for a year or less. Long-term borrowing is usually done by issuing government bonds.

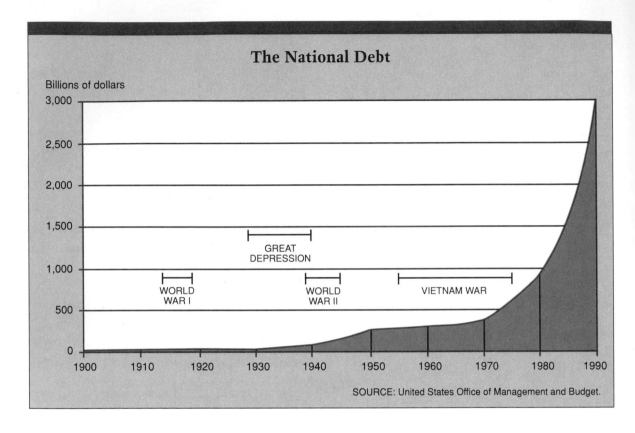

The National Debt

Billions of dollars

GREAT
DEPRESSION

WORLD
WAR I

WORLD
WAR II

VIETNAM WAR

SOURCE: United States Office of Management and Budget.

The Problem of the National Debt

The federal government has borrowed huge amounts of money in recent years to try to balance its budget. To do so, it has issued several kinds of government bonds. You may be familiar with one of these kinds of bonds—**savings bonds.**

Everyone who owns savings bonds or other federal bonds has loaned money to the government. Each year the government must pay interest on these bonds, and some of the bonds themselves must be paid off. These payments add to the cost of government and to our national debt. The chart on this page shows you how our national debt has grown over time.

How large a debt can our federal government owe? By law, the federal government can borrow only as much as Congress votes to permit. Congress has established a **debt limit** for the federal government. The federal government must keep its borrowing within this debt limit unless Congress votes to raise the limit to a higher level.

Public Money Is a Public Trust

Handling government money is very complex. It is also of extreme importance to the nation's well-being. It is necessary to keep careful records, or accounts, of where every dollar comes from and how it is spent.

To make sure that public funds are spent according to law and can be fully accounted for, all governments provide for an audit of their accounts. An **audit** is a careful examination, or study, by a trained accountant, of every item of income and expenditure. The auditor checks to make sure every cent is accounted for and every expenditure was properly authorized.

The expenditures of local governments are usually audited by a department of the state government. Expenditures of local school districts are examined by auditors from the state Department of Education or by an independent auditing firm. In our state governments, the audit is usually made by an independent agency of the state under the direction of the comptroller. All federal expenditures are checked by the General Accounting Office, an agency of the legislative branch of the federal government.

Citizen Responsibility

The whole subject of taxes, public funds, and the national debt is a difficult one for many Americans to understand. Yet the well-being of the American nation depends on how wisely our governments handle public funds. If wise policies of raising and spending money are to be followed, the citizen must make an attempt to understand these subjects.

 SECTION 3 REVIEW

Define budget, balanced budget, deficit, surplus, savings bonds, debt limit, audit

Identify Internal Revenue Service (IRS), treasurer, comptroller, Office of Management and Budget (OMB)

1. **Summarizing Ideas** Describe the preparation of the federal budget.
2. **Identifying Ideas** Name three safeguards that are used to prevent mismanagement of public funds.
3. **Expressing Ideas** Why does the federal government have such a large debt?
4. **Understanding Ideas** (a) Why do our governments borrow money? (b) How do they borrow money?
5. **Drawing Conclusions** What does "public money is a public trust" mean?

Thinking Critically The President has asked you to reduce the national debt. Will you increase government revenues, decrease expenditures, or both? Explain your answer.

Government costs a great deal of money. This money must be provided by our citizens. Each of us shares the costs of government. Over the years, the costs of the services of government have increased greatly.

Money for our government is raised by taxes, fees, fines, special payments, and borrowing. There are many kinds of taxes. Americans pay taxes on personal incomes, property, purchases, imported goods, corporate profits, gasoline, and many other things. Our federal, state, and local governments all collect a share of these taxes.

There are agencies to collect this money and others to see that it is spent properly. The executive branches of our governments work closely with the legislative branches to plan government spending and money raising.

Our governments also borrow large sums to help pay their expenses. Federal borrowing has created a large national debt. The public debt is a problem that concerns all Americans. As taxpayers, we must make sure our money is used wisely.

CHAPTER 12 SUMMARY

SOCIAL STUDIES SKILL
Reading A Circle Graph

The federal government collects over $1 trillion in revenue every year (a trillion is $1,000 billion). It uses the money to pay for the hundreds of programs and services it performs for citizens. Because the government handles so much money, it can be difficult to visualize how the huge government budget operates. Where does all of this money go?

One effective way to visualize this information is to use a circle graph. Like other graphs, circle graphs summarize large amounts of information in one easy-to-read diagram.

Every circle graph equals 100 percent of something. The circle graph on this page, for example, represents 100 percent of the federal government's expenses for one year. Each part of the graph represents a part of those expenses. Since national defense accounts for 26 percent of the government's expenses, 26 percent of the circle—about one fourth—is colored to represent this expenditure. Larger expenses take up more space in the circle; smaller expenses take up less space.

How to Read a Circle Graph

To read a circle graph effectively, follow these guidelines.
1. **Determine the subject matter of the graph.** Read the title of the graph to determine the subject and purpose of the graph.
2. **Study the labels.** Circle graphs usually have many labels. The labels indicate the main divisions, or categories, into which the circle has been divided.
3. **Analyze the data.** Compare the sizes of the various sections in the graph. The size of each section is determined by the percentage of the total it represents. The larger the section, the greater the percentage of the total that section represents.

4. **Put the data to use.** Use the data to draw conclusions about the subject of the graph.

Applying the Skill

Use the circle graph below to answer the following questions.
1. **(a)** What is the federal government's largest expense? What is its second largest expense? **(b)** What percentage of the federal budget is devoted to interest payments?
2. What conclusions can you draw about government spending priorities?
3. What are the advantages and disadvantages of using a circle graph?

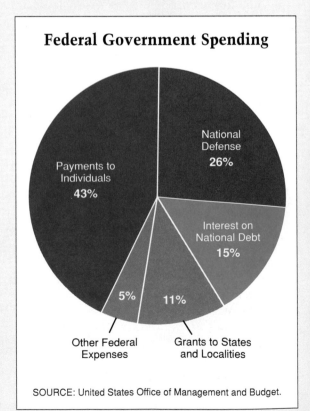

Federal Government Spending

Payments to Individuals 43%

National Defense 26%

Interest on National Debt 15%

5% Other Federal Expenses

11% Grants to States and Localities

SOURCE: United States Office of Management and Budget.

CHAPTER 12 REVIEW

Reviewing Terms

On a separate sheet of paper, supply the term that correctly answers each question.

1. In which kind of budget do expenditures equal revenue?
2. What term means the order of importance of government spending?
3. What is the term used for the payment made for the use of money?
4. What term refers to a tax collected on imported goods?
5. What term is used for the tax based on the amount of a person's income?
6. What must businesses and citizens pay to help support the costs of government?
7. What term refers to a plan for raising and spending funds?
8. Which tax is based on the profits made by corporations?
9. What is the chief agency that helps the President prepare the federal budget?
10. What is government income called?
11. Which federal agency is responsible for the collection of income taxes?

Using Thinking Skills

1. **Understanding Ideas (a)** What are some of the ways governments raise money? **(b)** Explain why it is necessary for our governments to borrow money.
2. **Expressing Ideas (a)** Why have the costs of government increased? **(b)** How is the federal budget prepared?
3. **Summarizing Ideas** What are the rules our governments attempt to follow when they set up taxes?
4. **Drawing Conclusions** Identify the causes of the federal government's debt.
5. **Identifying Ideas** Identify three safeguards that are in place to prevent the misuse of public funds.
6. **Contrasting Ideas (a)** What is the advantage of a protective tariff? **(b)** What is a disadvantage of a protective tariff?

7. **Seeing Relationships** Explain the relationship between government spending and government priorities.

Practicing Civics Skills

Understanding a Circle Graph The figures below show the main sources of revenue for the federal government in 1990. Present this information in the form of a circle graph. Remember to label each category clearly and to title the graph. Then compare the various categories and draw some conclusions about the sources of federal government revenue.

Source	Percentage
Individual Income Taxes	41
Social Security Taxes	34
Corporate Income Taxes	10
Borrowing	8
Excise Taxes	3
Other Sources	4

Being a Good Citizen

1. Conduct library research to prepare a report on the federal budget deficit. Why has the deficit grown? What are some negative effects of the deficit? Are there any advantages to deficit spending?
2. Organize the class into two teams to debate the following resolution: *Resolved: The sales tax is unfair to people who have smaller incomes.*
3. Work with other students to prepare a collage or photo essay that illustrates the results of government spending in your community. You might wish to include images of schools, parks, fire and police stations, and roadways.
4. Contact community officials to find out what local taxes and fees are paid by citizens in your area. Find out also how your local government decides how to spend the revenue. Report your findings to the class.

Reviewing the Facts

1. **(a)** What are political parties? **(b)** What are the advantages of the two-party system we have in the United States?
2. **(a)** What are interest groups? **(b)** How do lobbyists help interest groups?
3. **(a)** Why do our governments need money? **(b)** From what source does the federal government obtain most of its money?
4. **(a)** What is propaganda? **(b)** How does the use of propaganda in a free society differ from the use of propaganda in a totalitarian society?
5. **(a)** What are taxes? **(b)** What are some principles of taxation our governments attempt to follow?
6. **(a)** What is a budget? **(b)** How is the federal government's budget prepared?

Using Critical Thinking

1. **Seeing Relationships (a)** How do voters learn about the opinions of political candidates? **(b)** How has television influenced Presidential campaigns?
2. **Summarizing Ideas** List and describe six kinds of propaganda techniques.
3. **Identifying Roles (a)** What are the functions of political parties in the United States? **(b)** What is the role of a precinct captain in a political party?
4. **Evaluating Information (a)** Why do we have public opinion polls? **(b)** What things should be considered when evaluating the results of a poll?
5. **Organizing Ideas (a)** How do governments raise money? **(b)** What mechanisms are in place to prevent public funds from being misused?
6. **Contrasting Ideas (a)** How do primary elections differ from general elections? **(b)** How do open primaries differ from closed primaries?
7. **Expressing Ideas** How do priorities affect government spending?

8. **Understanding Ideas (a)** Briefly describe the general organization of political parties in the United States. **(b)** How do political parties nominate Presidential candidates?
9. **Comparing Ideas (a)** What is the difference between a regressive tax and a progressive tax? **(b)** Give an example of each kind of tax.
10. **Drawing Conclusions** Why does the federal government spend so much money on interest payments?

Applying What You Know

1. Contact local organizations to find out if volunteers are needed to help with voter registration drives. Offer to help encourage people to register and vote. Share your experiences with the class.
2. Conduct a poll of students in your school. Design the poll and try to obtain a representative sample. You may wish to poll students about school policy or about political events in your community, in your state, or in the nation.
3. Create circle graphs that illustrate the revenue and expenditures of your community government. One circle graph should show revenue and the other circle graph should show expenditures. Display your graphs in the classroom.

Expanding Your Knowledge

Archer, Jules, *Winners and Losers: How Elections Work in America*, Harcourt Brace Jovanovich. Summarizes the election process in the United States and encourages your participation even before you are old enough to vote.

Miller, Stephen, *Special Interest Groups in American Politics*, Transaction Books. Traces the growth of special interest groups throughout the history of the United States.

Citizenship: Home, School, Community

UNIT 5

Citizenship and the Family

Chapter Sections

1 The Changing Family
2 Law and the Family
3 Your Family and You

Chapter Focus

In the first four units of this textbook, you have learned about the ways in which our various governments—national, state, and local—are organized to carry on our public business. However, much of the success of our governments depends upon the willingness of each American citizen to carry out his or her duties and responsibilities.

Children first learn how to be good citizens within the family setting. A **family** is a group of people who are related by blood, marriage, or adoption and who live together and share economic resources.

The family is the basic social unit in every society in the world. Although it takes many different forms around the globe, the family in every society is responsible for **socialization**, or teaching children the basic skills, values, beliefs, and behavior patterns of the society.

As children grow, they are further socialized by teachers, friends, and the mass media. Even so, the family remains the most significant influence in their lives. One of the important things children learn from their families is what it means to be a citizen.

Study Guide

As you begin to learn about the family and its influence on citizenship, look for answers to the following questions:
★ How has the family changed over time?
★ How does the law protect family members?
★ Why is citizenship in the family important?

 The Changing Family

The people who settled our country believed in strong family ties and the importance of a good family life. Americans continue to believe in these things. Over the past several decades, however, the family has been undergoing many changes. As a result, the family now appears in many different forms in the United States.

Some American families contain two parents and children. Others have one parent and one or more children. Still other families are made up of married couples who have no children. Some families are formed when divorced people marry and blend children from their previous marriages into their new marriage. And sometimes three generations of a family all share a home. The fact that the American family can exist in many forms is a testimony to its strength.

The Colonial Family

How different was the colonial family from the family of today? Since much of the country at that time was rural, most American families lived and worked on farms. Colonial families also tended to be much larger than they are now.

Children were economic assets to the colonial family, for many hands were needed to do all the work required on a farm. Older boys worked alongside their father. They learned how to plow the soil, plant seeds, and harvest the crops. They also learned to care for the animals, repair barns and fences, and do the daily chores necessary on a farm. Daughters learned from their mother how to cook and sew, make soap and candles, can fruits and vegetables that they themselves grew, and preserve meat.

Life on the early American farm was hard. There was little time for play or schooling. Sometimes farm children attended a one-room schoolhouse. Most, however, learned the alphabet and numbers at home.

The early farm family was the basic work unit in the colonies. It produced most of what the family needed in order to survive. The family depended on all its members to do their part. As children grew up and were married, they did not always move away from home. Often they brought their wives or husbands with them to live on the family farm.

In these large families, everybody lived and worked together. As a man grew older, he took on lighter chores while his son or son-in-law did more of the heavier work. As a woman grew older, she too spent less time on heavy household chores. She gave more time to sewing or looking after the grandchildren.

Young or old, family members contributed what they could and received whatever care they needed. Because of this need to work together, a strong spirit of cooperation and family pride developed.

The Move to Cities

During the 1800's, American life began to change fairly rapidly. One hundred years ago, seven of every ten Americans lived on farms or in rural areas. Today only one in four

On the farms of rural America a hundred or more years ago, all members of the family had to pitch in to get the work done. Even toddlers had their jobs.

Americans lives in a rural area. This change came about because of the remarkable progress in science and technology that took place during the past hundred years.

Americans soon found use for the new discoveries and inventions. These led to the building of large factories in many urban, or city, areas. The factories needed many workers. At the same time, the development of better farm machinery meant that fewer people were needed to work on the farms. Farm families began to move to urban areas to seek jobs in the factories. This movement of Americans away from the farms to the cities resulted in changes in family life.

The City Family

Life in the cities was much different for families than farm life had been. For one thing, families could no longer spend as much time together as they once had. Fathers now had to work long hours outside the home to earn money to buy the things they had once produced on their own farms. And, until child labor laws were passed in the 1930's, many young children worked in city factories to earn money for their families.

On the farm, the family tended to be a self-contained, self-sufficient unit. Family members were economic producers, and the family was largely responsible for the educational and religious training of the young. Thus the family tended to be the major influence in the lives of children. In the cities, however, the family had to share these responsibilities with other institutions.

The public schools, for example, took on the major responsibility for educating children. Families began to share religious instruction with churches, synagogues, and other houses of worship. And the family became a unit of consumers rather than a unit of producers. In other words, the family in the city had to earn money to buy what farm families could make or grow on their own farms.

Today, the family continues to be a critical influence in the lives of children, but now teachers, friends, and the media are important influences, too. The family has changed in other ways. Families today are smaller than families of the past. In addition, more women work outside the home than ever before. And the family now takes so many different forms that there no longer is a "typical" American family.

The Changing American Family

Family life has changed a great deal since the time most Americans lived on farms. Social scientists who study the family are interested in the ways in which the family continues to change. They have noted a number of trends in recent years. Among these trends are delayed marriage, two-earner marriages, one-parent families, and remarriage.

Delayed Marriage. The average age at which men and women get married has been rising steadily for several decades. In 1960, for example, the average age at first marriage for women was 20.3 years. The average age for men was 22.8. By 1989, the average age at first marriage had risen to 23.6 for women and 25.9 for men.

According to social scientists who study the family, there are several reasons for **delayed marriage,** or marrying at older ages. First, there has been a growing acceptance of singlehood as a life-style. Second, young people have been delaying marriage in order to finish their educations and start their careers. This is especially true for women. And, third, there has been a large increase in the number of couples who live together without being married. Although most people who live with someone eventually get married, living together contributes to delayed marriage.

In addition to delaying marriage, couples are delaying having children. In the past, married women usually had their first baby when they were in their twenties. Today, it is very common for women to have their first child after the age of 30. Couples who delay childbearing usually wait until they are well-established in their careers.

Two-Earner Families. In the past, husbands usually provided the sole income in the family. In recent years, however, there has been an increase in the number of **two-earner families,** or families in which both partners work. This increase is due to the fact that large numbers of married women now work outside the home. The percentage of women who work outside the home has been rising steadily since about 1940. In that year, only about one in seven married women were in the labor force. Today, more than half of all married women work outside the home at least part time.

Married women work for the same reason that married men work—economic necessity. Also, as more women pursue higher education, more of them want to put their skills to use in the labor force. And large numbers of women are finding success in fields once considered the domain of men—fields such as business, engineering, medicine, and law. Social scientists also note that it is more acceptable now than in the past for married women to work outside the home.

Along with the increase in the number of working women has come an increase in the amount of time that husbands devote to child care and household tasks. Although women still have the major responsibility for these tasks, more men than ever before are sharing these responsibilities with their wives. Social scientists have found that men who share household tasks and child care with their wives tend to be younger and have more education than men who do not share.

One-Parent Families. Another trend noted in recent years is a large increase in the number of **one-parent families.** One-parent families are formed through divorce, widowhood, adoption by unmarried people, and births to unmarried women.

Most one-parent families in the United States are the result of divorce. About 25 percent of American families with children under the age of 18 now are one-parent families. In nine out of every ten of these families, the mother is the head of the family.

Although every family has difficulties, the one-parent family is subject to special stresses. For example, one-parent families are much more likely than two-parent families to be poor. In fact, about a third of all one-parent families currently live in poverty. Also, parents in one-parent families must take care of all the responsibilities usually shared by husbands and wives in two-parent families.

Remarriages. Although the United States has one of the highest divorce rates in the world, Americans continue to believe very strongly in marriage and the family. Social scientists who study the family have found that 80 percent of people who get divorced marry again within five years. More than 40 percent of the marriages occurring today are **remarriages.** This means that one or both of the partners has been married before.

Very often in remarriage, one or both of the partners bring children from their previous marriages into the new marriage. These new families are known as **blended families,** or step-families. A number of scientific surveys have studied the relationships between step-parents and step-children. Most surveys have found these relationships to be happy ones.

As you can see, the American family has undergone a number of changes in recent years. Many of these changes are in response to our constantly changing society. The strength of the family is shown by its ability to adapt to these changing times. The American people know that the family is the foundation upon which our nation rests.

 SECTION 1 REVIEW

Define family, socialization, delayed marriage, two-earner families, one-parent families, remarriages, blended families

1. **Understanding Ideas** How did family life in the cities differ from life on the farm?
2. **Summarizing Ideas** Summarize the trends in family life discussed in the section.

Thinking Critically You work for a large company. Your co-workers ask you to urge management to provide a child care center. Accept or refuse their request, and tell why.

② Law and the Family

As you have read, there are many different kinds of families in the United States today. Although all families share some things in common, life within the family unit is affected by a number of factors.

For example, family life may differ depending on whether you live in a big city, a suburb, or a small town. Your family life also may be affected by your racial, cultural, and religious background. Each racial, cultural, and religious group has its own rich heritage and traditions that it brings to family life. Family life also may be affected by such factors as income and age at marriage.

Although life within the family may vary quite a bit, all families are subject to certain laws. These laws are designed to benefit all.

State Laws About Marriage

Because the family is so important to our nation, many laws have been passed to protect it. These laws have been passed by state legislatures, because it is the state governments that have the power to regulate family law. **Family law** regulates marriage, divorce, and the duties of parents and children.

The more than 2 million marriages that take place each year must meet the laws of the state in which they are performed. State laws, for example, have established the earliest age at which young people may marry.

Most states require young people to be at least 18 in order to be married without parental consent. In many states, boys and girls may be married at 16 with the consent of their parents. In a few states, the couple also needs the consent of the court. Some states allow people to marry at younger ages. As you will remember from your reading, the average age at which young people are marrying has been increasing for several decades.

About half our states require a **waiting period** of one to five days from the time a couple applies for a marriage license until the license is issued. This waiting period allows the couple to "think it over." The time is intended to discourage hasty marriages.

All but a few of the states also require that a young man and woman applying for a marriage license take a **blood test** to show that they are in good health. This examination of the blood checks for diseases that can be passed on to another person.

Can You Guess?

- **Why is a wedding ring usually worn on the third finger of the left hand?**
- **Why do wedding guests throw rice at the bride and groom after the ceremony?**

Answers are on page 594.

All states require that marriages be performed by such civil officials as a justice of the peace, judge, or mayor, or by such religious officials as a minister, priest, or rabbi. Witnesses must be present at the ceremony to testify that a legal marriage was performed.

State Laws Protect Family Members

When the marriage ceremony is completed, the newly married couple is considered a family unit. Husband and wife now have certain rights guaranteed by law. If the rights of the husband or wife are neglected, the courts may be asked to step in.

Most cases of nonsupport, physical abuse, desertion, and other marital problems are tried in a domestic relations court. Usually, before a case comes to trial, the court and the lawyers will recommend that the couple consult a marriage counselor to see if they can work out their problems.

Children, too, have certain legal rights as members of the family. If a child is not given proper care by the parents, the law can step in to protect the child. Every state requires doctors and other people to report instances of **child abuse.** Children who are abused, or mistreated, mentally or physically may be taken from their parents by the state.

They may be placed in a **foster home**—the home of people who are unrelated to the child but who agree to act as his or her parents. The state pays the foster parents to care for the child. Parents who abuse their children may also have criminal charges filed against them. Sometimes parents who cannot take care of a child may ask the state to place the child in a foster home for a while.

If a child's parents die, a judge may appoint a relative or close family friend to act as a guardian to care for the child. A **guardian** is a person appointed by a state court to look after individuals who are not yet adults, or who for some reason are unable to care for themselves.

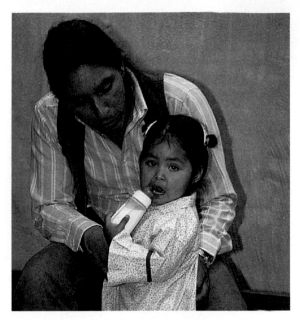

As this picture shows, most family relationships are loving and caring. When problems develop, though, we can count on state laws to protect family members.

Sometimes the guardian will **adopt,** or legally establish, the child as his or her own. If no relative or friend can be found to act as a guardian, the state may put the child up for adoption.

State Laws About Separation

Marriage is a legal act recognized by law. A marriage can be officially ended only by the action of a state court. If a couple cannot get along together, they can take their problems into a state court. The judge will hear both sides of the argument and make a decision.

In some cases, the judge may decide that a **legal separation** is the answer. This means that the marriage is to continue, but that the couple will separate and live apart. The judge weighs the financial situation of the partners and decides how support payments are to be made. In cases of legal separation, it is possible for the partners to return to living together.

(continued on page 268)

Focus on Freedom

The Freedom of Belief

The United States has always been a haven of religious freedom. Many of the people who have settled in the United States came here to escape religious persecution in their own countries. Even today, people come to our country because it offers them the freedom to worship as they choose. This freedom is guaranteed by the First Amendment to the Constitution.

Religion in the United States

The First Amendment states that "Congress shall make no law respecting an establishment of religion, or prohibiting the free exercise thereof." Although they sound simple, these 16 words guarantee Americans many things.

This amendment guarantees the separation of church and state. In other words, Congress may not establish a national religion and may not support one religion over another.

The First Amendment also gives Americans the freedom to belong to any religion they choose. There are now more than 1,300 religious groups in the United States, all free to worship as they wish. (The largest of these groups are shown in the chart on the next page.) Americans also may choose not to join a religious group or practice a religion.

Many cases concerning the interpretation of this First Amendment right have been brought before the Supreme Court. Two of the most interesting cases involve high school students.

"A Position of Neutrality"

In 1962, Ellory Schempp was a senior at a public high school in Abington, Pennsylvania. Each day before announcements were read over the loudspeaker, the principal of Schempp's school read a passage directly from the Bible without comment. Schempp, however, was a member of a church that objects to reading the Bible without interpretation. He thought it was wrong for the principal to read religious material that violated his faith, so he complained about the Bible readings.

When the school district refused to halt the Bible readings, Schempp and his family sued. In 1963 the case went before

The freedom to worship as we choose has always been one of the foundations upon which our nation is based. This freedom is guaranteed to Americans under the First Amendment to the Constitution.

the Supreme Court. The Justices ruled that Bible readings in the public schools are a violation of the First Amendment. "In the relationship between man and religion," Justice Tom C. Clark wrote for the Court, "the State is firmly committed to a position of neutrality."

A Student's Request

Like Schempp, Bridget Mergens was a senior in a public high school when she started on a course that would lead all the way to the Supreme Court. In 1985 Mergens asked the principal of her Omaha, Nebraska, school if she and her friends could meet after school to discuss the Bible. The principal refused her request, maintaining that to allow a Bible group to meet on school grounds would violate the separation of church and state.

Mergens argued that it was wrong to compare voluntary student clubs with enforced religious activities. The school board disagreed, however, and in 1990 the case reached the Supreme Court. The Court ruled that religious clubs may meet on public school grounds as long as they are not sponsored by the school. According to the Court, schools that allow extracurricular activities cannot discriminate against student groups on religious, political, or philosophical grounds.

The Debate Continues

The place of religion in the public schools has been the subject of long and intense debate. Some people believe that schools should encourage religion and prayer. Others maintain that the separation of church and state is a fundamental constitutional guarantee that must be protected. The debate is likely to continue.

Questions to Consider

1. Why did Schempp sue his school district?
2. How did the Court rule in the Mergens case?
3. Should public school teachers lead students in prayer? Why or why not?

Religious Groups in the United States*

Group	Total Members
Roman Catholic	53,496,862
Baptist	26,101,469
Methodist	12,656,593
Lutheran	7,985,237
Moslem	6,000,000
Jewish	4,300,000
Eastern Orthodox	4,241,478
Latter-Day Saints	4,194,286
Pentecostal	3,645,525
Presbyterian	3,345,180
United Church of Christ	1,662,568
Churches of Christ	1,623,754
Christian Church (Disciples of Christ)	1,086,668
Christian Churches and Churches of Christ	1,071,995
Jehovah's Witnesses	773,219
Christian Methodist Episcopal	718,922
Adventist	696,194
Reformed	585,121
Church of the Nazarene	543,762
Salvation Army	434,002
Polish National Catholic	282,411
Christian & Missionary Alliance	244,296
Churches of God	239,058
Mennonite	233,958
Wesleyan	185,641
Unitarian Universalist	173,167
Evangelical associations	120,930
Independent Fundamental	120,446
Friends	111,311
Baha'i	110,000
Buddhist	100,000

*Groups of 100,000 or more.

SOURCE: *World Almanac and Book of Facts, 1990.*

State Laws About Divorce

The final, legal ending of a marriage is called **divorce.** Each state makes its own laws concerning divorce. Some states make it difficult to obtain a divorce by limiting the causes for which divorces are granted. Some grounds for divorce in these states are desertion, mental and physical cruelty, felony conviction, drug addiction, and adultery.

Beginning in the 1970's with California, many states began to offer what is called **no-fault divorce.** Under this system, people seeking divorce do not have to charge their partners with grounds such as those mentioned. Instead, couples simply must state that their marriages have problems that cannot be resolved.

All couples who divorce must make decisions, often through their lawyers, about the division of property, custody of children, visitation rights, and spouse support and child support payments. These decisions are reviewed by a judge. If the judge finds that the decisions are fair, the divorce agreement is approved. If the couple cannot agree on these issues, the judge will decide.

The United States has one of the highest divorce rates in the world. More than 1 million marriages in our country end in divorce each year. In over half of these divorces, the couple has children under the age of 18.

Social scientists who study the family note several reasons for our high divorce rate. First, the divorce process has become less complicated over the past few decades, and the cost of getting a divorce is lower. Second, as more women work outside the home, they are less likely to stay in unhappy marriages for financial reasons. And third, society generally has become more tolerant of divorce.

Some Americans believe that the best way to cut down on the number of divorces is to pass stricter marriage laws. Others believe that more preparation for marriage would result in better family life and lead to fewer divorces. Many high schools and colleges now offer courses in marriage and the family to help young people understand the realities of married life.

The stability of the family affects everyone involved. Therefore, laws are passed to protect marriage partners and their children. State agencies work to keep families together and provide funds to help in child care and family welfare. Laws, however, cannot do the whole job. The best way to guarantee a happy and productive family life is to encourage family members to share and work together for the good of their group.

 SECTION 2 REVIEW

Define family law, waiting period, blood test, child abuse, foster home, guardian, adopt, legal separation, divorce, no-fault divorce

1. **Summarizing Ideas** Describe the state laws that regulate marriage.
2. **Contrasting Ideas (a)** How do state laws protect children? **(b)** How does legal separation differ from divorce?
3. **Understanding Ideas (a)** What types of decisions must be made by couples who are planning a divorce? **(b)** Why does the United States have so many divorces each year?

Thinking Critically You head a committee whose purpose is to suggest ways to reduce our high divorce rate. List three of your suggestions and explain why you think they will work.

 Your Family and You

The family continues to be the most important group in American society. It is the foundation upon which our nation is built. Regardless of whether a person's family is large or small, rich or poor, it performs many important functions for its members and for the nation.

The Family Serves the Nation

There are about 66 million families in the United States. We depend on these families to teach children many of the responsibilities they will have to face as adults. What are some of the family's chief functions as it teaches us these responsibilities?

1. The Family Ensures the Future of Our Nation. A country is only as strong as its people. The family helps keep the nation strong when it provides a home where children can be raised as securely and happily as possible.

2. The Family Educates Its Members. We learn many things from our families. It is in the home that children learn to walk, talk, and dress themselves. Families also teach us to get along with others and to share in the work of the household.

3. The Family Teaches Us the Rules of Good Behavior. The child's earliest ideas of right and wrong are taught in the home. We learn how to behave from the other members of our family.

4. The Family Helps Us Manage Our Money. The family earns and spends money to provide food, clothing, and a place to live for its members. The family should encourage children to learn to manage money, to save, and to share financial responsibilities.

5. The Family Trains Us to Be Good Citizens. The family has the responsibility of helping children learn to respect the rights of others and to understand what their responsibilities as useful citizens will be.

Good Citizenship at Home

Carrying out the functions of the family requires effort by everyone. A home is more than just four walls, a roof, floors, windows, and doors. When Americans think of home, they picture a special place where the family lives together in safety, comfort, and affection. The word **home** means the familiar place that members of the same family share.

The relationship between brothers and sisters can be a rewarding experience. Both can learn patience, kindness, cooperation, and caring.

The ideal home is loving and secure. Of course, no family can ever live up to the ideal all the time. Any group of people living together will disagree at times and need to find ways to solve their differences.

Using common sense and considering another person's point of view help prevent serious family conflict. Remember that each member of the family is a person worthy of respect. Each person has rights. If someone's rights are respected, that person is more likely to respect the rights of others in return.

Members of a family should try to take a sincere interest in one another's activities. They should take every opportunity to discuss the events of their day and to share their feelings. Sharing problems and events of interest teaches family members to give and receive praise, advice, support, and criticism.

Solving Conflicts

Even family disagreements can benefit individual members. Arguments, if kept in hand, can teach you how to present your ideas effectively and help you understand the other person's point of view.

Compare this picture to the one on page 262. Obviously, it is still necessary—and often fun—for family members to work together to meet their needs.

Conflicts can occur between parents and children or among the children in a family. These disagreements require members of the family to make compromises, to give a little and take a little. One of the signs of a well-adjusted family is that members of the family try to work together to find solutions to the irritating problems of everyday living before they grow into big, emotional crises.

By talking over ideas with members of the family, you learn to be understanding and patient. This is important in getting along with other people—friends, classmates, teachers, neighbors, and later, co-workers.

The Problem of Family Funds

One problem many families have is deciding how to spend the family's money. Adults worry about earning enough money to pay for all the things the family needs and wants. They are concerned about the best way to feed, clothe, and shelter the family. The children in the family want money for school lunches, transportation, supplies for hobbies, tickets to the movies, and many other things that seem important at the time.

There are just so many dollars to be divided among the various members of the family. When each person cannot have everything that he or she wants, compromises must be worked out. Doing your share in handling family funds will help you to learn about spending and saving money. Learning to manage money now will be a valuable skill to you as an adult.

The Family Budget

Many families operate on some kind of a budget. The very thought of a budget scares some people. When they think of a budget, they picture a complicated bookkeeping system with column after column of figures. They also believe it usually means "pinching pennies" and denying good times to all members of the family.

A budget should not scare anyone. A budget is simply a plan for spending the family's money. In fact, if a budget is carefully planned and faithfully followed, it can help to reduce the family worries about money matters.

No one else can tell your family how to budget its money. They may make suggestions and explain a little about handling money. However, your family's own special interests and needs require that your family work out its own spending plan.

The first step is to gather facts. The next step is to make a plan based on these facts and to cooperate in carrying it out. The starting point in all budgets is the total amount of money available to spend. Most families have a fixed amount of income. They must keep their spending within this income.

First on your budget would be certain **fixed expenses.** These are expenses that occur regularly and must be paid. There may be rent on an apartment or mortgage payments on a house. There is also the cost of food. This is one of the most important items in the budget. There may also be such regular payments as insurance and telephone bills. The remaining money could pay for clothing, medical expenses, amusements, and other items. You would probably want to set some money aside for savings. A plan would help you spend this money wisely.

Preparing for the Future

You can help your family follow its budget plan. One important way is to help prevent waste in your home. Try not to ask for things that upset the budget. Talk to your parents or guardian before you agree to do things that cost money. Do not insist upon doing things your family cannot afford.

If you receive a regular allowance or earn some money on your own, draw up your own budget. Decide how much you need for transportation, lunches, and other fixed expenses. Then, if you can, set aside some money for future expenses or emergencies.

Remember, too, that your home is the best place in which to learn about home man-

agement. Handling money is just one skill you will need for the future. By learning to get along with your family, you are preparing yourself for the day when you manage your own home.

 SECTION 3 REVIEW

Define home, fixed expenses

1. **Composing an Essay** Write a short essay that discusses the important functions performed by the family.
2. **Understanding Ideas (a)** Why is it important to respect the rights of other family members? **(b)** Why is it important for family members to make compromises?
3. **Identifying Roles** What role can you play in helping your family manage its money?

Thinking Critically You have been invited to give a televised speech on "Citizenship in the Family." Write a draft of your speech.

The American family is the foundation on which our nation's future depends. It is the group in which young citizens learn valuable lessons that stay with them for the rest of their lives.

As our nation has changed, so has family life. We have changed from a nation of farm families who provided for most of their own needs to a nation of city dwellers who must buy most of the products they need. There no longer is a typical American family. People are marrying at older ages, and there have been large increases in the number of two-earner families, one-parent families, and remarriages.

To protect the family, states pass laws regulating marriage, divorce, and the rights of parents and children. The practice of family law has grown as the stresses of modern life have caused family difficulties to increase. Among the problems that have arisen are legal separation, divorce, and abuse.

Many solutions have been offered for keeping the family together. There may be no one answer. However, those who achieve a satisfactory family life work hard at it. You can help your family by cooperating, being willing to make compromises, and staying within the family budget.

CHAPTER 13 SUMMARY

SOCIAL STUDIES SKILL
Using Television as a Resource

New York, 1929. *Engineers focus a camera on a statue of cartoon hero Felix the Cat. In Kansas other engineers see a face flicker on a tiny screen called a viewer. It's Felix—America's first television star.*

The Moon, 1969. *A camera outside the lunar capsule sends pictures back to Earth. Over 500 million people all over the world hold their breath as astronaut Neil Armstrong steps onto the moon.*

In the 40 years between these two events, television became the nation's main source of news and entertainment. Today, over 98 percent of American households have television sets. Because so much of our news comes from television, it is important to watch it with a critical eye. Fortunately, most news programs follow definite formats. Once you become familiar with these formats, it will be easier for you to interpret what you see and hear.

How to Use Television as a Resource

To get the most from television news, follow these guidelines.

1. **Listen for the important events of the day.** Regularly scheduled news programs shown each evening are set up like a newspaper. The opening stories are the headline news, or the most important events of the day. In this portion of the program, you are given the hard facts, along with film clips and on-location reports.

2. **Distinguish between straight news and features.** Features are human-interest stories, meant to amuse and entertain you. This portion of the program usually follows the straight news. Features often appeal more to the emotions than to the mind.

3. **Watch the close of the program.** News programs usually close with sports and weather reports. Sometimes, though, the last report is a commentary. A commentary is a journalist's own interpretation of an event.

4. **Learn to recognize types of news programs.** In addition to the evening news, there are other types of news programs. The most popular are news magazines and documentaries. A news magazine usually studies several issues in one program. A documentary always focuses on a single issue or topic for the entire program.

Applying the Skill

Use the television schedule below to answer the following questions.

1. On which programs would you expect to find a report on the arrival of a foreign official in the United States?

2. **(a)** Which program is an example of a news magazine? **(b)** Which programs are examples of documentaries?

7:00 (2,4,7) NEWS

    (9) BEST OF NATIONAL GEOGRAPHIC: "Season of the Cheetah."

8:00 (2) 60 MINUTES: Includes segments about the volunteer army, economic growth in the Southwest, and a cross-country bicycle trip.

    (4) CHARLIE BROWN SPECIAL: "The Great Pumpkin."

    (7) NFL FOOTBALL: Los Angeles Raiders vs. Minnesota Vikings.

    (9) NATIONAL AUDUBON SOCIETY: "Greed & Wildlife: Poaching in America."

Reviewing Terms

On a separate sheet of paper, supply the term from the list below that correctly answers each question.

blended family
home
family law
foster home

delayed marriage
family
socialization
blood test

1. What term refers to teaching children the basic skills, values, beliefs, and behavior patterns of society?
2. What do social scientists call the tendency to get married at older ages?
3. What is another term for a step-family?
4. What do we call the familiar place that members of the same family share?
5. What regulates marriage, divorce, and the duties of parents and children?
6. What term is used for the home of people who are unrelated to a child but who agree to act as the child's parents?
7. What do we call a group of people who are related by blood, marriage, or adoption and who live together and share economic resources?
8. What is required to show that applicants for a marriage license are in good health?

Using Thinking Skills

1. **Seeing Relationships (a)** How was family life affected by the move to the cities? **(b)** Explain why the average age at marriage has been increasing in recent years.
2. **Organizing Ideas (a)** How are blended families formed? **(b)** How are one-parent families formed?
3. **Expressing Ideas (a)** How do states protect children from abuse? **(b)** How does the no-fault system of divorce differ from the traditional system? **(c)** Give three reasons for our high divorce rate.
4. **Summarizing Ideas** Summarize the five ways in which the family serves the nation.

5. **Drawing Conclusions (a)** What are the special stresses to which one-parent families are subject? **(b)** Why do most states have a waiting period between the time a couple applies for a marriage license and the time the license is issued?
6. **Evaluating Ideas (a)** How does a budget help manage a family's income? **(b)** How can we practice good citizenship at home?
7. **Understanding Ideas (a)** What accounts for the increase in the number of married women who work outside the home? **(b)** How has this increase affected the amount of time that husbands devote to household tasks?

Practicing Civics Skills

Evaluating a News Program Prepare a written report on a television news program. Use the following questions as a guide.

1. **(a)** What news stories does the program cover? **(b)** What features does it cover?
2. **(a)** How much time is devoted to sports and weather? **(b)** Does the program include a commentary? If so, what is the topic?
3. In your opinion, are all the stories reported fairly? Explain.

Being a Good Citizen

1. Organize the class into groups to conduct interviews with religious leaders, police officers, judges, marriage counselors, and citizens. Ask this question: "How can home life be improved in our community?"
2. Conduct research and write a report on one of the following: family life in colonial America; marriage laws in the Soviet Union; child care in the United States.
3. Watch several television programs that focus on two-parent families and several that focus on one-parent families. Do the stresses faced by two-parent families differ from those faced by one-parent families?

CHAPTER 14

Citizenship in School

Chapter Sections

1 The American School System
2 The Best Education for You
3 Developing Skills in Thinking

Chapter Focus

A senator is preparing a speech. A surgeon is about to operate. An auto mechanic is preparing to repair a car. What do these people have in common? They are about to show the practical effects of their education. If they have really profited from their education, the senator will make an effective speech, the surgeon will save a life, and the mechanic will keep the car running smoothly.

The future of our nation depends, in large part, on our system of education. America's schools and colleges must help train our citizens to meet the challenges of a complicated and rapidly changing world.

Today almost every occupation requires some special training. The progress our nation must make in science, social science, engineering, and technology depends upon well-educated citizens prepared to contribute to these fields. You can make a difference in our nation through your dedication, training, and hard work.

Study Guide

As you begin to learn about America's schools and the opportunities they offer you, look for answers to the following questions:

★ How did our school system begin, and what is it like today?
★ What are some of the American values in education?
★ What goals guide our schools, and how can you get the most from your education?
★ How do we develop skills in thinking?

1 The American School System

There are about 60 million students enrolled in public and private schools and colleges in the United States. The cost of running these educational enterprises has now risen to more than $300 billion a year, or about $5,000 per student. Almost 7 million teachers, administrators, and staff handle the day-to-day tasks of education. It is obvious that Americans place a high value on education.

The Purposes of Education

The American people are proud of the progress and achievements of their educational system. There are two main reasons for this great interest in education.

1. Schools Exist to Serve in the Development of Each Individual American Citizen. From the earliest days of our nation, Americans have placed great value on the individual. The first purpose of education is, therefore, to serve the individual. All citizens should be given the opportunity to study and learn in order to develop their own talents and abilities.

The Declaration of Independence sets forth the American belief "that all men are created equal; that they are endowed by their Creator with certain unalienable rights; that among these are life, liberty, and the pursuit of happiness." Over the years, Americans have come to believe that all citizens—all races and both men and women—should have equal opportunities to succeed through equal access to education.

2. Schools Serve in the Development of the American Nation. The welfare of all Americans depends on the willingness and ability of all individuals to use their talents for the welfare of the entire nation. The aim of education is to teach Americans how to make important contributions to our society.

Education stresses the need for good citizenship. Our schools try to show how the welfare of each citizen and the welfare of the nation depend on all Americans learning to work together for the common good.

Beginnings of Our School System

Our system of education has been growing for over 300 years. The first important step was taken in Massachusetts in 1647. A law was passed there requiring all towns except very small ones to set up public schools.

The purpose of this law was to make sure all children learned to read the Bible, so that they would not fall into evil ways. This law provided for every town of 50 families or more to hire a schoolteacher, who would be paid out of town funds. By doing this, Massachusetts shifted the responsibility for schooling from the home to the community as a whole.

In many of the other colonies, however, education of the young was neglected. Children of the wealthy were sent to private schools or taught by tutors. In contrast, children of poor parents often were put to work at an early age and given little or no schooling.

It was not until the first half of the 1800's that leaders such as Horace Mann began to demand free public schools for all children. The gradually developing public school

Artist Winslow Homer shows us what an American country school looked like more than a hundred years ago. Students of different ages all studied in the same room.

system, however, did not include black Americans. Many of them were slaves, and very few received an education.

Many Americans in those days were opposed to free public schools. Some taxpayers did not want to pay to educate other people's children. Owners of private schools argued that free public schools would ruin their businesses. Some people who ran church-supported schools claimed that education should be under the control of the church and the home.

Supporters of public education, on the other hand, argued that a democratic society requires a citizenry that can read and write. By the time of the Civil War, the struggle for public, tax-supported schools was beginning to be won. Most Northern states and some Southern states had set up public school systems. These school systems, however, were usually limited to elementary schools. There were very few high schools in the United States in 1850. It was not until the period after the Civil War that a system of public secondary schools, or high schools, began to be set up in the United States.

The Educational Ladder

Most Americans spend many years getting an education. There are several levels in the American system of education. Our schools range from nursery schools for young children to universities for adult higher education.

Nursery Schools. Many American children attend nursery school, or preschool. Nursery school is usually attended by children three and four years old. In these schools, children learn to play and get along with other children. Most nursery schools are private. However, some communities support nursery schools as part of their public school system. The federal government also grants funds for preschool programs in some communities.

Kindergartens. Many public school systems start with kindergarten classes for five-year-old children. The word "kindergarten" is German and means "garden for children." Kindergarten children spend a year learning how to get along with others and preparing for first grade. In some areas, they begin learning to read and write and to recognize numbers.

Elementary Schools. Most children enter the first grade of elementary school at the age of five or six. In elementary school students learn the basics of education—reading, writing, and arithmetic. The curriculum is also enriched by such subjects as history, science, health, art, music, and physical education. Children attend elementary school for from five to nine years, depending on how the school system is arranged.

Junior High Schools. Grades 7, 8, and 9 usually make up the junior high school. Many school systems have given up junior high schools in favor of middle, or intermediate, schools. Middle schools usually include grades 5 or 6 through 8. Some are only for grades 7 and 8.

High Schools. Students who have completed the first eight or nine grades enter high school. There are generally three kinds of high schools. Academic high schools prepare students for college. Technical and vocational high schools enable students to learn a trade or occupation. Comprehensive high schools offer college preparatory work as well as vocational courses. About 85 percent of all American girls and boys ages 14 through 17 are enrolled in public high schools.

Higher Education

The need for higher education in the United States has grown with advances in knowledge. Many jobs now require college and university training. Therefore, many high school students feel it is important that they continue their education.

Junior Colleges. The growing demand for higher education is being met in part by two-year **junior colleges.** These schools are sometimes called **community colleges.** They are often supported by taxpayers and offer courses free or at low tuition to local high school graduates. Courses include training for specialized fields and preparation for more ad-

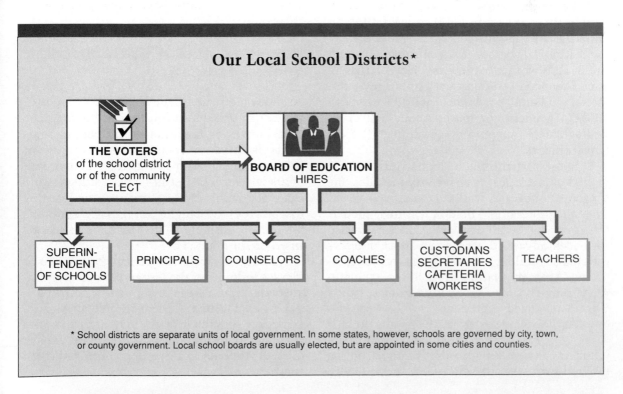

Our Local School Districts*

THE VOTERS
of the school district
or of the community
ELECT

BOARD OF EDUCATION
HIRES

SUPERINTENDENT OF SCHOOLS

PRINCIPALS

COUNSELORS

COACHES

CUSTODIANS SECRETARIES CAFETERIA WORKERS

TEACHERS

* School districts are separate units of local government. In some states, however, schools are governed by city, town, or county government. Local school boards are usually elected, but are appointed in some cities and counties.

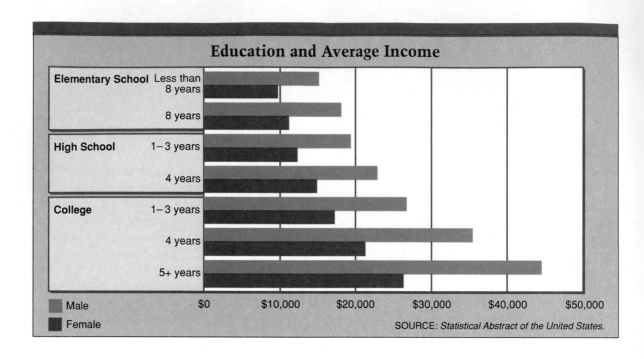

Education and Average Income

Elementary School	Less than 8 years
	8 years
High School	1–3 years
	4 years
College	1–3 years
	4 years
	5+ years

$0 $10,000 $20,000 $30,000 $40,000 $50,000

Male
Female

SOURCE: *Statistical Abstract of the United States.*

vanced study. Many junior college graduates transfer to four-year colleges or universities.

Colleges and Universities. Altogether there are some 2,000 colleges and universities in the United States. Most are co-educational. That is, they are open to both men and women students. They range in size from small **colleges** with only a few hundred students to large institutions with 100,000 students or more. About half of all colleges are supported by state or local governments.

Some institutions of higher learning are called universities. A **university** includes one or more colleges as well as graduate programs in some professional field of learning, such as business, medicine, and law. A university also provides advanced studies in most subjects offered in college, including history and biology. After graduation from college, the student may go on to **graduate school** to study for an advanced degree.

As you can see from the graph on this page, it pays to stay in school and get as much education as you can. In addition to becoming a well-educated person, your income will

likely increase. This is true for both men and women. However, at every educational level, women traditionally have made less money than men.

Special Education

American citizens believe in equal opportunities through education for everyone. In the past, however, students with special needs were isolated in separate classrooms or schools. Today, the law demands that students with special needs—gifted students and students with physical, mental, or learning disabilities—be taught in regular classrooms whenever possible. This practice is called **mainstreaming.**

Many disabled students go to regular classes for most of the day and then work with specially trained teachers for a few hours each day or each week. Others receive special instruction for much of the day and then join regular classes in such things as art and music. Gifted students receive special enrichment instruction.

American Values in Education

Our school system has developed the way it has because the American people value education highly. Some of the traditional values that have developed over the years are:

1. Public Education Should Be Free. There should be no hidden charges to prevent any citizen from receiving a good education at public expense. Public education in the United States costs local taxpayers more than $150 billion a year. This amount includes educational expenditures by the federal government of about $24 billion.

2. Schooling Should Be Equal and Open to All. No one should be discriminated against because of race, sex, religion, or financial status.

3. Public Schools Should Be Free of Any Creed or Religion. Our schools are open to all Americans regardless of their religious beliefs. The Supreme Court has held that no special prayer or Bible reading shall be allowed during the school day. However, private religious schools are permitted to exist outside the public school system.

4. Public Schools Should Be Controlled by the State and Local Governments Within Which They Are Located. Local school boards run the public schools under laws passed by the state legislature. State boards or departments of education assist local schools but do not give orders to district boards. Actual control of the schools rests with the local school district, where the people know the local needs.

5. Attendance at School Should Be Compulsory. Each state compels school attendance by young people, usually between the ages of 7 and 16. Parents may not decide to keep their children out of school.

6. Schooling Should Be Enriching and Not Limited to the Basics. Schools should be places where young people can grow in mind, body, and spirit. Sports, clubs, social events, and creative arts are a part of each person's education. Schools should be lively places where individuals are encouraged to develop to their greatest potential.

Problems of Today's School System

Americans have long believed that education is the backbone of democracy. Because education is so important to our nation and its citizens, we must all be aware of the problems that face our educational system and work toward solving them.

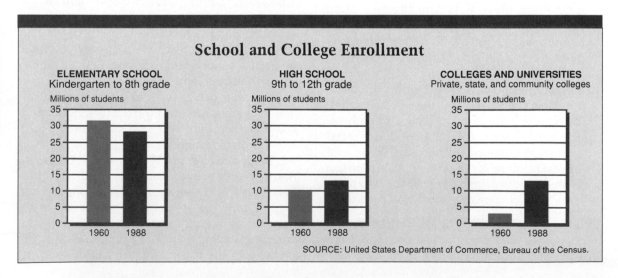

School and College Enrollment

SOURCE: United States Department of Commerce, Bureau of the Census.

One issue that currently challenges our educational system is the need for educational reform. Test scores show that American students are falling behind the students of other industrial nations in science, math, and reading. Some people fear that this will make it difficult for our nation to compete economically in the global community. In addition, American technology is advancing so rapidly that our own economy increasingly needs highly skilled, well-educated workers.

To help our youth meet the challenges of the future, states all across the nation are instituting educational reforms. Among these reforms are increased emphases on math, science, and reading, and stricter requirements for graduation from high school.

Our educational system has also been challenged in recent years by an increase in violence in the schools. In some places, teachers must spend more time trying to maintain discipline than they do teaching. This threatens the learning environment for everyone.

★ SECTION 1 REVIEW

Define junior colleges, community colleges, colleges, university, graduate school, mainstreaming

1. **Expressing Ideas** What are the two main purposes of education in the United States?
2. **Composing an Essay** Write a short essay describing the history of public education in the United States.
3. **Summarizing Ideas (a)** Describe the main levels on the American educational ladder. **(b)** Why is it important to get as much education as you can? **(c)** How has special education changed in recent years?
4. **Understanding Ideas (a)** List six American values in education. **(b)** Describe two problems that challenge American education.

Thinking Critically You head a panel designed to encourage students to stay in school. What will be your recommendations?

② The Best Education for You

Luck has been defined as being in the right place at the right time. What we sometimes forget to add is that the lucky person is also able to see opportunities and make good use of them. This is true in school and in studying, too. You must be alert in order to take advantage of the opportunities offered in school. What are these opportunities?

What Your School Has to Offer You

Some years ago, a group of teachers and school officials listed the goals of education that American schools should try to achieve. The statement they prepared is called "The Seven Cardinal Principles of Secondary Education." As you study these goals, or principles, try to think how your school works to achieve them. Ask yourself if you are taking advantage of the opportunities offered under each heading.

1. Using Basic Learning Skills. One of the main goals of our schools is to teach each student the skills of reading, writing, and arithmetic. In addition, schools teach certain other skills that help students learn and study. These learning skills include public speaking, organizing and expressing ideas, using a dictionary, and doing research. They also include the ability to read and interpret maps, graphs, charts, pictures, and cartoons.

You can use these skills to great advantage in many different courses in school. You will discover that you will continue to use these skills throughout your life.

2. Learning to Work with Others. Many of your school activities require you to work with other students. This cooperation is good practice in helping you work with members of your family. It will also help you work with other people in your community now and in the future. Furthermore, your experience in working with others will be very useful when you have a job.

3. Health Education. Most schools have a program in health education to teach students to develop good health habits. Health education usually also offers programs of physical activities, including sports and athletics. You will benefit from the exercise these programs provide. Moreover, the theory and practice learned in school will help you take good care of your health and keep physically fit throughout your life.

4. Training for Your Life's Work. Your school provides the educational foundation on which your special job training will be based. Your school also tries to help you prepare for job opportunities after you graduate. Employers want and need well-educated workers. Schools make it possible for you to become a desirable employee. By taking advantage of your education, you can prepare for a job in which you can both contribute to your nation and find satisfaction.

5. Active Citizenship. To help you to become a good citizen, your school seeks to develop your interest in your community. It teaches you about the history of your nation, its institutions, and the problems it faces today. Your classes and school activities help develop in you a sense of loyalty, love of country, good judgment, and willingness to do your fair share.

6. Considerate Behavior. In addition, your school tries to teach students to adapt to accepted standards of behavior. It tries to develop in all students a feeling of consideration for their families, teachers, classmates, friends, and all members of the community. Your school stresses, too, the importance of respecting the privacy and property rights of other citizens.

7. Wise Use of Leisure Time. Your school also tries to teach you to enjoy good books, art, and music so that they may enrich your life. Your teachers encourage you to take up interesting hobbies and to take part in such school activities as athletics, dramatics, glee club, or band.

By encouraging you to undertake such activities, your school is trying to help you to find a hobby or special interest to enjoy now and in the future. In this way, your school helps prepare you to make good use of your spare time throughout your lifetime.

Getting the Most Out of School

If you are to make the best use of the opportunities your school offers, you will need to remember the goals your school is trying to reach. Your years in school are very important. The success you enjoy in school and the study and learning habits you develop will help determine the kind of person you will be later in life. What kinds of study and learning habits should you try to develop?

One of the first and most important study habits all students must learn is the wise use of time. The well-organized student finds time in his or her daily schedule for study, school activities, exercise, relaxation, and the proper amount of sleep. Just as your family budgets
(continued on page 284)

The students in this chemistry class know the value of a good education. The things they are learning in school will prepare them for their lives as adults.

CITIZENSHIP
IN ACTION

Senior Volunteers

Ruth Givens teaches French. Charles Wauneka teaches mathematics. Anna Chavez helps Spanish-speaking children learn English. These jobs aren't unusual—but the people who do them are. All three are retired people who work each week as volunteers in the public schools of Houston, Texas. No one pays them. They work for fun and because they enjoy helping.

VIPS-SENIORS

None of these three volunteers had ever taught before joining Houston's VIPS-SENIORS program. VIPS stands for Volunteers in Public Schools. The program is run by the Houston Independent School District. The SENIORS part of the program has drawn more than 1,000 older citizens. Its aim is to encourage retired people to share their skills with students.

Ruth Givens is a grandmother who loves French. While raising her own children, she had studied French in her free time. Now she helps others learn to speak French. Ruth tutors seventh graders in French in a middle school.

Charles Wauneka is a retired sales executive. He works two days a week helping to teach math in an elementary school. At first Charles thought he would have difficulty explaining the importance of numbers to young students. Soon, though, he found that teaching mathematics "is more personally rewarding than anything I have ever done."

Anna Chavez retired from a job in a food-processing plant. Now, as a full-time school volunteer, she uses her ability to speak both Spanish and English fluently. Anna's goal is to encourage young people to learn. She regrets that she did not discover her love for teaching earlier. However, she says that "now I can give the students the time they need."

Time for Success

VIPS-SENIORS began in 1976 with a grant—money donated for a special project. The program was so successful that

Older Americans have a lifetime of knowledge to share with young people.

when the grant ran out, Houston businesses and foundations contributed money so that the project could continue.

Time given to individual students is the key to the VIPS-SENIORS success, says one teacher in the program. "Who but senior volunteers can give a student two hours of undivided attention each week?"

Volunteers choose the hours they want to work and the kind of work they prefer. If they like, they can serve as "living historians." These volunteers are interviewed by students three times a year—usually about life in their childhood communities or about some special period or event in their lives.

Many volunteers end up doing more than they planned. Some have given slide shows or put together cultural programs. A number of volunteers have gone back to college to become teachers. As one retired volunteer said, "After I realized how much I enjoyed teaching, I decided to become better prepared."

Everyone benefits from the work done by volunteers.

Thinking It Over

1. Why do you think the Houston school district wanted to use older citizens in its volunteer program?
2. What benefits might a retired person receive from being a school volunteer?
3. Why might a student want to interview a "living historian"?

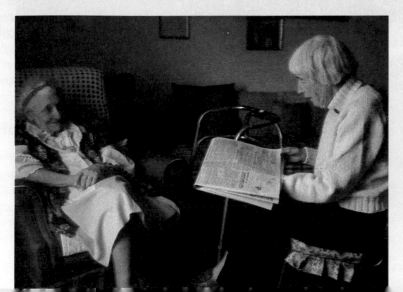

Retired people also volunteer their time to help other senior citizens.

3 Developing Skills in Thinking

One of the main purposes of education is to help people learn how to think. The dictionary tells us that to think is to form ideas in the mind. This sounds simple enough, but how do we form these ideas? We think mainly with facts. When faced with a problem, thinking people consider all the facts. They then consider all possible solutions and decide which solution seems best to them. How do we obtain the facts with which we do our thinking? We learn them.

How We Learn

Almost everything we do—the way we act, think, pass along information, even the way we show emotion—is learned. People learn in many ways. However, all learning is the result of some kind of **experience,** or things that happened in the past.

The simplest kind of learning is the result of experience that involves the motor nerves—those nerves that control our muscles. For example, a person who touches a hot stove will pull back the hand because of the pain. Next time, that person will avoid hot stoves. Now suppose that while the person was reaching for the stove, someone said "Hot!" in a sharp tone. In the future, if near a hot stove, the person will draw back a hand whenever someone says "Hot!" This kind of learning is called **conditioning.**

Much of our behavior, or the way we act, is conditioned. People learn to do things because they expect to be rewarded or to gain satisfaction. Children will wash their hands before meals if they expect to receive praise or a hug. They will continue to behave in the desired way if they are rewarded occasionally. Behavior that is repeated often usually becomes a **habit**—an action that is performed automatically.

People also learn by copying, or imitating, others. Young children imitate their parents or guardians and other members of the family. They try to act and think like them. They repeat their family's opinions and habits. As adults, people often imitate their friends and others they admire.

Learning in School

Much of what we know is also learned by looking and listening. Every day of our lives we learn through our senses and take in different kinds of information. However, in our complex society, there is so much information that it has to be organized, or arranged in groups, in order to be usable. A large part of the organized information we learn is taught in school and in books.

Besides facts, schools teach students how to make the best use of information by comparing and analyzing facts, putting the facts together, and drawing conclusions. We also are taught where to find information.

Our ability to learn depends on our maturity, experience, and intelligence. It also depends on how highly motivated we are. **Motivation** is something within people that stirs them and directs their behavior.

How We Think

Thinking is a complex process. It involves our awareness, understanding, and interpretation of what we see and know. We are thinking when we solve problems by considering all the solutions we know. Every time we make a decision, we solve a problem.

Sometimes we try to find an answer to something and cannot come up with it, no matter how hard we try. Then, suddenly, the answer will spring to mind. This is called **insight.** The answer seems to come out of nowhere. Actually, it comes to mind only after we have studied the problem and ruled out several possible answers. Without realizing it, people often take what they know about something else and apply it to the subject they are studying.

Occasionally our solutions are original. The ability to find new ways of thinking and doing things is called **creativity.** Everyone can think creatively. We have other thinking abilities, too. Our abilities to reason, question, and weigh information are ways of thinking.

Critical Thinking

The kind of thinking we do in order to reach decisions and solve problems is called **critical thinking.** This type of reasoning, or clear thinking, includes a number of different steps. There is no simple way to learn the truth about an issue or solve a problem. The search for truth on many subjects is long and hard. Yet all Americans must seek answers to problems that face us and our nation every day. How can we learn to think clearly in order to make up our minds?

Defining the Problem. The first step is to make sure that the problem or question is clear in your mind. That is, you need to make certain that you fully understand it and any terms that might be involved. You may find it helpful to write down the problem to which you wish to find the answer. If it is a difficult one, you might outline the main ideas. See if you can find the relationships between the ideas. Are some of the ideas causes and others effects?

Distinguishing Fact from Opinion. Once the problem is clear to you, you can look for evidence that will help you understand and judge the issues involved. What are the facts? It may surprise you to discover that there are often disagreements over facts. One side may say one thing, and the other side may claim something very different. Therefore, it is important in critical thinking always to distinguish between fact and personal opinion, or judgment.

To illustrate how difficult it is to determine what is fact, let us look at the following

Although computers now have an important place in American education, they cannot replace the human ability to think critically.

For individuals to receive a good education, they must have a great deal of help—from experienced people and from a variety of learning materials.

facts really fit the problem. You must learn to judge which side of the argument the facts seem to support.

Reaching a Conclusion. After you have weighed the evidence, you can reach your own judgment, or conclusion. Try to keep an open mind. Remember that if new evidence is found, it may be necessary to change your conclusion.

Sometimes there is more than one possible answer to a question or solution to a problem. In trying to decide which solution you favor, you may want to test how each solution might work. You may do this by mentally checking the facts against each possible solution. If you still cannot make a decision, you might try to imagine the question or problem in a real-life setting. See which of the possible solutions would work best in such a situation. Knowing which solution would be most appropriate to the circumstances is an important part of making decisions and solving problems.

example. A newspaper reporter may write that a famous actor "angrily pounded on a neighbor's door until it was broken." The fact that the door pounding took place can be proved. Several eyewitnesses may have seen it. Yet was the actor really angry? This is the reporter's judgment. The actor may have pounded on the door not in anger, but to warn the neighbor of a fire.

A person's emotions, such as anger or happiness, are difficult to check or measure accurately. It is important, therefore, to know whether you are dealing with facts or information colored by emotions.

Weighing the Evidence. In thinking through a problem, it also is important to learn to weigh all the evidence. Are the facts used by the speaker or writer really the important ones you need to know? Are these all the facts you need to know, or are important facts still missing? Have you studied all the tables, graphs, maps, and other available sources and helps? In learning to think clearly, you also must learn to judge whether the given

Who Influences Your Thinking?

Clear thinking also demands that you realize how other people influence your thinking. How much are you influenced by what others say or do?

No one can do our thinking for us. However, other people do help determine what we think. Our families, teachers, and friends have a great influence on our opinions. Sometimes we are influenced by some well-known person we admire. We often listen carefully to what a famous person says. As you recall, we also get ideas from the mass media. Many of these ideas are propaganda. That is, they are used to try to influence us.

Sometimes people think and behave in certain ways because they are members of particular groups in our society. In a labor dispute, for example, an employer may have a different opinion from that of a worker. Few people are able to be impartial, or completely objective, all the time.

People sometimes have opinions that are biased, or favor one side. All of us have certain fixed feelings, or prejudices. **Prejudice** is an opinion not based on a careful and reasonable investigation of the facts. We must be careful not to be ruled by our own prejudices or those of others.

Thinking for Yourself

You live in a nation that values the freedom of independent thought. Take advantage of this freedom to learn how to think for yourself. Study the way that you make decisions. Learn how to gather information and how to interpret it. Most important, believe in yourself enough to arrive at your own conclusions.

Our republic can work only if citizens are willing to think for themselves and not simply accept what others tell them. Your school can help you think clearly. By trying harder to examine the facts given to you in class and to make up your own mind, you will learn the skills you need to vote wisely, understand current issues, and solve local problems.

SECTION 3 REVIEW

Define experience, conditioning, habit, motivation, insight, creativity, critical thinking, prejudice

1. **Seeing Relationships (a)** How do we learn through experience? **(b)** What role does insight play in the thinking process?
2. **Summarizing Ideas** Describe the steps involved in learning to think critically.
3. **Understanding Ideas (a)** What is the difference between a fact and an opinion? **(b)** Explain why it is important to learn how to think for yourself.

Thinking Critically The Secretary of Education has asked you to give a televised speech entitled "The Importance of Education in Today's World." Write a draft of your speech.

The American educational system has developed in many ways during the history of our nation, and it continues to grow. The American people value a free public education for all.

Your school tries to teach many worthwhile things. It teaches you the basic skills of learning. It offers a variety of subjects. Education also prepares you to be a good citizen in your family and in the nation.

One of the most important skills you learn in school is the ability to read well and understand what you read. Schools also help people think clearly and make judgments. Everyone must learn to gather and study the facts, weigh the evidence, and consider alternative solutions before reaching a conclusion.

In learning to think for yourself, you need to consider how opinions are formed. For example, you may sometimes be influenced by people you admire. You must also be aware that some people are biased because of the kind of work they do or because of the groups to which they belong. As an American, you must learn the skills needed to be able to think for yourself.

CHAPTER

14

SUMMARY

CITIZENSHIP SKILL
Distinguishing Fact from Opinion

One of the keys to evaluating what you read and hear is the ability to distinguish between fact and opinion. A fact is something that can be proved true. In other words, facts can be counted, measured, or documented in some way. Opinions, on the other hand, are personal beliefs about what is true. Because people often use facts to back up their opinions, it is important to learn how to distinguish between the two. Once you learn this skill, you will be better able to evaluate the information you read and hear on a daily basis.

How to Distinguish Fact from Opinion

To distinguish fact from opinion, follow these guidelines.

1. **Determine if the information can be proved.** You can begin to identify facts by asking the same questions a reporter uses to write a good news story. If the information answers the questions *who, what, when, why,* or *how,* it probably contains facts. Next, determine if these facts can be documented in any way, perhaps through other sources.

2. **Notice how the facts are used.** Keep in mind that a single word often can change a statement from fact to opinion. Certain phrases, such as "In our judgment . . . ," or "I think that . . ." clearly signal that an opinion is about to be given.

3. **Be on guard against "loaded" words.** Loaded words are words that carry an emotional appeal, such as *beautiful, boring, exciting, extremely,* and *most important.* The minute you spot such descriptive words, you have found an opinion. Do not allow loaded words such as these to color your judgment about the facts.

Applying the Skill

Read the campaign flier shown below. Then use the flyer to complete the following activities.

1. **(a)** Identify the loaded words in the following sentence: "Janice Green is a dedicated educator who has served successfully on the school board for more than 12 years." **(b)** How might these loaded words affect a person's interpretation of the facts?

2. Imagine that you are a reporter for your local newspaper. What facts from the flier would you include in your news story?

3. Use the facts contained in the flier to write an editorial supporting Janice Green.

JANICE GREEN FOR CITY COUNCIL

Janice Green is determined to improve our city. If elected Green will:

★ increase the number of buses running during rush hour. Thirty percent of public buses do not run during rush hour.

★ ensure that our city taxes are reasonable. Over the past ten years, city taxes have been increased six times.

★ add to and improve facilities for the elderly. At present, there are over 100 persons waiting to take part in this city's programs for the elderly.

Janice Green knows our city well. She is a dedicated educator who has served successfully on the school board for more than 12 years.

Elect **JANICE GREEN.** She will make this a better city in which to live.

CHAPTER 14 REVIEW

Reviewing Terms

On a separate sheet of paper, supply the term from the list below that correctly completes each sentence.

graduate school
creativity
junior college
conditioning

critical thinking
mainstreaming
prejudice
study helps

1. The kind of thinking one does in order to reach decisions and solve problems is called _____ _____.
2. An institution that offers advanced degrees to college graduates is a _____ _____.
3. _____ is the practice of putting students with special needs into regular schools and classes.
4. _____ is the ability to find new ways of thinking and doing things.
5. Learning that is the result of a reward system or of experience involving the motor nerves is called _____.
6. _____ is an opinion that is not based on a careful and reasonable investigation of the facts.
7. _____ _____ are the parts of a textbook that help you learn the material in the text.
8. A _____ _____ is a two-year college.

Using Thinking Skills

1. **Contrasting Ideas (a)** Why were some Americans in the 1800's opposed to public education? **(b)** Why argument did supporters of public education offer for their views?
2. **Seeing Relationships (a)** Explain how schools serve both the individual and the nation. **(b)** Why is it important to get a good education?
3. **Summarizing Ideas** Describe each level of the American educational ladder.

4. **Identifying Ideas (a)** Identify six American values in education. **(b)** Why do the problems facing education challenge us all?
5. **Composing an Essay** Write an essay that describes the goals of American schools.
6. **Understanding Ideas (a)** What can you do to get the most from your textbooks? **(b)** What are some of the ways in which we learn?
7. **Expressing Ideas (a)** Explain the steps you must take to practice critical thinking. **(b)** Why is it a good idea to take notes?

Practicing Civics Skills

Identifying Fact and Opinion Read the following paragraph. Then answer the questions.

"Americans are better educated today than ever before. According to recent statistics, nearly 75 percent of all people over the age of 25 have high school diplomas. An impressive 20 percent hold college degrees. To set even higher records, I think each state should require students to attend school until they reach the age of 25."

1. **(a)** Which sentences are statements of opinion? **(b)** Which sentences are statements of fact?
2. What loaded words are found in the paragraph?

Being a Good Citizen

1. Organize the class into groups to interview school officials, family members, and business people concerning their opinions of the importance of education in today's world.
2. Research and write a report on the history of public education in the United States. Share your findings with the class.
3. Make a time budget, or schedule, for your day. Include in your schedule a regular time for study, recreation, meals, travel, work, household tasks, and sleep. See if it helps you to improve your study habits.

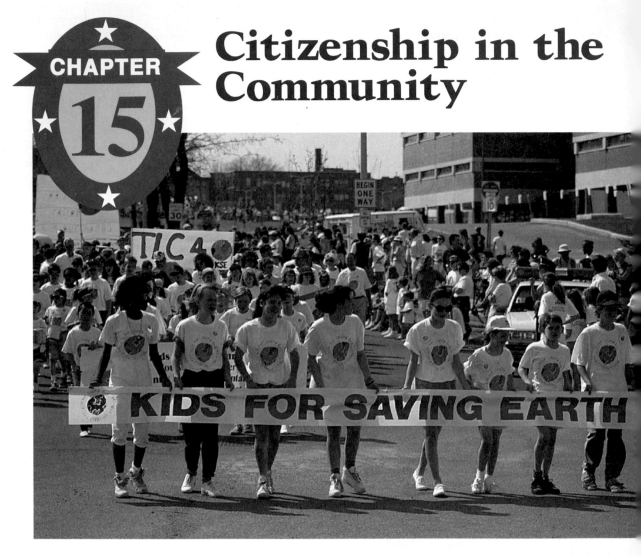

Citizenship in the Community

CHAPTER 15

Chapter Sections

Chapter Focus

There are very few people in the world who do not enjoy being with other people. Most people find life easier, richer, and more interesting when they can share it with others. We also need other people to provide us with the goods and services that we cannot provide for ourselves.

The early settlers in America found that their lives were easier if they settled near other people. They often depended on their neighbors for help or protection. Working together was an absolute necessity. Building a barn or harvesting crops often required help from others. Moreover, social affairs provided a much needed break from the toils of settlement life.

Ever since our country began—and indeed, ever since the beginning of human history—people have lived and worked together. The community plays a vital role in the lives of all American citizens.

By **community,** we mean a group of people having common interests who live in the same area and are governed by the same laws. You, along with every other American citizen, live in a community.

Study Guide

As you begin to learn about communities, look for answers to the following questions:

★ How do communities develop, and what kinds of communities exist?

★ What special advantages do people enjoy by living in communities?

★ What do people do to make life better in their communities?

1 Many Kinds of Communities

From the beginning, American settlers tried to pick out locations for their settlements that had natural advantages. Farmers were attracted to the fertile river valleys and later to the plains. Those interested in commerce knew that a place with a good harbor would help them build a prosperous trade. A natural dam site along a river would provide power for factories. A bend in the river provided a good landing place for riverboats. Even today a warm sunny climate, beautiful sandy beaches, or snowcapped mountains may encourage the growth of a tourist center or manufacturing area.

Crossroads Settlements

As American settlers moved farther inland, they often settled where two main roads crossed. A **crossroads** was generally a good place to sell supplies to travelers. An enterprising settler built an inn at the crossroads. A blacksmith found business there shoeing horses and repairing wagons. Farmers came to this small settlement to trade. In time the crossroads settlement grew and became a thriving city.

Transportation Centers

Our young nation depended largely on boats for transportation. The location of America's waterways therefore helped determine the location of our cities. The largest cities in the American colonies were deep-water ports on the Atlantic coast. Boston, New York, Philadelphia, and Charleston were such cities.

Most of our large inland cities grew up at lake ports or along major rivers. St. Paul and Minneapolis, for example, are located at easy-to-reach stopping points on the upper Mississippi River. New Orleans prospered because it was at the mouth of the Mississippi River. Goods coming down the river were reloaded onto oceangoing vessels at the port of New Orleans. These cities became important **transportation centers** because of their location on major bodies of water.

The coming of the railroad also helped our cities grow. After 1840 railroad lines were built to connect various parts of our nation. They soon contributed to the further growth of our towns and cities. Railroads also created new cities. Inland cities that were not on rivers or lakes grew up as railroads provided a new and speedy method of transportation. Indianapolis, Dallas, and Denver grew prosperous because they were located along busy railroad lines.

Today, Americans depend heavily on automobiles for transportation. New communities have grown up along our highways. In the open countryside, land is less expensive than in the city. For that reason, families can more easily afford to live there. On this land, new industrial plants have been built that do not have to be near railroad or water transportation. Trucks carry goods to and from them over modern highways. New communities have grown up around these plants to house the workers and provide services for them.

Resources and Climate Help Communities Grow

The United States is a nation with rich natural resources. It has a temperate climate in which vigorous activity is possible. Its broad, navigable lakes and rivers and long coastline furnish many good ports and harbors. Our nation also has vast stretches of fertile soil, adequate rainfall, good pasture land, and abundant forests. Beneath the soil are rich deposits of uranium and other metals, petroleum, and coal.

Climate and natural resources have encouraged the growth of many American communities. Duluth, Minnesota, for example, is a port on Lake Superior. It owes much of its growth to the great iron deposits located nearby in the Mesabi Range.

As you read in Chapter 1, communities in the South and West, called the Sunbelt, have been growing rapidly. For example, one of the fastest growing cities in the country is Ocala, Florida. Its warm climate and growing economy have attracted large numbers of people from other parts of the United States, especially the North.

Southern California's pleasant climate also has attracted large numbers of people. Not only is the California climate pleasant, it is favorable too for growing a wide variety of crops.

Many New England communities were settled near waterfalls. The early textile mills needed water power to turn machines that spun thread and wove cloth. Many settlers in the Middle West moved there because of the rich, fertile soil—one of nature's most important resources.

Our nation still has many rural communities, like this one in the Green Mountains of Vermont. In recent years, some rural communities have grown.

America's Rural Communities

As you read in Chapter 1, a **rural area** is a region of farms and small towns. When you travel along our nation's highways, you see many different kinds of rural communities. One way to classify them is by their size. Another way is to notice the various kinds of buildings located in the community and the way in which the people make their living.

Rural Farm Communities. The people who live and work on farms make up America's smallest kind of community—the rural farm community. In most parts of the United States, you will pass farm after farm as you travel through the countryside. All parts of the United States have farms. However, farms differ from region to region because of the climate.

In Pennsylvania, for example, you will see farms on which a variety of crops are grown. These farms usually also raise some pigs, cows, and chickens, and are called mixed farms. In Wisconsin you will see a large number of dairy farms. Farther west, in Wyoming, you will see large ranches, or farms that specialize in raising cattle or sheep.

In the South, you will pass tobacco, soybean, and cotton farms. West of the Mississippi River, you will see large wheat farms. In the Imperial Valley of California, there are farms that grow fruits and vegetables for city markets. In Hawaii you will see sugarcane and pineapple plantations.

Today there are about 2 million farms in the United States. Some farms are near others. Or they are near main highways or roads. Other farms are isolated and are a long distance from their nearest neighbors.

Small Country Towns. There is also another kind of rural community—the small country town. It has a population of less than 2,500 people and is located in a rural area, usually near open farmland. Most country towns have served as places where farmers could buy supplies and where rural people could shop, go to the movies, and send mail. They have also been marketing centers for farm crops.

During the 1930's, many of the rural areas of our country experienced severe droughts and hard economic times. As a result, these areas lost population as farmers moved to the cities. Recently, however, some rural areas have begun to grow again. The newcomers are not farmers, but workers who commute to new factories and businesses built in the countryside. This means that there are now two rural Americas. One is the old rural community. The other is the rural area with farms and also businesses that have left the city.

Suburbs

As you have read, a town, village, or community located on the outskirts of a city is called a **suburb.** People who live in the suburbs often work in the city. Each morning they travel from their homes to their city offices or other places of employment.

Today more than 100 million Americans live in suburbs. They often travel to the city to work, but prefer to live in a community with more open space.

There are several reasons why many Americans wish to live in the suburbs. Suburbs are smaller than cities, and some people prefer life in a smaller community. Others want their children to grow up in a community with more open spaces, trees, and places to play. They want a house with a backyard. Some families want to get away from city crowds, noise, and traffic.

Suburbs make it possible for such people to live away from the city even though they earn their living in the city. However, suburbs have been growing rapidly and are beginning to experience some problems.

Urban Areas

Suburbs and all other towns and cities of 2,500 or more people are called **urban areas.** Urban areas vary greatly in size. For example, the population of the town of Fayette, Alabama, is 5,260. This makes Fayette an urban area. Another urban area in our country is the New York City area. New York City has a

San Francisco, California, like many of our nation's large cities, is a city of contrasts. It includes private homes, tall office buildings, theaters, hotels, and restaurants.

population of about 18 million. Most urban areas have populations between the sizes of Fayette and New York.

About three quarters of all Americans today live in urban communities. Those who live in the large cities are near theaters, restaurants, museums, and other cultural advantages that cities offer. They enjoy the hustle and bustle of city living. Recent studies show, however, that the suburbs are growing faster than the cities. More than half the urban population lives outside the central cities. A number of large cities actually showed a loss in population.

Metropolitan Areas

Certain American cities, such as New York, Dallas, Chicago, and Los Angeles, have become so large that each one is known as a **metropolis.** If you fly over a metropolis, you will find it hard to tell where the giant city ends and the surrounding towns and suburbs begin. In fact, there really is no dividing line. The settled area seems to have no end. For this reason, as you have read, a big city and its surrounding towns and suburbs are referred to as a **metropolitan area.** The metropolitan area of Chicago, Illinois, for example, includes several fairly large cities in neighboring Indiana, such as Gary, Hammond, and East Chicago.

There is evidence that someday soon several of our metropolitan areas, particularly those along the Atlantic coast around Boston, New York, Philadelphia, Baltimore, and Washington, will grow into a single metropolitan area. A name has been given to this type of giant urban area. It is a **megalopolis.** Three of the largest megalopolises in the nation are BosWash (Boston to Washington), ChiPitts (Chicago to Pittsburgh), and SanSan (San Francisco to San Diego).

★ SECTION 1 REVIEW

Define community, crossroads, transportation centers, rural area, suburb, urban areas, metropolis, metropolitan area, megalopolis

1. **Understanding Ideas (a)** How did transportation help determine the location of many American communities? **(b)** How do resources and climate help determine the kind of community a settlement will become?
2. **Summarizing Ideas (a)** Describe both of the "two rural Americas." **(b)** How do they differ?
3. **Comparing Ideas (a)** Why do some people choose to live in the suburbs? **(b)** What are some advantages to city living?

Thinking Critically Imagine you are a farmer in the 1930's. Because of drought, you are seeking work in the city. How will your new life in the city differ from what you have known on the farm?

② Communities Have Many Purposes

At the beginning of this chapter, a community was defined as "a group of people having common interests who live in the same area and are governed by the same laws." What are some of their common interests? Also, how does the community serve its people?

Living and Learning in a Community

One of the most important things communities do is teach us how to live and work together. Our first lessons in living with others are learned in the home. The family, as a small community, teaches us important lessons in sharing. As we grow up, we also learn from teachers, schoolmates, and friends.

The people of our communities teach us to talk and behave the way we do. They teach us values. The food we like, our respect for the law, the kind of person we want to be, and a hundred other things are learned by living with the people of our community.

Communication in Communities

We continue to learn as long as we live. Almost every day, we share information with others. This passing along of information, ideas, and beliefs from one person to another is known as **communication.** One

Did you know that...

George Washington, Benjamin Franklin, and Paul Revere all served in volunteer fire companies? In fact, it was Franklin who started the nation's first volunteer fire company. Members of the community were trained to work the equipment and were ready to rush to a fire as soon as they heard the alarm bell.

Not until the mid-1800's did large American cities begin to hire professional firefighters. Many smaller communities continued to be protected by volunteers—as they are today. Now the equipment of volunteer fire companies is modern and efficient, but the spirit of working together in the community is as old as our nation.

reason people live in communities is to be able to communicate with each other easily. The problems people face seem to be made easier if they can talk them over with someone else. Life is also more pleasant if we can hear about the latest happenings in the neighborhood and learn new ideas from other people in the community.

Every community has a number of important means of communication. We have already mentioned the most common one—conversation. Such modern inventions as the telephone, computer, radio, and television have increased our ability to learn and share information. We also communicate in writing through letters and notes.

One of the most important means of communication is the newspaper. Newspapers tell us about happenings all over the world. They also give us news of our own communities, such as what laws are passed, who is running for office at election time, and when public meetings will be held. In addition, newspapers tell us about births, marriages, and deaths in

Communities often provide recreation areas, like this park. Community funds and community employees maintain these areas for all to enjoy.

our community. Books and magazines are other important means we use to communicate ideas and facts.

Communities Help Us Enjoy Life

One important reason people form communities is to enjoy the company of other people. Nearly every American city and town has movie theaters, bowling alleys, skating rinks, parks, and other places of recreation that are open to the public. **Recreation** is relaxation or amusement by playing or doing something different from one's usual activities. Many of our larger cities have professional baseball, football, hockey, and basketball teams whose games are eagerly followed by sports fans.

Many recreational facilities are maintained at public expense. Taxes support public playgrounds, athletic fields, picnic grounds, basketball courts, and golf courses. There are also worthwhile activities sponsored by groups of citizens willing to volunteer their own time and money. The YMCA, YWCA, YMHA, Boy Scouts, Girl Scouts, Campfire Boys and Girls, Big Brothers, Big Sisters, and 4-H Clubs are examples of groups that help the members of the community enjoy playing and learning together.

Communities Help Us Use Our Free Time

Many communities have learned to take advantage of an unusually good climate or geographical location. They have promoted and developed these advantages not only for their own residents but also to attract tourists. Lake communities and seaside towns have developed boating, water skiing, and swimming as special attractions. Rural communities have made the most of the hunting and fishing opportunities in their areas. Other communities have featured skiing, horseback riding, and hiking.

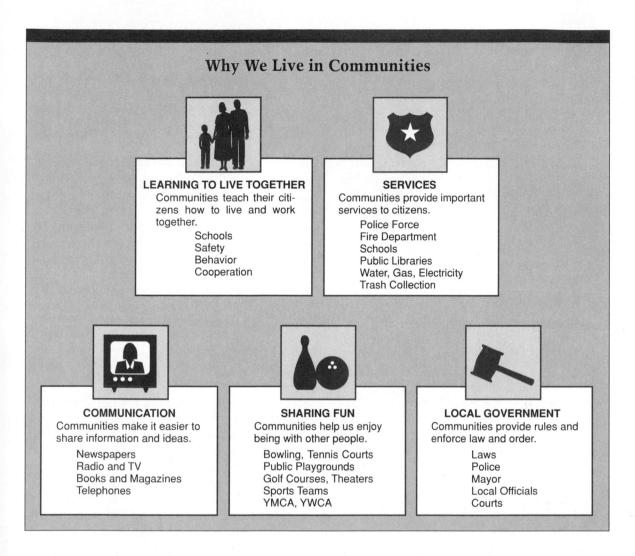

Why We Live in Communities

LEARNING TO LIVE TOGETHER
Communities teach their citizens how to live and work together.

    Schools
    Safety
    Behavior
    Cooperation

SERVICES
Communities provide important services to citizens.

    Police Force
    Fire Department
    Schools
    Public Libraries
    Water, Gas, Electricity
    Trash Collection

COMMUNICATION
Communities make it easier to share information and ideas.

    Newspapers
    Radio and TV
    Books and Magazines
    Telephones

SHARING FUN
Communities help us enjoy being with other people.

    Bowling, Tennis Courts
    Public Playgrounds
    Golf Courses, Theaters
    Sports Teams
    YMCA, YWCA

LOCAL GOVERNMENT
Communities provide rules and enforce law and order.

    Laws
    Police
    Mayor
    Local Officials
    Courts

Several purposes are served by good community recreational facilities:

1. Good recreational facilities provide worthwhile ways for Americans to use their leisure time. They give people something interesting and healthful to do.

2. Good recreational facilities help members of the community keep physically fit. Well-run swimming pools, playgrounds, and recreation centers encourage good health habits and help members of the community build healthy bodies.

3. Recreation often expands our knowledge. A recreation center may help us develop new interests and hobbies. A community stamp club or coin club, for example, can teach us much about history and geography.

4. All of us benefit from recreation by relaxing and having fun in the company of others. Recreation helps us to "re-create" ourselves—to feel like new people.

Communities Provide Many Services

One of the reasons communities have been established is to provide services to their citizens. There are certain things the people of a community, working together, can do more effectively than each can do separately. A good police force helps ensure our safety. Fire protection is a critical community service. Public schools are another valuable community service.

People living as neighbors also need pure water, an efficient sewer system, regular trash removal, and dependable gas and electric service. Sometimes the people of a community join together and vote to have services furnished by their local government in return for the taxes they pay. In other cases, some services are provided by private companies.

Communities Provide Local Government

In the United States, communities of all sizes serve their citizens by providing local government. When people live together, some kinds of laws and regulations are needed. Suppose that several neighbors get into an argument over where the boundary that separates their property is located. If there were no laws or local government, they might use force to settle their difficulties. Fortunately, though, our communities provide a local government with courts, judges, and law enforcement officers that help us maintain good order in our neighborhoods.

 SECTION 2 REVIEW

Define communication, recreation
1. **Summarizing Ideas (a)** How do communities influence what people learn? **(b)** What methods do people use to communicate with each other?
2. **Understanding Ideas (a)** How do communities help citizens to enjoy their lives? **(b)** List and describe four ways that community recreation facilities help us.

Thinking Critically You have been hired to make suggestions about the expansion of services in your community. What new services do you think would benefit the people of your community? Explain your answer.

 **Citizens Serve Communities**

Communities depend on **cooperation**—people working together for their common benefit. Communities serve their citizens. In return, their citizens should serve them. Some citizenship services are compulsory. For example, members of the community must obey the laws or pay the penalty. Young citizens must attend school. In most matters, however, communities rely on their members to respect the rights of others simply because it is the correct thing to do.

Your Communities

Each of us lives in a number of different communities. We profit from their services, and we owe certain duties in return. In many ways our family is a kind of community. The obligations of cooperation and respect for members of our family—the smallest community we live in—have already been mentioned. This cooperation should extend to people living in our immediate neighborhood. Finally, it should extend to the larger communities of our town or city, state, and nation.

Every community faces problems that must be solved if life in that community is to be as pleasant as it can be. These problems can be solved if every member of the community takes an interest in them.

How Americans Improve Their Communities

Groups of concerned citizens are doing something about their problems. Take the example of Las Vegas, New Mexico, a town of about 15,000 people. For years Las Vegas streets

The citizens of Boston reclaimed and restored run-down and unused warehouses to create this pleasant area of shops and restaurants, called Quincy Market.

were run-down and its sidewalks in need of repair. The town had few recreation centers. Nevertheless, the citizens of Las Vegas were proud of their community. Finally some of them decided to act to improve Las Vegas.

The mayor headed the community's improvement program. A new gymnasium was added to the high school. A community swimming pool was built. The people of the town began to feel that Las Vegas was a good place to call home. As streets and sidewalks were rebuilt, the town began to show new signs of life. Several more projects were planned to continue Las Vegas's program of improvement.

Each year other American communities face their problems and do something about them. For example, the citizens of Decatur, Illinois, undertook a program to improve their downtown areas, clear slums, and reduce traffic jams. Decatur cleared and rebuilt a large part of its business district.

In similar fashion, the city of Worcester, Massachusetts, established a successful new program consisting of better schools, playgrounds, museums, and retirement homes. Across the nation, cities such as Baltimore,

Philadelphia, Houston, Denver, and St. Paul have rebuilt old areas.

The people of Pittsburgh, Pennsylvania, also took a critical look at their city. They were not pleased with what they saw. The smoke from the steel mills and factories was so thick that Pittsburgh was known as "the Smoky City." The traffic jams were awful. The central city was run-down.

The people of Pittsburgh voted to spend the money needed to improve their city. New skyscrapers were built. A successful campaign reduced the smoke in the air. More roads were built, a new water system was planned, and parks and recreation centers were added. Proud of what they had done, the citizens of Pittsburgh learned that their city must continue to plan and build and change if it is to meet their needs in the future.

Community Volunteers

Another way citizens can improve their communities is by becoming volunteers. As you recall, a **volunteer** is someone who offers to work without pay. Many Americans do not

These citizens have volunteered to help clean up the Colorado Trail.

realize just how much work in our society is done by volunteers. They help the sick, the poor, the disabled, and the elderly. They collect money for charities. In some areas, volunteers put out fires and drive and assist in ambulances. Volunteers also help in schools, libraries, museums, sports groups, and many other organizations.

Communities rely on the help of volunteers because no government can know all the needs of local areas. Volunteers also help provide services a community might not otherwise be able to afford. It is up to all of us as citizens to help keep our communities healthy, clean, and safe.

Small and Large Volunteer Groups

The United States has many different kinds of volunteer groups. Some are small local groups. Others are large national organizations that depend upon local volunteers to carry out their work. A small group may be formed for specific purposes, such as cleaning up the neighborhood. After the problem is solved, the group breaks up. Some areas, however, have permanent neighborhood groups

that get together regularly to discuss their community needs.

Many towns, cities, and counties have permanent volunteer groups. They include hospital volunteers, volunteer firefighters, student-parent-teacher associations, and various community action groups. Such groups rely on the help of citizens of all ages. Some high school students, for example, take senior citizens to doctors' appointments. Retired people, in turn, may spend a few hours each week helping out in libraries, in hospitals, and in other community facilities.

Some groups require that volunteers take short courses to learn specific skills, such as carrying a stretcher or working special equipment. Those people who take part in these programs have the satisfaction of performing a valuable service for their community. They also learn useful new skills.

Among the large national volunteer groups are the League of Women Voters, the American Cancer Society, the American Red Cross, the Scouts, and the Little League. These associations are supported by money from private contributors and depend on the services of volunteers. A large group such as the Red Cross has millions of volunteers working for it. Local branches of these organizations are usually started by concerned citizens. Community members can support these groups with time, ideas, and money.

Good Citizens Make Good Communities

Right now you are an active member of your local community. You attend its schools and enjoy its parks and playgrounds. You are protected by its police and fire departments. You depend on it to provide you with many other services. Someday you may work and raise a family in your community. It is important, therefore, that you be a good citizen in your local community.

It is also important that you be a good citizen in the other communities in which you live. These communities include your state and your country. Remember that you are also a member of the global community— the community of all people in the world. To be a good global citizen, you must learn about the events happening around the world.

Because you enjoy the benefits of all the communities of which you are a member, you have certain duties and responsibilities to those communities. These range from picking up litter to offering your services as a volunteer. In order for communities to continue to benefit citizens, citizens must make contributions to their communities. It is up to you to take pride in your communities and practice good citizenship wherever you are.

 SECTION 3 REVIEW

Define cooperation, volunteer

1. **Expressing Ideas** Explain how a person lives in several communities at the same time.
2. **Understanding Ideas** What problems are faced by American communities?
3. **Seeing Relationships (a)** How do volunteer groups help to improve communities? **(b)** How is good citizenship related to good communities?

Thinking Critically Identify at least three problems in your community. Make a list of activities you and your classmates can participate in to help solve these problems.

The United States is a nation of many communities. These communities differ greatly in size and population. However, they have many common problems wherever they are located—in rural or in urban areas.

Communities serve many important purposes. They help us enjoy living with other citizens, get a good education, and earn a good living. The prosperity of a community depends upon its location, climate, natural resources, industrial possibilities, and hardworking citizens.

Many communities are meeting their problems through a planned program of improvement. Cities such as Pittsburgh and Houston have attracted many different industries and built cleaner and more beautiful cities.

Much work remains to be done in our nation's communities. Citizens can help to improve their communities by becoming volunteers and by fulfilling the responsibilities of citizenship.

CHAPTER 15 SUMMARY

DEVELOPING ★ CIVICS SKILLS

LIFE SKILL
Working in Groups

Chances are that you will work with some group of people nearly every day for the rest of your life. That group may be your family, your classmates, your friends, or your co-workers. Whatever group you find yourself in, it is important that you know how to work effectively as a group member. This knowledge will make your group more effective and make your time with the group much more enjoyable.

How to Work in a Group

To work effectively in a group, follow these guidelines.

1. **Make sure that group members understand the group's task.** Groups are usually formed to accomplish a particular task. For example, your teacher may organize the class into groups to complete a project for class. It is important that the members of each group understand the group's goal, or purpose. If they do not, the resulting confusion can interfere with achieving that goal.

2. **Create an agenda for the group meeting.** An agenda is an itemized plan of the topics to be covered in the meeting. An agenda is useful for keeping group members on task. The agenda for the first meeting of a group might include the election of the group's leader, a discussion of the group's goals, and the assignment of tasks.

3. **Choose a leader for the group.** Because groups are made up of many people, it is often helpful to have a leader. The leader can help keep the group's discussion focused on the group's goal. The leader can also make sure that all of the items on the group's agenda are covered. Equally important is the leader's role in making sure that all group members have the opportunity to contribute their ideas.

4. **Be a good communicator.** Communication in a group means both speaking and listening. Organize your thoughts before you speak so that you are sure about the ideas you want to contribute. Do not interrupt other members of the group. Speak clearly so that you will be understood by everyone. When other group members are speaking, listen closely to what they have to say. Take notes.

5. **Compromise to reach a decision.** Groups are made up of a number of people who usually have different ideas about how things should be done. How do groups agree on what action to take? The answer is that group members compromise in order to reach an agreement. For people to compromise, each side needs to make sure the other side gets something in return. This way all members of a group will accept a proposal even though it might not completely satisfy everyone. As you have learned, compromise is a vital part of the democratic process.

Applying the Skill

Use what you have learned about working in groups to answer the following questions.

1. Why is it important to know how to work with a group of people?
2. Why is compromise vital to the achievement of group goals?
3. Why is having a leader helpful for a group?
4. What qualities do you think an effective group leader should have?
5. Identify a group of people you have worked with recently. The group may have been at home, at school, or elsewhere. Did the group follow the guidelines on this page? If it did, explain how this benefited the group. If your group did not follow these guidelines, explain how it differed.

304   *Unit Five   Citizenship: Home, School, Community*

Reviewing Terms

On a separate sheet of paper, supply the term from the list below that correctly completes each sentence.

crossroads   megalopolis
metropolitan areas   suburb
community   urban areas

1. A _____ is a community located on the outskirts of a city.
2. _____ _____ are communities with populations of at least 2,500.
3. The place where two main roads meet is known as a _____.
4. A group of people who have common interests, live in the same area, and are governed by the same laws is a _____.
5. A giant urban area consisting of many cities that have grown together is a _____.
6. _____ _____ are large cities and their surrounding towns and suburbs.

Using Thinking Skills

1. **Expressing Ideas (a)** Why do people live and work in communities? **(b)** How is what people learn influenced by living in communities? **(c)** Name several communities a person lives in at the same time.
2. **Seeing Relationships (a)** What problems must many communities in our country work to solve? **(b)** What have community members done to solve these problems? **(c)** How is good citizenship related to solving community problems?
3. **Summarizing Ideas (a)** What role did transportation play in determining the location of some early American communities? **(b)** Explain how natural factors can influence the development of a community.
4. **Understanding Ideas** In what ways are volunteer groups essential for the success of a community?
5. **Contrasting Ideas** How do the "two rural Americas" differ?

6. **Comparing Ideas (a)** What are some advantages to living in the suburbs? **(b)** Why do some people choose to live in cities?

Practicing Civics Skills

Reaching a Compromise Imagine that your civics class has raised $300 to improve one of the parks or recreational areas in your community. A class committee has been formed to determine how to spend the money. Some students in the group think the money should be used to plant trees. Others want to buy picnic tables and benches. A few group members argue that purchasing more trash cans would help cut down on the litter problem.

Before the group can reach a decision on how to spend the money, these differences of opinion must be settled. Answer the following questions to help you arrive at a decision that would be accepted by all of the committee members.

1. **(a)** What is the main area of agreement among the committee members? **(b)** What is the main area of disagreement?
2. What compromises might be accepted by each group (those who want to plant trees, those who want to buy tables and benches, those who want to buy trash cans)?
3. What decision might be accepted by all of the committee members?

Being a Good Citizen

1. Work with a group of other students to create a history of your community. Conduct library research to locate appropriate historical materials. Also interview people who have lived in your community for many years.
2. Invite a newspaper reporter to your class to discuss some of the important issues in your community.
3. Conduct library research to find out why your community was founded where it is. Report your findings to the class.

Reviewing the Facts

1. **(a)** What is a family? **(b)** How do families serve our nation?
2. **(a)** What are the main purposes of education? **(b)** Through what levels may one progress on the American educational ladder?
3. **(a)** What is a community? **(b)** How do communities influence their members?
4. **(a)** What is a volunteer? **(b)** Why are volunteers important to the success of a community?
5. **(a)** What is critical thinking? **(b)** List and describe the steps you must take to be a critical thinker.
6. **(a)** What is divorce? **(b)** What do social scientists identify as the reasons for the high divorce rate in our country?

Using Critical Thinking

1. **Seeing Relationships (a)** Why did families move from farms to cities? **(b)** How did this move affect family life in the United States?
2. **Understanding Roles (a)** What can you do to get the most out of your classroom experiences? **(b)** How can you help yourself do well on tests?
3. **Summarizing Ideas (a)** What are some of the important problems faced by American communities? **(b)** What steps are community members taking to help solve these problems?
4. **Understanding Ideas (a)** How did transportation and natural resources influence the growth of American communities? **(b)** Why were some people in the 1800's opposed to free public education?
5. **Composing a Paragraph** Identify and discuss one of the challenges facing American education today.
6. **Composing an Essay** Write a short essay that discusses the American family from colonial times to the present.

7. **Expressing Ideas (a)** Why do people live in communities? **(b)** Why do people choose to live in cities? **(c)** What are the advantages to life in the suburbs?
8. **Comparing Ideas (a)** How does insight differ from creativity? **(b)** How does college differ from graduate school?
9. **Organizing Ideas (a)** What laws regulate marriage in the United States? **(b)** How do state governments protect children?
10. **Drawing Conclusions** Why is it important to be a good citizen in your family, school, and community?

Applying What You Know

1. Based on what you know about the changing American family, write an essay describing what you think family life will be like in the year 2010.
2. Collect several product advertisements from magazines and newspapers. Identify which statements in each advertisement are facts and which are opinions. Then tabulate the results and write an essay that discusses the use of opinion in advertising.
3. Work with a group of students to organize a recycling program for your school. Organize the group, elect a leader, and follow the guidelines given in Chapter 15 to help your group make its project a success.
4. Make a bulletin-board display of photographs from magazines to show the American family in all of its various forms.

Expanding Your Knowledge

Burns, Marilyn, *I am Not a Short Adult: Getting Good at Being a Kid*, Little, Brown. A thoughtful and humorous discussion of a teenager's life with family, in school, and in the community.

Gay, Kathlyn, *The Changing Families: Will the United States Be Ready for the Year 2000?* Franklin Watts. A look at some of the problems encountered by families.

The American Economy

UNIT 6

Our American Economic System

Chapter Sections

Chapter Focus

The United States is one of the richest nations in the world. Most Americans enjoy a high standard of living. A nation's **standard of living** is the well-being of its population based on the amount of goods and services they can afford. On the average, we have more money to spend—and more goods to buy—than the people of most other nations.

What makes all this possible? There are a number of reasons for our economic success. First of all, the United States is a land of great natural resources. We have timber, minerals, energy resources, a good climate, and fertile soil in abundance. In addition, we always have had energetic and inventive people.

Furthermore, our system of government has ensured the right of private enterprise— that is, the owning and operating of businesses by individuals rather than by the government.

It has protected the rights of individuals to own property and to make a profit. Finally, the United States has developed an economic system in which most of its people can find work and seek financial success.

A nation's economic system, or **economy,** is the nation's method of using its resources to care for the needs and wants of its people. An economic system includes the production and distribution of goods and services, buying and selling, jobs, money, investments, and all the decisions these things require. Our economic system has enabled the United States to become a rich and powerful nation.

Study Guide

As you begin to learn about our economy, look for answers to the following questions:
★ How is freedom essential to our economy?
★ What are the various ways in which Americans organize their businesses?
★ What are the factors of production, and how do they affect business decisions?

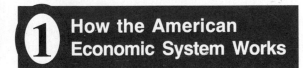

1 How the American Economic System Works

The American government is based on certain principles of freedom. We enjoy free speech and freedom of religion. We vote in free elections. We can do as we choose if we do not interfere with the freedom of others. That is why our nation is a free nation.

Our Economic Freedoms

We also enjoy important economic freedoms. It is because of these freedoms that our economic system is called a free economy. Let us examine some of these economic freedoms.

Freedom to Buy and Sell. Americans are free to buy and sell any legal product and service. Shoppers can go from store to store looking for the best quality goods and services at the lowest price. If the price seems too high, the buyer is free to go somewhere else to buy the product. Producers are free to sell goods and services at prices they think buyers will pay. If people do not buy a product or service, the producer is free to change the price or to sell something else. We use the term **free market** to refer to this exchange between buyers and sellers who are free to choose. The role of the government in our free market is limited.

Freedom to Compete. Businesses in the United States compete with one another for customers. That is, each business firm tries to get people to buy what it has to offer. Customers are free to shop where they wish. In this system of **free competition,** buyers show which goods they favor every time they make a purchase. If shoppers do not buy a product, producers will make something else or go out of business. Therefore, producers make what they think the public will buy.

Freedom to Earn a Living. American workers are free to compete for the best jobs their training qualifies them to perform. They also may bargain with their employers for higher wages, better benefits, and better working conditions. They are free to leave their jobs and find better ones. Or they may go into business for themselves.

Freedom to Earn a Profit. As you recall, a **profit** is the income a business has left after expenses. The **profit motive,** or desire to make a profit, is essential to our free economic system. It is the reason that people start and run businesses. It is also the reason that people **invest** in, or put money into, various businesses and valuable articles. People are motivated to start businesses and to invest because they believe they will make a profit.

Freedom to Own Property. Americans have the right to own and use their own land, personal belongings, and other kinds of property. The free market and free competition would not work if we did not also have private ownership of property. All Americans are free to do as they like with their own money. They may spend, save, or invest it. They may buy buildings, land, tools, and machines. These forms of property may be used to produce goods and services. That is, Americans may start their own businesses and use them to earn profits. They may employ others to work for them.

Americans also have the right to profit from their ideas and inventions. They can protect this right by copyrighting what they write and by patenting their inventions. A **copyright** is the exclusive right, granted by law, to publish or sell a written, musical, or art work for a certain number of years. A **patent** gives a person the exclusive right to make and sell an invention for a certain number of years. The right to own and use property of all kinds is guaranteed in the Constitution.

The Free Economy in Action

Our nation, like every other nation, must face a basic economic fact: people's wants and needs are greater than the resources available to satisfy them. In other words, there are never enough resources to meet all of our wants and needs. This problem of limited resources is called **scarcity.** Scarcity forces us to choose which wants and needs to satisfy with our available resources. How do we decide how to use our limited resources?

Under the American economic system, these decisions are made in the free market. That is, people are free to produce, sell, and buy whatever they choose. They are free to work for whomever they wish, including themselves. Of course, businesses would not last long if they produced things that no one wanted. Thus, it makes sense for businesses to supply what consumers demand.

Supply and Demand

You are already familiar with supply and demand. You know, for example, that a rare baseball card is more expensive than one that everyone has. A rare card costs more because the demand for it (the number of people who want it) exceeds the supply (the number of the cards that actually exist).

The American economy as a whole works in a similar way. Businesses supply goods and services, people demand them, and the balance of supply and demand determines the prices of the goods and services. In fact, the relationship between supply and demand is so predictable that economists have identified rules that it follows. These rules are called laws.

The **law of supply** states that businesses will provide more products when they can sell them at higher prices and fewer products when they must sell them at lower prices. The **law of demand** states that consumers will demand more products when they can buy them at lower prices and fewer products when they must buy them at higher prices.

The supply of products in our economy and the demand for those products balance each other to provide consumers with what they need and want and to provide businesses with profits. It also affects the price we pay for products.

Let us use videocassette recorders (VCRs) to see how the laws of supply and demand work. If businesses produce more VCRs than they can sell, they may lower the price to increase demand. If this does not increase demand, businesses will produce fewer VCRs to match the demand.

On the other hand, if people demand more VCRs than businesses have supplied, businesses will raise the price because they know people want the VCRs. They will also make more VCRs to meet the demand.

What Is Capitalism?

Our American economic system is sometimes called **capitalism.** Another name for it is the capitalistic system. The money Americans invest in business is called **capital.** This is

Freedom in Our American Economy

FREEDOM TO EARN PROFITS

FREEDOM TO OWN PROPERTY

FREE COMPETITION AMONG BUSINESS FIRMS

FREE COMPETITION AMONG WORKERS

FREE MARKET

money that Americans do not spend on living expenses but, instead, save to invest in buildings, machines, and other forms of property used to produce goods and services.

Capital is not only the money that people invest. It is also what people buy with it—tools, buildings, machines, or anything that means they own part or all of a business. Anyone who owns such things is a **capitalist.**

For example, the tools owned by a self-employed electrician are capital. The electrician had to save in order to buy them. The tools are used to produce things people want or to provide services people want. The machines that turn out automobile bodies are part of the capital of an automobile manufacturing company.

As you can see, the electrician is a capitalist on a small scale. The automobile manufacturer is a capitalist on a large scale. If you own a few shares of stock in an automobile company, or other type of company, you are also a capitalist. These shares of **stock** mean that you own part of the company. You had

to save the money to invest in this stock. You did not spend the money to pay for living expenses or to have a good time.

People work and invest in order to get ahead financially and improve the quality of life. Because many people are doing this, our economy produces the vast number of goods we all enjoy. New and better products are constantly being offered for sale. Business people who supply Americans with the products and services they want, at a price they are willing to pay, usually make a profit. Therefore, our capitalistic system works for the benefit of the American people as a whole.

Our Free Enterprise System

American business people are basically free to operate their own businesses in the way they think is best. They do not depend on some government official to tell them how to do it, as business managers do in Cuba, for example. Americans depend upon their own

Our free enterprise system has made available a wide range of products and services from which American citizens can choose.

enterprise—that is, their own ability and energy. For this reason, our economic system is sometimes called a **free enterprise system.** Freedom in our economy offers enterprising business people the opportunity to enjoy success and profits.

American business owners take many risks. They are free to earn profits. But they are also required to take the losses if they make mistakes. They may produce a new product and find that customers do not want it. Or they may produce their products inefficiently and have to charge more than people are willing to pay for them. If they make mistakes, they may be forced out of business. If their businesses fail, they may lose all their capital. As a rule, though, efficient businesses earn profits in our economic system.

The Rise of Big Business

From their very beginnings, American businesses have been privately owned, with business decisions made by their owner or owners. During the early years of our nation's history, most businesses were small. Even then, some shippers, importers, and manufacturers became wealthy. But it was not until the late 1860's that big businesses began to develop in the United States.

These businesses benefited from America's new technology. For example, they used machines that were powered by steam or, later, by electricity. By placing these machines in factories, where large numbers of workers were employed, businesses were able to produce large quantities of goods at lower prices. The owners of these businesses made huge profits. Some owners, however, hoping to make great fortunes and gain economic power, used business practices that would be considered unfair or illegal today.

Monopolies

Unfair business practices harm our free economy. They may interfere with the free market and affect the prices people have to pay for goods and services. Therefore, it is important to understand these practices.

One unfair practice used by big business owners in the late 1800's and early 1900's was the forming of monopolies. A company has a **monopoly** if it is the only firm selling a product or providing a service. If there is no competition for the product or service, and if it is something people really need (such as food), the monopolist controls the price. People will be forced to pay the price that is asked if they want the product or service.

The **merger** is one way of trying to form a monopoly. A merger occurs when two or more companies in the same industry combine to become one company. If all the companies in an industry merge, a monopoly will be formed. There no longer will be real competition in the industry.

Another way to create a monopoly is to form a **trust.** That is, several companies in a similar industry place their stock in the hands of a board of trustees. Even though each company remains a separate business, the trustees make sure the companies no longer compete with one another. If all the companies in an industry became part of the trust, a monopoly would be created. In this way they could charge prices that would prevent smaller companies from entering the industry.

Let us look at an example of a monopoly. Suppose that a large coffee company decides to lessen its competition by buying up all the small coffee companies or forcing them out of business. The large coffee company might do this by lowering its prices below the cost of production.

Soon all the other companies would have to lower their prices to compete and stay in business. Every coffee firm would be selling coffee at a loss. Because the big company has more capital than the small companies, it can afford to lose money longer than they can. The small companies would be forced to sell out, merge with the big company, or go out of business altogether.

The big company would now be a monopoly. It alone would produce all the coffee on the market. Moreover, it could sell this coffee at any price. Since there would be no other companies selling coffee, people would have to buy their coffee from the big company at the price charged, or drink something else.

The Importance of Big Business

It is a mistake to think that all large companies are monopolies or even have the power to act like monopolies. Today, most big businesses in the United States have to face competition from other big companies and from foreign producers. Also, if the company's profits are high, there is always the possibility that this will encourage other companies to enter the industry. Competition would be quickly restored.

The fact that a company is big does not mean that it makes huge profits or that it abuses its power. A company should be judged by its actions, not by its size. Big businesses are essential to our economy. It would not be the same without them.

Many of the goods and services we need cannot be produced efficiently by small companies. To produce steel, electricity, automobiles, and ships, for example, large and very expensive capital equipment is needed. The term "economies of scale" is used to describe the situation in which things can be produced more efficiently and cheaply by larger and larger companies.

In some industries today, a few large companies account for most of the production and sales. If these companies should get together and agree on how much to produce and what to charge for their product, they might be abusing their size and power. As you will see, there are laws to prevent this.

The Government as Referee

The referee of a basketball or football game makes sure that the teams observe the rules. In the same way, the federal government enforces rules to protect the American system of free enterprise.

To prevent monopolies, Congress has passed antitrust and antimonopoly laws. The Sherman Antitrust Act of 1890 was passed to help prevent monopolies. It was strengthened by the Clayton Act of 1914, which forbade practices that would lessen competition. The Antitrust Division of the Justice Department and the Federal Trade Commission are responsible for enforcing these laws.

In recent years, the government and the American people have been trying to decide whether to regulate business combinations known as conglomerates. A **conglomerate** is formed by the merger of businesses that produce, supply, or sell a number of unrelated goods and services. For example, a single conglomerate may control communication systems, insurance companies, hotel and restaurant chains, and other types of businesses.

The government watches mergers carefully to make sure that conglomerates do not gain too much control over an industry or part of the economy. If a conglomerate gains so much power that it threatens the operation of our free economy, the government may step in as referee.

In some industries, monopolies are legal. These legal monopolies are **public utilities,** companies that provide essential services to the public. Electric companies are examples of public utilities. Their capital equipment is so expensive that it would be wasteful to have more than one company trying to provide the same service in the same area. Therefore, one company is allowed to have a monopoly. The government regulates public utilities to make sure they provide adequate services at reasonable prices.

Comparing Economic Systems

As you have learned, the freedom of consumers and business people is essential to our economy. However, our economic system has grown large and complicated. As a result, the federal government sometimes acts as referee and makes some economic decisions. The government now makes many more economic decisions than it did 100 years ago. It is still correct, however, to call our economy a free economy or a free enterprise system because most economic decisions are still made by individuals.

In an economy like that of Cuba, for example, the opposite is true. Most economic decisions are made by government officials who head huge planning agencies. Individuals are left with only a few decisions to make.

The government of China is now in the process of instituting economic reforms. For example, workers who meet certain quotas are sometimes allowed to sell their surplus at a profit.

The government decides what goods and services should be provided. Workers are told what jobs they must take. Young people are told what jobs to train for. The government manages nearly everything.

For these reasons and others, we say that Cuba has a command economy. A **command economy** is the opposite of a free economy. In a command economy, the government owns almost all of the capital, tools, and means of production. The government tells the managers and workers in factories and on farms what and how much to produce. Most economic decisions are thus made by the government, instead of by individuals in the free market.

Our economy is free, but it does have some features of a command economy. For example, the government regulates businesses to make sure that working conditions are safe. Because the United States has features of a command economy in its mostly free system, some people now describe our system as a **mixed economy.**

✔ SECTION 1 REVIEW

Define standard of living, economy, free market, free competition, profit, profit motive, invest, copyright, patent, scarcity, law of supply, law of demand, capitalism, capital, capitalist, stock, free enterprise system, monopoly, merger, trust, conglomerate, public utilities, command economy, mixed economy

1. **Expressing Ideas** List and describe five important economic freedoms.
2. **Seeing Relationships** What does the problem of scarcity force us to do?
3. **Summarizing Ideas** Describe the way in which supply and demand operate in our free economy.
4. **Identifying Roles** (a) What role does the government play in the operation of the economy? (b) Why are most monopolies illegal? (c) Why are some legal?

Thinking Critically Imagine you live in a nation that has a command economy. How does your life differ from someone who lives under a free economic system?

② How American Business Is Organized

More than 100 years ago, a young clerk in a small New York town decided to try out a new idea for increasing his store's business. He gathered several small items from the store's shelves and placed them on a table near the entrance. Then he put up a sign: "Everything on this table, 5 cents each." Customers who came into the store to buy thread or cloth began to stop at the table for a bag of clothespins, an eggbeater, or some other item that caught their eye.

The young man then decided to open his own store and to sell only five- and ten-cent items. Unfortunately, his new store was not a success. He lost all the money he had saved and borrowed to start the business. He did not give up, however. He borrowed the money he needed to buy new goods and start over again. This time his business was a success.

The young man with the new idea was Frank W. Woolworth. With the profits from his successful business, he soon opened another store, and then another and another. When he died in 1919, Woolworth had established more than 1,000 five-and-ten-cent stores in the United States and Canada. Woolworth became a wealthy man because he had a good idea and the business ability to make it succeed.

The Single Proprietorship

There are more than 19 million business firms in the United States today. Over 13 million are small businesses owned by one person. They include gas stations, grocery stores,

In the United States, more than 200,000 grocery stores are single proprietorships. This owner works many hours to keep his store operating at a profit.

beauty shops, drugstores, and other businesses that serve people who live nearby. These small businesses, owned by one person, are called **single proprietorships.**

You probably already know some of the advantages of going into business for yourself. Single proprietors are their own bosses. They decide the hours the businesses will be open and how the businesses will be run. Because they are the owners, they take all the profits.

On the other hand, there are disadvantages to being a single proprietor. Owners have to furnish all the money needed to rent or buy the buildings their businesses use and the equipment needed to run them. If they require help, they have to be able to pay the salaries of employees. Owners are hard-working people. They can hire others to help them. However, they alone are responsible for the success or failure of their businesses.

If their businesses fail, proprietors must face the losses. Workers may lose their jobs. Proprietors, however, may have to sell everything they own to pay their business debts.

The Partnership

In the United States each year, many small businesses are started and many others go out of business. Some small businesses fail because the single proprietor lacks enough capital or the business ability to earn a good profit. For such reasons, the owner of a small business sometimes seeks another person to become a part owner of the business.

They then form a **partnership,** which gives the business a greater amount of capital and a better chance of success. In a partnership, there is more than one person to provide capital, share responsibility, furnish ideas, and do the work. The partners also share the risks. If the business fails, the partners share responsibility for the debts.

Any two or more persons can form a business partnership. Usually they sign an agreement setting up the partnership. Unwritten partnership agreements, however, are legal and are recognized by the courts. There are a few large and wealthy American businesses that are organized as partnerships. However, most partnerships are small.

You often can recognize a partnership from the name of a business firm: Kim and Jackson, Contractors; Reilley, Cortes, and Clark, Attorneys. If the abbreviation ''Inc.'' does not appear after the names, the business is probably a partnership. ''Inc.'' is an abbreviation, or short form, of ''incorporated.'' It means the business is organized as a corporation, a third form of business organization.

The Corporation

Just what is a corporation? Establishing a big business requires large sums of money—to buy land, build offices and factories, purchase tools and machinery, and employ workers. A big business can seldom be set up by an individual or even by a number of partners. Another form of business organization is needed. This form of business organization is called a **corporation.**

The corporation is the most common form of business organization for most of our nation's large companies and for many smaller ones. The corporation is a permanent organization. It is unlike proprietorships and partnerships, which end when their owners die. Corporations play a vital part in our American economy. How does a corporation work? Its most important features are these:

1. Corporations Raise Money by Selling Stocks, or Shares of Ownership. Each share of stock represents a part of the ownership of the corporation. The people who buy these stocks are called **stockholders.**

Suppose that a new corporation is organized with a capitalization of $1 million. This means that the corporation has the legal right to accept $1 million in the form of capital from investors. It could do this, for example, by selling 10,000 shares of its stock at $100 a share. Each purchaser of a single share of stock would then own one ten-thousandth of the company.

When profits are divided each year, each owner of a single share would get one ten-thousandth of the profits. Corporation profits paid to stockholders are called **dividends.** Some stockholders own several shares. A few stockholders own many shares. Each stock-

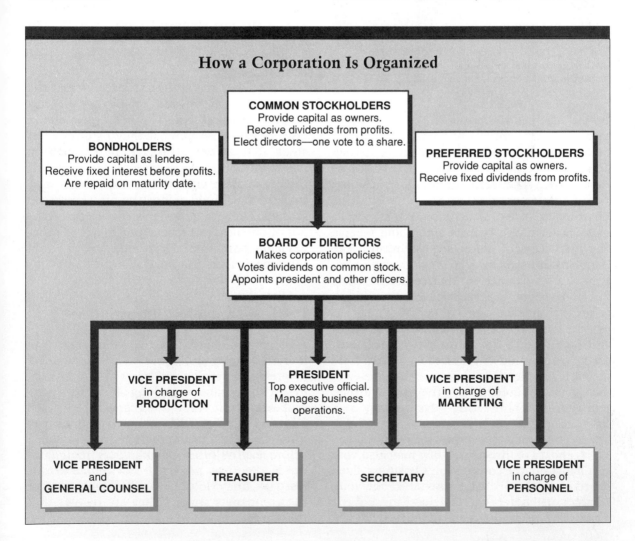

How a Corporation Is Organized

COMMON STOCKHOLDERS
Provide capital as owners.
Receive dividends from profits.
Elect directors—one vote to a share.

BONDHOLDERS
Provide capital as lenders.
Receive fixed interest before profits.
Are repaid on maturity date.

PREFERRED STOCKHOLDERS
Provide capital as owners.
Receive fixed dividends from profits.

BOARD OF DIRECTORS
Makes corporation policies.
Votes dividends on common stock.
Appoints president and other officers.

VICE PRESIDENT
in charge of
PRODUCTION

PRESIDENT
Top executive official.
Manages business
operations.

VICE PRESIDENT
in charge of
MARKETING

VICE PRESIDENT
and
GENERAL COUNSEL

TREASURER

SECRETARY

VICE PRESIDENT
in charge of
PERSONNEL

This hectic scene takes place every business day on the floor of the New York Stock Exchange, where millions of shares of stock are bought and sold.

holder receives a share of the profits in proportion to the amount of stocks owned.

2. The Corporation Receives Its Rights to Operate from a State Government. The state grants the business firm a **charter,** or grant, of incorporation. This charter recognizes the corporation's right to carry on business, sell its stock, and receive the protection of state laws. In return, the company must obey state regulations in regard to its organization, the reports it makes public, the taxes it pays, and the way in which it sells its stock to the public.

3. The Directors of the Corporation Are Elected by the Stockholders. Every corporation is required by law to hold at least one meeting of its stockholders each year. All stockholders have the right to attend and address this meeting—even if they own only one share.

At this annual meeting, the stockholders elect a board of directors. They may also vote on changes in the corporation's business. Each share of stock entitles its owner to one vote. Major stockholders therefore cast most of the votes. The **board of directors,** representing the

stockholders, meets during the year to make decisions about the corporation.

4. The Board of Directors Chooses Those Who Manage the Corporation. Those people who manage the affairs of the corporation are its **executives.** The top executives are elected by the board of directors. They include the president of the company, vice presidents, secretary, and treasurer. The president usually picks the other major assistants. Together, all these officials are called the **management** of the corporation.

5. Individuals Are Not Responsible for the Debts of the Corporation. Corporations, as you recall, are owned by the stockholders. The money received from the sale of stock becomes the corporation's capital. The purchase of shares gives the stockholders the right to receive a part of the company's profits.

But what if the business fails? Are the stockholders responsible for paying the corporation's debts? No. The most that stockholders may lose is what they paid for their stock. This is the advantage the corporation has in gathering large amounts of capital. If the corporation fails, owing many debts, neither the stockholders nor the officers are responsible for its debts. If a corporation goes out of business, its assets (property and other valuables) are sold. The money raised from this sale is then used to pay off the debts.

Preferred and Common Stock

A corporation may issue two kinds of stock—preferred stock and common stock. Owners of **preferred stock** take less risk when they invest their money. As long as the company makes a profit, they are guaranteed a fixed dividend every year. The corporation must pay these dividends to the preferred stockholders before paying other stockholders their dividends. Because preferred stockholders take less risk, they do not usually have a vote in the company's affairs. They are owners, but they have no voice in managing the company.

Owners of **common stock** take more risk when they invest their money. They receive dividends only if the company makes good profits. Why, then, would anyone want to risk buying common stock? There are three main advantages in owning common stock:

1. If the company's profits are high, owners of common stock may receive higher dividends than owners of preferred stock.

2. If the company's profits are high, the market price, or selling price, of the common stock usually increases. This means stockholders can sell their shares, if they wish, for more than they paid for them.

3. Common stock owners have a vote in electing the board of directors and in deciding certain company policies.

Corporate Bonds

Even with the sale of preferred and common stocks, corporations sometimes need additional large sums of money to expand operations. In such cases, one method corporations use is the issuing of **bonds.**

The issuing of bonds is a method of borrowing money. Bonds are certificates stating how much the original purchaser paid. They also declare the percentage of interest on this amount that the corporation will pay the bondholder each year. **Interest,** as you have read, is the percentage paid to individuals or banks for the use of their money. The company must pay the interest on its bonds before it pays dividends to stockholders. This interest must be paid whether or not the company earns any profits for the year.

If the company cannot repay the money borrowed from bondholders by the date stated on the bonds, the holders of the bonds may take over the business. They may close the corporation and sell its property to raise the money owed them. Or they may decide to keep the business in operation, perhaps with new management. They may do this in the hope that the corporation soon will be able to pay back the amount owed on the bonds.

SECTION 2 REVIEW

Define single proprietorships, partnership, corporation, stockholders, dividends, charter, board of directors, executives, management, preferred stock, common stock, bonds, interest

1. **Evaluating Ideas (a)** What are the advantages and disadvantages of a single proprietorship? **(b)** Why might people choose to enter into a partnership?
2. **Understanding Ideas (a)** List the five main features of a corporation. **(b)** Why is the corporation well suited to large industries?
3. **Contrasting Ideas (a)** How does preferred stock differ from common stock? **(b)** Why do corporations issue bonds?

Thinking Critically You plan to start your own business. Will you organize as a single proprietorship, a partnership, or a corporation? Explain the reason for your choice.

3 How Business Decisions Are Made

You now know that Americans can run a business as individual proprietors, members of a partnership, or managers of a corporation. No matter how a business is organized, its success depends mainly upon decisions about the use of four things: land, capital, labor, and management. These are called the **factors of production.**

Production Requires Land

Suppose that Maria Morano decides to start a bakery business. She will need a place to conduct her business. That is, she needs land. Every business enterprise requires land.

(continued on page 324)

CITIZENSHIP
IN ACTION

Students Run a Business

Running a business isn't easy. It takes thought, hard work, and patience. It also requires the ability to enjoy a challenge. That's what Rosa Furvo and Jonathan Banks think, and they should know. In their sophomore year in high school, Rosa and Jonathan learned the responsibilities of running a business. Rosa worked as president of a company, factory worker, and door-to-door salesperson. Jonathan was company treasurer, package handler, and salesperson.

A Junior Achievement Company

Rosa and Jonathan did all those jobs in a Junior Achievement Company. With other students they formed a manufacturing company and ran it from beginning to end. Their company was one of hundreds around the United States that are formed each year as part of Junior Achievement (JA).

Junior Achievement is a national organization whose goal is to teach high school students about the free enterprise system. Each year more than 200,000 students learn how to organize, run, and liquidate (shut down) a business. Businesses

In secondary school Junior Achievement programs, a business executive teaches students about running a business.

Students in a Junior Achievement company work together to organize their business.

usually follow the school calendar. Students meet once a week for three hours on their own time for about 15 weeks.

Rosa and Jonathan's company was named Double-M—for Double the Money! It made and sold desk lamps and decorated T-shirts. In order to raise money to buy materials and run the business, the students sold stock in their company. They sold 130 shares, mostly to family and friends, at $1 a share.

After the stocks were sold, the students elected company officers and divided up the jobs. They also chose the products they wanted to sell and settled on prices. Help came from two sources. One source was national JA materials that, among other things, explain how to decide on a price. The materials point out typical manufacturing and sales costs. The most common costs include raw materials and supplies, salaries and sales commissions, office or factory rentals, and bank charges. The materials also discuss how much the students should add to the selling price in order to keep the price competitive yet enable their company to make a profit.

The second source of help was an adult adviser who sat in on the company meetings. JA advisers are local business people who volunteer their time. Usually it is such advisers who start JA programs in the community and keep them going. They ask local industries to donate funds to pay for a space where the student companies can meet and work. In Rosa and Jonathan's home town, three companies worked side by side in a former bakery that the advisers rented.

Meeting the Challenge

Most people who start their own businesses don't have to learn how to do several jobs in a few weeks. What was it like for students who had to learn all those new jobs so quickly?

As president of Double-M, Rosa had a lot of work to do. She learned that "the president really has to get out and work. She or he can't just sit back and watch."

As treasurer, Jonathan had to learn to give financial details his constant attention. "It's so easy to forget to write down a few cents here and a few cents there. But it makes a difference in the long run."

All the members of the company cooperated in decorating the T-shirts and making the desk lamps. Rosa had the extra duty of seeing that things ran smoothly. She set up an assembly line to make the products. "Organization is the key to working on an assembly line," she discovered. "Jobs have to be done in the correct order to keep things rolling."

When the products were ready, all company members became salespeople. They found door-to-door selling the most effective way of making sales. By May most of the products were sold, except for a half dozen desk lamps. The students worked extra hard and thought up new ways of trying to sell the lamps quickly, so that they could close down the company by the end of the school year.

Liquidating the Company

The students ended their business by publishing an annual report and closing their record books. They were able to declare a profit—as most JA companies do. This meant that they not only returned the $1 that each stockholder had invested but also paid a dividend. A dividend is the share of the profit each stockholder receives in return for having taken a risk.

How did Rosa and Jonathan feel about having spent so much time on their JA company in addition to their regular

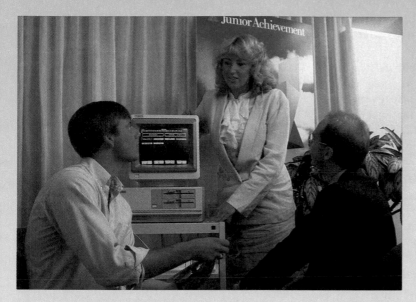

With the help of business executives and computer simulations, students learn economic decision making.

schoolwork? Both agreed that the experience had more than repaid all their effort. "We learned a lot and are ready to go again," they said.

Thinking about what they learned with Double-M, Jonathan and Rosa think the company might have done better with less expensive products. "We should have chosen something cheaper to sell. Our material costs were high. Spending $5 just for the desk lamp ran up our price."

Thinking It Over

1. What are the advantages and disadvantages of learning to do several jobs in the same company?
2. Why is it necessary to keep track of all the money that is made and spent in a company?
3. What are some of the things you might take into account in deciding what product to sell?
4. Do you think running a Junior Achievement company is a good way to learn about the free enterprise system? Why or why not? How else might a person learn how our economic system works?

The word **land** includes more than a place to locate a store, factory, or office. It also includes all the natural resources that come from the land. The wheat used to make flour for Maria Morano's bakery comes from the land. The wood for her bread racks comes from trees grown on the land. All the raw materials needed to produce goods of all kinds come from the mines, fields, and forests that are a part of the land.

Our nation's total supply of actual land is limited. In some places land is so scarce that there are many businesses in every city block. People who wish to start new businesses must decide on location.

Maria Morano, for example, must decide whether or not to own the property on which her business will be located. She can buy either a piece of land with a building on it or land on which she can build. Or she can pay rent for a building. **Rent** is what a person pays to use land or other property belonging to someone else.

Rents and land prices are higher in crowded business areas where land is scarce than in less densely populated areas. Maria Morano must decide which location will give her the most profit. If she pays a high rent or price for land, she will be nearer customers.

If she goes to the edge of town where land or rent is cheaper, customers will have to travel farther to get to her bakery. Morano must also make decisions about the quality and costs of the flour and other raw materials she will use.

Production Requires Capital

Maria Morano will also need such equipment as mixers and ovens. She may rent her equipment. Or, if she has enough money, she may buy it. As you can see, Morano cannot go into business without money. Her decision to rent or buy equipment will depend on how much capital she has available and how she wants to use it. Capital, you recall, is money used to pay for tools and other capital goods such as trucks, machines, office equipment, and factory buildings.

How will Morano obtain the capital she needs? Perhaps she will decide to go ahead alone and set up her business as a single proprietorship. To do so, she must have saved some money as capital. If she does not have enough, she may ask the bank for a loan.

If the bank officials decide that Morano is a good risk, they will give her a loan. They will think she is a good risk if she can prove

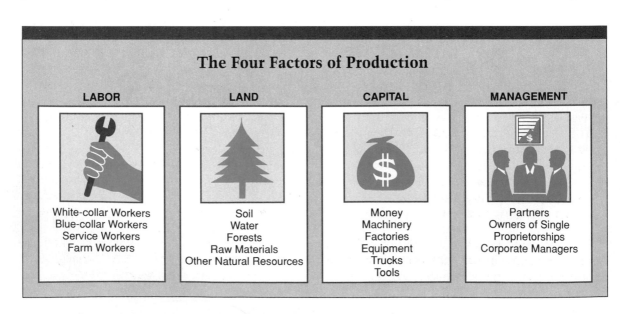

The Four Factors of Production

LABOR	LAND	CAPITAL	MANAGEMENT
White-collar Workers Blue-collar Workers Service Workers Farm Workers	Soil Water Forests Raw Materials Other Natural Resources	Money Machinery Factories Equipment Trucks Tools	Partners Owners of Single Proprietorships Corporate Managers

that she has good ideas for a business and is likely to pay back the loan. If Morano takes out a loan, she will have to pay interest.

Perhaps Morano will decide instead to seek one or more partners who are willing to invest in the bakery business. Or she may decide to set up her business as a corporation and sell stock to raise capital. She would do this if she decided to go into the bakery business on a large scale.

Production Requires Labor

All human effort used to produce goods or services is called **labor.** However, the word "labor" often is used to mean workers as opposed to owners and the people who manage companies. The workers in businesses, industries, and on farms usually earn wages. **Wages** are the money earned by workers each hour. They are paid on either a daily or a weekly basis. Those who manage companies generally are paid salaries. **Salaries** are fixed incomes paid twice a month or monthly.

If Maria Morano does her own work, the amount of bread and rolls she can produce in her bakery will be limited. If she hires more labor, her production will be greater. She will then have more goods to sell.

The money Maria Morano gets for the additional bread and rolls should be at least enough to pay the wages of the new workers. If it is more than enough, she will increase her profits. If it is not enough to pay the workers' wages, she will have to discharge them, lower their pay, or find some way of increasing their productivity. **Productivity** is the amount a worker produces in an hour.

Production Requires Good Management

The decisions made by Maria Morano must be made by all business owners, or **entrepreneurs** (ahn·truh·pruh·NURS). Then, after the business is started, they must make

Three of the four factors of production can be seen in this pencil factory. Can you tell which three factors they are? What is the fourth factor of production?

countless decisions such as how to distribute the product, how much to charge for it, and whether to hire more people.

Those who operate businesses are called **managers.** The group of managers of a single business, you will recall, is called its management. Their decisions determine whether the business will succeed. If management makes the wrong decisions, the business may fail. If management makes wise decisions, the business will usually prosper.

When managers make decisions, they take risks. If business people did not take risks, the average standard of living in the United States would not be so high. Because Thomas Edison and other business people took risks, for example, Americans were among the first people to enjoy the benefits of electricity. Because Henry Ford and others took risks, Americans had the first low-priced, mass-produced cars. Because David Sarnoff and hundreds of others took risks, Americans enjoy radio and television.

These people were successful. Their decisions turned out well. Many other people, however, were not successful. Why, then, are Americans willing to take business risks?

JAMESTOWN, INC.

the first permanent settlement in the 13 American colonies was sponsored by a corporation? A group of English investors formed a corporation called the London Company to send settlers to America. The profits made by the settlers were to be distributed as dividends. In 1607 the settlers sent by the London Company founded Jamestown, Virginia.

Jamestown made history, but unfortunately it did not make much money for the corporation. At first all of the land was owned by the London Company. Only when the individual settlers were allowed to own land themselves did the colony begin to succeed.

Management and Profits

Management takes risks because it hopes to produce profits. What are profits, and how are they determined?

The money a firm receives from the sale of its goods or services is called **gross income.** Out of gross income, the firm must pay the costs of making and distributing its product.

The cost of materials and supplies used in the business must be paid. Rent must be paid. If the business owns its own land and buildings, property taxes must be paid. Machines wear out. So money must be put aside to repair machinery or replace it. If the busi-

ness has borrowed money, interest must be paid. Workers and those who manage the business must be paid. Even if single proprietors do all the work themselves, the salary they pay themselves is a business cost.

If the business firm has been well managed, and if other conditions are right, money will be left over after all the costs have been paid. The amount left over is called **net income.** What happens to this net income? Part of it will go to pay income taxes. Some may be set aside in a bank to meet future business needs. The rest is profit. As you may recall, profit is money remaining after all the firm's obligations have been met. In a corporation, profits are distributed among the stockholders as dividends.

Government's Role in Business

As you have read, government has a role in our free enterprise system. Our government does not tell business people what they must do. However, it does influence business in many ways. For example, government acts as a referee to make sure that big corporations do not destroy the competition of small businesses. Our Constitution protects the rights of private property. Federal laws protect our right to buy and sell in a free market. Other laws protect the right of business people to take risks to make profits.

Many agencies of the federal government help businesses. One agency, the Small Business Administration, helps small businesses as they compete in our economy.

In some ways the federal government acts as an overseer of our economy. There are laws that ensure that women and members of minority groups are not unfairly kept from getting jobs. Laws protect the health and safety of workers and prevent pollution of the environment. Laws protect consumers from dishonest practices and harmful products.

The government plays many other roles in business. It tries to help business by providing information that managers can use in planning their production levels, sales, and costs. It sometimes provides loans and other types of assistance to businesses. The government also tries to keep the economy running smoothly.

Some people say that the government has gone too far in doing its job as overseer. For example, tens of thousands of pages are needed to print all the regulations issued by the federal government. Some regulations are considered necessary. Some regulations, however, may add to the costs of doing business without providing much benefit to the people. Moreover, businesses usually raise their prices in order to cover the costs of meeting government regulations.

Achieving the right balance of government activity is not easy. The question of how much government regulation is necessary is much debated. As a citizen in our free economy, you will help decide this issue.

 SECTION 3 REVIEW

Define factors of production, land, rent, labor, wages, salaries, productivity, entrepreneurs, managers, gross income, net income

1. **Seeing Relationships (a)** Explain how people consider the factors of production when starting and running a business. **(b)** How is good management related to profits?
2. **Contrasting Ideas (a)** How do wages differ from salaries? **(b)** What is the difference between net income and gross income?
3. **Identifying Roles (a)** Describe the ways in which the government plays a role in business. **(b)** Why do some people think government has overregulated business?

Thinking Critically You are starting a business and have a limited budget for advertising. How will you go about making potential customers aware of your new business?

The American economy, or economic system, is based on ideas of personal freedom. As Americans, we are free to choose our own jobs, work for others, or go into business for ourselves. We are free to buy and sell the goods and services we wish.

The American economic system is known as capitalism, or as a free enterprise economy. This means that it is based on a free market, free competition, private ownership of property, and the right to make a profit on business activities. Government does not tell business what to do. It acts as a referee in our economic system. The free American economy based on capitalism is clearly different from a system like that of Cuba, which is based on a command economy.

American business firms may be organized as single proprietorships, partnerships, or corporations. A corporation usually is owned by many people. These people own shares of stock in the corporation. The money they pay to buy the stock is the capital that the corporation uses to engage in business.

Business owners must make decisions about their use of the four factors of production—land (which includes raw materials), capital, labor, and management. In the American economy, most of these decisions are freely made by business people as they seek to earn profits.

CHAPTER **16** SUMMARY

LIFE SKILL
Understanding a Warranty

When you pay for a product, you expect it to work properly. The best way to ensure this is to deal only with businesses that back up their products with a warranty. A warranty is a written guarantee of the condition of a product. A warranty tells what the manufacturer of the product will do if the product is defective. Usually, the company will promise to repair or replace the product or refund your money. Not all companies issue warranties. Those that do offer various guarantees. Therefore it is very important that you become familiar with warranties.

How to Understand a Warranty

To use a warranty effectively, follow these guidelines.
1. **Distinguish between the two kinds of warranties.** By law, a warranty must carry one of two labels—"full" or "limited." A full warranty promises that the company will pay the total cost of repair. A limited warranty covers only part of the expense. If the warranty is limited, you should find out what the limitations are. You may want to shop around to find the product with the best guarantees.
2. **Determine the length of the warranty period.** Normally, the longer the warranty period, the better the quality of the product.
3. **Find out what the warranty does and does not cover.** Most warranties cover parts and labor. Remember, however, that there are often limits to warranties. Make sure you read the fine print to find out what is *not* covered.
4. **Fulfill your obligations under the warranty.** In order to take advantage of the guarantees in a warranty, you are often required to complete certain tasks. For example, you generally must provide proof of purchase when requesting warranty service. You may have further obligations as well. Find out

what these responsibilities are, and make sure you fulfill them.

Applying the Skill

Use the warranty shown below to answer the following questions.
1. **(a)** Is the warranty a full warranty or a limited warranty? **(b)** For how long is the warranty valid?
2. **(a)** When does the warranty begin? **(b)** Who pays for labor after 90 days?

LIMITED WARRANTY TO ORIGINAL PURCHASER
CAR RADIO/CAR STEREO

- This Hi-Tech product is warranted against manufacturing defects for the following period:

PARTS	LABOR
1 YEAR	90 DAYS

- Hi-Tech will repair or replace at no charge, any part(s) found to be defective during the warranty period.
- This warranty period starts on the date of purchase by the original owner.
- The warranty repairs must be performed at a Hi-Tech authorized service station. A list of Hi-Tech authorized service centers can be obtained at any Hi-Tech dealer.

OBLIGATIONS OF THE ORIGINAL OWNER

- The dealer's original bill of sale must be kept as proof of purchase and must be presented to the Hi-Tech authorized service station.
- Transportation to and from the service center is the responsibility of the customer.

EXCLUSIONS OF THE WARRANTY

- This warranty does not cover accident, misuse, or damage caused by improper installation.
- This warranty is valid only on products purchased and used in the United States.

CHAPTER 16 REVIEW

Reviewing Terms

On a separate sheet of paper, copy the paragraph below. Then fill in each blank, using the correct term from the following list.

bonds
corporations
stock
command
partnership

common
economy
proprietorship
preferred

The American (1) _____, or economic system, is based on freedom. Unlike the (2) _____ economy of Cuba, for example, businesses in the United States arc free to make their own economic decisions. One of the most important decisions businesses face is how to organize. Smaller firms tend to organize as a sole (3) _____ or as a (4) _____. Larger firms usually form (5) _____. These businesses raise money by selling (6) _____ to individuals. People buy either (7) _____ stock, which guarantees a dividend but provides no voting rights, or (8) _____ stock, which provides voting rights but does not guarantee a dividend. If these companies wish to borrow money, they may issue (9) _____.

Using Thinking Skills

1. **Identifying Roles** What roles does the government play in the economy?
2. **Understanding Ideas** What does the problem of scarcity force us to do?
3. **Contrasting Ideas (a)** How do stocks differ from bonds? **(b)** What are the advantages of owning common stock? **(c)** What are the advantages of owning preferred stock?
4. **Expressing Ideas** How do supply and demand operate in a free economy?
5. **Summarizing Ideas (a)** What are the characteristics of a free economy? **(b)** How does a free economy differ from a command economy? **(c)** Why is the United States economy called a mixed economy?

6. **Seeing Relationships (a)** What are the four factors of production? Give an example of each. **(b)** Explain how business decisions are based on these factors.
7. **Drawing Conclusions (a)** Discuss the three ways in which American businesses are organized. **(b)** Which type of organization is best suited for large industries? Why?

Practicing Civics Skills

Writing a Warranty A good way to learn about warranties is to write your own. Reread the discussion about warranties on page 328. Then choose a product for which to write a warranty. As you write the warranty, keep in mind that the warranty should protect the purchaser without putting too much of a burden on the manufacturer. Write your warranty so that it answers the following questions often asked by a careful buyer.

1. Is this a full or a limited warranty?
2. **(a)** On what date does the warranty begin? **(b)** When does the warranty expire?
3. **(a)** What does this warranty cover? **(b)** What is not covered by the warranty?
4. What must I do if something goes wrong with the product?

Being a Good Citizen

1. Invite a local business owner to tell the class how he or she established a business. Ask the owner about the challenges faced by business owners in our economy.
2. Prepare a bulletin board that compares free, mixed, and command economies.
3. Work with a group of other students to identify the major concerns of businesses in the United States today. Some students should interview local business leaders, others should read business magazines, and still others should read the business section of your local newspaper. Compile your findings into a report for the class.

CHAPTER 17

How Our Goods Are Produced and Distributed

Chapter Sections

Chapter Focus

One of the outstanding features of the American economic system is its ability to produce. Just about any product you might want to buy is made in our nation. In recent years, the United States has produced nearly $4 trillion worth of goods and services a year! This is more than any other nation in the world.

The dollar value of what we produce is called the **Gross National Product (GNP)**. It is figured by adding up the dollar value of all goods and services produced in the United States during the year.

Economists—the people who study the economy—use the GNP as one measure of how well our economy is performing. If the GNP rises year after year, the nation's economy is doing well generally. If the GNP for any one year falls, the economy probably slowed down during that year.

There are also other ways of judging the health of an economy. The number of unemployed people, the number of business failures, and the amount of tax income produced by the nation all help tell us about the well-being of the economy.

Our economy has been relatively strong for over two centuries. Much of its strength lies in the way American products are made, distributed, and eventually purchased.

Study Guide

As you begin to learn about how our goods are made and how they reach consumers, look for answers to the following questions:
★ What is mass production, and why does it work so well in our free economy?
★ How do businesses distribute goods?
★ How can you become a wise consumer?

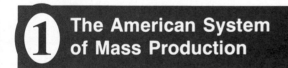

1 The American System of Mass Production

During one recent year, the United States produced nearly 12 million automobiles, trucks, and buses. In a single year we produced over 880 million tons (798 million metric tons) of coal, over 130 million tons (118 million metric tons) of steel, and more than 230 million tons (209 million metric tons) of corn. Millions of other goods are produced each year in our nation. What makes this huge production possible?

Mass Production

There are many factors that make the United States capable of such an enormous output. One is mass production. **Mass production** means huge amounts of goods being made rapidly by machines to supply the needs and wants of the nation's large population. Mass production requires many big machines and vast amounts of power. American inventors have developed machines that can make, or help make, almost any product that you can imagine.

One of the first inventors to make mass production possible was Eli Whitney. (You may remember him as the inventor of the cotton gin.) In 1798 Whitney signed a contract to make muskets, or guns, for the United States Army. He promised to manufacture 10,000 guns in two years. The promise seemed impossible to keep. This was because up to that time guns had been made by hand, one by one. To prove that he could keep his promise, Whitney agreed to show some government officials how he planned to make so many guns so quickly.

From a box, he took ten gun barrels, ten triggers, ten stocks, and ten locks for exploding the gun powder. He asked the officials to choose one of each of these parts. Whitney then took the four parts and quickly put together a finished musket. To show that the parts were all alike, he continued to put together muskets until all ten were completed. He had made ten identical guns from a box containing identical parts. Moreover, he was able to do this very rapidly.

Eli Whitney's methods have become the basis of all mass production, from radios and sewing machines to automobiles and tractors. What are these methods?

1. Use of Machine Tools. Whitney developed **machine tools,** or machinery carefully built to turn out parts that were exactly the same. Instead of boring each gun barrel by hand, for example, he made a machine that did nothing but bore gun barrels, all in the same way.

2. Use of Standard Parts. Each of Whitney's machine tools made parts that were exactly alike, called **standard parts.** That is, any Whitney gun barrel would fit any gun made by Whitney. Other parts were all alike and would fit any of the guns. This was a great advantage. If a part wore out, it could easily be replaced by a new standard part.

3. Use of Division of Labor. Barrels, triggers, stocks, and locks for Whitney's guns were made by different groups of workers, each operating a separate machine. No one worker made a complete gun. The whole job was divided among the various workers. In this **division of labor,** each worker was a specialist at part of the job. Specialization made the entire process go faster.

The use of machine tools, standard parts, and division of labor helped increase production. Yet the early machines used by Whitney and others were small and inefficient. Many machines used in factories today are enormous and highly efficient.

Large Machines Require Great Power

For many years, Americans used the force of falling water, or water power, as the source of energy to operate their machines. Early factories were therefore located near streams. Dams were built to hold back water so that it could be released when necessary to turn water wheels. As these big wheels turned, their power was used to run machines within the factory.

Then a great change took place. James Watt, a Scottish engineer, invented a practical steam engine. This invention became more and more popular in the United States. Soon steam power began to replace water power.

Steam power continued to be the leading source of industrial power during the 1800's. In the late 1800's, several new sources of power were developed. For instance, the internal combustion engine used the power released by exploding gasoline. It was often used to run small machines. The main use of the internal combustion engine, however, was in the automobile.

The source of power that really made modern mass production possible was electricity. In the late 1800's the work of Thomas Edison made practical the widespread use of electricity. At first it was used mainly for lighting. As time went on, it was used in many other ways. American families today use electricity to run their toasters, fans, refrigerators, air conditioners, washers, dryers, vacuum cleaners, radios, and television sets. Today nearly every American factory uses electricity as its source of power. In addition, scientists are constantly searching for even better sources of power.

Mass Production in an Automobile Factory

One of the best ways to understand modern mass production is to visit an automobile manufacturing plant. Suppose you were to go to Detroit, Michigan, to make such a visit. What would you see?

When you first enter the factory, it may take a few minutes to get used to all the activity and noise. As you look about, you begin to see how Eli Whitney's methods of manufacturing are still used by American industry.

As an engine block moves by, a team of workers goes to work on it. First a huge machine tool bores dozens of holes into the block, all in one operation. As the block moves along, workers fit pistons, valves, and bolts into the holes. The block has become an internal combustion engine. Other teams of workers fasten carburetors, ignitions, and

Can You Guess?

- One of our Presidents was a celebrated inventor. Who was he?
- An 1893 invention that helps us get into and out of our clothes was first marketed as a "clasp locker or unlocker for shoes." What is it?
- Chewing gum, first manufactured for sale in 1872, has a long history. Who were the first people to use it?

Answers are on page 594.

Foundations of Modern Mass Production

MACHINE TOOLS
to make
standard parts

STANDARD PARTS
to make identical
products

DIVISION OF LABOR
to speed production
along the assembly line

SOURCE OF POWER
to operate machinery
cheaply and efficiently

other parts to the engine. One automobile engine after another is made in this way, each exactly alike.

How does modern mass production use Whitney's methods? Think about what you have just seen in the automobile plant. You saw a machine tool used to produce identical parts—in this case, bored engine blocks for cars. You saw many examples of the division of labor. Each worker does a special job and has become highly skilled. You saw many standard parts, such as valves, being used. Each valve fits exactly into a hole in the engine block. Each wire fits into a part where it belongs. Eli Whitney's ideas for making guns really started something important!

The Assembly Line

One feature of modern mass production is different from Whitney's day. That feature is the **assembly line.** How does the assembly line work?

Let us watch it again in our visit to the automobile plant. Starting with just the frame, the car moves along on a very large **conveyor belt.** The belt slowly moves many car frames at a time through the factory.

As the car frame moves slowly along the assembly line, the four wheels are added to the frame. Then the engine, transmission, windshield, steering wheel, and gears are added. Seats, door panels, and lights are put on next. The car moves on to the paint shop. There it is spray-painted and dried. It is finally driven off the assembly line and tested. The car is now ready to be shipped to an automobile dealer's showroom. There customers may look at it, test drive it, and buy it.

How do the various parts arrive at the assembly line just in time to become parts of the finished automobile? At the beginning of your tour, you recall, you saw an engine being made. This engine was not then on the main assembly line. It was on a side line, or **feeder line.** The engine's movement along the feeder line was timed so that the engine was completed just as the feeder line met the main assembly line.

The engine was then lowered into place in the car from its overhead conveyor belt. In this way, feeder lines are used to assemble many parts of the car and bring them to the main assembly line exactly when and where they are needed.

Your imaginary visit to an automobile plant should have helped you understand the

This American automobile plant includes many features of modern mass production. Here automobiles are shown moving along a robot welding assembly line.

mass production methods that are used in nearly all of our large industries. The automobile industry, while important, is just one of our nation's many large industries.

Bread from a bakery is made in a similar way. Flour and other ingredients are dumped into huge mixers from overhead bins. Conveyor belts running from the storage rooms supply the bins. After the loaf is shaped, it is carried on a conveyor belt through a block-long oven. By the time it reaches the other end of the oven, the bread is baked.

The finished loaf travels through another machine that slices and wraps it. Still another machine packs loaves in boxes. A conveyor then transports the boxes to trucks for delivery to stores.

Mass Production in the World

Mass production was first developed in the United States, but it has spread to other nations. European nations have made use of it for years. Japan has adopted and perfected methods of mass production.

Cuba also uses mass production methods. But it has not been as successful as other nations. One reason may be that in Cuba, as you recall, the government controls the economy. Property is not privately owned. People are not free to start their own businesses as they wish. They cannot decide what prices to charge or the amount of goods and services to produce. This kind of economy—a command economy—does not have the same incentives, or motives, that a free economy has. The lack of a profit motive particularly discourages people from working hard or producing more.

A free economy stimulates business people to take risks. When there is no incentive to make a profit by taking a risk, people may be less inclined to take risks. What, for example, was Eli Whitney's incentive? He invented a new method of production because he hoped to profit from it. So did all the other business people who adopted and perfected our system of mass production.

Business people must be quick to grasp new ideas. To remain competitive, they must be ready to change from old ways to new ways.

They must do this even if it means rebuilding factories and buying costly new machinery.

SECTION 1 REVIEW

Define Gross National Product (GNP), mass production, machine tools, standard parts, division of labor, assembly line, conveyor belt, feeder line

Identify economists

1. **Identifying Roles** Describe how Eli Whitney introduced mass production.
2. **Understanding Ideas (a)** What are the three main features of mass production? **(b)** How has the source of power for American factories changed since the early years of our nation?
3. **Summarizing Ideas** Describe the mass production methods used by the American automobile industry.
4. **Seeing Relationships** How does the profit motive affect the American economy?

Thinking Critically You work in the automobile factory described in this section. What would you say are the advantages and disadvantages of working on the assembly line?

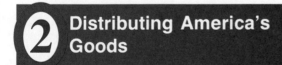

Distributing America's Goods

American industry and business produce goods and services that supply our needs. Yet production is only one part of supplying our needs. The other is **distribution.** After goods are produced, they must be distributed to the people who want them.

Distribution has two sides: transportation and marketing. **Transportation** is essential for bringing goods from the places where they are made to the places where people can buy or use them. Getting people to buy the goods is called **marketing.**

Transporting America's Goods

In such a vast land as the United States, transportation has always been important. Early in our history, the American people learned that a good system of transportation was necessary to bring together, or unify, the nation. As a result, young America went through a long period of road, canal, and railroad building. This made it possible for American businesses and industries to transport their goods to all parts of the nation.

American industry was greatly helped by the growth of railroads. Railroads that fanned out all over the nation helped create a single, huge market for products. Long freight trains rolled from coast to coast carrying raw materials, machine tools, standard parts, and countless other products. The railroads brought up-to-date products to every American city, to most towns, and within reach of farms. They brought business people a means of rapid travel and communication.

Railroad Transportation Today

Railroads were the nation's chief method of transporting passengers and freight for nearly a century. In the mid-1900's, however, railroads found it difficult to compete with other means of transportation—trucks, buses, automobiles, and airplanes. In the 1960's and 1970's, many railroads went out of business. Railroads carried a smaller percentage of passengers and freight.

Some experts think our railroads cannot become profitable unless they modernize. The tracks and equipment of many railroad lines in the United States are in poor condition. Also, our trains are not as speedy as more modern trains in some nations. For example, Amtrak's Metroliner Service trains travel between New York and Washington, D.C., at speeds of up to 125 miles (201 kilometers) an hour. But the newest trains in France travel at speeds of 230 miles (370 kilometers) an hour.

Railroads, though, are still an important part of our transportation system. They are needed to carry bulk cargo, such as coal and grain. They carry passengers. They give people jobs. Trying to save the railroads, Congress created a new national rail passenger system called Amtrak in 1970. Organized with funds from the federal government, Amtrak is working hard to improve the nation's railroads.

Air Transportation

Today railroads must compete with other forms of transportation. In passenger transportation, for example, the airlines have grown rapidly. In 1950 railroads carried more than 6 percent of the passengers traveling between cities. Airlines carried less than 2 percent. By 1990, the airlines had more than 15 percent of passenger traffic. The railroads had less than 1 percent. Modern research, equipment, and management methods have made airlines in the United States among the best and safest in the world.

Airlines now carry all first-class mail between American cities over a certain distance apart. They are also important in transporting freight. Airlines can carry all kinds of freight—from small packages to large industrial machinery and autos—with great speed.

Our Highway System

The automobile is the leading means of transportation in the United States. Private automobiles carry about 85 percent of passengers—more than all other kinds of transportation combined. More than 140 million cars are registered in the United States. That is about one vehicle for every two persons.

Rapid highway transportation depends on good roads. To speed motor traffic, our nation has built a great highway system. We now have more than 3.9 million miles (6.3 million kilometers) of roads.

Some of our highways are toll roads. Drivers must pay a toll, or fee, to use these roads. Other roads are freeways, which are free of

Railroads helped make possible the tremendous growth of American industry. Today railroads remain an important part of our nation's transportation system.

charge. More and more of the recently built roads are limited-access superhighways. Limited access means that cars can enter the highways only at certain points. Superhighways have several lanes and higher speed limits. The interstate highway system provides a network of highways that reaches every part of the nation.

Buses, cars, and trucks can be seen on our highways at all hours. Cars create the heaviest traffic. Trucks carry 75 percent of the nation's freight. Heavy traffic on highways and roads has caused a number of problems. Among them are traffic jams, accidents, air pollution, and heavy use of oil—a nonrenewable resource. Among the steps being taken to solve these problems are lower speed limits, stricter auto emission laws, smaller cars, and better public transportation.

Mass Marketing

Selling goods in large quantities is called **mass marketing.** This kind of large-scale selling is well illustrated by the modern supermarket. The **supermarket** is a huge store that sells thousands of different kinds of products of nearly every brand. At first the supermarket was mainly a food store. Now it also often sells medicines, auto supplies, compact discs and tapes, clothes, hardware, and many other products.

The customer pushes a cart up and down the aisles, selecting articles. When the customer has finished shopping, he or she rolls the cart to the checkout counter. There a cashier rings up the purchases on a cash register or scans them with a special laser device.

Another example of mass marketing is the **department store.** This is a large store that has many separate sections for selling different kinds of goods.

The type of marketing that is used in supermarkets and department stores is called **self-service.** It is an efficient and inexpensive way to sell goods because it is labor-saving. Self-service is a modern method of marketing.

It may seem hard to believe today, but the term "supermarket" did not even exist 50 years ago. Now supermarkets such as this one are a common sight.

Fifty years ago, storekeepers hired clerks to sell the goods. Each clerk waited on only one customer at a time. In today's self-service stores, many customers can shop at the same time, and one clerk can help many more people.

Standard packaging also adds to the efficiency of the self-service system of marketing. Goods come from the factory already wrapped. Crackers, for instance, are sealed in double wrappers and sold in boxes. Sugar comes in boxes or bags of different weights. Steaks, chops, and other meats are cut in convenient sizes and wrapped in plastic. Years ago crackers came in a barrel. They were weighed out for each customer. Sugar also was scooped out of a barrel. It was poured into a paper bag and weighed for each customer. Today few items have to be weighed or measured in the store.

(continued on page 340)

Foxfire—A Class Project Becomes a Big Business

Can a group of teenagers in a rural high school start a successful magazine? They can, and they did. Students in Rabun County High School in northeastern Georgia publish a magazine that is read throughout the country.

Creating a Magazine

The idea for the magazine started with Eliot Wigginton during his first year as an English teacher in Rabun County High School. He wanted to find a way to help his students learn language arts skills. He also wanted to help them understand their own backgrounds and the community in which they live. Only by knowing how their community actually works, he believed, could they become committed to its future and help plan appropriate methods for improving the community.

A magazine put out by the students seemed to be an ideal way to fulfill these goals. Moreover, publishing a magazine would give students the opportunity to create and run a business. From the start the plan was for students to do all the work—everything from raising money to writing articles and preparing material for the printer.

Eliot Wigginton (right) and his students publish *Foxfire* four times a year.

The contents of the magazine were drawn from the students' own community, which is in the Appalachian Mountains—an area with a rich culture and heritage. The articles included stories about the people of the community. Older citizens told students about their experiences and what they had learned from them. Relatives and neighbors also demonstrated, step by step, many traditional skills such as woodcarving, weaving, and building a log cabin.

The class named their magazine *Foxfire,* after a lichen, or mosslike plant, that glows in the dark. The students went from door to door asking for contributions to help them pay the printer for the first issue. They collected $440, enough for 600 copies of the magazine. When they sold those copies, they had enough money to print the next issue. In a short time the magazine paid for itself.

The Magazine Is a Success

The students published *Foxfire* four times a year, and readers kept asking for it year after year. Soon the magazine was known throughout the country. Articles from the magazine were collected in *The Foxfire Book,* which sold more than 3 million copies. Many other *Foxfire* books have followed. A classroom project had turned into a huge success!

Many years have passed since *Foxfire* was started in 1966. New groups of students have taken over, and the magazine has branched into new fields. Income from the magazine and books pays for college scholarships and enables *Foxfire* to hire students to work during the summer. Today more than half the staff members are former students who returned after graduating from college. These staff members also work at the high school. They help students continue to publish the magazine and books, and help them produce daily shows about the community for the local cable television station. Students also produce and market a series of record albums and conduct environmental studies in the region. When the operation needed more space, the students were able to buy land and move and reconstruct 24 traditional log buildings.

The magazine continues to be popular. One reason for its success is that it is filled with useful information. It explains, for example, how to use common items to make quilts, toys, and baskets. Readers have learned about blacksmithing and well digging.

The students who worked on the magazine discovered that the people of their community possessed a vast amount of information that was appreciated by millions of other Americans. The success of *Foxfire* encouraged students in other communities to start similar projects. Similar magazines are now being published in high schools all across the country.

Many older citizens demonstrate their traditional handicrafts for *Foxfire.*

Thinking It Over

1. How does *Foxfire* make use of the special human resources of the Appalachian region?
2. What do you think students might learn about business by putting out magazines such as *Foxfire?*

Another feature of mass marketing is the **one-price system.** This term means that the selling price is stamped or coded on every item. The one-price system was first used by Wanamaker's department store in Philadelphia, Pennsylvania, more than 100 years ago. Now it is a standard practice everywhere. Before the one-price system, customers often bargained with salespeople to try to get the price down a little. Imagine how much time a shopper would spend in buying the week's groceries if he or she had to bargain for every item instead of paying the price marked on the product! Americans do, however, tend to bargain for big ticket items such as houses and automobiles.

Shopping Malls and Centers

An outgrowth of the supermarket has been the **shopping mall,** or **shopping center.** This is a large cluster of different kinds of stores, partly or completely surrounded by a big parking area. The center of the mall or shopping center is usually a food supermarket or a large department store. There may also be a drugstore, shoe store, hardware store, restaurant, and dozens more stores and shops of various kinds.

The mall or shopping center is an example of highly efficient marketing. Customers can drive in, park their cars, and buy almost everything they need. Many stores can afford to sell goods at lower prices because so many goods are being sold so rapidly in the shopping center.

Chain Stores and Specialty Shops

Many of the stores in a shopping mall or center are chain stores. A **chain store** is owned and operated by a company that has many of the same kind of stores. The company may purchase its goods directly from the factory or farm. Or it may own its own factory or farm. The chain store can get its products at lower cost because it buys or produces goods in large quantities.

Many stores are independent. That is, they do not belong to a chain of stores. Many such stores are **specialty shops.** They sell only certain kinds of goods or offer a particular kind of service. They may sell only women's or men's clothing, books, or toys and games.

These small, independent stores often offer special services not provided by larger stores. For instance, smaller stores often handle special products for which there is not a great demand. These locally owned stores are important to most communities. The business people who own and operate them make an important contribution to the prosperity of their community.

Wholesalers and Retailers

Products may pass through several hands from the time they leave the factory to the time they reach the customer. A factory often sells goods in large quantities to a **wholesaler.** This business person owns a large warehouse where goods can be stored. The wholesaler sells to **retailers.** A **retail store** is one that sells directly to the public.

Wholesalers are often called distributors. They perform a service in linking the factory and the retailer. In the end, of course, the customer must pay for this service. Chain stores, large department stores, and supermarkets often have their own warehouses. They have no need for distributors. Therefore, sometimes they can offer goods at lower prices.

The distribution and marketing of goods, whatever methods are used, cost a great deal of money. Sometimes it costs as much to market a product as it did to make it. Inefficient marketing may add to the price you pay for a product. Just as in mass production, efficiency in mass distribution reduces the prices of the things you buy.

Advertising

Mass marketing of goods would not be possible without advertising. **Advertising** tells people about products and tries to persuade some of them to buy these products. It speeds up the movement of goods from factories to the public.

In the competition between producers of similar products, advertising often makes the difference between the success of one product and the failure of another. Some people say this is bad. They say it would be better and less wasteful not to have so many products. Others say that competition among mass producers, marketers, and advertisers helps to keep quality high and prices low.

National advertising makes it possible for producers to sell their products all over the country. They do this by getting people to recognize their products by their brand names. A **brand name** is usually a widely advertised and distributed product. When customers shop, they may choose a product with a brand name they have heard about most favorably or most often. By using national advertising, small producers may be able to grow into large national producers. Then they can mass produce their products for a larger market at lower costs.

Shoppers are sometimes confused by advertising, especially when several producers claim that their product is best or most effective. Yet advertising is a useful way for a producer to inform shoppers about a new product. In the next section, you will learn how you can get good value for your money in the American system of mass production and mass marketing.

 SECTION 2 REVIEW

Define distribution, transportation, marketing, mass marketing, supermarket, department store, self-service, standard packaging, one-price system, shopping mall, shopping center, chain store, specialty shops, wholesaler, retailers, retail store, advertising, brand name

1. **Seeing Relationships (a)** Why is transportation essential to our economic system? **(b)** How did the growth of America's railroads affect businesses and the economy?
2. **Summarizing Ideas** How has America's transportation system changed over time?
3. **Composing an Essay** Write an essay that explains mass marketing.
4. **Contrasting Ideas** What roles do wholesalers and retailers play in our economy?

Thinking Critically You have just left a debate on the role of advertising in our economy. One side argued that advertising is necessary and beneficial. The other side argued that it is unnecessary and harmful. Outline the arguments made by each side.

③ You, the Consumer

Each one of us is a consumer, or customer. A **consumer** is one who buys or uses goods and services. As consumers, all of us play an extremely important part in the American free economic system.

Each year business firms spend more than $100 billion to get us to buy their products. They run advertisements in newspapers and magazines, on billboards and posters, over radio and television. They think up clever slogans they hope we will remember. They know that some of us will buy the product whose slogan appeals to us. Often the slogan has nothing to do with the quality or the usefulness of the product.

Some shoppers are **impulse buyers.** They buy just because they see something they think they want. They like the slogan or the advertising skit on television. So they buy the product. They buy without thinking about the price or about the real usefulness of the product. Other people buy intelligently. Anyone can learn to buy intelligently.

Learning Where and When to Buy

There are a number of ways in which consumers can get the most for their shopping dollars. For example, wise food shoppers study the food advertisements in the local newspaper. They find out which stores are having special sales. At certain times of the year, for example, chicken may be priced very low. At other times, certain fruits and vegetables may be bargains.

By watching for sales, you can often buy clothing, books, furniture, hobby supplies, hardware, and other articles at reduced prices. Some people never pay the full price for an article. They stock up when the price is low.

A low price on an item, however, does not always mean the item is a bargain. Fur-niture, automobiles, television sets, and even houses are often advertised as bargains. Yet a bargain is not a bargain if it is something you cannot really use or if it is poorly made. It is not a bargain if the one you already have is just as good as a new one.

How to Judge Price and Quality

Wise shoppers must be able to judge the quality of a product. They also must know how they plan to use it. Of the many goods and services available, shoppers must make sure that they choose those that are best suited to their own needs. Many consumers solve the problem by shopping only at well-known stores that guarantee the quality of anything they sell. Others learn how to shop at various stores and look for real bargains.

Many people buy articles by brand name. They trust certain business firms. They believe that all products bearing the brand names of these firms must be of good quality. This may or may not be true. Large nationwide firms, as you have read, sell their products under brand names. They spend billions of dollars making consumers aware of these names. One way to be sure of the quality of a product is to study its label carefully.

How to Study Labels

Labels are placed on foods, clothing, and other articles in order to protect you, the consumer. Our governments require that certain kinds of information be included on these labels to help consumers judge the quality of the products they buy.

There are a number of federal laws on labeling. For example, the Food, Drug, and Cosmetic Act provides that all packages of food, as well as medicines and some cosmetics, must state all the things these products contain. The Wool Products Act requires that labels on clothing state how much wool the clothing contains.

Shopping at sales is an excellent way to buy something you need at a reduced price. But remember, the wise consumer is always a careful shopper.

The Truth in Packaging and Labeling Act requires businesses to supply certain information on the packages of the goods they sell. This information includes the name and address of the manufacturer, the contents of the package, and the weight or quantity of the items in the package.

Some of our state and local governments require that every package of meat carry information about its contents. If it is hamburger, for example, the package must name the part of the animal from which the ground meat comes. It also must state whether anything besides meat has been added.

Many products, such as bread, milk, and cheese, must be stamped with a date. This is the date by which the product must be sold or used. Dating a product ensures that it will be fresh when purchased.

Some laws require **unit pricing.** That is, the price tag must show how much money is being asked a unit—for an ounce or a gram, for example. A 10-ounce (283-gram) can of peaches would be a better buy than a can at the same price with only 8 ounces (227 grams). Larger sizes often are a better bargain because they have a lower price per unit. This is not always true, however. You must read labels carefully to get the best bargain.

Unless people are able to read labels intelligently, the labels will be of no help to them. Beware of a term such as "highest quality." These words sound good. Yet they often have no real meaning. A label stating that a piece of clothing is "pre-shrunk" means little. The label does not tell you how much the piece of clothing is likely to shrink when it is washed. If the label says "Sanforized," however, you know the clothing will not shrink more than 1 percent. The word "Sanforized" is a standardized term that has this meaning in the clothing industry.

Organizations That Help Consumers

Sometimes people find that a product has been falsely labeled or advertised. If you believe you have been misled by an unfair business practice, you should first try to seek satisfaction from the business that sold you the product or service. If you are still not satisfied, you should get in touch with the local **Better Business Bureau.** There is one in or near most communities. This organization gives advice and assistance to people who believe they have been cheated or treated unfairly by a business firm.

The federal government also protects the consumer. The Federal Trade Commission, for instance, has the power to bring to court any business firm that uses false or misleading advertising or false labeling. The National Institute of Standards and Technology tests and grades many products. The Department of Agriculture inspects and grades meat, poultry, and certain other foods sold in interstate commerce. The United States Postal Service sees that business firms do not use the mails to cheat the public. The Consumer Product Safety Commission checks products to be sure they will not cause injuries.

A number of cities also have commissioners or departments of consumer affairs. They publish consumer advice and issue warnings to business firms that violate consumer laws. The firms are brought to court if they persist in cheating consumers.

There are a number of private organizations that help consumers. These include Consumers' Research and Consumers Union. These organizations test and rate nearly every product the public buys. They publish the results of their tests in magazines and special reports. A visit to the library to examine their publications will help you compare various brands of the same product. In this way you can learn which is best for your own needs and which is the best buy.

Problems Caused by Consumers

Consumers often accuse businesses of misleading advertising, poor service, and inferior products. Sometimes, however, consumers cause problems for businesses.

Shoplifting, for example, costs businesses billions of dollars each year. Some people damage the store owner's property or demand refunds for merchandise they have already used or abused. Items in motels, hotels, and restaurants are frequently stolen or damaged. Sometimes people fail to pay for purchases obtained on credit.

These people are not professional criminals. They seem to think their actions are unimportant. They often argue that the business—especially if it is a big business—can afford the loss. However, they may be hurting other consumers because these dishonest acts add to the costs of doing business. The prices of products and services may have to be increased to help cover the losses.

The variety of products available in the United States means that consumers have a chance to compare quality and price before making a purchase.

Pay Now or Later?

When you buy something, you may pay cash. You also may charge it. Or you may buy it on the installment plan. Just what are the advantages and disadvantages of buying merchandise in these three ways?

The person who pays cash is likely to be a careful buyer. Since the buyer must pay the full amount at the time of purchase, he or she is likely to think carefully before handing the money to the sales clerk. In addition, a person with cash is sometimes able to buy a product for a lower price than someone who has to rely on credit. He or she may be able to shop in a store that sells products at a reduced price for cash only.

On the other hand, suppose you find a real bargain on something you need. However, you do not have the cash on hand to pay for it. At such times, a charge account can be of help. A **charge account** is an easy form of credit that stores grant to many of their customers. A charge account can usually be obtained by people who have a steady job and a record of paying their bills on time. A charge account permits customers to buy now and pay later. That is, they can make their purchases during the month but not pay for them until the end of the month, or whenever they get the bill from the store.

If customers fail to pay their bills when they are due, the store may close their charge accounts. Such customers become bad credit risks. As a result, they may find it difficult to obtain a charge account somewhere else. Stores share information about customers. This enables them to find out whether a person is a good credit risk.

Pros and Cons of Charge Accounts

There are advantages to using charge accounts. What are some of them?

A charge account makes it easy for you to keep track of what you have bought and

Shopping Tips for Consumers

Before you buy:

Think about what you need and what product or service features are important to you.

Compare brands. Ask for word-of-mouth recommendations and look for formal product comparison reports. Check your local library for magazines and other publications that contain product comparisons.

Compare stores. Look for a store with a good reputation and plan ahead to take advantage of sales. Check with your local Better Business Bureau (BBB) to find out if the company is reputable.

Read warranties to understand what you must do and what the manufacturer must do if you have a problem. Read contract terms carefully. Make sure all blank spaces are filled in before you sign a contract. Ask the sales person to explain the store's return or exchange policy.

After you buy:

Read and follow the instructions on how to use the product or service.

Read and understand the warranty. Keep in mind that you may have additional warranty rights in your state. Keep all sales receipts, warranties, and instructions.

If trouble develops, report the problem to the company as soon as possible. Keep a file of your efforts to resolve the problem. It should include the names of the individuals you speak with and the date, time, and outcome of the conversation. Also, keep copies of the letters you send to the company and any replies they send to you.

SOURCE: United States Office of Consumer Affairs.

what you paid for various articles. You do not have to carry large amounts of cash with you when you go shopping. If you have a charge account, it is easier for you to return purchases you decide you do not want. Charge account customers often receive notices of sales before the sales are advertised in the newspapers. As you can see, there are important advantages to using charge accounts.

"IT'S THE SAME OLD STUFF
BUT IN A BIGGER AND
BETTER BOTTLE!"

Advertising plays a major role in informing consumers about products being sold. Why is it important to pay careful attention to all advertisements?

Most important, though, when you have charge accounts and pay your bills regularly, you establish a good credit rating for yourself. A **credit rating** tells how reliable customers are about paying their bills. A good credit rating is essential when you want to take out a bank loan or buy a house.

There are also disadvantages in having a charge account. What are some of them?

Charge account customers often pick up the telephone and order what they want to buy without shopping around for the best values available. These customers may buy things on impulse that they do not need. They also may find themselves paying more for the things they buy. Stores that sell for cash often sell items for less because they do not have to hire clerks or pay for computers to keep charge account records.

Stores that allow charge accounts usually charge high interest on unpaid balances. If the bill is not paid by the due date (usually 10 to 30 days after the customer receives the bill), most stores add a percent of the unpaid balance to the bill. The interest is often over 19 percent a year. Many American consumers have gone bankrupt because they have used charge accounts unwisely.

Buying on the Installment Plan

There is another way for consumers to buy goods without paying the full amount in cash when they make their purchases. They can use the **installment plan.** In this system of buying, the buyer uses cash to pay part of the purchase price. This money is called the **down payment.** The rest of what the buyer owes is called the **balance.** This is paid in small equal payments, or **installments,** over a period of weeks, months, or years. The installment plan allows a buyer to have the use of a product while paying for it.

Automobiles, houses, refrigerators, furniture, and other large items are often bought on the installment plan. The purchaser signs a written contract with the seller. The contract states how much the installment payments must be and how often they must be paid. It also states that the article still belongs to the seller.

If the customer does not make payments on time or complete the necessary number of installment payments, the seller can **repossess,** or take back, the article. When this happens, the purchaser loses the article. He or she also loses the amount of money that has already been paid.

Buying an article on the installment plan increases its cost. In addition to the regular price, a **carrying charge** as well as interest on the unpaid balance is included in the installment payments.

If you should ever think of buying something on the installment plan, you may find it cheaper to borrow the money from a bank. You can then pay cash for the article and pay the bank back in installments. This is called **installment credit.** Banks usually charge only interest, and not an additional carrying charge, for installment loans. The interest paid to the bank may be less than the combined carrying charge and interest under an installment plan.

Whether you buy an article under an installment plan or installment credit, it is wise to make as large a down payment as possible. Also it is wise to pay off the balance as quickly as possible.

The American system of mass production makes possible the wide variety of goods and services Americans can buy. The easy availability of all these products enables the American people to enjoy a high standard of living.

Mass production is made possible by machine tools, standard parts, and the division of labor. It requires great sources of power to run the machines. These elements of mass production are organized in an assembly line on which the products move as they are manufactured.

CHAPTER 17 SUMMARY

Once products are manufactured, there must be a good system of distribution—transportation and marketing. Railroads, trucks, ships, and airplanes transport goods from factories, farms, and warehouses. They take them to places where consumers can buy them. Our mass marketing system includes many kinds of stores and service organizations. It also requires the labor of many workers.

As consumers, or customers, each of us has an important role to play in our economy. In knowing how to judge price and quality and in buying wisely, we help manufacturers and retailers know how they can serve us best. By making use of the consumer organizations that serve us and by learning the best ways to pay for goods, whether with cash or on credit, we get good value for our money.

LIFE SKILL
Reading a Label

You go to the supermarket to buy, among other things, a can of sliced peaches. That seems simple enough. But when you get to the aisle that has canned fruit, you see at least a dozen different brands of canned sliced peaches. Which brand should you buy?

One way to help you make this decision is to read the label attached to each can. As you learned in this chapter, labels are placed on products to help and protect you, the consumer.

How to Read a Label

To read a food label effectively, follow these guidelines.

1. **Identify the ingredients.** Federal law requires food companies to list the ingredients in each package of food. Further, the ingredients must be listed in the order of their amounts. The main ingredient appears first, and the ingredient used in the least amount appears last. If there are foods you wish to avoid, such as foods that contain large amounts of sugar, reading the list of ingredients will help you choose a product.

2. **Determine the nutritional value of the food.** The federal government requires that food labels tell consumers how many servings are in the container, the size of a serving, and the number of calories and the amount of protein, carbohydrate, and fat in each serving. Labels must also tell consumers what percentage of their recommended daily allowance (RDA) of vitamins and minerals will be filled by one serving of the food. As a rule, you should strive to buy nutritious food.

3. **Locate other information on the label.** You can often learn other things from what is listed on food labels. The name of the food company, for example, might help determine whether you buy a particular product.

4. **Be a comparison shopper.** Comparing labels for ingredients and nutritional content will help you make intelligent buys.

Applying the Skill

Use the food label shown below to answer the following questions.

1. **(a)** What is the main ingredient in the can? **(b)** Which ingredient is found in the smallest amount?

2. **(a)** What percentage of your recommended daily allowance (RDA) of vitamin C is supplied by one serving of the canned peaches? **(b)** What percentage of your daily requirement of calcium will a serving supply?

3. **(a)** Why do you think the number of calories in one serving would interest some people? **(b)** What else can you learn from this label?

Sliced Peaches

NUTRITION INFORMATION PER SERVING

SERVING SIZE . . . . 4 OZ.	PROTEIN 1g
SERVINGS PER CONTAINER . . . 2	CARBOHYDRATE . . . 12g
CALORIES 50	FAT 0

PERCENT OF U.S. RECOMMENDED DAILY ALLOWANCE (U.S. RDA)

VITAMIN A 10	NIACIN 4
VITAMIN C 6	CALCIUM . . . ., *
THIAMINE (B₁) . . . . *	IRON . . . . *
RIBOFLAVIN (B₂) . . . . *	

*CONTAINS LESS THAN 2 PERCENT OF U.S. RDA OF THESE NUTRIENTS.

INGREDIENTS: PEACHES, WATER, CONCENTRATED PEAR JUICE, CONCENTRATED APPLE JUICE, AND CONCENTRATED GRAPE JUICE.

STERLING FRUIT COMPANY
LA GRANGE, IL. 60525 U.S.A.

Reviewing Terms

On a separate sheet of paper, supply the term from the list below that correctly completes each sentence.

economists
mass production
wholesalers
standard parts
marketing

consumers
mass marketing
retailers
transportation

1. _____ buy goods directly from the manufacturer to sell to stores.
2. People who buy goods and services are known as _____.
3. The rifles made by Eli Whitney had _____ _____ so that any part would fit any rifle.
4. Distribution has two sides: _____ and _____.
5. _____ sell goods directly to the public.
6. Making a large amount of goods with machines for a large population is called _____ _____.
7. _____ _____ means selling goods in huge quantities.
8. People who study the economy are called _____.

Using Thinking Skills

1. **Composing a Paragraph** Write a paragraph that identifies and explains the three main features of mass production.
2. **Contrasting Ideas (a)** What are the advantages and disadvantages of charge accounts? **(b)** What are the advantages and disadvantages of installment plans?
3. **Organizing Ideas (a)** In what ways does the federal government help consumers? **(b)** How do other organizations help consumers? **(c)** What can consumers do to become wise buyers?
4. **Identifying Roles** How did Eli Whitney help make mass production possible?

5. **Seeing Relationships** What are the roles of wholesalers and retailers in getting goods from manufacturers to consumers?
6. **Expressing Ideas (a)** Explain how our transportation system is vital to our economy. **(b)** How has the transportation system in our country changed over the years?
7. **Understanding Ideas** What are some characteristics of mass marketing?

Practicing Civics Skills

Comparing Consumer Information Find two brands of the same food product. The product may be canned, frozen, or boxed. Compare the information provided on the labels, and answer the following questions.

1. **(a)** How many servings are in each container? **(b)** What is the serving size of each?
2. **(a)** How are the ingredients in each brand similar? **(b)** How do the ingredients differ?
3. Which brand provides the most vitamins and minerals?
4. If you had to choose one of the brands, which one would you buy? Why?

Being a Good Citizen

1. Organize the class into committees to visit manufacturers, retail stores, freight companies, wholesalers, and the local Chamber of Commerce. Each committee should report on local methods of production and distribution.
2. Invite a member of your local Better Business Bureau or a consumer protection group to class. Ask the speaker about the group's activities and goals, and find out how you can become an informed consumer.
3. Imagine that you are trying to sell a new product called "Brand X." Brand X can be any product you wish. Prepare a magazine advertisement that will make people want to buy your product.

CHAPTER 18

How Americans Manage Their Money

Chapter Sections

1 **Money and Credit**
2 **Banks and Banking**
3 **Saving and Investing**
4 **Insurance Against Hardship**

Chapter Focus

In this chapter, you will read about a subject that interests everyone—money! Money is one of the most useful devices ever invented. Without it the whole process of mass production, marketing, and consumption (what we buy) would grind to a halt. Without money we would have to depend on barter. **Barter** is the swapping of one product for another. Barter was used in early societies before money became the basis of trade.

Barter was often difficult. Imagine that you are a shoemaker living in the days when barter is the chief method of trade. You have more shoes than you can use, but how can you obtain other things you need? You will have to swap shoes for them.

You take several pairs of shoes and set out for the marketplace. You may need flour, chickens, a shirt, a dress, and a broom. When you get to the market, you meet a miller who has flour to sell. But the flour is packed in huge sacks, and all you want is a small sack. The miller is willing to trade a large sack of flour for all your shoes. You agree to the trade.

You now try to trade flour for the things you want. You trade some flour for a broom. You meet a butcher who has chickens but who does not want flour. The butcher would like to trade chickens for some pottery. So you find someone who has pottery and needs flour. Then you return to the butcher and swap your pottery for his chickens.

By this time, it is late evening. You are too tired to try to find a dress or a shirt. As you return home, tired and discouraged, you think to yourself that there must be a better way of doing business. In this chapter, you will learn about that better way.

Study Guide

As you begin to learn about how Americans manage their financial affairs, look for answers to the following questions:

★ How do currency, checks, and credit serve the economy?
★ What kinds of banks exist in the nation?
★ Why are saving and insurance important for Americans?

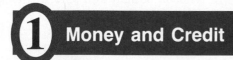

At various times and in various places, people have used many different things for money. Cows, pigs, guns, playing cards, furs, salt, olive oil, big stones, knives, tobacco, copper, iron, wampum beads, shells, rings, silver, and diamonds have all been used for money.

What Is Money?

Money is something that sellers will take in exchange for whatever they have to sell. Buyers can exchange it for whatever they want to buy. Money is thus a medium, or means, of exchange.

To a banker, the term "money" may include checks, bank accounts, and other kinds of writing on pieces of paper. You will read later about some of these kinds of money. For now, think about the "jingling money" and "folding money" that people carry in their pockets or purses. Another term used for these kinds of money is **currency.**

Paper bills and coins do not get their value as means of exchange just because the government prints them or stamps them out of metal. Money in these forms has value only because it will buy something. For a nation's currency to be worth something, the nation's economy must produce something for its people to buy. One reason the United States can produce so much is that American citizens are able to buy what is produced. American currency is also valuable in the world's markets because our nation produces so much.

Every Nation Has Its Currency

Every nation has its own supply of currency. In all nations, currency is alike in four important ways. What are the four common features of currency?

1. Currency must be easy to carry and must take up little space. People must be able to carry it with them for everyday use.

2. Currency must be based on a system of units that are easy to multiply and divide. That is, it should not take too long to figure out the number of coins and bills needed to exchange for any article.

3. Currency must be durable, or last a long time. It should not wear out too quickly or fall apart. People must be able to keep currency until they are ready to spend it.

4. Currency must be made in a standard form and must be guaranteed by the nation's government. In this way, the nation's citizens can be certain that their coins and bills will be accepted by everyone else in exchange for goods and services.

The currency used by Americans is issued, or made, by the federal government. All United States paper money and coins are considered **legal tender.** That is, the law requires that every American accept this money as payment in exchange for all goods and services.

Coins and Paper Money

You may recall that one of the weaknesses of the nation under the Articles of Confederation was the lack of a standard currency. The Constitution solved this weakness by granting to Congress the sole right "to coin money, regulating the value thereof. . . ." In 1792 a **mint,** or plant where coins are made, was opened in Philadelphia. This mint and one in Denver now make most coins for general circulation. Mints in San Francisco and West Point, New York, make commemorative, or special occasion, coins.

Coins are sometimes called "hard money" because they are usually made of hard metal. In the United States, five coins are used: pennies, nickels, dimes, quarters, and half dollars. These coins are parts of one dollar. Dollar coins have not been made since 1981.

For many years, the value of a coin was decided by the amount of metal it contained. A silver dollar, for example, yielded about a dollar's worth of silver when melted down. In the past, many Americans would accept only hard money. They thought it was more valuable and reliable than paper money.

Coins now make up about 6 percent of our total money supply. Coins are used mainly for small purchases and to make change. And they no longer contain gold or silver. All coins are alloys, or mixtures, of metals. Pennies are copper-coated zinc. Nickels, dimes, quarters, and half dollars are alloys of copper and nickel.

Why do Americans accept coins that are not made of gold or silver? They accept them because they have faith in the United States government. They know that the coins will be accepted as legal tender when they are presented at stores, banks, or elsewhere. They also know that the government has a supply of gold and silver bullion, or bars. This bullion is kept in a depository at Fort Knox, Kentucky. It could be used to pay our debts with foreign nations. It also helps to strengthen our nation's financial position.

Most of the money issued by the government today is paper money. It is printed in Washington, D.C., at the Bureau of Engraving and Printing of the Treasury Department. Bills are printed in denominations of $1, $5, $10, $20, $50, and $100. Bills in denominations of $2, $500, $1,000, $5,000, and $10,000 are no longer issued, but some are still around.

Checks

Very little of what is bought and sold in the United States is paid for with either coins or paper money, the currency you have been reading about. Many Americans make greater use of another kind of money. This is the money represented by checks. A **check** is a written and signed order to a bank to pay a sum of money from a checking account to the person or firm named on the check.

Most of our total money supply, more than 70 percent, is in the form of bank deposits. Bank deposits are the figures in checking accounts. These figures represent the amount of credit in a person's or business firm's account. **Credit** is what the bank owes the person or the firm. The person or business firm spends money out of this account by writing a check.

Can You Guess?

Whose face appears on a $1 bill, a $5 bill, a $10 dollar bill, and a $20 bill?

Answers are on page 594.

The check is just a piece of paper. It is not legal tender because it is not guaranteed by the federal government. Most sellers, however, will accept a check that has been written by a responsible person or firm. The person or firm who writes the check maintains the account by depositing cash or checks—such as paychecks—from other persons or firms.

Many people never see most of their money because they use this kind of credit. What they see instead is a column of figures the bank sends them on their monthly statement. This **statement** tells them how much credit they have in their account.

Charge Accounts and Credit Cards

A charge account is a method by which a store extends credit to customers. Customers receive charge cards, which allow them to buy things without paying cash at the time of purchase. The amount of the purchases is simply added to their charge accounts. Customers then receive a monthly bill.

The customer writes a check for all or part of the bill, keeping in mind that interest is charged on the unpaid portion. The store deposits the check in its own bank, which sends the check to the customer's bank. The customer's bank subtracts the amount from the customer's account. No currency changes hands. (Banks do not actually collect from each other check by check. They use computerized systems that handle checks.)

Credit cards are a substitute for money. Credit cards are issued by banks and other major lending institutions. Examples of credit cards include American Express®, VISA®, and MasterCard®. Thousands of stores and other businesses now accept credit cards in place of currency or checks.

The customer shows the credit card when making a purchase. The store or business then charges the credit card company. The credit card company pays the store or business and charges the customer. As with charge cards,

These coins have just been made at a government mint. This machine counts them and places them in bags for shipment throughout the nation.

the customer pays all or part of the credit card bill with one check once a month. Interest charges, which often are quite high, are added to the unpaid portion of the monthly bill. Again, no currency will change hands.

Credit in Business

Credit is used instead of currency in most sales involving large amounts of goods. Wholesale grocers may order half a truckload of canned goods, for example. They promise to pay for this order at the end of the month or, sometimes, within 90 days. Because they have good credit, the wholesalers can get the canned goods right away.

If they can sell the canned goods before their debt is due, the wholesalers will have the money they need to repay their debt.

Are we becoming a "cashless society"? This woman uses a credit card to pay for a purchase. When the bill arrives, she probably will pay it by check.

Credit gives wholesalers a chance to do a larger amount of business than they could do if they had to pay for the goods immediately.

Credit, however, is sometimes used unwisely. Suppose business people use credit more often than they should. When the time comes for them to pay their bills, they find themselves in trouble. They cannot pay the bills they piled up by using credit. Then their **creditors**—those people to whom they owe money—may force them to sell their businesses to pay their debts.

Credit in the Family

Credit can also be an advantage to the average American family if used wisely. Emergencies occur in most families. Sometimes a product or service is needed immediately. The family washing machine, for example, may break down. A new one may be needed. If the family does not have enough money in the bank to pay for it, a new washing machine can usually be obtained on credit.

If the family plans to pay within a few weeks, it needs only **short-term credit.** On the other hand, the family may need several months to pay for the machine. If so, it will plan to pay a certain amount each month until the total has been paid. This **long-term credit,** as you recall, is also called installment credit. Most American families use this kind of credit to make large purchases, such as homes, automobiles, or furniture.

Like some business people, families may use credit unwisely. Suppose a family buys so much on credit that it cannot afford to make the payments. What will happen? The stores may take back their products. Or, the debts may be so high that the family has no choice but to declare personal bankruptcy. Declaring bankruptcy can hurt the family's credit rating for years.

Credit in the Overall Economy

Credit, as you have seen, plays several important roles in the buying and selling of goods and services that go on all the time in our free market. It also plays an important role in the successful operation of the American economy as a whole.

In a healthy economic system, the supply of money must increase or decrease in relation to the general condition of the economy. When production picks up and business is brisk, there must be plenty of money available to consumers. Otherwise, goods that are produced could not be sold. In that case, production would have to slow down again. Free-flowing money in the form of credit makes it possible for customers to buy whenever there are goods to be sold.

If too much money is available when production slacks off, prices may go too high. That would happen because there would be more money to spend than there were goods to buy. Customers would try to outbid each other to get the limited supply of goods. But with our credit system, when production drops, banks may extend less credit to customers. Therefore, buying slows down.

Our American society is made up, for the most part, of honest people. As a result, the widespread use of credit has become possible as a means of exchange. If buyers and sellers could not trust each other, credit would not be possible.

 SECTION 1 REVIEW

Define barter, money, currency, legal tender, mint, check, credit, statement, credit cards, creditors, short-term credit, long-term credit

1. **Summarizing Ideas** Describe the four common features of every nation's currency.
2. **Identifying Ideas** (a) List the coins and denominations of bills issued by the government. (b) Why do Americans accept coins that are not made of gold or silver?
3. **Expressing Ideas** (a) Why are checks not legal tender? (b) Why do sellers accept them?
4. **Understanding Ideas** Explain how the American system of credit works.

Thinking Critically Some people want to abolish the penny. How would this affect our economy?

② Banks and Banking

A thousand years ago, money was a problem just as it is for many people today. In fact, money was even a problem for the wealthy. They had a difficult time finding a safe place to keep their money. Carrying it made them the target of thieves. Even hiding it in their homes did not guarantee its safety.

How Banking Began

In most communities, however, there were goldsmiths who kept their wealth heavily guarded. Because their gold was so valuable, the goldsmiths kept it in strong, sturdy safes.

In time, the townspeople began to bring their money to the goldsmiths for safekeeping. Before long, local goldsmiths found themselves in the money-keeping business. They began to charge a small fee for this service.

Eventually, the goldsmiths added money-lending to their money-keeping service. Townspeople who needed money began to come to the goldsmiths for loans. In return for the loans, they signed a paper promising to repay the money by a certain date and to pay interest for using the money.

Borrowers also guaranteed their loans by promising to give their property to the moneylender if the loans were not repaid on time. Property used to guarantee that a loan will be repaid is called **collateral.** These practices started by the early moneylenders developed into the banking system we know today.

What Is a Bank?

Banks are familiar sights in every American town and city. A **bank** is a business establishment that deals in money and credit. Banks safeguard the deposits of customers, and provide them with a convenient means of paying bills. Banks also make loans to customers, usually in the form of checks or credits to their checking accounts.

Most people rely on banks for their checking and savings. Money deposited in a checking account is called a **demand deposit.** That is, the bank must give depositors their money back when the depositors request it by writing checks. Depositors usually do not earn interest on regular checking accounts.

Money deposited in a savings account is called a **time deposit.** Most banks require depositors to keep the money in their accounts for some period of time. Savings accounts pay interest to depositors, but the amount of interest paid depends on the type of account.

An increasingly popular type of account combines checking and savings—the negotiable order of withdrawal (NOW) account. With a NOW account, the customer can write checks and receive interest on the money in the account. Most NOW accounts, though, require depositors to keep a certain minimum balance in the account.

A bank chartered under state laws is a **state bank.** One chartered under federal laws is a **national bank.** The type of charter determines whether the bank is supervised by state or federal officials. It also determines many of the rules that guide the bank.

Kinds of Banks

There are four main kinds of banks in the United States: commercial banks, savings and loan associations, mutual savings banks, and credit unions. Although the differences among these banks have blurred in recent years, some important differences remain.

Commercial Banks. The largest banks in the United States are **commercial banks,** which offer a full range of services. Commercial banks offer checking, savings, and NOW accounts. They make loans to individuals and businesses. They issue credit cards and manage retirement accounts. They also have trust departments that help customers manage property and invest money.

Accounts in commercial banks are insured by a government agency called the **Federal Deposit Insurance Corporation (FDIC).** Each depositor is insured up to $100,000. This means that if a bank cannot give its depositors their money, the FDIC will, but only up to $100,000 per depositor.

Like corporations, commercial banks are owned by stockholders who buy shares in the bank. Shareholders receive cash dividends from the profits made by the bank.

Savings and Loan Associations. Banks known as **savings and loan associations** were originally begun in the mid-1800's to help people buy homes. They still account for a large percentage of home mortgage loans. In recent years, though, federal regulations have allowed them to expand their services to include many of those offered by commercial banks. In addition to loans, customers can open checking, savings, and NOW accounts and can get credit cards.

Deposits in savings and loans are insured by the **Federal Savings and Loan Insurance Corporation (FSLIC).** Like the FDIC, the FSLIC insures depositors up to $100,000.

By law, depositors own the savings and loans. As shareholders, depositors elect a board of directors to handle the day-to-day operations. Shareholders also benefit from any profit made by the savings and loans through interest paid to their accounts.

Mutual Savings Banks. Banks known as **mutual savings banks** were begun in the early 1800's to encourage savings by people who could make only very small deposits. Today these banks offer a variety of services, including home loans. Most mutual savings banks are located in the New England and Middle Atlantic states.

As with commercial banks, deposits in mutual savings banks are insured by the FDIC. Accounts are insured up to a maximum of $100,000.

Each mutual savings bank is run by a board of directors. Members of the board, rather than depositors, elect the people who will take their places on the board. The bank passes on its profits to depositors in the form of interest.

Credit Unions. Most **credit unions** are established by people who work for large businesses or who are members of the same labor union. Credit unions are owned and run by their members. When members make deposits, they buy shares in the credit union that pay interest. These deposits are pooled to make low-interest loans available to members. Depositors also may write checks, which are called "share drafts."

Deposits in credit unions are insured by a government agency called the **National Credit Union Administration (NCUA).** Each account is insured up to a maximum of $100,000.

George McClain Gets a Bank Loan

What really happens when a person borrows money from a bank? Consider the example of George McClain, who owns and operates a small gas station. George needs $5,000 to buy some new equipment. He goes to a commercial bank to speak to a loan officer. After listening to George, the loan officer tells him that he probably will get the loan. But George must show that he is a good credit risk.

George then brings in his business records, which show that his gas station makes a profit. George also points out that he owns his home, and that he has no large business debts. All this convinces the bank that George McClain will be able to repay the loan. The bank then agrees to make the loan and to consider George's house as collateral.

Many loans made by commercial banks are short-term loans. They are to be paid back in 30, 60, or 90 days. George McClain receives a short-term loan of $5,000, due in 90 days. However, he does not receive any currency or even a check. What he gets is a credit in his checking account.

George does not get the full $5,000 credit. The bank takes out, say, $125 in advance as

the interest it is charging for the loan. George receives a credit of $4,875 in his checking account. Deducting the interest on a loan in advance is known as **discounting.**

After he receives his loan, George McClain buys his new equipment. George begins to take in more money because his gas station can now offer better service.

The equipment company, richer now by George's borrowed credit, uses the money to expand its business. In fact, with George's check and the checks of other customers coming in, the equipment company may borrow money from a commercial bank for its own expansion. In this way, credit circulates throughout the American economy.

McClain Renews His Loan

What happens when the loan is due at the end of the 90-day period? If George McClain's business has done well enough, he can now

Many small business owners like this one depend on bank loans to help them start their businesses.

repay the loan. But suppose the new equipment was late in arriving, or business did not increase quite as fast as expected. George may have to go to the bank and ask that his loan be renewed, or continued. If the bank agrees, George will not have to repay the loan for another 90 days.

Usually a bank will renew a loan to a person like George McClain, whose credit is good. George, of course, will have to pay interest again on the loan renewal.

Suppose, however, that bank officials think George has done a poor job managing his business with the new equipment. They may decide he is no longer a good risk and may refuse to renew the loan. George must then find some way to repay the loan at once. In order to save his house, which is the collateral for his loan, he may have to sell his car or other possessions. He may even have to sell his business. As you can see, a loan

involves a risk both for the bank and for the person who borrows the money.

Government Regulation of the Banking System

There was a time when banks were allowed to do business just about as they wished. They sometimes loaned money without enough collateral. They sometimes did not keep enough money in reserve. Under these conditions, rumors might spread that the bank was shaky. Depositors would start "a run on the bank"—that is, panic, go to the bank, and demand all their money. Sometimes so many depositors withdrew their money that the bank had no funds left. As a result, other depositors lost their money.

Bank failures happened so often in our nation's history that the federal government finally stepped in with a plan to regulate banking. In 1913 Congress established the **Federal Reserve System.** All national banks were required to belong to this system. State banks might join the system if they wished, and many did.

For many years, the Federal Reserve had direct control only over its member banks. For example, only the member banks had to keep part of their deposits on reserve with the "Fed," as the system is called. Then in 1980 a law was passed stating that all banks had to meet the Fed's reserve requirements.

People applying for a bank loan must speak to a loan officer, who will then approve or deny the loan.

The Federal Reserve System

This is how the Federal Reserve System is set up. The United States is divided into 12 Federal Districts. There is a large Federal Reserve Bank in each district. The Federal Reserve Banks do not usually do business with individuals or business firms. Instead, they act as the bankers for the federal government and for other banks.

The Federal Reserve Banks serve two main purposes. First, the federal government uses the Federal Reserve Banks to handle its own banking needs. The Secretary of the Treasury deposits the funds of the United States government in these banks. Then the Secretary writes checks on the federal government's account, just as an individual does who has a checking account. The Federal Reserve Banks also handle the sale of bonds issued by the government. Most United States currency is put into circulation through the Federal Reserve System.

Second, the 12 Federal Reserve Banks provide services to the state and national banks and help control our banking system. Even banks sometimes have to borrow money. A member bank can go to the Federal Reserve Bank in its district and borrow money in order to increase its own reserve. The member bank then is able to make more loans or investments. The bank must pay interest on these loans. The rate of interest charged by the Federal Reserve is called the **discount rate.**

The Federal Reserve at Work

The Federal Reserve System is managed by a seven-member **board of governors** in Washington, D.C. Each member is appointed by the President, with the consent of the Senate, for a single 14-year term. The board of governors makes most of the major decisions for the Federal Reserve System.

A healthy economy must have enough money and credit in circulation, but not too much. Through its influence over the banking system, the Fed tries to keep the right amount of money in circulation. When our economy is growing, we need more money in circulation. Remember, money is simply a useful tool that helps us exchange goods and services efficiently. If more goods and services are being produced, more money is needed.

If the supply of money grows faster than the supply of goods, prices will rise. To prevent this, the Federal Reserve may try to slow down the growth of the money supply or even take money out of circulation.

If the Federal Reserve wants to speed up our economic growth, it will put more money into circulation. It will usually do this by purchasing government bonds from banks or others holding these bonds. Then these banks or people have more money to spend or lend, and the money goes into our economy. To take money out of circulation, the Federal Reserve does the opposite. It sells government bonds back to banks or people. After buying these bonds, individuals or banks have less money to spend or lend.

SECTION 2 REVIEW

Define collateral, bank, demand deposit, time deposit, state bank, national bank, discounting, discount rate.

Identify commercial banks, Federal Deposit Insurance Corporation (FDIC), savings and loan associations, Federal Savings and Loan Insurance Corporation (FSLIC), mutual savings banks, credit unions, National Credit Union Administration (NCUA), Federal Reserve System, board of governors

1. **Summarizing Ideas** Summarize the four main types of banks.
2. **Understanding Ideas (a)** Why did Congress establish the Federal Reserve System? **(b)** Discuss the responsibilities of the Fed.

Thinking Critically You are a bank loan officer. What do you ask loan applicants?

Saving and Investing

Most of us want money in order to spend it. But we do not have to spend it right away. One of the features of money is that it can be kept and spent at some future time. Most people try to keep some money in case they have unexpected expenses. Keeping money by setting it aside is called **saving.** Saving is important for individuals and for our nation.

Why People Save

Almost everyone saves, or tries to save. Families try to put aside money for their children's education or to buy a house. They try to save money to meet emergencies, such as medical and hospital bills, loss of a job, or other unexpected difficulties. People try to save money for their retirement years. Saving is an important part of knowing how to manage money wisely.

There are several ways to save money. Some kinds of saving make it possible for people to get together enough money to pay for expensive items, such as vacations, clothing, and household appliances. True, the American credit system allows us to obtain expensive goods and services without paying cash for them at the time of purchase. Yet even in our credit system, the customer often must make a fairly large down payment.

The largest purchases most persons ever make are houses and cars. To buy a house, you must first pay a sizable part of the total cost as a down payment. Builders may advertise, "Only 10 percent down—pay the rest as rent." But 10 percent of the cost of a $75,000 house is $7,500. The average family has to save a long time to accumulate $7,500.

Used-car dealers may advertise, "No money down, drive it home today!" But without a down payment, the monthly payments on a car may be higher than the buyer can afford. The smaller the down payment, the greater the amount of interest and the larger the monthly payments. The extra interest will also make the total cost of the car higher. Learning to save and practicing saving throughout life is wise for everyone.

Owning our own home figures prominently in the American Dream. Careful attention to saving is one way to help make that dream become a reality.

How People Save

There are various ways to save money, of course. You can hide your money under a mattress, put it in a cookie jar, or keep it in a piggy bank. Most Americans find that there are better ways to save money.

1. Many Americans Save by Putting Money in the Bank. They put aside a regular amount each week in a savings account at a bank. Or whenever they make extra money, they put it in their savings account instead of spending it. The bank pays interest on money deposited in a savings account. By

SAVINGS ACCOUNTS	STOCKS AND BONDS	INSURANCE
		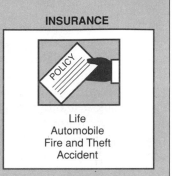
Regular Savings Accounts NOW Accounts Certificates of Deposit Money Market Accounts	Government Bonds Corporate Stocks Corporate Bonds	Life Automobile Fire and Theft Accident

saving in this way, a person's money earns more money for him or her. The money is always there to be withdrawn when it is needed.

Regular savings accounts are also called "passbook accounts" because depositors receive a small book in which their transactions are recorded. Regular savings accounts usually do not require a minimum balance. Some banks, though, charge a monthly service fee if the account falls below a certain amount or if no transactions have occurred within a certain length of time.

2. Many Americans Save by Buying Bonds. You probably remember that when you buy a bond, you are lending money to the business or government that issues the bond. When the bond reaches maturity, you get the money back. In the meantime, your money is earning interest. Agencies that issue bonds include the United States government, many state and local governments, as well as large corporations.

United States government bonds, as well as the bonds of most states, localities, and corporations, are a safe form of savings. In most cases, bondholders receive regular interest payments.

One form of bond, the United States savings bond, does not pay interest until it is cashed in. For example, a savings bond bought for $100 earns $100 in interest after a certain number of years. The purchaser who paid $100 for a bond gets back $200. Meanwhile, the buyer's money is safe because the United States government will always repay its debt. However, the interest rate for savings bonds is not as high as it is for many other kinds of investments.

3. Many Americans Save by Buying Stocks. You read about common stocks and preferred stocks in Chapter 16. There are regular organizations that buy and sell stocks for their customers. These organizations are called **brokerage houses.** The people they employ are called **brokers.** Each brokerage house is a member of a **stock exchange.** Millions of shares of stock are bought and sold every working day at the stock exchange.

Anyone can buy stocks by getting in touch with a brokerage house. However, people need to know a great deal about the stock market before they buy stocks. There are both safe stocks and risky stocks.

People who buy common stocks are taking a chance. They hope their investment will earn more money—perhaps much more—than it would earn in a savings account or a bond purchase. Annual stock dividends may be higher than interest payments would be. Also, if the value of a stock rises in the stock exchange, the customer may sell that stock, take a profit, and buy a new stock. However, the stock may pay small dividends or none at all. Moreover, its value on the stock market may fall.

To reduce the amount of risk in stock purchases, some people buy shares in **mutual funds.** These funds are managed by people who are familiar with stock market conditions. Mutual fund managers buy many different stocks. Therefore, the risk in any one stock is not so great. By buying a share in a mutual fund, the purchaser owns a small piece of a large number of stocks.

4. Many Americans Save by Buying Insurance. There are many kinds of insurance. Some of them are, in part, forms of saving. A private life insurance policy, for example, may be "surrendered" for its cash value after a certain number of years. You will read more about insurance in Section 4.

5. Other Ways of Saving. In recent years, Americans have been able to save in other ways, too. They have been investing in certificates of deposit and money market funds. These often pay higher rates of interest than regular savings deposits and bonds.

Certificates of deposit (CDs) are issued by banks and other financial institutions. Savers invest a certain amount of money for a specified period of time. The amount of money invested in a CD may range from $250 to $100,000. The interest to be paid when the CD matures is set at the time of purchase and remains constant. Most people buy six-month CDs, but longer time periods are also available. Usually the longer the money is invested, the higher the interest paid on the CD. Investors who withdraw any money before the end of the specified period of time lose a percentage of the interest.

Money market funds, like mutual funds, buy types of investments that most individuals could not purchase alone. Savers can withdraw their money at any time. However, money market funds do not guarantee a specified amount of interest. The rate of interest can either rise or fall. Moreover, this form of saving is not insured by the government.

People also have been buying gold, silver, jewels, paintings, and other precious items as a form of saving. They hope the value of these things will rise sharply. If they do, the owners may make more money than people who put their savings in stocks, bonds, or savings accounts. However, they get no interest on these holdings. Also, the value can go down as sharply as it can go up.

Savings in Our Economy

Saving by individual citizens is absolutely necessary in our free economy. What happens to the money that Americans have in savings accounts, bonds, stocks, and other forms of saving? That money is used to help expand our nation's economy. You have read that continued growth of production is important to a nation's economy. How is continued growth of production made possible?

Continued growth is possible only if factories and other means of production are continually expanded. How does this happen? The means of production expand only when there is capital available to pay for new factories, machine tools, and other capital goods. You read about capital in Chapter 16.

Where does capital come from? It comes from savings. Suppose you have $10. You spend $5 of it and put the other $5 in a bank. The $5 you spend represents goods that you consume. That is, you spend the money for something you want. But you do not consume the $5 you put in the bank. It is money that can be used for another purpose. It can be invested. The bank can use this money to make loans to business people.

Using Savings to Invest

Saving and investing are not the same thing. Money in a piggy bank is saved, but is not invested. Money you deposit in a savings account in a bank is both saved and invested. It is saved by you. It is invested by the bank.

When you buy stocks, bonds, or CDs you are both saving and investing.

When you invest, you turn money into capital. What the money buys is not consumed. It is used to produce goods and services. Thus, investing money results in the production of goods and services. This production results in more profits.

The ability of the American people to save large amounts of money, and the ability of our economic system to invest this money, help keep our nation prosperous. The ability of our free economy to raise large amounts of capital has made it possible for American

business firms to build huge factories that turn out vast amounts of goods.

Business firms also save in order to raise part of their own capital. The managers of most corporations put aside a certain part of their companies' profits before they pay dividends to stockholders. This money is then put back into their business in the form of new capital.

The new capital helps businesses invest in new machines or expand their factories. It also helps businesses establish new branches or add new lines of products to what they already produce. This new capital for

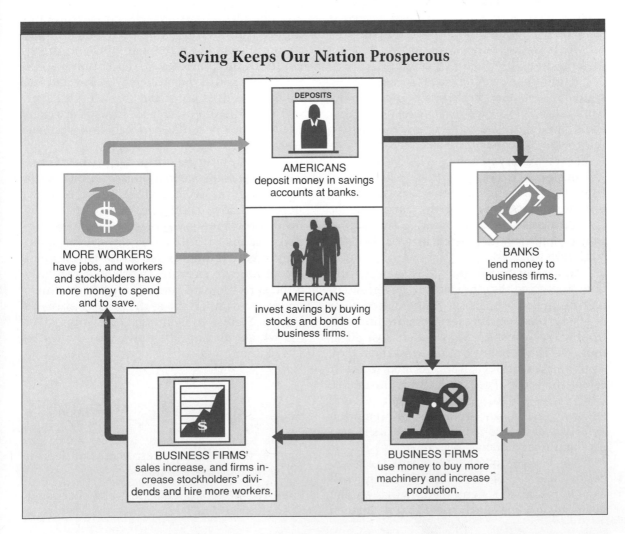

Saving Keeps Our Nation Prosperous

DEPOSITS

AMERICANS
deposit money in savings accounts at banks.

AMERICANS
invest savings by buying stocks and bonds of business firms.

MORE WORKERS
have jobs, and workers and stockholders have more money to spend and to save.

BANKS
lend money to business firms.

BUSINESS FIRMS'
sales increase, and firms increase stockholders' dividends and hire more workers.

BUSINESS FIRMS
use money to buy more machinery and increase production.

expansion is in addition to the money set aside to replace older buildings and equipment when they wear out.

Making Saving Safe

When people put their money into a bank, they want to know their money will be safe. They want to know they will be able to get it back when they ask for it. Also, when people buy stocks or bonds, they want to feel they are not taking unnecessary risks.

For these reasons, our federal and state governments have passed laws to regulate the activities of those institutions that handle the savings of others. All banks must receive a state or federal charter to operate. Our governments charter only banks that are properly organized and have enough capital.

After a bank is chartered, it is inspected regularly by state or federal officials. The bank's directors are responsible for seeing that their bank obeys all banking laws. Also, you may recall, all banks must keep reserve funds in Federal Reserve Banks.

In spite of these regulations, banks sometimes fail. The officials of the bank may make unwise investments, and the bank may be forced to close. What happens to the savings that people have deposited in a bank if the bank fails?

Insuring Savings. Most savings are now protected by the federal government. During the 1930's, many banks closed their doors because businesses were in financial trouble. As a result, many people lost all or most of their savings. Congress then took steps to protect depositors. As you recall, it established the Federal Deposit Insurance Corporation (FDIC). Similarly, the Federal Savings and Loan Insurance Corporation (FSLIC) was formed to protect deposits in savings and loan associations.

You can tell whether your bank is a member of the FDIC or the FSLIC. The bank will display prominent signs in its windows and in its advertising. Each bank that is insured by the FDIC or the FSLIC contributes to an insurance fund held by the government. If any member bank fails, all depositors will be paid the amount of their deposits in the bank up to $100,000.

Regulating Stock Exchanges. Also in the 1930's, Congress established the **Securities and Exchange Commission (SEC)** to ensure that all offerings of stocks and bonds on the nation's stock exchanges would be honest. In the past, people sometimes sold "watered-down" stock. This was stock that did not fully represent the value claimed for it. There were many other stock "dodges," or tricks, by which dishonest people cheated the public.

The regulations of the Securities and Exchange Commission were established to put a stop to such practices. The SEC constantly monitors the practices of the nation's stock exchanges and of the brokers who buy and sell stock. This does not mean that all stocks are safe investments or that all brokers are honest. A company can be perfectly honest, meet all the SEC's rules, and still fail.

Regulating Savings Organizations. All the nation's savings organizations come under state or federal government supervision. Insurance companies are regulated by state governments. Savings and loan associations are also regulated by laws. Even company credit unions must allow government accountants to examine their books regularly to be sure they are being run properly. Since saving is so important to the prosperity of the United States, it is in the best interest of the whole nation that individual savings be safeguarded.

SECTION 3 REVIEW

Define saving, brokerage houses, stock exchange, mutual funds, certificates of deposit (CDs), money market funds

Identify brokers, Securities and Exchange Commission (SEC)

1. **Understanding Ideas (a)** Discuss the reasons that people save money. **(b)** Why is saving necessary even with our system of credit?
2. **Summarizing Ideas** Describe the five ways in which Americans can save money.
3. **Seeing Relationships** How does saving help American businesses?
4. **Identifying Roles (a)** How does the federal government help protect bank depositors? **(b)** How does the federal government protect people who buy stock?

Thinking Critically You just won $250 in an essay contest on "How to Use Money Wisely." What will you do with the money?

4 Insurance Against Hardship

Life is full of risks and uncertainties. There is the chance of illness or accident. There is the possibility of losing one's job. A person's house could burn down or be destroyed by earthquake or flood. A motorist could be involved in an accident and be sued for thousands of dollars by someone injured in the accident. A parent might die, leaving the spouse with young children to support. There is the uncertainty of old age, when a person may not be able to work and earn a living.

Our economic system includes arrangements that protect people, at least in part, against such risks and uncertainties. These protections are called **insurance.**

What Is Insurance?

Suppose you thought you might suffer a loss of $100,000 from some cause. Would you be willing to pay a small sum—say $750 each year—just to make sure you did not run this risk? That is what insurance is. It is a system of paying a small amount to avoid the risk of a large loss.

The small amount a person pays for this protection is called the **premium.** Premiums may be paid yearly or at regular times throughout the year. The large loss against which a person is insured is the **principal sum.** The contract that gives this kind of protection is an **insurance policy.**

Private insurance is voluntary. That is, individuals and companies choose to pay for it. **Social insurance** is required by state and federal laws. Individuals and companies must pay for social insurance programs.

Private Insurance

There are many different kinds of private insurance companies. Altogether, they write insurance policies covering almost every possible kind of risk.

How can insurance companies do what they do? How can they take small amounts of money from people, yet pay them a large sum if hardship occurs to them? The reason

Without a health and accident insurance policy, this girl's family would have had to pay all the medical expenses for her broken leg themselves.

is simple. Not everybody has a hardship. You may pay premiums on accident insurance all your life. Yet you may never collect a cent because you never have an accident. You cannot, however, be sure you will never have an accident. Most people consider it wise to buy insurance against such a risk.

A large insurance company has millions of policyholders who pay their premiums regularly. Part of this money goes into a reserve fund. State laws specify how much of a reserve fund a company must maintain. The amount depends on the kind of insurance the company issues and the number of policyholders it has.

When someone has a hardship of the type specified in the company's policies, payment of the principal sum is made from the reserve fund. Even with millions of policyholders, there may be only a few thousand payments out of the reserve fund each year.

Except for money held in reserve funds, insurance companies invest the premiums they collect. They buy stocks and bonds and make other forms of investment. The dividends, interest, and other income from the investments pay the expenses of these companies and earn profits for their shareholders.

Their investments help provide the capital needed in our economy.

Life Insurance. The main purpose of **life insurance** is to provide the policyholder's family with money in case the policyholder dies. In this way, the family is protected from financial hardship. The person named in the policy to receive the money upon the policyholder's death is called the **beneficiary.**

Two kinds of life insurance are term insurance and whole life insurance. **Term insurance** covers only a specified period of time. This insurance is often chosen by couples who have young children or very high bills. Because it expires at the end of the specified term, it is relatively inexpensive. But it will allow the surviving spouse to care for the children and pay off large debts. **Whole life insurance** covers the policyholder throughout his or her life, and is more expensive.

Disability Income and Health Insurance. There are many forms of insurance that make regular payments to policyholders if they are injured in an accident or become too ill to work. **Disability income insurance** may cover total disability or partial disability or both. Some policies cover

A home is the biggest investment that most people make in their lifetime. They often take out insurance that will pay for unexpected damage to it.

all kinds of accidents, even breaking a leg by slipping on the soap in the bathtub. Other kinds of policies cover only accidents on common carriers—that is, on airplanes, trains, buses, and other means of public transportation. In case of death, the beneficiary receives the principal sum.

Health insurance makes regular payments to policyholders when they cannot work because of illness not caused by an accident. Health insurance premiums are higher than disability premiums because people are more likely to become ill than they are to become disabled.

Hospitalization insurance pays part of a policyholder's hospital expenses. Other insurance plans pay doctors' bills, dentists' bills, and other medical expenses. The premiums for these kinds of insurance are often paid in part by the policyholders and in part by their employers.

Property Insurance. For people who own a home, property insurance is probably the greatest single investment. If the home should burn down, they might be financially ruined. For this reason, most homeowners carry some form of property insurance. **Fire insurance** is the most common form. Americans buy fire insurance on their factories, stores, offices, and other places of business, as well as on their homes.

In addition, many people take out **homeowners' insurance.** This covers a person's home not only for fire but also for many other kinds of risks—windstorm, hail, flood, theft, burglary, and legal liability.

Liability Insurance. Suppose someone comes to your door on an icy day and falls coming up the steps. The person breaks a leg and has to go to the hospital. You are legally liable, or responsible, because the accident happened on your property—even if you did not invite the person or put the ice there. You might even have posted a sign by your door saying "Warning—Ice—Slippery." It makes no difference.

You are legally liable for the injury to that person. He or she can sue you in court and collect payment, called damages. **Liability insurance** can protect property owners from high costs in cases of this kind.

Sometimes doctors are sued by patients who claim they have been neglected or incorrectly treated. Doctors performing extremely risky operations are most often involved in such cases. To protect themselves, doctors purchase **malpractice insurance,** or professional liability insurance

Automobile Insurance. The most common form of property and liability insurance is the kind that automobile owners buy. **Automobile liability insurance** covers automobile owners in case their cars kill or injure other people or damage property. About half of all states require all automobile owners to have liability insurance before they are able to register a car. Most automobile insurance policies also protect the owner from loss by fire or theft.

Insurance Against Dishonesty. Among the many kinds of private insurance are some that protect people against losses caused by burglars, embezzlers, and swindlers. Business firms, stores, banks, and homeowners carry burglary insurance. Banks and other businesses that deal in valuable documents carry forgery insurance.

Companies that handle money pay to have their employees **bonded.** This means the company is repaid if an employee disappears with the company's money. Such policies also cover embezzling, which occurs when an employee steals from the company by making false entries in the company's records.

Social Insurance

The business failures of the 1930's caused much hardship and suffering among the American people. Many business firms and factories closed down. Millions of men and women lost their jobs. Banks failed, and thousands of persons lost their life savings. Money they had counted on for old age was gone.

To meet the problems of this troubled period, called the Great Depression, President Franklin D. Roosevelt recommended many new laws. Congress passed most of them. Together these laws were called the New Deal. Some of the new laws brought immediate assistance to needy people. Other laws, looking to the future, offered protection against severe economic risks and hardships.

Government programs that are meant to protect individuals from future hardship are called social insurance. They make certain forms of insurance compulsory, or required, for nearly all the nation's people. In this way, almost everyone can receive its benefits.

An important program of social insurance was adopted by Congress and President Roosevelt in the Social Security Act of 1935. The act set up an insurance system called **Social Security.** It has three major parts: old-age, survivors, and disability insurance; unemployment insurance; and workers' compensation.

Old-Age, Survivors, and Disability Insurance. The basic idea of this type of insurance is simple. People pay a percentage of their salaries each month while they work in order to get back cash benefits when they most need them. During the years when workers earn money, they and their employers make contributions to a fund. When workers retire, or if they become disabled and their earnings stop, they receive payments from the fund as long as they live.

If workers die before reaching retirement age, their families receive survivors payments. A payment is made for each child under 18 and for the widow or widower. Payments for children stop when they reach the age of 18.

Paying for Social Security. Monthly contributions under the Social Security Act are paid equally by workers and by their employers. The contributions actually are a tax, because they are compulsory, or required. The program was made compulsory because Congress wanted as many American citizens as possible to be spared some of the financial hardship they had experienced during the Great Depression.

Today the Social Security program extends to workers in almost every industry, business, and profession. Self-employed people must also participate. They pay the entire contribution themselves.

Receiving Social Security. The benefits paid by Social Security have gradually increased since 1935. The amount of the required contribution also has increased. The amount that workers and employers pay depends on how much money the workers earn each year. The benefits received by workers when they retire is based on their average earnings over a long period of time. Retired workers, their survivors, and disabled workers receive monthly Social Security checks.

Benefits under the Social Security program provide a cushion against the worst hardships caused by the disability, death, or retirement of the wage earner. But the benefits are not large. Those people who can afford to do so supplement their social insurance by buying private insurance of various kinds.

Unemployment Insurance. The problem of unemployment was extremely serious when the Social Security Act was passed in 1935. At that time, between 12 and 15 million Americans were unemployed. Most of them had lost their jobs because of the depression in the economy. The Social Security Act of 1935 contained a plan to help future workers who lost their jobs because of circumstances beyond their control. This plan is called the unemployment insurance program.

To receive benefits, unemployed workers must register with a state employment office. They report periodically to the office to see if it can help them find suitable jobs. If the job search is unsuccessful, unemployed workers begin to receive weekly benefits based on their average earnings over the previous year. The amount paid varies from state to state, but most provide benefits for up to 26 weeks. The amount received is small, but it helps families support themselves while the workers are looking for jobs.

The unemployment insurance program is financed by employers. Federal law requires

How the Social Security Law Works

| THE FEDERAL GOVERNMENT administers | THE FEDERAL GOVERNMENT sets standards and makes contributions to | STATE GOVERNMENTS administer and pay part of cost |

Retirement and Old-Age Insurance Program and Health Insurance Program

Contributions by

Employers

Workers

Self-employed Workers

Used for

Disability and Survivor Payments

Retirement Payments

Hospital Care*

*A voluntary medical insurance plan also covers doctors costs.

Unemployment Insurance Program and Workers' Compensation Program

Contributions by

Employers

Used for

Unemployment Insurance Benefits

Workers' Compensation

Public Assistance Programs

Maternal and Child Health

Disabled Children

Child Welfare

Aid to the Aged

Aid to Dependent Children

Aid to the Blind

Aid to the Disabled

Medical Help for the Aged

People pay Social Security tax during the years they are working. They hope that it will save them from financial hardship when they retire.

all businesses that employ at least one worker to pay a special tax to the federal government. The state governments pay unemployment insurance benefits out of the money collected by the federal government.

Workers' Compensation. The workers' compensation program is designed to help people who have job-related injuries or who develop an illness as a result of their jobs. The program pays their medical costs and helps replace lost income. It also pays death benefits to the survivors of workers killed on the job. In return for these benefits, workers give up their right to sue their employers for compensation for their injuries.

The benefits received by workers vary by state and depend on the kind of disability the worker has and how long it lasts. The benefits also depend on the worker's weekly salary.

Workers' compensation is administered by the state or a private insurance company.

In some states, administration is shared by a state agency and a private insurance company. Employers in most states are required to participate in the program and to pay the entire cost of it.

Medicare and Medicaid. The federal government has also set up programs to help elderly and poor Americans pay their medical expenses. In 1965 Congress passed the health insurance program known as **Medicare.** This program helps American citizens who are 65 years of age and older to pay for hospital care and for some nursing home care. The Medicare program also includes a voluntary medical insurance plan to help older citizens pay their doctors' bills.

The **Medicaid** health insurance program was also passed by Congress in 1965. Under this program, the federal government provides money to help the states pay the medical costs of poor people.

SECTION 4 REVIEW

Define insurance, premium, principal sum, insurance policy, private insurance, social insurance, life insurance, term insurance, whole life insurance, disability income insurance, health insurance, hospitalization insurance, fire insurance, homeowners' insurance, liability insurance, malpractice insurance, automobile liability insurance, bonded

Identify beneficiary, Social Security, Medicare, Medicaid

1. **Seeing Relationships** (a) Upon what principle is insurance based? (b) Why is insurance important to the financial well-being of all Americans?

2. **Understanding Ideas** How can insurance companies cover large risks for small premiums?

3. **Contrasting Ideas** Describe the major differences between social insurance and private insurance.

4. **Composing a Paragraph** Write a paragraph that explains how businesses can insure themselves against dishonesty.

5. **Drawing Conclusions** Why did President Roosevelt recommend Social Security as part of the New Deal legislation?

Thinking Critically You sell insurance and have been asked to speak to a local homeowners' association about the importance of homeowners' insurance. Write a draft of your speech.

Money is a medium of exchange. We give it in return for goods and services. Most modern money has no value in itself. We value it because the government guarantees it. We also value it because sellers will accept it in exchange for the things we want to buy.

Very little of what is bought and sold is paid for with coins or paper money. Checks are written to pay for most of our trade. Banks play a key role in the process of paying by check. Banks are safe places in which to keep money. They also provide the checking service that transfers balances from one account to another when checks are written to pay for goods and services. Banks also help businesses and individuals by making loans.

The Federal Reserve System helps regulate banking in our nation. Federal Reserve Banks are the banks in which the federal government keeps its funds. They also are the banks for other banks. They help regulate the use of credit in our economy. The Federal Reserve System tries to keep our money supply at the right level.

When money is saved, it may be invested. That is, it may earn more money for the investor. The money we put in savings accounts, for instance, is usually invested by the bank.

Our federal and state governments help protect our savings and investments by regulating banks, insurance companies, and the sale of stocks and bonds. Insurance companies, as well as the federal government, issue policies that may help protect us from most of the financial hazards of life.

CHAPTER

18

SUMMARY

DEVELOPING CIVICS SKILLS

LIFE SKILL
Writing a Check

As you know, checks are a convenient way to make purchases and pay bills. Before opening a checking account, you should decide which type of account is right for you. A regular checking account typically does not require you to keep a minimum balance in your account. Usually, though, the bank will deduct a monthly service charge, and you will have to pay for your checks. Also, the money you have in your account does not earn interest.

The NOW account is actually a checking and savings account all in one. You can write checks and receive interest. In return for interest and free checks, however, the bank usually requires you to maintain a certain balance.

No matter what type of checking account you choose, a signed check represents the money you have in your account. For this reason, it is important that you follow certain procedures when you write a check.

How to Write a Check

To write a check, follow these guidelines.

1. **Examine your checks.** Most checks are printed with the account owner's name in the upper left corner. Near the bottom left side of the check, you will see a series of numbers. The first part is the bank's identification number. The second part is your checking account number.

2. **Remember to date your checks.** Near the check number is a place for you to write the date. Be sure you write the correct date.

3. **Tell the bank whom you want them to pay.** In the center of the check are the words "Pay to the Order of" and a blank space. By filling in the blank, you tell the bank who to pay.

4. **Write the amount of the payment twice.** Notice that you must write the amount of the check twice—once in figures and once in words.

5. **Sign your checks.** Signing your name authorizes the bank to carry out your wishes. Banks will not accept unsigned checks.

Applying the Skill

Use the sample check shown below to answer the following questions.

1. **(a)** To whom is the check written? **(b)** What did Paul buy? **(c)** How much did he pay?
2. **(a)** What is the name of Paul's bank? **(b)** Where is his bank located?

PAUL W. ROGERS   NO. 257

September 9   19 90   4-0/210

PAY TO THE ORDER OF Bill's Sport Shop $48.80/100

Forty eight and 80/100 ————————— DOLLARS

Urban National Bank
524 PACIFIC AVENUE
PORTLAND, OREGON 97204

MEMO tennis racket   Paul W. Rogers

⑈ 02800 108 ⑈: 0791 02064 ⑈ 0171

CHAPTER 18 REVIEW

Reviewing Terms

On a separate sheet of paper, supply the term from the list below that correctly answers each question.

collateral
demand deposit
social insurance
barter

time deposit
broker
private insurance
creditor

1. What term refers to property that one uses to guarantee that a loan will be repaid?
2. Which type of insurance is voluntary?
3. What term is used for the person to whom one owes money?
4. What is the money that depositors put in savings account called?
5. Which type of insurance is required by state and federal laws?
6. What term refers to the swapping of one product for another?
7. Which term refers to a person who sells stock and bonds?
8. What is the money that depositors put in a checking account called?

Using Thinking Skills

1. **Summarizing Ideas** (a) What are the four common features of money? (b) Why were mutual savings banks originally established?
2. **Composing an Essay** (a) Write a short essay discussing the ways in which Americans can save. (b) Write a short essay discussing the importance of insurance.
3. **Seeing Relationships** (a) How does saving help keep our economy prosperous? (b) Describe the main purposes of the Federal Reserve Banks.
4. **Understanding Ideas** (a) Discuss the importance of credit in our free economy. (b) Explain how using credit unwisely can hurt businesses and families.
5. **Expressing Ideas** Describe the chief advantage and disadvantage of using checks over other forms of money.

6. **Identifying Roles** Who owns each of the following types of banks: commercial banks, savings and loans, credit unions?
7. **Drawing Conclusions** (a) Why did Congress establish the Social Security system? (b) How does Workers' Compensation help workers?
8. **Contrasting Ideas** (a) Explain the difference between the FDIC and the FSLIC. (b) What is the difference between Medicare and Medicaid?

Practicing Civics Skills

Writing a Check Draw a personal check, using the same basic design as the one on page 372 of your textbook. Be sure to print your full name at the top and the name and address of a local bank at the bottom.

After you have finished drawing your check, show how you would fill it out if you were buying an $8.50 cassette tape at the Oak Park Record and Tape Store.

Being a Good Citizen

1. Conduct library research and write a report on one of the following topics: the history of money in the United States; the current crisis of the savings and loans; the daily operations of the New York Stock Exchange; types of money used in other countries. Share your findings with the class.
2. Organize the class into groups. Each group should choose one well-known stock from the financial pages of the newspaper. Check the price of this stock each day for one month. Note whether the stock market price goes up or down. Then see if you can find any news articles to explain the rise or fall.
3. Draw a map of the United States showing the 12 Federal Reserve Districts. Display the maps in the classroom and discuss how the Federal Reserve Banks serve their member banks.

CHAPTER 19

Our Economy Faces Challenges

Chapter Sections

1 Coping with Inflation
2 Boom or Bust
3 Labor and Management

Chapter Focus

The United States is a very rich nation. Yet our economic system continues to face some serious challenges. The average American is earning more money than ever before, but the money buys fewer goods and services. The reason is that prices have been going up faster than wages. Therefore, it is sometimes difficult to plan for the future. Many people worry that their money may buy fewer products next year than this year.

Our economy has grown tremendously since our nation was founded, but its growth has not been steady. Throughout most of our history, business has been good. At these times, more goods and services have been produced than ever before. Then things have slowed down. Some businesses have failed, and fewer goods and services have been produced. These ups and downs in our economy have caused problems for businesses, consumers, workers, and the government.

In order to produce goods and services, businesses need labor. That is, they need workers. Workers, in turn, need jobs. Management does the hiring. As you can see, workers and managers need each other. Yet labor and management sometimes disagree. Our entire economy can be hurt when production stops because labor and management cannot settle their differences.

Study Guide

As you read about the challenges that face our economy, look for answers to the following questions:

★ What is inflation, and how does it cause problems for people?

★ How does the federal government try to control the business cycle?

★ What can labor and management do to help each other and the economy?

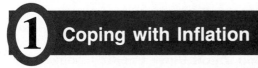

1 Coping with Inflation

One of the most important challenges facing the American economic system is inflation. Many different explanations for inflation have been given. We will look at some of them in this section. Briefly, **inflation** means a rise in the prices of most goods and services. If your income is not rising as fast as prices, you will be able to buy fewer things.

For example, suppose you work during the summer to buy a new bicycle that you saw in a store window. The price was $180. After earning the $180, you find that the price is now $200. You are the victim of inflation. Your money will buy less than before.

Inflation Affects Everyone

People often talk about rising prices. Perhaps they had to change their plans to take a va-

cation or buy a television set because the price rose too high. Inflation causes problems for many people. Inflation is especially serious for people living on fixed incomes. Their incomes stay the same while prices go up.

Let us look at the case of Sara Golden, an elderly woman who retired in 1980. Golden worked hard all her life. When she retired, she received a pension from the company for which she had worked. She also received some money from the government's Social Security program. In all, she received $200 a week. At the time, this was enough to meet her needs.

However, since 1980 prices have increased greatly. Now Golden can barely afford to pay her rent, buy food, and meet her other needs. In fact, it would take over $300 today to buy the same goods and services her $200 bought in 1980.

Consider another example of how inflation hurts people. Ten years ago, the Harvin family built a new house. It cost them $40,000. They took out a fire insurance policy for $40,000. They thought that if their house ever burned down they would be able to build a new one with the insurance money.

This year their house was destroyed by fire. The Harvins collected $40,000 from the insurance company, but this was not enough to build a new house. To build a similar house now would cost $80,000. The price of lumber, electric wiring, plumbing, and everything else it takes to build a house has increased.

Inflation and Savings

Inflation also hurts savers. Many people put their savings into savings accounts or invest in government savings bonds. In this way they earn interest on their savings. They hope that in the future they will be able to use the money they have saved to send their children to college, buy a new car, travel, or retire comfortably. Some people may be hoping to use their savings to start their own business.

Even though they are earning interest on their savings, however, savers may be losing

Some Causes of Inflation

Economists often give different reasons for rising prices. One major cause of inflation that they cite is "too much money, too few goods." If people have increasing amounts of money to spend but the supply of goods is not increasing as fast, prices will rise. This is because shoppers will be competing with each other for the scarce supply of goods.

It is almost like an auction. People at an auction offer to pay higher and higher prices for the object being sold. The supply of an item being auctioned is limited. Therefore, the price keeps going up as more people try to buy it.

Let us look more closely at some of the possible causes of inflation.

Too Much Money. In Chapter 18 you learned how the Federal Reserve tries to control the amount of money and credit in our economy. Some economists believe the major cause of inflation is the circulation of too much money. They think the Federal Reserve has put too much money into our economy. As people spend this additional money, they cause prices to rise.

Too Much Bank Credit. Some economists blame the banks for making too many loans. This has the same effect as putting more money into the economy. People and business firms borrow from the banks and then spend what they have borrowed. Up go the prices.

Government Spending. As you know, the government spends many billions of dollars each year. It spends for roads, dams, education, assistance for farmers, military bases, pollution control, and many other things. Soldiers, members of Congress, federal judges, postal workers, and many others who are employed by the government must be paid. Much of the money spent by the government comes from taxes paid by individuals and business firms. The government also borrows some of the money it spends.

Many people believe the government is borrowing and spending too much. Govern-

One of the most serious consequences of inflation in recent years has been the increase in the number of people in our nation who are homeless.

money. For instance, suppose the Garcia family put $1,000 in a savings account ten years ago. Today they have about $1,700 in their account because the $1,000 has been earning interest. That is, their money has been increasing by about $5\frac{1}{4}$ percent a year. Prices, however, have been increasing at a much faster rate.

Suppose the Garcias had planned to use the money to pay for their daughter Gloria's first year in college. Ten years ago, this would have cost $1,000 at the college Gloria wants to attend. Now it costs over $2,000 a year to attend that college. The money the Garcias saved is not enough, even though it has been earning interest.

ment borrowing, like bank loans to individuals, puts more money into our economy and helps raise prices. Government spending puts money into the economy but does not add to the supply of goods available for sale to the public.

Consumer Spending. We, as consumers, share some of the blame for inflation. Many people borrow money to buy things they cannot afford and do not really need. On the average, Americans save only a very small part of their income. Too little saving and too much spending by consumers may be partially responsible for inflation.

Low Productivity. Productivity, as you recall, means the amount a worker produces in an hour. For example, suppose you work in a factory making pens. You produce ten pens in an hour. Your boss sells the pens for $1 each, or a total of $10. Your productivity is ten pens, or $10. The most your boss can afford to pay you is $10 an hour.

Suppose, however, you demand $11 an hour. To meet this demand, your boss must raise the price of the pens. Your boss has to pay you 10 percent more. Yet you are not producing 10 percent more pens. Many economists believe the most important reason for inflation is that wages have been rising faster than workers' productivity.

Other Possible Causes. The price of energy sources, such as oil and gas, has gone up sharply in recent years. This has caused the price of nearly everything else to go up because we use energy to produce all goods and services. For instance, the cost of attending college has risen partly because of higher energy prices. It takes a great deal of fuel to heat college buildings. (You will learn more about the energy problem in Chapter 25.)

Sometimes nature creates inflation problems. Storms, droughts, or floods may destroy crops. This causes shortages of farm crops and raises the price of food.

In Chapter 16 you learned about monopolies. If one firm gets a monopoly of a product or service, it might be able to raise the price. Suppose several companies in an industry get together and decide to set one price for that industry's product. The price of the product will probably rise.

Controlling Inflation

It is not easy to control inflation. One reason is that the steps necessary to control it can be unpleasant for many people. Let us go back over each possible cause of inflation and examine some possible ways of stopping it.

Control Money and Credit. The Federal Reserve could try to keep the money supply from growing too quickly. It has to be careful, however. If the Federal Reserve cuts our money supply too sharply, business may decline. People will have less to spend, and

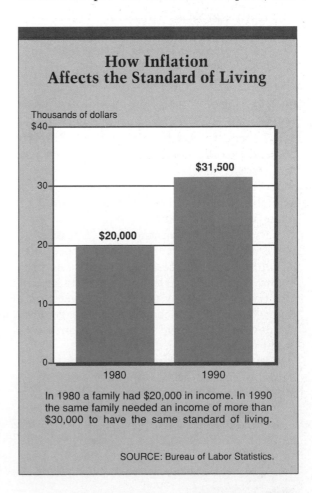

How Inflation Affects the Standard of Living

Thousands of dollars

$20,000 (1980)

$31,500 (1990)

In 1980 a family had $20,000 in income. In 1990 the same family needed an income of more than $30,000 to have the same standard of living.

SOURCE: Bureau of Labor Statistics.

"I DECIDED TO GET UP AND EAT THIS TONIGHT — TOMORROW IT'LL COST MORE!"

courtesy of Rothco

The speaker here seems to have given up hope that he can do anything to control inflation. What is his solution for coping with the problem of inflation?

business firms will have lower profits. They might then lay off some of their workers.

To control credit, the Federal Reserve could try to prevent banks from making too many loans. At the same time, however, it must make certain there is enough credit available for loans to businesses that want to make wise investments.

Reduce Government Spending. Government could reduce wasteful spending. It could halt unnecessary government programs. Many believe the government should also try to spend only the money it gets from taxes. With a balanced budget, the government would not have to borrow money and could work toward reducing its debt.

Increase Saving. Consumers could help by cutting their spending and saving more of their incomes. They should use credit only for buying things they really need.

Increase Productivity. If the total amount produced each hour increases, the supply of goods will be increased. Business managers should try to run their factories more efficiently. Workers should learn to do their jobs better and make fewer mistakes. If workers' productivity increases, they can get higher pay without helping to cause inflation. Some economists suggest that wages should not increase faster than productivity increases.

Other Steps. Many economists believe we need to conserve fuel and other energy sources. They suggest that people drive less often or that they share rides in order to save gasoline. Oil and electricity can also be saved by keeping houses cooler in winter and warmer in summer. By using less of these energy sources, we can help hold down their prices.

 SECTION 1 REVIEW

Define inflation

1. **Understanding Ideas** What are some consequences of inflation?
2. **Seeing Relationships** Identify and explain several possible causes of inflation.
3. **Identifying Roles** What could the federal government and individuals do to try to control inflation?

Thinking Critically Imagine you are retired and living on a fixed income. What are some ways you can cope with increasing prices?

 Boom or Bust

Although Americans enjoy a high standard of living, our economy does not always behave the way we want it to. Sometimes we have a period of prosperity, called a boom. During a boom, business is good. Jobs are plentiful, and profits are high. Then business slows down. Some companies begin to lose money, and many workers find themselves without jobs. The nation enters a period of hard times, known as a bust. This tendency—to go from good times to bad, then back to good times again, and so on—is called the **business cycle.** Let us look more closely at the ups and downs of the business cycle.

The Business Cycle

The chart on this page shows the various parts of the business cycle. When the economy is booming, the Gross National Product (GNP) is increasing. (As you recall, the GNP is the total amount of goods and services produced by our economy in one year.) This period of growth is called **expansion,** because the economy is expanding, or growing.

The expansion of the economy during a boom is generally good: most people have jobs and businesses are doing well. However, expansion can cause some problems. One of the problems that often accompanies a boom is inflation.

During these periods of prosperity, most people have jobs and good incomes. People have money to spend, causing the demand for goods and services to increase. Prices rise as customers compete with each other to buy scarce products.

The costs of doing business also increase during a period of economic expansion. Businesses have to pay higher prices for raw materials and transportation. They may also have to increase the wages of their workers in order to keep them, since jobs are more plentiful. Wages, payments for raw materials, transportation, rent, and interest on money borrowed are the **costs of production.** When inflation makes these costs rise, business firms may have to increase the prices of their products in order to pay these costs and still make a profit.

At some point, the expansion of the economy and the inflation that goes with it stops. When this happens, the business cycle has reached a **peak,** or high point.

After the economy peaks, business activity begins to slow. This slowdown is the opposite of an expansion, and is called a **contraction.** If the contraction becomes severe enough, a **recession** may occur. During a recession, businesses fail, more people are unemployed, and profits fall.

When the economy reaches its lowest point, it is said to be in a **trough,** or low point. Can you see how a trough is the opposite of a peak? When the trough is especially low, times are very hard, and economists say the economy is in a **depression.** During a depression, the number of people without jobs is high. Unemployed people cannot buy many goods and services, so businesses suffer. Many businesses close down.

Usually, troughs are not so low as to throw the economy into a depression. Some people lose jobs and businesses fail, but the economy soon bounces back. The economy begins to grow again. Business activity increases, more people have jobs, and another period of expansion occurs as the business cycle continues.

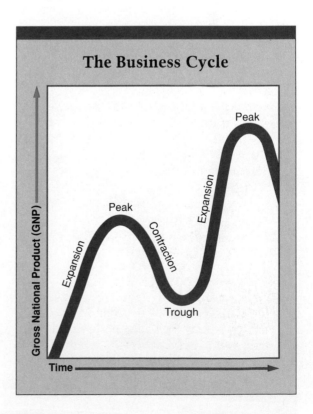

The Business Cycle

The Great Depression

The worst depression in our nation's history took place during the 1930's. This period, as you have read, is known as the **Great Depression.** The first sign of trouble came in October 1929, when the prices of stocks fell sharply. Many banks failed, and people lost their savings.

By 1932 business was producing only half as much as it had produced in 1929. Thousands of businesses closed down. Farm prices were lower than ever before. By 1933 about one in every four American workers had lost their jobs. Most of these people had families to support. Unable to repay their mortgages, many people lost their homes. Farmers had to leave their land. These are only some

During the Great Depression millions of Americans were unemployed, and tried to make a living any way they could. This was a common sight on streets then.

of the many severe hardships people suffered during the Great Depression.

Old Theories of the Business Cycle

Before the Great Depression of the 1930's, most economists believed the business cycle should be left alone. They thought the government should not step in and try to stimulate the economy, control inflation, or end unemployment.

Most economists believed the problems that came with the business cycle would cure themselves. If prices rose too high, people would stop buying goods and services until the prices came down again. Also, high prices and attractive profits would convince some people to go into business. The supply of goods and services would therefore increase. This would prevent prices from rising.

Many economists also thought that recessions could not last very long. Workers who lost their jobs would soon be willing to accept lower wages. Businesses would then be able to hire people for lower pay. Other costs of production also would be low. This would encourage businesses to produce more. As businesses expanded and increased their spending, they would help other businesses. Soon new businesses would be started. The economy would improve. Salaries would be raised and more people would be hired. People would buy more, and so on. Then came the Great Depression. The old theories did not seem to work.

Government Efforts to Help

Wages were very low during the Great Depression. Millions of unemployed people were willing to accept any pay, no matter how low, rather than be without work. Yet businesses did not hire them. Moreover, businesses did not expand because there was no point in producing more goods when few people had

Does this look like a desert sandstorm? It is really farmland that was turned into a "Dust Bowl" by drought. During the 1930's many farmers lost their land.

enough money to buy them. To the surprise of the economists, the Great Depression did not end in a fairly short time. It went on year after year.

Finally, many people were willing to have the government step in and do something to try to improve the economy. As you recall, President Franklin D. Roosevelt established a program known as the **New Deal.** Under this program, unemployed workers were hired by the government to do useful work, such as creating parks and building schools. Young people could join the Civilian Conservation Corps. They worked on projects to restore our forests and other natural resources. Homeowners and farmers could get loans to help pay their mortgages.

You may remember from Chapter 18 that the Federal Deposit Insurance Corporation (FDIC) was set up to insure bank deposits. The Social Security System was established to give regular payments to retired citizens and help others in need. Unemployment insurance was created to provide workers with some money when they lost their jobs.

Many of the measures established during the Great Depression have remained in effect.

However, they have not put an end to the business cycle. We still have periods when business is slow. The number of unemployed people has remained high during both good and bad periods. Furthermore, inflation continues to cause prices to rise, so that it costs us more to live each year. Economists once believed that prices always fell during a recession. During the 1970's, however, we continued to have inflation, even during serious recessions.

Government and the Business Cycle

There are several remedies that the federal government has tried in an effort to control the business cycle. For one, the government has changed its **fiscal policy,** or program for taxing and spending. If the economy is going into a recession, for instance, the government may reduce the amount of taxes that individuals must pay. Lower taxes give people more money to spend. Increased spending encourages businesses to produce more, which leads to the creation of more jobs.

Government efforts to put people back to work in the 1930's were portrayed by the American artist William Gropper in this painting called "Building a Dam."

During recessions the government may step up its own spending. It buys more goods and hires more people to work for the government. In the past, it has built public projects, such as bridges and dams. The government also may give larger payments to the unemployed, the poor, and the elderly.

The government has also tried to control the business cycle by changing its **monetary policy,** or money policy. This policy is handled by the Federal Reserve System. As you recall, Federal Reserve Banks serve as banks for other banks. They try to control the amount of money in the economy. If we are entering a recession, the Federal Reserve may increase the money supply by making it easier for banks to lend money to businesses at lower interest rates. It is hoped that this will encourage businesses to expand, thus creating more jobs and income.

If we are in a boom period, these actions may be reversed. When inflation becomes too high, the federal government may raise taxes and reduce its spending. The Federal Reserve may make it harder for banks to lend money to businesses. This decreases the amount of money in the economy.

At times the government has used direct controls over the economy. In 1971, for example, a **wage-price freeze** was attempted. Most prices and wages could not be raised for several months, and then only a little. However, the freeze was soon lifted because it did not work very well.

We have not yet learned how to control the economy. Some economists believe it does not have to be controlled. They think the government should keep out of the economy. They also believe programs begun under the New Deal have contributed to inflation. Other economists believe the government can help the economy. They say that without government actions, inflation would have been worse. They claim that government efforts have helped to prevent the occurrence of another Great Depression.

The debate will no doubt continue as economists, government leaders, and the American people try to deal with inflation and keep our economy healthy.

 SECTION 2 REVIEW

Define business cycle, expansion, costs of production, peak, contraction, recession, trough, depression, fiscal policy, monetary policy, wage-price freeze

Identify Great Depression, New Deal

1. **Composing a Paragraph** Write a paragraph that explains the business cycle.
2. **Seeing Relationships** Discuss the relationship between the Great Depression and the New Deal.
3. **Identifying Roles** How does the government try to control the business cycle?

Thinking Critically Imagine that you own a small store. How does your knowledge of the business cycle help you to run your business effectively?

3 Labor and Management

One day you will join the working population of our nation. You may be part of the labor force—perhaps a worker in the computer or automobile industry. Or you may be part of management—one of the owners or managers of a business. Therefore, it is important to understand the relationship between labor and management.

Working Conditions in the Past

In the early days of our nation, many Americans were self-employed. They worked for themselves on small farms or in their own workshops or stores. They then sold the goods they produced to neighbors and friends. Most businesses were small. They employed only a few workers, or wage earners. Wage earners usually worked side by side with the owner of a business. They knew the owner personally.

If workers were not satisfied, they could speak to the owner and ask for better wages or improved working conditions. If the owner refused, they could quit their jobs. They could work elsewhere because industry was growing and the nation was expanding westward. There was little labor-saving machinery. Most of the time, there were more jobs than workers. Therefore, employers often considered it important to treat their employees fairly.

Between 1800 and 1850, working conditions for many wage earners changed greatly. Large factories were built, using machines to make products. Many of these factories employed hundreds of workers, including many young children.

In these new factories, relations between employers and workers were different. Factory managers and owners had little or no contact with their workers. The working day was long—12 or even 16 hours. Wages usually were low. Working conditions were often poor, but workers could do little to improve them. When the western lands began to be filled in by settlers, it became more difficult for dissatisfied workers to leave their jobs and start on their own.

The Rise of Labor Unions

As American businesses continued to expand between 1850 and 1900, the number of workers also increased. American workers began to organize in groups, hoping to improve wages and working conditions. These organizations of workers became known as **labor unions.** Several small labor unions had been established on a local basis earlier. However, local unions were not always successful in dealing with employers. Workers came to believe they needed national union organizations in order to be powerful enough to deal with employers as equals.

Between 1850 and 1900, the growing labor unions wanted the right to bargain with employers for better wages, shorter hours, and improved working conditions. The unions worked hard to show that the best way for workers and employers to settle differences was through collective bargaining.

In **collective bargaining,** representatives of a labor union meet with representatives of an employer and try to reach an agreement. The terms of the agreement are put into a written contract. This **labor contract** is signed by the employer and the officers of the union.

The labor contract details the agreed-upon wage rates and working conditions. The agreement is for a fixed period of time. It usually is one, two, or three years. When the contract nears its ending date, representatives of the union and the employer sit down again and bargain for a new contract.

Methods Used by Labor

In the earlier days of union organization, collective bargaining often broke down. Sometimes employers refused to bargain at all. The **strike** came to be the chief method used by labor unions to try to force business owners to bargain with them. In a strike, union members walk off the job if employers do not agree to meet labor's demands. Production then stops, and the company loses money.

What is to prevent a company from hiring other workers when there is a strike? The strikers try to prevent this by **picketing.** Picketing strikers walk back and forth, often carrying signs, in front of company buildings. They discourage other workers from entering and taking over their jobs. Workers who cross picket lines and enter the buildings in order to work during the strike are called scabs. Sometimes fights have broken out between strikers and scabs. The law now limits the use of scabs by employers.

Instead of striking, workers sometimes stay on the job but work much more slowly than usual. This union action is called a slowdown. Any kind of slowdown, or action short of a strike, is called a **job action.** The union, for example, may tell its members to follow all written orders to the letter and to check and recheck their work. This job action slows down production and costs the company money. Sometimes it gains as much for the union as a strike would.

Methods Used by Employers

Most early business owners looked upon union workers as troublemakers. Organizations of employers were formed to oppose the growing power of labor. Sometimes employers hired new workers who were not members of the union. They took over the jobs of workers who were on strike. Private police were sometimes hired by employers to see that the picketing strikers did not prevent other workers from entering the plant. A period of conflict and struggle, which sometimes turned violent, began between employers and labor.

Employers used other methods to fight the unions. They made up blacklists containing the names of workers who were active in the labor unions. They sent these blacklists to other companies and asked them not to hire anyone whose name was listed.

Employers also found a way to fight labor slowdowns. They closed the factory and "locked out" the workers. The lockout prevented workers from earning wages. With no income, workers were soon forced to agree to go back to work.

The Closed Shop Versus the Open Shop

Early labor leaders quickly realized that unions needed money to succeed. To raise money, unions began to charge their members union dues, or fees. This money was used by

Strikes, such as this one in New York City, have been an effective way for workers to make their demands known to management.

the unions to pay their officials. During strikes or lockouts, it helped feed union members and their families.

In order to gather strength, the early labor unions tried to enroll every worker as a union member. It became the aim of the unions to establish a closed shop in every factory. In a **closed shop,** workers cannot be hired unless they first become members of the union. The employers did not like the idea of a closed shop. They insisted upon an open shop in every factory. In an **open shop,** anyone can be hired. Workers do not have to be union members or join the union.

Much later, a third type of shop was organized, the union shop. In a **union shop,** an employer can hire any worker, union or nonunion. But within a short period of time, usually about 30 days, new workers must join the union in order to keep their jobs.

Today there is also a fourth type of shop, called the agency shop. In an **agency shop,** a worker cannot be forced to join the union, but he or she must pay union dues anyway. The unions believe workers should help pay for the protection they get from unions. If the union fights for higher pay and better conditions, nonmembers also benefit.

Many states have passed **right-to-work laws.** In these states, no one may be forced to join a union. That is, only the open shop is legal. Both union members and nonunion members may work in the same company.

The AFL Versus the CIO

Early unions were organized according to jobs or occupations. All members of the same skilled trade joined together in a **craft union,** or **trade union.** The carpenters throughout the nation, the plumbers, the bakers, and so on, each had their own union.

In 1886 some craft unions formed a large organization called the American Federation of Labor (AFL). Under the leadership of Samuel Gompers, the AFL grew into a powerful
(continued on page 388)

Focus on Freedom

A Noble Gathering

The city of Birmingham, Alabama, was rocked in the spring of 1963 by massive demonstrations that captured the attention of people throughout the world. The demonstrators were African Americans and their supporters who gathered in Birmingham to protest decades of racial injustice. Primary among their concerns were segregation laws that denied them equal access to jobs and the chances for economic success.

Leading the demonstrators was the Reverend Martin Luther King, Jr., who called Birmingham "the country's chief symbol of racial intolerance." King believed that effective demonstrations in this southern city could lead to sweeping changes in the laws that denied equality to black Americans.

King was right. The events of 1963 helped pave the way for important civil rights legislation. But these events could not have occurred without a fundamental freedom guaranteed to all Americans in the Constitution of the United States. That freedom is "the right of the people peaceably to assemble," and it is guaranteed by the First Amendment.

A Permit to Demonstrate

In April 1963, King and his supporters sent representatives to request a demonstration permit from the city of Birmingham. They needed the permit to demonstrate legally.

The city's Commissioner of Public Safety, Eugene "Bull" Connor, denied the request personally. Other city officials agreed with Connor's decision. They cited an ordinance that allowed them to stop a gathering if they believed it would disturb "the public welfare, peace, safety, health, decency, good order, morals or convenience" of the city.

Two days later, the demonstrators tried again. They requested a permit to demonstrate "against the injustices of segregation and discrimination." Again, Connor saw to it that the request was denied. He telegrammed the protest leaders, "I insist that you and your people do not start any picketing on the streets in Birmingham, Alabama."

The leaders of the protest felt certain that city officials were using the ordinance as an excuse to deny them their civil rights. They knew that their cause was just, though, and they proceeded with the march anyway.

The police in Birmingham, Alabama, used fire hoses on these protestors in an effort to keep them from demonstrating on the streets of Birmingham.

An Appeal for Justice

The police wasted no time in arresting the protest leaders, who were soon tried, convicted, and sentenced to prison. When the case went to the Alabama Supreme Court, the convictions were upheld.

The leaders of the protest were not satisfied with the state court's decision. One of the leaders, Fred L. Shuttlesworth, represented all of the demonstrators when he appealed his conviction to the United States Supreme Court. He charged that the city had violated his constitutional right to gather with others in peaceful demonstration.

In 1969, the Supreme Court heard the case. The Court agreed that the city ordinance was applied unfairly and that the demonstrators had indeed been denied their right to assemble. Arguing that "fundamental rights" were at stake, the Court maintained that the city of Birmingham had acted "to deny . . . the right of assembly and the opportunities for the communication of thought."

Protecting the Right to Assemble

Martin Luther King's vision of a nation with equality for all people was given new promise with the demonstrations of 1963. These demonstrations prompted President John F. Kennedy to seek sweeping federal civil rights legislation aimed at social, political, and economic justice for all. But the achievements of the 1960's and beyond could not have been realized without the freedom of citizens to work together for change. Our continuing fight for equal justice for all people requires that we protect our First Amendment right of assembly.

These marchers in Birmingham, Alabama, used their First Amendment right of assembly to make the entire nation aware of injustice.

Questions to Consider

1. Why do you think the protestors were denied a permit to demonstrate?
2. What was the result of Shuttlesworth's appeal to the United States Supreme Court?
3. How is the freedom of assembly related to the freedom of speech?

labor group. Each craft union in the AFL had its own officers and its own local branches throughout the nation. Each union worked to improve conditions for members in its own craft. However, these craft unions joined with other unions in the AFL to strengthen their bargaining power.

As our nation's factories and businesses grew in size, some labor leaders argued that a new type of union should be formed. They thought unions should include unskilled workers as well as craft workers. These leaders pointed out that mass production methods had weakened the power of craft unions. They insisted that all workers in an industry, such as those in steel, automobiles, and coal mining, should be members of the same union, no matter what kind of jobs they had. This kind of union is an **industrial union.**

Industrial unions grew rapidly during the 1930's. Industry after industry—steel, automobiles, electrical equipment, rubber—was organized by labor leaders. Led by Walter Reuther and others, the industrial unions took members away from some of the craft unions. In 1936 the industrial unions formed one large organization called the Congress of Industrial Organizations (CIO).

Workers in many industries found it difficult to choose between the CIO and AFL. In many cases, the leaders of the AFL or the CIO called a **jurisdictional strike.** This is a strike to see which union group will represent the workers. The rivalry between the two large union organizations continued for many years. An agreement was finally reached in 1955. Then the AFL and CIO joined together in a single labor organization, the AFL-CIO.

Today the AFL-CIO is the largest American labor group. It has a membership of more than 14 million workers. Not every union belongs to this large combination of unions. Some very large unions have decided to be independent. The leaders of these independent unions do not agree with all the policies of the leaders of the AFL-CIO. American unions are not completely united. There is still some rivalry among them.

Union Problems

Individual unions sometimes have problems with one another as well as with employers. Perhaps two unions want to organize the workers in the same company. In that case, there will be a contest to see which union can get more workers to join. This may cause confusion on the part of the workers. They may even decide not to join either union.

Sometimes there are problems within a particular union. Many unions are called national unions because they have members in all parts of the nation. They are divided into smaller groups called local unions. Sometimes the locals disagree with the leaders of the national organization. They may think the national leaders are trying to control them or are not giving them enough support.

Recent Union Organization

During the 1960's, the most successful attempts to organize workers occurred among hospital workers and among the migrant workers who harvest farm produce. The person who organized the union for farm workers is Cesar Chavez. Today, Chavez continues to speak out for the rights of farm workers and other working people.

During the 1970's, the labor movement made gains among the people who work for our governments. In spite of laws that prohibit strikes against government, some strikes by teachers, police, air traffic controllers, and other public workers have taken place.

In recent years, unions have not grown as rapidly as they did in the past. By 1990, about 124 million workers were in the labor force. Yet only about 19 million belonged to unions. Thus, only about 15 percent of all workers were union members.

The fact that the percentage of union members is small does not mean that American unions are weak. Many of our major industries are unionized. Strikes in these industries could cause serious problems.

Congress Passes Labor Laws

Over the years, Congress has passed a number of important laws dealing with labor-management relations. It has done so for several reasons. One reason is that Congress wants to protect the public. When workers go out on strike, the whole country may suffer. For example, a strike by coal miners might cause a serious coal shortage in our nation. A strike by truck drivers might halt the delivery of some kinds of foods.

Congress has passed laws to prevent employers from using unfair practices in dealing with workers. It has also tried to make unions act fairly in their disputes with employers. Congress has also tried to stop dishonest actions by some union leaders and to ensure that unions are run democratically.

These are some of the major labor laws passed by Congress.

1. National Labor Relations Act. This law, usually called the Wagner Act, was passed by Congress in 1935. It guarantees the right of all American workers to join the union of their choice. The law also provides ways of settling disputes between labor unions and employers.

An independent government agency, the **National Labor Relations Board (NLRB),** was set up under this act. It judges the fairness of the activities of unions and employers toward each other. The NLRB also conducts elections within a company when a union wants to organize the workers. The workers vote to decide which union they want. They can also vote to have no union at all.

2. Labor-Management Relations Act. This law, which is usually called the Taft-Hartley Act, was passed in 1947. It revised the Wagner Act in several ways. The Taft-Hartley Act allows the President of the

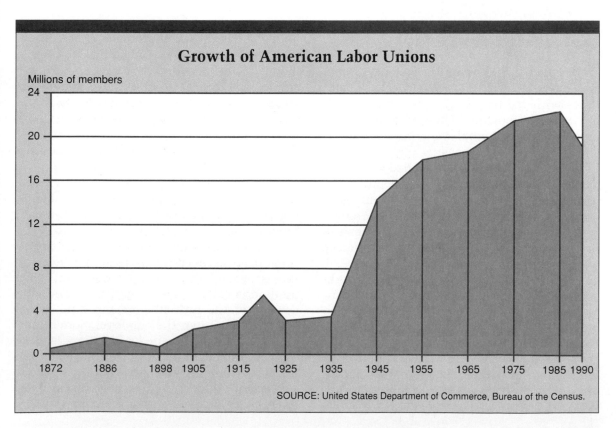

Growth of American Labor Unions

Millions of members

SOURCE: United States Department of Commerce, Bureau of the Census.

United States to order any union to postpone a strike for 80 days when such a strike would threaten the national welfare. During this "cooling-off" period, a fact-finding commission may meet and recommend a settlement. At the end of the 80 days, the union may strike if no settlement is reached.

The Taft-Hartley Act also forbids the closed shop and condemns featherbedding. Featherbedding occurs when a union forces employers to hire more workers than are needed. In addition, the law enabled states to pass right-to-work laws.

3. Landrum-Griffin Act. This law was passed in 1959 to prevent certain abuses by union officials. It prohibits persons with criminal records from serving as union officials for five years after their conviction. It also requires unions to file reports of their finances with the Secretary of Labor each year. The law says that union members have the right to a voice in union affairs.

Labor Relations Today

Over the past 100 years, as you have seen, employers and workers have struggled, sometimes with the help of government, to work out new relationships. The attitudes of most union leaders and employers today are different from those of the past.

Modern union leaders realize that companies must make profits. If the union demands such high wages that a company goes out of business, jobs will be lost. Therefore, some modern unions even help companies find new business or develop more efficient ways of operating.

Modern employers know that their workers must have good wages and working conditions. Well-paid workers are better able to buy the goods and services they produce. Some companies are sharing a certain portion of the profits with their workers. Others are letting workers decide on their work schedules or giving them a voice in how the work is to be done. Such actions make workers

more satisfied with their jobs. They then produce more goods, are absent less often, and feel more needed.

Today's Collective Bargaining

Most disputes between employers and unions are settled peacefully. Yet in spite of improved labor-management relations, there are many strikes each year. You read about strikes in the newspapers or hear about them on radio or television. In 1985 even the major league baseball players went out on strike!

When a strike does occur, both sides may suffer. Workers lose money during a strike because they are not getting their wages. The company, too, loses money when it has to shut down because of a strike. Other people also are hurt by strikes. For example, during the baseball strike many small businesses located near the ballparks lost most of their customers.

Often a strike will not be settled until both sides agree to compromise. That is, each side gives up some of the things it has demanded. During collective bargaining, for example, the company may agree to give a greater wage increase than it originally offered. The union may agree to drop its demand for a six-hour day and accept a seven-hour day. Thus both sides will be able to feel that they have won.

Unions and employers prefer to settle their differences through collective bargaining. If they are unable to reach an agreement, however, they may call for help. A third party who is an expert on labor-management relations may be asked to examine both sides of the issue and recommend a solution. This method is called **mediation.** The recommendations of the mediator are not binding on either the union or the employer. Sometimes a different method, called **arbitration,** is used instead. In this case, the decision of the arbitrator is binding on both sides.

When collective bargaining takes place today, both sides must think about ways to increase productivity and protect profits. The decisions of labor and management have a powerful influence on our nation's prosperity and on its future.

 SECTION 3 REVIEW

Define labor unions, collective bargaining, labor contract, strike, picketing, job action, closed shop, open shop, union shop, agency shop, right-to-work laws, craft union, trade union, industrial union, jurisdictional strike, mediation, arbitration

Identify National Labor Relations Board (NLRB)

1. **Understanding Ideas** Why did workers form labor unions during the 1800's?

2. **Identifying Roles (a)** What methods do labor unions use to get business owners to agree to their union demands? **(b)** In the early days, what methods did employers use to fight strikes?

3. **Contrasting Ideas (a)** Why did labor unions support closed shops? **(b)** Why did businesses support open shops?

4. **Expressing Ideas (a)** How has the federal government helped American workers? **(b)** Write an essay that discusses the history of the AFL-CIO.

Thinking Critically You work as a nurse in a large metropolitan hospital. You and the other nurses are unhappy with your pay, but the hospital will not increase your wages. If you go on strike, there will not be enough people to help the patients. Should you strike? Justify your decision.

Our American economy is one of the most productive in the world. As citizens, however, we must be aware of the challenges facing our free enterprise system.

One major problem is inflation. During a period of inflation, prices are generally rising. A dollar one year will not buy as much as it bought the year before. People are hurt by inflation if their incomes do not rise as fast as prices rise.

The business cycle is another problem. Our economy goes through a period of good times, called a boom. Then it slows down, and we have a recession or depression, called a bust. Inflation sometimes becomes worse during the boom period. Businesses fail and unemployment increases during the period of recession or depression. The government has tried various methods to control the business cycle, but no method has been completely successful.

Our economy also suffers when labor and management cannot settle their differences peacefully. The public can be hurt if a major strike prevents an industry from providing an important product or service. The government often tries to help settle labor-management disputes that will hurt the public. Most unions and companies solve their problems by themselves. Some union leaders and employers are cooperating for the good of all.

CHAPTER 19 SUMMARY

SOCIAL STUDIES SKILL
Reading a Line Graph

Do you consider yourself a victim of inflation? Are the prices of the things you need and want to buy continually increasing? Most Americans answer "yes" to these and similar questions. Suppose you are tired of always paying more for goods and services, and you want Congress to take action to curb inflation. How would you make this point to your representatives in a simple yet dramatic way? An excellent way would be to use a line graph.

As you have learned, graphs help people understand data by condensing large amounts of information into easy-to-understand diagrams. By looking at a graph, you get a quick visual image of the basic information you need.

How to Read a Line Graph

To read a line graph effectively, follow these guidelines.

1. **Determine the subject matter of the graph.** Read the title of the graph to determine the subject and purpose. This will give you a good general idea of what you will learn from the graph.
2. **Study the labels.** Line graphs usually have two labels. One label runs across the bottom of the graph. This label identifies the data on the horizontal axis. The other label sits on top of the line running up and down. This label identifies the data on the vertical axis of the graph.
3. **Examine the indicator line.** The purpose of a line graph usually is to show changes in amounts over time. It does this with an indicator line. By following the indicator line from left to right, you are following the amount indicated on the vertical axis through time. In the line graph on this page, for example, the indicator line shows you how the price of gasoline has changed over the years.

4. **Put the data to use.** Use the graph to draw conclusions about the data. Try to identify trends and make generalizations.

Applying the Skill

Use the line graph below to answer the following questions.

1. **(a)** What was the trend in gasoline prices between 1974 and 1988? **(b)** During what years did the price change most significantly?
2. **(a)** What was the average price of a gallon of gasoline in 1980? **(b)** What was the average price one year later?
3. **(a)** To whom might the graph on this page be interesting? Why? **(b)** Why is a line graph better than a bar graph for showing this kind of data?

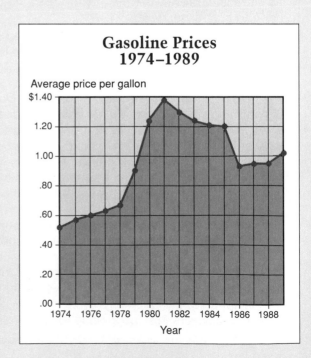

Gasoline Prices 1974–1989

CHAPTER ⑲ REVIEW

Reviewing Terms

On a separate sheet of paper, supply the term from the list below that correctly answers each question.

strike	inflation
fiscal policy	labor unions
business cycle	depression
recession	monetary policy

1. Which term refers to a rise in the prices of most goods and services?
2. What is a period of very hard economic times called?
3. What do economists call the tendency of the economy to go from boom to bust and back again?
4. What is the term for the government's program for taxing and spending?
5. Which term refers to the government's program that affects the nation's money supply?
6. What are organizations of workers called?
7. Which term refers to workers walking off the job in protest?
8. What is a slowdown in the economy called?

Using Thinking Skills

1. **Composing an Essay** Identify and explain actions that people and the government can take to help control inflation.
2. **Identifying Roles** (a) How do labor unions try to achieve their goals? (b) When are mediation and arbitration used?
3. **Seeing Relationships** (a) Why were many people opposed to government involvement in the economy before the Great Depression? (b) What was the government's response to the Great Depression?
4. **Summarizing Ideas** Explain how the government has taken action to help workers.
5. **Understanding Ideas** (a) What are some possible causes of inflation? (b) What effects does inflation have on consumers?

6. **Expressing Ideas** Describe what life was like during the Great Depression.
7. **Organizing Ideas** How does the government try to control the business cycle?
8. **Drawing Conclusions** (a) Why do workers form unions? (b) Why do unions strike?
9. **Contrasting Ideas** (a) How do booms differ from busts? (b) Why do prices tend to rise during good economic times?

Practicing Civics Skills

Interpreting a Graph Use the line graph on page 389 to answer the following questions.

1. Based on reading just the title, what do you think you will learn from this graph?
2. What data does the vertical axis represent?
3. (a) About how many people belonged to labor unions in 1900? (b) About how many labor union members were there in 1985?
4. (a) Which period of time shows the most dramatic increase in labor union membership? (b) What trends can you identify in labor union membership?
5. Based on this graph, what do you expect to happen to membership in American labor unions in the next 10 years?

Being a Good Citizen

1. To gain an understanding of labor-management relations, organize the class into two groups. One group will represent workers, and the other group will represent management. The two groups are in a labor dispute and are in the process of reaching a settlement. One student will serve as mediator. Each side should base its position on an actual case.
2. Collect newspaper articles on a current strike. Prepare a report on the causes, effects, and outcome of the strike.
3. Conduct research on one of the great labor leaders in American history, and write a report about the leader's life and work.

Careers for Americans

Chapter Sections

Chapter Focus

As an American citizen, you must be prepared to find your place in a world where changes are constantly taking place. The modern world is a world of space travel, satellites, miracle medicines, personal computers, frozen foods, air conditioners, giant-screen televisions, and a thousand other wonders. You may be certain, too, that still more changes are on the way. What job opportunities will you find in this changing world?

In the early days of our nation, choosing a job was not difficult. In those days, nine out of ten Americans lived and worked on farms. Only one American in ten lived and worked in a town or city. Job opportunities in towns and cities were limited. This situation was slow in changing. As recently as 100 years ago, there were still only a few hundred different kinds of jobs from which people could choose to make their living.

Today, of course, the situation is different. Now there are thousands of careers from which Americans may choose. As one of the workers upon whom our nation's future will depend, you will want a career in which you can do your best. You will be happiest and most successful if you are doing what you like and what you can do well.

Chapter Focus

As you begin to learn about career opportunities and the world of work, look for answers to the following questions:

★ How does one choose a career?
★ What kinds of careers exist, and how much education and training do they require?
★ What career opportunities will there be in the future?
★ What can you do to prepare yourself for the world of work?

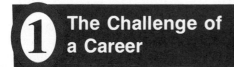

1 The Challenge of a Career

One of the most important things you will have to decide in your life is the kind of work you want to do. Work can be enjoyable, or it can be unpleasant. Thus it is important to find the kind of work that best suits you and for which you are best qualified. The satisfied worker is the person who has a job that fits his or her special needs.

Freedom to Choose a Job

Citizens of the United States have freedom of job choice. They are free to choose the occupation they wish to enter. No government official tells them where, when, and how they must apply for a job. You will learn how important freedom of choice is when you decide on a career. You will be free to pursue any

kind of work that suits your interests, intelligence, and abilities.

You need not follow the same occupation as your father or mother. You are free to plan your own future. Young Americans have the right to set their own goals. They are free to gain as much success in their jobs as their own abilities and opportunities allow.

The freedom to decide which job to take is sometimes limited by the economic situation. During times of high unemployment, people may have to settle for less than their first choices. Yet they still have freedom to succeed in the jobs they have or to change jobs when the chance comes. These freedoms do not guarantee happiness or prosperity. However, they do give Americans a chance to succeed in their chosen careers.

Personal Values and Choosing a Job

The way in which people use their freedom of choice depends on their **personal values**— the things they believe to be most important in their lives. Someone whose main purpose is to earn as much money as possible will seek an occupation that pays well. Another person may consider helping others to be most important. He or she may feel happy only in a service career. Such a person may become a teacher, health worker, or social worker. Personal values play a strong part in determining a person's choice of jobs.

Try to think of the reasons people work. It may help you understand why it is so important to find a job that will best meet your special needs. Perhaps you are thinking that the reasons are clear—most people work to earn money for food, clothing, and shelter.

Many Americans, however, are not content simply to meet basic needs. They want more. They want new cars, compact disc players, washing machines and dryers, and many other things that are now part of our nation's high standard of living. They want to be able to afford vacations and recreational activities

One of the most rewarding careers a person can pursue is that of teacher. Our nation is going to need more of these dedicated professionals in the years to come.

in their free time. Someday they want to be able to retire comfortably.

In addition to the money a job pays, many people think a job should offer other rewards. They believe a job should allow them to do something important. A job should also give them a chance for advancement. Some people get into the habit of working at a particular job and find it a comfortable way to go through life. Others have a real desire to do something new and different. These men and women regard work as a challenge. They would not be happy at a routine job.

The Best Job for You

Before making a decision about a job, everyone should take a good, hard look at his or her own qualifications. How can you decide which job is right for you?

With your abilities, talents, interests, and skills, there are probably many different jobs you can do. That is why it is sometimes difficult to discover which one would be best.

As you begin to study about jobs, you may narrow your choices to those occupations that have a special appeal for you. But do not make the mistake of narrowing your choices too soon. You may discover new and rewarding job opportunities as you get deeper into the subject and learn more about occupations that interest you.

The most important step in deciding upon a career is to get to know yourself. Does this surprise you? Even though you may think you already know yourself quite well, you should take another look. You should try as honestly as possible to discover your abilities, interests, and skills.

If you think about it, you can see why an honest study of yourself is useful when considering a career. It helps you to be practical and to understand your strengths as well as your weaknesses.

For example, if you are afraid of speaking in front of groups, you will have to overcome this fear if you want to be a lawyer or a teacher. Can you do that? Perhaps you can. Many people have. But be frank with yourself. Admit that you have weaknesses as well as strengths. If you balance your job choices against your abilities and interests, you will be more likely to make a wise job decision.

How Your School Years Help You

To succeed in today's rapidly changing world, you will need the best education you can get. Employers want young men and women who read well, write clearly, and have learned as much as possible in school. Employers know that the educated person is easier to teach, is better able to meet new situations, and usually tries harder to get ahead.

Making sure that you get a good education benefits everyone—you, your employer, and your country. A good education is certainly worth all of your efforts. As you learned in Chapter 14, your years of education pay off in hard cash. On average, the more years of schooling people have, the higher their incomes. Education does not guarantee success. But it certainly improves your chances for earning a better income during your lifetime.

Perhaps more important than money, though, is the personal satisfaction that comes from knowing that you have given your best effort. Moreover, each person has the potential to make unique contributions to the world. Doing less than your best only short-changes everyone.

Some students find school difficult and decide to drop out. Dropouts believe that when they quit school and go to work they will be getting a head start in earning money. Leaving school, however, is the worst thing to do if you really are interested in a good income. It is true that dropouts can begin to earn money sooner than students who remain in school. But most dropouts earn low wages, since they can obtain only the lowest-paying jobs. They do not have the education or skills needed for most of today's occupations.

Furthermore, dropouts often find themselves without work. With every year that passes, a person who does not finish high school will find it harder and harder to earn a living. To make matters worse, many tasks that were once done by unskilled workers are now being done by machines.

The Kinds of Workers Employers Want

Employers usually want workers who have a good general education. If special training is required in a certain industry, it is sometimes given on the job. When hiring a secretary, for example, an employer wants someone who types well and does neat work. The employer also seeks a person who can spell accurately, follow directions, and develop new skills. When hired, the secretary is not expected to know much about the company's products. Such things can be learned on the job.

A young person hired as a clerk in a small grocery store may become the store manager if he or she has a good education and is able to solve practical problems. The employer knows that the clerk can learn how to manage the store while working.

The young man or woman who does well at a job builds on information and skills

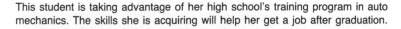

This student is taking advantage of her high school's training program in auto mechanics. The skills she is acquiring will help her get a job after graduation.

Can You Guess?

Several American Presidents began their careers in areas outside of politics. Can you match the Presidents in the left column with their careers listed in the right column?

Andrew Johnson   Actor
Warren Harding   College professor
Woodrow Wilson   Tailor
Herbert Hoover   Journalist
Ronald Reagan   Engineer

Answers are on page 594.

Answers are on page 594.

learned in school. The best way, therefore, to prepare for your future job—no matter what it may be—is to get everything you can from your school years.

Beginning Your Career Choice

You may be asking yourself, "Since American business is changing so rapidly, how can I be sure what job to prepare for and what kind of education to seek?" Fortunately, you do not need to make your job choice right now. If you stay in school, you have several more years in which to study job possibilities before you make your decision.

The first thing you need to do to prepare yourself is study various occupations and get some idea of the type of work each one involves. Then consider the personal qualities each occupation requires, such as originality, patience, or mechanical ability. Once you have done this, examine your own interests and abilities. See how well they fit in with different kinds of jobs.

Gradually you will begin to focus on one job (or perhaps several) that may be best for you. When you have made your choice or choices, you will want to begin preparing for your career. The next four parts of this chapter will help you start thinking about the job you want to work at in the future.

SECTION 1 REVIEW

Define personal values

1. **Expressing Ideas** Why is the freedom of job choice important?
2. **Summarizing Ideas** Discuss the reasons why people choose certain kinds of jobs.
3. **Composing a Paragraph** Why is getting to know yourself important in choosing a career?
4. **Understanding Ideas (a)** Why should you stay in school? **(b)** What problems do drop-outs face?

Thinking Critically You own a business and want to hire a new manager. What qualities should your new manager have?

2 The World of Work

You are already familiar with many of the career opportunities in your community. In your daily life, you have had a chance to see a number of workers in action. You have learned about jobs from your family and friends. Perhaps you have worked at some part-time jobs. All these experiences have helped you become acquainted with the world of work. Now it is time to examine the various fields of work in a systematic way.

Occupations may be divided into many different categories. These categories are determined by the Bureau of the Census and the Bureau of Labor Statistics, and may change over the years. We will now examine four categories of workers: white-collar workers, blue-collar workers, service workers, and farm workers.

White-Collar Workers

The largest group of workers in our nation today is white-collar workers. **White-collar workers** are those people who are in the professions or who do technical, managerial, sales, or administrative support work.

Professionals. Jobs that require many years of education and training, and in which the work is mental rather than physical, are called **professions.** Examples of **professionals** include doctors, nurses, lawyers, architects, teachers, and dentists.

In the field of science, professional workers include chemists, biologists, botanists, geologists, and many other specialists. In the business world, there are professional workers such as accountants, economists, computer programmers, and engineers. Among the professionals in the arts are writers, painters, conductors, composers, and entertainers.

As our economy has changed and grown, the demand for professional workers has also grown. Among today's fastest growing fields are those in the computer, nursing, and engineering professions.

Technicians. Jobs done by **technicians** require some specialized skill in addition to a solid, basic education. Among the best known of these skilled workers are medical laboratory technicians, medical X-ray technicians, physical therapists, and dental hygienists. Other technicians are employed in radio and television, the film industry, manufacturing, and computer industries.

A high school education is the foundation upon which the technician builds. Some technicians learn their skills on the job. Many people take special courses in colleges or in technical or vocational schools.

Managers, Administrators, and Executives. The people in charge of large businesses and corporations are known as **managers** or **administrators.** They also are called **executives** because they execute, or carry out, the operations of the business or corporation.

American businesses are now experiencing stiff competition from other nations of the world. If our nation is to remain competitive in the global economy, American businesses must have experienced, well-educated, and well-trained people on whom they can rely.

The owners of American businesses know that their success depends upon good management. They work hard to hire, train, and develop managers. Intelligent, hard-working executives are needed as heads of departments, branch offices, research divisions, and special projects. Government, too, needs executives to keep the nation's affairs running smoothly. In every community there are many opportunities for those people who wish to manage small businesses.

A person with executive ability has a good chance for success in our free economy. Special training is needed, however, if one is to become a successful executive. Today many of our top executives are college graduates who studied management in university business schools. Large businesses often have their own executive training programs.

Many managers and executives are self-employed workers. They prefer to work for themselves. They take risks and hope to profit

Advances in the technology of computers have opened up many new careers in recent years.

from their own efforts. Self-employed workers are often owners of small businesses, builders, or contractors.

Managers and executives, however, are not the only self-employed people. Many professionals, such as doctors, dentists, and lawyers, work for themselves. So do many writers, painters, musicians, and other kinds of workers.

Administrative Support and Sales Workers. Bookkeepers, secretaries, office clerks, and word processors are examples of **administrative support workers.** They do

These workers are employed in the shipbuilding industry. The work they do requires skills developed through observation, training, and practice.

much of the paperwork required to keep American businesses and industries operating smoothly. According to the Bureau of Labor Statistics, our nation will need many more of these workers in the years ahead.

People who sell goods and services are **sales workers.** Sales workers may be clerks in retail stores. They may sell from door to door. Or they may sell to other businesses, to institutions, or to governments.

Sales workers are much in demand. Many get their training on the job. The skills these workers need do not require long periods of training and may be learned by intelligent, hard-working individuals. Other sales workers, such as real estate agents, insurance agents, and specialized sales representatives, often have college educations. Some workers are required to take special courses and pass state examinations.

Blue-Collar Workers

Workers who hold jobs that require manual labor are known as **blue-collar workers.** They work in construction, steel, petroleum, transportation, manufacturing, mining, and many other industries. Since the mid-1950's, the percentage of blue-collar workers in our country has decreased.

Craft Workers. People who work in trades or handicrafts are **craft workers.** They include carpenters, electricians, machinists, bricklayers, plumbers, printers, bakers, auto mechanics, painters, patternmakers, shoemakers, and construction workers.

The most important requirement for workers in crafts, or trades, is manual ability. That is, they must be able to do accurate and sometimes difficult work with their hands. They must also be good at practical mathematics. In some cases, they must have great physical strength to do parts of their jobs.

To train for a craft, the new worker usually serves an **apprenticeship,** or fixed period of on-the-job training. An apprentice receives an income while learning. The length of on-the-job training varies according to the job. Some industries and unions reduce the amount of apprenticeship time by giving credit for job training courses completed in high school or trade school.

When apprentices have learned their craft, they receive a certificate of completion of apprenticeship. After gaining some job experience, these people may become master craft workers and receive the highest wages in their trade.

Each craft has its own labor union. The number of people admitted into the crafts each year is limited by union rules, the needs of the industry, and the available supply of trained workers. Some craft workers, such as plumbers and electricians, must pass state examinations and receive licenses in order to practice their crafts.

The future holds many opportunities for young people who can work with their hands as well as their heads and who can become skilled in the crafts. In the past, craft jobs were held almost entirely by men. Women now work in almost all of the trades.

Operators. People who operate machines or equipment in factories, mills, industrial plants, gas stations, mines, and laundries are called **operators.** Other factory workers, such as those people who inspect, assemble, and package goods, are included in this group. Drivers of trucks and buses are also operators.

Many operators get their training on the job. Their work usually does not require long periods of training because they often repeat the same task many times. The qualities employers look for are dependability, good health, and some manual skill. Because a job does not require long periods of training does not mean that anyone can handle it. A good truck driver gains skill only after many years. This skill comes with practice, good judgment, and being in good physical condition.

Some operators face an uncertain future. The number of machine operators in American industry has declined as factories have come to rely more on automation.

Laborers. There are and probably always will be jobs calling for little or no training. Workers without special skills are often employed to mix cement, carry bricks, dig ditches, and handle freight and other heavy loads. Workers who do this type of heavy physical work are called **laborers.**

The demand for laborers will grow more slowly than the demand for other types of workers in the years ahead. Automation increasingly is replacing muscle power. More and more, machines are used to mix cement, dig ditches, load freight, and do many other jobs requiring heavy manual labor.

Service Workers

Today one of every seven employed Americans is a service worker. **Service workers** provide the public with some needed assistance. One type of service worker provides protection services. In this group are firefighters, police officers, and security guards. Another category provides health services. Among these workers are paramedics, dental and nursing assistants, and orderlies.

Another group of service workers is employed by business firms that sell services rather than products. These business firms are called **service industries.** They include hotels, restaurants, dry cleaners, laundries, barbershops, and hair salons.

Some service industry jobs require a college education or training courses. Others teach the needed skills on the job. There are many career opportunities in service industries because much of the work cannot be automated.

Farm Workers

The need for farm workers has decreased greatly during this century. **Farm workers** are people who own, manage, or work on a farm, even an unpaid member of a farm family. Today only one of every 34 workers is a farm

There is always plenty of work to do on a farm. On this apple orchard, for example, many farm workers are needed to help out at harvest time.

worker. Experts predict that the need for farm workers will continue to decline.

 SECTION 2 REVIEW

Define professions, apprenticeship, service industries

Identify white-collar workers, professionals, technicians, managers, administrators, executives, administrative support workers, sales workers, blue-collar workers, craft workers, operators, laborers, service workers, farm workers

1. **Seeing Relationships** Why do professions require years of education and training?

2. **Classifying Roles** Identify three occupations in each of the following categories: professional, technical, administrative support, craft.
3. **Understanding Ideas** What training must workers have to become master craft workers?
4. **Drawing Conclusions** Why has the demand for laborers decreased over the years?

Thinking Critically Rather than work for a company or corporation, you have decided that you would rather be self-employed. Discuss the advantages and disadvantages of self-employment.

③ Opportunities Unlimited

Whether a person is a professional, technician, craft worker, service worker, or laborer, there are opportunities for advancement. For example, young men and women who complete a high school commercial course might start their careers as word processors, filing clerks, or bookkeepers. By attending special night school classes, they may later qualify for better paying positions.

They might study accounting, for example, and learn how to keep business financial records. Skilled accountants are needed by management as part of the business team. If young men and women are prepared, they will be ready when the right opportunity presents itself.

Government Jobs

Our nation's largest employer is the United States government. Over 3 million Americans work for the federal government, not counting those people who serve in the armed forces. Federal employees perform a wide range of jobs.

Some workers deliver the mail, care for war veterans, or protect us against counterfeiting. Others run the national parks, forecast the weather, or inspect food and medicines to make sure they are pure. Many thousands of clerks, word processors, and secretaries are also required to carry out the everyday business of the United States government.

Applicants must take a test to qualify for most federal jobs. The tests are called **civil service examinations.** They are announced when government job openings occur. The jobs go to those people who receive the highest test scores on the examinations.

State and local governments also employ many different kinds of workers. Like federal employees, state and local workers usually are chosen on the basis of their civil service examination scores. Notices of job openings in federal, state, and local governments are sent to school counselors. You also may see these notices on post office bulletin boards or in local newspapers.

Opportunities in the Armed Forces

With the recent emphasis upon a volunteer army, careers in the military are being made more attractive. Salaries have been raised, and there is a greater choice of occupation.

A high school diploma is helpful in qualifying for most good jobs in the armed forces. High school graduates may receive technical training in the armed forces for such jobs as electronic technician, radar operator and technician, medical equipment technician, and motor mechanic. They may also be trained as surveyors, printers, or medical technicians.

As you have read, our nation has four officer training schools. To qualify for the Army, Navy, Air Force, or Coast Guard academies, you must be a high school graduate. Applicants must be recommended by their United States senator or representative. They must also pass scholastic and physical tests.

(continued on page 408)

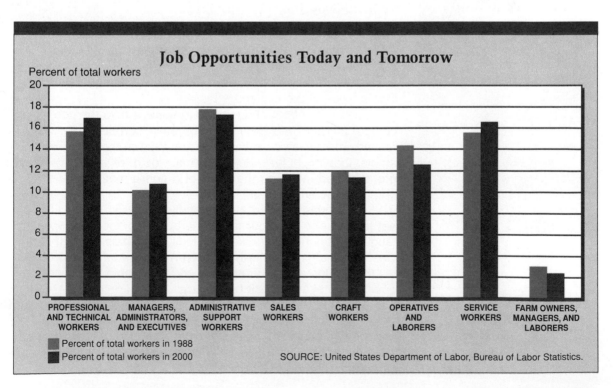

Job Opportunities Today and Tomorrow

Percent of total workers

Categories: PROFESSIONAL AND TECHNICAL WORKERS; MANAGERS, ADMINISTRATORS, AND EXECUTIVES; ADMINISTRATIVE SUPPORT WORKERS; SALES WORKERS; CRAFT WORKERS; OPERATIVES AND LABORERS; SERVICE WORKERS; FARM OWNERS, MANAGERS, AND LABORERS

Percent of total workers in 1988
Percent of total workers in 2000

SOURCE: United States Department of Labor, Bureau of Labor Statistics.

CITIZENSHIP IN ACTION

Getting a Jump on Careers

Would you know how to get a monkey to take its medicine? Or how to interest a six-year-old in the alphabet? Could you run a television news show? Each of these tasks requires a special talent—one that could help you choose a career someday.

Janice Buhl, Cassandra Cole, and Mark Shichtman began their career search even before finishing high school. Janice worked in a zoo. Cassandra started a school on the back porch of her home. Mark started his own news show on cable television. Each of them learned the skills mentioned above—and much more!

"Housekeeping" at the Zoo

The high school in Honolulu, Hawaii, that Janice attended offered a special class in zoo work. Since Janice had always been interested in animals, she signed up for the course. It required one zoo class a week at the high school and two mornings a week at the city zoo.

Each year about 25 juniors and seniors take the zoo course. Students are asked to keep daily journals of their zoo-related work. They do many different tasks at the zoo. For example, they might help clean elephant teeth for a display. One group helped massage the limbs of a gorilla that had been paralyzed by an accident.

Janice was amazed at the variety of jobs in a zoo. One of her jobs was to take tour groups through the zoo. Her work taught her about many different kinds of animals—birds, reptiles, and mammals. She had to learn enough information to tell the groups about the animals and to be able to answer the questions they might ask her.

After she graduated from high school, Janice took a part-time job at the zoo. Her work as an assistant to the animal keeper was much like housekeeping. She helped feed the animals and clean their pens and cages. When an animal became sick, she helped treat it.

Part-time jobs can help teenagers make career choices.

At first, one of Janice's biggest problems was figuring out how to give medicine to a sick animal. Then she learned that one of the best ways is to "make use of the animal's eating habits." She found that many animals keep their appetites unless they are very sick. One favorite monkey, she remembers, "always ate as if it were starving. When it became sick, I put a pill in a banana, and the monkey—Jake, we called him—was in such a hurry to eat that it never noticed the medicine."

Janice learned a lot about zoos and animals. She learned, too, that she wants to make working with animals her career. "It will be wonderful," she says, "to be paid for doing something I enjoy so much."

Reporting the News on Television

Appearing on television became routine for Mark Shichtman. His news show—*Kids News*—appeared every Thursday afternoon. It was seen in thousands of homes in New York City.

Mark became a TV news reporter when he was in the fifth grade. He approached a cable television company with the idea for a news program by and for young Americans. The

Personal fulfillment is an important part of job satisfaction.

These teenagers learned that work can also be fun.

Television journalists play an important role in bringing us the news.

company agreed, and before long Mark and several friends were television stars. By the time they reached eighth grade, their classmates were teasing them about their "fame."

Kids News reported on a wide range of events. Mark and the other members of the news team got most of their stories from newspapers or from other television news shows. Each reporter was responsible for a special area. They covered local, national, and international news. Other features included a weather forecast and a sports report. A special feature of the show was "Citiline," which explored what was happening for kids in New York.

Modern camera and videotape equipment now make it possible for students who are interested in news gathering to go out and cover stories directly—that is, to film stories as they are happening. Students interested in making a career on television will certainly have a jump on most people their age.

A School of Her Own

Cassandra Cole took a different approach to her career search. She knew at the age of 12 that she wanted to teach.

Becoming a teacher requires commitment, dedication, training, and hard work.

She decided then and there to open her own summer school in her home in Chicago, Illinois.

Cassandra's parents agreed to let her use the porch and yard for the summer, provided she kept them clean. Cassandra then gathered materials to use in the school, signed up some students, and went to work. The school was such a success that Cassandra kept it going summer after summer.

The school was free, but each student had to have his or her parents' permission to attend. Cassandra's goal was to help younger children do well during the regular school year. There were usually 15 students. To make sure they got the attention they needed, Cassandra's teenage cousin helped with the teaching.

The classes were held from 12:30 to 3:00 on weekday afternoons. A typical day began with the class reciting the Pledge of Allegiance. The first subject was reading, followed by spelling. After a break for juice, the students studied mathematics. The afternoon ended with a game like Bingo, in which the winner got a prize or a star. After the homework assignments were passed out, students were asked to help clean up.

Cassandra expected the students to do all their homework. The teacher did homework too. On Saturday afternoons Cassandra went to the library to choose books and records for the students to use during the week.

Cassandra's own teachers praised her initiative and leadership skills. Her summer school was written about in newspapers and magazines, and the class appeared on a local television program. What did Cassandra think about her success? She said that someday "I might like to have my own nursery school."

These students are benefiting from Cassandra's determination to be a teacher.

Thinking It Over

1. Identify some of the talents a person might need to work in a zoo.
2. Why do you think Cassandra's teachers admired her?
3. Do you think Mark sometimes needed adult help in preparing his weekly news show? Why or why not?
4. Do you have any special interests that might lead to a possible career for yourself? Explain.

Workers in High Demand

The United States Department of Labor constantly studies job opportunities in our nation. Each year it reports where men and women are working and what jobs they are doing. This department also studies the job needs of our nation. What skills are needed right now? What will be needed ten years from now?

In a study made in 1990, the Department of Labor estimated that through the 1990's the demand would be high for the following categories of workers:

Accountants
Building custodians
Carpenters
Cashiers
Child care workers
Computer analysts
  and programmers
Cooks and chefs
Electrical and
  electronics
  engineers
Executives
Food service
  workers
Gardeners
General managers
General office
  clerks
Home health
  workers
Kindergarten,
  elementary, and
  secondary school
  teachers
Lawyers
Maintenance
  repairers
Medical assistants
Practical nurses
Receptionists
Registered nurses
Stock clerks
Sales workers, retail
Secretaries
Security guards
Truck drivers
Waiters and
  waitresses

Nurses contribute a great deal to the quality of medical care in the United States. Nursing provides job opportunities for men and women alike.

Keep in mind that the need for a particular type of worker may be greater in some parts of the nation than in others. This study is for the nation as a whole. Local needs often reflect a demand for certain kinds of workers.

Other kinds of workers, too, are almost always in demand. For example, law enforcement officers and members of the medical profession are usually needed. Also, remember that in all jobs there is a constant turnover because of promotions, job changes, or retirements. These events almost always create a job opening. The well-prepared person will be ready to seize this type of job opportunity when it occurs.

Equal Employment Opportunity

In your study of career opportunities, you may have noticed in newspaper classified advertisements the phrase "An Equal Opportunity Employer." This means that the employer does not discriminate against job applicants because of their sex, age, race, skin color, religion, or ethnic background.

Congress passed the Civil Rights Acts of 1964 and 1968 to help end discrimination in hiring and in wage rates (see page 547). These acts have opened up new job opportunities for women and minority groups. An **Equal Employment Opportunity Commission,** appointed by the President, upholds fair employment standards. Several states have similar laws and commissions to enforce them.

Women continue to fight for the right to be considered for any job. Today women are members of Congress, generals, judges, doctors, scientists, airline pilots, cab drivers—indeed, few fields are not open to women now. In industry, distinctions between women's and men's jobs are breaking down.

American businesses are urging women to study for scientific and technical jobs that once were open only to men. The Women's Bureau of the Department of Labor has predicted that our nation's future needs for technical and scientific workers cannot be met unless more women enter these fields.

Fields traditionally dominated by women are now opening their doors to men. The profession of nursing is a field in which men as well as women are urgently needed. Many men are lending their talents to kindergarten and elementary school teaching. And more men are finding job satisfaction as secretaries and word processors.

Periods of Unemployment

As you read in Chapter 19, there are times when our economic system goes through a recession or depression. At such times many people are out of work. Others are working but cannot find jobs in their chosen fields.

The young person studying careers should remember that there have always been periods of unemployment. It is wise to have more than one interest and if possible to develop skills in more than one area of work. You might want to consider job possibilities from the point of view of security before you make a final decision.

In the early days of computers, the people who ran them were mostly men. Today women are entering the computer field in growing numbers.

 SECTION 3 REVIEW

Define civil service examinations

Identify Equal Employment Opportunity Commission

1. **Composing an Essay** Write an essay on government and military job opportunities in the United States.
2. **Classifying Ideas** List ten jobs that will be in demand through the 1990's.
3. **Seeing Relationships** (a) What does the phrase "An Equal Opportunity Employer" mean? (b) Explain how job opportunities are opening up for men and women.

Thinking Critically How will you answer when a job interviewer asks, "What will give you the most job satisfaction?"

4 Learning More About Careers

You are probably discovering that you know a great deal more about careers and jobs than you thought you did. For one thing, in your earlier studies you often have read about the careers of famous men and women. However, no single book, even one on careers, can give you all the information you need about various jobs. You may have to spend a lot of time hunting in different places to get the facts you need in order to choose the job that is best for you.

Reading About Careers

One of the best ways to learn about jobs is to read the many available books, magazines, and pamphlets on the subject. Explore your library, the newsstands, and any literature you may have at home. Your local state employment office has a number of booklets about careers in your community. Usually, these booklets may be obtained free of charge. Since large business firms are always on the lookout for good employees, many of them put out interesting brochures that contain useful job information.

Another source of information about jobs is the United States Department of Labor. It publishes a book entitled *Occupational Outlook Handbook*, an important reference for job seekers.

Reading about career opportunities in order to find a job field that interests you is like doing detective work. One clue leads to another as the job picture becomes clearer. You may find a clue in a novel or biography. Then you may find another bit of evidence in a newspaper column or magazine article. You are acting as a detective in solving the problem of your own career.

As you read about jobs, of course, you must remember your own interests, needs, and abilities. You should also try to keep an open mind. You may discover a career you never thought about before.

Watching Others at Work

Reading about jobs will help you gather many facts about them. But why not take a closer look by investigating job opportunities in your community? Through school-sponsored trips, you can find out a great deal about jobs available in factories, offices, and stores in your locality. Someone in your family may be able to arrange for you to visit his or her place of employment. You can also learn about jobs as you go about your daily affairs. Observe the work of bus drivers, police officers, teachers, salespeople, office workers, and others you meet each day.

You will gain more from watching people at work if you go about it in a carefully planned manner. Take notes on what you learn. Ask questions. Interview people who are working at jobs that interest you. Ask them what they like best and what they like least about their work. Talk about jobs with your family, friends, and counselors. Discussing your thoughts with others will help make many ideas clearer in your own mind.

Learning by Working at a Job

One good way to discover more about careers is to get a job. For many students, responsibilities at home make getting a job impossible. Some students, though, work at part-time or summer jobs. You can learn something from any job.

Baby-sitting, for example, may lead you to think about a future job in a child care center. If not, it will at least give you a chance to learn more about people. Baby-sitting can also teach you why being prompt and dependable is important in any job. Being a newspaper carrier, supermarket clerk, gasoline station attendant, or movie usher are

Here are just four of the hundreds of jobs you might choose. What kinds of work does each involve? What kinds of skills does each job require?

other ways you can get to know what working is like.

Do not overlook hobbies as a means of finding out what you like to do and can do well. Many people have turned their hobbies into their life's work. Hobbies may help you determine whether you have special talents. You can then begin to think about jobs that require similar abilities.

Another good way to explore your abilities is to take an active interest in school life. Try writing for the school newspaper. Manage a team. Serve on a class committee. Help decorate for school dances. Sell tickets for local events. These and other activities will give you a chance to see whether you enjoy writing, managing, selling, decorating, or some other skill that you may be able to use later in a job.

Job Questions to Ask Yourself

As you consider your future career, you can avoid guesswork if you ask yourself the seven important questions listed on the next page. Your answers should indicate whether you are making a wise choice.

1. What Kind of Work Will I Do in This Job? Will I be working alone or with other people? Will I be working mostly with my hands or with my mind? What skills will I need to develop in order to do the job well? Does the job involve a lot of study and careful planning, or does it involve repeating the same task?

2. What Personal Qualifications Does the Job Require? How important in this job are neatness, promptness, dependability, and pleasant personality? Must I be able to follow directions? Will I be expected to give directions and to lead others? Does the job call for strong muscles?

3. How Much Education and Training Does the Job Require? Must I be a college graduate? Is a graduate school degree necessary? Is any specialized training required? Is a period of apprenticeship needed for the job? If so, how long does it last?

4. Are Job Opportunities in This Field Good? Are there many openings now? Is this a growing field of work? Will there be more openings when I am ready to look for a job? Is this the kind of career in which I can develop my abilities and move ahead?

5. What Salary Does the Job Pay? Is the starting salary only the first step toward a higher income? What training must I have to receive salary increases? Will I be satisfied with the **salary range** (beginning salary, possible raises, and highest salary) that the work offers? What other benefits, such as insurance, sick pay, retirement benefits, and pleasant working conditions, are available?

6. How Do I Feel About This Job? Do I believe this is a job worth doing? Will I be making a contribution to the community? Will I be happy with the kinds of people who may be working with me?

7. Where Will I Have to Live and Work for This Kind of Job? Will I have to move to another part of the country? Does the job require that I travel a lot? Will I have

Working on a school newspaper is just a hobby for these students now. But if they like the work, they may choose careers in the news field.

to live in a large city? Are most workers in this field employed in factories, on farms, in offices, or in their own homes?

A Sample Job Quiz

Why is it so important to ask yourself these questions—and to find the answers to them? You probably have guessed the reason. It is one of the best ways to find out whether the job you are considering is the right job for you.

Suppose that Rita Sanchez, a ninth grade student, is interested in a job as a medical laboratory technician. The following seven questions should help Rita decide whether she wants that kind of career.

Question 1: What kind of work will I do in this job?

Answer: Medical technicians usually work with doctors in the laboratories of hospitals and clinics. Medical technicians perform tests that help doctors decide how to treat illnesses. They take blood tests, for example, and report the results of these tests. They help prepare various tests that doctors give patients to check for many illnesses.

Question 2: What personal qualifications are required?

Answer: The medical technician must be a dependable, accurate person who is interested in science. He or she must be intelligent, careful, and able to follow directions. He or she must also have good eyesight and skillful hands.

Question 3: How much education and training does the job require?

Answer: At least three years of college are required, plus a year of special training in a hospital to learn laboratory procedures.

Question 4: Are job opportunities in this field good?

Answer: There is a shortage of medical technicians. Well-trained workers will have no trouble getting jobs. The work can lead to a job in medical research, to ownership of an independent laboratory, or to a job as a laboratory supervisor.

Question 5: What salary does the job pay?

Answer: The starting salary of a college-trained medical technician is about $18,000. It can be more or less than this, depending on the exact nature of the job. Also, salaries vary in different parts of the country. Salaries increase with experience.

Question 6: How do I feel about this job?

Answer: Medical technicians do interesting and important work. They help the sick get well again.

Question 7: Where will I have to live and work for this kind of job?

Answer: The medical technician works in the hospitals, medical centers, private laboratories, clinics, and doctors' offices that are located in most communities. The worker can live anywhere within commuting distance of the job.

This job quiz should help the person who is deciding whether or not to become a medical technician. It should also give you and the rest of your class a good idea of the work done by a medical technician.

Using the seven questions listed above, you and your classmates can work out quizzes for any occupations that interest you.

 SECTION 4 REVIEW

Define salary range

1. **Expressing Ideas (a)** Describe the ways in which you can get information about careers. **(b)** How is finding out about careers like doing detective work?
2. **Seeing Relationships (a)** How are part-time jobs helpful in choosing a career? **(b)** Explain why hobbies are useful in deciding what kind of work you might like to do in the future.
3. **Summarizing Information** What are the seven important questions to keep in mind when considering a job?

Thinking Critically Outline your personal plan for choosing a future career.

5 Learning More About Yourself

Some jobs may interest you because they seem exciting and glamorous. Many young people think about becoming singers, actors, or professional athletcs. But many of them discover that succeeding in these jobs is too difficult. Or they learn that they are more interested in some other job.

Of course, if you decide that you have what it takes to be a success in one of these fields, you should work as hard as you can to get into it. However, if you study your interests and abilities and discover you are more likely to succeed in some other occupation, you would be wiser to choose that career.

To learn about yourself is not easy. It is difficult for most of us to look at ourselves honestly and to judge our own qualifications. It is worth the effort, though, if we finally are able to get a true picture of ourselves. We must also learn how we appear to other people. Often other people can help us see ourselves better and discover the kind of person we are. What are some ways in which we can learn to know ourselves?

Preparing to Apply for a Job

When the time comes to look for your first job, you will probably have to fill out a **job application.** This is a printed form on which you are asked to supply important information about yourself. Your job application helps the employer decide if you are the right person for the job.

Large businesses and corporations have **personnel workers** whose job it is to hire or recommend new employees. Personnel workers examine job applications and interview people to determine the best-qualified applicant for the available job.

You will probably find it helpful to practice filling out a job application. Then, when you apply for a job later on, you will know what type of information you will be asked to supply.

You can practice writing out job applications in several ways. Perhaps you can fill out a real application used by a local business firm. Or you can prepare an outline of important facts about yourself. Many students prefer to write short autobiographies, including the chief facts about their lives. No matter which you choose, you will find it useful in filling out a job application.

What Employers Want to Know

To prepare your own job application, you should know what information employers need when they are seeking a new employee. In general, they will want to know the following facts about you.

1. Your School History. Your school record tells the employer a lot about you. List the subjects you have taken in the last two years and the grades you received. Then look at the reasons for these grades. What do grades mean? Perhaps you have high marks in English because you enjoy expressing yourself through writing. This may show that you should consider an occupation in which you can use your writing talent. On the other hand, you may have poor grades in mathematics. Does this mean you should not even consider a job that requires mathematical ability? Not necessarily!

Grades do not always tell the whole story. Some students who have gotten low marks in mathematics may be late in discovering their ability in this subject. Perhaps they had trouble understanding number concepts in their earlier math courses. After special effort, they may be catching up in their studies. They may now be on their way to mastering math and getting higher grades. As you see, low grades in any subject are not necessarily a sign that the student cannot learn that subject. Low marks frequently indicate lack of effort rather than lack of ability.

Perhaps in listing your subjects and grades you should include a third column entitled "Reasons for the Grades." This column will help you judge your own abilities and interests. It will also tell you how well you have used them up to now.

2. Your Health Record. Good health is an important qualification for any job. Some occupations even require that workers have special physical qualifications. Sometimes good eyesight is essential. A medical technician, surgeon, or jeweler, for instance, needs good eyesight. You will want to examine your health record and review your program for keeping fit.

There are many job opportunities, however, for disabled citizens. The history of American business and industry contains countless stories of disabled people who have found great success. As just one example, Thomas Edison, the great inventor, was deaf. Yet his life was filled with outstanding contributions. Americans believe that everyone should have an equal chance to succeed. To this end, recent civil rights legislation has made it illegal for employers to discriminate against disabled Americans.

3. Your Outside Activities. Make a list of your hobbies, the school offices you have held, sports in which you take part, school organizations to which you belong, and your part-time and summer jobs. After you have completed this list, take another look at it. Does it show many different activities? What part of each did you like best? This review can tell you and an employer a great deal about your potential job skills.

4. Your Special Interests. The things that interest you now may also point the way to the future. List all your interests that you think might help you make a career choice. Check back on the subjects you liked best in school. See if your interests helped you do well in these subjects. Finally, review your hobbies and your part-time work activities to see which interests they emphasize.

A future employer will know and understand you better if he or she is aware of your special interests. These interests will tell the employer whether you prefer indoor or outdoor work, whether you would rather work alone or with others, or whether you want to be a leader or a follower. Your interests help determine your job needs.

Study Your Test Record

Tests are another means of helping you understand yourself and your abilities. Every test you take in school measures certain skills. You have probably already taken tests that show how well you study, how accurately you remember what you read, and how well you express yourself. Go back over your test scores and consider the reasons for these scores. They should reveal your ability to do certain things. Here are some of the strengths such tests seek to measure.

Motor Skills. Certain tests are used to determine how well people can use their

The young people shown here are developing their motor skills. The skills required to repair a bicycle could lead to profitable careers in the future.

Art classes such as this one give students the chance to develop their talents and abilities. These students might pursue careers in art.

hands—their **motor skills.** They measure how fast individuals can do things with their hands. They also check how accurately they do things. Certain other tests determine how well people can handle and arrange small objects. You can understand why good motor skills are useful to a watchmaker or a worker assembling small electronic equipment.

Number Skills. One of the most common tests measures a person's ability to work quickly and accurately with numbers. Such **number skills** are essential to bookkeepers, carpenters, and accountants. Most scientists also need to be skilled in using numbers.

Perceptual Skills. How well can you picture things—that is, see them in your mind? In order to read a blueprint, for example, you must be able to picture in your mind the way a building will look when finished. You must be able to see depth and width in a flat drawing. The ability to think in this way is a part of **perceptual skills.**

Language Skills. A teacher explaining an idea to students, a salesperson talking to a customer, and a parent describing to a child how to draw all have skills in using language. An editor, an advertising specialist, and an executive in a business firm must be skilled in using written language. Many kinds of tests check these abilities, called **language skills,** or linguistic ability.

Special Talents. Some tests include sections that try to discover whether a person has artistic and creative talent. Sometimes there is also a section that measures the ability to organize and present facts. People can use these special talents in many different kinds of jobs. Publishing companies and advertising agencies, for example, need designers and writers.

Personal Relationships. There are tests to check how well you handle personal relationships—how well you get along with others. This is important in many jobs. Teachers should rank high in this skill. So should salespeople, receptionists, and other workers who deal with many people.

Interests and Aptitudes. There are certain other tests you take in school that can help you to know yourself better. These are called interest tests, or **aptitude tests.** They are easy to take and reveal interesting things about you. Your teacher or counselor will help explain the results of these tests and the meaning they have for you.

Such tests probably will not tell you the exact job you should look for. No test can map out the future for you. What these tests are supposed to do is help you discover your abilities and interests. Then it is up to you to match what you have discovered about yourself with what you have learned about various job opportunities.

By now you probably have made a good start in getting to know yourself better. As you study jobs that interest you, compare your opportunities with your abilities. Your present aim should be to choose a general field of work—a type of work rather than a specific job. Leave the way open so that you can change to another kind of work if you need to do so. Remember, a person's first job choice may not be the final one.

 SECTION 5 REVIEW

Define job application, motor skills, number skills, perceptual skills, language skills, aptitude tests

Identify personnel workers

1. **Drawing Conclusions** Why it is a good idea to practice filling out job applications?
2. **Seeing Relationships (a)** Why is your school history important to employers? **(b)** Why do employers ask about a person's health record? **(c)** What can your special interests tell your future employer?
3. **Summarizing Ideas** Discuss the various types of skills that tests seek to uncover.

Thinking Critically The President of the United States has asked you to deliver a televised speech to the American people. The title of the speech is to be "Our Nation's Future Depends on the Workers of Tomorrow." Write a draft of your speech.

All young Americans must plan for their future careers. There are many job opportunities for young people. But these opportunities keep changing. You must get up-to-date information on jobs if you are to make a wise career choice.

In considering job possibilities, you should know about the work done by people in the professions and by managers, technicians, service workers, craft workers, operators, and farm workers. The choice of your career must be made by you alone. However, there are certain general guides that you may find helpful. You can read widely about jobs, explore jobs in your community, interview workers, and work at a part-time job.

An important step in deciding upon a career is to learn more about yourself. Your school and health records, your special interests, your outside activities, and your work experience will be of interest to prospective employers.

You can prepare yourself now so that you will know what employers look for when hiring new workers. Learn about jobs that are available, not only in your community but throughout the country. Use your school years wisely. The skills and knowledge you acquire in school will help you for the rest of your life.

LIFE SKILL
Reading a Help Wanted Ad

Choosing an occupation is one of the most important decisions you will ever make. You will therefore want to find a job that you would enjoy doing on a year-round basis.

The best source of information on jobs available in your community is the classified section of your newspaper. The classified section contains the help wanted ads listing employment opportunities in your local area.

Sometimes it is helpful to look through more than one newspaper. This will be easy for you if you live in an area where more than one newspaper is published. No matter what newspaper you consult, however, keep in mind that the Sunday paper usually contains the largest selection of help wanted ads.

How to Read a Help Wanted Ad

To get the most from help wanted ads, follow these guidelines.

1. **Become familiar with the organization of the ads.** Most help wanted ads in the classified section follow the same general organization. First they are divided into major categories such as "Accounting, Bookkeeping," "Engineering," "Medical," "Office, Clerical," "Professional," and "Sales." Then within each of these categories, jobs are listed roughly in alphabetical order by type. This information usually runs across the top of each ad to help you spot job possibilities.

2. **Read the ads carefully.** When you see an interesting ad, read it carefully. If you do not have the required training or experience, think about how you can get it. Also, carefully study any promises made in the ad. What is the salary? Are benefits such as vacations or health insurance discussed? The answers to these and other questions will help you decide whether or not you might want to ap-

ply. Pay special attention to ads placed by employment agencies, or businesses that charge money to fill a position. The company that has the job opening often pays the agency fee, but not always. Sometimes it is the successful applicant who must pay the agency's fee.

3. **Do not limit yourself.** Remember not to limit yourself to only one of the major headings in the help wanted section. You may find that the job you are looking for is listed under more than one category.

Applying the Skill

Read the help wanted ad shown below and answer the following questions.

1. **(a)** What qualifications are needed for this job? **(b)** Who is advertising the position? **(c)** Is there any fee involved?
2. What features are used to attract applicants?
3. **(a)** If you wanted to apply for the job, how would you go about it? **(b)** What other information should you ask about?

RECEPTIONIST
ART GALLERY

$225/fee paid

Bright energetic H.S. grad. to handle front desk and busy phones. Typing 55 w.p.m.

Neat appearance and punctuality a must. Knowledge of modern art would be useful. Excellent vacations and fringe benefits. Immediate hire.

Winston Agency   724-3791

An Equal Opportunity Employer

Reviewing Terms

On a separate sheet of paper, supply the term from the list below that correctly completes each sentence.

service workers   personnel workers
motor   personal values
craft workers   blue-collar
white-collar   perceptual

1. Carpenters, auto mechanics, electricians, and bakers are examples of _____ _____.

2. _____ _____ workers are those who are in the professions or who do technical, managerial, sales, or administrative support work.

3. Picturing how a finished building will look by examining a blueprint is an example of a _____ skill.

4. _____ _____ include police officers, paramedics, and barbers.

5. A test that tries to determine how fast you can do things with your hands is a test of your _____ skills.

6. Workers who hold jobs that require manual labor are called _____ _____ workers.

7. The attitudes and principles people believe to be most important in their lives are called their _____ _____.

8. People whose job it is to hire or recommend new employees are called _____ _____.

Using Thinking Skills

1. **Seeing Relationships (a)** What is the relationship between personal values and job choice? **(b)** How can an honest study of yourself help you in choosing a job?

2. **Comparing Roles (a)** What is the difference between a craft worker and an operator? **(b)** Explain the difference between an administrator and an administrative support worker.

3. **Expressing Ideas (a)** Why is it important to get as much education as you can? **(b)** Why is dropping out of school harmful if you want a good income?

4. **Identifying Opportunities (a)** Identify ten jobs in which the demand will be high through the 1990's. **(b)** What evidence shows that the distinctions between men's and women's jobs are breaking down?

5. **Summarizing Ideas** Summarize the seven questions you should ask yourself when considering your future career.

6. **Identifying Ideas (a)** What types of information do employers want to know about job applicants? **(b)** How can people practice writing job applications? **(c)** What types of strengths do tests in school measure?

7. **Understanding Ideas (a)** What kinds of careers are available from the government? **(b)** How do applicants qualify for government jobs? **(c)** How do applicants qualify for military officer training schools?

Practicing Civics Skills

Analyzing Job Descriptions Make a list of the jobs that interest you. Choose one of these and write a "Help Wanted" ad for that position. Be sure to research the training and experience needed for this kind of work. Learn what salary and benefits the job might offer.

Being a Good Citizen

1. Organize the class into groups to conduct interviews with people in the community who hold various types of jobs. Find out what the person you interview likes most about the job and what he or she likes least.

2. Consult your school librarian for a list of reference sources students can study to find out about various jobs.

3. Look in the "Help Wanted" section of your local newspaper for several jobs that interest you. Practice your job hunting skills by writing letters of application.

Reviewing the Facts

1. **(a)** What is the Federal Reserve System? **(b)** What two purposes does it serve?
2. **(a)** What are white-collar workers? **(b)** What are blue-collar workers? **(c)** What type of workers usually serve apprenticeships?
3. **(a)** What are stocks? **(b)** What are bonds? **(c)** How does saving help the nation's economy?
4. **(a)** What are standard parts? **(b)** Why are standard parts important to mass production?
5. **(a)** What is a labor union? **(b)** List and describe three labor laws passed by Congress.

Using Critical Thinking

1. **Seeing Relationships (a)** How does scarcity affect nations? **(b)** How do personal values affect job choice?
2. **Identifying Roles (a)** What kind of work is done by personnel workers? **(b)** What do stock brokers do? **(c)** How did Eli Whitney contribute to the development of mass production in the United States?
3. **Understanding Ideas (a)** Explain why businesses and families must use credit wisely. **(b)** How can individuals and the government help stop inflation?
4. **Summarizing Ideas (a)** Discuss the importance of getting a good education. **(b)** Explain why dropping out of school is harmful to the individual.
5. **Composing an Essay** Write a short essay that describes the three main parts of the Social Security program.
6. **Expressing Ideas (a)** What is a business cycle? **(b)** How does government attempt to control the business cycle?
7. **Comparing Ideas (a)** How does a closed shop differ from an open shop? **(b)** How do perceptual skills differ from motor skills?
8. **Composing a Paragraph** Write a paragraph that explains how important our transportation system is to the economy.

9. **Organizing Ideas (a)** Describe the advantages and disadvantages of charge accounts. **(b)** Describe the advantages and disadvantages of installment plans.

Applying What You Know

1. Make a bulletin-board display of photographs from newspapers and magazines that show the four factors of production. Use the bulletin boards as the basis for a class discussion on the decision-making process of business owners.
2. Imagine that you have just purchased a microwave oven for the sum of $130. Draw a picture of the check that you wrote to pay for your purchase. Now write a warranty for the product.
3. Research and prepare a written report on the contributions of one of the following Americans: Andrew Carnegie, George Washington Carver, Cesar Chavez, Henry Ford, Samuel Gompers, Lewis Latimer, Mary Elizabeth Lease, Cyrus McCormick, J. P. Morgan, Jan Matzeliger, Elizabeth Lucas Pinckney.
4. Consult *The Statistical Abstract of the United States* to find out how the average price of a house has changed since 1980. Use this information to draw a line graph.

Expanding Your Knowledge

Antell, Gerson, and Harris, Walter, *Economics for Everybody*, Amsco. Case studies explain how our economic system works.

Dahlstrom, Harry, *Don't Let People Rip You Off*, Dahlstrom. Discusses how you can become a wise consumer.

Fitzgibbon, Dan, *All About Your Money*, Macmillan. Discusses how to earn money, how to budget money wisely, and where to invest money.

Reed, Jean, *Resumes That Get Jobs*, Arco. Explains the steps of job hunting, with a focus on writing effective resumes.

The United States in Today's World

UNIT 7

CHAPTER 21 ★ Establishing Our Foreign Policy

UNITED KINGDOM • UNITED STATES • YUGOSLAVIA • ZAMBIA • UNION OF SOVIET SOCIALIST REPUBLICS

Chapter Sections

1 **Conducting Our Foreign Relations**
2 **Working for Peace**
3 **The United Nations**

Chapter Focus

The United States is a leader among the nations of the world. Our country has long been a haven for people who seek freedom. Our military has come to the assistance of peaceful countries threatened by powerful neighbors. And our Constitution has served as the model for the constitutions of many other countries.

As a world leader, the United States has accepted a great deal of responsibility. Many countries turn to us for advice and help. Other countries are opposed to American ideals, and could threaten our country and our friends. Helping our friends and guarding against potential enemies are enormous responsibilities.

Moreover, we are living in an increasingly complex and dangerous world. Many countries now have nuclear weapons. A large-scale war could threaten civilization.

Dramatic changes in the countries of Eastern Europe in recent years have raised new questions. More than ever, the leaders of the world are seeking ways to improve relations among nations and bring about peace.

As a world leader, the United States devotes a great deal of energy to addressing these international concerns. Thousands of American officials participate in the work of foreign policy. Our ultimate goal is a peaceful and free world in which the people of all nations can prosper.

Study Guide

As you begin to learn about our country's relations with the other countries of the world, look for answers to the following questions:

★ What roles do the executive and legislative branches play in establishing and conducting our foreign policy?

★ What is the chief goal of our foreign policy, and how do we try to achieve it?

★ What is the United Nations, and how does it try to improve life for all people?

1 Conducting Our Foreign Relations

The plan that our nation works out for dealing with other nations is called our **foreign policy.** The purpose of this policy is to maintain peace, trade, and friendship throughout the world. The way in which this policy is carried out and its success or failure affects our **foreign relations.** That means it affects the way we get along with the governments of other nations.

In carrying out its foreign policy, the United States depends on a number of people. Government officials make contact with the leaders of other nations. Businesses and corporations carry on foreign trade, which affects our foreign relations. Even United States tourists traveling in other nations may influence the attitude of other people toward our nation.

How does the United States government establish our foreign policy?

The President and Foreign Relations

President Harry S. Truman once said, "I make American foreign policy." By this he meant that the President is responsible for the conduct of our nation's foreign policy. Although assisted by officials of the Department of State and other advisers, the President is responsible for the major decisions. Article II, Section 2, of the Constitution of the United States gives the President the following powers concerning foreign relations:

1. Military Powers. As Commander in Chief of the armed forces of the United States, the President makes recommendations to Congress concerning the size of the military and the kinds of weapons we need. Only Congress can declare war, but the President can order troops, planes, and warships into the world's trouble spots. However, the War Powers Act requires troops sent abroad to be recalled within 60 days unless Congress approves the action.

2. Treaty-Making Powers. Written agreements, or treaties, with other nations are an important part of our foreign relations. With the advice and consent of the Senate, the President has the power to make three kinds of treaties.

Peace treaties are agreements to end wars. Peace treaties spell out the terms for ending the fighting. They must be consented to by all sides in the conflict. **Alliance treaties** are agreements in which nations promise to help defend each other in case of attack. The United States has established alliances with many nations of the world. **Commercial treaties,** or **trade treaties,** are agreements by two or more nations to trade with each other on favorable terms.

All treaties must be approved by a two-thirds vote of the Senate. However, our nation sometimes reaches agreements with other

The President meets often with other leaders. President Reagan, for example, met often with Great Britain's former Prime Minister Margaret Thatcher.

power of **diplomatic recognition.** That is, the President may decide whether to recognize the government of a foreign nation. To recognize a foreign government means to establish official relations with that government. Sending an American ambassador to that country and receiving that nation's ambassador means that official recognition has taken place.

The President may refuse to recognize a government whose foreign policies are considered unfriendly or dangerous to the United States or its allies. For many years, the United States refused to recognize the communist government of China. Recognition was granted in the 1970's. The two countries then exchanged ambassadors.

Sometimes it is necessary to break off relations with a foreign nation. Breaking off relations means ending all official dealings with that nation. In breaking off relations, the United States recalls our ambassador, and the other nation's ambassador returns home. The United States broke off relations with Iran in 1980 when American diplomats were held hostage there. Breaking off relations is a very serious move. It occurs rarely, and only when two nations are unable to settle a serious dispute.

In establishing and carrying out our foreign policy, the President may call upon any department of the government for assistance. The President also hires foreign policy experts to assist in this important responsibility. These policy-making experts are part of the Executive Office of the President.

nations without the signing of treaties. The President of the United States and the leader of a foreign government may meet and come to a mutual understanding. This is known as an **executive agreement.** The agreement is then announced in a joint statement to the people of the two nations. Or the leaders may exchange official letters or notes in which they spell out details of their agreement. Executive agreements have been used much more often in recent years.

3. Diplomatic Powers. The President, again with the approval of the Senate, appoints **ambassadors** to represent the United States in foreign nations. The President also receives ambassadors from other nations.

The right of the President to receive ambassadors from foreign nations includes the

The Department of State

The President establishes foreign policy. The Department of State is the principal organization for carrying out that policy. It also acts as "the eyes and ears of the President" in obtaining information upon which our foreign relations are based.

The Department of State is headed by the Secretary of State, who is appointed by the

President with the approval of the Senate. The Secretary of State reports directly to the President and is assisted by a deputy secretary, undersecretaries, and many assistant secretaries.

The Secretary of State advises the President and supervises the activities of American ambassadors. The ambassadors are our nation's major representatives in other nations. They are stationed in the capital cities of most foreign nations.

In a few smaller nations, American representatives are known as **ministers.** In many foreign cities, American representatives who are known as **consuls** help American business people and travelers. Ambassadors, ministers, and consuls, with their assistants, are members of our **diplomatic corps.**

Members of the diplomatic corps work for friendly relations with the nations in which they are stationed. They report to the Secretary of State on any events of importance that are happening there. Their reports are sent in secret code. Or they may be carried by special messengers called **couriers.** Sometimes ambassadors or ministers will hurry to Washington to meet with the Secretary of State or the President on some special problem.

Information obtained in this way helps the President and advisers to decide on our policy and actions toward other countries. American consuls also send regular reports on business and trade conditions. These reports help American businesses plan their operations in foreign countries.

The Department of Defense

An important source of military information for the President is the Department of Defense. The Secretary of Defense advises the President on troop movements, placement of military bases at home and abroad, and development of weapons.

The Secretary of Defense and the President receive advice on military matters from the Joint Chiefs of Staff. The Joint Chiefs include a chairperson and the highest-ranking military officer of the Army, Navy, Air Force, and Marines. All these officials are appointed by the President.

Agencies Assist the President

Every other department of the executive branch of our government also becomes involved in foreign policy at various times. The Secretary of Agriculture, for example, keeps the President advised of available surplus foods that may be sent to a needy nation. The Secretary of the Treasury handles the financial transactions relating to assistance to other countries. The Secretary of Health and Human Services supplies information essential to medical assistance for foreign lands. Other executive departments assist in their fields of specialization.

In addition to the assistance and the advice provided by the regular departments, Congress has established a number of specialized agencies to help establish and carry out our nation's foreign policy. You are already familiar with some of these specialized agencies from your study of Chapter 6.

The **Central Intelligence Agency (CIA)** is responsible for gathering secret information essential to our national defense. The CIA also helps keep the President informed about political trends in various nations.

(continued on page 428)

Can You Guess?

- Who was the first American President to win a Nobel Peace Prize?
- Who was the first American President to travel to Europe while in office? (Hint: He was also the second President to win a Nobel Peace Prize.)

Answers are on page 594.

Bill of Rights

A Dream of Democracy

The early morning hours of June 5, 1989, were pierced by the sounds of gunfire in downtown Beijing, the capital of China. With the gunfire came other noises: wailing sirens, rumbling tanks, and, worst of all, the sounds of tens of thousands of people fleeing in terror.

These people were ordinary citizens who had gathered in Beijing's Tiananmen Square to call for democratic reforms in China's communist government. Over the previous seven weeks, more than one million people had gathered to proclaim with one voice their dream of democracy.

Tensions grew in Tiananmen Square as it became clear that the government had no intention of responding to the citizens' pleas. The government finally ended the seven-week-old demonstration brutally: they ordered units of the Chinese army to clear the square. Firing on their fellow citizens, the army injured thousands of people and killed over 1,000 more.

What had prompted so many people to risk their lives? This question was answered by a demonstrator a few days before the massacre. He said simply, "We want the rights Americans have."

One of the rights Americans cherish and the Chinese bravely sought is guaranteed to us by the First Amendment to the Constitution. This right is freedom of the press.

A Call for Truth

The people of China had grown increasingly frustrated in the months leading up to the Tiananmen Square massacre. They believed that the Chinese communist government was corrupt, and that government decisions served the leaders rather than the nation and its people.

An end to government corruption, however, was not all the protestors sought. Their most deeply felt desire was for democracy, and they knew that the first step toward democracy is the creation of a free press. The protestors believed that an open and honest exchange of ideas would expose government corruption and pave the way for democratic reforms.

The Chinese students constructed this "Goddess of Liberty," based on our Statue of Liberty, to symbolize their dream of freedom and democracy.

The Power of the Press

China, like most communist countries, has a long history of suppressing the news. Typically, the government censors reporters and uses the news media as a pipeline for government propaganda. By controlling the press, communist leaders also stop critics of the government from telling the truth to the public. Controlling the press is the key to controlling a nation's people.

The protestors in Beijing knew the power of the press. And they knew that a government that fears a free press is a government that fears the truth. Among the protestors' strongest supporters were Chinese journalists. For years, these men and women had been forced to report only what the government wanted them to say. With great courage, many of them reported on the protests in Tiananmen Square, only to have the government quickly censor them.

The Truth Is Revealed

The communist leaders of China tried to keep the news of the massacre from reaching the rest of the world. They warned foreign journalists who were in China not to report on the protests. Government leaders banned all live broadcasts from China. But the tactics that had censored reporters in China could not stop the foreign journalists from reporting the news of the massacre to a shocked and outraged world.

Reporters from the United States, a country founded on the ideal of free expression, went to great lengths to tell the story of Tiananmen Square. The bravery of these journalists and their dedication to the truth proved the power of the press. Without our American free press, we never would have known about the hunger of others for democracy.

Over one million Chinese citizens gathered in Tiananmen Square in 1989 to proclaim the need for changes in the Chinese communist government. Because of our First Amendment right to a free press, Americans were able to witness this historic plea for democracy.

Questions to Consider

1. Why were Chinese citizens protesting in Tiananmen Square?
2. How did the Chinese government respond to the protestors in Tiananmen Square?
3. How do the events surrounding the protest illustrate the power of a free press?

President George Bush meets often with his Cabinet members and advisers to decide on important foreign policy issues.

The **National Security Council (NSC)** is part of the Executive Office of the President. Its members are the President, the Vice President, and the Secretaries of State and Defense. The chairperson of the Joint Chiefs of Staff and the director of the Central Intelligence Agency attend all NSC meetings. The NSC was created to help coordinate American military and foreign policy.

The **United States Information Agency (USIA)** helps keep the world informed about the American way of life and about American points of view on world problems. It does this through information centers set up in 127 countries around the world. The USIA also publishes booklets, distributes films, and sponsors "Voice of America" radio programs. It was formerly called the International Communications Agency.

The **Arms Control and Disarmament Agency** seeks to prevent dangerous weapons-building races. It does so by negotiating with other nations and seeking to reach agreements on arms limitations.

Another group established to influence our foreign relations is the **Agency for International Development.** It provides technical and financial assistance to developing nations. This agency has provided billions of dollars worth of modern machinery, raw materials, food, fuel, medical supplies, and loans to help the world's peoples. The agency also provides money and technical assistance during emergencies resulting from floods, epidemics, and other disasters.

Congress and Foreign Relations

The President leads our nation in dealing with world affairs. Congress also plays a major role. It is essential that the President work closely with leaders in both houses of Congress when deciding on foreign policies. It is the responsibility of the Senate Foreign Relations Committee and the House Committee on Foreign Affairs to make important recommendations to Congress and the President on questions of foreign relations.

1. Approval Powers. The Senate, as you know, must approve all treaties between the United States and other nations by a two-thirds vote. What happens if the Senate refuses to approve a treaty?

After World War I, President Woodrow Wilson wanted the United States to join the League of Nations. A provision for joining this peace-keeping organization was included as a part of the Treaty of Versailles that ended World War I. However, a powerful group of senators opposed membership of the United States in the League of Nations. These senators wanted the United States to stay out of European affairs and to concentrate on solving its own problems. They eventually succeeded in preventing a two-thirds majority vote in the Senate in favor of the treaty. As a result, the United States did not approve the Treaty of Versailles or join the League of Nations.

The Senate also must approve the appointment of all ambassadors by majority vote. The President's nominations are almost always approved.

2. War-Making Powers. Under the Constitution of the United States, as you recall, only Congress can declare war. Over the years, however, Presidents have sent troops to fight in foreign countries without a declaration of war. In 1973 Congress passed the War Powers Act. This act limits the President's power to commit troops abroad without the approval of Congress.

3. Financial Powers. As you have read, both houses of Congress must approve all expenditures of public funds. This too gives Congress power in foreign affairs. All spending for national defense, for example, must be approved by Congress. The President may recommend that a new weapon be built or that our armed forces be expanded. Unless Congress votes for the necessary money, however, these policies cannot be carried out.

SECTION 1 REVIEW

Define foreign policy, foreign relations, peace treaties, alliance treaties, commercial treaties, trade treaties, executive agreement, ambassadors, diplomatic recognition, ministers, consuls, diplomatic corps, couriers

Identify Central Intelligence Agency (CIA), National Security Council (NSC), United States Information Agency (USIA), Arms Control and Disarmament Agency, Agency for International Development

1. **Understanding Ideas (a)** What are the purposes of our foreign policy? **(b)** How do businesses and tourists affect our foreign relations?
2. **Identifying Roles (a)** List and describe the three basic foreign relations powers of the President of the United States. **(b)** How do the Department of State and the Department of Defense assist the President in conducting foreign affairs?
3. **Seeing Relationships (a)** What are the executive agencies that help the President of the United States carry out our nation's foreign policy? **(b)** How can Congress check the President's activities in international affairs?

Thinking Critically List and explain three ways you think our country can promote peace, trade, and friendship throughout the world.

Working for Peace

The fact that so many departments and agencies of our government devote so much time to foreign affairs indicates its importance to us. The chief goal of our foreign policy is to maintain peace in the world. Government officials work to achieve this goal in a number of ways.

Diplomacy

The process of conducting relations between nations, as you recall, is called **diplomacy.** It is used to prevent war, negotiate an end to conflicts, solve problems, and establish communication between nations. As you know, the President is our nation's chief diplomat.

To carry out this role, Presidents make frequent use of **personal diplomacy.** That is, they travel to other countries to meet with foreign leaders. They also confer with foreign leaders and ambassadors in the United States. One example of personal diplomacy is the **summit.** This is a meeting with the heads of other nations, or heads of state, as they are sometimes called. Summit conferences first became popular during World War II, when Allied leaders met several times to discuss wartime strategy.

Diplomacy is also carried out by other government officials. For example, State Department officials often represent the President in trying to settle conflicts between other nations. In recent years, American diplomats have flown back and forth between different nations so often that this kind of peace-seeking has become known as **shuttle diplomacy.**

Our Many Alliances

The United States has alliances with many individual nations, such as Japan, South Korea, and the Philippines. It has also established alliances with several large groups of nations.

The **North Atlantic Treaty Organization (NATO)** includes the following 16 nations: the United States, Belgium, Canada, Denmark, France, Great Britain, Greece, Iceland, Italy, Luxembourg, the Netherlands, Norway, Portugal, Turkey, Spain, and Germany. NATO was created in 1949 to establish a united front against the threat of aggression by the Soviet Union in Europe and the Middle East. The members of NATO have agreed that "armed attack against one will be considered an attack on all."

President Bush and Soviet President Mikhail Gorbachev have used summits to establish effective communications between their two nations.

In recent years, however, changes in the policies of the Soviet Union and its allies have lessened the threat of attack. As a result, NATO is in the process of deciding what role it will play in the coming years.

Australia, New Zealand, and the United States are joined in an alliance called **ANZUS,** established in 1951. Its purpose is to protect the mutual interests of the member nations.

In the Western Hemisphere, the United States and most of the nations of Latin America formed the **Organization of American States (OAS)** in 1948. The goal of the OAS is to defend the member nations and work for peace.

Foreign Aid

Our nation also uses foreign aid to help achieve its foreign policy goals. **Foreign aid** is a government program that provides economic and military assistance to other nations. Our country first gave large amounts of foreign aid during World War II. After the war, the nations of Europe needed help. People needed food, clothing, housing, and jobs.

In 1947 the United States Secretary of State, George Marshall, proposed a plan to help the nations of Europe rebuild their factories, farms, homes, and transportation systems. Congress agreed that these nations needed American help. It granted $13 billion for aid under the **Marshall Plan.** By 1952 the economies of Western Europe had recovered to a remarkable degree. Marshall Plan aid, having done its job, was ended.

Since World War II, the United States has given or loaned about $1 trillion in aid to nations around the world. Some of this aid has been in the form of grants, or gifts. In recent years, it has more often been in the form of low-interest loans. A large part of American foreign aid is managed through the Agency for International Development.

In the past few years, about one percent of our federal budget has been spent on foreign

Peace Corps volunteers work in many countries throughout the world. This volunteer is explaining to people in Ecuador the dangers of tooth decay.

aid. More than 50 nations have received military assistance to help them maintain their independence. Economic assistance has been given to help new nations in Africa and Asia become self-supporting. Foodstuffs, such as wheat, corn, and rice, have been sent from the United States to help feed the hungry people of the world.

Another kind of foreign aid has been provided by individual Americans. President John F. Kennedy established the **Peace Corps** in the early 1960's to send volunteers into countries that requested help. Peace Corps volunteers in such fields as teaching, farming, medicine, and industry have worked in countries throughout the world.

American foreign aid sometimes takes the form of food for the victims of famine. Here food has been sent to starving people in Africa's Sahara.

Questions About Foreign Aid

Should the United States continue to spend one percent of its federal budget on foreign aid? Should it spend more? Should it spend less? Foreign aid has always been a controversial subject. There are many arguments for and against foreign aid.

Those who favor foreign aid point to the necessity of assisting developing nations. If we do not help, they say, these nations may turn for aid to countries that are unfriendly to the United States. Supporters of foreign aid argue, too, that our wealthy nation should not watch people starve without offering assistance. The foreign aid we have given in the past, they say, has helped build stronger nations and has contributed to world peace. They also point out that most of the foreign aid money is spent by foreign nations to buy American goods and services.

Those people who oppose giving foreign aid claim that it is wasteful and that it takes money out of our nation. They also argue that we should not bear so many of the world's burdens. Some critics believe that too much aid is in the form of military assistance. They question whether this kind of aid helps peace. Critics also oppose giving foreign aid to countries that are dictatorships or that violate the human rights of their citizens.

Foreign Trade

Trade is another important part of American foreign policy. Early in American history, our nation began to collect taxes on certain imported goods. These taxes, or tariffs, were intended to protect American industries from foreign competition. As you read in Chapter 12, such taxes are called **protective tariffs.**

Tariff rates were set high enough so that the prices stores had to charge for imported goods were equal to, or higher than, the prices of similar goods made in the United States.

A protective tariff helps American manufacturers. Yet it also means American consumers must pay more for what they buy.

Many nations have used protective tariffs. This sometimes causes difficulties in relations among nations. When an importing nation raises its tariffs, an exporting nation loses business. Sometimes when one nation raises its tariffs, other nations do the same. These "tariff wars" harm international trade.

To improve world trade, the United States and many other nations have joined in a General Agreement on Tariffs and Trade (GATT). This agreement helps encourage **free trade,** or trade not restricted by tariffs and other trade barriers. We have also made **reciprocal trade agreements** with other countries. Under these agreements, both sides consent to lower certain tariffs.

Congress has given the President power to raise or lower tariffs when it is believed the change will be in the national interest. This power makes it possible for the President to take prompt action in lowering tariffs when certain materials or products are in short supply and imports need to be encouraged. Tariffs may also be raised to discourage certain imports. The President may raise all tariffs and then work out lower reciprocal rates with individual nations.

Balance of Trade

Foreign trade involves both what our country sells to other countries, or **exports,** and what we buy from them, or **imports.** The difference in value between the nation's exports and imports is called the **balance of trade.** In recent years, the United States has suffered serious trade deficits. This means more dollars are going out of the country to buy foreign goods

Trade is an important part of our nation's foreign relations. Each year we export American-made products and import goods from around the world.

than are coming into the country from those who buy American goods. The deficit creates problems for our economy.

Much of the deficit is caused by the increase in the price of oil, or petroleum. The price of most oil imported by the United States is set by members of the **Organization of Petroleum Exporting Countries (OPEC).** It consists of the major oil-exporting countries. The cost of a barrel of oil rose from $2.50 in 1970 to about $14.00 in 1989.

Another major cause of the trade deficit is the rising productivity of other countries. Japan, for example, has increased its productivity faster than the United States. As a result, American consumers can buy Japanese goods at a lower price than they must pay for similar goods made in the United States.

 SECTION 2 REVIEW

Define diplomacy, personal diplomacy, summit, shuttle diplomacy, foreign aid, protective tariffs, free trade, reciprocal trade agreements, exports, imports, balance of trade

Identify North Atlantic Treaty Organization (NATO), ANZUS, Organization of American States (OAS), Marshall Plan, Peace Corps, Organization of Petroleum Exporting Countries (OPEC)

1. **Identifying Roles** In what ways does the President carry out the role of our nation's chief diplomat?
2. **Understanding Ideas** What are the purposes of our alliances with other nations?
3. **Summarizing Ideas** Summarize the arguments for and against American foreign aid.
4. **Identifying Ideas** Why has the United States had a trade deficit in recent years?

Thinking Critically You are the Secretary of State. The President has asked you whether the United States should provide foreign aid to a country whose government violates human rights. What is your answer, and why?

3 The United Nations

In 1941 President Franklin D. Roosevelt met with Winston Churchill, the prime minister of Great Britain, to discuss the aims of the Allies in World War II. The meeting was held on a ship in the Atlantic Ocean off the coast of Newfoundland. The agreement reached by these two leaders was known as the **Atlantic Charter.** This document stated the following principles:

1. No nation should try to gain territory as a result of the war.

2. All peoples should have the right to choose the kind of government they want.

3. All nations should have the right to trade and secure raw materials.

4. The peoples of the world should be able to live free from fear or want.

5. Nations in the future should not use military force to try to settle their international disputes.

The principles set forth in the Atlantic Charter have continued to guide the nations of the world in their search for peace.

Forming the United Nations

In 1945 representatives from 50 nations met in San Francisco to form an organization that would stress peaceful coexistence and cooperation among all the nations of the world. This organization is called the **United Nations (UN).** In its constitution, or charter, the nations pledged to save the people of the future from war. They also agreed to support basic human rights, including the equal rights of men and women and of large and small nations. They promised, as well, to live together in peace as good neighbors.

Today the United Nations is an international organization with more than 150 permanent members. Its headquarters is located in New York City.

How the United Nations Is Organized

The United Nations is organized into six main divisions. You can see the organization of the United Nations in the chart on page 436 of your textbook. The six divisions are described briefly below.

1. General Assembly. The body that discusses, debates, and recommends solutions for problems that come before the United Nations is called the **General Assembly.** Each member nation has one vote in the General Assembly. All important issues, such as decisions on matters concerning world peace, adding new members, or passing the budget, must be agreed upon by a two-thirds majority in the Assembly. Other issues are decided by a simple majority vote.

The Assembly meets annually. Its sessions begin on the third Tuesday in September. If necessary, it may be called into emergency session at any time. The Assembly elects its own president and makes its own rules of procedure.

2. Security Council. The body mainly responsible for keeping the peace is the **Security Council.** It is composed of 15 members. There are five permanent members: the United States, the Soviet Union, Great Britain, France, and China. Ten temporary members are chosen by the General Assembly for two-year terms. The 15 countries are each represented by one delegate.

All measures that come before the Security Council must receive the vote of 9 of the 15 members in order to pass. However, if one of the permanent members of the Council votes against it, or vetoes it, the measure is automatically defeated.

To help prevent war, the Security Council may call upon quarreling nations to work out a peaceful settlement. If any nation refuses to negotiate or refuses the Council's offer to help settle the dispute, the Council may take action. It may call upon all members of the United Nations to break off relations and end all trade with the offending nation.

The United Nations was founded by 50 nations in 1945. Today the flags of most nations of the world fly outside UN headquarters in New York City.

If all else fails, the Security Council may recommend that United Nations members use military force against an aggressor nation or nations. When North Korea invaded South Korea in 1950, the Council asked members of the United Nations to send troops to help South Korea. The United States and 15 other nations responded.

3. International Court of Justice. Member nations may take disputes about international law to the United Nations law court—the **International Court of Justice.** They do not have to do so, but many disputing nations have voluntarily agreed to come before the Court. It is also known as the **World Court.**

The Court consists of 15 judges from various nations who are elected for nine-year terms by the General Assembly and the Security Council. The Court's decisions are made by majority vote. The Court meets at The Hague, in the Netherlands. It may be called upon by members to decide such matters as boundary disputes, debt payments, and interpretations of the UN Charter.

4. Economic and Social Council. The General Assembly elects representatives from 54 nations to serve as members of the **Economic and Social Council.** This group conducts studies on such important topics as the use of narcotic drugs, human rights, and international trade. It may then make recommendations to the General Assembly.

5. Trusteeship Council. Certain islands and other areas of the world that were once colonies are supervised by the **Trusteeship Council.** It assists these areas to prepare for self-government. The United States and other nations act as trustees and are responsible for the progress of the trustee areas. Trustees make an official report to the Trusteeship Council each year. The council also sends committees to trustee areas to inspect conditions there.

6. Secretariat. The day-to-day activities of the United Nations are carried out by the **Secretariat.** This division has a staff of more than 9,000 clerks, typists, guides, translators, research experts, technicians, and administrators.

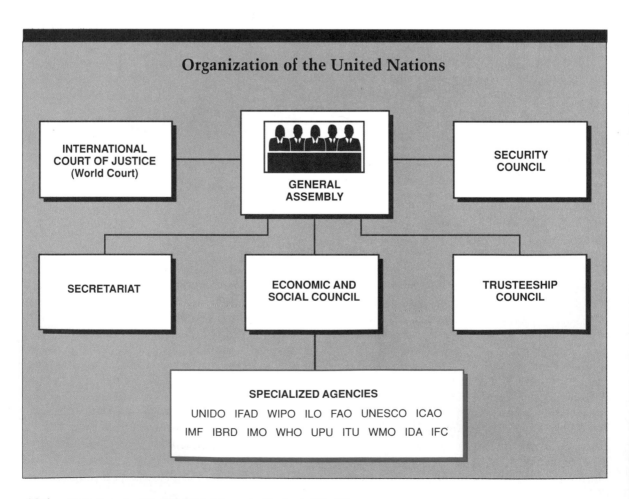

Organization of the United Nations

INTERNATIONAL COURT OF JUSTICE (World Court)

GENERAL ASSEMBLY

SECURITY COUNCIL

SECRETARIAT

ECONOMIC AND SOCIAL COUNCIL

TRUSTEESHIP COUNCIL

SPECIALIZED AGENCIES

UNIDO IFAD WIPO ILO FAO UNESCO ICAO

IMF IBRD IMO WHO UPU ITU WMO IDA IFC

The person in charge of the Secretariat is the **Secretary General,** who is elected by the General Assembly for a five-year term. The Secretary General is the chief executive of the United Nations. The Secretary General prepares the agenda for the meetings of the General Assembly, Security Council, Trusteeship Council, and Economic and Social Council. The Secretary General is also responsible for carrying out the decisions of these bodies. The Secretary General may bring before the United Nations any problems that threaten world peace.

The United Nations Depends Upon Cooperation

The United Nations has no armed forces of its own. Without the cooperation of its members, it cannot keep the peace. At certain times it has obtained soldiers from its members to carry on a "police action." Usually it relies upon moral persuasion, or a sense of obligation on the part of its member nations, in settling disputes.

In other words, the United Nations is not a supergovernment that can force its will upon its members. The United Nations has become a kind of "town meeting" of the world. There all nations have an opportunity to express their points of view about conditions that threaten the peace.

One of the best examples of cooperation among nations that has resulted from the United Nations is the United Nations Children's Fund, or UNICEF. At its first meeting, the United Nations decided to do something for the children of the world. UNICEF was set up as a special United Nations committee to help care for sick and hungry children throughout the world.

Specialized Agencies

Much of the work accomplished by the United Nations is carried out through its many specialized agencies. These agencies have worked to improve the lives of people in many parts of the world.

Each agency is independent of the main body of the United Nations. The Economic and Social Council is responsible for ensuring that the United Nations and the many specialized agencies work together to help the people of the world. What are some of these specialized agencies, and what do they do?

WHO. The World Health Organization (WHO) is fighting a worldwide battle against disease. The weapons used in this battle are medicine, insect sprays, vaccines, sanitation programs, water purification, and health education. WHO has a great victory to its credit. A worldwide vaccination program conducted by WHO succeeded in eliminating smallpox from the world.

FAO. The Food and Agriculture Organization (FAO) helps nations grow more and better food for their people. For example, FAO has helped develop a special kind of disease-resistant rice in India. It has introduced steel plows in developing nations. FAO experts are helping many nations with forest planting, soil conservation, irrigation, and improvement of farming methods.

UNESCO. The United Nations Educational, Scientific, and Cultural Organization (UNESCO) was established to extend educational opportunities everywhere in the world. People who cannot read or write are often unable to learn new and better ways of doing things. UNESCO has sponsored programs to set up schools in developing nations. In addition, it encourages people to protect and develop their traditional cultures.

In recent years, however, UNESCO has been the center of controversy. A major problem is the attempt by some nations to use the agency for political purposes. Because of the problem within UNESCO, the United States withdrew from the agency in 1984.

IBRD. The International Bank for Reconstruction and Development (IBRD), usually called the World Bank, makes loans and gives technical advice to help nations improve

The World Health Organization brings medical care to people in remote areas of the world. It has helped improve the health of millions of people.

their economies. It is assisted by two other agencies, the International Development Association (IDA) and the International Finance Corporation (IFC). The IBRD has loaned more than $15 billion a year to developing nations.

ITU. The International Telecommunication Union works to promote international electronic communication. The ITU establishes international regulations and conducts research to improve communication.

Other Specialized Agencies. If you study the chart of the United Nations organization, you will see that there are many other specialized agencies. They include the International Labor Organization (ILO), which attempts to improve the welfare of the world's workers. The World Meteorological Organization (WMO) keeps a world weather watch to obtain data for long-range weather forecasting. The International Civil Aviation Organization (ICAO) promotes safety in air transportation. The International Monetary Fund (IMF) promotes world trade.

Other specialized agencies of the United Nations are the Universal Postal Union (UPU), the World Intellectual Property Or-

ganization (WIPO), the Intergovernmental Maritime Organization (IMO), the United Nations Industrial Development Organization (UNIDO), and the International Fund for Agricultural Development (IFAD).

Arguments For and Against the United Nations

Some Americans are critical of the United Nations. They believe that the United States pays more than its fair share of the costs of operating the organization. They point out that the many small nations can outvote the large nations in the General Assembly. They argue that the organization has failed to create a permanent police force to prevent military attacks and stop trouble.

On the other hand, some Americans believe the United Nations is the world's best hope for peace. They note that it has frequently succeeded in leading quarreling nations to the conference table. They do not believe the lack of a United Nations police force is a problem. They argue that such a force, over which we would have no control, would be unacceptable to our nation or any other world power. Those in favor of the United Nations claim that creating a forum in which all nations can be heard is a good way to encourage world peace.

SECTION 3 REVIEW

Identify Atlantic Charter, United Nations (UN), General Assembly, Security Council, International Court of Justice, World Court, Economic and Social Council, Trusteeship Council, Secretariat, Secretary General

1. **Seeing Relationships** Why was the United Nations formed?
2. **Organizing Ideas** Briefly describe the organization of the United Nations.
3. **Identifying Roles** List and describe the activities of several of the specialized agencies of the United Nations.
4. **Summarizing Ideas** What are the arguments for and against the United Nations?

Thinking Critically You are Secretary General of the United Nations. Representatives of several countries have suggested that the United Nations create an army to enforce its decisions. Will you support their idea? Explain your position.

The plan our nation follows in dealing with other nations is called our foreign policy. The goals of American foreign policy are peace, prosperity, and friendship. To keep the peace and advance American interests, we send ambassadors, ministers, and consuls to represent us in other nations. We in turn receive representatives from other nations.

The President is responsible for conducting our foreign relations. The President is assisted by personal advisers, the Department of State, and other departments and agencies of the executive branch.

Congress, too, is concerned with foreign affairs. It votes the money needed to carry out the nation's policies. The Senate must approve all treaties and the appointments of representatives to foreign lands.

The United States plays a large role in the world today. The President and officials of the State Department engage in personal diplomacy with world leaders. Alliances with other nations serve mutual defense and security needs. Foreign aid helps developing nations grow and protect themselves. The United States carries on trade with other nations and promotes the flow of goods among nations.

The United Nations provides an organization in which nations may discuss serious problems and work out reasonable solutions. The specialized agencies of the United Nations work to serve the needs of the people of the world. The future of this world organization depends upon the willingness and ability of nations to work together in peace.

SOCIAL STUDIES SKILL
Reading a Table

The United States shares the globe with 169 other countries, and we have some kind of relationship with virtually every one of them. Nearly every nation has received some kind of American aid at one time or another. We trade with most nations, and have alliances, agreements, and treaties with many more. Keeping track of the many types of relationships we have with so many countries can be very confusing. How can you make sense of it all?

One effective way to clarify large amounts of information is to use a table. Like a graph, a table condenses a great deal of data into a format that is easy to read and understand.

How to Read a Table

To read a table effectively, follow these guidelines.

1. **Determine the purpose of the table.** Read the title of the table to determine the subject and purpose of the table. This will give you a good general idea of what you will learn from the table.
2. **Study the headings.** Tables have several headings. Each vertical column has its own heading. There are also headings to the left of each horizontal row. Read the headings, and make sure you know which row or column each one refers to. Also make sure you understand the meaning of each label before you attempt to use the table.
3. **Analyze the information.** To locate specific facts on a table, you simply look down a vertical column and across a horizontal row. Where the column and row intersect, or meet, is where you will find the data you need.
4. **Put the data to use.** Use the table to draw conclusions about the data. Try to identify any trends or make any generalizations about the information. You should look

for trends down each column and along each row.

Applying the Skill

Use the table below to answer the following questions.
1. What years does the table cover?
2. What is the meaning of the minus signs ($-$) in the "Balance" column?
3. What was the United States balance of trade in 1985? What was it in 1987?
4. **(a)** Do you see any trend in the value of United States exports in the years covered by the table? Describe it. **(b)** Do you see any trend in the amount of goods the United States imports? Describe it. **(c)** How has the United States balance of trade changed during the years covered by the table?
5. How might government officials put the information in this table to use?

United States Balance of Trade
1983–1988
(in billions of dollars)

YEAR	EXPORTS	IMPORTS	BALANCE
1983	200.5	258.0	$-$ 57.5
1984	217.9	325.7	$-$107.8
1985	213.1	345.3	$-$132.2
1986	217.3	370.0	$-$152.7
1987	254.1	406.2	$-$152.1
1988	322.2	440.9	$-$118.7

Reviewing Terms

On a separate sheet of paper, copy the paragraph below. Then fill in each blank, using the correct term from the following list.

foreign policy   treaties
couriers   foreign relations
executive agreements   diplomatic corps

As a world power, our (1) _____ _____, or the way we get along with other governments, are very important. To improve them, we have developed a (2) _____ _____ to maintain peace, trade, and friendship throughout the world. To carry out this policy, the President has the power to make (3) _____, or written agreements, with other nations. The President also has the power to make (4) _____ _____ with the leaders of other countries. Our representatives in other countries make up the (5) _____ _____. In order to communicate with the Secretary of State and the President, these representatives sometimes use (6) _____, or special messengers.

Using Thinking Skills

1. **Understanding Ideas (a)** Why does the United States enter alliances with other countries? **(b)** Why does the United States provide foreign aid? **(c)** What are the basic arguments for and against foreign aid?
2. **Summarizing Ideas (a)** What are some of the objections people have to the United Nations? **(b)** What are the major arguments in support of the United Nations?
3. **Drawing Conclusions (a)** What are the goals of our foreign policy? **(b)** How does the diplomatic corps support this policy?
4. **Seeing Relationships (a)** What is the purpose of the United Nations? **(b)** How does the United Nations strive to achieve its goal?

5. **Identifying Roles (a)** Describe the President's powers as chief diplomat. **(b)** How does the executive branch help the President carry out foreign policy? **(c)** What is Congress's role in foreign policy?
6. **Classifying Ideas (a)** What types of treaties does the United States make with other countries? **(b)** What happens if the Senate does not approve a treaty?
7. **Composing a Paragraph** How do private citizens affect our foreign relations?

Practicing Civics Skills

Creating a Table The estimated figures below come from a United Nations study of world population. Organize this information into a table entitled "World Population Growth: 1990–2025." On the basis of your table, what conclusions can you draw about population changes in the coming years?

1990: Africa—645 million; Asia—3,057 million; Europe—500 million; Latin America—453 million; North America—275 million; Oceania—27 million; Soviet Union—291 million

2025: Africa—1,643 million; Asia—4,467 million; Europe—527 million; Latin America—787 million; North America—347 million; Oceania—40 million; Soviet Union—367 million

Being a Good Citizen

1. Conduct library research and contact the Peace Corps to find out about the history, goals, and work of this organization.
2. Conduct a mock meeting of the United Nations. Organize the class into groups representing countries. Choose a current issue and conduct research to find out each country's position on the issue.
3. Write an essay on the role the UN has played in an international conflict. Then evaluate the effects of its participation.

CHAPTER 22

Changing Foreign Policies for Changing Times

Chapter Sections

Chapter Focus

More than 200 years ago, Thomas Jefferson headed the State Department, with its staff of about half a dozen people and a budget of about $6,000. Today more than 25,000 people work in the State Department. Their budget exceeds $3.5 billion a year.

About 50 years ago, the United States had diplomatic relations with 60 nations. It was tied by treaties to only a few nations, and just a few hundred American troops were stationed in other nations. Today the United States has relations with more than 160 nations. It is tied to many nations by treaties. In addition, hundreds of thousands of American troops are now stationed overseas.

The United States has come a long way since its beginning in the late 1700's, when it was a small and weak nation. In those days many European nations wondered if the young American nation would even survive. What has enabled the United States not only to survive, but to become a world leader?

Study Guide

As you begin to learn about how American foreign policy has changed over time, look for answers to the following questions:
★ How did American foreign policy develop in the early years of our nation?
★ What was the Cold War, and how did it affect our foreign policy?
★ What recent world events are causing us to rethink our foreign policy?

1 The Development of American Foreign Policy

Our foreign policy has helped the nation grow. For many years the policy that worked best for our nation was to avoid involvement in the affairs of other nations. This policy of staying out of foreign affairs worked as long as the United States was somewhat isolated from the rest of the world.

Over time, however, transportation and communication systems improved. These developments allowed us to communicate and trade with other countries much more often. Because we had become more closely tied to other countries, we became interested in and involved with world affairs.

Isolationism

When our nation began, it was deeply in debt and struggling to build its economy. It was busy looking for solutions to many domestic problems. Most of the leaders of the new government thought that the United States

should concentrate on its own development and stay out of foreign affairs. This belief that the United States should avoid becoming involved in foreign concerns is known as **isolationism.**

At no time in our history has the policy of isolationism been an easy one to follow. Even in the late 1700's, President Washington found it difficult to practice this policy. To the north of the United States was the British colony of Canada and a troubled border situation. To the south and west lay Spanish territory. It blocked American expansion westward and threatened American commerce on the Mississippi River. When American ships ventured east into the Atlantic as they had to do to keep trade alive, they were stopped and seized by ships of the British or French navy.

The War of 1812

Finally, in 1812, it seemed that war with Great Britain could not be avoided. Americans claimed that Great Britain was turning the Indians on our western frontier against us, occupying forts on our soil, and taking American sailors off our ships. This was the time, they said, to take the British colony of Canada and make it a part of the United States.

The War of 1812 with Great Britain ended in a stalemate—neither side won a clear-cut victory. However, the peace treaty that ended the war led in time to improved relations with Great Britain. Most important, the War of 1812 won a new respect for the United States among the nations of Europe. For nearly 100 years following the war, the United States was able to stay out of European conflicts and build up the nation at home.

The United States and Canada

The War of 1812 also marked a turning point in our relations with Canada. American attempts to invade Canada during the war had

President James Monroe (center) meets with his Cabinet to develop an American policy prohibiting further European interference in Latin America.

proved unsuccessful. After the war, Canada, under Great Britain, and the United States began to build forts along their border and station fleets of warships on the Great Lakes. This was the kind of situation that could lead to border incidents and perhaps to war.

The leaders of both nations wisely decided to act to ensure the peace. In 1817 they met to talk over their differences and sign a treaty of friendship. The result was the **Rush-Bagot Agreement.** This treaty provided that the United States and Great Britain would settle their disputes with each other by peaceful means. As proof of their desire for peace, the two nations agreed that the boundary between the United States and Canada should no longer be fortified.

The friendly spirit of the Rush-Bagot Agreement has shaped our relations with Canada ever since. Today, the border between our two countries is the longest unfortified na-tional border in the world. Our neighbor to the north is one of our strongest allies.

The Monroe Doctrine

Most of the nations of Latin America, the region south of the United States, won their independence from Spain in the early 1800's. Yet Spain and its European allies were determined that Spain should win back its American colonies. For a while it looked as though Europe was about to interfere in the affairs of the new Latin American nations. The United States government decided that we had to take a stand to prevent the new Latin American nations from being conquered again by Spain or by any other European nation.

President James Monroe used his annual message to Congress in 1823 to let the world know what the United States thought about this matter. He declared that any attempt by European nations to interfere in the affairs of any nation in the Western Hemisphere would be considered by the United States to be an unfriendly act. He promised that we would not interfere in European concerns or those of European colonies already established in the Americas. But he also declared that the Americas were no longer open to colonization by European nations.

This policy came to be known as the **Monroe Doctrine** (see page 539). A foreign policy doctrine sets forth a new policy of action with respect to other nations. It is a statement of United States policy and is not necessarily an agreement with any other nation. The Monroe Doctrine set the course of our relations with Latin America as well as with Europe for many years.

The United States and Latin America

At first the nations of Latin America welcomed the support of the United States. As "watchdog of the Western world," the United States helped settle boundary disputes between Latin American countries. When certain European countries threatened to use force to collect debts owed by Latin American countries, the United States acted to prevent such interference. When Cuba rebelled against Spain in 1898, the United States declared war on Spain and easily defeated the Spanish fleet.

President Theodore Roosevelt strengthened the Monroe Doctrine in 1904. He declared that in the future the United States would take on the role of police officer of the Western Hemisphere. If Latin American countries could not manage their own affairs, the United States would step in. This policy became known as the **Roosevelt Corollary** to the Monroe Doctrine. A corollary is something that follows as a normal result.

Americans in growing numbers then began to invest money in Latin American companies. When these investments were threatened by internal disorders, the United States sometimes sent troops to keep the peace. Our policy in Latin America became known as **dollar diplomacy.**

The Good Neighbor Policy

In some ways, the actions of the United States in Latin America helped the nations there. However, these actions also stirred up bad feelings because they insulted the national pride of Latin American nations. Latin American leaders declared that the United States had turned from protector to oppressor. As a

Under the Good Neighbor Policy of President Franklin D. Roosevelt, the United States sought to improve relations with Latin America.

result, the United States took steps to improve its relations with Latin America.

In the 1920's the United States stated that the Monroe Doctrine would no longer be used to justify United States intervention in the internal affairs of any neighbor. In 1929 President Franklin D. Roosevelt announced the **Good Neighbor Policy.** This policy opposed armed intervention by the United States in Latin American affairs. Also, it emphasized friendly agreements. In 1948 nations of the Western Hemisphere joined together to form the Organization of American States (OAS).

The End of Isolationism

In 1914, when World War I broke out in Europe, the United States attempted to stay out of the conflict. President Woodrow Wilson announced a policy of **neutrality.** That is, the United States would neither assist nor favor either side. This policy was difficult to maintain. It became impossible when German submarines began to sink American merchant ships without warning and without regard for the safety of the passengers. In response to a war message by President Woodrow Wilson, Congress declared war on Germany in 1917.

President Wilson stated that our aim in fighting the war was to help "make the world safe for democracy." The victory of the Allies brought hope for peace. Wilson centered his hopes in a new international organization called the **League of Nations.** The League promised to solve disputes in a friendly fashion and go to war only as a last resort.

As you may recall, a provision for joining the League of Nations was submitted to the Senate as a part of the treaty ending World War I. Many Americans, however, including some powerful senators, opposed United States membership in the League. They feared that if the United States joined the League, our nation would be drawn into European conflicts. The spirit of isolationism was still strong. It helped keep the United States out of the League of Nations.

The beginning of World War II found the United States again in a neutral position. Con-

President Woodrow Wilson (in top hat) hoped to keep the United States out of World War I. He finally concluded that neutrality was impossible.

gress passed Neutrality Acts in the mid-1930's forbidding the sale of arms, or weapons, to warring nations. In 1939 the United States did agree to sell arms, but only on a "cash and carry" basis. The arms had to be carried in foreign ships. Soon the United States became the "arsenal of democracy," supplying arms needed by the Allies.

Once again our neutrality and the isolationist views of some Americans did not keep us out of war. The bombing of Pearl Harbor by the Japanese on December 7, 1941, shocked the American people. They realized that isolationism in a worldwide conflict was impossible (see page 543). The United States declared war on Japan and, soon afterward, on Germany and Italy.

While World War II was still being fought, plans were underway for a postwar organization of nations to keep the peace. In 1945, as you have read, Americans joined the people of three fourths of the world in forming the United Nations.

 SECTION 1 REVIEW

Define isolationism, neutrality

Identify Rush-Bagot Agreement, Monroe Doctrine, Roosevelt Corollary, dollar diplomacy, Good Neighbor Policy, League of Nations

1. **Seeing Relationships (a)** Why did the United States follow a policy of isolationism in its early history? **(b)** Why was it difficult to maintain this policy?
2. **Understanding Ideas (a)** Why was the War of 1812 a turning point in American foreign policy? **(b)** Why did our country adopt the Good Neighbor Policy?
3. **Expressing Ideas** Explain why our country did not remain neutral during the two World Wars.

Thinking Critically You have just left a public debate on whether the United States should return to a policy of isolationism. Write down the arguments stated by each side.

2 The Cold War and Containment

During World War II, the United States and the Soviet Union were allied in fighting Nazi Germany. Soon after the war ended, however, relations between the two nations changed and they came into conflict. What caused this change? The roots of the conflict were in the two nations' very different economic systems and forms of government. The United States has always been a representative democracy while the Soviet Union, at that time, was a communist nation.

What Is Communism?

The ideas behind modern communism come mainly from a German writer named Karl Marx. He believed that factory owners, or capitalists, throughout the world were getting rich by treating workers unfairly. With another writer, Friedrich Engels, Marx wrote a book called the *Communist Manifesto.*

In this book, Marx and Engels proposed a new economic system called **communism.** They argued that in the future the workers, called the **proletariat** (pro·la·TER·ee·at), would take over factories and businesses. Under communism, said Marx, the proletariat in all nations would own or control all the means of production—the land, capital, and labor. Private individuals—capitalists, that is— would not be permitted to own or control the means of production in order to make profits. Later Marx expanded these ideas in another book called *Das Kapital* (from the German word for capital).

According to Marx, the proletariat would run the government. Everything from raw materials to finished products would be owned by the government in the name of the workers. In the process, capitalism would be overthrown, by force and violence if necessary. The workers would establish a "dictatorship of the proletariat" throughout the world. Marx argued that communism thus would be both an economic and a political system.

Communism in the Soviet Union

In 1917 Russia became the first nation to adopt communism. Russia's ruler, the czar, was overthrown and a communist government was established under Vladimir Ilich Lenin. Russia became the Union of Soviet Socialist Republics (USSR), or the Soviet Union. Lenin was succeeded by Joseph Stalin, and a new, harsh period began. Stalin established a communist dictatorship that completely controlled the Soviet Union.

For decades, the Communist Party of the Soviet Union was all-powerful. The communist government made all of the economic decisions for the nation. It owned and managed all of the nation's industries and farms. It also controlled many aspects of the Soviet citizens' lives.

Most people, for example, had little choice concerning the type of job they held,

the education they received, or even where they could travel or live within the country. For years, no political party except the Communist Party was allowed to exist. There was no free press to tell the truth to the people. Journalists reported only what the government told them to report. As you can see, the Soviet people had little control over their own lives and their nation's government.

The people of the Soviet Union suffered other hardships under the Communist Party. For example, through enforced programs, the government drove the citizens to make the Soviet Union a modern industrial nation. In so doing, citizens had to do without many consumer goods. In 1912, the Soviet Union ranked fifth among the industrial powers of the world. By 1950, the country ranked second, surpassed only by the United States.

However, the standard of living in the Soviet Union was much lower than the standard of living in the United States. Shortages of many basic goods, including food, caused widespread hardship and suffering. People often spent long hours waiting in lines just to get enough food to feed their families. In recent years, however, conditions in the Soviet Union have begun to change. You will learn about these changes later in this chapter.

In the Soviet Union, the government strictly controlled the press for decades. The people received the news only from the government news agency, Tass.

The Spread of Communism

After World War II, hopes were high that the Soviet Union and the United States, allies in the war, would remain friends. It was hoped that the Soviet Union would share the ideals expressed in the Atlantic Charter and the Charter of the United Nations. Everywhere, people of all nations hoped that the world might now find a way to live in peace.

These hopes were soon shattered. During World War II, the Soviet Union occupied large parts of Poland and Rumania. After the war, in country after country in Eastern Europe, leaders of political parties opposed to communism were jailed, forced to flee, or assassinated. Within a few years, communist governments were set up in Poland, Romania, Bulgaria, Hungary, Czechoslovakia, Albania, and East Germany. In this way, the Soviet Union turned the nations along its borders into **satellite nations**—nations that take orders from another country.

Soviet leaders maintained that they were taking these actions so that the Soviet Union would never again be attacked by Germany or any other nation or nations of Western Europe. But leaders in the United States and Western Europe thought Soviet leaders had more in mind than defense of their own country. They believed the Soviet Union, with its great new military strength, would try to impose Soviet-dominated communist governments wherever in the world it could.

Only the fear of American nuclear bombs, some believed, prevented Soviet forces from trying to overrun all of Western Europe and Great Britain. At that time, only the United States had nuclear weapons.

The Cold War Begins

With the satellite nations of Eastern Europe under its control, the Soviet Union tried to increase Soviet power in the eastern Mediterranean Sea and the Middle East. The Soviet Union wanted an ice-free route for Soviet ships into the oceans of the world. It also wanted influence in the oil-rich lands of the Middle East.

Troops from the Soviet Union had occupied part of Iran, with its rich oil fields, during World War II. Instead of being withdrawn after the war, troop strength was increased. A Communist Party was encouraged in Greece. Turkey was faced with a demand for a Soviet naval base within its territory. The United States and other noncommunist nations saw these southward thrusts of Soviet power as severe threats to their security and to world peace.

Thus, soon after World War II, much of the world was caught up in what was called the **Cold War.** On one side was the Soviet

Union and its satellite nations. On the other side was the United States and other noncommunist nations. Both sides in the Cold War used propaganda, spying, alliances, foreign aid, and all other methods of conflict short of actually starting an all-out war that might destroy the world.

Waging the Cold War while also trying to win it were the major problems of American foreign policy in the 35 or 40 years after World War II, as you will see.

The Policy of Containment

The President of the United States in the immediate postwar period was Harry S. Truman. He warned the Soviet Union that it must get out of Iran. He was successful. The Soviet Union removed its troops. President Truman then asked Congress to provide military equipment and economic aid to Greece and Turkey to help them resist Soviet influence. Because of this aid, Greece and Turkey did not become satellites of the Soviet Union.

The success of American aid to Greece and Turkey encouraged our government to give similar aid to other European nations. This policy of helping free nations resist communist aggression became known as the **Truman Doctrine.**

The idea behind this policy came to be known as **containment.** The purpose of containment was to prevent Soviet communism from spreading. The forces of the Soviet Union

The 1948 Berlin airlift brought needed food and supplies to people trapped in West Berlin.

land routes through East Germany. In June 1948 the Soviet Union closed these routes. That is, it started a blockade of Berlin.

Soviet strategy in closing East German routes into Berlin was to force the noncommunist occupation forces to leave. They planned to make the city a communist center. The German people living in the British, French, and American sections of the city, called West Berlin, were cut off from food and coal. They faced cold and starvation.

The United States and Great Britain took prompt action. They began a massive airlift of fuel, food, clothing, and other vital items. Airplanes were loaded with supplies and flown into the city. Day after day, in all kinds of weather, American and British planes landed in West Berlin. More than 250,000 flights brought huge amounts of needed goods into West Berlin. Planes landed every 45 seconds. The Soviet strategy failed. The Soviet Union agreed to reopen the land routes.

were to be "contained" within the area they had occupied up to 1948. American policymakers expected, however, that the Soviet Union would test American commitment to the policy.

The Berlin Blockade

The first real test of containment came in 1948 in Berlin. At the end of World War II, Germany was divided into two separate nations. East Germany became a communist nation. West Germany became a republic. The city of Berlin, although located in East Germany, was not part of that nation.

Berlin was occupied by troops of four nations—France, Great Britain, the United States, and the Soviet Union. Each nation controlled a part of the city. Even though Berlin was within the area of Germany controlled by the Soviet Union, the noncommunist nations had free access to the city over special

Communism Wins in China

After World War II, a full-scale civil war broke out in China. In 1949 the government led by Chiang Kai-shek (JEEANG ky·shek) was defeated by Chinese communists. Chiang's forces fled to the island of Formosa (now called Taiwan), off the mainland of southern China. There they set up a government in exile, called Nationalist China.

The communists held the mainland—known as the People's Republic of China. The first head of the People's Republic of China was Mao Zedong (MOU DZUH·DOONG).

The United States refused to recognize the People's Republic of China. Instead, our nation provided economic and military aid to Nationalist China. With the support of the United States and other noncommunist nations, Nationalist China was allowed to remain a member of the United Nations. In 1971, however, Nationalist China was expelled from the United Nations and replaced by the People's Republic of China.

The Cuban Missile Crisis

The Cold War between the United States and the Soviet Union took a dangerous turn when the Soviet Union developed its own nuclear weapons during the 1950s. Leaders of both countries recognized that a **balance of power,** or situation in which countries are about equal in strength, was developing. The two nations, each seeking to gain the upper hand, continually tested each other for weaknesses. The most dangerous of these tests took place in October 1962.

The event took place on the island of Cuba, about 90 miles (145 kilometers) south of Florida. There, in 1959, Fidel Castro had set up a communist government.

In October 1962 President John F. Kennedy was informed that the Soviet Union was building secret missile bases in Cuba. These missile bases, if finished, would have been a threat to the United States and to other parts of the Western Hemisphere.

President Kennedy demanded that the Soviet Union remove its missiles from Cuba immediately. To force the Soviet Union to agree, President Kennedy declared that our nation was prepared to take whatever steps might be required, including military force.

As a first step, the American government announced that it would not allow the delivery of more offensive weapons—weapons of attack—to Cuba. The Navy sent destroyers to stop and search foreign ships bound for Cuba. The Air Force flew over the Atlantic to locate and photograph ships on their way to Cuba. Army troops were put on the alert.

As a result of this show of American military strength and determination, the Soviet Union backed down. It agreed to remove Soviet long-range missiles from Cuba and to take down the missile launching sites.

From that time on, Soviet and American leaders truly understood how dangerous the Cold War had become. They continued to pursue their own interests and search for each other's weaknesses. However, they were careful to avoid situations that could develop into a third world war, which would be a nuclear war certain to destroy much of the world.

The Korean Conflict

This did not mean that the United States did not ever get involved in war. The wars, though, were limited ones. A **limited war** is fought without using a nation's full power, especially nuclear weapons.

The two wars our country has fought since World War II took place in Asia. They both occurred in countries that had been divided into communist and noncommunist halves. The first of these two wars was fought in Korea.

As a result of an agreement reached after World War II, the nation of Korea, which juts out of eastern Asia into the Pacific Ocean, was divided into communist North Korea and noncommunist South Korea. In June 1950 the army of North Korea invaded South Korea in a surprise attack. Its goal was to reunite both parts of Korea as a communist nation. North Korea was equipped with Soviet weapons and assisted by Chinese communists.

In late 1951 the two sides in the Korean conflict drew a line across a map of Korea and agreed to stop firing across it. Nevertheless, the war dragged on.

The United States government called upon the United Nations to halt the invasion. The Security Council of the UN, with the Soviet Union absent, held a special session. It voted to send military assistance to the South Koreans.

Led by troops from the United States, combat forces sent by 15 other members of the United Nations helped defend South Korea. The Korean conflict lasted three years. By July 1953 the conflict had reached a point where neither side could win a clear-cut victory. The two sides agreed that Korea would remain divided into communist North Korea and noncommunist South Korea. Since then tensions between the two Korean nations have continued.

Involvement in Vietnam

Under agreements passed in 1954, several French colonies in Southeast Asia—Vietnam, Laos, and Cambodia—became independent. Vietnam, like Korea, was divided into a communist northern half and a noncommunist southern half. The agreements called for elections to be held throughout Vietnam in 1956 to reunite the country.

When the elections did not take place, war broke out in South Vietnam in the late 1950's. Communist forces in the south were supported by troops, supplies, and other assistance from North Vietnam. The North Vietnamese received military supplies from the Soviet Union and Communist China.

American officials feared that if South Vietnam fell to the communists, other nations of Southeast Asia—Laos, Cambodia, and Thailand—might also fall. But how should these new forces of communism be contained? The United States began to send economic aid and military advisers to South Vietnam.

Gradually the United States became more deeply involved. In 1964, at the request of President Lyndon B. Johnson, Congress passed the Gulf of Tonkin Resolution. It gave the President the power to take all necessary ac-

tions in Vietnam. It was not, however, a declaration of war. American combat troops soon were sent into action in South Vietnam. By 1969 more than 500,000 Americans were fighting there.

Perhaps no other conflict in American history brought more heated debate than Vietnam. Those in favor of stronger military action argued that America's honor and position of world leadership were at stake. Opponents of the war maintained that its cost in lives and money was not justified.

Finally, in January 1973, a peace agreement was announced. After more than eight years of war, with almost 60,000 Americans killed and more than 350,000 wounded, and at a cost of over $150 billion, the war came to an end for the United States. Despite the agreement, however, fighting continued in Vietnam. In 1975 the communists launched a new offensive and South Vietnam fell. The communists now ruled all of Vietnam.

 SECTION 2 REVIEW

Define communism, proletariat, satellite nations, containment, balance of power, limited war

Identify Cold War, Truman Doctrine

1. **Composing a Paragraph** Write a paragraph that explains Karl Marx's ideas about communism.
2. **Identifying Ideas (a)** What caused communism to spread through Eastern Europe? **(b)** How did the Cold War begin? **(c)** What did the United States and the Soviet Union do to try to win the Cold War?
3. **Summarizing Ideas (a)** How did the United States respond to the blockade of Berlin? **(b)** How did the United States respond to the Cuban missile crisis?

Thinking Critically You are an adviser to President Kennedy during the Cuban missile crisis. What actions do you recommend that the President take?

New Trends in American Foreign Policy

In recent years, the American people and their leaders have been rethinking foreign policy. The problem has been to work out new policies for a rapidly changing world. New foreign policies are especially needed to meet developments among the communist nations and the newer developing nations.

The Split in the Communist World

For many years after World War II, communism was viewed by Americans as a single political and economic movement that threatened to take over the rest of the world. The Soviet Union controlled the countries of Eastern Europe and some of central Europe.

In Asia, as you have read, the Soviet Union and Communist China assisted North Korea in its aggression against South Korea. They also supported North Vietnam in its attempt to seize control of South Vietnam. The Soviet Union backed Fidel Castro in Cuba and his attempts to spread communism in Latin America. Some African nations also came under the influence of the Soviet Union.

As the years passed, however, it became clear that communism was not a single worldwide movement. American policymakers learned that a foreign policy that works with one communist country might not work with another communist country. They understood that each country must be treated differently.

The End of the Cold War

As you have learned, the foreign policy of the United States was dominated in the years after World War II by the Cold War with the Soviet Union. Much of the rest of the world was also

Since becoming President of the Soviet Union, Mikhail Gorbachev has instituted dramatic social and economic reforms in that country.

involved in the Cold War as these two world powers sought to influence other countries and make them allies.

Recently, however, dramatic changes in the Soviet Union and in its satellite nations of Eastern Europe have ended the Cold War. New leadership and new policies, serious economic problems, pressure from the free world, and growing dissatisfaction among the people have worked to overturn many communist governments.

In 1985, Mikhail Gorbachev became the leader of the Communist Party in the Soviet Union. Gorbachev was known as a reformer. But no one was certain what policies he intended to establish for the Soviet Union and its satellite nations.

Perestroika and Glasnost

By 1987 the direction in which Gorbachev was intending to lead the communist world became clear. Gorbachev had announced two important new policies. One is **glasnost** (GLAS nost), or "openness." Through glasnost, Gorbachev is seeking to free the Soviet nation and its satellites from many political and intellectual controls. For example, the press has been given greater freedom.

The second important policy established by Gorbachev is **perestroika** (per is TROY ka) or "reform." Perestroika is aimed at improving the faltering Soviet economy. The Soviet Union's economy has lagged behind that of the United States for years. Under perestroika, the Soviet Union is moving toward a free economic system. Government controls on the economy have been relaxed, and free enterprise is being encouraged.

Changes in Eastern Europe

The changes occurring in the Soviet Union are being reflected in its satellite nations in Eastern Europe. For decades, these countries were under the strict control of the Soviet government. On a number of occasions, the Soviet Union had even sent troops into these countries to enforce its rule.

Under Mikhail Gorbachev, however, this policy changed. Gorbachev sent clear signals to the satellite nations telling them to assert a greater degree of independence. By 1988 it became clear that Gorbachev's reform programs would take many years to complete. The countries of Eastern Europe were encouraged to promote these reforms. A feeling of great change was in the air.

In 1989 the promise of change became a reality. Over the course of the year, the communist governments in the Eastern European countries of Bulgaria, Czechoslovakia, East Germany, Hungary, Poland, and Romania began to fall. Only the satellite nation of Albania maintained strict Communist Party rule.

The most dramatic symbol of the disintegration of the communist world was the tearing down of the Berlin Wall. As you recall, part of the German city of Berlin was controlled by communist East Germany and part of it was controlled by democratic West Germany. In 1961 the communists constructed a fortified wall along the border to keep people from escaping to freedom in the West. The wall soon came to symbolize the division between the communist and free worlds. When it was destroyed, in 1989, the broken wall came to symbolize the end of the Cold War.

Changing Relations with the Soviet Union

The recent and dramatic changes in the Soviet Union and Eastern Europe have enabled the United States and the Soviet Union to end the Cold War. The foreign policy of the United States has therefore changed. Instead of trying to win the Cold War, American foreign policy now is aimed at reducing nuclear weapons. We also are helping the Soviet Union and the countries of Eastern Europe move closer to the ideals of freedom, democracy, and free enterprise upon which our nation is built.

Relations with Less Developed Countries

Since the 1960's, American foreign policy has been increasingly concerned with an important group of countries. These countries, located in Latin America, Asia, and Africa, are known as **less developed countries (LDCs).**

The less developed countries all have very different cultures, languages, and customs. What makes them similar is that they generally have agricultural economies, shortages of food, generally low incomes, and high birth rates.

Most of these countries are former colonies of European nations. They won their independence in the years following World

War II. Many of the colonial powers created problems in the areas they occupied that have made it difficult for these young countries to develop their economies.

About three fourths of the world's population lives in LDCs. A major goal of American foreign policy is to encourage economic development in these countries. We also encourage these countries to create or maintain democratic governments and to maintain friendly relations with the United States.

Relations with the Middle East

The Middle East is the name given to the area of southwest Asia and northwest Africa. It includes the countries of Egypt, Israel, Iraq, Iran, Saudi Arabia, and several others.

The United States has tried to have good relations with all of the nations of the Middle East. At the same time, however, we have been the chief supporter of Israel. Israel is surrounded by Arab nations. Because of differences in religion and culture, and because of boundary disputes, Israel has fought several wars with its neighbors since its creation as a nation in 1948.

Our policy of supporting Israel has often angered Arab nations. But the United States continues to try to encourage negotiations among the countries of the Middle East to make it a peaceful region.

The Middle East is especially important to the United States and the rest of the world because it contains most of the world's oil. Because the Middle East is an unstable region, the flow of oil from this region has sometimes been disrupted. This causes serious problems for the economies of countries that depend on Middle Eastern oil, like the United States.

A good example of the instability of the Middle East is the invasion of the country of Kuwait by Iraq in August 1990. The government of Iraq, led by the dictator Saddam Hussein, claimed that Kuwait was stealing oil from Iraq. Iraq used this as an excuse to invade Kuwait and take over its rich oil fields. There

These American soldiers marching in Saudi Arabia were sent to that nation in 1990 to protect the Middle East from Iraq's aggression.

was fear that Iraq would also invade Saudi Arabia.

The United States led the members of the UN in condemning Iraq's actions. The United States sent troops to Saudi Arabia to protect that nation and the rest of the Middle East from Iraq. The goal of this action and general United States policy in the region is to protect the world's oil supplies and to promote peace among Middle Eastern countries.

Relations with South Africa

Located at the southern tip of the continent of Africa, the country of South Africa is
(continued on page 458)

CITIZENSHIP IN ACTION

Felicia's Year in the United States

Felicia de Rosado stood up and raised her baton. As the band played the national anthem of Colombia, South America, she felt great pride in her homeland. However, her pride was mixed with a little homesickness.

Promoting International Understanding

Felicia was directing a high school band in Maplewood, New Jersey—a long way from home. She had left Colombia to spend her junior year as an exchange student in the United States. The student exchange program is sponsored by American volunteers as a step toward forming a better understanding among nations.

The spring concert at which Felicia directed the band was one of the high points of her year in the United States. During her stay she took part in many American activities. She even played soccer. At home in Colombia, she said, "Girls play basketball and volleyball, but soccer? Never!" However, Felicia had to give up soccer because the band took up so much time. But the band was her first love.

Two Different Cultures

At first Felicia found it difficult to get used to American ways. "Everything was so different, although English was my biggest frustration." She had studied English in high school in Colombia. "However, I suddenly had to think quickly in English and find the correct words to make myself understood. It wasn't easy."

She found the customs different, too. One of the practices she had trouble adjusting to was dating. In Colombia, "we don't go out with just one person at such a young age. We go many more places with groups of friends."

The Block family, with whom Felicia lived in Maplewood, also had to get used to her ways. "Felicia was always cooperative, but we could tell when things upset her. She wasn't used to doing jobs like drying dishes and cleaning her room," said Viola Block. "In Colombia her family has servants." The Block family also was struck by Felicia's amazement at the many "ordinary" household appliances that Americans own—vacuum cleaners, washing machines, freezers, and calculators. Very few people own these items in Colombia.

Felicia and the Block family think their year together helped each better understand the other's country. For Felicia, the year in the United States was "a wonderful experience, something I'll never forget. No one who visits here just for a few weeks could learn so much." She also made many friends with whom she hopes to keep in touch. Through their friendship, they feel they have formed a bond of understanding between two very different countries.

Thinking It Over

1. What do you think Felicia's friends in the United States learned about Colombia from getting to know Felicia?
2. Do you think foreign exchange programs for students can help form a better understanding among nations? Explain.

Relations with Communist China

China is the largest nation in the world and houses about one fifth of the total world population. In recent years, it has become increasingly important in world affairs.

Because it is so large, any actions that China takes are important to the rest of the world. Recently, the United States has sought to improve relations with communist China. We have sought to increase exchanges of journalists, students, and scholars. We have also sought to increase the amount of trade we conduct with China.

Our attempts to improve relations with China, however, were dealt a blow in 1989. The communist Chinese government brutally ended demonstrations of Chinese citizens who were calling for democratic reforms. The United States condemned the action, but we are still seeking ways to improve relations with the large and powerful nation of China.

Relations with Latin America

The United States has been concerned about the spread of communism to some Latin American countries. The communist government of Fidel Castro has remained firmly in control in Cuba. Moreover, the Cuban government has tried to spread communism to other Latin American countries.

Another issue that causes tensions in our relations is the smuggling of illegal drugs from Latin America into the United States. Recently, the United States has assisted many Latin American nations in trying to control the illegal drug trade.

In 1989, the United States invaded Panama in part to help stop the flow of drugs. The dictator of Panama, Manuel Noriega, had been indicted on drug trafficking charges in the United States. The United States invasion of Panama drove Noriega from power. He was brought to the United States to stand trial for the crimes of which he was accused.

Although Manuel Noriega went into hiding when President Bush sent troops into Panama, the dictator was caught and arrested on drug trafficking charges.

unique in the world. Under a system called **apartheid** (a PART hayd), which means "apartness," the country's white minority has ruled the country's nonwhite majority for decades. The government of South Africa, controlled by whites, has maintained a system that calls for a strict separation of races.

Many Americans have demanded that our government take action to help the nonwhite people of South Africa. The United States has condemned apartheid. Responding to international pressure and growing internal unrest, the South African government announced important reforms in 1990. It legalized nonwhite political parties and opened the way for the dismantling of apartheid. The nonwhites of South Africa still face oppression, but changes are under way.

Understanding Foreign Policy

The basic goal of American foreign policies—to promote peace, trade, and friendship throughout the world—does not change. The ways in which we try to achieve this goal, however, change with the changing times. New problems, such as nuclear proliferation (the spread of nuclear weapons), challenge American foreign policymakers. New problems require new solutions. As an American citizen, it is your responsibility to stay informed about United States foreign policy.

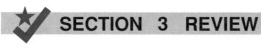

★✓ SECTION 3 REVIEW

Define glasnost, perestroika, less developed countries (LDCs), apartheid

1. **Identifying Ideas** What important lesson did the United States learn about communist countries in the years after World War II?
2. **Composing an Essay** Write a brief essay discussing the changes in relations between the United States and the Soviet Union since World War II.
3. **Identifying Roles** How did Soviet President Mikhail Gorbachev help to end the Cold War?
4. **Organizing Ideas (a)** Why is the Middle East important to the United States? **(b)** What are the chief concerns of the United States in Latin America?

Thinking Critically Imagine you are President of the United States. You want to stop the flow of illegal drugs from Latin America. What should you do?

Through the years, the United States has moved from a policy of isolationism to deep involvement in world affairs. In the present century, our nation has fought in two world wars.

After the end of World War II, the world was dominated by two opposing groups of nations. The communist nations were determined to spread their ideas and their form of government throughout the world. Noncommunist nations, led by the United States, opposed the spread of communism. The worldwide struggle between communist and noncommunist nations, using every means short of all-out war, became known as the Cold War.

The United States began a policy of containment. Its aim was to resist the spread of communism. The United States fought limited wars with communist forces in Korea and Vietnam.

In recent years, significant changes in the Soviet Union and in Eastern Europe have led to the end of the Cold War. The United States is seeking to improve relations with communist countries while encouraging them to become more free and democratic.

Less developed countries are very important in American foreign policy. Most of the people of the world live in LDCs. United States policy seeks to improve life for these people.

American foreign policy is complicated and continually changes to meet new international challenges. American citizens must study international relations carefully and use their influence for the peaceful solution of international problems.

CHAPTER 22 SUMMARY

DEVELOPING
★ CIVICS
SKILLS

SOCIAL STUDIES SKILL
Using Primary Sources

Primary sources are written by people who actually saw or participated in historical events. Primary sources of information differ from secondary sources of information. Secondary sources are usually written after an event has taken place. They are often written by an author using primary sources.

Both primary and secondary sources provide important facts. But only primary sources allow you to see events through the eyes of the people who experienced them. They not only provide information about the event, but also give you glimpses of the attitudes, feelings, and concerns of people who lived in the past.

How to Use a Primary Source

To use a primary source effectively, follow these guidelines.

1. **Understand the background of the source.** To get the most information from a primary source, you must understand who wrote it and the conditions under which it was written. As you read, ask yourself if the author was biased in some way. Learn what was going on in the world when the source was written. Answering these and similar questions will help you decide if the source is reliable.

2. **Read the source carefully.** Make certain you understand what the author is saying. Look up the definitions for words you do not know, and read the source several times until you feel confident you understand its meaning. As you read the source, be sure to identify all facts, or statements that can be proven true. Also note any statements that give you insight into the opinions of the author and the period in which the author lived.

3. **Draw conclusions from the source.** Use your careful reading of the source to draw

conclusions about the topic or event discussed in the source.

Applying the Skill

The primary source on this page is part of a speech written by President George Washington as he was about to leave office in 1796. Use it to answer the following questions.

1. Why might this speech be a good source of information on early American foreign policy?
2. **(a)** What is the basic message of this part of George Washington's speech? **(b)** What arguments does President Washington use to support his position? **(c)** Based on the secondary information in this textbook, why might Washington have taken this position?

> *The great rule of conduct for us is to extend our commercial relations with foreign nations, but to have as little political connection with foreign nations as possible. Let us fulfill our previous commitments. Here let us stop.*
>
> *Europe's interests have little relation to ours. It is engaged in frequent controversies that are not important to us. Thus it is unwise for us to let artificial ties involve us in Europe's politics.*
>
> *Our distance from Europe permits us to pursue a different course. Why give up the advantages of our special situation? Why entangle our peace and prosperity in the web of European ambition, rivalry, interest, and whim?*
>
> *It is our true policy to steer clear of permanent alliances with any foreign nation.*

CHAPTER 22 REVIEW

Reviewing Terms

On a separate sheet of paper, supply the term from the list below that correctly answers each question.

glasnost	isolationism
perestroika	neutrality
apartheid	Cold War

1. Which term refers to a policy of staying out of international affairs?
2. What is South Africa's policy of racial separation called?
3. Which term refers to the new programs of economic reform in the Soviet Union?
4. What was the rivalry between the United States and the Soviet Union in the years after World War II called?
5. What term refers to a policy of refusing to take sides in a conflict?
6. Which term refers to the new policy of openness in the Soviet Union?

Using Thinking Skills

1. **Organizing Ideas** (a) What caused the Cold War? (b) What caused the Cold War to end?
2. **Summarizing Ideas** (a) What was the main purpose of the Truman Doctrine? (b) Why did the United States participate in the Korean War? (c) Why did the United States send troops to Vietnam?
3. **Understanding Ideas** (a) Why did the United States adopt the Monroe Doctrine? (b) What was Latin America's response to the Monroe Doctrine?
4. **Identifying Ideas** (a) Why did the United States follow a policy of neutrality in the years leading up to World War I and World War II? (b) Why did this neutrality end?
5. **Seeing Relationships** (a) Why did the United States seek to stay isolated from world affairs in its early years? (b) Why did this policy change?
6. **Expressing Ideas** What are the basic aims of American foreign policy?

7. **Drawing Conclusions** Why was the War of 1812 a turning point in American foreign policy?
8. **Composing a Paragraph** Discuss the history of United States relations with the country of Canada.
9. **Composing an Essay** Discuss how the Cuban missile crisis and the blockade of Berlin relate to the Cold War.

Practicing Civics Skills

Analyzing a Primary Source Read this passage from President Truman's address to Congress in 1947. Then answer the questions.

> Our victory in World War II was won over countries that sought to impose their will and their way of life upon other nations. The peoples of a number of countries have recently had totalitarian regimes forced upon them against their will.
>
> I believe that it must be the policy of the United States to support the peoples who are resisting control by armed minorities or by outside pressures. We must assist free peoples to work out their own destinies in their own way.

1. (a) How had the nation's foreign policy changed since President Washington's time? (b) What statements in President Truman's speech help to explain possible reasons for this change?
2. Why might President Truman's speech be a good source of information on American foreign policy in the 1940's?

Being a Good Citizen

1. Create a file of current concerns in United States foreign policy. Read newspapers and magazines to keep your file current.
2. Hold a class discussion on United States policy toward one or more of the following countries: South Africa, the Soviet Union, China, Israel, Mexico.

Reviewing the Facts

1. (a) What is foreign policy? (b) How does foreign policy differ from foreign relations?
2. (a) What is communism? (b) What was the United States foreign policy response to the spread of communism in the years after World War II?
3. (a) What was the Monroe Doctrine? (b) Why was it replaced by the Good Neighbor policy?
4. (a) What was the Cold War? (b) What events caused the Cold War to end?
5. (a) What are the basic goals of American foreign policy? (b) What are some ways in which the United States has tried to achieve these goals?
6. (a) What is isolationism? (b) What caused the United States to end its policy of isolationism?
7. (a) What is the United Nations? (b) What are some of the activities pursued by the United Nations?

Using Critical Thinking

1. **Identifying Ideas** (a) Why does our country provide foreign aid? (b) What are the arguments for and against providing foreign aid to other countries?
2. **Comparing Points of View** (a) Why was the United Nations organized? (b) What are the arguments in support of the United Nations? (c) Describe the objections some people have to this organization.
3. **Expressing Ideas** Why can it be said that the United States has several foreign policies rather than one foreign policy?
4. **Organizing Ideas** (a) Why did the Cold War begin? (b) What are some of the major events of the Cold War? (c) How did the Cold War involve countries other than the United States and the Soviet Union?
5. **Drawing Conclusions** Explain how American citizens can affect our nation's relations with foreign countries.

6. **Understanding Ideas** (a) Why is the Middle East so important to the United States? (b) What is American foreign policy toward less developed countries? (c) Describe two important issues in our relations with Latin America.
7. **Summarizing Ideas** How did the Korean War and the conflict in Vietnam relate to the Cold War?
8. **Seeing Relationships** (a) Explain why the United States forms alliances. (b) Why does our country sign trade treaties?
9. **Identifying Roles** (a) What is the role of the President in foreign policy? (b) How does the executive branch help the President in this role? (c) What role does Congress play in American foreign policy?

Applying What You Know

1. Conduct library research to find out what types of governments exist in the countries of Africa. Create a table to organize this information.
2. Read firsthand accounts of the fighting in two of the wars in which the United States has been involved. Summarize these accounts for the class, and identify how the fighting differed in the two conflicts.

Expanding Your Knowledge

Fincher, E.B., *Mexico and the United States: Their Linked Destinies*, Crowell. Examines the relations the United States has with its neighbor to the south.

Goode, Stephen, *Foreign Policy Debate: Human Rights and American Foreign Policy*, Franklin Watts. Discusses how human rights issues affect American foreign policy.

Pratt, J.W. et. al., *A History of United States Foreign Policy*, Prentice-Hall. Provides discussions of the critical events in the historical development of the foreign policy of the United States.

Meeting the Challenges of the Future

UNIT 8

CHAPTER 23

Improving Life for All Americans

Chapter Sections

1 **Improving Our Communities**
2 **Ensuring Rights for All**
3 **Protecting Our Health and Safety**

Chapter Focus

The American people have always worked to improve life for themselves and their children. Today, Americans continue to seek more opportunities—better jobs and education, better pay, and a chance to develop their own interests.

Throughout most of our nation's history Americans have tried to improve their standard of living by moving to the cities, which offered more and different kinds of jobs. Gradually, however, this population movement has begun to shift. The 1980 census showed that, for the first time in more than 100 years, the rural areas of our nation were growing faster than the urban areas.

Many of our cities have serious problems. Overcrowding, crime, lack of affordable housing, and loss of jobs have led many people to leave the cities. Today our communities are working hard to improve conditions, but there is still work to do.

Our nation was founded on the ideal of equal rights and opportunities for all. But many of our citizens have been denied basic American rights and freedoms during much of our history.

The challenges of improving our communities and ensuring rights for all citizens—while protecting the health and safety of our population—must be met if we are to improve life for all Americans.

Study Guide

As you read about how citizens can work to improve the quality of life in our country, look for answers to the following questions:

★ What problems are facing American cities, and what can be done to solve these problems?
★ How have citizens worked toward ensuring equal rights for all Americans?
★ What is wellness, and what can Americans do to achieve it?

1 Improving Our Communities

The United States contains many different kinds of communities. They vary from small rural towns and villages to huge, sprawling cities. Today more than three fourths of all Americans live in or around large cities. Many of these urban areas face serious problems. They include poor housing, run-down transportation systems, and crime. Such problems exist not only in our cities but also in suburbs and rural areas. They are found in communities throughout the world as well.

The problems of our communities affect all of us. Finding solutions to these problems and making our communities more pleasant places in which to live are important issues to all Americans.

The Growth of American Cities

America began as a rural country with small, scattered settlements. All American cities and towns were once small communities. Those that grew into cities usually spread over the surrounding countryside in a typical pattern. Most cities have spread outward, away from the original settlement. If you were to draw a diagram showing how the typical city grew, it would look like a target. As you can see on the diagram on page 466, the old downtown area would be in the center. It would be surrounded by several circles, each larger and larger as you go outward from the center.

The old central part of the city usually is the downtown business center. Here you find stores, office buildings, factories, and warehouses. Sometimes modern hotels and luxury apartment houses also are located in the downtown section. Yet areas in and around it are often run-down.

The next circle outward from the downtown area is occupied by apartment buildings, small private homes, and neighborhood shops and stores. These buildings are often built side by side with little or no space between them.

The next circle is sometimes called the greenbelt. Houses with yards and lawns, trees, and shrubbery are often found in this section. The greenbelt usually lies only partly within the city boundaries. It also extends beyond city lines, where it is called the suburbs. Suburbs, as you recall, are small, independent communities that surround a city.

On the edge of the greenbelt is the rural-urban fringe. This is where the city meets the countryside. There are often farms and small towns in this area. The rural-urban fringe may stretch as far away as 50 to 100 miles (80 to 160 kilometers) from the downtown center.

In recent years, many factories, businesses, and stores have moved from the cities into the rural areas. These industries and businesses left the cities because country areas often offer cheaper land, lower taxes, better housing, less crowded traffic and parking conditions, and other advantages.

The Move of Middle-Income Families

As you may remember, a large city with its surrounding area of suburbs and small towns is known as a metropolitan area. Although the number of metropolitan areas has been growing, the centers of our cities have been losing population. More people have moved out of the central cities than have moved in. By 1970 more people were living in the towns and suburbs of metropolitan areas than were living within city limits.

Why are people leaving the cities? There are many reasons. Some people seek fresh air, sunshine, and neighborhoods with yards. The number of crimes in some cities is so high that many people are afraid to live there.

Some Americans have left the cities to avoid paying high rents and city taxes. Others seek better schools and an escape from urban noise, grime, and bustle. People also move to be near the new jobs that are opening up in the suburbs as businesses move there.

How Many American Communities Grew

NEARBY SMALL TOWNS

SUBURBS

APARTMENT BUILDINGS

PRIVATE HOMES

PRIVATE HOMES

ORIGINAL DOWNTOWN CENTER

SMALL STORES

SMALL STORES

TWO-FAMILY DWELLINGS

SUBURBS

NEARBY SMALL TOWNS

This shift of people to the suburbs has had serious effects on American cities. For the most part, those who move are middle-class or upper-middle-class families. Many of these people still work in the city and use its services. Those who travel from suburban homes to city places of business are called commuters. Commuters often pay little or no tax to the city government.

Furthermore, since the federal government's financial aid to cities is based on urban population figures, the cities lose federal aid when people leave. As residents move out, urban areas lose federal funds for housing, schools, transportation, public assistance, and other services. Cities also lose voters when people move to the suburbs. This means a loss of representatives in state government and in Congress.

The Problem of Slums

As people shifted to the suburbs, the older areas of many cities became slums. A **slum** is a run-down section of the city where the buildings are neglected and families live crowded together.

Life is often difficult for people living in slums. In these crowded areas, the rates of disease and death are high. Compared with other sections of the city, slums have higher proportions of school dropouts, unemployed people, and criminals. Worst of all is the feeling of hopelessness. Slum dwellers often have no jobs and little hope for the future.

Slums create problems for everyone, not just for those who live in them. For instance, slums cost everyone money. The number of fires is greater in slum areas. More police officers are also needed to protect these areas because they tend to have more crime than other neighborhoods. More of the city's money must be spent on health needs, public assistance, child care, and other services in slum areas than in any other part of the city. Thus all the people in the city help pay the cost of allowing slums to exist.

Planning to End Slums

American cities have tried several plans to end slums. Some communities have been replacing slum dwellings with **public housing projects.** These are apartment houses built with public funds. The rents in these projects are low, and the apartments are open primarily to low-income families.

Another plan to end slums calls for redeveloping, or completely rebuilding, the center of the city. Sometimes large new, public buildings are constructed on the site of the torn-down buildings to form a civic center. Facilities are provided for business conferences, concerts, sporting events, and public exhibits. Private corporations are often encouraged to take part in the redevelopment project or even to plan it. Usually better housing for those people whose homes are torn down is provided nearby.

A third plan to end slums is to restore and maintain the buildings in the area. Buildings that can be saved are repaired by their owners. Sometimes owners get financial help from the city. Buildings that cannot be repaired are torn down. They are replaced with new dwellings or with parks and playgrounds.

The programs you have just read about are called **urban renewal programs.** Usually they are planned and carried out by local agencies with financial support from the federal government.

Some urban renewal programs have achieved great success. Many new schools, libraries, hospitals, and other community centers have improved the lives of local residents. These community improvements have also helped revive business in former slum areas, providing jobs and incomes for many people. Philadelphia, Chicago, St. Louis, and New York City, for example, have had successful urban renewal programs.

Unfortunately, urban renewal programs are very expensive. And many of the programs have been failures. When run-down areas are redeveloped, people are moved to make room for the new development. Often, as you have

Large metropolitan areas have grown up throughout the nation. Many people living in suburbs commute from their homes to their jobs in the cities.

read, they are relocated to public housing projects. Over time, however, many of these projects become unhealthy and dangerous.

America's Homeless Citizens

One of the most pressing and difficult problems facing America's cities today is **homelessness.** For the first time since the Great Depression of the 1930's, many American citizens do not have a place to live.

There have always been homeless people in the United States. The majority of these have been single men. Another large group is made up of people who have mental problems. What has brought homelessness to the attention of the American people in recent years is the fact that a growing percentage of the homeless population is made up of families. Because more and more families are becoming homeless, children now make up about one fourth of the homeless population.

Being homeless makes life very difficult. Many homeless people spend nights in shelters set up to house the homeless. But these places fill up quickly, forcing many people to seek shelter elsewhere. In addition, some shelters for the homeless are unsanitary and dangerous places. Because of this, many homeless people spend nights in bus stations, under bridges, on benches—any place they can sleep. Because they have no home, they are forced to carry their few possessions with them. Poverty is a constant companion, and jobs

for people who have no permanent address are few.

One of the main reasons for the increase in homelessness in the United States is the lack of affordable housing. Across the country the price of housing has increased dramatically in recent years. Moreover, millions of low-cost apartments and houses have been lost in the past ten years. These buildings are abandoned, or, more often, converted to high-cost housing. Recent cutbacks in federal funding of programs designed to provide low-cost housing have added to the problem.

Homelessness in America is a problem that challenges our nation. Many private groups have set up shelters and programs to help the homeless, but the number of homeless continues to grow. More and more city governments have recognized the problem and are working to establish shelters and more low-cost housing. Notable entertainers have held concerts and other benefits to help homeless Americans.

The federal government also is attempting to ease the problem. In 1987, Congress passed the Homeless Assistance Act, authorizing about $1 billion in financial aid for the homeless. Most of this money is reserved for emergency shelters and other services needed by the homeless. Among these services are educational programs for homeless children and job training for homeless veterans.

What "irregularity" do you suppose the "zoning commission" has found? Do you believe communities should have zoning laws? Why or why not?

courtesy of The Chicago Tribune—New York News Syndicate, Inc.

"THE ZONING COMMISSION WOULD LIKE TO POINT OUT AN IRREGULARITY!"

Zoning Laws

American communities have acted not just to solve old housing problems but also to prevent new problems. Many local governments, for example, have passed **zoning laws.** Such laws regulate the kinds of buildings that may be put up in a zone, or particular area. Only certain types of buildings or businesses are allowed in each zone.

Towns and cities also pass laws that builders must follow in making new structures safe and attractive. To keep track of these new buildings, local governments require builders to obtain permits before they start working. Other laws require owners to keep their buildings comfortable and in good repair. As a result, buildings that are being worked on, as well as all apartment houses, office buildings, and other buildings open to the public, are inspected regularly to make sure local regulations are followed. Such laws are part of an area's **building code.**

Suburban Problems

Suburbs and other small communities also have problems to solve. If you go for a drive in the country, notice some of the things you pass. You will probably see new communities with attractive homes. You may also pass old, run-down homes or poorly built stores. Other common sights may be gas stations, signs and billboards, junkyards, and drive-in snack stands—many of which were built without careful planning. Such conditions are often called suburban blight.

As suburbs and other communities have grown in size and population, some of them have had problems of water supply, trash removal, sewage disposal, increasing crime, and high taxes. Like the large cities, these communities have established programs to redevelop their run-down areas. They too have tried to prevent problems through zoning laws and community action.

The Transportation Tangle

"Dirty, inefficient, debt-ridden!" These are the words increasingly used to describe mass transit. **Mass transit** includes various forms of public transportation, such as subways, buses, and commuter railroads. All of them are plagued with problems. Fewer passengers. Poorer service. Increased fares. What is causing the crisis in mass transit? Is there a remedy?

The movement of large numbers of city workers to the suburbs is one cause of the decline of mass transportation. Many suburban commuters prefer to drive their cars, even though highways leading into the city are choked with traffic. The loss of riders has caused mass transit systems to lose money.

Rising payroll and maintenance costs on mass transit lines are another problem. Higher operating costs mean higher fares. Higher fares mean a further drop in the number of passengers. As service becomes worse, still other passengers take to the highways or, if possible, walk or bicycle to work.

Another transportation difficulty has been caused by dependence on the automobile. In many communities, residents prefer to use automobiles rather than mass transit. Because of poor planning, some of these places suffer from enormous traffic jams, lack of parking spaces, and air pollution. Also, superhighways and large parking garages take up space that could be used for buildings.

These problems, plus the increasing cost of gasoline, have caused some cities to make plans for building or modernizing their mass transit systems. For example, BART (Bay Area Rapid Transit), which began running in 1972, links San Francisco with nearby communities. A new subway system was also built in Washington, D.C.

Various solutions have been suggested for transportation troubles. Most of these solutions involve some degree of tax support and help from the federal government.

Despite their many problems, mass transit systems are essential to every large city. They are as vital as the highways and airlines that connect the city with the rest of the nation and the world. They must be made to succeed if cities and their surrounding communities are to flourish.

Planning for the Future

So many people have moved out of the inner, or central, city to the suburbs and rural areas that a number of problems have been created in the entire metropolitan area. How, for

Have you ever been caught in a scene like this? What steps do you think communities can take to avoid traffic jams?

example, can essential services, such as water supply, trash removal, electric power, and mass transportation, be provided for such great numbers of people living throughout the metropolitan area?

Many counties, cities, and towns have community planning commissions that work to improve conditions. Some large groups of cities also have regional planning groups, which study the problems of the entire area. These regional groups sometimes are made up entirely of private citizens.

All planning groups employ experts to help them. Among the specialists they consult are traffic engineers, population specialists, economists, and health experts. Landscape architects and scientists are also asked to study the land and its uses.

One kind of problem that often requires regional planning is transportation. The streets of the city and the roads of the suburbs are a part of one system. Therefore, many cities and suburbs have formed **metropolitan transit authorities.** Representatives from the city and suburban communities are included in the transit authority. These groups study traffic problems and work to solve them.

Similar groups are working to solve the other problems that face American communities. Among these problems are pollution, drug abuse, overcrowding, crime, poor school systems, and the high cost of services.

Poverty is also a problem that can devastate the lives of many city dwellers. People who live in poverty have shorter life expectancies, are ill more often, and have fewer opportunities for education and jobs.

Solutions to the problems of our communities are not always easy to find or carry out. Many solutions would require a lot of money. Yet money alone is not the answer. Our communities also need imaginative planning. Above all, they need citizens who are willing to do their part and accept their responsibility to make our communities better places in which to live.

SECTION 1 REVIEW

Define slum, public housing projects, urban renewal programs, homelessness, zoning laws, building code, mass transit, metropolitan transit authorities

1. **Composing a Paragraph** Write a short paragraph to explain the pattern by which many of our American communities have grown.
2. **Seeing Relationships** (a) Why have many middle-income families moved away from the cities? (b) What have been the results of this migration?
3. **Organizing Ideas** (a) What actions have cities across the nation taken to reduce slums? (b) How effective have these actions been?
4. **Expressing Ideas** (a) Identify and explain the basic cause of homelessness in the United States. (b) What are some of the problems city planning commissions are working to solve?

Thinking Critically Imagine you have just been elected mayor of a large city. During your campaign, you promised to help the homeless people of your city. Now that you are mayor, what actions will you take?

② Ensuring Rights for All

The quality of life in our communities depends not just on beautiful buildings, well-kept parks, and efficient services. It requires, too, that all Americans have equal rights and opportunities. These rights, of course, are guaranteed to all citizens by the Constitution of the United States. Yet, in spite of this guarantee, Americans have not always shared these rights equally. Many groups of Americans have had to work hard to win their rights as citizens.

Our Rich Cultural Heritage

As you read in Chapter 1, people from all over the world have settled in our country and contributed to its heritage. As group after group came to the United States, they brought with them different languages, ideas, and customs. For instance, almost every language in the world is spoken somewhere in the United States. Also, the special holidays, foods, clothing, and other customs of many different groups add a special richness to the lives of all Americans.

Our country's many different groups are proud of their varied backgrounds. Sometimes, however, because of their different customs and beliefs, they have misunderstood each other. This has happened not only in our country but in every land throughout history.

Minority Groups

People whose ways are different from others are often referred to as **minority groups.** The word "minority" in this case does not necessarily mean that the group is outnumbered. Rather, it means that it is not the group in power. It also means that the group is set apart from other people in the society because of race, nationality, language, customs, or religion.

Minority groups often have met with prejudice and discrimination. **Prejudice** is an unfair opinion, not based on facts, of members of a particular group. **Discrimination** refers to unfair actions taken against people because they belong to a particular group. Prejudice and discrimination have been present throughout human history. In the United States, too, some Americans have looked upon others who were "different" from them with fear and distrust.

These feelings, as well as acts of discrimination, were not uncommon in the early years of our nation. For example, American Indians were often treated badly by the settlers from Europe. Some English settlers did not welcome the early Scotch-Irish and Germans. In later years, some Americans were unfriendly to newly arriving Catholics from Ireland and Germany. Still later, these people looked with distrust on the new immigrants from southern and eastern Europe.

Throughout our nation's history, African Americans have suffered greatly as a result of prejudice and discrimination. Also, Mexican Americans and other Spanish-speaking Americans as well as Asian Americans often have faced resentment and hostility.

All of the minority groups you have been reading about are ethnic groups. An **ethnic group** is a group of people of the same race, nationality, or religion who share a common and distinctive culture and heritage.

In recent years women, older Americans, and people with physical and mental disabilities also have been regarded as minority groups. These groups have not been set apart by language, race, or religion. Yet many of these people believe that they, too, have not been given their full equal rights.

The Struggle for Equal Rights

As you may recall, the rights of citizenship that all Americans are entitled to are called **civil rights.** They include the right to vote and the right to equal treatment under the law. Civil rights also include the right to be considered for any job for which one is qualified. Civil rights mean, too, the right to use and enjoy public places and facilities.

The struggle for equal rights is an old one. For more than 200 years, African Americans were forced to live in slavery. Although slavery was ended after the Civil War, most blacks were denied their rights as free Americans. Laws in many states caused blacks to be treated as second-class citizens.

Some of the southern states passed laws to prevent black Americans from voting. These states also passed **segregation laws.** As you have read, these laws segregated, or separated, black Americans. There were separate schools for blacks, separate parks, separate drinking fountains, and other separate facilities. Black Americans could not buy homes in certain sections of a community. They were not allowed to work at certain jobs.

Black Americans in the North were also denied full civil rights. The northern states did not actually pass laws that took away the civil rights of black citizens. However, black Americans in the North also had trouble finding jobs. They were forced to live in areas where only blacks lived and where schools were inferior to those attended by white students.

African Americans have worked to achieve equal rights for many years. One of the earliest groups formed to help in this struggle was the **National Association for the Advancement of Colored People (NAACP)**, founded in 1909. The NAACP remains a visible force today.

An important step toward obtaining equal rights for all Americans was made in 1954. In that year, as you read in Chapter 7, the Supreme Court gave its landmark decision in the case of *Brown v. Board of Education of Topeka*. The Court ruled that segregation in public schools was a denial of equal rights to black citizens.

The Civil Rights Movement

After the *Brown* decision, the struggle for equal rights grew even stronger. It has come to be known as the **civil rights movement.** Americans who supported the civil rights movement were opposed to laws that denied African Americans equal rights.

Can You Guess?

One of our Presidents had a serious physical disability. Who was he?

Answer is on page 594.

In 1963 more than 200,000 Americans staged a "March on Washington." They came from all over the nation to urge the passage of civil rights laws.

Under our American form of government, citizens can express their **dissent**—their disagreement with a law—in many ways. People involved in the civil rights movement used many different methods of dissent. For example, they wrote letters, made phone calls, and sent telegrams to their elected lawmakers. They wrote books and made speeches. Supporters of the civil rights movement also organized mass demonstrations. During a **demonstration,** dissenters march in public carrying signs, singing songs, and making speeches (see page 546).

The right of all Americans to express their dissent against laws in these and many other ways is protected by our Constitution. However, people do not have the right to break the laws while expressing their dissent.

Sometimes, though, citizens have used some or all of these forms of dissent, but without results. Is there anything more that citizens can do to change a law they think is wrong or unjust?

During the civil rights movement, and at other times in the past, some Americans have shown their dissent by intentionally disobeying laws they believed to be wrong. This practice is called **civil disobedience.**

As you know, people who disobey a law must face the consequences. Supporters of the civil rights movement who disobeyed a law they objected to knew they could be arrested. They hoped that their willingness to lose their freedom would make other people look more closely at the opposed law. Perhaps others would help get the law changed. Activists generally used civil disobedience only when other tactics failed.

Progress in Civil Rights

Large numbers of Americans have taken part in the civil rights movement. It has had a great impact on our nation. In response to demands
(continued on page 476)

Rosa Parks—The Woman Who Kept Her Seat

Should a person who has a seat on a bus be forced to give up the seat to someone else? On December 1, 1955, Rosa Parks of Montgomery, Alabama, stayed seated after being told to move to the back of the bus. She was arrested.

A Policy of Segregation

At that time many parts of the South had laws that called for segregation, or separation, of blacks and whites in public places. Black Americans and white Americans had to use separate restaurants, schools, and even water fountains. They rode the same buses and trains, but they were not allowed to sit together. Under the policy of Montgomery's bus company, the first four rows of the bus were reserved for whites. If the white section filled up, blacks had to give up their seats.

On the evening that Rosa Parks refused to move to the back of the bus, all the seats in the white section were taken. When more white passengers boarded the bus, the driver ordered Rosa Parks and three other black riders to move. Rosa was tired after sewing hems on dresses in a department store

Rosa Parks is fingerprinted after being arrested for not giving up her seat.

After the end of the Montgomery bus boycott, a policy of "first come, first seated" became the law.

all day. She stayed seated. The bus driver called a police officer, and Rosa was taken to jail.

This was not the first time a black person had been arrested for keeping a seat on a Montgomery bus. Less than a year before, a 15-year-old girl had refused to move and was led away in handcuffs. The incident caused only a brief stir.

In 1955, however, the attitudes of many Americans were beginning to change. The year before, the United States Supreme Court had ruled that segregation in public schools was unconstitutional. As a result of that decision, black Americans became more determined to fight for their rights.

The Montgomery Bus Boycott

Rosa Parks was a respected member of her community, a college graduate, and an active member of her church. Immediately after her arrest, the black community of Montgomery went into action. "This is no time to talk," black leaders decided. "It is time to act." They asked all black people in the city to boycott the buses—that is, to stop riding them—until the bus company started a "first come, first seated" policy. The boycott won wide support. Black citizens of Montgomery walked or shared rides.

Rosa Parks decided not to pay the fine the court had set for her. Her lawyer appealed, and the case reached the United States Supreme Court. In 1956 the Court ruled that segregation on buses was unconstitutional. The bus boycott ended, although the struggle for equal rights continued. Martin Luther King, Jr., the 27-year-old black minister who led the boycott, went on to become one of the best-known leaders of the national civil rights movement.

The bus boycott, led by Rosa Parks and Martin Luther King, Jr., was an early victory for the civil rights movement.

Thinking It Over

1. Why do you think the black leaders of Montgomery decided to boycott buses as a way to win equal rights?
2. Explain why you think Rosa Parks did not pay her fine.
3. In your opinion, was Rosa Parks right to act as she did? Explain your answer.

Annual festivals, such as this Cinco de Mayo (May 5th) festival in Texas, are one way in which members of minority groups show pride in their cultural heritage.

The voting rights of minority groups were further strengthened by various voting rights acts and by the Twenty-fourth Amendment to the Constitution. This amendment, ratified in 1964, prohibits the use of poll taxes or other taxes as a requirement for voting.

Extending Equal Rights to Other Groups

In recent years the progress made by African Americans has encouraged other minority groups. As a result, these groups have also worked to end discrimination.

Hispanic Americans. Hispanic Americans are the fastest growing minority in the United States. This Spanish-speaking group includes Mexican Americans, Puerto Ricans, Cubans, and people from Central and South America. Spanish-speaking Americans, like African Americans, have suffered discrimination in many areas of life.

Hispanic Americans have become increasingly united in their efforts to gain better working and living conditions. In addition, many parents have also urged that public schools teach in Spanish as well as in English. A number of laws have guaranteed educational, voting, and other rights to our Spanish-speaking citizens.

Native Americans. Native Americans make up one of the country's smallest ethnic minorities. For most of our nation's history, the federal government considered American Indians to be conquered peoples with their own governments. As a result, they were long denied many of the civil rights guaranteed to all Americans. For example, American Indians could not vote until 1924, when they were granted American citizenship. Since the 1960's, protests, court cases, and lobbying efforts have brought about many changes and improvements in the treatment of American Indians.

Women. Many women have joined together to work for equal rights. From the earliest period in our nation's history, women

for equal rights, Congress passed several civil rights laws. These civil rights laws established the following six principles to guarantee the rights of American minority groups.

1. The right to vote cannot be denied because of race or color.
2. Discrimination in public schools must be ended.
3. The right to work or belong to a union shall not be denied because of race or color.
4. Any business open to the public, such as restaurants and theaters, shall be open equally to all people.
5. Public places of amusement, such as parks and swimming pools, shall be open to all people.
6. Discrimination in the rental or sale of houses is forbidden.

have not had the same rights as men (see page 540). For many years women could not own property. Most women could not vote until the Nineteenth Amendment to the Constitution was passed in 1920. They also did not enjoy the same educational and career opportunities as men.

In recent years our federal and state governments have passed laws guaranteeing women equal rights. Many businesses have hired women in occupations formerly reserved for men. However, some professions and unions still admit very few women. Also, women do not always get the same pay as men doing the same jobs. As a result, the movement for equal rights for women continues strong today.

Senior Citizens. As you may recall, the population of the United States is "growing older" every year. Today, about 30 million Americans are age 65 and over. As the number of senior citizens has increased, so have their demands for equal rights.

The elderly of our country, like other minority groups, have faced discrimination. This discrimination is based on the unfounded belief that senior citizens, because they are not young, are unproductive. Unfortunately, this prejudice has cost our country a great deal. Senior citizens, with their wealth of experience, are particularly able to make valuable contributions to our society.

Recently more people have begun to recognize that older Americans are a great national resource. This recognition largely came through the efforts of organizations such as the American Association of Retired Persons. The Gray Panthers have been especially active on behalf of older Americans.

Disabled Americans. People who have disabilities have suffered from discrimination as well. In recent years, disabled Americans have organized nationwide groups to fight for an end to discrimination in employment, housing, transportation, and many other areas of life. They won an important victory in 1990 when Congress passed the Americans With Disabilities Act. This law extends the provisions of the Civil Rights Act of 1964 to American citizens who have disabilities.

Working Together for Equal Rights

Much has been accomplished in moving toward the goal of equal rights for all American citizens. However, many groups are still working toward fuller civil rights and opportunities throughout the nation.

Our nation was founded and made free and strong through the efforts and contributions of the many different groups that settled here. Over the years, many of these groups have struggled to secure their lawful rights. It is up to all of us as responsible citizens to uphold the laws that guarantee these rights.

Modern technology, such as this Braille computer, has allowed many disabled Americans to contribute their skills and talents to the labor force.

SECTION 2 REVIEW

Define minority groups, prejudice, discrimination, ethnic group, civil rights, segregation laws, dissent, demonstration, civil disobedience

Identify National Association for the Advancement of Colored People (NAACP), civil rights movement

1. **Understanding Ideas** Explain how African Americans were discriminated against prior to the civil rights movement.
2. **Composing an Essay** Write a short essay identifying the methods of dissent and the accomplishments of the American civil rights movement.
3. **Summarizing Ideas** Summarize the problems faced by each of the following groups: Hispanic Americans, Native Americans, women, senior citizens, and disabled Americans.

Thinking Critically Describe three things citizens can do to help protect the rights of all Americans.

3 Protecting Our Health and Safety

Being healthy means more than not being sick. The World Health Organization of the United Nations defines **health** as "a state of complete physical, mental, and social well-being and not merely the absence of disease or infirmity." Many people also refer to this state of well-being as **wellness.**

Everyone has the responsibility to look after his or her own wellness. However, the lack of wellness in individuals can affect an entire community. The welfare of our communities and our nation depends on the wellness of our citizens. For this and other reasons, the health and safety of the people of our country are of concern to all Americans. How does our government promote wellness?

The Federal Government and Health

The Department of Health and Human Services has one of the largest budgets in the federal government. It spends billions of dollars a year on health programs alone. The department also advises state and local governments and distributes federal funds to local health programs.

One of the most important agencies of the department is the United States **Public Health Service.** It carries on medical research in such fields as cancer and heart disease. The Public Health Service makes sure our nation's water supplies are pure. In addition, it works with foreign governments to prevent the spread of disease and maintains the largest medical library in the world.

Three important agencies are under the direction of the Public Health Service. They are the Food and Drug Administration, the Health Services and Mental Health Administration, and the National Institutes of Health. These three agencies serve the public in many ways.

State Public Health Departments

Each state has a department of public health. Its function is to see that health laws are carried out in every part of the state. This department has broad powers covering every city, town, village, and rural community.

State public health departments assist local boards of health in several ways. They work with local boards when cases of communicable diseases, such as measles or flu, are especially numerous. They provide laboratory services for doctors and local health authorities who need help in diagnosing disease. State health departments regularly publish bulletins and pamphlets containing useful information for the general public. They also provide medicines and vaccines for the prevention of various diseases.

State public health departments have other duties as well. They must examine all plans for public buildings. They inspect all public buildings and factories and other workplaces to make sure they are safe and have satisfactory air quality and sanitary conditions. Also under the supervision of these departments are state water systems and the disposal of garbage and sewage.

The Community Guards Our Health

Nearly every American city and town has a local health department to enforce rules of sanitation and cleanliness. It also offers help in the prevention and cure of disease. This department keeps records of cases of disease and acts to stop disease from spreading.

The health departments in most cities have laboratories that test foods to make sure they are pure. They inspect all restaurants and other places that perform services that could affect someone's health.

Most communities have local hospitals that are supported in part by local funds. Some communities also have public clinics where medical care is offered free or at a small cost.

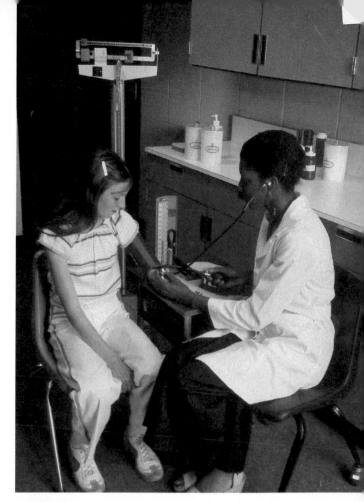

Federal, state, and local levels of government all offer public health services. What public health services are available in your community?

The Drug Problem

Widespread use of legal and illegal drugs has become a serious problem for people concerned with health and safety in American communities. We live in a society where drugs are a part of everyday life for many people. The medicine chest in the average American home usually contains many different kinds of drugs. Depending on their use, they may be helpful or harmful.

Drugs are prescribed by physicians in the treatment of disease. When taken as directed, they benefit people. Drugs also are used in self-medication. If used correctly, they may be helpful. However, some people take drugs for the wrong reasons. They take drugs to seek

a new thrill, to forget, or for "kicks." This use of drugs is called **drug abuse.**

Drug Abuse

Most of the drugs used by drug abusers are habit-forming. Drug abuse can cause serious health problems and can have other side effects. For example, a drug abuser will show poor judgment when driving. Continued use of drugs causes the users to become **addicts,** or slaves to the habit. Addicts must have the drug or they suffer headaches and pains in the stomach, muscles, and bones. As their dependence on the drug grows, they require stronger and stronger doses of most drugs in order to get the effect they desire.

The quality of drugs sold illegally by "pushers" is not regulated. Therefore, the drugs may be too strong or mixed with something harmful. When this happens, individuals may take too strong a dose, or overdose. They may imagine terrible things are happening to them and have to be hospitalized. An overdose may also lead to death.

Much of the increase in crime in the United States is related to the illegal sale, possession, and purchase of drugs. Often needing hundreds of dollars a day to buy illegal drugs, the addict may turn to crime. A large proportion of the crimes of mugging, shoplifting, and burglary are committed by habitual drug users in search of money.

Drug addiction alone is not a crime, but an illness. Both public and private hospitals have programs for treating and curing addicts. Private groups also run special centers where addicts may live while being cured. However, drug addiction is often difficult to cure. The best way to treat drug abuse and addiction is to prevent it. Therefore, public health officials run many programs to educate students, school officials, and parents.

The Problem of Alcohol

Many people do not think of alcohol as a problem. Yet too much alcohol can be harmful to health. In fact, alcohol is a drug. It, like many drugs, is habit-forming. More than 15 million Americans are problem drinkers. These problem drinkers are called alcoholics. They suffer from a disease called **alcoholism.**

The costs to our country of alcohol abuse are tremendous. Alcohol is a factor in about half of all fatal automobile accidents. Thousands of people die each year from physical ailments brought on by drinking too much. Many crimes are committed by people who have been drinking. People who drink too much put a serious strain on family relationships. They also have trouble keeping jobs.

It is important to remember that alcohol, like other drugs, can be very dangerous to your health and well-being. The best way to avoid the dangers of alcohol is not to use it.

The Problem of Smoking

Since the early 1950's, scientists have studied the lives and health of people who smoke. They have reported that smokers run great risks of lung cancer, respiratory ailments, and heart disease. So powerful was their evidence that Congress in 1970 passed a law banning cigarette advertisements from television.

A federal law also provides that every pack of cigarettes and every cigarette advertisement shall carry a warning. As Americans have become more aware of its dangers, smoking increasingly has been banned or limited in public places. Recent reports have suggested that nonsmokers may be harmed by inhaling the smoke of nearby cigarettes.

Smoking, too, is habit-forming. Tobacco products contain an addictive drug called nicotine. Once a person starts smoking, it is difficult to stop. The best way to prevent the smoking habit is not to begin.

Surgeon General's Warnings on Cigarette Packages

- Smoking causes lung cancer, heart disease, emphysema, and may complicate pregnancy.

- Quitting smoking now greatly reduces serious risks to your health.

- Smoking by pregnant women may result in fetal injury, premature birth, and low birth weight.

- Cigarette smoke contains carbon monoxide.

The AIDS Epidemic

In 1981, a deadly disease showed up in the United States for the first time. This disease is **acquired immune deficiency syndrome (AIDS).** In just a few years, a few hundred cases turned into an epidemic, or a disease affecting large numbers of people. By the late 1980's, the United States Surgeon General had identified AIDS as our country's most serious health problem.

AIDS is a worldwide problem. The World Health Organization estimates that there currently are about 600,000 AIDS cases worldwide. By the year 2000, that number is expected to reach 8 million cases.

AIDS is caused by a virus called human immunodeficiency virus, or HIV. HIV destroys the body's ability to fight off illness. As a result, people with AIDS have no protection against diseases such as cancer and pneumonia.

Although there have been advances in the treatment of the disease, there is no cure for AIDS. Medical researchers have been working on the problem since it was discovered. The federal government and other organizations have devoted millions of dollars to research on AIDS. Researchers, however, believe it may take years of intensive work before a vaccine or a cure for AIDS is developed.

People who contract AIDS may not show any signs of being sick for many years. Thus, it is difficult to know exactly how many people are infected with HIV. But it is certain that the disease is spreading rapidly.

Currently, it is estimated that 1.5 million American citizens are infected with HIV and will eventually become sick. AIDS cases have been reported in all 50 states. At present, more than 3,000 new cases are being reported in the United States each month.

Medical researchers originally identified homosexual men as the group most likely to contract AIDS. The group with the second-highest risk was identified as users of illegal intravenous drugs (drugs that are injected with a needle). While these groups still account for

Reported Cases of AIDS in the United States

Year	Number of Cases
1981	199
1982	744
1983	2,117
1984	4,445
1985	8,249
1986	13,166
1987	21,070
1988	31,001
1989	35,238

SOURCE: Centers for Disease Control.

the largest number of reported AIDS cases, researchers have found that AIDS is spreading to other groups in the population.

How AIDS Is Transmitted

The AIDS virus is transmitted through blood and other body fluids. Most people who contract AIDS are infected with the virus through sexual contact or by using needles that were used by people who carry the virus. Pregnant women who have the AIDS virus can pass it on to their unborn children. Before 1985, recipients of blood transfusions sometimes contracted the virus by receiving infected blood. Today, our nation's blood supply is checked carefully to avoid this type of transmission.

People sometimes think that they can catch the AIDS virus by associating with people who have the disease. In fact, there is no evidence that a person can catch AIDS through casual contact. Medical research has established that casual social contact—at school, in restaurants, in swimming pools—does not pose any threat of infection.

The Danger of Accidents

Every American wants to live in a community in which it is safe to live, work, and play. Yet each year about 70 million Americans are injured in accidents. About 11 million of these people must remain in bed for at least one day after the accident. More than 400,000 more people are permanently disabled, and more than 100,000 Americans die from accidents each year.

What kinds of accidents cause so much suffering? Automobile accidents, misuse of electrical equipment, and drownings are among the leading categories of accidents in the United States. Many of these accidents take place at home or on the job. The rest take place on highways, in schools, in parks, and in other public places.

Safety on the Highway

Most of the nation's serious accidents occur on our nation's streets and highways. Nearly 2 million people are injured each year in the United States in accidents involving motor vehicles. About 50,000 people are killed in these automobile accidents.

Around half of these deaths involve alcohol. That is, drinking and driving contribute in some way to about 25,000 deaths each year. In recent years, local and state governments have responded to the growing public outcry over drinking and driving by passing stricter drunk driving laws.

The main cause of automobile accidents is speeding. For this reason, law enforcement officials devote much time and energy to catching people who exceed the speed limit. Police issue tickets, and, in many states, drivers with a certain number of tickets lose their driver's license.

Government officials also promote safety on the highway by encouraging the use of seat belts. In recent years, many state governments have passed laws that require everyone to wear their seat belts. Experts estimate that 10,000 lives could be saved each year if everyone wore their seat belts. In addition, many state governments have also passed child-restraint laws, which require children riding in cars to be placed in specially designed child seats or harnesses.

These government measures save lives. But the burden of highway safety still rests with individual citizens, who must be depended on to act responsibly on our nation's roadways.

Fight Against Fire

More than 3 million fires occur in the United States each year. These fires cause the deaths of about 6,000 people annually and cost about $6 billion in property damage.

What causes all of these fires? Most are caused either by carelessness or by defective equipment. Thus, most fires that have occurred in the United States could have been prevented. In fact, the best way to fight a fire is to prevent it from happening. Every citizen has the responsibility to follow common-sense rules of fire prevention in the home, at school, at work, in the community, and while outdoors.

One of the best ways to avoid the hazards of fire is for people to install smoke detectors. A **smoke detector** is a small device that sounds a loud alarm the moment it detects smoke. This early warning can help everyone in the building escape safely. Most communities in the United States now require that smoke detectors be installed in newly constructed homes and office buildings.

Can You Guess?

Fire trucks are equipped with many different tools and supplies. How many of these things can you name?

Answers are on page 594.

Safety Is a Serious Business

Safety is a serious, life-and-death business. Fortunately, many accidents can be prevented. The key to preventing accidents is education. All American citizens have the responsibility to learn and follow the common-sense rules of safety. The more citizens know how to prevent accidents—and know what to do should an accident occur—the safer our country will be for everyone.

 SECTION 3 REVIEW

Define health, wellness, drug abuse, addicts, alcoholism, acquired immune deficiency syndrome (AIDS), smoke detector

Identify Public Health Service

1. **Composing a Paragraph** Write a paragraph that explains how government promotes the health of the American people.
2. **Identifying Ideas (a)** Why does the use of drugs, including alcohol, concern all Americans? **(b)** What are some dangers of smoking cigarettes?
3. **Expressing Ideas (a)** Why is AIDS considered to be the country's number-one health problem? **(b)** Explain how the AIDS virus is transmitted.
4. **Summarizing Ideas** Explain what you can do to prevent accidents on the highway and at home.

Thinking Critically You are a city council member. A citizen's group has proposed an ordinance to ban smoking in all public places. Will you support the group's proposal? Explain your position.

Americans have always tried to improve their way of life. Early in our nation's history, for example, men and women began moving to the cities to find new and more interesting jobs. There they hoped to make a better life for themselves and their children.

As time passed, however, and our population continued to grow, Americans began leaving the large cities. They moved out into smaller towns and suburbs. For the most part, the problems of our nation's cities are responsible for this movement of the American people.

The centers of many of our cities have deteriorated. Many areas have become slums. Mass transportation has declined. As the population of many small towns and suburbs has grown, these areas have developed similar problems. Many communities across the country are working hard to improve conditions.

Our communities are made up of many different minority groups. These groups have contributed much to the richness of our society. Unfortunately, many groups have been victims of prejudice and discrimination. They have had to struggle to achieve their full civil rights, and their struggle continues.

The wellness of people in our communities is very important. There are many things that each person can do to safeguard his or her health and safety and that of others. For example, you can learn about the causes of alcoholism and drug abuse, help prevent accidents, and seek safety training.

CHAPTER 23 SUMMARY

CITIZENSHIP SKILL
Comparing Points of View

As a citizen, you are free to make choices and take stands on issues. During your lifetime, you will face hundreds of questions like these: Who will you vote for? Which proposals do you support? What should be done about a problem?

Different people will have different answers to these types of questions. Comparing the different points of view about a situation will enable you to make a fair, reasonable, and well-informed decision.

How to Compare Points of View

To compare points of view effectively, follow these guidelines.

1. **Identify the issue.** Before you can compare points of view, you must understand the issue. Often, it helps to put the issue in the form of a question. For example, the issue in an argument or discussion about who should be elected governor might be phrased as "Who should be governor of our state?"

2. **List the arguments used by each side.** Listing the arguments side-by-side on a piece of paper will help you compare each side's argument on a point-by-point basis.

3. **Examine the evidence.** Just because someone gives a reason for a position does not mean the position is a valid one.

4. **Distinguish between facts and opinions.** When comparing points of view, it is useful to compare facts and to ignore opinions.

Applying the Skill

Compare the points of view given below. Then answer the following questions.

1. What issue is being discussed?
2. **(a)** What arguments does each person use to support his or her point of view? **(b)** What evidence does each person use to support these arguments? **(c)** What are the opinions?
3. Express your own point of view on the issue under consideration.

VALERIE'S POINT OF VIEW: There is nothing more important than saving lives on American highways. The best way to do this would be to require car makers to install air bags in all new cars. Air bags are better than seat belts: people can ignore or disconnect seat belts, but they can't defeat air bags. Government studies show that deaths from auto accidents would drop as much as 30 to 55 percent if all cars were equipped with air bags. This is a large percentage. Studies done by the insurance industry also show that air bags save lives. The sooner the government acts, the sooner more American lives would be saved.

LUIS'S POINT OF VIEW: Air bags are expensive, and would add hundreds of dollars to the price of a car. If the government required air bags to be installed in all new cars, American consumers would lose their choice as to whether to pay extra for air bags. Moreover, according to auto industry studies, it can cost as much as $2,000 to restore an air bag after it has been used. Who can afford that? And what if the air bag inflated accidentally? That could cause an accident. The cost and risk of air bags are things American consumers should have a choice about: the government should not require that air bags be installed in new cars.

Reviewing Terms

On a separate sheet of paper, copy the paragraph below. Then fill in each blank, using the correct term from the following list.

prejudice	civil disobedience
dissent	civil rights
minority groups	demonstrate
discriminate	

America was founded on the ideals of freedom and equality. Unfortunately, many citizens have been and continue to be denied their (1) _____, or rights of citizenship. (2) _____, or an unfair opinion of certain groups of people, has led some Americans to (3) _____, or unfairly treat, groups of people. The people treated unfairly are members of (4) _____, those people not in power in our society. To win the fight for rights, citizens express their (5) _____, or disagreement, with laws and unfair practices in many ways. They march, or (6) _____. They contact public officials. If all else fails, citizens may use (7) _____ and knowingly break a law to call attention to their cause.

Using Thinking Skills

1. **Understanding Ideas** What is the best way to prevent accidents and to ensure the safety of American citizens?
2. **Expressing Ideas (a)** What problems has the movement of middle-income families away from cities caused? **(b)** What are some of the actions cities have taken to combat these problems?
3. **Identifying Roles** How do our governments promote wellness?
4. **Identifying Ideas** What problems does discrimination cause for minority groups?
5. **Organizing Ideas (a)** What is the goal of the civil rights movement? **(b)** What tactics do people active in the civil rights movement use to achieve their goals?

6. **Composing a Paragraph** Explain why so many Americans are homeless.
7. **Seeing Relationships (a)** What are the costs to our nation of illegal drug use? **(b)** What are some effects of alcohol abuse? **(c)** What are some effects of smoking?
8. **Drawing Conclusions** Why is AIDS considered this country's number-one health problem?

Practicing Civics Skills

Comparing Points of View Read the letters to the editor that appear on the editorial page of your local newspaper. Clip out two letters that express different points of view on the same issue. Then answer the following questions:

1. What is the main issue in the letters?
2. **(a)** What arguments are made in each letter? **(b)** How are the arguments supported?
3. Do the letters contain opinions? If so, what are they?
4. **(a)** With which letter do you most agree? **(b)** Do you have a point of view that differs from both of the letters?

Being a Good Citizen

1. Contact a local civil rights organization and invite a representative to speak to your class on the topic "Current Challenges to the Civil Rights Movement."
2. Work with a group of students to organize a Safety Awareness Day in your school or home. Contact the fire department, the Red Cross, and similar organizations to obtain information about good safety habits.
3. Conduct research to find out about homelessness in your community. Determine approximately how many people are without homes, what your local government and private organizations are doing to help homeless citizens, and how individuals can contribute to the effort. Report your findings to the class.

CHAPTER 24

You and the Law

Chapter Sections

1 **Crime in the United States**
2 **The Criminal Justice System**
3 **Treating Juvenile Crime**

Chapter Focus

One of our most important duties as citizens, as you know, is to obey our nation's laws. Unfortunately, every period of history has had its own special kinds of crime to fight. Long ago Americans worried about horse theft and cattle rustling. Today we are trying to find ways to deal with computer crime, drug abuse, and street gangs.

Yet new types of criminal activity are only a small part of the total problem facing Americans and people throughout the world. Offenses in almost all categories of crime are increasing at an alarming rate. The need to find solutions is urgent.

Americans are worried about the increase in crime. They are concerned too about protecting the civil rights of those people suspected of committing a crime. Americans have debated the proper role of the police, the justice of the court and prison systems, and the treatment of juvenile offenders.

Study Guide

As you begin to learn about crime in America, look for answers to the following questions:

★ What is crime, and how are crimes categorized?
★ What are the causes and costs of crime?
★ How does the criminal justice system operate in the United States?
★ How does the juvenile justice system operate?

1 Crime in the United States

The Federal Bureau of Investigation (FBI) is our main source of information on crime in the United States. According to the FBI, serious crime in the United States has quadrupled since 1960. In recent years, more than 13 million serious crimes have been reported each year. Americans have become increasingly alarmed by the extent of crime in the United States.

What is considered a crime? A **crime** is any act that breaks the law and for which a punishment has been established. The FBI identifies 29 types of crime. These crimes range from the most serious crimes, such as murder, to the least serious crimes, such as minor traffic violations.

These 29 types of crime are categorized in various ways. We will look at five categories of crime: crimes against persons, crimes against property, victimless crimes, white-collar crimes, and organized crimes.

Crimes Against Persons

Crimes against persons are violent crimes, acts that harm or end a person's life or that threaten to do so. The most serious of such crimes is **murder.** Murder is the willful killing of one person by another person. More than 20,000 murders are committed in the United States each year.

The most common type of violent crime is **aggravated assault.** Aggravated assault is any kind of physical injury that is done intentionally to another person. Such assault is often committed during the act of robbing someone. The FBI records more than 800,000 cases of aggravated assault each year.

Another type of violent crime is **forcible rape.** Forcible rape is the sexual violation of a person by force and against the person's will. According to the FBI, a forcible rape takes place every six minutes in the United States.

Crimes Against Property

Most crimes committed in the United States are crimes against property. This type of crime includes actions that involve stealing or destroying someone else's property. The forcible or illegal entry into someone's home or other property with the intention to steal is called **burglary.** More than 3 million burglaries a year were reported in recent years.

Larceny is the theft of property without forcible or illegal entry. Examples of larceny are theft of an outboard motor, stealing from a cash drawer, and shoplifting. If the property is worth over a certain amount of money (which varies from state to state), the theft is called **grand larceny.** A theft of goods valued under this amount is called **petty larceny.**

The theft of automobiles, or **motor vehicle theft,** is a common crime against property and a serious national problem. More than 1 million cars are reported stolen each year. Many cars are taken by organized gangs that resell them or strip them and sell the parts. Other cases involve young people who risk arrest to steal the cars, drive them for a while, and then abandon them.

Robbery is a crime that involves both property and persons. It may be defined as taking something from a person by threatening the person with injury. The robber may demand "your money or your life" and back

Each year thousands of people are arrested in the United States for the crime of arson. The effects of arson are felt by the whole community.

up the threat with a weapon. About half a million robberies take place in our country each year. Most of them are done with firearms. A murder committed during a robbery, even if unplanned, may be punished by life imprisonment.

Another kind of crime against property is **vandalism,** or the willful destruction of property. **Arson** is the destruction of property by setting fire to it. The damaging of schools and other public buildings and property by vandalism and arson has been increasing over the years. These forms of crime hurt all the citizens in a community.

Victimless Crimes

Some crimes, such as gambling and the use of illegal drugs, are known as **victimless crimes.** In such crimes there is no victim whose rights are invaded by another. These crimes mainly harm the lawbreakers themselves. Nevertheless, victimless crimes are

harmful to society. The sale and possession of illegal drugs increases the death rate and often leads to other types of crime, such as robbery. Gamblers who lose their money may turn to stealing and other crimes.

White-Collar Crimes

Crimes committed by white-collar workers on the job are called **white-collar crimes.** They range from stealing paper clips to embezzlement and fraud. **Embezzlement** is taking for one's own use money that has been entrusted to one's care. **Fraud** is taking someone else's money or property through dishonesty. A person may commit fraud by charging for services that were not done, for example.

As the number of white-collar workers has increased, so has the number and seriousness of crimes they commit. Theft by employees and businesses costs far more than street crime. Experts estimate that white-collar crime accounts for losses of about

$200 billion a year. One insurance company found that 30 percent of all business failures each year are from employee dishonesty.

Many of the most recent types of white-collar crime involve the use of computers. Today nearly all large businesses and government offices use computers. They are used to keep track of bills and records, payroll, inventory, and other financial matters. Some people have used computers to commit electronic theft, fraud, and embezzlement.

Organized Crime

When most people think of criminals, they think of individuals who act on their own to commit crimes. This is not always the case. Some criminals are part of organized crime. That is, they belong to a **crime syndicate,** or a large organization of professional criminals.

Organized crime syndicates specialize in providing illegal goods and services, such as gambling, drug trafficking, prostitution, and loan-sharking (lending money at extremely high interest rates). Often these crime syndicates engage in legitimate business pursuits that serve as a front for their illegal activities.

Such criminals are difficult to catch. They often use terror tactics, blackmail, and violence to keep people from going to the police.

The Rising Crime Rate

National statistics of criminal offenses are collected from local police departments by the FBI. The findings are published each year as a part of *Crime in the United States—Uniform Crime Reports*. These reports show that every year the number of almost every type of crime increases.

We do not know how many crimes are actually committed each year. Police statistics do not include all crimes. One reason is that citizens often do not report crimes to the police. We can be sure that the crime rate is much higher than the statistics show.

The Causes of Crime

No one really knows why people commit crimes. There have been many theories. The causes usually given for crime and its increase are poverty, unemployment, and certain trends in society.

Poverty. The most common explanation for crime is probably poverty. Many poor people live in slums, where there is overcrowding, poor education, and unstable family life. Under these conditions, many people do not get the training they need for better jobs. In such an environment, people often feel helpless and angry. Some people break the law in an attempt to "get even" with society for the kind of life they have.

Unemployment. Unemployment is another probable cause of crime. When economic conditions are unfavorable and people lose their jobs, some of them may turn to robbery or commit other crimes against people or property.

Permissive Society. Some experts think a permissive society contributes to the increase in crime. They say many parents spoil their children and permit them to do anything they want. These children sometimes find it difficult to control their behavior when they are older and do not get what they want. They have not learned to act responsibly in their own lives and toward others.

Other people believe our courts are too permissive. They say judges often are too lenient with convicted criminals.

Population Shifts. Some experts point to two other reasons for the increase in crime—the large percentage of young people now in the population and urbanization.

Many kinds of crime are committed mainly by young people. Today people between the ages of 15 and 24 account for over half of all the arrests in the United States. Most of those arrested are young men. Also, more offenses have always been committed in cities than in rural areas. Since the United States has become a nation of cities, it is not surprising that crime is on the increase.

One of the costs of crime is fear. As a result of the increase in crime, many people have taken precautions to protect their lives and property.

The Costs of Crime

Whatever its causes, crime is a problem that must be solved if people are to live in safety and without fear. Crime harms everyone. The cost to society is over $60 billion a year. More than $29 billion is spent on public law enforcement alone. Not included in these figures are private sums that are spent for insurance and for crime prevention services and equipment.

There are psychological costs as well. Among the highest costs are the pain and suffering of its victims. The constant worry by those who live and work in high-crime areas also must be taken into account.

Can we end crime? We can start by trying to lower the number of illegal acts committed. This can be done if all citizens take precautions to ensure their safety and protect their property. Also, each citizen should support those officials who are trying to prevent crime and bring criminals to justice.

SECTION 1 REVIEW

Define crime, murder, aggravated assault, forcible rape, burglary, larceny, grand larceny, petty larceny, motor vehicle theft, robbery, vandalism, arson, victimless crimes, white-collar crimes, embezzlement, fraud, crime syndicate

1. **Expressing Ideas** (a) What is our main source of information about crime in the United States? (b) Provide evidence to show that crime has been on the increase.
2. **Summarizing Ideas** (a) What are crimes against persons? (b) What are crimes against property? (c) Give two examples of each.
3. **Seeing Relationships** (a) Explain why victimless crimes are harmful to our society. (b) Why has white-collar crime been increasing in recent years?
4. **Composing an Essay** Write a short essay describing the possible causes of crime.

Thinking Critically Your local Chamber of Commerce has asked you to give a speech to the community. The title of your speech will be "How Citizens Can Protect Themselves Against Crime." Write a draft of your speech.

2 The Criminal Justice System

Our society depends on responsible citizens. It needs people who obey the law and who go about their daily tasks in a peaceful and orderly fashion. To help achieve this goal of "domestic tranquillity," police forces have been established at the local, state, and national levels.

Keeping the peace requires more than hiring efficient police officers. Once arrested, the accused must be tried and, if found guilty, punished. The three-part system of police, courts, and corrections needed to bring criminals to justice is known as the **criminal justice system.**

The Role of the Police

The police have a number of duties. These are to protect life and property, prevent crime, seek out and arrest those people who violate the law, protect the rights of the individual, maintain peace and order, and control the flow of traffic on streets and highways.

It is not a police officer's job to punish lawbreakers or to decide who is guilty or not guilty. Deciding questions about guilt and innocence is the function of courts of law. Good police officers try to use their trained judgment about whom to arrest and on what grounds. They try to avoid the use of undue force and to be patient in the face of insults and threats of personal injury. They try to act as peacemakers, advisers, protectors, and friends, as well as law enforcers.

The job of police officers is not an easy one. It can also be a discouraging one because of overcrowding and other problems in the American court system.

The Training of Police Officers

Modern police officers are carefully selected and trained. Before they are hired, they are fully checked and investigated. They must pass aptitude and intelligence tests, as well as civil service examinations or similar written tests. In addition, they must pass rigorous physical and psychological examinations. Most cities require police officers to be high school graduates. In recent years some cities have been seeking college graduates.

New police officers attend special police academies. They learn about law, community relations, evidence, arrest procedures, and recordkeeping. They also receive on-the-job training that includes the use of weapons and other physical skills. They are taught how to deal calmly with the public, how to handle emergencies, and how to give first aid. When trouble occurs, they must be ready to arrest suspects, prepare reports for the courts, and appear in the courts as witnesses.

Police Patrols Help Prevent Crime

New police officers may begin their careers by "walking a beat," or patrolling an assigned area. Many experts believe that such foot patrols are an effective way to prevent crime in the cities, especially at night. Officers on foot patrol can cover a territory carefully. They also can get to know the people who live and work in the neighborhood.

Most communities cannot afford all the foot patrol officers they need. They add to the strength and mobility of their force by using patrol cars. Radio-equipped police cars can be sent to any part of the city when trouble is

Did you know that...

for a long time American cities had no paid police officers? Some cities, however, were served by volunteer patrols called "watch and ward" societies. Their members walked the streets on the lookout for criminals and fires. New York City organized the first paid police force in 1844. Other cities and towns soon followed.

The police had many different nicknames. The most common, *cop* (from *copper*), may have come from the Latin word *capere*, "to catch." Or it may have started with the copper buttons worn by early police officers. The name *fuzz* goes back to the 1930's and probably comes from the word "fussy."

Police officers walking a beat are often an effective way to prevent crime. They get to know the people in the neighborhood and are welcomed by them.

From Arrest to Sentencing

A police officer must have **probable cause** to arrest a suspect. This means that a crime must have been committed and that the officer must have seen it or gathered enough evidence to make an arrest. If the suspect has not been seen committing the crime, an arrest warrant may be necessary. An **arrest warrant** is an authorization by the court to make the arrest.

All crime suspects are entitled to due process and must be informed of their rights before they are arrested. They must be told that they have the right to remain silent and to have a lawyer present during all questioning. They also must be told that anything they say can be used against them in a court of law. If a suspect is not given this information when arrested, any statements he or she makes cannot be used as evidence in court.

After an arrest, the suspect is taken to the police station for **booking.** That is, a record of the arrest will be made. An officer will write down the name of the suspect, the time of the arrest, and the charges involved. The suspect will be fingerprinted and photographed.

Preliminary Hearing. Usually within the next 24 hours, a **preliminary hearing** will be held. During this procedure a judge must decide if there is enough evidence to send the case to trial. If there is not, the judge can dismiss, or drop, the charges against the suspect. If the charges are not dropped, the judge must decide whether or not to set bail.

Bail, as you recall, is money the suspect posts as a guarantee that he or she will return for trial. The amount of bail is determined by the seriousness of the offense.

If the offense is minor, the judge may agree to release the suspect on his or her **own recognizance,** that is, without bail. This usually is done if the suspect lives in the community and has a good reputation. It is assumed from this that the suspect will appear in court for the trial.

Indictment. Next a formal charge must be made. In some states, a grand jury hears the evidence in order to decide whether

reported or suspected. Cruising patrol cars often catch lawbreakers in action.

The main job of the police officer is to prevent crime. The well-trained officer knows the danger signs that invite crime—burned-out street lights, open doors, broken windows. By preventing crime, police officers save lives, money, and property. They also make the community a better and safer place in which to live.

When a crime is committed, the police officer's job is to round up suspects, collect evidence, and recover property whenever possible. The officer must also take care to protect the rights of suspects and witnesses.

to send the case to trial. If the grand jury does find probable cause, the suspect is **indicted,** or charged formally with the crime.

Arraignment. The accused person then goes before a judge to be **arraigned.** That means the accused enters a plea of guilty or innocent of the charge. If the person pleads guilty, no trial is necessary.

Trial. If the accused person pleads innocent to the charge, the case goes to trial. The **defense** is the accused person's side of the case. The government's side of the case is the **prosecution.** The defense and prosecution lawyers choose the jurors for the trial from a large group of people. Both lawyers have the right to question prospective jurors and to reject those people they believe to be prejudiced against their case.

After the jury has been selected, the prosecutor and the defense lawyer make opening statements to the jury. Each lawyer outlines the facts he or she will try to prove.

Then the prosecutor presents the case against the **defendant,** or accused person. Witnesses are sworn in, questioned by the prosecutor, and cross-examined—that is, questioned by the defense attorney. Next the defense presents its case. The defendant may choose whether or not to testify. Under the Constitution, no defendant can be forced to testify against himself or herself.

After all the evidence has been presented by each side, each lawyer makes a closing statement that summarizes his or her arguments. Before the jury leaves the courtroom to reach a **verdict,** or decision, the judge tells them what they can and cannot consider in reaching their verdict.

The defendant is always presumed to be innocent. It is the job of the prosecution to prove that the accused person is guilty beyond a reasonable doubt. If there is any reasonable doubt of guilt, the jury must find the defendant not guilty. Usually the jury must reach a unanimous verdict. As you have read, if the defendant believes that an error was made in the conduct of the trial, he or she may appeal the verdict.

Sentencing. If the defendant is found guilty, the judge must decide the **sentence,** or punishment. Usually the law sets a minimum (least) and maximum (most) penalty for the type of crime that has been committed. In some cases the judge may suspend the sentence. This means the defendant will not have to go to prison at all. The past record and reputation of the defendant will greatly influence the judge's sentence.

Plea Bargaining

Many cases in the United States never go to trial. They are taken care of quickly by **plea bargaining.** This means that the accused person is allowed to plead guilty to a lesser offense than the original charge. The penalty is therefore lighter than it would be if the accused were tried before a jury and found guilty of the more serious crime.

(continued on page 496)

Under the Constitution, all persons accused of a crime are entitled to due process. When arrested they must be informed of their rights immediately.

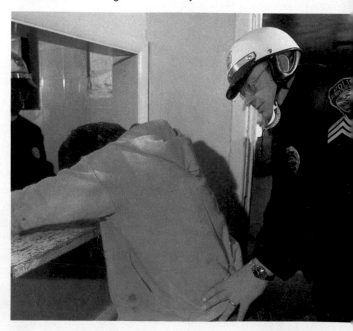

Focus on Freedom

Justice for All

When the founders of our nation wrote the Constitution, they sought to secure the blessings of liberty and justice for all Americans. The Bill of Rights was added to the Constitution to protect the rights and freedoms of all citizens.

One of these rights is guaranteed by the Sixth Amendment. It is the right of an accused person "to have the assistance of counsel," or the help of an attorney. Before the 1960s, however, people on trial in state courts had to pay for their own attorneys. State courts were required to provide counsel for defendants who could not afford it only in cases in which the death penalty was involved.

As a result, many poor people were tried without adequate representation. But one man's fight for justice has ensured that all Americans, rich or poor, now can have the help of counsel if they want it. That man is Clarence Gideon.

Clarence Gideon Is Arrested

In 1961, someone broke into a pool hall in Florida and stole money and food from a vending machine. Clarence Gideon, a Florida resident, was arrested for the crime. Gideon, because he was penniless, asked the state court to appoint free legal counsel for his defense. The court refused, saying that in cases such as Gideon's, only federal courts were required to provide counsel. Gideon then had only two choices: hire a lawyer on his own or represent himself in court. Because he had no money, Gideon was forced to serve as his own attorney.

Although he was determined to convince the jury of his innocence, Gideon did not have any legal expertise. The prosecution, a professional attorney, easily won the case. The court found Gideon guilty of the crime and sentenced him to five years in prison.

Not satisfied with the state court's decision, Gideon spent his long hours in prison studying law books and legal procedures. Using what he learned from his determined study, Gideon sent a handwritten petition to the Supreme Court, asking the Court to review his case. The Court granted Gideon's request.

All Americans, rich or poor, are entitled to have the help of an attorney if they want it.

A Landmark Case

Gideon argued that the state court, by refusing to appoint a lawyer for his defense, had denied him his Sixth Amendment right to the assistance of counsel. The Justices of the Supreme Court, in a unanimous decision, agreed. Justice Hugo Black wrote the decision for the Court. Black wrote that "any person hauled into court, who is too poor to hire a lawyer, cannot be assured a fair trial unless counsel is provided for him. This seems to be an obvious truth."

As a result of the Supreme Court's decision, Gideon won the right to have a new trial in Florida. This time the state court, following the Supreme Court's ruling, appointed a lawyer to defend Gideon. He was found innocent of the charge and was given his freedom.

Clarence Gideon's fight for justice required hard work and dedication, but Americans everywhere benefited from his struggle.

The Right to Counsel

When Gideon won his case before the Supreme Court, he struck a blow for the rights of all Americans. As a result of this landmark decision, many other people who were convicted without counsel won the right to new trials. And since the time of Gideon's case, state courts have been required to provide public defenders, or free counsel, for the poor.

Through his untiring quest for justice, Clarence Gideon proved that our Constitution is a document that serves all Americans. Gideon knew, as the framers of our Constitution knew, there can be no justice without equal justice for all.

Questions to Consider

1. How did the Florida state court respond to Gideon's request for a court-appointed lawyer?
2. How did the Supreme Court rule on Gideon's case?
3. What were the results of the Supreme Court's decision?

Many people support the use of plea bargaining. They say the practice keeps the courts from becoming overloaded with cases. Without it, they say, the number of judges and courts would have to be greatly increased. Critics argue that plea bargaining allows criminals to avoid adequate punishment. Opponents of plea bargaining also say it encourages accused persons to give up their constitutional right to a trial.

Punishing Lawbreakers

People who break the law and are found guilty of their crimes must be punished. The methods used to punish lawbreakers are called **corrections.** The corrections system in the United States generally includes imprisonment, parole, and capital punishment.

Imprisonment. While some less serious crimes may be punished by fines or suspended sentences, more serious crimes are typically punished by imprisonment. People generally agree that lawbreakers should be removed from society for a period of time. Although most people believe in imprisonment as a fair punishment for crime, they disagree on the purpose imprisonment serves.

Some people see the purpose of imprisonment as retribution, or revenge. These people believe that society has the right to make the criminal pay for his or her crimes.

Other people view imprisonment as a deterrence to crime. This means that the threat of a prison term will discourage people from breaking the law.

A third view of imprisonment is that it serves as a means of rehabilitation. People who hold this view believe that the purpose of imprisonment is to reform criminals and return them to society as law-abiding citizens.

Still other people view imprisonment as a means of social protection. People who are imprisoned cannot commit additional crimes or pose a threat to people or property.

Parole. After serving only a part of their sentences, prisoners may become eligible for **parole,** or release. People are paroled on the condition that they obey certain rules and keep out of trouble. Parole generally is granted only to those prisoners who behave

Cameras are forbidden in many courtrooms. Therefore the mass media often hire artists to show the jury and other courtroom scenes.

Prison sentences punish criminals and remove them from society for a time. Some prisons offer training programs to help people get jobs after their release.

 SECTION 2 REVIEW

Define criminal justice system, probable cause, arrest warrant, booking, preliminary hearing, own recognizance, indicted, arraigned, defense, prosecution, verdict, sentence, plea bargaining, corrections, parole, capital punishment

Identify defendant

1. **Identifying Roles** (a) Describe the roles played by police officers. (b) How do people become police officers?
2. **Summarizing Ideas** (a) Summarize the main steps a suspect must go through before being sentenced or set free. (b) Summarize the arguments for and against capital punishment.
3. **Understanding Ideas** (a) Discuss four views of the purpose of imprisonment. (b) How does the parole system work?
4. **Contrasting Ideas** What are the arguments for and against plea bargaining?

Thinking Critically Discuss the qualities you think police officers should have.

well in prison and who show signs of being rehabilitated.

A parole board reviews each application for parole very carefully and makes a decision on it. When a prisoner is paroled, he or she must report regularly to a parole officer. Parole usually lasts until the end of the maximum part of the sentence.

Capital Punishment. The harshest punishment for crimes committed in our nation is **capital punishment**—putting the criminal to death for serious crimes. Some people oppose capital punishment, or the death penalty. They believe it violates the Eighth Amendment's prohibition against "cruel and unusual punishments." Other people say the death penalty is a just punishment, especially for a person who has committed a murder. In 1976 the United States Supreme Court ruled that capital punishment as a penalty for murder is constitutional. Each state passes its own laws about capital punishment.

 Treating Juvenile Crime

Young people are responsible for a large number of our nation's crimes. They commit many of the crimes against property, such as burglary, larceny, vandalism, arson, and automobile theft, and many of the more serious crimes. The rate of crime among those between the ages of 15 and 24 has jumped considerably since the early 1980's.

Juvenile Delinquency

Every state has special laws for dealing with young offenders. The ages to which these laws apply vary from state to state. Most states define **juveniles** as people under 18. Some set

Programs like the Police Athletic League work to bring police officers and young people into close contact. Why might police departments want such programs?

the age as low as 16 and others as high as 21. Juveniles become **delinquents** when they are found guilty of breaking a law.

Statistics show that young people commit many of the serious crimes reported to the police. Some, however, commit minor offenses that bring them into conflict with society. Juveniles who stay out late at night, who prove to be unmanageable by their parents, or who repeatedly run away from home may be termed unruly. The laws concerning unruly behavior vary from community to community. But in communities where such behavior is unlawful, a young person who is repeatedly unruly may be turned over to the juvenile authorities.

Causes of Juvenile Delinquency

Why do some young people break the law and become unruly, while most live law-abiding and useful lives? According to experts who have studied the problem, there is no single answer. All individuals are complicated. Their behavior, whether it be good or bad, may have many causes. Following are some of the more important causes of juvenile delinquency. Some of these are the same as for crime in general.

1. Poor Home Conditions. Many juvenile delinquents come from homes in which parents take little responsibility for their children. Often one parent has permanently left and the other is rarely at home. Youngsters whose parents are alcoholics or drug addicts may spend a lot of time on the streets, where they get into trouble.

2. Poor Neighborhood Conditions. The poorer areas in our cities frequently have a higher rate of crime than other areas. People who live crowded together in poverty often feel hopeless and angry. Many young people in these areas get into trouble while seeking outlets for their frustration or unhappiness. Some young people view delinquency and crime as their only way out of poverty.

3. Membership in Gangs. Some young people who get into trouble are members of neighborhood gangs. It is natural for a young person to want to be with a group and take part in group activities. If the group turns against the community and breaks the law, it becomes a bad influence.

4. School Dropouts and Unemployment. When young people have nothing to do, no place to go, and no money to spend, they may be headed for trouble. A person who drops out of high school is not necessarily headed for a life of crime. Nevertheless, a number of studies have shown that unemployed youths with little skill and training often become delinquents.

5. Alcohol and Drugs. Laws forbid the sale of alcoholic beverages to anyone under a certain age. They also ban the sale of habit-forming drugs to anyone who does not have a prescription from a doctor. Yet many young people manage to get hold of these substances. Under the influence of alcohol or drugs, they frequently do things that they would not do under normal circumstances. People addicted to drugs, who need money to pay for their habit, often turn to crime—sometimes violent crime.

6. Problems of Mental Health. Some young people get into trouble because of mental and emotional problems. They need help. Delinquents are often unhappy people. Deep down inside, they may be afraid of the world or think that society is against them.

Treatment of Juvenile Delinquents

Before the late 1800's, juveniles at least 14 years old were held responsible for the crimes they committed. They were put on trial in adult criminal courts and sentenced to prison and even death. However, during the 1870's reformers began working to change the way young offenders were treated. They said very young people were not really responsible for their actions. Instead of being punished as adults, juveniles needed to be given special understanding.

As a result, many communities set up a juvenile court system. Its purpose was not to punish but to save children from the harmful environment in which they lived. The reformers also hoped to reeducate delinquents by giving them care, treatment, discipline, and responsible supervision.

Instead of trials, juvenile courts hold hearings, which may be attended only by parents or guardians and people directly involved in the case. The reason for the hearings is to determine the guilt or innocence of juveniles. The meetings are informal, and the records of them are kept secret. The purpose of a separate court system for juveniles is to do what is best for the young people involved. For many years it was believed that their parents and court officials would protect their rights. Sometimes, though, juveniles were denied equal protection under the law.

In 1967 a Supreme Court decision brought major changes to the juvenile justice system.

One way to stay out of trouble is to take part in sports. These young people have found a way to play basketball on the street where they live.

Some juvenile offenders are placed on probation. Probation officers stay in close touch with the juvenile offenders assigned to report to them. These dedicated professionals work to keep young offenders out of further trouble with the law.

The Supreme Court ruled that juveniles accused of breaking the law have the same rights of due process as adults. That is, juveniles have the right to be informed of the charges brought against them, to be represented by a lawyer, to confront and question all witnesses, and to refuse to testify against themselves in court. However, the Supreme Court also ruled that juveniles accused of crimes do not have the right to a jury trial or to bail. Nevertheless, a number of states allow young people to be tried before juries.

Punishing Juvenile Delinquents

After hearing all of the evidence, the judge must decide the guilt or innocence of the juvenile offender. If the juvenile is found guilty, several outcomes are possible. For example, the judge may order that the juvenile be placed in a foster home. Or in serious cases, the judge

may have the youth confined to a juvenile correction facility.

One type of correction facility for people under the age of 18 is a training school. Youthful offenders placed in **training schools** usually stay there from six to nine months. Juveniles who are confined for shorter periods of time usually are sent to **juvenile detention centers.** The main goal of both of these types of facilities is to rehabilitate, rather than punish, the young offenders.

Another possible outcome for the juvenile offender is **probation.** Probation is a time period during which a person guilty of an offense is given an opportunity to show that he or she can reform. Offenders placed on probation must obey strict rules, such as being home by a certain time each night and avoiding bad influences. They also must report regularly to a probation officer.

In deciding on a course of action, the judge considers the offense and the home and background of the juvenile offender. The judge takes into account the facts of the case as well as the recommendations of social workers, teachers, relatives, and former employers before deciding the proper punishment.

Serious Crimes by Juveniles

In recent years, there has been an increase in the number of serious crimes committed by young people. As a result, many Americans are demanding that juvenile offenders be tried as adults. Under the traditional juvenile justice system, a young person who commits a brutal murder may be on the street again after only a few years in a juvenile correction facility. In spite of the good intentions of correction officers, that juvenile may not be reformed. He or she may commit another serious crime soon after being set free.

In response to the public demand for protection, some states have begun to punish juveniles convicted of serious crimes as they would punish adults. Some people want to get rid of juvenile courts completely.

Juvenile Decency

Most of our nation's young people are good citizens who stay out of serious trouble. They obey the law and the rules of society. Criminologists—scientists who study crime and the behavior of criminals—give the following suggestions to young people who want to avoid trouble with the law.

1. Do not get started on drugs. Those who try drugs often end up in criminal courts and correction facilities or jails.

2. Stay in school and get the best education possible. It will keep you busy and increase your chances for a good job.

3. Avoid acts of vandalism and arson. These are not the proper ways to express discontent, frustration, or hostility.

4. Have the courage to say no when friends suggest illegal acts.

5. Try to live a full life, with plenty of physical activity and interesting hobbies. The person who is busy doing challenging things does not get bored and turn to criminal activities as an outlet.

 SECTION 3 REVIEW

Define training schools, juvenile detention centers, probation

Identify juveniles, delinquents

1. **Composing an Essay** Write an essay describing the possible causes of juvenile delinquency in our nation.
2. **Summarizing Ideas** (a) How has the treatment of juvenile offenders changed over the years? (b) Why are juveniles tried in special courts?
3. **Understanding Ideas** What happens when juveniles are charged with breaking the law?

Thinking Critically You head a campaign to discourage young people from using drugs. How will you go about this task?

Americans want and need to be protected from crime. Such protection is one of the services governments provide for their citizens. However, crime has become an increasingly serious problem in our nation. Many more offenses are committed, and several new types of crimes have appeared. The financial and psychological costs of crime are alarmingly high. The FBI has identified 29 types of crime.

The American criminal justice system operates to protect everyone, even those people who have been accused of committing criminal actions. Police officers are trained to deal with the public, handle emergencies, and control situations that may lead to crime. They must also inform suspects of their rights. From the moment of arrest, all people suspected of crimes are entitled to the due process of law.

Although most of the nation's young people are law-abiding citizens, juvenile delinquency has become an increasingly pressing problem. A large percentage of offenses are committed by young people. Juveniles who commit crimes sometimes continue a life of crime. Therefore, special courts have been set up to deal with the problems of juvenile delinquents.

CHAPTER

24

SUMMARY

SOCIAL STUDIES SKILL
Doing Library Research

Throughout your school career, you will be called upon to do research on many different topics. Your school library and your local public libraries contain a wide collection of fact-filled reference books especially designed to help you research any topic. All reference books contain facts, but the type of facts varies with the reference. Choosing the right reference book will save you a lot of time.

How to Do Library Research

To do library research effectively, follow these guidelines.

1. **Reacquaint yourself with encyclopedias.** Most students are already familiar with encyclopedias. These reference books contain articles on a wide range of topics. Most encyclopedias consist of several volumes in which topics are arranged alphabetically. Some, however, have all their information in only one or two volumes.

2. **Become familiar with almanacs.** A handy source of both historical and up-to-date facts is an almanac. Here you will find statistics on everything from crime to Presidential elections. One particularly useful almanac is the *World Almanac and Book of Facts.* Like all almanacs, this reference book is updated every year and presents much of its information in tables, graphs, and charts.

3. **Consult the sources on people.** If you are looking for information on well-known people, you might go to a biographical dictionary. This reference book summarizes the key events and dates in a person's life. For important people in American history, consult the *Dictionary of American Biography.* For famous people in the present, consult dictionaries such as *Who's Who in America* or *Current Biography.*

4. **Sharpen your geography skills.** To locate maps and statistics on the United States or other parts of the world, use an atlas. An atlas is a book of maps. In addition to maps, atlases provide interesting facts and figures, including information on geography, population, and climate.

5. **Be aware of current events.** Whenever you want current information on a topic, refer to the *Readers' Guide to Periodical Literature.* This useful reference book records all of the articles that have appeared in many popular magazines. To find articles on a particular topic, turn to that subject heading in the Guide. If an article on the topic has been published, it will be listed along with the name, date, and page numbers of the magazine in which it appeared.

6. **Consult your most valuable resource.** Your most valuable resource is the librarian. This trained professional can help you find the best reference materials for your needs. Do not hesitate to consult with the librarian before you begin your research.

Applying the Skill

Use what you have just learned about reference books to answer the following questions.

1. **(a)** Where would you look to find out how many cases of arson occurred in the United States in recent years? **(b)** Where would you find Billy the Kid's real name?

2. **(a)** What would be the best source of information on the history of the juvenile justice system? **(b)** Where would you find recent articles on crimes involving handguns?

3. You are writing a report on crime and want to show crime figures on a map of the United States. Where would you find a map you could use?

Reviewing Terms

On a separate sheet of paper, supply the term from the list below that correctly completes each sentence.

fraud   prosecution
probation   robbery
larceny   defense
embezzlement

1. Taking for one's own use money that has been entrusted to one's care is called _____.

2. The accused person's side of a court case is called the _____.

3. Taking something from a person by threatening the person with injury is called _____.

4. The government's side of a court case is called the _____.

5. _____ is a time period during which a person guilty of an offense is given an opportunity to show that he or she can reform.

6. _____ is taking someone else's money or property through dishonesty.

7. _____ is the theft of property without forcible or illegal entry.

Using Thinking Skills

1. **Summarizing Ideas** Summarize the five categories of crimes discussed in the chapter.
2. **Seeing Relationships (a)** Why do we think the crime rate is higher than the statistics show? **(b)** How have attitudes toward juvenile offenders changed in recent years?
3. **Expressing Ideas (a)** What can be done to help lower the increasing crime rate? **(b)** What should young people do to avoid getting in trouble with the law?
4. **Identifying Ideas (a)** What may a judge do if he or she finds a juvenile guilty of a crime? **(b)** How does a training school differ from a juvenile detention center?

5. **Composing a Paragraph (a)** Write a paragraph explaining how poverty may contribute to crime. **(b)** Write a paragraph explaining how dropping out of school may contribute to juvenile delinquency.
6. **Organizing Ideas** Describe what happens to a criminal suspect from the time of arrest until the time of sentencing.
7. **Understanding Ideas (a)** How do people become police officers? **(b)** What rights do all criminal suspects have?
8. **Identifying Points of View (a)** Describe four points of view concerning imprisonment. **(b)** Why is capital punishment controversial?

Practicing Civics Skills

Using Library References Reread the information on page 502 of your textbook. Then decide which reference you would use to find the answer to each of the following questions.

1. **(a)** What was the crime rate in your state last year? **(b)** In what state did Supreme Court Justice Sandra Day O'Connor first practice law?
2. **(a)** When was the FBI founded? **(b)** What kinds of problems do police officers face?
3. When was William Howard Taft Chief Justice of the United States?

Being a Good Citizen

1. Organize the class into groups to visit a local courthouse. Each group should observe an actual trial. Note the ways in which the rights of the accused are protected. Compare your group's observations with the observations of other groups.
2. Invite a local police officer to talk about law enforcement in your community.
3. Organize the class into groups to research current newspaper and magazine articles on the things citizens across the country are doing to fight crime. Write a brief summary of each article to share with the class.

CHAPTER 25

Saving the Earth

Chapter Sections

1 **Understanding Ecology**
2 **The Problem of Pollution**
3 **Energy for Today and Tomorrow**
4 **Protecting Our Future**

Chapter Focus

Late December 1968: American astronaut James Lovell, halfway to the moon, looked out the window of his spacecraft. There among the stars he saw a round ball, a planet. One side of it was in shadow. The other side was streaked with color—blue, brown, green, and white. It was beautiful. It looked, he said, "like a grand oasis in the vastness of space."

Lovell, with a grin, asked if this planet might be inhabited. The other astronauts laughed. Of course it was inhabited. It was the planet earth. For the first time in history, humans could view the entire world from a great distance. The earth could be seen as a "spacecraft" among the stars. We are all riding on it, passengers together, dependent upon it for all the necessities of life.

The earth has been good to us. It has provided us with air to breathe, water to drink, food to eat, and materials to make our lives easier. Over the years, these natural resources have been taken for granted, as though they could never be used up. However, now we know that the natural resources of the earth are not limitless. They need protection, especially from humans.

Study Guide

As you read about how "Spaceship Earth" can be protected from its passengers, look for answers to the following questions:

★ What is ecology, and what can we learn from it?

★ What kinds of pollution exist today, and what can be done to reduce pollution?

★ What types of energy are available to us, and which types offer promise for the future?

★ What can governments, private organizations, and individuals do to protect our planet?

 Understanding Ecology

The world around us is our **environment.** It is made up of layers of air, water covering about three fourths of the surface of the globe, and land. We depend on our environment for everything we need to live. Every part of the environment is important to all of us.

What happens, however, when our environment changes? Each day, new buildings go up. Highways are built. Jet planes streak through the skies. These changes can be helpful. They can also create serious problems.

What Is Ecology?

All living things depend on each other for survival. The study of the relationship of living things to each other and to their environment is called **ecology.**

Human beings and animals, for example, depend on green plants for the oxygen they breathe. Plants take carbon dioxide out of the air. They then break it down into carbon and oxygen. The plants use the carbon to make their own food. The pure oxygen, which they cannot use, is released back into the atmosphere. Human beings and animals breathe in this oxygen, which they need to live. They breathe out carbon dioxide, and the cycle begins again. Without green plants and the oxygen they supply, no animal or human being could live.

There are many other ways in which living things depend upon each other. Bacteria feed on fallen leaves, causing them to decay. This decaying matter enriches the soil, so that more plants and trees can grow. They in turn supply food for many animals, such as rabbits, squirrels, deer, and many kinds of birds. Some birds eat insects that feed on the plants. Tiny marine animals called plankton live in marshes and wetlands and provide food for shrimp, oysters, and minnows. These in turn become food for larger fish and make possible the great schools of herring, tuna, salmon, and other seafood so important to human beings.

In such ways, all living things, including people, are like links in a chain. Take away one link of the chain and all living things depending on that link will suffer. Reduce the number of forests and fields in the world, and the wild bird population also will be reduced. Without enough birds to eat them, insects will multiply too quickly. Increase the number of insects, and more crops will be damaged.

Reduce the wild areas of the country, and eagles, hawks, coyotes, mountain lions, and other animals who live in them will no longer have a home. Without these natural enemies, other animals, such as mice and deer, will increase too quickly. With too many plant-eating animals, not enough plants will decay to enrich the soil and hold moisture. Later there will be fewer plants, and the plant eaters too will suffer.

These are only a few simple examples. Perhaps you can think of others. The way in which all living things, including human beings, depend on one another is referred to as the **balance of nature.** The study of this complex subject, ecology, is of great importance to us. People sometimes upset the balance of nature without realizing that their activities can have harmful side effects. We must all learn that our actions have consequences.

America's Early Environment

Long before any European settlers came here, the North American continent was a land of great natural wealth and beauty. This part of the world had moderate climates, with plenty of sunshine and a good supply of rain in most places. Trees grew thick and tall in the forests. The plains were covered with wild grasses. The river valleys were fertile and green. Many kinds of wild animals lived in harmony with each other.

America's abundance was the result of natural forces that had been at work for thousands of years. The sun, wind, and rain had worn away huge rocks and reduced them to soil. Melting snow had formed streams that carried soil down from the mountains into the valleys. Huge rivers were formed. These rivers dug out great channels and canyons and deposited more soil in their paths.

Plants then grew in this soil, and when they decayed their leaves and roots enriched the soil. As the soil was built up, trees were able to take root and grow. Some of these trees grew in rocky places. Their roots helped break up the rocks and make more soil. Their leaves decayed and built up the soil even more. Then other trees took root and huge forests were born as a result.

These great forests provided protection and food for many kinds of animals. Other animals, such as the great herds of American bison (buffalo), grazed on the open plains. Various species of birds, insects, and animals kept each other in balance. Each plant or animal took what it needed from the environment. In turn it contributed to the needs of other living things.

At this time, people also were part of the balance of nature. The Indians hunted animals for food and used the hides for clothing and

Water, green plants, trees, and deer and other wildlife all have their place in the balance of nature. How have people upset nature's balance over the years?

shelter. Hunting with spears or bows and arrows, they rarely killed more than they needed to feed themselves. The Indians had great respect for the earth and for the other creatures with whom they shared it.

Upsetting America's Ecology

The early European settlers were amazed by the natural wealth of America. In Europe most of the land was divided up and had been farmed for hundreds of years. There were few forests and little wild game left. No wonder the fertile land, the forests, and the wildlife of America seemed unlimited to the early European settlers.

America's forests were so thick with growth that settlers in the East first had to clear away the trees in order to grow crops. They used some of the wood to build their houses and furniture. They burned what they did not need. Then they started sending lumber back to Europe. The tallest and straightest trees were used to make the masts of great sailing ships.

As the number of settlers to America increased and the demand for wood grew, more and more forests were cut down. No new trees were planted in their place. If people wanted more wood, there were many more forests to the west.

But as settlers destroyed the forests they destroyed something more. As the trees disappeared, so did much of the wildlife that depended on them for food and shelter. Many other wild animals were killed by settlers, not only for food but also for their furs or for sport.

Beavers were trapped by the millions because beaver hats were popular in Europe. Whole herds of buffalo were shot for hides or for sport, and their meat was left to rot. Other animals and birds of prey, including foxes, bears, mountain lions, owls, hawks, and eagles, were shot as pests because they sometimes attacked livestock.

Destroying these animals upset the balance of nature. These creatures fed mostly on

The cutting down of vast timberlands in the past greatly changed American ecology. Today more care is taken to replant forests as trees are cut.

other animals, including mice and snakes. Soon mice and other small animal populations began to grow unchecked. Another result of the thoughtless killing of so many animals was that some species, including the American eagle, were almost destroyed. The American eagle and other endangered species are now protected by special laws.

Farming the Land

The land cleared for farming was at first very fertile. This rich soil produced wonderful crops of vegetables, wheat, oats, corn, cotton, and tobacco. However, when the farmer planted a crop and harvested it, nothing was

Science and technology have helped make American farmland the most productive on earth. Contour farming has prevented great amounts of soil from washing away.

left to decay and rebuild the soil. As the land was farmed year after year, the supply of plant food in the soil was used up and nothing was put back.

In the West, cattle ranchers and sheepherders took the land for granted too. Their huge herds ate all the plants on the prairies they roamed. Without plants to hold water, the land dried out. Much good grassland was ruined in this way. People seemed to think that new land would always be available.

By the early 1900's, our vast continent was filling up with people. There was no longer a seemingly endless supply of land. Farmers were plowing up more and more of the flat grasslands on the Great Plains. Then in the 1930's, the plains went through a long dry period. With no grass growing, vast amounts of rich soil were blown away by the wind. A few years later, all that was left was a barren "dust bowl."

In the 1930's, President Franklin D. Roosevelt urged Congress to pass a program to conserve the nation's farmlands. Under this program, called the **soil bank,** landowners were rewarded if they did not farm some of their land. They were paid to grow trees or grass on it instead. This ensured that a supply of good land would be left for the future.

Modern Agriculture

The population of the United States was increasing. New farmland was scarce. Old farmland was wearing out. Some of the land was no longer farmed at all. How were all the new people to be fed?

The answer came from modern science and technology. Farmers learned how to keep the soil from being worn out. They could prevent topsoil from washing or blowing away by many different techniques. Some farmers tried a method called **contour farming.** By plowing across slopes instead of up and down, they prevented the soil from being worn away.

Many farmers built drainage channels, small dams, and terraces—flat, level spaces on the slopes. Other farmers planted **cover crops,** such as clover, soybeans, and hay, because they hold the soil better than other crops. They also practiced **crop rotation,** planting different crops on the land each year. Crop rotation helps to keep the soil from wearing out so quickly.

Chemical Fertilizers and Pesticides

With the help of science, farmers can now grow more food on less land. This increase in productivity was made possible by the use of chemical fertilizers and pesticides.

Fertilizers are special plant foods that make crops grow faster and bigger. The most important fertilizers are nitrates, which contain nitrogen. Nitrates can be mixed with water and pumped into the ground, or they can be spread as powder to soak in with the next rain. When a field is fertilized with nitrates, plants grow so quickly that much more food can be harvested. Nitrates are now used by almost all farmers in the United States. They are used as well by home gardeners on their lawns and flower beds.

Pesticides are special chemicals that kill insect pests and weeds. Many insects attack food plants, and they can ruin a farmer's entire crop. Weeds lower crop production. The use of chemical pesticides has dramatically reduced crop losses to insects and weeds. Pesticides are also used by individuals to control insects and weeds in their lawns and gardens. Currently, there are thousands of different chemical pesticides in use.

Unfortunately, the widespread use of chemical fertilizers and pesticides may have negative consequences for the environment. The chemicals sometimes get into the food we eat. Chemicals that are not absorbed by the crops may pollute the soil and water. Because of this, some people are supporting **organic farming,** or farming without the use of artificial substances. By using natural substances and certain farming practices to increase crop yields and control pests, farmers can avoid the use of chemicals.

Overpopulation—A Threat to Our Resources

Our farmers have proved that they can produce enough food to feed the present population of the United States, with some left over for export. But will they still be able to do so in the future, as more and more farmland is covered with cities, dams, highways, and other kinds of development?

Consider too the increasing problems of living space, water supply, and disposal of trash and waste, as more and more people crowd the earth. How many people can the United States and the rest of the world hold and still provide a decent standard of living for all?

The increase in the world's population has been called a population explosion. It took more than a million years for the human population to reach 1 billion, by the year 1850. However, it took only 80 years to arrive at the second billion, in 1930. Today, the world's population is over 5 billion. If it keeps increasing at the same rate, the world's population will reach 6.3 billion by the year 2000—and 8.2 billion 20 years after that.

This rapid growth greatly concerns the United States. At present, food must be sent to many nations because they cannot feed all their people. Even with this help, nearly 15 million people die from hunger-related causes each year.

The population of the United States is growing, but not rapidly. It is increasing at less than 1 percent a year. In the late 1980's, there were more than 3 million births and about 2 million deaths a year. Thus the natural increase in our population was about 1 million a year. In addition, about 600,000 immigrants came to live and work in the United States each year during this same period.

Even if our nation continues at this relatively low rate of growth, we will have nearly 270 million people by the year 2000. The people we have now are already using up our resources at an alarming rate. Where will the United States be able to find the resources to provide a high standard of living for so many more people? This is a serious challenge Americans face for the future.

★ SECTION 1 REVIEW

Define environment, ecology, balance of nature, soil bank, contour farming, cover crops, crop rotation, fertilizers, pesticides, organic farming

1. **Expressing Ideas** Explain how living things depend on their environment and each other.
2. **Seeing Relationships (a)** How have human beings upset the balance of nature? **(b)** Describe the advantages and disadvantages of using chemical fertilizers and pesticides.
3. **Identifying Ideas (a)** Why is the world's population growth called an "explosion"? **(b)** Why is overpopulation a problem?

Thinking Critically You work with a group of citizens devoted to preserving America's natural areas. What activities will you pursue?

② The Problem of Pollution

Our natural resources are precious. Unfortunately, however, many people have taken the air, land, and water around us for granted. They have polluted our environment.

Pollution occurs when we cause any part of our environment to become dirty or contaminated—made unfit for use. Pollution can destroy plants and animals and can upset the balance of nature. Among the countless living creatures that pollution harms are the ones who cause it—human beings.

Why Do People Pollute?

Pollution may occur when we get rid of something we do not want. Harmful unburned gases from our automobile engines are added to the air. Unwanted smoke and gases from factories, power plants, and home furnaces go up millions of smokestacks and chimneys. Ashes, soot, and gases are carried far and wide by the wind and make the air unhealthy to breathe. People throw away tires, bottles, cans, and even old automobiles along the highways and in streams. Chemical plants and steel mills pour their wastes into rivers, lakes, and oceans.

Why do people pollute their environment? They do it because they started doing it long ago when the damage caused by dumping was less evident. For example, an early town used a piece of swampland as its dump. There was plenty of other land, so hardly anyone was aware of this small-scale damage to the environment.

An early factory was built beside a river. The factory owners dumped waste into the river. The river did not belong to anyone in particular, and few people complained. When there were fewer towns and factories scattered throughout our vast land, not many people worried about these methods of getting rid of unwanted waste.

Causes of Pollution

Since the early history of our nation, however, three things have happened that have made these practices unsuitable. First, our population has grown enormously. Each person produces garbage, sewage, and other kinds of waste. The more people we have, the more garbage we produce. As long as our population continues to grow, so will the problem of disposing of our waste.

Second, our economy has developed such enormous capacity that we manufacture and use more and more goods each year. Americans use more than 180 million automobiles, trucks, and buses to move people and goods from place to place. Billions of cans, bottles, and other packages are used each year and then thrown away.

Third, new inventions have led to products that complicate our trash disposal problem. Plastics and some chemicals do not decay and, if burned, may pollute the air. Detergents may upset the natural balance in streams and lakes.

These are only a few of the new and old products that cause trouble in our environment. Because our economy gives us so much, we must dispose of mountains of trash. We must also control tons and tons of waste that may pollute the air and water.

Air Pollution

The air we breathe is a unique mixture of nitrogen, oxygen, carbon dioxide, and small amounts of other gases. It is a **renewable resource.** That is, it can be replaced. Under good conditions, nature can clean the air of germs that are breathed into it by people, or of dirt and harmful gases put into it by furnaces, factories, and automobiles. In recent years, however, the pollution in the air sometimes has become so great that nature cannot get rid of it.

As a result, the air over many of our cities sometimes is filled with **smog**—a combination of smoke, gases, and fog. Smog burns the eyes, causes coughing, and is dangerous for anyone with a breathing ailment.

Automobiles in the United States pour more than 50 million tons of pollutants into the air each year. However, automobiles are by no means solely responsible for our bad air. Nearly 21 million tons of pollutants are spewed into the atmosphere by the fuel we burn to heat our homes and to power the generators for electricity.

Furthermore, each year almost 25 million tons of pollutants come from factories. In some parts of the country, factories are the worst polluters of all. In addition, more than 5 million tons of ashes and gases enter the

(continued on page 514)

Factories produce many goods that we enjoy. Unfortunately, some factories also produce unwanted by-products—air pollution, ground pollution, and water pollution.

CITIZENSHIP IN ACTION

"For Future Generations"

You may never have heard of Closter, New Jersey. But what happened in this small suburb of New York City has echoed throughout the United States and in many other nations around the world. As you will see, the town of Closter is home to a group of citizens who have made it their goal to save our planet.

Kids Against Pollution

Kids Against Pollution (KAP) was founded by a group of civics students and their teacher at Tenakill School in Closter in 1988. From the original 19 members, KAP has grown to include more than 800 chapters in the United States and in several foreign countries. KAP members have testified before local and state governments, served as witnesses before the Environmental Protection Agency, proposed an amendment to the Constitution, and even made presentations at the United Nations.

What has prompted so many young citizens to do so much? One eighth-grade KAP member gave this answer: "I want my generation to be known as the one that did something about the environment."

Other KAP members agree. Distressed by what they saw as the spoiling of the environment, the original KAP group decided to do something about it. They immediately formed KAP and adopted as their motto a simple yet moving phrase: "Save the Earth, Not Just For Us, But For Future Generations."

Working Hard to Make a Difference

The first action of the newly formed group was to petition their school district to stop using plastic foam products. (Plastic foam, or polystyrene, can be dangerous to the environment. It takes up space in landfills, cannot decay, and can give off toxic fumes when burned in trash incinerators.) The school dis-

Members of Kids Against Pollution have testified to Congress about their environmental concerns.

trict was impressed by KAP's logical and poised presentation, and agreed with the students' proposal. KAP had won its first victory.

The many victories that have followed KAP's early success have not been won as easily. The students learned that changing long-standing practices—like changing people's minds—is hard work. But KAP members believe strongly that we must save the planet from pollution, and that their hard work is well worth the effort.

KAP's balloon protest is a good example. A hospital was planning to use helium-filled balloons as part of a promotion. When KAP members learned of the plan, they were upset. They were afraid that some of the balloons might land in the sea and kill the sea animals that tried to eat them. The kids of KAP sprang into action.

KAP members from several chapters organized a large demonstration to urge the hospital not to use balloons. They spent long hours researching the effects of balloons on the environment and organizing the demonstration. But KAP's hard work and dedication paid off. Hospital administrators listened to the facts and agreed not to use the balloons.

Since its beginning, Kids Against Pollution has organized and participated in hundreds of similar projects, all aimed at helping our planet. KAP efforts have even caused change as far away as Europe and Asia. But this worldwide movement of young people all started with one civics class in one small town in the United States.

The members of KAP are doing everything they can to ensure that the world is a clean and healthy place to live, now and in the future.

Thinking it Over

1. What is the goal of Kids Against Pollution?
2. What are some activities KAP members have organized to help achieve this goal?
3. Do you think young people can make a difference in saving the earth? Explain your answer.

atmosphere each year from the burning trash dumps and waste incinerators that are near almost all our cities and towns.

Effects of Air Pollution

Each year it costs government and business about $30 billion to try to control and reduce air pollution. The pollutants eat away metal, damage crops, and waste our resources.

Air pollution has also led to the creation of acid rain. **Acid rain** occurs when pollution from burning gas, oil, and coal mixes with water vapor in the air to form acid. This acid then falls to earth with snow and rain. Acid rain kills trees and makes lakes and ponds unable to support life. Some of the lakes in the eastern United States are now so polluted that they can barely support life. Acid rain has caused damage in Canada as well.

Furthermore, changes in the makeup of the air, some scientists say, are affecting the earth's climate. Harmful gases and tiny particles of foreign matter are increasing in the upper atmosphere. When the sun's rays strike these particles, the rays are scattered back into space. It will not take long, these scientists say, for this process to cut down the amount of sunlight that reaches the earth. The effect of this will be to reduce plant life and eventually to threaten all life on earth.

Our Water Supply

Water, like air, is essential to life on our planet. Protecting our planet and ourselves requires us to protect our water supply.

All fresh water comes from clouds—as rain, snow, or other precipitation. It sinks into the earth, follows underground routes, and forms underground pools. Excess water runs into rivers, lakes, and oceans. Eventually it evaporates into the atmosphere, to fall again. This process is called the water cycle.

Underground water reserves are one of the keys to life on the land. Underground water

nourishes plants. Bubbling out in wells and springs, it helps supply the water needs of people and animals. A good supply of underground water is assured when trees, plants, and grasses cover the earth's soil. The roots of trees and other plants help keep the soil moist. They slow the flow of water. Trees and plants give off moisture into the atmosphere to help keep the water cycle working.

When trees and other plants are removed from large areas of land, the rain tends to rush down slopes instead of sinking slowly into the ground. That has happened in many parts of the United States. The level of water under the ground, the water table, is slowly sinking. As a result, our nation's supply of usable water is decreasing.

Yet we are using more water than ever before. Some scientists say that every day we take twice as much from ground water reserves as what flows in. This situation is made worse because we are rapidly polluting much of our surface water—the water of rivers, lakes, and reservoirs.

Water Pollutants

Anything in the water that makes the water less useful or less healthful is a pollutant. Water pollution can be classified into five different types: chemical, sewage, thermal, silt, and crud.

Chemical pollutants come mainly from industrial plants. In fact, industry—factories, mills, and mines—accounts for more than half of all water pollution. Insect sprays and artificial fertilizers used in agriculture are also major causes of chemical water pollution. There are other forms of chemical pollution. For instance, many detergents we use contain substances called phosphates. These phosphates make detergents act more quickly. However, they also pollute the waters in much the same way fertilizers do.

Sewage comes mainly from cities and other communities that dump waste, including that made by people, into lakes and streams. Water pollution also comes from sewage treatment plants and from septic tanks.

Thermal pollution occurs when industries use cold water from a stream or lake to cool their products, then pump the warmer water back into the body of water. Steel plants, nuclear power plants, and others pump warmed water into streams. The temperature of the water, raised in this manner, may kill fish and other marine life. Algae, or tiny water plants, may grow in the warmer water and begin to smell. Thermal pollution upsets the balance of nature that helps renew the purity of fresh water.

Silt is soil, sand, or mud that has washed into streams. Silt comes mainly from sloping land that does not have enough trees or other plants to hold the soil in place. Silt pollution often is caused by improper mining and agricultural practices, road building, and earth moving.

Crud, usually a slang word, can also refer to trash, such as old tires, bottles, and other used items. Such things become crud when they are thrown by thoughtless people into our streams, lakes, and rivers, as well as onto the land.

Cleaning Our Water

Curing water pollution requires two steps. First, we must make an effort to use water wisely. Americans waste huge amounts of water each year. If we used less water, there would be less polluted water to be returned to the environment.

The second step in curing water pollution is to rid the water we do use of all impurities before it is returned to the ground, streams, lakes, and oceans. Purification of polluted water, however, is a costly process.

Americans use about 400 billion gallons (1,514 billion liters) of water each day. More than three fourths of this water becomes sewage. All of this sewage will have to be treated to make our water pure.

Facts About Our Environment

More than three fourths of all Americans consider themselves to be environmentalists, but there is still much work to be done.

★ Americans generate more garbage per person than the citizens of any other country. Each year Americans throw out about 160 million tons of garbage—more than 1,000 pounds for every man, woman, and child.

★ Each year, Americans throw away, among other things: about 16 billion disposable diapers, 240 million tires, 1.6 billion pens, 2 billion razors and blades, 365 million cigarette lighters, and 45 billion paper and plastic cups.

★ The United States recycles about 10 percent of its garbage. Another 10 percent is burned. Most of the remaining garbage is dumped into landfills.

★ More than 1,200 hazardous waste sites have been identified in the United States—an average of 24 per state.

★ More than 1 million tons of toxic chemicals are released into the air over our country each year.

★ The United States spends more than $80 billion annually in efforts to control pollution.

★ The United States Coast Guard reports as many as 12,000 "oil polluting incidents" in United States waters each year.

★ The United States contains less than 5 percent of the world's population but uses more than 60 percent of the world's resources.

★ The national bird of the United States—the bald eagle—is an endangered species.

Ground Pollution

The ground of the United States, like its air and water, has become seriously polluted. Littering is a major cause of ground pollution. In many areas of our country, it is impossible to walk very far without seeing trash that someone has thoughtlessly tossed on the ground.

In the United States, about 80 percent of garbage is deposited in sanitary landfills.

Sanitary landfills are huge pits dug in the ground as a place to store garbage. The garbage is supposed to decompose, much as leaves on the forest floor decay. Unfortunately, recent discoveries have shown that garbage does not decompose as rapidly as once thought.

Moreover, landfills often leak toxic materials into the surrounding soil. Another problem with landfills is that no one wants to live near them. Thus, as existing landfills become full, it is growing more difficult to locate places to build new ones.

Responding to Pollution

The huge amounts of garbage produced in our country have led many communities to begin recycling programs. **Recycling** is the process of turning waste into something that can be used. For example, aluminum cans can be melted down and the metal used to produce new cans. If we recycled more of our garbage, the pollution problem in our country would be greatly reduced.

Working Together to Fight Pollution

There is no single solution to the many serious problems of pollution. And no single person or government will be able to solve these problems. Cooperative efforts among governments, private organizations, and individuals are needed.

Polluted air and water from one country may drift into the air and water of another country. Thus, the problem of pollution calls for international cooperation. Recently, governments have been working together to seek solutions to this international problem.

Individuals, too, are taking steps to help the environment. People who recycle their trash, for example, make an important contribution to the environment.

Everyone in the world depends on our environment for life. The future of the earth as a home for human beings depends on how well all of us work together to control the problem of pollution.

 SECTION 2 REVIEW

Define pollution, renewable resource, smog, acid rain, sanitary landfills, recycling

1. **Identifying Ideas** (a) Why have people polluted the environment? (b) What three developments have increased pollution?
2. **Seeing Relationships** (a) What are some harmful effects of air pollution? (b) Why is it important that we have a clean water supply? (c) How would recycling help the ground pollution problem?
3. **Identifying Roles** Why must countries work together to solve pollution problems?

Thinking Critically You are your community's recycling coordinator. How will you encourage residents to recycle their trash?

3 Energy for Today and Tomorrow

Today most Americans are aware of the problems of pollution and the need to protect our natural resources. Until recently, however, many Americans believed our country's resources would last forever. Ever since the European settlers arrived in America, people have been using up the land and its resources faster and faster. Besides cutting down the forests, Americans have covered the land with cement and asphalt. They have also stripped mountains bare for coal, copper, silver, gold, and other minerals.

The United States has about five percent of the world's population. However, it uses about 60 percent of the world's natural resources. This places a heavy burden on the earth's limited supplies.

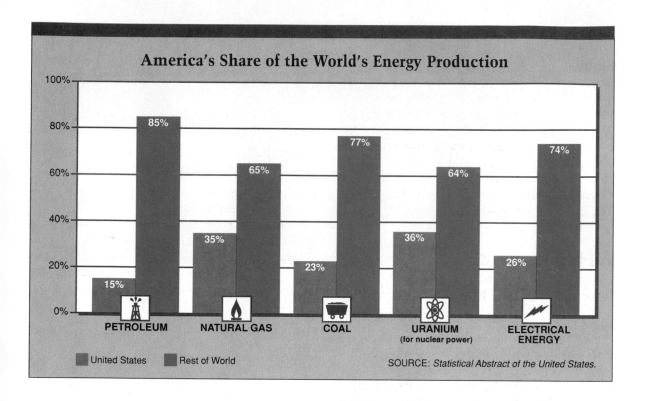

America's Share of the World's Energy Production

	PETROLEUM	NATURAL GAS	COAL	URANIUM (for nuclear power)	ELECTRICAL ENERGY
United States	15%	35%	23%	36%	26%
Rest of World	85%	65%	77%	64%	74%

SOURCE: *Statistical Abstract of the United States.*

Our Energy Resources

Among the natural wealth we are using up quickly are our **energy resources.** These resources—mostly coal, petroleum, and natural gas—furnish the power for doing the nation's work. Between 1950 and 1970, we doubled the amount of energy used in running our machines. That means that we used up a large amount of our energy resources. Some of these fuels were also imported. The United States is not the only industrial nation in the world to use up energy at a fast rate. Moreover, developing nations around the world are now demanding a greater share of the world's energy resources.

Unless we take steps now, we will soon be without valuable energy resources. These fuels are limited. They also are **nonrenewable resources.** That is, they can be used only once. Without these valuable energy resources, our way of life would be in danger. Our factories would stop running. Our homes would be dark and cold. Our transportation systems would come to a halt. Our national defense system would be in danger. To understand better why this would happen, let us examine the energy situation.

Oil for Industry

The energy source we depend on most is petroleum, or oil, as it is commonly called. It lies deep within the earth in great pools. These pools were formed from microscopic plants and animals that lived millions of years ago. They were covered with mud, rocks, and water. After centuries of decay and pressure from the earth, petroleum, an energy source of great value, was formed.

Pumped to the surface and refined, petroleum furnishes the energy to heat our homes, the gasoline to run our cars and trucks, and the lubricating oil to grease the wheels of industry. It also is the basis of a great variety

For the first time in their history, Americans are actively working to conserve oil. What steps can you take to help in the effort to save energy?

of by-products, such as plastics, fertilizers, dyes, and many different chemicals.

However, only a certain amount of oil is left in the ground. When it is all used up, there will be no more. The United States was for many years the leading oil-producing nation in the world. Yet by the late 1980's, we were behind the Soviet Union in oil production. Moreover, we had to import about half of our oil supply.

Some experts think the world's existing oil supply will run out early in the next century. Of course, discovery of new oil deposits will give us an additional supply. To help in the search for more oil, the federal government has leased drilling sites off our coastlines to oil companies. These companies seek oil beneath the ocean floor.

Conserving Oil

Another way for Americans to stretch our available oil resources is through conservation. **Conservation** is the safeguarding of our natural resources by using them wisely. The growing popularity of smaller cars has helped to save oil. These smaller cars travel more miles per gallon of gas than larger cars. Many

industries have installed new machinery that requires less energy to run, thus conserving oil.

Homeowners must also do their part to conserve heating oil. Lowering home temperatures, insulating attics and walls, and putting in storm windows and doors are some ways to save oil. It would also help if certain industries would stop using oil and substitute coal and other fuels. In the meantime, our nation must find new resources to take the place of oil before it runs out.

A Shortage of Natural Gas

The second most widely used fuel in the United States is natural gas. It is usually found with petroleum. At one time, natural gas was burned off as it came out of the oil well. However, this clean-burning fuel found favor with homeowners and industry. It began to be used in even larger amounts. Over half the homes in our nation are now heated with gas. Industry relies on gas for about one third of its energy needs.

During the 1960's, energy experts began warning that our natural gas supplies were running low. Production began to fall around

1974, creating a shortage of natural gas. Some producers blamed the gas shortage on the low price of natural gas. They claimed producers were unwilling to spend money to find new sources because the price was too low to make a profit.

The federal government had been keeping the price of natural gas lower than the world price. The availability of cheap fuel and the belief that the nation's resources would last forever led people to become wasteful. Now Americans no longer can afford to use our fuel supplies so carelessly.

To encourage Americans to save energy resources, the government decided to gradually lift price controls on natural gas. Still, even if new sources of natural gas are found, our needs can be met for only a while. We must continue to use what we have now wisely and seek new energy sources.

Coal for the Future

The United States is fortunate in having a large supply of coal. We are thought to have enough coal to last for hundreds of years. The problem is that much of this coal lies deep in the earth where it was formed millions of years ago. Getting this coal out of the ground is difficult and dangerous, even with improved methods and machines. Coal is also expensive to transport.

Other deposits of coal lie near the surface and can be reached by stripping off the soil on top. The coal is then scooped up by machines. This **strip mining** has been severely criticized for its effects on the environment. It often leaves ugly scars on the land. Without trees or plants to hold it together, the soil washes down the hills and into streams. It muddies the water and sometimes clogs waterways.

To help solve this problem, Congress passed a strip mining act in 1977. It requires mining companies to re-cover the area with soil, plants, and trees after they have removed the coal. This policy has been opposed by

some people. They say it is too costly and raises the cost of coal.

Coal is looked upon by many as the best energy source for the near future—until other sources have been discovered or developed. To use coal, many industries will have to convert from oil and natural gas. However, it is difficult to burn coal without polluting the air. Researchers are looking for ways to prevent this from happening. They are trying to change coal into gas and oil so it will burn cleaner and more efficiently. In the meantime, many industries have installed expensive "scrubbing" equipment to prevent polluting materials from reaching our air.

Using Nuclear Energy

Nuclear plants were in operation in all regions of the United States by the early 1980's. Nuclear reactors run on a small amount of fuel. They produce large amounts of energy very efficiently. But nuclear reactors face unique problems. The use of nuclear energy is therefore very controversial.

Many people object to the building of more nuclear power plants. They are concerned about radioactivity and thermal pollution. Radioactivity is the giving off of rays that are dangerous to health. Nuclear plants can upset the balance of nature.

Public confidence in nuclear energy was shaken severely in 1979 by an accident at the nuclear-powered electric plant at Three Mile Island in Middletown, Pennsylvania. Because of a series of human and mechanical errors, the radioactive core of the reactor started to overheat. This caused some radioactive gas to escape into the air.

It was days before the danger of an explosion at Three Mile Island ended. The accident caused many Americans to question the wisdom of building more nuclear power plants. It also led them to question our ways of disposing of nuclear wastes. The wastes from nuclear plants remain radioactive and hazardous for thousands of years. We must find ways to store or treat these waste materials so that they will not be dangerous to the earth and to people in the future. We also need to find ways to make nuclear plants safer to operate.

Energy from the Sun

One of the most promising new sources of energy for the future is energy from the sun—**solar energy.** The sun gives off an enormous amount of energy, which cannot be used up anytime soon. Research on this type of energy is still in the beginning stages. However, solar energy has already proved to be a clean, efficient way to heat and cool specially constructed homes and offices.

To encourage the study and use of solar energy, the federal government has given grants to business, universities, and individuals. This clean and plentiful source of power holds great promise for the future.

Alternative Sources of Energy

The continuing energy shortage and the pollution caused by our current energy sources has convinced many Americans that action is needed to avoid serious problems. We can no longer assume that our nation has an endless supply of energy. Therefore, private industry, government agencies, and university research centers have all been engaged in the search for new and practical sources of energy.

One possible source being investigated is geothermal energy. Scientists are trying to use the heat from deep within the earth to produce energy. They are also studying ways to expand our use of hydroelectric power—energy from water, including the movement of ocean tides and waves.

A small number of people use gasohol as fuel for their cars. Gasohol is made from gasoline and ethanol, or alcohol. Other possible sources of energy being investigated are more efficient windmills and the conversion of manure into methane gas. Some communities are burning biomass and changing it into energy. Biomass is the leftover or unused parts of plants and animals. It includes garbage and plants, shells, bushes, stems, and so on. These and other ideas must be studied if Americans are to have enough energy for the future.

Energy and the Environment

Americans must be careful about how our new energy resources are developed. Each time we develop an area, we may upset its ecological balance. Development, of course, continues to be necessary for the well-being

In the 1970's Americans truly realized that gasoline supplies had become limited. What does this cartoon say about the possible causes of the shortage?

from *Herblock On All Fronts* (New American Library, 1980)

"Who Was Navigating, Anyhow?"

of our nation. Today, however, Americans are determined that in the future our development will not harm the environment, as it often did in the past.

Even though our nation needs new sources of energy, many Americans do not want new nuclear plants, mines, or dams to be built near areas where they live. Nor do Americans want oil drilling sites off their coastal shores. Too many oil spills from tankers and barges have ruined our beaches. Millions of tons of oil a year have leaked into the oceans from tankers, barges, oil rigs, and coastal installations.

Because of the harm that has been done to the environment, the federal government and some states and local communities have passed laws to control new development. They require developers of some new plants, mines, and installations to study the effects their developments will have on the environment. Before any work can begin, they must prove they will meet the standards that have been set.

Development Versus Conservation

Some Americans are worried about the high costs of keeping our environment clean. They argue that the new safeguards and equipment make it too costly to build new plants or carry out new development. In order to have the energy and raw materials we need, some people think we must continue to use the land and its resources as we have been doing. They believe it may even be necessary to relax some of the standards we have set in recent years for a cleaner environment.

Conservationists, on the other hand, say that continuing to pollute the environment or upset the balance of nature is dangerous. Their study of ecology has convinced them that what affects our land and its wildlife will eventually affect us. They also remind us that conservation is not a miserly saving of resources for some future time. It is "wise use" now.

SECTION 3 REVIEW

Define energy resources, nonrenewable resources, conservation, strip mining, solar energy

1. **Identifying Ideas** What are some ways that oil and natural gas have been conserved?
2. **Contrasting Ideas** What are the advantages and disadvantages of burning coal and using nuclear energy?
3. **Composing a Paragraph** Write a paragraph identifying several promising alternative sources of energy.
4. **Summarizing Ideas** Summarize the arguments for and against continuing to use resources the way we have in the past.

Thinking Critically You are the Secretary of Energy, and you must decide how to spend limited research funds. To which alternative source of energy will you devote the most research money? Explain your answer.

4 Protecting Our Future

Over 100 years ago, in 1872, our government set aside a portion of northwestern Wyoming as a national park. Its forests, rivers, waterfalls, geysers, hot springs, and wildlife became the property of all Americans. The land was to remain in its natural state, to be enjoyed as a place of beauty and an area for outdoor recreation. The region was named Yellowstone National Park—the first national park in the world. Since then 49 other national parks have been created.

Early Conservation Efforts

The National Park Service of the United States is only one of many agencies that help to preserve the natural resources of our country. Early in the 1900's, President Theodore

Roosevelt called a conference of the governors of the states to consider how best to conserve our land and resources.

The National Forest Service was established to supervise vast areas of our forest land to help conserve its timber. Later, laws were passed to limit the amount of oil and minerals that could be taken from the ground each year. Laws governing grazing practices helped stop the destruction of grasslands. The United States Department of Agriculture and state governments encouraged and helped farmers use soil conservation methods.

Under President Franklin D. Roosevelt, a program of soil banks was established. Land was set aside to be improved and renewed. Dams were built in our nation to irrigate farmlands and control floods. The dams also provide electricity and recreation areas.

These efforts, however, did not stop waste and pollution. By the 1950's, large numbers of concerned citizens began to point out that

an environmental crisis was at hand because of our misuse of resources. Today we know that firm conservation measures are needed.

The Federal Government and Conservation

The United States Congress has passed a number of laws to reduce pollution and restore the environment. The following are the most significant of these acts.

The National Environmental Policy Act. This 1969 act is sometimes called the Environmental Bill of Rights. It set up the Council on Environmental Quality to advise the President and oversee the nation's pollution controls. As a result of advice from this body, stricter laws were passed regulating pesticides, oil spills, and ocean dumping.

The 1969 act also provides that every federal agency must make and publish an environmental impact statement. This document must describe the expected effects on the environment of any project to be undertaken with federal assistance.

Clean Air Acts. The first clean air act was passed in 1955 and has been amended and strengthened several times, most recently in 1990. The clean air acts provide funds for research and set standards to be met by all industries and buildings. They make it possible for the government to reduce certain forms of air pollution. The automobile industry, for example, was told it must develop engines that give off reduced amounts of exhaust pollution.

Water Pollution Control Acts. As early as 1899, Congress passed a law making it a crime to dump refuse into any navigable waterway. This law was not strictly enforced until recent times. It has been strengthened by the Water Quality Act of 1965. This law sets standards of water quality for the interstate and coastal waters of the United States.

Again in 1966 and 1969, clean water acts were passed by Congress. Under these acts, the federal government has helped local communities build sewage treatment plants. In

Oil spilled from tankers or offshore wells can wash up on nearby beaches. Here, a volunteer is helping to clean an oil-soaked bird.

1972 a law was passed to limit the discharge of wastes into our waters in the future.

Other Acts of Congress. Americans have become very aware of the problems of using and disposing of chemicals. These substances pollute our land, water, and air in ever-increasing amounts. Some chemicals are toxic, or poisonous. To protect our health, Congress passed the Resource Recovery and Conservation Act in 1976. It enables the government to check the use of chemicals by industry in all stages of production.

Americans in favor of a better environment have also brought pressure on Congress to preserve the beauty of the land and conserve its wildlife. The National Wild Rivers Act and the Wilderness Act set aside areas of land to be kept in their natural state for the pleasure of people.

Hundreds of plants and animals in the United States alone are threatened with extinction. Endangered species acts have listed wildlife, such as the whooping crane and the Utah prairie dog, that should be protected. Laws have been passed to keep them from dying out and to help them multiply.

The United States is also concerned with saving wildlife in other parts of the world. Our federal laws forbid the importation of the feathers and skins of many animals for use in clothing and in other unnecessary ways.

Did you know that...

early conservation efforts saved the buffalo from extinction? The buffalo, or American bison, once roamed freely throughout the American West. According to one estimate, there were at least 100 million buffalo on the Great Plains as late as 1866. But then came thousands of hunters and the railroads. Mass killing of the herds followed. In 1889 a buffalo census revealed a shocking fact—there were only about 550 buffalo left.

A special society was formed in 1913 to protect the animals. As a result, the buffalo population steadily increased. By 1933 there were 4,000 buffalo. Today about 15,000 buffalo live on lands set aside for them by the United States government.

The Environmental Protection Agency

Many federal bureaus that deal with pollution and other ecological problems have been organized under an independent agency, called the **Environmental Protection Agency (EPA).** It reports directly to the President of the United States.

The EPA includes several offices responsible for controlling water and air pollution. It also oversees the management of solid wastes and radiation. In addition, the EPA deals with pesticide problems and carries out studies of ecological systems.

State and Local Activities

Every state government and most local governments in the nation have established laws that help provide better environments for their citizens. These laws range from provisions for the preservation of the state's natural resources and scenic beauty to local laws governing the disposal of trash.

Some states have taken giant steps forward by studying large areas and starting programs to preserve or restore their ecological balance. Oregon, for example, has made its entire Pacific shoreline public property. It also has a program to preserve its natural beauty.

Why is it important to conserve natural areas like this one? What can you do to help safeguard our nation's remaining wilderness areas?

New York has set up the Department of Environmental Conservation, with powers to set and enforce standards for purer air and water.

Local communities have acted to preserve the environment as well. Many communities regulate the amount of pollution released by factories. More cities are encouraging recycling. These and similar actions are largely the result of growing citizen concern about the environment.

Earth Day

The most dramatic example of citizen involvement is Earth Day. **Earth Day,** April 22, is an unofficial holiday dedicated to caring for the earth.

The first Earth Day, in 1970, was the largest organized political demonstration in history. About 20 million Americans participated in Earth Day activities, ranging from neighborhood cleanups to massive demonstrations. The government responded with a number of laws to protect the environment.

More than 200 million people around the world took part in Earth Day 1990. These people—and millions more—have made caring for our planet an important part of their lives.

The Individual's Role in Conservation

Federal, state, and local laws cannot guarantee that our environment will be saved. Private organizations of environmentalists cannot do the job alone. The future of our nation and our planet depends on the cooperation of individuals. The task of saving the earth begins with you, the citizen. Only through your action to save the environment can we have hope for the future.

Here are some steps you can take now to help conserve America's resources:

1. Prevent waste of all kinds in your home and school. Do not waste food, water, electricity, or anything else.

2. Take part with your class in a conservation project, such as tree planting, cleaning up streams, or picking up litter.

3. Take an interest in the natural resources you find all around you in your community. Study ways in which they might be used more wisely.

4. Participate in recycling projects. Newspapers, cans, bottles, and other materials can be reused in new products. Find out about companies in your area that accept such materials, and join in collection projects.

5. Be careful of fires when in a forest or wooded area. Put out your campfire with water. Then shovel dirt on the site to make sure it is out.

6. Do not destroy wildlife or damage forests or other public places. Vandalism is a serious crime against the environment.

7. Obey laws against open burning, littering, pollution, and other crimes against the environment.

8. Keep informed on ecological problems in your area. Make your opinions known by writing to your governmental representatives. Attend meetings and support petitions for a better environment.

9. Make it a point to take pleasure in the beauty of the natural world.

10. Start thinking about what you can do to help keep the world a fit place for people, including you!

SECTION 4 REVIEW

Identify Environmental Protection Agency (EPA), Earth Day

1. **Summarizing Ideas (a)** Describe the efforts made by the federal government to reduce pollution and restore the environment. **(b)** What are some duties of the Environmental Protection Agency?
2. **Identifying Ideas** Give some examples of state and local regulations that have helped the environment.
3. **Seeing Relationships** How has citizen involvement helped our environment?

Thinking Critically The President has appointed you to be the new head of the Environmental Protection Agency. Identify the three top priorities of your agency. Then explain how you plan to achieve these goals.

The United States is rich in natural resources. Yet many of our practices have upset nature's balance. Air, water, and ground pollution are among our greatest problems. Getting rid of pollution will be costly, but the cost must be met.

To understand the effects of pollution, we must understand ecology—the study of nature's balance and the relationship between all parts of the environment. Damage to any part of nature may result in damage to all of it, including humans.

Unwise development of land and the misuse of natural resources have resulted in the destruction of some wildlife and scenic areas. They also have upset the balance of nature. Problems have been caused by oil spills, careless mining and land use, the use of chemical pesticides and fertilizers, and other human activities. In addition, we face shortages of natural resources, especially of energy sources such as oil and natural gas. Besides conserving these resources, Americans are turning to other energy sources, such as nuclear power, solar power, and geothermal energy.

To protect our nation's future, federal, state, and local laws have been passed to ensure the wise use of natural resources. However, it is up to individual citizens to do their share and to work toward a better environment, now and for the future.

CHAPTER 25 SUMMARY

SOCIAL STUDIES SKILL
Reading a Map

Maps are flat diagrams of all or part of the earth's surface. Maps can show roads, political boundaries, natural features, and many other kinds of information. Like charts and graphs, they are excellent ways to organize data. You can often learn as much by studying a map for a few minutes as you can by reading for hours.

How to Read a Map

To read a map effectively, use the following guidelines.

1. **Read the title of the map.** Reading the title of the map will alert you to the kinds of information you can learn from the map.
2. **Study the map's legend.** Examine the legend, or key, to learn what the symbols and colors on the map mean.
3. **Use the scale and the compass rose.** The scale of a map tells you how distances on the map compare with the actual distances on the surface of the earth. The compass rose on a map indicates direction.
4. **Note all labels on the map.** The names of important geographic features and key terms often appear on the map.
5. **Use the map's information.** Learn as much as you can from the map.

Applying the Skill

Answer the following questions.

1. What does the legend of this map tell you?
2. **(a)** In what part of the United States does most acid rain fall? **(b)** Which cities experience severe acid rain?
3. **(a)** How far is it from Miami to Boston? **(b)** Which direction would you travel to go from Atlanta to Chicago? **(c)** Which city in the western part of the country has acid rain?

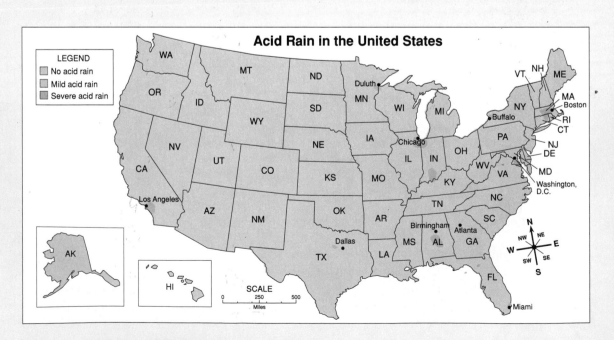

Acid Rain in the United States

LEGEND
☐ No acid rain
☐ Mild acid rain
☐ Severe acid rain

SCALE
0   250   500
Miles

Reviewing Terms

On a separate sheet of paper, supply the term from the list below that correctly answers each question.

environment   pollution
ecology   recycling
organic farming

1. Which term refers to the world around us?
2. What is turning waste products into something usable called?
3. Which term refers to the growing of crops without the use of chemical fertilizers or pesticides?
4. Which term refers to the study of the relationship among living things and their environment?
5. Which term refers to the contamination of the environment?

Using Thinking Skills

1. **Drawing Conclusions** (a) What problems do sanitary landfills present for our nation? (b) Explain how an increase in the amount of waste we recycle could help the environment.
2. **Understanding Ideas** Explain why people in our nation are concerned about the effects of overpopulation.
3. **Summarizing Ideas** Why is ecology important to us all?
4. **Identifying Roles** (a) Why has the government set up national parks? (b) What have state and local governments done to improve the environment?
5. **Identifying Ideas** What three factors make pollution more of a problem now than in the early years of our country?
6. **Expressing Ideas** (a) Describe the problems associated with coal and nuclear plants as energy sources. (b) How have people worked to conserve oil and natural gas? (c) Why is solar energy a promising energy source for the future?

7. **Seeing Relationships** (a) What actions of early American settlers interfered in the balance of nature? (b) Identify the farming techniques that have hurt the environment. (c) What developments in agriculture have helped the environment?
8. **Contrasting Points of View** Identify the arguments for and against conservation of natural resources.
9. **Organizing Ideas** (a) What are some causes of air pollution? (b) What are the different kinds of water pollution? (c) What effects do air and water pollution have on the earth's environment?

Practicing Civics Skills

Interpreting a Map Turn to the map of the United States on pages 530–531 of your textbook, and use it to answer the following questions.

1. (a) What symbols are identified in the map's legend? (b) What other symbols has the map maker used? (c) Why do you think Alaska and Hawaii have separate scales?
2. (a) What state lies north of North Carolina? (b) What state borders Alabama on the west? (c) Which ocean borders Florida?
3. (a) How far is it from Austin, Texas, to Santa Fe, New Mexico? (b) How long is Indiana's border with Ohio?

Being a Good Citizen

1. Work with other students to organize a mini-Earth Day in your class or school. Conduct activities to improve the environment and to alert local residents of the dangers facing our environment.
2. Locate a list of endangered species. Choose one of the species, and prepare a report on it to present to the class.
3. Contact a local environmental group and invite a speaker to give a presentation to your class.

Reviewing the Facts

1. (a) What is prejudice? (b) How is discrimination related to prejudice?
2. (a) What is plea bargaining? (b) What are the arguments for and against the use of plea bargaining?
3. (a) What is conservation? (b) What are the arguments in favor of conservation?
4. (a) What is wellness? (b) How do our governments promote wellness?
5. (a) What is homelessness? (b) Why has homelessness become a national problem in recent years?
6. (a) What is pollution? (b) Why have people polluted the environment?
7. (a) What is juvenile delinquency? (b) Why are special courts set up for juveniles?

Using Critical Thinking

1. **Organizing Ideas** (a) What is the goal of the civil rights movement? (b) How did the Supreme Court decision in *Brown v. Board of Education* affect the civil rights movement? (c) What is the purpose of civil disobedience?
2. **Identifying Roles** (a) What is the role of the police in the criminal justice system? (b) What is the goal of the prosecution in a criminal court case?
3. **Expressing Ideas** (a) Why do some people support organic farming? (b) What is the purpose of contour farming?
4. **Comparing Points of View** Why is capital punishment considered to be a subject of controversy?
5. **Understanding Ideas** How have cities tried to solve the problems of slums?
6. **Identifying Ideas** (a) What role have private organizations and individuals played in conservation? (b) Why must the countries of the world cooperate to solve the problems of pollution? (c) What are the responsibilities of the Environmental Protection Agency?

7. **Seeing Relationships** (a) What is the relationship between poverty and crime? (b) What is the relationship between juvenile delinquency and dropping out of school?
8. **Composing a Paragraph** Write a paragraph describing the problems created for cities by the move of middle-income families to the suburbs.

Applying What You Know

1. Locate two articles or editorials on capital punishment: one arguing for the death penalty and one arguing against it. Compare the two. Identify and list the arguments and evidence used by each author. Which is more convincing? Why?
2. Conduct library research and write a report on the history of Earth Day. Find out who started Earth Day, what famous people have participated in Earth Day activities, and what the organizers of Earth Day have planned for the future.
3. Locate a current map of the rain forests of the world. Then locate a map that shows what parts of the world had rain forests in the past. Study the two maps. Then write a paragraph telling what you have learned.

Expanding Your Knowledge

Currie, Elliott, *Confronting Crime: An American Challenge*, Pantheon. The author looks at the challenges presented to our country by the increasing amount of crime.

Earth Works Group, *50 Simple Things You Can Do to Save the Earth*, Earth Works Press. A list of practices you can follow in your everyday life that will help save the planet.

Kozol, Jonathan, *Rachel and Her Children: Homeless Families in America*, Fawcett. Looks at the growing problem of homeless families in the United States.

Reference Section

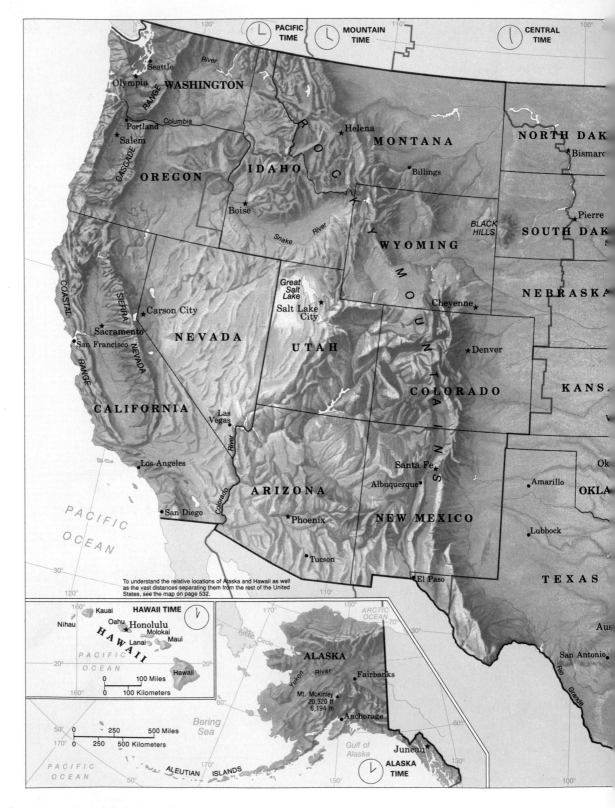

PACIFIC
TIME

MOUNTAIN
TIME

CENTRAL
TIME

120°

110°

100°

Seattle
River
Olympia
WASHINGTON

RANGE

Portland
Columbia
Salem

CASCADE

OREGON

IDAHO

Boise

Snake
River

ROCKY

Helena

MONTANA

Billings

WYOMING

MOUNTAINS

BLACK
HILLS

NORTH DAK

Bismarc

Pierre

SOUTH DAK

Cheyenne

NEBRASKA

COASTAL

SIERRA

Carson City

Sacramento

San Francisco

NEVADA

Great
Salt
Lake

Salt Lake
City

UTAH

NEVADA

RANGE

CALIFORNIA

Las
Vegas

River

Denver

COLORADO

KANS

Los Angeles

Santa Fe

Albuquerque

Amarillo

OK

OKLA

San Diego

Colorado

ARIZONA

Phoenix

NEW MEXICO

Lubbock

Tucson

30°

120°

El Paso

110°

TEXAS

To understand the relative locations of Alaska and Hawaii as well
as the vast distances separating them from the rest of the United
States, see the map on page 532.

Aus

San Antonio

160°

HAWAII TIME

150°

ARCTIC
OCEAN

70°

30°

Kauai

Oahu

Honolulu
Molokai

Nihau

HAWAII

Lanai

Maui

PACIFIC

OCEAN

20°

Hawaii

170°

Arctic Circle

Yukon

ALASKA

River

Fairbanks

Mt. McKinley
20,320 ft
6,194 m

Anchorage

60°

Rio

Grande

60°

160°

0   100 Miles

0   100 Kilometers

250   500 Miles

Bering
Sea

50°

0

170°

0   250   500 Kilometers

PACIFIC

OCEAN

50°

ALEUTIAN

ISLANDS

170°

150°

Gulf of
Alaska

Juneau

ALASKA
TIME

130°

100°

EASTERN
TIME

MAINE
★ Augusta

Duluth
SOTA
polis ★ St. Paul
VERMONT
★ Montpelier
NEW
HAMPSHIRE
★ Concord

WISCONSIN
Lake Superior
Lake Huron
MICHIGAN
Lake Ontario
Rochester
Albany ★
Boston
MASSACHUSETTS
Providence
RHODE
ISLAND
Hartford ★
CONNECTICUT
NEW YORK
Buffalo

Milwaukee
Madison ★
Lansing ★
Detroit
Lake Erie
Cleveland
PENNSYLVANIA
Harrisburg ★
Philadelphia
NEW
JERSEY
★ Trenton
New York

IOWA
★ Des Moines
Chicago
Gary
INDIANA
OHIO
★ Columbus
Pittsburgh
Baltimore
Wilmington
Dover
DELAWARE
Washington ★
Annapolis
MARYLAND

Kansas
City
ILLINOIS
Springfield ★
Indianapolis ★
Cincinnati
WEST
VIRGINIA
Charleston

St. Louis
River
Frankfort ★
Louisville
Charleston
Richmond
VIRGINIA
Norfolk
Chesapeake Bay
ATLANTIC

Jefferson
City
Ohio River
KENTUCKY
OCEAN

MISSOURI

NORTH
CAROLINA
Raleigh
Charlotte

★ Nashville
TENNESSEE

ARKANSAS
Memphis
Tennessee River
SOUTH
Columbia ★
CAROLINA

Little
Rock ★
Atlanta ★
Charleston

Birmingham
GEORGIA

Red River
ALABAMA
Jackson ★
Montgomery ★
Savannah

MISSISSIPPI
Mobile
Jacksonville
Tallahassee ★

Baton Rouge ★
LOUISIANA
New Orleans
FLORIDA
Orlando

Houston
Gulf of Mexico
Tampa

N

Miami

UNITED STATES: PHYSICAL

⊛ National capital
★ State capital
• Other city
━━ National boundary
── State boundary

Standard time zones are indicated by
clocks. (When it is 2 P.M. in western
Alaska, it is 6 P.M. along the eastern
coast of the United States.)

Albers Equal-Area Projection

500 Miles
250
0
0   250   500 Kilometers

THE WORLD: POLITICAL

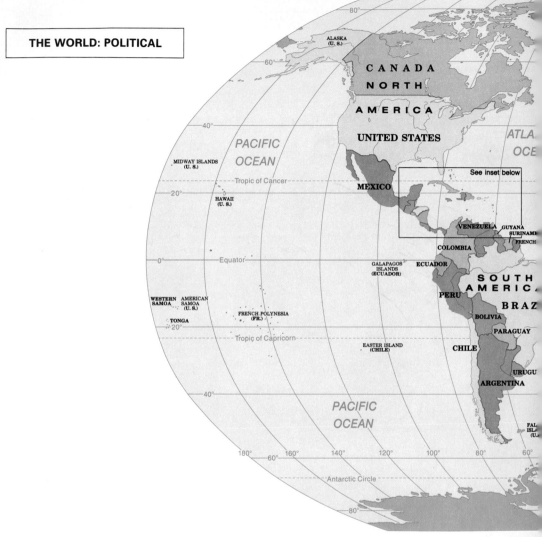

ALASKA (U. S.)

CANADA

NORTH

AMERICA

UNITED STATES

ATLA.

OCE

PACIFIC OCEAN

MIDWAY ISLANDS (U. S.)

See inset below

MEXICO

Tropic of Cancer

HAWAII (U. S.)

VENEZUELA   GUYANA
SURINAME
FRENCH

COLOMBIA

Equator

GALAPAGOS ISLANDS (ECUADOR)

ECUADOR

SOUTH

AMERIC.

PERU

BRAZ

WESTERN SAMOA   AMERICAN SAMOA (U. S.)

BOLIVIA

FRENCH POLYNESIA (FR.)

TONGA

PARAGUAY

20°

Tropic of Capricorn

EASTER ISLAND (CHILE)

CHILE

URUGU

ARGENTINA

40°

PACIFIC OCEAN

FAL ISL (U.

180°   160°   140°   120°   100°   80°   60°

60°

Antarctic Circle

80°

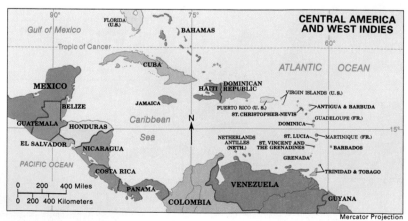

90°   75°

FLORIDA (U.S.)

Gulf of Mexico

BAHAMAS

Tropic of Cancer   60°

CUBA

ATLANTIC   OCEAN

CENTRAL AMERICA AND WEST INDIES

MEXICO

HAITI   DOMINICAN REPUBLIC

VIRGIN ISLANDS (U.S.)

BELIZE

JAMAICA

PUERTO RICO (U. S.)

ANTIGUA & BARBUDA

GUATEMALA   HONDURAS

Caribbean

ST. CHRISTOPHER-NEVIS

GUADELOUPE (FR.)

DOMINICA

EL SALVADOR   NICARAGUA

Sea

NETHERLANDS ANTILLES (NETH.)

ST. LUCIA   MARTINIQUE (FR.)

ST. VINCENT AND THE GRENADINES

15°

BARBADOS

PACIFIC OCEAN

N

GRENADA

COSTA RICA

TRINIDAD & TOBAGO

0   200   400 Miles

PANAMA

VENEZUELA

0   200   400 Kilometers

COLOMBIA

GUYANA

Mercator Projection

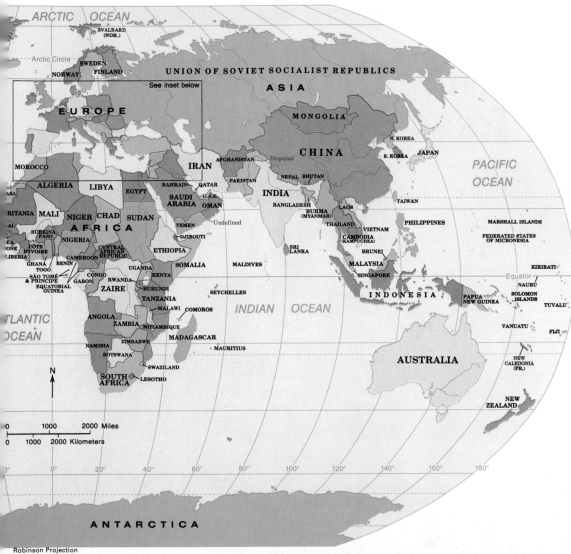

ARCTIC OCEAN

SVALBARD (NOR.)

Arctic Circle

SWEDEN
NORWAY FINLAND

EUROPE

See inset below

UNION OF SOVIET SOCIALIST REPUBLICS

ASIA

MONGOLIA

MOROCCO

IRAN

N. KOREA
JAPAN
S. KOREA

PACIFIC OCEAN

CHINA

ALGERIA LIBYA

EGYPT

BAHRAIN QATAR
SAUDI U.A.E.
ARABIA OMAN

AFGHANISTAN Disputed
PAKISTAN
NEPAL BHUTAN

INDIA

TAIWAN

RITANIA MALI
NIGER CHAD
SUDAN

BANGLADESH

BURMA
(MYANMAR)

PHILIPPINES

MARSHALL ISLANDS

FEDERATED STATES
OF MICRONESIA

AL
EA
ONE
LIBERIA

BURKINA
FASO
CÔTE
D'IVOIRE

AFRICA

NIGERIA

YEMEN

DJIBOUTI

Undefined

THAILAND

VIETNAM

CAMBODIA
(KAMPUCHEA)

BRUNEI

GHANA
TOGO
BENIN

CAMEROON

CENTRAL
AFRICAN
REPUBLIC

ETHIOPIA

SRI
LANKA

MALDIVES

MALAYSIA
SINGAPORE

KIRIBATI

SÃO TOMÉ
& PRÍNCIPE
EQUATORIAL
GUINEA

CONGO
GABON

ZAIRE

UGANDA
RWANDA
BURUNDI

KENYA

SOMALIA

INDONESIA

PAPUA
NEW GUINEA

NAURU
SOLOMON
ISLANDS

Equator

TANZANIA

SEYCHELLES

TUVALU

ANGOLA
ZAMBIA

MALAWI COMOROS

MOZAMBIQUE

INDIAN OCEAN

VANUATU

FIJI

ATLANTIC
OCEAN

NAMIBIA
BOTSWANA

ZIMBABWE

MADAGASCAR

MAURITIUS

AUSTRALIA

NEW
CALEDONIA
(FR.)

N

SWAZILAND

SOUTH
AFRICA LESOTHO

NEW
ZEALAND

1000 2000 Miles
1000 2000 Kilometers

0° 0° 20° 40° 60° 80° 100° 120° 140° 160° 180°

ANTARCTICA

Robinson Projection

15° NORWAY SWEDEN
0°

EUROPE

UNITED
KINGDOM

DENMARK

0 250 500 Miles
0 250 500 Kilometers

IRELAND

NETH.

UNION OF
SOVIET SOCIALIST
REPUBLICS

POLAND

ATLANTIC
OCEAN

BELGIUM

GERMANY

CZECHOSLOVAKIA

LUXEMBOURG

LIECHTENSTEIN
AUSTRIA HUNGARY

FRANCE SWITZ.

ROMANIA

45°

MONACO

ITALY

YUGOSLAVIA
SAN MARINO

Black Sea

Caspian Sea

ANDORRA

CORSICA
(FR.)

VATICAN CITY BULGARIA
ALBANIA

PORTUGAL

SARDINA
(ITALY)

GREECE

TURKEY

SPAIN

SICILY
(ITALY)

MALTA

CYPRUS SYRIA

LEBANON

IRAQ IRAN

ISRAEL

JORDAN

KUWAIT

MOROCCO

TUNISIA

Mediterranean Sea

ALGERIA

LIBYA

EGYPT

SAUDI ARABIA

30°

N

Mercator Projection

Abbreviation	Country
DEN.	—DENMARK
FR.	—FRANCE
NETH.	—NETHERLANDS
NOR.	—NORWAY
PORT.	—PORTUGAL
SWITZ.	—SWITZERLAND
U.A.E.	—UNITED ARAB EMIRATES
U.K.	—UNITED KINGDOM
U.S.	—UNITED STATES

Map of the World **533**

Living Documents: A Treasury of Freedom

Important documents and great speeches have shaped the American nation. These documents have fashioned the ideals of American citizens and have influenced the country's character as a land of freedom and democracy.

The ideas included in LIVING DOCUMENTS: A TREASURY OF FREEDOM focus on the freedoms to which the United States is dedicated and that American citizens cherish. Learning about these documents helps keep alive our country's commitment to individual freedom.

The Mayflower Compact
Patrick Henry's Speech Before the Virginia Convention
Nathan Hale's Speech
Thomas Jefferson's First Inaugural Address
The Monroe Doctrine
The Seneca Falls Declaration
The Gettysburg Address
The Emancipation Proclamation
Franklin D. Roosevelt's Four Freedoms
Brown v. Board of Education of Topeka
John F. Kennedy's Inaugural Address
I Have a Dream
The Civil Rights Act of 1964
The Voting Rights Act of 1965
The American's Creed

The Mayflower Compact

On November 11, 1620, the tiny ship—the *Mayflower*—carrying the Pilgrims to the New World reached shore. The ship was far off its course, and the Pilgrims had no charter to settle in New England or to form a government. Faced with the need to form a government, the Pilgrim leaders wrote the Mayflower Compact. This document created a government based on cooperation and the consent of the governed.

November 11, 1620

In the name of God, Amen. We whose names are underwritten, the loyal subjects of our dread [revered and feared] sovereign Lord King *James,* by the grace of God, of Great Britain, France, and Ireland, King, Defender of the Faith, etc., having undertaken for the glory of God, and advancement of the Christian faith, and honor of our king and country, a voyage to plant the first colony in the northern parts of Virginia, do by these presents [this document] solemnly and mutually in the presence of God, and one of another, covenant [promise] and combine ourselves together into a civil body politic [group organized for government] for our better ordering and preservation and furtherance of the ends aforesaid; and by virture [authority] hereof, to enact, constitute, and frame such just and equal laws, ordinances [regulations], acts, constitutions, and offices from time to time, as shall be thought most meet [fitting] and convenient for the general good of the colony unto which we promise all due submission and obedience.

In WITNESS whereof we have hereunto subscribed our names at Cape Cod, the eleventh of November, in the year of the reign of our sovereign Lord King James of England, France, and Ireland the eighteenth, and of Scotland the fifty-fourth. *Anno Domini, 1620.*

[Signed by forty-one men on the *Mayflower*]

Patrick Henry's Speech Before the Virginia Convention

Patrick Henry had attended the First Continental Congress as a delegate from Virginia. He returned to Virginia believing that war would soon break out with Great Britain. Soon after his return, Patrick Henry addressed the Virginia Convention, which was meeting to consider the situation in the colony. There he delivered his most famous speech—a rousing call to liberty and freedom, which continues to inspire Americans today.

March 23, 1775

Mr. President: No man thinks more highly than I do of the patriotism, as well as abilities, of the very worthy gentlemen who have just addressed the House. But different men often see the same subjects in different lights; and, therefore, I hope that it will not be thought disrespectful to those gentlemen if, entertaining as I do, opinions of a character very opposite to theirs, I shall speak forth my sentiments freely and without reserve. This is no time for ceremony. The question before the House is one of awful moment [importance] to this country. . . .

It is in vain, sir, to extenuate [prolong] the matter. Gentlemen may cry peace, peace. But there is no peace. The war is actually begun! The next gale that sweeps from the north will bring to our ears the clash of resounding arms! Our brethren are already in the field! Why stand we here idle? What is it that gentlemen wish? What would they have? Is life so dear, or peace so sweet, as to be purchased at the price of chains and slavery? Forbid it, Almighty God! I know not what course others may take; but as for me, give me liberty or give me death!

Nathan Hale's Speech

Nathan Hale, a captain in the American Revolutionary Army, volunteered for a secret mission behind the British lines. Pretending that he was a Dutch schoolmaster, Hale slipped into British-held territory. As Hale returned to the American lines, he was captured by the British and condemned to die by hanging. Before his death Hale made a brief speech, which has since served as an inspiration to all American citizens.

September 22, 1776

The cause for which I am dying I did not take up in an idle moment. I was born in it, as are all my countrymen. If the belief in man's right to freedom is held in any other place on earth, I have not heard of it. I am proud to have lived in the country where freedom is a reality. Living, it has been my privilege to fight for it. In death I shall hold it forever. If I were to be born a thousand times, I would choose no other life but service to American freedom. I have only one sorrow. I only regret that I have but one life to lose for my country.

Thomas Jefferson's First Inaugural Address

Thomas Jefferson, a Republican, won the Presidency in the election of 1800, defeating the Federalist candidate. Jefferson's inauguration marked the first time that the power to govern passed peacefully from one political party to another. Jefferson's Inaugural Address is one of the great speeches of all time. In it he reassures his Federalist opponents, and he advocates the ideals of limited government and representative democracy.

March 4, 1801

Friends and Fellow Citizens: . . .

All . . . will bear in mind this sacred principle, that though the will of the majority is in all cases to prevail, that will to be rightful must be reasonable; that the minority possess their equal rights, which equal law must protect, and to violate would be oppression. Let us, then, fellow citizens, unite with one heart and one mind. . . . And let us reflect that, having banished from our land that religious intolerance under which mankind so long bled and suffered, we have yet gained little if we countenance [allow] a political intolerance as despotic, as wicked, and capable of as bitter and bloody persecutions. . . . But every difference of opinion is not a difference of principle. We have called by different names brethren of the same principle. We are all Republicans; we are all Federalists. If there be any among us who would wish to dissolve this Union or to change its republican form, let them stand undisturbed as monuments of the safety with which error of opinion may be tolerated where reason is left free to combat it. . . .

Let us, then, with courage and confidence pursue our own Federal and Republican principles, our attachment to union and representative government. . . .

Relying, then, on the patronage of your good will, I advance with obedience to the work, ready to retire from it whenever you become sensible how much better choice it is in your power to make. And may that Infinite Power which rules the destinies of the universe lead our councils to what is best, and give them a favorable issue for your peace and prosperity. . . .

The Monroe Doctrine

The Monroe Doctrine is not a law passed by Congress. It is a statement of policy made by President Monroe in a State of the Union Address to Congress. The Monroe Doctrine is one of the most important documents in the nation's history. It has influenced American foreign policy to the present time. The Monroe Doctrine asserts the nation's dedication to freedom, and warns foreign nations that the Americas are closed to colonization.

December 2, 1823

. . . [It is] a principle in which the rights and interests of the United States are involved, that the American continents, by the free and independent condition which they have assumed and maintain, are henceforth not to be considered as subjects for future colonization by any European powers. . . .

. . . We owe it, therefore, to candor and to the amicable relations existing between the United States and those powers to declare that we should consider any attempt on their part to extend their system to any portion of this hemisphere as dangerous to our peace and safety. With the existing colonies or dependencies of any European power, we have not interfered and shall not interfere. But with the governments who have declared their independence and maintained it, and whose independence we have, on great consideration and on just principles, acknowledged, we could not view any [interference] for the purpose of oppressing them, or controlling in any other manner their destiny, by any European power in any other light than as the manifestation of an unfriendly disposition toward the United States. . . .

The Seneca Falls Declaration

The first women's rights convention met in 1848 in Seneca Falls, New York. At that convention, the delegates adopted a series of resolutions stating their belief in the equality of men and women. The document appeals to the principles of freedom and equality set forth in the Declaration of Independence. The Seneca Falls Declaration states the delegates' determination to strive for legal recognition of women's equality with men.

July 19, 1848

When, in the course of human events, it becomes necessary for one portion of the family of man to assume among the people of the earth a position different from that which they have hitherto occupied, but one to which the laws of nature and of nature's God entitle them, a decent respect to the opinions of mankind requires that they should declare the causes that impel them to such a course.

We hold these truths to be self-evident: that all men and women are created equal; that they are endowed by their Creator with certain inalienable rights; that among these are life, liberty, and the pursuit of happiness; that to secure these rights governments are instituted, deriving their just powers from the consent of the governed. . . .

RESOLUTIONS

Resolved, That all laws which prevent woman from occupying such a station in society as her conscience shall dictate, or which place her in a position inferior to that of man, are contrary to the great precept of nature, and, therefore, of no force or authority.

Resolved, That woman is man's equal—was intended to be so by the Creator, and the highest good of the race demands that she should be recognized as such. . . .

Resolved, That it is the duty of the women of this country to secure to themselves their sacred right to the elective franchise. . . .

Resolved, That the equality of human rights results necessarily from the fact of the identity [sameness of essential character] of the race in capabilities and responsibilities. . . .

The Gettysburg Address

In November 1863, President Abraham Lincoln dedicated the national cemetery at Gettysburg, Pennsylvania. Just four months earlier, Gettysburg had been the scene of one of the bloodiest battles of the Civil War. Lincoln's brief speech, *The Gettysburg Address,* has inspired generations of Americans. It reaffirms Americans' dedication to liberty and to the equality of all, and continues to inspire citizens today.

November 19, 1863

Four score and seven years ago our fathers brought forth on this continent a new nation, conceived in liberty, and dedicated to the proposition that all men are created equal.

Now we are engaged in a great civil war, testing whether that nation, or any nation so conceived and so dedicated, can long endure. We are met on a great battlefield of that war. We have come to dedicate a portion of that field as a final resting place for those who here gave their lives that that nation might live. It is altogether fitting and proper that we should do this.

But, in a larger sense, we cannot dedicate—we cannot consecrate—we cannot hallow—this ground. The brave men, living and dead, who struggled here, have consecrated it far above our poor power to add or detract. The world will little note nor long remember what we say here, but it can never forget what they did here. It is for us, the living, rather, to be dedicated here to the unfinished work which they who fought here have thus far so nobly advanced. It is rather for us to be here dedicated to the great task remaining before us—that from these honored dead we take increased devotion to that cause for which they gave the last full measure of devotion; that we here highly resolve that these dead shall not have died in vain; that this nation, under God, shall have a new birth of freedom; and that government of the people, by the people, for the people, shall not perish from the earth.

The Emancipation Proclamation

President Lincoln issued the Emancipation Proclamation on January 1, 1863. Before that time, the Civil War was fought mainly to save the Union. After that time, the war also became a crusade to end slavery. Many historians believe the Proclamation greatly helped the Union cause. The Proclamation expresses the commitment of the United States government to freedom. It has been a source of inspiration for Americans to the present day.

January 1, 1863

WHEREAS on the twenty-second day of September, A.D. 1862, a proclamation was issued by the President of the United States, containing, among other things, the following, to wit:

"That on the first day of January, A.D. 1863, all persons held as slaves within any state or designated part of a state, the people whereof shall then be in rebellion against the United States, shall be then, thenceforward, and forever free; and the executive government of the United States, including the military and naval authority thereof, will recognize and maintain the freedom of such persons and will do no act or acts to repress such persons or any of them, in any efforts they may make for their actual freedom.

"That the Executive will on the first day of January aforesaid, by proclamation, designate the states and parts of states, if any, in which the people thereof, respectively, shall then be in rebellion against the United States; and the fact that any state or the people thereof shall on that day be in good faith represented in the Congress of the United States by members chosen thereto at elections wherein a majority of the qualified voters of such states shall have participated shall, in the absence of strong countervailing [opposing] testimony, be deemed conclusive evidence that such state and the people thereof are not then in rebellion against the United States. . . ."

Franklin D. Roosevelt's Four Freedoms

President Franklin D. Roosevelt gave a State of the Union Address to Congress in January 1941. In his address, Roosevelt warned the nation about the war that was raging around the world. Roosevelt also stated four freedoms to which the United States was committed. These four freedoms inspired Americans during World War II, and the four freedoms remain at the heart of our nation's policies—foreign and domestic.

January 6, 1941

I address you, the members of the Seventy-seventh Congress, at a moment unprecedented in the history of the Union. I use the word "unprecedented," because at no previous time has American security been as seriously threatened from without as it is today. . . .

Every realist knows that the democratic way of life is at this moment being directly assailed in every part of the world—assailed either by arms, or by . . . propaganda . . .

In the future days, which we seek to make secure, we look forward to a world founded upon four essential human freedoms.

The first is freedom of speech and expression—everywhere in the world.

The second is freedom of every person to worship God in his own way—everywhere in the world.

The third is freedom from want—which, translated into world terms, means economic understandings which will secure to every nation a healthy peacetime life for its inhabitants—everywhere in the world.

The fourth is freedom from fear—which, translated into world terms, means a world-wide reduction of armaments to such a point and in such a thorough fashion that no nation will be in a position to commit an act of physical aggression against any neighbor—anywhere in the world. . . .

This nation has placed its destiny in the hands and heads and hearts of its millions of free men and women; and its faith in freedom under the guidance of God. Freedom means the supremacy of human rights everywhere. Our support goes to those who struggle to gain those rights or keep them. Our strength is in our unity of purpose.

To that high concept there can be no end save victory.

Brown v. Board of Education of Topeka

Brown v. Board of Education of Topeka is a landmark decision in the struggle for equality. In this decision, the Supreme Court struck down segregation in the public schools. In doing so, the Court overturned the "separate but equal" doctrine set up in the case of *Plessy v. Ferguson.* The Court's decision in *Brown* inspired Americans to continue the struggle for equality, and has helped to make the United States a nation where all are equal.

May 17, 1954

[In this case,] segregation was alleged to deprive the plaintiffs of the equal protection of the laws under the Fourteenth Amendment. . . .

The plaintiffs contend that segregated public schools are not "equal" and cannot be made "equal," and that hence they are deprived of the equal protection of the law. . . .

In approaching this problem, we cannot turn the clock back to 1868 when the [Fourteenth] Amendment was adopted, or even to 1896 when Plessy v. Ferguson was written. We must consider public education in the light of its full development and its present place in American life throughout the Nation. . . .

We come then to the question presented: Does segregation of children in public schools solely on the basis of race, even though the physical facilities and other "tangible" factors may be equal, deprive the children of the minority group of equal educational opportunities? We believe that it does. . . .

We conclude that in the field of public education the doctrine of "separate but equal" has no place. Separate educational facilities are inherently unequal. Therefore, we hold that the plaintiffs . . . are, by reason of the segregation complained of, deprived of the equal protection of the laws guaranteed by the Fourteenth Amendment. . . .

John F. Kennedy's Inaugural Address

John F. Kennedy, at age 43, was the youngest President ever elected in the nation's history. His Inaugural Address is one of the greatest speeches ever delivered. In it, President Kennedy challenges Americans to join in a "struggle against poverty, disease, and war itself." Kennedy's address inspired "a new generation of Americans" and continues to inspire citizens today. Americans still reach for the goals set forth by President Kennedy.

January 20, 1961

My Fellow Citizens:

We observe today not a victory of party but a celebration of freedom—symbolizing an end as well as a beginning—signifying renewal as well as change. For I have sworn before you and Almighty God the same solemn oath our forebears prescribed nearly a century and three-quarters ago. . . .

We dare not forget today that we are the heirs of that first revolution. Let the word go forth from this time and place, to friend and foe alike, that the torch has been passed to a new generation of Americans—born in this century, tempered by war, disciplined by a hard and bitter peace, proud of our ancient heritage—and unwilling to witness or permit the slow undoing of those human rights to which this nation has always been committed, and to which we are committed today at home and around the world.

Let every nation know, whether it wishes us well or ill, that we shall pay any price, bear any burden, meet any hardship, support any friend, oppose any foe to assure the survival and the success of liberty.

This much we pledge—and more. . . .

And so, my fellow Americans: Ask not what your country can do for you—ask what you can do for your country.

My fellow citizens of the world: Ask not what America will do for you, but what together we can do for the freedom of man.

Finally, whether you are citizens of America or citizens of the world, ask of us here the same high standards of strength and sacrifice which we ask of you. With a good conscience our only sure reward, with history the final judge of our deeds, let us go forth. . . .

I Have a Dream

Dr. Martin Luther King, Jr. symbolizes the dream of equality for all Americans. In 1963 Dr. King addressed more than 200,000 Americans—black and white—at the March on Washington, the largest rally for racial equality in the nation's history. Dr. King's speech, made to the huge crowd assembled before the Lincoln Memorial, sets forth his dream of a nation where all American citizens are truly equal and free.

August 28, 1963

I say to you today, my friends, that in spite of the difficulties and frustrations of the moment I still have a dream. It is a dream deeply rooted in the American Dream.

I have a dream that one day this nation will rise up and live out the true meaning of its creed: "We hold these truths to be self-evident: that all men are created equal. . . ."

I have a dream that my four little children will one day live in a nation where they will not be judged by the color of their skin but by the content of their character. . . .

I have a dream today.

This is our hope. This is the faith with which I return to the South. With this faith we will be able to cut out of the mountain of despair a stone of hope. With this faith we will be able to change the jangling discords of our nation into a beautiful symphony of brotherhood. With this faith we will be able to work together, to pray together, to struggle together, to go to jail together, to stand up for freedom together, knowing that we will be free one day.

This will be the day when all of God's children will be able to sing with new meaning "My country 'tis of thee, sweet land of liberty, of thee I sing. Land where my fathers died, land of the pilgrim's pride, from every mountainside, let freedom ring. . . ."

When we let freedom ring, when we let it ring from every village and every hamlet, from every state and every city, we will be able to speed up that day when all of God's children, black people and white people, Jews, Protestants, and Catholics, will be able to join hands and sing in the words of the old Negro spiritual, "Free at last! free at last, thank God almighty we are free at last!"

The Civil Rights Act of 1964

The Civil Rights Act of 1964 is landmark legislation. The act prohibits discrimination on the basis of race, color, religion, or national origin. Under the terms of this act, discrimination is outlawed in the exercise of voting rights, and in public places, public education, and employment practices. This act supported the principles set forth in the Fourteenth and Fifteenth amendments and helped our nation toward the goal of equality for all Americans.

July 2, 1964

VOTING RIGHTS

No person acting under color of law shall in determining whether any individual is qualified under State law or laws to vote in any Federal election, apply any standard, practice, or procedure different from the standards, practices, or procedures applied under such law or laws to other individuals within the same county, parish, or similar political subdivision who have been found by State officials to be qualified to vote. . . .

DISCRIMINATION IN PLACES OF PUBLIC ACCOMMODATION

All persons shall be entitled to the full and equal enjoyment of the goods, services, facilities, privileges, advantages, and accommodations of any place of public accommodation, as defined in this section, without discrimination or segregation on the ground of race, color, religion, or national origin. . . .

EQUAL EMPLOYMENT OPPORTUNITY

It shall be an unlawful employment practice for an employer—
to fail or refuse to hire or to discharge any individual, or otherwise to discriminate against any individual with respect to his compensation, terms, conditions, or privileges of employment, because of such individual's race, color, religion, sex, or national origin; or
to limit, segregate, or classify his employees in any way . . . because of such individual's race, color, religion, sex, or national origin. . . .

The Voting Rights Act of 1965

The Voting Rights Act of 1965 strengthened the Civil Rights Act of 1964. This act extends the prohibition of voting discrimination to federal, state, and local elections. It also outlaws the use of literacy tests as a way of preventing people from voting. This act increased the number of people who were eligible to vote, thus making the United States a more democratic nation. Extensions of this act ensure that its guarantees remain in effect.

May 26, 1965

To assure that the right of citizens of the United States to vote is not denied or abridged on account of race or color, no citizen shall be denied the right to vote in any Federal, State, or local election because of his failure to comply with any test or device in any State. . . .

The phrase "test or device" shall mean any requirement that a person as a prerequisite for voting or registration for voting (1) demonstrate the ability to read, write, understand, or interpret any matter, (2) demonstrate any educational achievement or his knowledge of any particular subject, (3) possess good moral character, or (4) prove his qualifications by the voucher of registered voters or members of any other class. . . .

Section 12. (a) Whoever shall deprive or attempt to deprive any person of any right . . . shall be fined not more than $5,000, or imprisoned not more than five years, or both.

The American's Creed

The American's Creed was written during World War I by William Tyler Page, who was the clerk of the House of Representatives. It includes phrases from the Constitution, the Declaration of Independence, and famous speeches. The Creed was adopted by the House of Representatives in 1918 as the "best summary of the political faith of America." The American's Creed states principles that all American citizens cherish.

1918

I believe in the United States of America as a government
   of the people, by the people, for the people;
whose just powers are derived from the consent of the
   governed;
a democracy in a Republic;
a sovereign Nation of many sovereign States;
a perfect Union, one and inseparable;
established upon those principles of freedom, equality, justice, and humanity for which American patriots sacrificed
   their lives and fortunes.

I therefore believe it is my duty to my country to love it;
to support its Constitution;
to obey its laws;
to respect its flag;
and to defend it against all enemies.

American Presidents

1
George Washington
1732–1799
Elected from: Virginia
In office: 1789–1797

6
John Quincy Adams
1767–1848
Elected from: Massachusetts
National-Republican
In office: 1825–1829

2
John Adams
1735–1826
Elected from: Massachusetts
Federalist
In office: 1797–1801

7
Andrew Jackson
1767–1845
Elected from: Tennessee
Democrat
In office: 1829–1837

3
Thomas Jefferson
1743–1826
Elected from: Virginia
Democratic-Republican
In office: 1801–1809

8
Martin Van Buren
1782–1862
Elected from: New York
Democrat
In office: 1837–1841

4
James Madison
1751–1836
Elected from: Virginia
Democratic-Republican
In office: 1809–1817

9
William Henry Harrison
1773–1841
Elected from: Ohio
Whig
In office: 1841

5
James Monroe
1758–1831
Elected from: Virginia
Democratic-Republican
In office: 1817–1825

10
John Tyler
1790–1862
Elected from: Virginia
Whig
In office: 1841–1845

11
James K. Polk
1795–1849
Elected from: Tennessee
Democrat
In office: 1845–1849

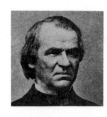

17
Andrew Johnson
1808–1875
Elected from: Tennessee
Republican
In office: 1865–1869

12
Zachary Taylor
1784–1850
Elected from: Louisiana
Whig
In office: 1849–1850

18
Ulysses S. Grant
1822–1885
Elected from: Illinois
Republican
In office: 1869–1877

13
Millard Fillmore
1800–1874
Elected from: New York
Whig
In office: 1850–1853

19
Rutherford B. Hayes
1822–1893
Elected from: Ohio
Republican
In office: 1877–1881

14
Franklin Pierce
1804–1869
Elected from: New Hampshire
Democrat
In office: 1853–1857

20
James A. Garfield
1831–1881
Elected from: Ohio
Republican
In office: 1881

15
James Buchanan
1791–1868
Elected from: Pennsylvania
Democrat
In office: 1857–1861

21
Chester A. Arthur
1830–1886
Elected from: New York
Republican
In office: 1881–1885

16
Abraham Lincoln
1809–1865
Elected from: Illinois
Republican
In office: 1861–1865

22
Grover Cleveland
1837–1908
Elected from: New York
Democrat
In office: 1885–1889

23
Benjamin Harrison
1833–1901
Elected from: Indiana
Republican
In office: 1889–1893

29
Warren G. Harding
1865–1923
Elected from: Ohio
Republican
In office: 1921–1923

24
Grover Cleveland
1837–1908
Elected from: New York
Democrat
In office: 1893–1897

30
Calvin Coolidge
1872–1933
Elected from: Massachusetts
Republican
In office: 1923–1929

25
William McKinley
1843–1901
Elected from: Ohio
Republican
In office: 1897–1901

31
Herbert C. Hoover
1874–1964
Elected from: California
Republican
In office: 1929–1933

26
Theodore Roosevelt
1858–1919
Elected from: New York
Republican
In office: 1901–1909

32
Franklin D. Roosevelt
1882–1945
Elected from: New York
Democrat
In office: 1933–1945

27
William H. Taft
1857–1930
Elected from: Ohio
Republican
In office: 1909–1913

33
Harry S. Truman
1884–1972
Elected from: Missouri
Democrat
In office: 1945–1953

28
Woodrow Wilson
1856–1924
Elected from: New Jersey
Democrat
In office: 1913–1921

34
Dwight D. Eisenhower
1890–1969
Elected from: Pennsylvania
Republican
In office: 1953–1961

35
John F. Kennedy
1917–1963
Elected from: Massachusetts
Democrat
In office: 1961–1963

36
Lyndon B. Johnson
1908–1973
Elected from: Texas
Democrat
In office: 1963–1969

37
Richard M. Nixon
1913–
Elected from: California
Republican
In office: 1969–1974

38
Gerald R. Ford
1913–
Elected from: Michigan
Republican
In office: 1974–1977

39
Jimmy Carter
1924–
Elected from: Georgia
Democrat
In office: 1977–1981

40
Ronald W. Reagan
1911–
Elected from: California
Republican
In office: 1981–1989

41
George Bush
1924–
Elected from: Texas
Republican
In office: 1989–

Our 50 States

The number in parentheses is the order in which each state was admitted to the Union. For the original 13 states, this is the order in which each state approved the Constitution. Population figures are based on preliminary estimates of the 1990 census. The nickname of each state is in *italics*.

 Alabama (22)
Admitted to Union: 1819
Capital: Montgomery
Population: 4,040,587
Heart of Dixie

 **Colorado** (38)
Admitted to Union: 1876
Capital: Denver
Population: 3,294,394
Centennial State

 **Alaska** (49)
Admitted to Union: 1959
Capital: Juneau
Population: 550,043
The Last Frontier

 **Connecticut** (5)
Admitted to Union: 1788
Capital: Hartford
Population: 3,287,116
Nutmeg State

 **Arizona** (48)
Admitted to Union: 1912
Capital: Phoenix
Population: 3,665,228
Grand Canyon State

 **Delaware** (1)
Admitted to Union: 1787
Capital: Dover
Population: 666,168
First State

 **Arkansas** (25)
Admitted to Union: 1836
Capital: Little Rock
Population: 2,350,725
Land of Opportunity

 **Florida** (27)
Admitted to Union: 1845
Capital: Tallahassee
Population: 12,937,926
Sunshine State

 **California** (31)
Admitted to Union: 1850
Capital: Sacramento
Population: 29,760,021
Golden State

 **Georgia** (4)
Admitted to Union: 1788
Capital: Atlanta
Population: 6,478,216
Peach State

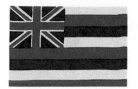

Hawaii (50)
Admitted to Union: 1959
Capital: Honolulu
Population: 1,108,229
Aloha State

Louisiana (18)
Admitted to Union: 1812
Capital: Baton Rouge
Population: 4,219,973
Pelican State

Idaho (43)
Admitted to Union: 1890
Capital: Boise
Population: 1,006,749
Gem State

Maine (23)
Admitted to Union: 1820
Capital: Augusta
Population: 1,227,928
Pine Tree State

Illinois (21)
Admitted to Union: 1818
Capital: Springfield
Population: 11,430,602
Prairie State

Maryland (7)
Admitted to Union: 1788
Capital: Annapolis
Population: 4,781,468
Free State

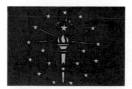

Indiana (19)
Admitted to Union: 1816
Capital: Indianapolis
Population: 5,544,159
Hoosier State

Massachusetts (6)
Admitted to Union: 1788
Capital: Boston
Population: 6,016,425
Bay State

Iowa (29)
Admitted to Union: 1846
Capital: Des Moines
Population: 2,776,755
Hawkeye State

Michigan (26)
Admitted to Union: 1837
Capital: Lansing
Population: 9,295,297
Wolverine State

Kansas (34)
Admitted to Union: 1861
Capital: Topeka
Population: 2,477,574
Sunflower State

Minnesota (32)
Admitted to Union: 1858
Capital: St. Paul
Population: 4,375,099
North Star State

Kentucky (15)
Admitted to Union: 1792
Capital: Frankfort
Population: 3,685,296
Bluegrass State

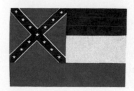

Mississippi (20)
Admitted to Union: 1817
Capital: Jackson
Population: 2,573,216
Magnolia State

Missouri (24)
Admitted to Union: 1821
Capital: Jefferson City
Population: 5,117,073
Show Me State

New York (11)
Admitted to Union: 1788
Capital: Albany
Population: 17,990,455
Empire State

Montana (41)
Admitted to Union: 1889
Capital: Helena
Population: 799,065
Treasure State

North Carolina (12)
Admitted to Union: 1789
Capital: Raleigh
Population: 6,628,637
Tarheel State

Nebraska (37)
Admitted to Union: 1867
Capital: Lincoln
Population: 1,578,385
Cornhusker State

North Dakota (39)
Admitted to Union: 1889
Capital: Bismarck
Population: 638,800
Sioux State

Nevada (36)
Admitted to Union: 1864
Capital: Carson City
Population: 1,201,833
Sagebrush State

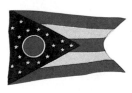

Ohio (17)
Admitted to Union: 1803
Capital: Columbus
Population: 10,847,115
Buckeye State

New Hampshire (9)
Admitted to Union: 1788
Capital: Concord
Population: 1,109,252
Granite State

Oklahoma (46)
Admitted to Union: 1907
Capital: Oklahoma City
Population: 3,145,585
Sooner State

New Jersey (3)
Admitted to Union: 1787
Capital: Trenton
Population: 7,730,188
Garden State

Oregon (33)
Admitted to Union: 1859
Capital: Salem
Population: 2,842,321
Beaver State

New Mexico (47)
Admitted to Union: 1912
Capital: Santa Fe
Population: 1,515,069
Land of Enchantment

Pennsylvania (2)
Admitted to Union: 1787
Capital: Harrisburg
Population: 11,881,643
Keystone State

Rhode Island (13)
Admitted to Union: 1790
Capital: Providence
Population: 1,003,464
Ocean State

Vermont (14)
Admitted to Union: 1791
Capital: Montpelier
Population: 562,758
Green Mountain State

South Carolina (8)
Admitted to Union: 1788
Capital: Columbia
Population: 3,486,703
Palmetto State

Virginia (10)
Admitted to Union: 1788
Capital: Richmond
Population: 6,187,358
Old Dominion

South Dakota (40)
Admitted to Union: 1889
Capital: Pierre
Population: 696,004
Coyote State

Washington (42)
Admitted to Union: 1889
Capital: Olympia
Population: 4,866,692
Evergreen State

Tennessee (16)
Admitted to Union: 1796
Capital: Nashville
Population: 4,877,185
Volunteer State

West Virginia (35)
Admitted to Union: 1863
Capital: Charleston
Population: 1,793,477
Mountain State

Texas (28)
Admitted to Union: 1845
Capital: Austin
Population: 16,986,510
Lone Star State

Wisconsin (30)
Admitted to Union: 1848
Capital: Madison
Population: 4,891,769
Badger State

Utah (45)
Admitted to Union: 1896
Capital: Salt Lake City
Population: 1,722,850
Beehive State

Wyoming (44)
Admitted to Union: 1890
Capital: Cheyenne
Population: 453,588
Equality State

The American Flag

The American flag is a symbol of our country. It is recognized instantly, whether it is a big banner waving in the wind or a tiny emblem worn on a lapel. The flag is so important that it is a major theme of our national anthem, "The Star-Spangled Banner." One of the most popular names for our flag is the "Stars and Stripes." It is also known as "Old Glory."

The Meaning of the Flag

The American flag has 13 stripes—7 red and 6 white. In the upper-left corner of the flag is the union—50 white stars against a blue background.

The 13 stripes stand for the original 13 states, and the 50 stars represent the states of our nation today. According to the United States Department of State, the colors of the flag are symbolic, too:

Red stands for courage.
White symbolizes purity.
Blue is the color of vigilance, perseverance, and justice.

Early American Flags

Before the United States declared its independence in 1776, the colonies used many different flags. A favorite colonial design of the southern colonies was a flag with a rattlesnake and the motto, "Don't Tread on Me." Another colonial symbol was the pine tree, which symbolized the strength and courage of New England. The first flag to represent all the colonies was called the "Continental Colors." It has 13 alternating red and white stripes and the British flag at the upper left (showing that the colonies belonged to Great Britain).

Adopting the Stars and Stripes

After the Declaration of Independence was adopted, the Continental Congress no longer wanted the British flag to be part of the American flag. On June 14, 1777, the Congress decided that the flag of the United States should have 13 red and white stripes and 13 stars "representing a new constellation." According to legend, a Philadelphia seamstress named Betsy Ross helped design this flag and made the first one. The story is probably not true, although she did make other flags.

After Vermont and Kentucky joined the Union in the 1790's, two additional stars and stripes were added to the flag. As you can imagine, adding a stripe for every new state would have created problems. So in 1818 Congress ruled that the number of stripes should remain at 13, with a star added for each new state.

Displaying the Flag

Our flag should not be displayed in bad weather. It should be displayed outdoors only from sunrise to sunset, except on certain occasions. In a few special places, however, the flag is always allowed to be flown day and night. When flown at night, the flag must be spotlighted.

Near a speaker's platform, the flag should occupy the place of honor at the speaker's right. When carried in a parade with other flags, the American flag should be on the marching right or in front at the center. When flying with state flags, the national flag must be at the center and the highest point. In a group of national flags, all should be of equal size and all should be flown from staffs of equal height.

The flag should never touch the ground, the floor, or water. It should not be marked with any insignia, pictures, or words. Nor should it be used in any disrespectful way—as an advertising decoration, for instance. The flag should never be dipped to honor any person or thing.

Saluting the Flag

The United States, like other countries, has a flag code, or rules for displaying and honoring the flag. For example, all those present should stand at attention facing the flag and salute it when it is being raised or lowered or when it is carried past them in a parade. A man wearing a hat should take it off and hold it with his right hand over his heart. All women and hatless men should stand with their right hands over their hearts.

The flag over the Capitol

Special Occasions

When the flag is flown upside down, with the stars at the bottom, it is a signal of distress. Flown at half-mast, it is a symbol of mourning. It may be draped over the casket of a person who has served in the United States armed forces. After the funeral, this flag is folded and given to a family member.

One of the best-known occasions for displaying the American flag was the first landing of Americans on the moon in July 1969. The astronauts placed a metal flag there because the moon has no atmosphere, and thus no wind. As far as we know, our flag is still there.

The flag on the moon

The Pledge of Allegiance

The Pledge of Allegiance was written by a Massachusetts magazine editor named Francis Bellamy in 1892. (The words "under God" were added in 1954.) These are the words:

> I pledge allegiance to the Flag of the United States of America and to the Republic for which it stands, one Nation under God, indivisible, with liberty and justice for all.

Civilians should say the Pledge with their right hands on their hearts. People in the armed forces give the military salute. By saying the Pledge of Allegiance, we promise loyalty ("pledge allegiance") to our nation and its ideals.

"The Star-Spangled Banner"

"The Star-Spangled Banner" is the national anthem of the United States. It was written by Francis Scott Key during the War of 1812. While being held aboard a British ship on September 13, 1814, Key watched the bombardment of the American Fort McHenry at Baltimore. The attack lasted for 25 hours. The smoke was so thick that Key could not tell who had won. Then the air cleared, and Key saw the American flag still flying over the fort. To express his joy, he wrote most of the words of the song in a few minutes on the back of an envelope. "The Star-Spangled Banner" is sung to music written by John Stafford Smith. In 1931 the United States Congress adopted "The Star-Spangled Banner" as our national anthem.

The Star-Spangled Banner

I

Oh, say can you see by the dawn's early
light

What so proudly we hail'd at the twilight's
last gleaming?

Whose broad stripes and bright stars
through the perilous fight,

O'er the ramparts we watched were so
gallantly streaming?

And the rockets' red glare, the bombs
bursting in air,

Gave proof through the night that our flag
was still there.

Oh, say does that star-spangled banner yet
wave

O'er the land of the free and the home of
the brave?

II

On the shore, dimly seen through the
mists of the deep,

Where the foe's haughty host in dread
silence reposes,

What is that which the breeze, o'er the
towering steep,

As it fitfully blows, half conceals, half
discloses?

Now it catches the gleam of the morning's
first beam,

In full glory reflected now shines in the
stream:

'Tis the star-spangled banner! Oh, long
may it wave

O'er the land of the free and the home of
the brave!

III

And where is that band who so vauntingly
swore

That the havoc of war and the battle's
confusion,

A home and a country should leave us no
more!

Their blood has washed out their foul
footstep's pollution.

No refuge could save the hireling and
slave

From terror of flight, or the gloom of the
grave:

And the star-spangled banner in triumph
doth wave

O'er the land of the free and the home of
the brave!

IV

Oh! thus be it ever, when freemen shall
stand

Between their loved home and the war's
desolation!

Blest with victory and peace, may the
heaven rescued land

Praise the Power that hath made and
preserved us a nation.

Then conquer we must, when our cause it
is just,

And this be our motto: "In God is our
trust."

And the star-spangled banner in triumph
shall wave

O'er the land of the free and the home of
the brave!

American Holidays

Holidays are special occasions usually marked by celebrations and vacations from school and work. Religious holidays are celebrated by people of various faiths. For example, Christians celebrate Christmas (marking the birth of Jesus) and Jews celebrate Rosh Hashanah (marking the beginning of the Jewish New Year). On legal holidays, banks, schools, and most government and business offices are closed.

National holidays usually commemorate, or remind people of, a special event in a nation's past. Strictly speaking, the United States has no official national holidays. It is up to the states, not the federal government, to determine which days will be celebrated. But the federal government influences these by designating the days to be observed in Washington, D.C., and by all federal employees. Along with New Year's Day (January 1) and Christmas (December 25), the following eight legal holidays are observed throughout the United States.

Martin Luther King's Birthday
(third Monday in January)

An act of Congress established the newest federal holiday—the birthday of Dr. Martin Luther King, Jr. Dr. King began the civil rights movement in 1955, working to end discrimination against African Americans. Dr. King led many peaceful protest marches in cities across the nation. Largely because of Dr. King's efforts, Congress passed the Civil Rights Act of 1964.

Dr. King's brilliant career was cut short when he was assassinated on April 4, 1968. After Dr. King's death, many people called for a national holiday to recognize his many accomplishments. The holiday became official in 1986.

Washington's Birthday
(third Monday in February)

February 22 is the day we think of as George Washington's birthday. However, he was actually born on February 11 according to the calendar in use in 1732, the year of his birth. In the 1970's the celebration of his birthday was changed to the third Monday in February. Some states in the nation observe this day as President's Day.

Cherries and hatchets are traditionally associated with the celebration of Washington's birthday. This is because of a legend made popular by an early biographer of Washington. As a young boy, according to tradition, George cut down his father's cherry tree. When questioned, George confessed, saying, "Father, I cannot tell a lie."

Memorial Day
(last Monday in May)

Originally, Memorial Day honored the soldiers who died in the Civil War. Today, the holiday honors all those Americans who died in all the wars in which the United States has fought. Memorial Day, sometimes called Decoration Day, was first celebrated on May 30.

Some states celebrate the holiday on the traditional day.

Independence Day
(July 4)

Fireworks, parades, and picnics mark this holiday, regarded as the birthday of our country. It commemorates the day in 1776 when the Continental Congress adopted the Declaration of Independence. Even then, John Adams, one of the leaders in the struggle for American independence, said of the day: "I am apt to believe that it will be celebrated by succeeding generations as the great anniversary festival." Time has proved John Adams to be right.

Labor Day
(first Monday in September)

A union leader, Peter J. McGuire, first suggested a holiday to honor working people. Various states observed the day in the 1880's. It has been celebrated by the whole nation since 1894. Labor Day is marked with parades or speeches honoring workers. It also has come to mean the end of summer and often is celebrated with a last day at the beach, a cookout, or community festivities.

Columbus Day
(second Monday in October)

On October 12, 1492, Christopher Columbus first reached the Americas. Today, we honor Columbus's first voyage to the New World on the second Monday in October. Parades and special banquets mark this holiday. The first Columbus Day was celebrated in New York City in 1792—the 300th anniversary of the voyage. Columbus Day has been celebrated as a federal holiday since 1920. The 500th anniversary of Columbus's voyage is celebrated in 1992.

Veterans Day
(November 11)

This holiday is unusual because it is also a special day in many European nations. Formerly called Armistice Day, it originally marked the armistice, or truce, that ended World War I on November 11, 1918. In 1954 the United States changed the observance to honor all the men and women who have served in the armed forces. Military parades are common on Veterans Day. Special services are also held at the Tomb of the Unknown Soldier in Arlington National Cemetery, near the nation's capital.

Thanksgiving Day
(fourth Thursday in November)

For hundreds of years, people have held autumn festivals to give thanks for a good harvest. The American celebration of Thanksgiving began with the Pilgrims in Plymouth Colony. They observed the first Thanksgiving in 1621 to mark the end of their first difficult year in America and the gathering of the harvest. Their celebration lasted three days. During that time the Pilgrims and their Indian guests feasted on wild turkey and venison.

Thereafter, many communities observed a day of Thanksgiving at various times in the fall. Finally, in 1863, President Abraham Lincoln declared that the day should be celebrated nationally. Thanksgiving Day is, above all, a time for family togetherness, commitment, and celebration.

American Symbols

The Statue of Liberty

At the entrance to New York Harbor, on Liberty Island, stands one of the best-known symbols of the United States—the Statue of Liberty. The official name of this colossal figure is *Liberty Enlightening the World*. Slightly over 150 feet (45 meters) tall, it is the largest statue ever made.

The statue was a gift from the people of France to the United States. It was presented as a symbol of friendship and in honor of the 100th anniversary of American independence. It was designed by Frédéric Bartholdi and constructed by Alexandre Eiffel.

The Statue of Liberty was built in Paris, taken apart, and then shipped to the United States in 214 crates. It was placed on a pedestal built with money raised by the American people. President Grover Cleveland dedicated it in 1886.

The statue represents a woman dressed in long flowing robes and wearing a crown with seven spikes. At her feet are the broken chains of tyranny. Her right arm holds a torch high in the air. In her left hand is a law book with the date of the Declaration of Independence, July 4, 1776. An elevator in the pedestal brings visitors to the foot of the statue. From there they may climb a narrow, spiral staircase to the statue's crown, which provides a beautiful view of New York Harbor.

The Statue of Liberty has long been a symbol of freedom for millions of immigrants to the United States. "The New Colossus," a poem by Emma Lazarus to welcome immigrants, was inscribed on a tablet in the pedestal in 1903. It ends with these lines:

Give me your tired, your poor,
Your huddled masses yearning to breathe free,
The wretched refuse of your teeming shore.
Send these, the homeless, tempest-tost to me,
I lift my lamp beside the golden door!

Over the years, rust and corrosion from weather and pollution have damaged the Statue of Liberty. By the early 1980's, the statue was badly in need of repair. In 1982 President Ronald Reagan formed a special commission of private citizens to oversee the statue's restoration. The project was funded by more than $230 million in private donations. Special rededication ceremonies took place in 1986.

The Liberty Bell

The Liberty Bell has been a symbol of American freedom ever since it rang on July 8, 1776, to announce the adoption of the Declaration of Independence. This giant bronze bell was made in England in 1752 for the State House (now Independence Hall) in Philadelphia. The bell's inscription—"Proclaim Liberty throughout all the land unto all the inhabitants thereof"—is from the Bible.

The Liberty Bell cracked soon after its arrival in Philadelphia and had to be recast. It rang at every anniversary of the Declaration of Independence until 1835. In that year it cracked again while tolling after the death of John Marshall, Chief Justice of the Supreme

Court. Finally, while ringing in honor of George Washington's birthday in 1846, the bell was damaged so badly that it could not be tolled again.

The bell was on display in Independence Hall until 1976. Then, in celebration of the nation's 200th anniversary, the bell was moved to its own glass building. There it is viewed by thousands of visitors each year.

The Great Seal of the United States

For more than 1,000 years, officials have used seals, or engraved stamps, as guarantees that documents are authentic. At one time kings even wore signet, or seal, rings. The Great Seal of the United States was adopted by the new nation in 1782. Today it is kept in the Department of State and is used only on certain important kinds of documents, such as treaties. Only the face of the seal is used to seal official documents. However, both sides of the seal appear on the back of the $1 bill.

The Face

The face of the seal shows an American bald eagle with raised wings. On its breast is a shield with 13 alternate red and white stripes representing the original states. In the eagle's right claw is an olive branch with 13 leaves and 13 olives. In its left claw are 13 arrows. These symbols indicate our nation's wish to live in peace, but also its ability to wage war. In the eagle's beak is a ribbon with the words *E Pluribus Unum*. This Latin phrase means "from many [states], one [nation]." Above the eagle's head are 13 stars surrounded by rays of light breaking through a cloud.

The Reverse

The reverse side of the Great Seal shows a pyramid made up of 13 layers of stone, representing the new nation. The base of the pyramid has a date in Roman numerals—

MDCCLXXVI (1776)—the year of the signing of the Declaration of Independence. The pyramid is guarded by an eye surrounded by rays of light. Above are the Latin words *Annuit Coeptis*, meaning "He [God] has favored our undertaking." Below is the phrase *Novus Ordo Seclorum*, which means "a new order of the ages."

The Bald Eagle

The bald eagle, which appears on the Great Seal, is the official emblem of the United States. This bird is not actually bald, but sometimes appears to be so because its head and neck are pure white. The eagle has symbolized official power since the days of ancient Egypt.

The bald eagle was chosen as the national bird of the United States in 1872. The choice was not unanimous, though. Benjamin Franklin would have preferred a native bird, the turkey, but he was overruled.

The Great Seal

Uncle Sam

The figure of Uncle Sam is an American symbol as widely recognized as our flag. He has symbolized the United States since the War of 1812.

During that war, a storeyard in Troy, New York, stamped the initials "U.S." on barrels of salted meat for American soldiers. The "U.S." stood for United States. Workers, though, jokingly claimed that the initials really stood for "Uncle Sam" (Samuel) Wilson, who managed the storeyard. The idea of equating Uncle Sam with the United States spread rapidly. After all, Great Britain, our opponent in the War of 1812, already had a personal symbol of its own—the figure of an English farmer, John Bull.

Uncle Sam as we know him today was first drawn in the 1860's by the American cartoonist Thomas Nast. The symbol of Uncle Sam usually has long hair and a white beard. His pants have red and white stripes, his stovepipe hat is decorated with stars, and he wears a cutaway coat.

The Donkey and the Elephant

Two well-known symbols—the donkey and the elephant—represent our nation's major political parties. They were first drawn as symbols of the Democratic Party and the Republican Party by the American cartoonist Thomas Nast.

The donkey was used for the first time as a political symbol by Andrew Jackson after his opponents in the 1828 Presidential election called him a "jackass." Later, Nast used the donkey in his cartoons to stand for the Democratic Party. The donkey soon became recognized as the symbol of the Democratic Party.

The elephant as a symbol of the Republican Party first appeared in a cartoon by Nast in *Harper's Weekly* in 1874. He used the elephant first to represent the Republican vote and then drew it often as a Republican symbol. It soon came to stand for the Republican Party.

Glossary

This Glossary contains many of the terms you need to understand in your study of civics. After each term there is a brief definition. The numbers in parentheses refer to the page on which each term is introduced in the textbook.

The definitions in this Glossary do not always provide you with all the information you may need about many of these terms. In most cases, however, your textbook provides a more complete discussion. Therefore, you may find it useful to turn to the page listed in parentheses to read more about any of the terms. Remember, this Glossary is included to help you. Develop the habit of using it as you continue your study of civics.

A

absolute monarch: all-powerful king or queen. (21)

acid rain: acid formed when air pollution mixes with water vapor. (514)

acquired immune deficiency syndrome (AIDS): fatal disease caused by a virus that destroys the body's ability to fight off illness. (481)

act (see **law**).

addict: slave to a habit, such as the use of drugs. (479)

administrative law: law made by government agencies. (140)

administrative support worker: person who handles the paperwork in an office. (400)

administrator (see **manager**).

adopt: legally establish a child as one's own. (265)

advertising: use of the mass media by businesses to inform people about products and to persuade people to buy them. (341)

Agency for International Development: government agency that provides technical and financial assistance to developing nations. (428)

agency shop: business in which a worker cannot be forced to join the union but must pay union dues anyway. (385)

aggravated assault: physical injury done intentionally to another person. (487)

alcoholism: addiction to alcohol (liquor). (480)

alien: person who lives in a nation but is not a citizen of that nation. (9)

alliance treaty: written agreement in which nations promise to defend each other in case of attack. (423)

ambassador: highest-ranking official representing a government in a foreign country. (126)

amendment: written change in the Constitution. (50)

American government: authority Americans have set up to help them rule their own affairs. (21)

Anti-Federalist: opponent of the Constitution who urged its rejection in 1787. (31)

ANZUS: alliance of Australia, New Zealand, and the United States. (431)

apartheid: system in South Africa that calls for complete separation of the races. (458)

appeal: right of a convicted person to ask a higher court to review his or her case. (142)

appeals court: court that reviews the decisions of a trial court. (176)

appellate jurisdiction: authority of some courts to review cases already tried in lower courts. (143)

apportionment: distribution of seats in the House of Representatives. (96)

apprenticeship: fixed period of on-the-job training. (400)

appropriation bill (or **money bill**): bill approving the spending of public money; must be introduced in the House of Representatives. (108)

aptitude test: test that indicates interests and abilities. (417)

arbitration: method of settling differences between labor unions and employers in which a third party's decision must be accepted by both sides. (390)

Arms Control and Disarmament Agency: agency that seeks to control weapons-building race. (428)

arraignment: process whereby an accused person enters a plea of guilt or innocence. (493)

arrest warrant: authorization by a court for police to make an arrest. (492)

arson: destruction of property by setting fire to it. (488)

Articles of Confederation: our first written plan of government, in effect from 1781 to 1789. (25)

assembly line: system in which individual workers do specialized jobs in making a product that is passed along on a slowly moving belt. (333)

Atlantic Charter: agreement between the United States and Great Britain in 1941 setting forth principles for the nations of the world to follow. (434)

Attorney General: chief legal officer of the nation or a state. (126)

audit: careful examination by an accountant of government or business expenditures. (254)

automobile liability insurance: insurance that protects automobile owners in case their cars kill or injure people or damage property. (367)

B

bail: money or property given to a court as a guarantee that an accused person will be in court at the time of trial. (81)

balance: remainder owed on a bill. (346)

balanced budget: budget in which income equals expenses. (253)

balance of nature: relationship of all living things to one another. (506)

balance of power: situation in which two countries are about equal in power. (451)

balance of trade: difference in value between a nation's imports and exports. (433)

bank: business that deals in money and credit. (355)

barter: swap one product for another. (350)

beneficiary: person to whom insurance is paid upon the death of the insured. (366)

Better Business Bureau: organization that helps people who have been treated unfairly by a business. (344)

567

bicameral legislature: lawmaking body consisting of two houses. (28)

bill: proposed law being considered by a lawmaking body. (101)

bill of attainder: law sentencing a person to jail without a trial. (106)

Bill of Rights: first ten amendments to the Constitution, which set forth basic rights guaranteed to all Americans. (77)

birth rate: number of births per 1,000 persons during one year. (11)

blended family: remarriage in which one or both partners brings children from a previous marriage into the new marriage. (263)

block association: organization of residents who work together to improve their neighborhood. (239)

block grant: federal funds given to state and local governments for broad purposes. (197)

blood test: test to show that marriage license applicants are healthy. (264)

blue-collar worker: person who holds a job requiring manual labor. (400)

board of directors: people who direct a corporation. (318)

board of education: group responsible for managing public schools in a community. (187)

board of governors: board appointed by the President to make decisions for the Federal Reserve. (359)

bond: certificate of debt issued by governments or corporations to persons from whom they have borrowed money. (246)

bonded: insured against loss or theft of funds by an employee. (367)

booking: record of an arrest. (492)

borough: term used by Alaska for a county (182); unit of local government similar to a town. (185)

brand name: widely advertised name of a product usually distributed over a large area. (341)

brief: written statement explaining the main points of one side's argument in a court case. (151)

broker: brokerage house employee who buys and sells stock. (361)

brokerage house: organization that buys and sells stocks for customers. (361)

budget: plan of income and spending. (169)

building code: local laws that regulate the construction and repair of buildings in a community. (469)

bureaucracy: government agencies and departments at all levels of government. (135)

burglary: illegal entry into a home with the intent to steal. (487)

business cycle: tendency of an economy to go from boom to bust and back again. (379)

C

Cabinet: leaders of executive departments who also act as advisers to the Chief Executive. (52)

calendar: listing of the order in which Congressional bills are to be considered. (110)

candidate: person who runs for election to public office. (205)

capital: money invested in business; also, property and equipment used to produce goods or services. (310)

capitalism (or capitalistic system): economic system based on private ownership of the means of production. (310)

capitalist: person who owns any part of a business, or capital. (311)

capital punishment: putting a convicted criminal to death for a serious crime. (497)

carrying charge: fee added to installment charges for bookkeeping and other costs. (347)

caucus: meeting of party leaders to determine party policy on proposed laws or to choose the party's candidates for public office. (100)

censure: formal disapproval of the actions of a Congress member by the other members. (99)

census: official count taken every ten years of the number of people in the United States. (11)

Central Intelligence Agency (CIA): government agency that gathers and studies information about foreign nations. (425)

certificate of deposit (CD): investment in which an amount of money invested for a specified period of time period earns a guaranteed rate of return. (362)

chain store: one in a group of similar stores owned and operated by the same company. (340)

charge account: form of credit that allows a store's customers to buy goods now and pay later. (345)

charter: plan of government granted by a state legislature to a local government (181); document permitting a business to form a corporation. (318)

check: written and signed order to a bank to pay a sum of money to a person or business. (352)

checks and balances: way in which the powers of government are balanced among three branches so that each branch can check, or limit, the power of the other two branches. (44)

chief burgess: head of a village or borough government. (188)

Chief Executive: President of the United States. (120)

Chief of State: role of the President as the symbol of the United States and its people. (123)

child abuse: mental or physical mistreatment of a child. (265)

circuit: one of the 12 judicial districts covered by a court of appeals. (145)

citizen: member of a nation. (3)

city: largest type of municipality. (188)

city council: lawmaking body of a city. (189)

city manager: official hired to run a city under the city manager plan. (192)

civics: study of what it means to be an American citizen. (3)

civil case: case involving disputes over money or property between two or more individuals or businesses. (173)

civil disobedience: intentional breaking of a law to show dissent. (473)

civil rights: rights guaranteed to all Americans. (84)

civil rights movement: struggle for equal rights for all Americans. (472)

civil service examination: test given to applicants for government jobs. (403)

civil township: division of a county for purposes of local government. (186)

closed primary: primary election in which only voters who are members of the party may vote for the party's candidates. (216)

closed shop: business in which only union members can be hired. (385)

cloture: vote to limit debate on a bill in the Senate. (112)

coalition: agreement between two or more political parties to work together to run the government. (208)

Cold War: worldwide political struggle that developed between the United States and the Soviet Union and their allies after World War II. (449)

collateral: property used to guarantee a loan will be repaid. (355)

collective bargaining: process in which representatives of a labor union and an employer work to reach an agreement about wages and working conditions. (384)

college: four-year institute of higher learning. (278)

command economy: economic system in which the government completely controls the nation's economy. (315)

Commander in Chief: role of the President as head of the armed forces. (121)

commercial bank: large bank that offers full service. (356)

commercial treaty (or **trade treaty**): written agreement between two or more nations to trade on favorable terms. (423)

commission: local government body that has both legislative and executive powers. (191)

commission plan: system of local government in which voters elect commissioners who head city departments and make and carry out the laws. (191)

committee: small group formed to consider bills. (101)

Committee of the Whole: entire House or Senate acting as one committee to discuss a bill. (112)

committee on committees: group within the Senate or within the House that names party members to standing committees. (102)

common law: customary law that develops from judges' decisions and is followed in situations not covered by statutory law. (140)

common stock: shares in a corporation that do not earn a fixed dividend but give stockholders a voice in managing the company. (319)

communication: passing of ideas, information, and beliefs from one person to another. (297)

communism: economic system based on the theories of Marx and Engels in which the means of production are owned by the government and the government decides what will be produced and where people will work. (447)

community: group of people who have common interests, live in the same area, and are governed by the same laws. (293)

commutation: change of a convicted person's sentence to one that is less severe. (123)

competition (see **free competition**).

compromise: agreement in which each side gives up part of its demands. (29)

concealed propaganda: propaganda presented as fact and whose source is kept secret. (228)

concurrent power: power shared by the federal government and the states. (41)

concurring opinion: statement written by a Supreme Court Justice who agrees with the majority but for different reasons. (151)

conditioning: learning that is the result of a reward system or of experience involving the motor nerves. (286)

confederation: loose association of states. (25)

conference committee: temporary committee made up of senators and representatives who try to reach an agreement on different versions of a bill. (102)

conglomerate: large company that controls many different kinds of smaller companies. (314)

Congress: lawmaking body of the federal government. (95)

congressional district: division of a state from which one representative is chosen. (96)

congressional immunity: freedom of Congress member from arrest while attending Congress or on official business. (98)

congressional township: division of the Northwest Territory in 1785 for purposes of survey and settlement. (186)

conservation: safeguarding of natural resources through wise use. (518)

constable: peace officer who enforces township laws. (186)

constituent: person represented by members of a lawmaking body. (107)

constitution: written plan of government describing the government's organization, purpose, basic laws, and the rights of the people. (22)

constitutional: within the limits and safeguards of the Constitution. (38)

Constitutional Convention: meeting in Philadelphia in 1787 at which the Constitution of the United States was written. (27)

constitutional law: law based on the Constitution and Supreme Court decisions. (140)

Constitution of the United States: plan of government approved in 1789 to be the supreme law of the land. (27)

consul: official who works to promote American trade in a foreign country and who helps Americans who do business there. (126)

consulate: office of a consul. (126)

consumer: person who buys or uses products and services. (342)

containment: American policy of preventing the spread of communism. (449)

contour farming: method of preventing soil erosion by plowing along natural land outlines. (508)

contraction: period of the business cycle during which the economy is slowing. (379)

conveyor belt: moving belt that carries products from one part of a plant to another. (333)

cooperation: working together for common benefit. (300)

copyright: exclusive right, granted by law, to publish or sell a written,

musical, or art work for a certain number of years. (310)

corporate income tax: tax on the profits of a corporation. (248)

corporation: business chartered by a state government and given power to issue stocks, own property, make contracts, and sue and be sued in court. (316)

corrections: methods used to punish lawbreakers. (496)

costs of production: business costs, such as wages, payments for raw materials, rent, transportation, and interest on borrowed money. (379)

council-manager plan: system of local government in which voters elect a city council to make laws and the council hires a city manager as the chief executive. (191)

council member-at-large: member of a local council who is elected by the voters of the community. (189)

county: subdivision of state government formed to carry out state laws, collect taxes, and supervise elections. (182)

county auditor: official who examines county financial records. (184)

county board: board of elected officials who head a county government. (183)

county clerk: official who keeps county records. (183)

county manager: official hired by a county board or elected by the voters to supervise the work of the county government. (184)

county prosecuting attorney: official who represents a county government in court. (184)

county seat: town or city in which a county government is located. (183)

county-township government: mixed form of government in which county and township officials work together to govern local affairs. (186)

county treasurer: official who takes care of county funds. (183)

courier: special government messenger. (425)

court-martial: trial of a person in the armed services accused of breaking military law. (146)

court of appeals: federal or state court to which a convicted person may take his or her case for review. (145)

Court of Military Appeals: appeals court for the nation's armed services. (146)

cover crops: crops with root systems that hold the soil. (509)

craft union (or **trade union**): union of skilled workers having the same skill. (385)

craft worker: person who works in a trade or handicraft. (400)

creativity: ability to find new ways of thinking and doing things. (287)

credit: amount of money a person or business has in a checking account. (352)

credit card: card issued by banks and businesses, used in place of money. (353)

creditor: person who is owed money. (354)

credit rating: record of how well a person pays bills. (346)

credit union: bank established by people with common interests to create a pool of money for low-interest loans. (357)

crime: any act that breaks the law and for which a punishment has been established. (487)

crime syndicate: large organization of professional criminals. (489)

criminal case: court case in which a person is accused by the state of breaking a law. (172)

criminal justice system: system of police, courts, and corrections used to bring criminals to justice. (490)

critical thinking: kind of thinking one does to reach decisions and solve problems. (287)

crop rotation: method of preventing soil depletion by planting different crops each year. (509)

crossroads: location where two roads meet. (293)

currency: coins and paper money. (351)

D

death rate: number of deaths per 1,000 persons during one year. (11)

debt limit: limit on the amount of money a government may borrow. (254)

Declaration of Independence: key document of American freedom, adopted on July 4, 1776, declaring the 13 colonies to be free and independent of Great Britain. (24)

deduction: expense taxpayers are allowed to subtract in figuring their taxable income. (247)

defendant: person accused of a crime in a court case. (493)

defense: accused person's side in a court case. (493)

deficit: amount by which a government's expenditures exceed income. (253)

delayed marriage: tendency to get married at older ages. (263)

delegate: representative chosen to attend the Constitutional Convention. Also, representative who attends the convention of a political party. (27)

delegated power: power given to the federal government by the Constitution. (41)

delinquent: juvenile who breaks the law. (498)

demand deposit: money deposited in a checking account, payable to the depositor on request. (356)

democracy: form of government in which the people of a nation rule directly or through elected representatives. (21)

Democratic Party: one of the two major political parties in the United States. (207)

demonstration: gathering in which people express dissent by marching, carrying signs, and making speeches. (473)

department store: large store with many separate sections. (337)

depression: sharp decline in a nation's business activity, during which many workers lose their jobs and many businesses close down. (379)

dictatorship: form of government in which all power is in the hands of one person or a group of persons. (21)

diplomacy: art of dealing with foreign nations. (122)

diplomatic corps: ambassadors and other representatives serving in foreign countries. (425)

diplomatic notes: written communications between heads of governments. (123)

diplomatic recognition: power of the President to decide whether to deal formally with the government of a foreign nation. (424)

direct democracy: form of government in which all the people meet together to make laws and decide what actions to take. (21)

disability income insurance: insurance that covers total disability, partial disability, or both. (366)

discounting: deducting interest on a loan before money is given to a borrower. (357)

discount rate: interest charged by Federal Reserve Banks on loans to member banks. (359)

discrimination: unfair actions taken against people because they belong to a particular group. (471)

dissent: disagreement with a law. (473)

dissenting opinion: statement written by a Supreme Court Justice who disagrees with the majority decision. (152)

distribution: process of getting goods from manufacturers to the people who want them. (335)

district court: lower federal court that has original jurisdiction in most cases involving federal laws. (143)

dividend: profit paid to corporate stockholders. (317)

division of labor: system in which each worker does a portion of a total job. (332)

divorce: legal ending of a marriage. (268)

dollar diplomacy: practice of sending United States troops into Latin American countries to protect American investments. (445)

double jeopardy: being tried a second time for the same crime. (79)

down payment: initial cash paid on an item bought on the installment plan. (346)

draft: policy requiring men to serve in the military. (87)

drug abuse: use of drugs for escape or excitement. (479)

due process of law: right of all people to a fair trial. (80)

E

Earth Day: April 22, unofficial holiday dedicated to caring for the earth. (524)

ecology: study of the relationship of living things to each other and their environment. (505)

Economic and Social Council: UN division that studies economic and social issues. (436)

economist: specialist who studies economics. (330)

economy (or economic system): nation's system for distributing available resources to satisfy the wants and needs of its people. (309)

elastic clause: Article 1, Section 8, of the Constitution, or the "necessary and proper" clause; allows Congress to extend its powers. (104)

elector: person elected by the voters in a Presidential election as a member of the Electoral College. (222)

Electoral College: group of people who cast the official votes that elect the President and Vice President. (222)

electoral vote: vote cast by the Electoral College for President and Vice President. (222)

embassy: official residence of an ambassador in a foreign country. (126)

embezzlement: taking money that has been entrusted to one's care. (488)

eminent domain: power of the government to take private property for public use. (80)

energy resources: substances that furnish power. (517)

entrepreneur: business owner. (325)

environment: air, water, and soil that make up the world around us. (505)

Environmental Protection Agency (EPA): agency concerned with environmental issues. (523)

Equal Employment Opportunity Commission: commission appointed by the President to uphold fair employment standards. (409)

estate tax: tax on all the wealth left by a person who has died. (251)

ethnic group: group of people of the same race, nationality, or religion who share a common culture and heritage. (472)

excise tax: federal tax collected on certain luxury items produced and sold in the United States. (249)

executive: person who manages the affairs of a business. (318)

executive agreement: mutual agreement between the President of the United States and the leader of a foreign government. (424)

executive branch: branch of government that carries out the laws. (43)

executive departments: departments in the executive branch of the federal government, the heads of which form the President's Cabinet. (125)

Executive Office of the President: executive offices and agencies that advise the President. (124)

executive order: order issued by a governor that sets up methods of enforcing laws. (169)

exemption: certain amount of money a taxpayer can subtract from taxable income. (247)

expansion: period during which the economy is growing. (379)

experience: something that happened in the past from which we learn. (286)

export: good or service sold to other countries. (433)

ex post facto law: law that applies to an action that took place before the law was passed. (106)

expulsion: removal of a person from Congress for serious misconduct. (98)

extracurricular activities: school activities in which students take part in addition to classes. (285)

extradition: legal process for returning criminals to the state from which they fled. (164)

F

factors of production: four means of production—land, capital, labor, and management. (319)

family: group of people who are related by marriage, blood, or adoption and who live together and share economic resources. (260)

family law: legal regulation of marriage, divorce, and the duties of parents and children. (264)

farm worker: person who owns, manages, or works on a farm. (401)

favorite sons or daughters: men or women in a state party, usually governors or senators, who are nominated for President by that state's delegates on the first ballot at the national nominating convention. (220)

Federal Deposit Insurance Corporation (FDIC): federal agency that insures the deposits of members up to $100,000 per depositor. (356)

federal government: our nation's national government. (40)

Federalist: supporter of the Constitution who urged its adoption in 1787. (31)

Federal Reserve System: United States banking system that handles the banking needs of the federal government and regulates the money supply. (358)

Federal Savings and Loan Insurance Corporation (FSLIC): federal agency that insures the deposits of members up to $100,000 per depositor. (356)

federal system (or **federalism**): American system of government in which the powers of government are divided between the national government, which governs the whole nation, and the state governments, which govern the people of each state. (29)

fee: government charge for certain licenses. (245)

feeder line: side line that supplies the main assembly line with parts. (333)

felony: serious crime, such as burglary, kidnapping, or murder. (172)

fertilizer: plant food that makes crops grow bigger and faster. (509)

filibuster: method of delaying action in the Senate by making long speeches. (112)

fine: money paid as penalty for breaking certain laws. (245)

fire insurance: property insurance that provides payment in case of fire damage. (367)

fiscal policy: government program of taxation and spending. (381)

fixed expense: expense that occurs regularly and must be paid. (270)

floor leader: party leader who works for the passage of bills. (100)

forcible rape: sexual violation of a person by force and against the person's will. (487)

foreign aid: government program of economic and military assistance to other nations. (431)

foreign policy: nation's plan for dealing with the other nations of the world. (121)

foreign relations: way in which a nation's foreign policies are carried out. (423)

foster home: home of people who are unrelated to a child but who agree to act as the child's parents. (265)

franking privilege: right of a Congress member to mail official letters free of charge. (97)

fraud: taking someone else's money or property through deceit. (488)

free competition: system in which business owners compete among themselves for customers. (309)

freedom of assembly: right to hold public meetings. (78)

freedom of petition: right to ask the government to take or not take certain actions. (78)

freedom of the press: right to express ideas in writing. (78)

freedom of religion: right to practice any religion or no religion at all. (77)

freedom of speech: right to express ideas and opinions as well as listen to the ideas and opinions of others. (77)

free enterprise system: economic system in which people are free to run their businesses as they see fit. (312)

free market: exchange between buyers and sellers who are free to choose. (309)

free trade: trade not restricted by tariffs and other trade barriers. (433)

full faith and credit clause: provision in the Constitution ensuring that each state will accept the decisions of courts in other states. (164)

G

General Assembly: division of the UN in which every member nation has a vote. (435)

general election: election in which the voters elect our leaders. (215)

general trial court: court that handles major criminal and civil cases. (173)

gift tax: tax on items received as gifts that are worth more than a certain amount. (251)

glasnost: policy of Mikhail Gorbachev that urges freedom from many political and intellectual controls in the Soviet Union. (454)

Good Neighbor Policy: policy of President Roosevelt that opposed armed intervention by the United States in Latin American affairs and emphasized friendly agreements. (446)

government: authority that acts on behalf of a group of people. (3)

governor: chief executive of a state government. (169)

graduate school: institute of higher learning that offers advanced degrees. (278)

grand jury: group that hears the evidence in a criminal case and decides whether there is enough evidence to bring the accused person to trial. (141)

grand larceny: theft of goods worth over a certain amount. (487)

grants-in-aid: federal funds given to state and local governments for specific purposes. (197)

Great Compromise: agreement made at the Constitutional Convention that all the states should have equal representation in the Senate and be represented in the House of Representatives according to their population size. (29)

Great Depression: period of great economic hardship during the 1930s. (380)

gross income: total amount of money a company receives from sales. (326)

Gross National Product (GNP): dollar value of all goods and services produced in a nation each year. (330)

guardian: person appointed by a state court to look after individuals who are not yet adults or who are unable to care for themselves. (265)

H

habit: action performed automatically. (286)

health (or **wellness**): state of complete physical, mental, and social well-being and not merely the absence of disease or infirmity. (478)

health insurance: insurance that provides payments to policyholders when they cannot work due to illness not caused by an accident. (367)

hearing: special meeting called by congressional committee to consider a bill. (109)

home: place that members of a family share. (269)

homelessness: situation of being without a place to live. (467)

homeowners' insurance: property insurance that provides payments for damage to one's home. (367)

home rule: power of a city to write its own municipal charter and to manage its own affairs. (189)

hospitalization insurance: insurance that pays part of a policyholder's hospital bills. (367)

House of Representatives (or **House**): lower house of Congress in which states are represented according to population. (95)

human rights: basic rights to which all people are entitled. (25)

I

ideal: belief or standard of conduct that people attempt to live up to. (3)

immigrant: person who comes to a nation to settle as a permanent resident. (7)

impeachment: formal charge brought against a government official. The House has the power to impeach the President and other high officials; an impeached official is tried by the Senate. (105)

implied power: authority not specifically granted to Congress by the Constitution but which is suggested to be necessary to carry out the specific powers. (104)

import: good or service purchased from another country. (433)

impulse buyer: person who buys on the spur of the moment without careful thought. (342)

independent agency: agency in the executive branch of the federal government formed by Congress to help enforce laws and regulations not covered by the executive departments. (133)

independent voter: citizen who registers to vote without becoming a member of a political party. (215)

indictment: formal charge against an accused person. (79)

industrial union: union consisting of all types of workers in an industry. (380)

inflation: rise in the prices of most goods and services. (375)

inheritance tax: tax on money and property received from an estate. (251)

initiative: process by which citizens of a state may propose a law by collecting signatures on a petition. (168)

insight: process by which people unknowingly take what they know about a subject and apply it to something else in order to find an answer. (286)

installment: payment made on a balance owed. (346)

installment credit: credit given by a bank in the form of a loan that can be paid back in installments. (347)

installment plan: system of buying in which the buyer makes a cash down payment and then pays the balance over a period of time. (346)

insurance: system of protection in which people pay small sums periodically to avoid the risk of a large loss. (365)

insurance policy: contract setting forth the agreement between the insured and the insurance company. (365)

interest: payment made for the use of loaned money. (246)

interest group (or **lobby** or **pressure group**): organization of people with common interests who try to influence government policies and decisions. (231)

Internal Revenue Service (IRS): federal agency that collects income taxes. (252)

International Court of Justice (or **World Court**): UN court that settles disputes involving international law. (435)

interstate highway system: system of highways that connects all parts of the country. (196)

invest: put money into businesses or valuable articles in hopes of making a profit. (309)

isolationism: policy of avoiding all involvement in foreign affairs. (443)

item veto: power of a governor to reject one part of a bill and approve the rest of it. (168)

J

job action: any kind of slowdown or work action short of a strike. (384)

job application: printed form on which job applicants must supply important information. (414)

Joint Chiefs of Staff: group made up of the highest-ranking officers from the Army, Navy, and Air Force that advises the President on military affairs. (127)

joint committee: committee made up of members of both houses of Congress to deal with matters of mutual concern. (101)

joint session: combined meeting of both houses of Congress. (99)

judicial branch: branch of government that interprets the laws and punishes lawbreakers. (44)

judicial review: power of the Supreme Court to determine whether a Presidential action or a law violates any provision of the Constitution. (150)

junior college (or **community college**): two-year college. (277)

jurisdiction: authority to interpret and administer the law. Also, extent or range of that authority. (143)

jurisdictional strike: strike to determine which labor union will represent workers in a particular industry. (380)

juror: member of a trial jury who judges evidence and determines the verdict in a court case. (141)

jury duty: responsibility of citizens to serve on a jury when called. (141)

Justice: member of the Supreme Court. (147)

justice of the peace: judge who presides over a state justice court, trying misdemeanors and some civil cases. (173)

juvenile: in most states, people under 18. (497)

juvenile detention center: correctional facility where juvenile offenders are confined for short periods of time. (500)

K

keynote speaker: person who gives the opening speech at a national nominating convention. (219)

L

labor: human effort expended to produce goods and services. (325)

labor contract: written agreement between a labor union and an employer that spells out workers' wages and working conditions. (384)

laborer: person who does unskilled or heavy physical labor. (401)

labor union: organization of workers formed to bargain for higher wages and improved working conditions and to protect workers' rights. (383)

land: factor of production, includes location and natural resources. (324)

language skills: ability to use spoken and written language. (416)

larceny: theft of property without forcible or illegal entry. (487)

law: rule of conduct enforced by government. (22)

law of demand: economic rule that states that consumers will demand more products when they can buy them at lower prices and fewer products when they must pay more for them. (310)

law of supply: economic rule that states that businesses will produce more products when they can sell them at higher prices and fewer

products when they must sell them at lower prices. (310)

League of Nations: international organization formed after World War I to resolve disputes. (446)

legal separation: situation in which a married couple agrees to live apart but remains married. (265)

legal tender: paper money and coins that Americans accept as payment for goods and services. (352)

legislative branch: branch of government that makes the laws. (43)

legislature: lawmaking body of government. (29)

less developed countries (LDCs): countries in Latin America, Asia, and Africa that generally have agricultural economies, shortages of food, generally low incomes, and high birth rates. (454)

liability insurance: insurance that protects an individual in case he or she is sued for damages. (367)

libel: written falsehoods that damage another's reputation. (78)

lieutenant governor: official who succeeds the governor if the governor dies, resigns, or is removed from office. (171)

life insurance: insurance that pays a beneficiary a guaranteed sum when an insured person dies. (366)

limited government: idea that the federal government must not be allowed to become too powerful. (42)

limited war: war fought without using a nation's full military power, especially nuclear weapons. (451)

literacy test: reading and writing test used as a requirement for voting. (215)

lobbyist: person paid to represent an interest group's viewpoint at congressional committee hearings and who tries to influence the votes of Congress members. (110)

long-term credit: advance of credit to be repaid over long period of time in installments. (354)

lower court: local court that hears minor cases. (173)

M

machine tools: machinery built to turn out identical parts. (331)

magistrate: district court official who hears evidence in a case and decides if the case should be presented to a grand jury. (144)

Magna Carta: English document signed in 1215 guaranteeing the rights of English citizens, on which many of the ideals expressed in the American Constitution are based. (28)

mainstreaming: practice of putting students with special needs into regular schools and classes. (278)

majority party: political party that has more members in Congress or in a state legislature. (100)

majority rule: system in which the decision of more than half the people is accepted by all. (40)

malpractice insurance: liability insurance for doctors. (367)

management: all officers who together run a business. (318)

manager: person who runs a business and decides how it should operate. (325)

marketing: ways of getting people to buy goods and services. (335)

marshal: official in each federal district court who makes arrests, delivers subpoenas, and carries out the court's orders. (144)

Marshall Plan: massive program of United States aid to postwar Europe. (431)

mass marketing: process of selling goods in large quantities. (337)

mass media: sources of information by which large numbers of people are reached. (227)

mass production: producing huge amounts of goods rapidly by machine to supply the needs and wants of many people. (321)

mass transit: public transportation, including buses, subways, and railroads. (469)

Mayflower Compact: document written in the New World by the Pilgrims to form a new government based on cooperation and the consent of the people. (39)

mayor: chief executive of a city government. (189)

mayor-council plan: system of local government in which voters elect a city council to make laws and a mayor to carry out laws. (189)

mediation: method of settling disputes between labor unions and employers through the use of a third party who offers a nonbinding solution. (390)

Medicaid: federal program that provides money to help the states pay the medical costs of poor people. (370)

Medicare: federal program of health insurance for people aged 65 and over. (370)

megalopolis: continuous urban area that includes many cities and extends over a vast area. (296)

merger: combination of two or more companies into one big business. (313)

metropolis: large central city in a metropolitan area. (296)

metropolitan area: large city and its nearby suburbs. (15)

metropolitan transit authority: group that studies traffic problems in its area and works toward solutions. (470)

migration: movement of people to different parts of the nation. (15)

minister: official sent to small country to represent the United States government. (126)

minority group: group not in power and set apart from other people in the society because of race, nationality, language, customs, or religion. (471)

minority party: political party that has fewer members in Congress or in a state legislature. (100)

mint: place where official coins are made. (352)

misdemeanor: less serious crime, such as a traffic violation. (172)

mixed economy: economic system that combines elements of free and command economies. (315)

moderator: official who presides over the part of a town meeting in which town business is discussed. (186)

monetary policy: government program that regulates the amount of money in the economy. (382)

money: means of exchange, usually coins and paper currency. (351)

money market fund: investment plan similar to mutual fund. (362)

monopoly: situation in which one company controls the production of a product or service. (312)

Monroe Doctrine: 1823 policy by President Monroe declaring that European nations should not interfere in the affairs of the Western Hemisphere. (445)

motivation: something within people that stirs them and directs their behavior. (286)

motor skills: ability to do things with one's hands. (416)

motor vehicle theft: theft of an automobile. (487)

multi-party system: political system in which many political parties play a role in government. (208)

municipal court: court in a large city that handles minor civil and criminal cases. (173)

municipality: local governmental unit that is incorporated by the state and has a large degree of self-government. (181)

murder: willful killing. (487)

mutual fund: investment plan that reduces risk to shareholders by investing in many different stocks. (362)

mutual savings bank: bank originally established to encourage saving by people who could make only very small deposits. (356)

N

National Association for the Advancement of Colored People (NAACP): group formed in 1909 to work toward obtaining equal rights for African Americans. (472)

national bank: bank chartered under federal law. (356)

National Credit Union Administration (NCUA): federal agency that insures deposits of members up to $100,000 per depositor. (357)

National Labor Relations Board (NLRB): independent government agency that judges the fairness of union and employee activities toward each other. (389)

national nominating convention: meeting held by the major political parties every four years to draw up the party platform and to choose the party candidates for President and Vice President. (210)

National Road: first federally financed road, extending from Cumberland, Maryland, to Vandalia, Illinois. (193)

National Security Council: top advisers to the President on matters concerning defense and foreign policy. (428)

native-born citizen: American born as a citizen of the United States. (8)

naturalization: legal process by which aliens become citizens. (9)

net income: money a company has left over after its costs have been paid. (326)

neutrality: policy of not favoring one side or the other in a conflict. (446)

New Deal: programs established during the Great Depression by President Roosevelt to relieve hardship and improve the economy. (381)

no-fault divorce: divorce in which a couple must state that their marriage has problems that cannot be resolved. (268)

nominate: select candidates to run for public office. (205)

nonrenewable resources: natural resources that can be used only once. (517)

North Atlantic Treaty Organization (NATO): alliance of 16 nations pledged to defend one another against aggression in Europe and the Middle East. (430)

Northwest Ordinance: law passed in 1787 that set up a plan for governing territories and forming them into states. (163)

number skills: ability to work with numbers. (416)

O

Office of Management and Budget (OMB): government agency that helps prepare the federal budget. (253)

one-parent family: family containing only one parent. (263)

one-party system: political system in which government control is held by a single political party and in which all other parties are banned. (209)

one-price system: system of mass marketing in which the price is stamped on every item. (340)

open primary: primary election in which voters may vote for the candidates of any party. (216)

open shop: business that employs both union and nonunion workers. (385)

operator: worker who operates machinery and other equipment or who inspects, assembles, and packs goods in a factory or who drives a truck, bus, or automobile. (401)

opinion: Supreme Court's written explanation of why it came to a particular decision (151); what people believe to be true. (227)

ordinance: regulation that governs a local governmental unit. (182)

organic farming: farming without the use of artificial substances. (509)

Organization of American States (OAS): mutual defense alliance made up of the United States and most of the nations of Latin America. (431)

Organization of Petroleum- Exporting Countries (OPEC): organization of major oil-exporting nations that sets the price of oil. (434)

original jurisdiction: authority of some courts to hold trials first in certain kinds of cases. (143)

own recognizance: legal responsibility for one's own behavior. (492)

P

pardon: official act by the President or by a governor forgiving a person convicted of a crime. (123)

parish: term used by Louisiana for a county. (182)

Parliament: lawmaking body of Great Britain. (28)

parole: early release from prison on certain conditions. (496)

partnership: business organization in which two or more persons share responsibilities, profits, and losses. (316)

party platform: written statement outlining a political party's views on issues and describing the program it proposes. (219)

party whip: assistant to the floor leader in each house of Congress who tries to persuade party members to vote for bills the party supports. (100)

passport: document issued by the State Department that permits Americans to travel abroad. (126)

patent: right given to one person to make and sell an invention for a certain number of years. (310)

Peace Corps: volunteer program founded in 1961 that sends Americans to foreign nations to help people learn needed skills. (431)

peace treaty: written agreement to end a war. (423)

peak: high point of the business cycle. (379)

perceptual skills: ability to picture things in one's mind. (416)

perestroika: policy of Mikhail Gorbachev aimed at improving the economy of the Soviet Union. (454)

personal diplomacy: process by which the President meets with foreign leaders and ambassadors. (430)

personal income tax: tax on the income a person earns. (247)

personal property: possessions such as money, stocks, and cars. (250)

personal values: attitudes and principles people believe to be most important in their lives. (395)

personnel worker: person who hires or recommends workers for a business. (414)

pesticide: chemical that kills insects and weeds. (509)

petty larceny: theft of goods worth under a certain amount. (487)

picketing: marching by workers in front of their workplace, often with signs urging others not to work or to buy the company's products. (384)

plank: each part of a political party's platform. (219)

plea bargaining: agreement between the prosecutor and defense in which the accused person pleads guilty to a reduced charge. (493)

pocket veto: one way the President can reject a bill passed by Congress. Any bill presented to the President within ten days before the end of the session is "pocket vetoed" if not signed before Congress adjourns. (113)

political action committee (PAC): political arm of an interest group that collects voluntary contributions from members and contributes it to political candidates and parties it favors. (238)

political party: organization of citizens who have similar views on issues and who work for the election of party members to office and for the passage of bills. (205)

polling place: place where citizens go to vote. (210)

poll tax: special tax that had to be paid in order to vote. (86)

pollution: contaminants of the earth, air, or water. (510)

poll watcher: party representative present at a polling place to see that an election is conducted fairly. (217)

popular sovereignty: government by consent of the governed. (39)

popular vote: total votes cast by individual voters in a Presidential election. (222)

Preamble: beginning of the Constitution, which describes its purposes. (39)

precedent: earlier court decision that guides later cases. (140)

precinct: local voting district in a county, city, or ward. (210)

precinct captain: political party leader in a local voting district. (210)

preferred stock: corporation stock on which fixed dividends are paid but which gives no vote in corporate affairs. (318)

prejudice: opinion not based on careful and reasonable review of the facts. (289)

preliminary hearing: procedure during which a judge decides if there is enough evidence to send a case to trial. (492)

premium: payment made for insurance protection. (365)

President: Chief Executive, or head, of the executive branch of the federal government. (117)

Presidential preference primary: primary election in which voters in a state select the Presidential candidate they wish their delegates to support at the party's national nominating convention. (219)

Presidential succession: order in which the office of President is to be filled if it becomes vacant. (119)

president *pro tempore*: official who presides over the Senate in the Vice President's absence. (100)

press secretary: Presidential assistant who represents the President to the news media and the public. (125)

primary election: election in which the voters of various parties choose candidates to run for office in a general election. (215)

principal sum: total amount for which a person is insured. (365)

priorities: order of importance of national needs. (243)

private insurance: insurance individuals and companies choose to pay to cover unexpected losses. (365)

probable cause: reason for an arrest, based on the knowledge of a crime and the available evidence. (492)

probation: sentence in which a person convicted of a crime does not go to prison but must follow certain rules and report to a probation officer. (500)

productivity: amount a worker produces in an hour. (325)

profession: job that involves mostly mental work and requires many years of education and training. (399)

profit: income a business has left after expenses. (249)

profit motive: hope of making money from business or investment. (309)

progressive tax: tax that takes a larger percentage of income from high-income groups than from low-income groups. (247)

proletariat: term used in communist theory for workers. (447)

propaganda: ideas used to influence people's thinking or behavior. (228)

property tax: local or state tax collected on real property or personal property. (250)

prosecution: government's side in a criminal case. (493)

protective tariff: tax on imported goods intended to protect American industries against foreign competition. (251)

Public Health Service: agency that conducts medical research and protects the health of Americans. (478)

public housing project: apartment houses for low-income families that are built with public funds and that charge low rents. (467)

public interest group: group seeking to promote the interests of the general public rather than just one part of it. (232)

public opinion: sum total of the opinions held concerning a particular issue. (227)

public opinion poll: survey taken to measure public opinion. (230)

public utility: legal monopoly that provides a public service. (314)

Q

quorum: minimum number of members who must be present before a legislative body can do business. (112)

quota: limit on the number of immigrants who may come to the United States each year. (7)

R

ratification: approval, such as of the Constitution in 1787 or of a constitutional amendment. (30)

real property: property that consists of land and buildings. (250)

recall: process by which voters may remove an elected official from office. (168)

recession: severe contraction in the business cycle. (379)

reciprocal trade agreement: agreement between nations to establish mutual tariff reductions on certain goods. (433)

recreation: relaxation or amusement. (298)

recycling: turning waste into something that can be used. (515)

referendum: method of referring bills to the voters for approval before they can become law. (168)

refugee: person who flees his or her homeland to seek refuge in another nation. (8)

register: sign up for military service (87); have one's name placed on the roll of registered voters. (215)

regressive tax: tax that takes a larger percentage of income from low-income groups than from high-income groups. (249)

regulatory agency: independent agency created by Congress that can make rules concerning certain activities and bring violators into court. (133)

remarriage: marriage in which one or both of the partners has been married before. (263)

renewable resource: any natural wealth that can be replaced. (511)

rent: payment for use of property. (224)

repeal: cancel or revoke. (51)

repossess: take back. (346)

representative: member of the House of Representatives. (95)

representative democracy (or **republic**): system of government in which the people elect representatives to carry on the work of government for them. (21)

representative town meeting: town meeting in which the people elect representatives to make decisions for them. (186)

reprieve: postponement in the carrying out of a prison sentence. (123)

republic: system of government in which the people elect represen-

tatives to carry on the work of government for them. (21)

Republican Party: one of the two major political parties in the United States. (207)

reserved power: power set aside by the Constitution for the states or for the people. (41)

retailer: business person who sells directly to the public. (341)

retail store: store that sells directly to the public. (341)

revealed propaganda: propaganda that openly attempts to influence people. (228)

revenue: income collected by the government to pay its costs. (244)

right to bear arms: right of Americans to own firearms. (79)

right to own private property: guarantee that private property will not be taken for public use without fair payment by the government. (80)

right-to-work law: law in certain states that forbid closed shops and make union membership voluntary. (385)

robbery: theft accompanied by the threat of force. (487)

roll-call vote: vote in Congress in which a record is made of how each member votes. (112)

Roosevelt Corollary: President Roosevelt's 1904 policy statement that the United States would help restore order if Latin American countries could not manage their own affairs. (445)

runoff election: election in which voters choose between the two leading candidates in a primary to determine the party's candidate in the general election. (216)

rural area: region of farms and small towns. (14)

Rush-Bagot Agreement: 1817 treaty by which the United States and Canada agreed to settle their disputes peacefully and that their shared border need no longer be fortified. (444)

S

salary: fixed income paid twice a month or monthly. (325)

salary range: lowest to highest earnings for a particular job. (412)

sales tax: state or city tax on items or services sold to the public. (249)

sales worker: person who sells goods or services. (400)

sanitary landfill: huge pit dug in the ground to store garbage. (516)

satellite nations: communist nations of Eastern Europe controlled by the Soviet Union. (449)

saving: putting money aside for future use. (360)

savings and loan association: type of bank originally established to help people buy homes. (356)

savings bond: certificate stating that the government has borrowed a sum of money and will pay interest to the bond's owner. (254)

scarcity: problem of limited resources. (310)

school district: special district set up to provide local schools. (187)

school tax: tax on property to support local public schools. (250)

search warrant: legal paper granted by a judge permitting police to enter and search a place where there is reason to believe evidence of a crime will be found. (79)

Secretariat: division of the UN that handles day-to-day activities. (436)

Secretary: official who heads an executive department in the federal government. (126)

Secretary General: chief executive of the United Nations. (437)

secret ballot: method of voting in which the voter casts a ballot in secret. (217)

Securities and Exchange Commission (SEC): federal agency that regulates the nation's stock exchanges and curbs dishonest practices. (364)

Security Council: UN body, composed of five permanent and ten temporary members, that deals with major issues affecting world peace. (435)

segregation law: law that forced African Americans to go to separate schools and to use separate public facilities. (152)

select committee: temporary House or Senate committee appointed to deal with an issue not handled by a standing committee. (101)

selectmen: men and women who manage a town's affairs between regular town meetings. (185)

self-incrimination: testifying against oneself. (79)

self-service: modern method of marketing in which customers select their own goods and bring them to cash registers. (337)

Senate: upper house of Congress in which each state is represented by two senators. (96)

senator: member of the Senate. (96)

seniority system: custom of giving leadership of committees to members of Congress who have served the longest. (102)

senior senator: senator from each state who has served the longest. (97)

sentence: punishment given to a person convicted of a crime. (493)

separation of church and state: division between religion and government, as specified by the Constitution. (77)

separation of powers: three-way division of power among the branches of the federal government. (43)

service industry: business that sells services rather than products. (401)

service worker: person who provides the public with some needed service. (401)

session: regular meeting of Congress. (99)

sheriff: chief law-enforcement official in some county governments. (183)

shopping mall (or **shopping center**): large cluster of stores surrounded by a parking area. (340)

short-term credit: advances of money to be repaid within a short period of time. (354)

shuttle diplomacy: peace-seeking method characterized by a diplomat flying back and forth between nations. (430)

single proprietorship: business owned by one person. (316)

slander: spoken falsehoods that damage another's reputation. (430)

slum: run-down section of a city where buildings are neglected and families live crowded together. (467)

small claims court: state court that hears civil cases involving small amounts of money. (176)

smog: combination of smoke, gases, and fog contained in air. (511)

smoke detector: device that sounds an alarm the moment it detects smoke. (482)

social insurance: insurance required under state and federal laws. (365)

socialization: process through which children are taught the basic skills, values, beliefs, and behavior patterns of society. (260)

Social Security: system of government insurance that provides benefits for retired people, disabled people, widows and widowers, and dependent children. (368)

Social Security tax: kind of income tax that is used mainly to pay income to retired people. (248)

soil bank: federal program started in the 1930's that paid farmers to enrich their land by growing trees or grass instead of farming some of their land. (508)

solar energy: energy from the sun. (520)

Speaker: presiding officer of the House of Representatives. (100)

special district: unit of local government set up to provide a specific service. (187)

special session: meeting of Congress called by the President. (99)

specialty shop: store that sells only certain kinds of goods or services. (340)

split ticket: ballot on which a person has voted for the candidates of more than one political party. (217)

standard of living: well-being of a nation's population, based on the amount of goods and services they can afford. (308)

standard packaging: practice of wrapping goods before they reach customers. (337)

standard parts: identical parts of a manufactured product that are mass produced and interchangeable. (321)

standing committee: permanent House or Senate committee that considers bills in a certain area. (101)

state auditor (or **comptroller**): official who ensures that no public funds are paid out of the state treasury without legal authorization. (171)

state bank: bank chartered under state laws. (356)

state legislature: general term for a state lawmaking body. (165)

statement: monthly report showing the amount of credit remaining in a bank account. (353)

State of the Union Address: yearly report of the President to Congress, as required by the Constitution, in which the nation's condition is described and programs and policies are recommended. (120)

state supreme court: highest court in a state. (176)

state treasurer: official responsible for handling all state funds, including the collection of taxes and payment of bills. (171)

statutory law: law passed by Congress and by lawmaking bodies of state or local governments. (139)

stock: share of ownership in a corporation. (311)

stock exchange: market where stocks are bought and sold. (361)

stockholder: person who owns stock in a corporation. (317)

straight ticket: ballot on which a person votes for all the candidates of one political party. (217)

strike: situation in which workers walk off the job and refuse to work

until disputed labor issues are settled. (384)

strip mining: stripping away the top layer of soil and removing the minerals underneath. (519)

strong-mayor plan: form of city government in which the mayor has strong executive powers not limited by the city council. (189)

study helps: parts of a textbook that help students learn it. (284)

subcommittee: division of a standing congressional committee that deals with specific issues in the area handled by the committee as a whole. (101)

subpoena: official court document ordering a person to appear in court. (144)

suburb: residential community near a large city. (14)

suffrage: right to vote. (85)

summit: meeting between the United States President and the heads of other nations. (430)

Sunbelt: region made up of states in the South and West. (15)

superintendent of public instruction: official responsible for carrying out the policies established by the State Board of Education. (171)

superintendent of schools: official appointed by a local board of education to manage the schools. (187)

supermarket: large store that sells food and other products. (337)

Supreme Court: highest court in the nation. Also, name given to the highest court in many states. (145)

surplus: amount by which income exceeds expenditures. (253)

T

tariff (or **customs duty**): tax on products imported from other countries. (251)

tax: payment of money citizens and businesses must make to help pay the costs of government. (244)

taxable income: amount of income, less deductions, on which individuals and businesses must pay taxes. (247)

tax collector: official who collects county taxes. (184)

technician: skilled worker who handles complex instruments or machinery. (299)

tenants' group: residents of an apartment house who work together to improve conditions in the building. (239)

term insurance: life insurance that covered a specified period of time. (366)

territorial court: federal court that administers justice to people in United States territories. (146)

territory: area that is eligible to become a state. (163)

third party: political organization in the United States other than the major parties. (208)

time deposit: money deposited in a savings account. (356)

toll: fee charged for use of a road or highway. (193)

totalitarian government: government that has total control over the lives of the people. (21)

town: unit of local government, usually larger than a village and smaller than a city. (184)

town meeting: form of government in which all citizens meet together to discuss the town's issues. (185)

township: local government unit that maintains local roads and rural schools within counties. (186)

township board of commissioners: elected officials who make laws for a township. (186)

township supervisor: elected head of a township. (186)

training school: correctional facility where juvenile offenders stay for a period of six to nine months. (500)

transportation: method of moving goods from manufacturers to the people who want them. (335)

transportation center: city that developed because of its accessibility by some means of transportation. (293)

treasurer: government official who sees that all federal tax money is kept safe and is paid out only as authorized. (252)

treaty: written agreement between nations. (121)

trial jury (or **petit jury**): people who hear evidence and decide the verdict in a court case. (141)

trough: low point of the business cycle. (379)

Truman Doctrine: United States policy of helping free nations resist communist aggression. (449)

trust: form of business organization in which several companies place their stock in the hands of trustees and no longer compete. (313)

Trusteeship Council: division of the UN that supervises former colonies and helps them prepare for self-government. (436)

two-earner family: family in which both parents work. (263)

two-party system: political system in which two major political parties have almost equal strength. (208)

U

unconstitutional: going against the Constitution, or beyond the powers granted by it. (150)

unicameral legislature: lawmaking body consisting of one house. (165)

union (see **labor union**).

union shop: business in which a non-union worker may be hired but must join the union within a certain period of time. (385)

United Nations (UN): organization formed to promote peace and cooperation among nations. (434)

United States attorney: district court official who is a lawyer for the federal government. (145)

United States Claims Court: federal court that hears cases involving money claims against the United States. (146)

United States Conference of Mayors: regular meeting of mayors to discuss city problems and their solutions. (197)

United States Court of International Trade: federal court that hears cases involving import taxes. (146)

United States Immigration and Naturalization Service: agency that oversees immigration and naturalization. (9)

United States Information Agency (USIA): government agency that informs the world about the American way of life. (428)

United States Tax Court: agency that hears appeals concerning payment of federal taxes. (146)

unit pricing: system of pricing that shows how much a product costs per ounce, gram, or other unit of measure. (343)

university: institution of higher learning that includes one or more colleges. (278)

unwritten Constitution: traditional ways of doing things in our government that are seldom written down or made into laws. (52)

urban area: city or large town. (14)

urban renewal program: program to redevelop a slum area. (467)

V

vandalism: willful destruction of property. (488)

verdict: decision of a jury. (141)

veto: refusal of the President or a governor to sign a bill. (45)

Vice President: second-highest official of the United States government. (118)

victimless crime: crime in which there is no victim whose rights have been invaded. (488)

visa: document that allows people from one nation to visit another nation. (126)

volunteer: person who works without pay to help others. (238)

voting machine: machine by which voters record their votes. (217)

W

wage: money earned by a worker each hour and usually paid weekly. (325)

wage-price freeze: policy to control inflation by prohibiting increases in most wages and prices. (382)

waiting period: time between application for a marriage license and granting of the license. (264)

ward: election district within a city or county. (189)

War Powers Act: law that requires troops sent abroad by the President to be recalled within 60 days unless Congress approves the action. (121)

warrant: order to pay out government funds (171); announcement of a town meeting. (185)

weak-mayor plan: form of city government in which most of the power is held by the city council and not by the mayor. (189)

white-collar crime: crime committed by a white-collar worker. (488)

white-collar worker: person in a profession or who does technical, managerial, sales, or administrative support work. (398)

whole life insurance: life insurance that covers the insured person's entire life. (366)

wholesaler: business person who buys from manufacturers and sells to retailers. (341)

write-in vote: vote cast for a candidate whose name must be written in by the voter. (216)

writ of *habeas corpus*: court order requiring that an accused person be brought to court to determine if there is enough evidence to hold the person for trial. (106)

Z

zoning law: local government regulation on the kinds of buildings that may be constructed in a certain area. (468)

Index

Italicized page numbers preceded by *c, d, m,* or *p* refer to a chart *(c)*, document *(d)*, map *(m)*, or picture *(p)* on the page. **Boldface** page numbers refer to definitions of important items. For a list of Civics Skills features, see page xi. For a list of charts and maps, see pages xii-xiii. See page xiv for a list of Citizenship in Action features. Focus on Freedom features are listed on page xiv.

INDEX

Acknowledgments

COVER: Bob Gelberg/Sharp Shooters.

TITLE PAGE: Scott Slobodian/Tony Stone Worldwide.

FRONT MATTER: page xv(tl), Emmet Collection 9398, Rare Books and Manuscript Division, The New York Public Library, Astor, Lenox and Tilden Foundations; xv(tr), The Granger Collection, NYC; xv(b), The Virginia Museum of Fine Arts, Richmond, Gift of Colonel and Mrs. Edgar W. Garbisch; xvi(bl), The Granger Collection, NYC; xvi(t), U.S. Department of Justice; xvi(br), The Bettmann Archive; xvii(tl, bl, br), The Granger Collection, NYC; xvii(tr), The Bettmann Archive; xviii(t), Frank Siteman/Taurus; xviii(bl), David M. Campione/Taurus; xviii(br), J. R. Laffont/Sygma; xix(t), Dirck Halstead/Gamma-Liaison; xix(c), Michael Lyon/TexaStock; xix(bl), L. L. T. Rhodes/Taurus; xix(bc), Geoffrey Hiller/Black Star; xix(br), Paul Fusco/Magnum; xx(t), J. Alex Langley/DPI; xx(bl, bc, br), The Granger Collection, NYC; xxi(t), The Corcoran Gallery of Art; xxi(c), Cynthia Johnson/Gamma-Liaison; xxi(b), Paul Conklin; xxii(bl, blc), The Granger Collection, NYC; xxii(brc, br), The Bettmann Archive; xxii(t), U.S. Senate, Legislative Records Branch; xxiii(tl), Paul Conklin; xxiii(tr), Dennis Brack/Black Star; xxiii(bl, brc), The Bettmann Archive; xxiii(blc), The Granger Collection, NYC; xxiii(br), Diana Walker/Gamma-Liaison; xxiv(t), The Bettmann Archive; xxiv(b), Dennis Brack/Black Star; xxv(tl), The Bettmann Archive; xxv(tc), U.S. Supreme Court; xxv(tr), Fourth Estate Press/Black Star; xxv(b), Gamma-Liaison; xxvi(t), Fred Ward/Black Star; xxvi(b), Hugh Talman/The National Archives; xxvii(t), The National Archives; xxvii(b), Dennis Brack/Black Star; xxviii(t), xxviii(b), The Granger Collection, NYC; xxix(t), Courtesy of A. E. Lear, Inc.; xxix(b), Courtesy of the Commission on the Bicentennial of the United States Constitution; xxx(t), Bob Llewellyn/Four By Five/SuperStock; xxx(bl), HBJ Photo by Leif Skoogfors/Woodfin Camp; xxx(bc), Philadelphia Orchestra; xxx(br), Paul Conklin.

UNIT ONE: page 1, Jonathan Wallen, courtesy of Harry N. Abrams, Inc.; 2, Dennis Hallinan/FPG International; 4, Jeffry W. Myers/Uniphoto Picture Agency; 5, Mike L. Wannemacher/Taurus; 6, Ronnie Kaufman/The Stock Market; 8(tl, tr, bc, br), HBJ Photos; 8(bl), HRW Photo by Stephen McCarroll; 9, Blair Seitz/Photo Researchers; 12(t), Jeffrey Jay Foxx/Woodfin Camp; 12(b), Southern Living/Photo Researchers; 13, The Bettmann Archive; 15, Matt Bradley/Tom Stack & Associates; 16, David R. Frazier; 20, The Granger Collection, NYC; 23(l), Patti McConville/The Image Bank; 23(r), Tom Myers/Photo Researchers; 24, The Bettmann Archive; 26, William S. Nawrocki; 29(l), The Bettmann Archive; 29(r), The Granger Collection, NYC; 31, 33, The Bettmann Archive; 38, David J. Carol/The Image Bank; 41, Dick Hanley/Photo Researchers; 46, 47, 48(t), 48(bl), 48(br), UPI/Bettmann Newsphotos; 49, Dennis Brack/Black Star; 51, Brown Brothers; 76, Paul Conklin; 78, Dick Hanley/Photo Researchers; 79, Hanson Carroll/Peter Arnold; 82, Paul Conklin; 83, Brad Markel/Gamma-Liaison; 84, The Bettmann Archive; 86, Charles Gupton/The Southern Light Agency; 87, HBJ Photo.

UNIT TWO: page 93, Marc Romanelli/The Image Bank; 94, G. Ahrens/SuperStock; 100, Dennis Brack/Black Star; 101, Paul Conklin; 106, Paul Conklin; 110, Hugo Wessels/Photopress; 116, B. Kulik/Photri; 118, UPI/Bettmann Newsphotos; 119, AP/Wide World Photos; 121, Wally McNamee/Woodfin Camp; 123, UPI/Bettmann Newsphotos; 126(l), The Granger Collection, NYC; 126(r), AP/Wide World Photos; 127, Paul Conklin; 128, The Bettmann Archive; 129(l), Sullivan/TexaStock; 129(b), Kennedy/TexaStock; 133, Luc Novovitch/Gamma-Liaison; 138, David M. Doody/FPG International; 141, John Neubauer; 145, Dawson Jones/Tony Stone Worldwide; 146, Chris Sorensen; 148, UPI/Bettmann Newsphotos; 150, The Bettmann Archive; 151, Gamma-Liaison; 153(l), The Bettmann Archive; 153(r), Bruce Roberts.

UNIT THREE: page 159, Mark E. Gibson; 160, Pro Pix/Monkmeyer Press; 163, Richard Wood/Taurus; 168, Paul Conklin/Uniphoto Picture Agency; 173, James L. Shaffer/PhotoEdit; 174, Paul Conklin; 175, Teri Gilman/Tony Stone Worldwide; 180, Sepp Seitz/Woodfin Camp; 185, Dick Hanley/Photo Researchers; 187, Ann Hagen Griffiths/Omni-Photo Communications; 191, Oscar Palmquist/Lightwave; 194, Porterfield-Chickering/Photo Researchers; 195, courtesy of Mark Woolley; 196, Marvin Ickow/Uniphoto Picture Agency; 197, John Running/Stock, Boston; 198, Wil Blanche/DPI.

UNIT FOUR: page 203, Dany Krist/Uniphoto Picture Agency; 204, Smithsonian Institution; 207(l), The Bettmann Archive; 207(r), 208, The Granger Collection, NYC; 212, Tom Myers; 213(t), Paul Conklin/Monkmeyer; 213(b), Robert Brenner/PhotoEdit; 214, Ken Hawkins/Sygma; 216, Wil Blanche/DPI; 218, Charles Gupton/The Stock Market; 220(l), A. Tannenbaum/Sygma; 220(r), Cynthia Johnson/Gamma-Liaison; 221, Cindy Charles/Gamma-Liaison; 226, Rogers/Monkmeyer; 232, Ken Hawkins/Sygma; 233, P. F. Gero/Sygma; 234, Joseph A. DiChello, Jr.; 235, Larry Lawfer/The Picture Cube; 238, Mary Kate Denny/PhotoEdit; 242, Richard Laird/FPG International; 244, Dirck Halstead/Time Magazine; 246, George Ancona, Inc./International Stock Photography, Ltd.; 248, Felicia Martinez/PhotoEdit; 253, HBJ Photo.

UNIT FIVE: page 259, Alan Carey/The Image Works; 260, M. Roessler/H. Armstrong Roberts; 262, The Bettmann Archive; 265, Len Berger/Berg & Associates; 266, The Granger Collection, NYC; 269, Freeman-Grishaber/PhotoEdit; 270, George Roos/Peter Arnold; 274, Richard Hutchings/Photo Researchers; 276, St. Louis Art Museum; 281, Flip Chalfant/The Image Bank; 282, Sybil Shackman/Monkmeyer; 283(t), VIPS-Seniors, Houston Independent School District; 283(b), Paul Conklin/Monkmeyer; 284, Hugh Rogers/Monkmeyer; 287, Robert Frerck/Odyssey Productions; 288, Arthur Sirdofsky; 292, Ed Bock/The Stock Market; 294, Peter Miller/Photo Researchers; 295, Frank Siteman/Stock, Boston; 296, Richard Choy/Peter Arnold; 298, 301, Peter Vadnai/Art Resource; 302, Todd Powell/ProFiles West.

UNIT SIX: page 307, Leo de Wys, Inc./Fridmar Damm; 308, Clyde H. Smith/FPG International; 312(l), Steven Dunwell/The Image Bank; 312(r), Cameramann International; 314, Herbert Lanks/Monkmeyer; 316, Ellis Herwig/Stock, Boston; 318, Randy Duchaine/The Stock Market; 320, 321, 323, courtesy Junior Achievement; 325, Guy Gillette/Photo Researchers; 330, Blair Seitz/Seitz and Seitz; 334, Dick Durrance II/Woodfin Camp; 336, HBJ Photo; 337, FPG International; 338(t, b), The Foxfire Fund, Inc.; 339(t), Lowell Georgia/Photo Researchers; 339(b), Michal Heron/Woodfin Camp; 343, MacDonald Photography/Unicorn Stock Photos; 344, Peter Vadnai/Art Resource; 350, Jerry Sarapochiello/Bruce Coleman, Inc.; 353, Jim Amos/Photo Researchers; 354, Larry Mulvehill/Photo Researchers; 357, Robert Frerck/Odyssey Productions; 358, Comstock/Jim Pickerell; 360, George Goodwin/The Picture Cube; 365, L. L. T. Rhodes/Taurus; 366, Fredrik D. Bodin/Stock, Boston; 370, Richard Weiss/Peter Arnold; 374, R. Kord/H. Armstrong Roberts; 376, Steven Baratz/The Picture Cube; 380, 381, The Bettmann Archive; 382, U.S. Department of the Interior; 385, Kim Keitt/Globe Photos; 386, 387, AP/Wide World Photos; 394, R. Kord/H. Armstrong Roberts; 396, John Running; 397, Jean-Claude Lejeune/Stock, Boston; 399, Palmer/Kane, Inc./The Stock Market; 400, Dick Durrance II/Woodfin Camp; 402, Doug Wilson/Black Star; 404, Ira Block/Woodfin Camp; 405(t), Nathan Benn/Woodfin Camp; 405(b), 406(t), Steven Borns; 406(b), 407, courtesy Cassandra Cole; 408, Jeff Dunn/The Picture Cube; 409, Ken Biggs/DPI; 411(tl), Frank Siteman/Rainbow; 411(tr), Michal Heron/Woodfin Camp; 411(bl), Owen Franken/Stock, Boston; 411(br), Yoram Kahana/Peter Arnold; 412, Tony Freeman/PhotoEdit; 415, Clyde H. Smith/Peter Arnold; 416, Bill Bachmann/f/Stop Pictures.

UNIT SEVEN: page 421, Steven E. Sutton/Duomo; 422, Christopher Morris/Black Star; 424, UPI/Bettmann Newsphotos; 426, AP/Wide World Photos; 427, Joe Japho/Picture Group; 428, Susan Biddle/The White House; 430, Gary Hershorn/Reuters/Bettmann Newsphotos; 431, Hermine Dreyfuss/Monkmeyer; 432, Carl Purcell/Agency for International Development; 433, James R. Holland/Stock, Boston; 435, Richard Choy/Peter Arnold; 438, Wernher Krutein/Photovault; 442, Andree Kaiser/Reuters/Bettmann Newsphotos; 444, 446, The Bettmann Archive; 448, Paolo Koch/Photo Researchers; 450, Walter Sanders/LIFE Magazine © Time Warner; 451, UPI/Bettmann Newsphotos; 453, Frank Fournier/Contact Stock Images; 455, J. Langevin/Sygma; 456(t), Jeffrey Jay Foxx/Woodfin Camp; 456(bl), Cary Wolinsky/Stock, Boston; 456(br), DPI; 457(t), Cary Wolinsky/Stock, Boston; 457(b), Jeffrey Jay Foxx/Woodfin Camp; 458, Reuters/Bettmann Newsphotos.

UNIT EIGHT: page 463, R. Allyn Lee/SuperStock; 464, Taylor Johnson; 467, Steven Proehl/Photo Researchers; 470, Peter Vadnai/Art Resource; 473, Fred Ward/Black Star; 474(t), AP/Wide World Photos; 474(b), AP/Wide World Photos; 475, UPI/Bettmann Newsphotos; 476, Sam C. Pierson, Jr./Photo Researchers; 477, James D. Wilson/Woodfin Camp; 479, Peter Vadnai/Art Resource; 486, Richard B. Levine; 488, Bruce Anspach/Art Resource; 490, Mike Mazzaschi/Stock, Boston; 492, Judy Gurovitz/International Stock Photography, Ltd.; 493, John Running/Stock, Boston; 494, Marc St. Gil/The Image Bank; 495, Flip Schulke/LIFE Magazine © 1964 Time, Inc.; 496, Marilyn Church; 497, Charles Gatewood; 498, Erik Anderson/Stock, Boston; 499, Joel Gordon/DPI; 500, Alvis Upitis/The Image Bank; 504, NASA; 506, W. J. Schoonmaker/National Audubon Society/Photo Researchers; 507, Porterfield-Chickering/Photo Researchers; 508, U.S. Department of Agriculture, HBJ Photo; 511, Kim Steele/Black Star; 512, 513, Charlie Archambault/U.S. News & World Report; 518, Hugh Rogers/Monkmeyer; 522, Michael Baytoff/Black Star; 524, Bill Weems/Woodfin Camp.

PRESIDENTS: page 550, (1) detail, painting by Gilbert Stuart, Metropolitan Museum of Art; (5) Metropolitan Museum of Art, Bequest of Seth Low; (all others) Library of Congress; 551, (12) Charles Phelps Cushing; (16) The Bettmann Archive; (all others) Library of Congress; 552, (29) Ewing Galloway; (31) Photo by Bachrach; (32) Franklin D. Roosevelt Library, Hyde Park, New York; (33) Charles Phelps Cushing; (34) Chase News Photo; (all others) Library of Congress; 553, (35) Henry Grossman; (36) Photo by Bachrach; (37) The White House; (38) courtesy of Gerald Ford's Office in Congress; (39) The White House; (40) UPI/Bettmann Newsphotos; (41) David Valdez/The White House.

END MATTER: page 559, Evan H. Sheppard/Folio, Inc.; 560, NASA; 565, U.S. Department of State.

Answers to "Can You Guess?"

Page 52: Nearly one million people a year view the Declaration of Independence and the Constitution.

Page 97: A person who holds office after his or her replacement has been chosen is called a lame duck. This person, like a lame duck, has little power.

Page 117: John F. Kennedy, at 43, was the youngest person ever elected President.

Ronald W. Reagan, at 69, was the oldest person ever elected President.

Page 167: The answers are:

Jefferson City, Missouri
Madison, Wisconsin
Jackson, Mississippi
Lincoln, Nebraska

Page 172: After winning its independence from Mexico in 1836, Texas was an independent republic until it became part of the United States in 1845.

Hawaii contains a former royal palace. The Iolani Palace, near Honolulu, was the residence of Queen Liliuokalani, Hawaii's last royal ruler.

Page 189: St. Augustine, Florida, is the oldest city in the United States. It was founded by the Spanish in 1565, on the site of an ancient Indian village.

Chicago, Illinois, has the tallest building in the United States—the Sears Tower, which is 1,454 feet high and has 110 stories.

New York City has more people than any other city in the United States.

Houston, Texas, is the location of the NASA Space Center.

Page 230: "Tippecanoe and Tyler Too" was used by William Henry Harrison in 1840. "Tippecanoe" referred to a victorious battle General Harrison had fought against the Indians at Tippecanoe Creek, Indiana, in 1811.

"Return to Normalcy" was used by Warren G. Harding in 1920. By "normalcy," Harding meant the way Americans had lived before World War I.

"A New Deal" was used by Franklin D. Roosevelt in 1932.

"I Like Ike" was used by Dwight D. Eisenhower in 1953. "Ike" was Eisenhower's nickname.

Page 252: Tobacco, legal tender in Virginia, Maryland, and North Carolina, was sometimes used to pay taxes.

Page 264: The wedding ring is worn on the third finger of the left hand because people used to believe that a vein or nerve ran directly from this finger to the heart.

Rice is a symbol of earth's bounty. Wedding guests originally threw rice at the bride and groom to show their wish that the couple would have children.

Page 285: The nation's first college (founded in 1636) was Harvard College (now part of Harvard University) in Cambridge, Massachusetts.

The nation's first coeducational college was Oberlin College in Ohio—founded in 1833.

The nation's first college for women was Mount Holyoke Female Seminary (now Mount Holyoke College)—founded in 1837.

Page 332: Thomas Jefferson was also an inventor. His inventions included the revolving chair, the revolving desk, and the seven-day clock.

The 1893 invention that helps us get into and out of our clothes is the zipper, invented by Whitcomb L. Judson to replace the buttons on high-button shoes.

The first people to use chewing gum were the American Indians, who collected chicle—the sap from certain trees. When making long journeys, they tucked pieces of chicle inside their cheeks to keep their mouths moist.

Page 352: George Washington's portrait appears on a $1 bill.

Abraham Lincoln's portrait appears on a $5 bill.

Alexander Hamilton's portrait appears on a $10 bill.

Andrew Jackson's portrait appears on a $20 bill.

Page 359: An average dollar bill lasts 18 months before it wears out.

If a piece is missing from paper money, the bill may still be worth something, depending on how much of the bill is left. If three fifths remain, the bill is worth its full value. If between two fifths and three fifths is left, the bill is worth half its value. But if less than two fifths of the bill is left, the bill is worthless.

When paper money wears out, it is collected by the Federal Reserve Banks. There, the bills are cut in two lengthwise. The halves are shipped (in separate batches) to the Treasury Department in Washington, D.C., where they are then burned.

Page 398: The answers are:

Andrew Johnson—Tailor
Warren Harding—Journalist
Woodrow Wilson—College Professor
Herbert Hoover—Engineer
Ronald Reagan—Actor

Page 425: The first President to win a Nobel Peace Prize was Theodore Roosevelt, in 1906, for helping to end the Russo-Japanese War of 1904–1905.

Woodrow Wilson was the first President to travel to Europe while in office. He went to France after World War I to meet with America's allies and draft a peace treaty. He was awarded the Nobel Peace Prize in 1919 for helping to end the war.

Page 449: "G.I." is an abbreviation of "government issue." It referred to equipment of the armed forces. "GI" also meant "government inductee" when applied to soldiers who were drafted. The term is no longer used because the army is now all-volunteer.

During World War II, over 2 million women worked in our defense industries. The term "Rosie the Riveter" was used to refer to these women. The name probably was first used to describe a woman working in an industry such as ship-building. There, "Rosie" sometimes used machines that drilled bolts, or rivets, into thick metal plates.

Page 472: In 1921, Franklin D. Roosevelt came down with polio, which left his legs paralyzed. Roosevelt helped found a national organization whose research led to the development of a successful antipolio vaccine.

Page 482: Some of the things that fire trucks carry are pike poles, axes, ropes, sledges, hoses, hammers, crow bars, power saws, and bolt cutters. Fire trucks also carry first-aid kits, oxygen tanks and masks, chemical fire extinguishers, and devices that remove smoke.